Research Anthology on Strategies for Using Social Media as a Service and Tool in Business

Information Resources Management Association
USA

Volume I

IGI Global
PUBLISHER of TIMELY KNOWLEDGE

Published in the United States of America by
    IGI Global
    Business Science Reference (an imprint of IGI Global)
    701 E. Chocolate Avenue
    Hershey PA, USA 17033
    Tel: 717-533-8845
    Fax: 717-533-8661
    E-mail: cust@igi-global.com
    Web site: http://www.igi-global.com

Library of Congress Cataloging-in-Publication Data

Names: Information Resources Management Association, editor.
Title: Research anthology on strategies for using social media as a service
  and tool in business / Information Resources Management Association,
  editor.
Description: Hershey, PA : Business Science Reference, [2021] | Includes
  bibliographical references and index. | Summary: "This book of
  contributed chapters provides updated information on how businesses are
  strategically using social media and explores the role of social media
  in keeping businesses competitive in the global economy by discussing
  how social tools work, what services businesses are utilizing, both the
  benefits and challenges to how social media is changing the modern
  business atmosphere,"-- Provided by publisher.
Identifiers: LCCN 2021016024 (print) | LCCN 2021016025 (ebook) | ISBN
  9781799890201 (hardcover) | ISBN 9781799890218 (ebook)
Subjects: LCSH: Social media--Economic aspects. | Marketing. | Branding
  (Marketing) | Customer relations. | Customer services--Technological
  innovations.
Classification: LCC HM742 .R4678 2021 (print) | LCC HM742 (ebook) | DDC
  302.23/1--dc23
LC record available at https://lccn.loc.gov/2021016024
LC ebook record available at https://lccn.loc.gov/2021016025

British Cataloguing in Publication Data
A Cataloguing in Publication record for this book is available from the British Library.

The views expressed in this book are those of the authors, but not necessarily of the publisher.

For electronic access to this publication, please contact: eresources@igi-global.com.

List of Contributors

Table of Contents

Volume II

Section 4
Utilization and Applications

Volume III

Section 5
Organizational and Social Implications

Volume IV

Section 6
Managerial Impact

Section 7
Critical Issues and Challenges

Preface

Since its conception, social media has become an integral part in how society communicates. As with the development of any other important piece of communication, business and industry must adapt to utilize this tool to reach its vast audiences to survive. Moreover, social media can be applied for internal processes for organizations and should be considered by human resources managers. Through this transition, it is essential for businesses to be aware of how to best utilize these tools and services in order to best promote themselves within the social sphere. The *Research Anthology on Strategies for Using Social Media as a Service and Tool in Business* provides these strategies for businesses to grow under this new era of communication.

Staying informed of the most up-to-date research trends and findings is of the utmost importance. That is why IGI Global is pleased to offer this four-volume reference collection of reprinted IGI Global book chapters and journal articles that have been handpicked by senior editorial staff. This collection will shed light on critical issues related to the trends, techniques, and uses of various applications by providing both broad and detailed perspectives on cutting-edge theories and developments. This collection is designed to act as a single reference source on conceptual, methodological, technical, and managerial issues, as well as to provide insight into emerging trends and future opportunities within the field.

The *Research Anthology on Strategies for Using Social Media as a Service and Tool in Business* is organized into seven distinct sections that provide comprehensive coverage of important topics. The sections are:

1. Fundamental Concepts and Theories;
2. Development and Design Methodologies;
3. Tools and Technologies;
4. Utilization and Applications;
5. Organizational and Social Implications;
6. Managerial Impact; and
7. Critical Issues and Challenges.

The following paragraphs provide a summary of what to expect from this invaluable reference tool.

Section 1, "Fundamental Concepts and Theories," serves as a foundation for this extensive reference tool by addressing crucial theories essential to understanding the concepts of social media in multidisciplinary settings. Opening this reference book is the chapter "The Role of Social Media in Public Involvement: Pushing for Sustainability in International Planning and Development" by Prof. Tooran Alizadeh of University of Sydney, Australia and Profs. Reza Farid and Laura Willems of Griffith

University, Australia. This chapter explores social media's potential to enhance public involvement to pursue sustainable practices on an international scale across planning and development projects. This first section ends with the chapter "Social Media and Social Identity in the Millennial Generation" by Prof. Guida Helal of American University of Beirut, Lebanon and Prof. Wilson Ozuem of University of Cumbria, UK, which focuses on theoretical implications and managerial implications. The concluding section offers some significant roles that social media and social identity may play in keeping up with the design and development of marketing communications programs.

Section 2, "Development and Design Methodologies," presents in-depth coverage of the design and development of social media strategy for its use in different applications. This section starts with the chapter "An Absorptive Capacity Perspective of Organizational Learning Through Social Media: Evidence From the Ghanaian Fashion Industry" by Profs. Richard Boateng, Edna Owusu-Bempah, and Eric Ansong from University of Ghana, Ghana, which examines the role social media has played on brand perceptions in the fashion apparel and accessories industry from a social identity theory perspective. This section ends with the chapter "CommuniMents: A Framework for Detecting Community Based Sentiments for Events" by Prof. Muhammad Aslam Jarwar of Quaid-i-Azam University, Pakistan & Hankuk University of Foreign Studies (HUFS), South Korea; Prof. Rabeeh Ayaz Abbasi of King Abdulaziz University, Saudi Arabia & Quaid-i-Azam University, Islamabad, Pakistan; Prof. Mubashar Mushtaq of Forman Christian College (A Chartered University), Pakistan & Quaid-i-Azam University, Pakistan; Prof. Onaiza Maqbool of Quaid-i-Azam University, Pakistan; Prof. Naif R. Aljohani of King Abdulaziz University, Saudi Arabia; Prof. Ali Daud of King Abdulaziz University, Saudi Arabia & International Islamic University, Pakistan; Prof. Jalal S. Alowibdi of University of Jeddah, Saudi Arabia; Prof. J.R. Cano of University of Jaén, Spain; Prof. S. García of University of Granada, Spain; and Prof. Ilyoung Chong of Hankuk University of Foreign Studies (HUFS), South Korea, which proposes a framework CommuniMents that enables us to identify the members of a community and measure the sentiments of the community for a particular event. CommuniMents uses automated snowball sampling to identify the members of a community, then fetches their published contents (specifically tweets), pre-processes the contents, and measures the sentiments of the community.

Section 3, "Tools and Technologies," explores the various tools and technologies used in the implementation of social media for various uses. This section begins with the chapter "Social Networking Data Analysis Tools and Services" by Prof. Gopal Krishna of Aryabhatt Knowledge University, India, which explains the methods and tools used for the analysis of the huge amount of data produced by social networks. This section ends with the chapter "Social Media as a Tool to Understand Behaviour on the Railways" by Prof. David Golightly of University of Nottingham, UK and Prof. Robert J. Houghton of Griffith University, Australia, which highlights important factors such as the broad range of issues covered by social media (not just disruption), the idiosyncrasies of individual train operators that need to be taken into account within social media analysis, and the time critical nature of information during disruption.

Section 4, "Utilization and Applications," describes how social media is used and applied in diverse industries for various technologies and applications. The opening chapter in this section, "Adoption of Web 2.0 Marketing: An Exploratory Study About the Nigerian SMEs," by Prof. Maryam Lawan Gwadabet of IT and Business School, Blue Sapphire E-Solutions ltd, Kano, Nigeria, explores the value which Web 2.0 marketing adds to the Nigerian SME's. The final chapter in this section, "An Evaluation of Toronto's Destination Image Through Tourist Generated Content on Twitter," by Profs. Hillary Clarke and Ahmed Hassanien of Edinburgh Napier University, Edinburgh, UK, evaluates the cognitive, affective, and conative components of destination image from the perception of tourists on social media.

Section 5, "Organizational and Social Implications," includes chapters discussing the impact of social media on society and shows the ways in which social media is used in different industries and how this impacts business. The first chapter, "An Empirical Evaluation of Adoption and Diffusion of New ICTs for Knowledge Sharing in IT Organizations," by Profs. Srinivasan Vaidyanathan and Sudarsanam S. Kidambi of VIT Business School, VIT University, Chennai, India, describes how knowledge is one of the most important assets in organizations which should be carefully managed and is continuously generated throughout an organization. The last chapter, "Fast-Fashion Meets Social Networking Users: Implications for International Marketing Strategy," by Prof. Tehreem Cheema of Clark University, USA, contributes to the existing literature on the influence of digital marketing on fast fashion, and it provides a number of pertinent marketing recommendations in regard to the practice of apparel retailers.

Section 6, "Managerial Impact," presents the uses of social media in industry and management practices. Starting this section is "Management and Marketing Practices of Social Media Firms" by Prof. Abdulaziz Alshubaily of University of Liverpool, Jeddah, Saudi Arabia, which examines the key variances in application and strategy between different social media management strategies and its effective marketing. Ending this section is "Tweeting About Business and Society: A Case Study of an Indian Woman CEO" by Profs. P. Vigneswara Ilavarasan, Ashish Kumar Rathore, and Nikhil Tuli of Indian Institute of Technology Delhi, India, which examines the social media content posted by a woman Indian chief executive officer (CEO) on Twitter.

Section 7, "Critical Issues and Challenges," highlights areas in which social media provides challenges for the industries utilizing it. Opening this final section is the chapter "E-Reputation in Web Entrepreneurship" by Profs. Sylvaine Castellano and Vincent Dutot of Paris School of Business, France, which gives to web-entrepreneurs the key elements in order to manage their e-reputation efficiently by presenting what e-reputation is, what its main components are, how to measure it, and what tools exist. The final chapter, "Ethical Dilemmas Associated With Social Network Advertisements," by Prof. Alan D. Smith of Robert Morris University, USA and Prof. Onyebuchi Felix Offodile of Kent State University, USA, explains the three hypotheses dealt with the interplay of online social networking, advertising effectiveness, gender and age trends, and remaining the interplay with positive comments of the use of the "like" function and its impacts on consumer behavior, as derived from the review of relevant operations literature and from applying the basic tenants of uses and gratification theory.

Although the primary organization of the contents in this multi-volume work is based on its seven sections, offering a progression of coverage of the important concepts, methodologies, technologies, applications, social issues, and emerging trends, the reader can also identify specific contents by utilizing the extensive indexing system listed at the end of each volume. As a comprehensive collection of research on the latest findings related to social media, the *Research Anthology on Strategies for Using Social Media as a Service and Tool in Business* provides researchers, instructors, social media managers, IT consultants, business managers, students, executives, practitioners, industry professionals, social media analysts, and all audiences with a complete understanding of the applications and impacts of social media. Given the vast number of issues concerning usage, failure, success, strategies, and applications of social media in modern industry, the *Research Anthology on Strategies for Using Social Media as a Service and Tool in Business* encompasses the most pertinent research on the applications, impacts, uses, and development of social media as a tool in business.

Section 1
Fundamental Concepts and Theories

Chapter 1
The Role of Social Media in Public Involvement:
Pushing for Sustainability in International Planning and Development

Tooran Alizadeh
University of Sydney, Australia

Reza Farid
Griffith University, Australia

Laura Willems
Griffith University, Australia

ABSTRACT

This chapter explores social media's potential to enhance public involvement to pursue sustainable practices on an international scale across planning and development projects. Using a case-study approach, the international institutions of the World Bank, UN-Habitat, Unilever, and World Business Council for Sustainable Development are investigated. The relationship between public versus the institutions' intake on sustainability is examined. Findings identify strong public push for increased sustainability in international development and show evidence of the ways in which international institutions respond to the public. Contributing to the social media research field, it offers an alternative application to the planning profession via e-planning. This could contribute to an extended form of public engagement through social media that goes beyond the limiting geographical borders of each local community, and assesses planning and development projects for their broader sustainability implications on an international platform.

DOI: 10.4018/978-1-7998-9020-1.ch001

INTRODUCTION TO ORGANIZATIONAL SUSTANIBALITY

The widely accepted definition of sustainable development/practice by Brundtland (1987) is development/practice that meets the needs of current generations without compromising the ability of future generations to meet their own needs. This has traditionally been interpreted on a local level, by analyzing local impacts and intergenerational equality. However, the rapid onset of globalization via multilateral trade negotiations over the last few decades has brought about an unprecedented increase in the local consumption of globally sourced goods and services. This definition of sustainable development detaches local planning, development, and resourcing from the issues of international inequality (AntonioDuro, 2012; Milanovic, 2011; Willard, 2009).

It is argued that the progress towards sustainable practice at an international level has been infrequent and inconsistent (Aras & David Crowther, 2009; Dyllick & Hockerts, 2002). Marsden (2000) outlines the wide variation in progress may be attributed to three distinct attitudes towards organizational uptake of sustainable practices:

- **Denial:** Placing responsibility on the government;
- **Reaction:** Acceptance as a contributor to the problem and taking guidance on solutions; and
- **Autonomous Action:** Recognition of power and proactive, independent acts.

Organizations in the reaction or autonomous response categories often utilize new forms of business models that have hybridized corporate and organizational strategy with sustainability and gained a competitive advantage in the market. The traditional business models, on the other hand, were mainly ruled by the economic system with only minor tradeoffs for social or environmental capital gain (Stubbs & Cocklin, 2008). Two major concepts arose in the literature in response to balancing this, namely 'corporate social responsibility' and 'corporate environmental responsibility/corporate sustainability' (Fernando, 2012; Montiel, 2008; Svensson & Wagner, 2010; Willard, 2009). In many cases though, the extent of these efforts are dictated by the organizations and vary greatly. Numerous international examples of over-consumption of local environmental resources, tax avoidance, and social injustices (Cerro Santamaria, 2013; Crane & Matten, 2016; Huang & Hsu, 2003) represent a disturbing level of ingenuity in the corporate sustainability agenda (Aras & Crowther, 2009). More recently, a growing line of critical scholarship has focused on the international corporations' philanthropic efforts, especially at the international level (Alizadeh, 2017; Gautier & Pache, 2015; McNeill, 2015; Paroutis, S., Bennett, M., & Heracleous, L., 2014). A particular focus has been on how firms have tried to influence national and urban governments, while engaging in providing philanthropic services (Kitchin, 2015). Critics argue that in many cases firms gain so much out of their involvement that do not fit with a pure pro bono, philanthropic model (Hack, 2013; McNeill, 2015). This line of argument suggests that new tools are required to bring organizations' international involvement with local projects to a global stage in a push for sustainable practice.

This chapter is an exploratory study into the potential of social media, as a new tool with the ability to give local level issues a global audience, in short time periods, to enhance public involvement and sustainable practices on an international scale across planning and development projects. Using a comparative case-study approach, the supply-demand relationship - on social media - for sustainable practice is examined. Building upon the literature, the chapter examines the virtually sourced data to discover how internationally renowned development and manufacturing organizations react to, or align with public request for sustainable practice. The results could open the door for an alternative form of public engagement through social media that goes beyond the limiting borders of each local community, and assesses planning and development projects for their broader environmental impacts on an international platform.

THE POTENTIAL OF SOCIAL MEDIA

Social media can be defined as an umbrella term, for blogs, wikis, social networks, and online communities; with the key feature of allowing users to connect (Carr & Hayes, 2015; Fieseler & Fleck, 2013). Some of the social media platforms are already incorporated in learning environments and currently affecting development policy through peer learning and by transforming social norms (Alizadeh, T., Tomerini, D., & Colbran, S., 2016; Denskus & Papan, 2013; Fieseler & Fleck, 2013; Willard, 2009). Social media are broad reaching and allow dispersed groups and individuals to form connections and share or promote information relating to common ideas, concerns, interests, or causes (LaRiviere, K., Snider, J., Stromberg, A., & O'Meara, K., 2012; Minton, E., Lee, C., Orth, U., Chung-Hyun, K., & Lynn, K., 2012; Walther & Jang, 2012). Social media has even been described as abstract forms of infrastructure for communities (Fieseler & Fleck, 2013), and is thought to be more accessible than traditional publications and discussions (Denskus & Papan, 2013). Social media, in particular, has played an important role in a number of civic uprisings around the word including but not limited to Arab Spring, the Occupy Movement, and recent presidential election campaigns in the US. This has prompted a new line of scholarship focusing on the role of social media in enabling participation, creating collective voice, and facilitating socio-political change (Comunello & Anzera, 2012; Howard & Parks, 2012; Kavada, 2015).

It is acknowledged that social media use is limited in some countries, but growing rapidly as cross-cultural platforms. Social media has also been shown as highly effective for reaching rural communities and developing countries with limited internet connectivity (Minton, E., Lee, C., Orth, U., Chung-Hyun, K., & Lynn, K., 2012; Willard, 2009). Increasing use is allowing local sustainability issues to gain international attention and support (Fieseler & Fleck, 2013; Mithas, S., Costello, T., & Tafti, A., 2011). It has been argued that the growing connections via social media may create relatively weak social ties (Ellison, N. B., Steinfield, C., & Lampe, C., 2007; Wellman, B., Haase, A. Q., Witte, J., & Hampton, K., 2001), but they seem sufficient for large enough networks of individuals with common concerns to gain enough power to challenge global superpowers (Willard, 2009).

The opportunities are possible due to social media platforms' participatory and interactive nature, which is also what separates them from the traditional forms of media (Barker, M. S., Barker, D. L., Bormann, N. F., & Neher, K. E., 2008; Minton, E., Lee, C., Orth, U., Chung-Hyun, K., & Lynn, K., 2012; Walther & Jang, 2012). In social media, the traditional producers of content engage with their receivers; and studies show that this eliminates the passive nature associated with traditional media (Fieseler & Fleck, 2013). Denskus and Papan (2013) found in their study that the active engagement provides opportunities for discussing and giving feedback on development issues and practices. The interactivity and user-generated content dominate social media, and provide avenues for bottom-up social movements and concerns (Dennis Linders, 2012; Juris, 2012; Waters, R. D., Burnett, E., Lamm, A., & Lucas, J., 2009). Fieseler and Fleck (2013) suggest that social media removes the formal hierarchy of society, and companies and organizations can no longer shield themselves from the involvement of stakeholders. Social capital is a means of empowerment, and social media can provide the necessary environment to create capital amongst users, empower stakeholders to raise their concerns through virtual cooperation (Scott & Liew, 2012; Tapscott & Williams, 2006).

In contrast to these possibilities of empowerment, there is also growing skepticism around the quality of online actions. Slacktivism or clicktivism has been recognized for its ability to draw attention to progressive causes; but questions of user validity, motivations for participation, and longevity in support stand and may lead to a reduction in perceived quality and therefore little overall impact on decision-making (McCafferty, 2011). Particularly in relation to the younger generations who are more enveloped in social media, participation in online campaigns has become too convenient and rarely translates into effective offline action (Vitak, J., Zube, P., Smock, A., Carr, C. T., Ellison, N., & Lampe, C., 2011). Moreover, concerns over the extent of cyber bullying across different social media platforms; and their special impact on vulnerable groups are growing (Best, P., Manktelow, R., & Tylor, B., 2014). Last but definitely not least, the growing role of social media in major terrorist organizations' operational strategy has brought the discussions to a new level (Klausen, 2015). The discussions are no longer simply about the power of social media to connect like-minded people; and to be influential. It is far more complicated.

Concerns about the role of social media in spreading fake news and also fake identities (accounts) on social media (Ferrara, E., Varol, O., Davis, C., Menczer, F., & Flammini, A., 2016) have broad implications on the legitimacy of citizen voice captured via the social media platforms; and raises skepticism about the level of trust that could be or should be put in the trends on social media. In response to growing concerns as such, different sectors (including governments, NGOs, and also private companies) have started developing social media strategies to capitalize on the opportunities and manage risks involved (Robin Effing & A.M.Spil, 2016; SergioPicazo-Vela, IsisGutiérrez-MartínezOpens, & Felipe Luna-Reyes, L., 2012).

Nevertheless, the complexity of the social media debates is, partially, due to its growing ability to connect people; and provide an alternative voice. It is recognized in some cases that within the virtual world of social media, corporations and governments – the officials in a sense - may not be the loudest voice, especially compared to the rising public disapproval of socio-political and environmental issues (Fieseler & Fleck, 2013; Walther & Jang, 2012). The dissatisfaction in the public realm by stakeholders and the community are frequently broadcasted over social media, in the direction of the responsible bodies (Jansen, B. J., Zhang, J. M., Sobel, K., & Chowdury, A. 2009). One of the powerful mechanisms of social media for gauging dissatisfaction and demand according to Walther & Jang (2012) is that of incidental aggregate user statistics, such as likes, shares, and retweets which are generally beyond the control of organizations and can represent mass evaluations of organizational reputation and dependability. In principle this can change the normal hierarchy and give the public the upper hand over authorities and decision makers.

However, as in traditional media, there is growing evidence of manipulating the public by green washing initiatives, or spearing false information on social media. In the context of this study – with attention to sustainability discussions - green washing is especially important. Following the Gulf of Mexico oilrig explosion and leak in 2010, the corporation responsible launched a traditional and online media campaign to superficially improve its environmental image. It is noted that while some met the campaign with skepticism, others showed approval and acceptance (Matejek & Gossling, 2014). More recently, in 2014, Nestle was accused of green washing for its customized recycling program, for Nespresso disposable coffee pods, which had only a negligible overall waste reduction impact. Unilever was also subjected to a Twitter campaign alleging that its role in a sustainable living online engagement platform did not accurately reflect the firm's true environmental impacts (Bowen & Aragon-Correa, 2014).

Examples like these, show that social media can also act as an avenue for organizational advertisement and in some cases misrepresentation, to gain public approval. It is, however, important to acknowledge that in response to green washing attempts on social media, online activism focused on 'green washing exposed' or 'against green washing' has also increased in the recent years (Lyon & Montgomery, 2013).

The literature also discusses the impacts of the social media on organizational credibility, reputation, and trustworthiness (Minton, E., Lee, C., Orth, U., Chung-Hyun, K., & Lynn, K., 2012; Walther & Jang, 2012). Transparency of an organization is highly related to its credibility, and a growing number of studies agree that the internet and social media are highly transparent and open spaces in comparison to the traditional media (Denskus & Papan, 2013; Fieseler & Fleck, 2013; Waters, R. D., Burnett, E., Lamm, A., & Lucas, J., 2009). Research has found that organizations and businesses can utilize social media in a variety of positive ways, including managing operations (Waters et al., 2009), educating and engaging with volunteers, donors, and stakeholders (Fieseler & Fleck, 2013; Waters, R. D., Burnett, E., Lamm, A., & Lucas, J., 2009), and observing and gathering information from interactions with consumers (Minton, E., Lee, C., Orth, U., Chung-Hyun, K., & Lynn, K., 2012). The research in this area also acknowledges the frequency of cases in which high-profile firms are being accused of misleading communications about environmental activities or performance; and the damaging impact on the credibility of managers and researchers of organizations (Bowen & Aragon-Correa, 2014).

Nevertheless, it is hoped that openness embedded in the way social media operates will eventually reduce the incidence of corporate green wash (Lyon & Montgomery, 2013). Here, there is an emphasis on the dynamic nature of social media which allows for both bottom-up and top-down community involvement; as public recognizes the opportunities for engagement. From a bottom-up perspective, there is growing research on the use of community led groups to organize and coordinate via social media in opposition to planning, policy, and manufacturing or development processes (Evans-Cowley, 2010; Maireder & Schwarzenegger, 2012). Shav-Ami (2013) argues that a new and incredibly powerful type of social movement has started through social media. This type of movement has the potential to strongly impact any activity that angers community members and is not necessarily geographically restricted. In a top-down engagement perspective also, there is a growing line of literature (Afzalan & Evans-Cowley, 2015; Evans-Cowley, 2012) that argues planners can greatly utilize social media based opportunities to mobilize and organize citizens. This is part of a bigger trend in the literature which supports the idea that online spaces, such as social media, can be used as public spheres to deliberative democracy (Hanson & Hogea, 2012).

METHOD

Case Studies

This study uses an exploratory case study approach. The case study organizations of the United Nations (UN) Habitat, World Bank, Unilever, and World Business Council for Sustainable Development (WBCSD) have been selected based on the recognition of their contribution to sustainable development or production, and their mission statement (Table 1). All four case study organizations self-declare sustainability as the core of their international development focus.

More importantly, these diverse four organizations represent different types of non-state actors recognized to have the most power in the international development (SparkNotes, 2014). The UN-Habitat and World Bank as Intergovernmental Organizations (IGOs) perform in partnership with national governments; World Business Council for Sustainable Development as an International Non-government Organization (INGO) operates by building international partnerships between non-government actors; and finally Unilever as a Multinational Corporation (MNC) is a business operating in multiple countries. The four case studies will provide great opportunities for this study to explore the potential role of the different international actor types in the promotion of sustainability at the international level. Due to their roles, these institutions have elements of both development and business practices. However, they are generally focused more towards one than the other. For example, IGOs most likely have development as their priority while a MNC focuses on production and business.

Having said this, we acknowledge that the four case study organizations have different levels of presence on social media. It would have been easier for our investigation if all case studies have had similar level of activities (e.g. Facebook and Twitter followers, posts and comments). Yet, the different levels of presence on social media could also be linked to the different levels of resources dedicated by each case study organization to their global outreach, which is per se worthy of investigation.

Table 1. Case studies' contribution to sustainable development, mission statement, and presence on Facebook and Twitter

Name	International Development Focus/Mission	Sustainability Reputation in the Literature	Social Media Following – Stage One*		Social Media Following- Stage Two*	
			Facebook	Twitter	Facebook	Twitter
World Bank	Poverty reduction and sustainable development	Stiglitz 1999; Stone 2000	1.34M	791K	2.33M	2.48M
Unilever	Increase quality of life and promote sustainable living	Smith 2009; Fernando 2012	2.77M	61.4K	3.66M	167K
UN-Habitat	Finance socially and environmentally sustainable towns and cities including provision of housing	Cobbett 2001; Mukhija 2006	23.4K	29.2K	61.8K	66.4K
WBCSD	Sustainable global business; balance with society and environmental	Dyllick & Hockerts 2002	3.9K	8.5K	7.6K	24.9K

K= Thousand M=Million *Accurate at time of collection – 24 July 2014, and 16 Aug 2017

Data Collection

Data collection for the study was conducted in two stages, using different data sources. Stage one of the study has already been published (Willems & Alizadeh, 2015). Yet, this chapter – including both stages - provides an opportunity to shed light on the social media usage pattern change in the recent years.

Stage One

In 2014, we conducted the first round of data collection mainly based on the institutions' Facebook pages. The focus on Facebook was based on its overall status as the most dominant social media of the time, and also driven by the fact that it was also the major social media outlet used by the case study institutions (see Table 1). To complement the data collected via Facebook, we also analyzed each organization' official website; and sent a questionnaire to their social media administration.

Facebook Pages

The official Facebook pages of the case study organizations were used as primary data source. Measuring reactions to Facebook content is difficult and debated. A study conducted by Cvijikj and Michahelles (2013) examined factors affecting online customer engagement with Facebook brand pages. The sample included posts obtained from 100 sponsored brand pages and utilised a data-mining tool to extract seven elements from each post including: (1) the message; (2) post media type; (3) number of likes; (4) number of comments; (5) number of shares; (6) creation time; and (7) time of last interaction (Cvijikj & Michahelles, 2013).

Even Facebook itself provides limited guidance on measuring reactions. Relevant examples of how Facebook officially gauges reactions include:

- Positive feedback is calculated based on the number of times audience took a desired action after seeing an ad, such as shared or liked it (Facebook, 2015).
- Negative feedback is based on the number of times audience hid an ad (Facebook, 2015).
- Post engagement is the number of people who have clicked, liked, commented on or shared a posts (Facebook, 2014).

Access to some measurements, such as post reach, hides, and clicks, is restricted to the page owner. As observed also, positive and negative measurement relates primarily to advertisements. Given that this chapter is exploring opportunities for community engagement, and the post reach measurements are not accessible, the quantitative measurement of post engagement including likes, comments and shares, is the most viable option.

This research structure (stage one) is similar to that of Cvijikj and Michahelles (2013), with a focus on assessing the engagement of Facebook users with official pages. We examined the official Facebook pages of the four case study organizations using content analysis. The last one hundred posts, on each Facebook page were cataloged for number of likes, shares, and comments.

Grounded theory was applied to qualitatively code the Facebook posts' content. Grounded theory method was adopted as it is attentive to issues of interpretation and does not bind itself too closely to longstanding assumptions (Suddaby, 2006). The grounded theory method utilizes flexible guidelines for data collection and analysis to construct theories grounded in the data themselves (Charmaz, 2006). Corbin and Holt (2005) discuss the fundamental steps of grounded theory that were taken at the stage one of this research to draw a theory out of data, including the constant flux between data collection and analysis:

- **Concept Identification:** On Facebook as posts are made, they spread throughout networks of people and accumulate feedback. A date was chosen which allowed sufficient time for posts to undergo this spread. Then, the 100 most recent posts from that date, from each case study were simultaneously collected in a one off collection. Due to the mechanics of Facebook, which allow observers to review past posts, this one off collection method is akin to observing and recording posts as they occur over multiple months. However, the method of recording upon occurrence poses the issue that it takes time for each post to receive feedback, as it spreads throughout the network. In contrast, the one off collection of previous posts has allowed sufficient time for posts to be observed by users and collect feedback. The posts underwent content analysis and the theme of each post was described. This theme description was based on open coding and a total of 44 minor themes were identified.

- **Data Reduction:** This followed the initial data collection and involved combining similarities in the 44 minor theme descriptions into 10 manageable categories, called subthemes. The subthemes included promotion, news, sustainable economics, equality, health, governance, community, resource management, sustainable urban planning, and environmental management. The ten subthemes were finally reduced to three major themes of economic, social, and environmental.

- **Theoretical Sampling:** Quantitative analysis of the data attached to the subthemes and major themes were examined in relation to one another. Emerging patterns were followed through new levels of data collection and analysis across the sources. Examples of the data which supported the emerging trends include viral Facebook posts, website information comparison to public Facebook comments, and questionnaire responses. It should also be noted that single posts were classed in multiple categories if there was evidence of several themes. This multiple theme coding denoted score frequency to be irrelevant unless calculated into a percentage over total category frequencies. This allowed each category to be recognized for its occurrence compared to other categories.

In order to address one of the repeated criticism of the grounded theory on the potential for bias based on individual researcher preconceptions of the themes and subthemes (Juliet Corbin & Strauss, 2014), this study went through careful examination of the steps taken. Initially, two individual researchers – both trained in grounded theory research – conducted the concept identification and data reduction steps – independent from each other. They then cross-examined each other's identified themes and subthemes to reduce the personal bias. The final sets of themes and subthemes were also examined by three researchers with extensive experience in grounded theory, to minimize the bias in this study.

Official Websites

The official websites correlating to each institution were also analyzed using content analysis. Once data patterns began to emerge from the primary Facebook analysis through grounded theory, the official websites were more closely examined to collect additional data as evidence of the patterns.

Questionnaire

Due to this being a case study research method, input from the case study organizations was desirable. A questionnaire was sent to the Facebook administrator of each institution's page via the Facebook message system.

The questionnaire was designed to gain insight into intentional institution strategies, attitudes, and responses towards demand or promotion of sustainable international development over social media. Due to the limited scope of the questionnaire distribution to the four institutions, responses could only be analyzed qualitatively. Verbatim quotes were matched to the patterns appearing in the content analysis of the Facebook pages.

Due to the size of these institutions, it was recognized that responses were not guaranteed. Where response was not received within a week, the questionnaire was resent through their official websites or to the personnel identified on their webpage as communication focal points. Despite the numerous attempts made via institutions' Facebook pages and their official websites, the UN- Habitat was the only case study organization that responded to the questionnaire. However, two out of three non-respondent organizations reacted to the questionnaire. The reasons given by Unilever and World Bank (passed up to head office/could not identify appropriate person with overview of all the issues) perhaps suggest a tension between horizontal and vertical management of the public relations in the organizations which could be the topic of investigation for another independent study. The fact that the questionnaire ignited some reactions from three out of four case study organizations suggests that the research was understood, and the questions did not seem problematic. At the end, we cannot really know the real reason behind the low response rate. It could be interpreted as a negative mark against the organizations' public engagement practices over social media; or it could be simply because they did not like our questionnaire enough to make it a priority. Whatever the reason, we decided to include the only response received from the UN-Habitat in our investigation; as it provided a unique window of opportunity to directly hear from one of the organizations. This could add another layer to our understanding of these institutions' approach towards sustainable practice.

Stage Two

Stage two of the data collection was conducted in 2017. The aim was to update the learning from stage one, and to investigate if the patterns observed in 2014 have changed at all. However, due to the fast pace of changes around the social media, an update of the research meant much more than just repeating the first stage of the study. First, the number of studies focused on social media analytics has grown dramatically over this short period of time; and research from a wide range of disciplines has started picking up the importance of analyzing the voices raised via the social media platforms (Batrinca & Treleaven, 2015; Khan, 2017). Second, there was a clear shift in the popularity of social media platforms and in particular the role that Twitter versus Facebook play in the public debates. Without getting into too much details of the elements contributing to the shifted role of Twitter versus Facebook, Table 1 shows a much faster growth rate of Twitter followers versus Facebook followers for the four case study institutions. This perused us to use Twitter as the main source of data collection in the stage two of our investigation in 2017.

In order to keep the two stages of data collection consistent and then comparable, we built on the findings from stage one to design data collection approaches for stage two. Results of stage one are elaborated in the later parts of the chapter. Nevertheless, as explained above, the data collected in stage one was categorized around three major themes of economic, social, and environmental; with special attention paid to how the three themes were promoted by the case study institutions; and then received by the public. We followed the same line of investigation in the stage two of the study, using Twitter data.

In order to do so, we extracted the latest 3200+ Twitter posts made by the four case study organizations (as the maximum number of tweets that, at this point of time, Twitter allows to be extracted for free), in a one off collection. Due to the mechanics of Twitter, which allow observers to review past posts, this one off collection method is akin to observing and recording posts as they occur over a longer period of time. Using data analytics, we then built a bank of all of the hashtags and their frequency used in the latest 1000 extracted Twitter posts per each case study. The hashtags with minimum two frequency then thematically analyzed around the three major themes of social, environmental, and economic – identified in the stage one of the study. The thematic analysis of the hashtags was conducted by two researchers to minimize the level of bias (similar to the technique adopted in the stage one of the study). The three theme based categories of hashtags (social, environmental, and economic) were then used to categorize the Twitter posts on the four case study institutions' official accounts. We, however, soon figured out that quite a sizeable number of Twitter posts did not use hashtags; and were being excluded from our investigation. So, in order to address the shortcoming, we extended our analysis by using hashtags as keywords. This basically resembled the context analysis adopted in stage one of the study; and meant that examples such as #budget vs. 'budget', #women vs. 'women', and # deforestation vs. 'deforestation' were equally accounted for in our data analysis. Moreover, in order to have a comparable sample size across the four case study institutions we continued the study to reach 1000 Twitter posts accounted for using the above technique. It should also be noted that, similar to stage one, single posts were classed in multiple categories if there was evidence of several themes.

The 1000 twitter posts, categorized under three major themes of social, environmental, and economic, were then further analyzed based on the engagement statistics – the level of reaction they received from the public. The public engagement analysis was based on the number of likes and retweets. At this point, Twitter does not allow for mass collection of comments made on the posts. So, this limited our chance of analyzing the direction of public reaction to the posts; whether it was positive or negative or mix. In order to alleviate this shortcoming, we identified the Twitter post on each institution's account that had gone viral by attracting the biggest public reaction (the largest number of likes and retweet). We then conducted a more in-depth analysis of the viral tweets to further understand the nature of public reaction.

RESULTS

Stage One

Initial data analysis of the subthemes allowed the researchers to identify which particular subthemes occurred most in each institution's Facebook posts (Table 2). It was noted that World Business Council went through sporadic periods of inactivity on Facebook, sometimes for multiple months, and therefore limited data was available for this case.

The following provides a theme overview and description, in the format of major themes, subthemes, and their descriptions:

- Economic Major Theme
  - **Promotion:** Any post, which aimed to acquire money or increase popularity, such as donation collection, events or project advertisement, product marketing, competitions, Twitter movements.
  - **News:** Any post, updating followers on recent institution news, information, or publications such as reports.
  - **Sustainable Business Practice:** Any post relating to making business processes and practices more sustainable (general advice for businesses and not just the case study institutions).

- Social Major Theme
  - **Equality:** Posts relating to increasing equality such as through humanitarian aid, gender and age equality, poverty reduction, education, and unemployment.
  - **Health:** Posts containing information on disease, healthcare, and safety.
  - **Governance:** Posts relating to governmental transparency, policy, war, peace, and reform.
  - **Community Building:** Posts relating to capacity building and community engagement.
- Environmental Major Theme
  - **Resource Management:** Posts relating to the management of resources such as water, natural resources, and food.
  - **Sustainable Urban Planning:** Posts containing information about sustainable transport, infrastructure planning, sustainable development, or land use management.
  - **Environmental Management:** Posts relating to managing and protecting environment including climate change, conservation, disaster and risk management, and pollution and energy waste reduction.

Table 2. Frequency of subthemes in each organization's Facebook posts

Subtheme	World Bank	UN-Habitat	Unilever	WBCSD
Promotion	13	11	9	9
News	16	47	35	9
Sustainable Economics	21	2	0	14
Equality	46	20	12	1
Health	4	0	17	2
Governance	6	5	0	3
Community	2	6	1	0
Resource Management	3	3	18	2
Sustainable Urban Planning	3	36	4	2
Environmental Management	3	15	34	4
TOTAL	117	145	130	46

Note: Frequency total greater than total posts as some posts contain multiple subthemes.

The next step of data analysis involved merging each organization's subthemes into major themes to gain a clearer overview. This was used to measure the supply and demand ratio of the posts, by comparing engagement statistics. The occurrence graph (Figure 1) represents the percentage of posts that related to each major theme by each organization. The popularity chart (Figure 2) was calculated by summing the number of likes, comments, and shares for each post, and then graphing the median of all summations separated by major theme. Average scores provided less accuracy than medians, as they were prone to distortion from viral posts.

The comparison between major theme occurrence (Figure 1) and popularity (Figure 2) shows that the interests of the organizations generally influence and cause a preference in the type of information presented in their posts. However, the public does not unconditionally support these interests. The public popularity data shows a relative balance for social, environmental, and economic information. There is also an increase in the popularity of social and environmental information when compared with its occurrence in the posts. This redistribution of information demand-supply suggests that the public may have interests and demands that are not being met, particularly in relation to environmental and social sustainability.

Figure 1. Comparison of case studies' major theme occurrence (via Facebook)

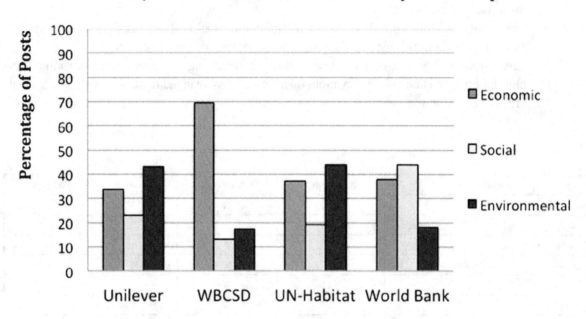

Figure 2. Comparison of case studies' major theme popularity (via Facebook)

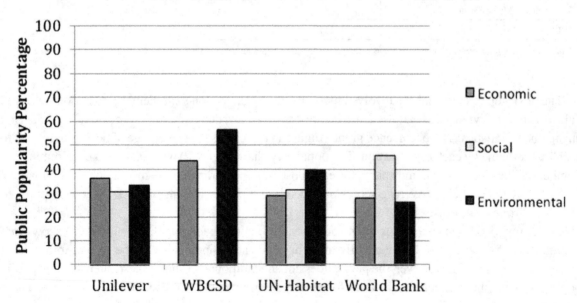

The questionnaire responses and official website comparisons provided further evidence of a publicly, and not necessarily an institutionally, driven demand. As described earlier, despite the numerous attempts, the questionnaire received a response from only one case study organization - the UN-Habitat. The UN-Habitat Social Media Focal Point's response to the question '*Does your organization identify as: Sustainable Enough, Good But Could Be Better, Not Very Sustainable, Not Sustainable At All?*', was '*Sustainable Enough*'. Similarly, when asked '*Does your organization aim to promote sustainability more/the same/less through social media than currently?*', the organization responded '*The same*'. These answers suggest that the organization (or at least its social media manager) is happy with the level of emphasis put on sustainable practice; and considers it a high standard model. This attitude suggests that the international development organization is not necessarily eager to promote sustainability to the public more than it has already been. This does not necessary align with the public demand; especially in respect to environmental and social dimensions of sustainability.

Comparisons between the institutions' official website information and the public comments on Facebook provided further evidence of the emerging pattern described above. A clear example of public demand versus the organizations' contentment is shown in the Unilever case. On their website, Unilever notes they have met their 100% sustainable palm oil sourcing goal by marking it as achieved. However, on their Facebook page a large number of posts were confronted with comments demanding things such as 'stop green-washing' and 'commit to going palm oil free'.

Examining viral posts reveals a tangential aspect of public demand. These are posts originally made by the organizations which attract enormous attention from the public and receive an amount of likes, comments, and shares that far exceeds the average counts. Viral posts reach a greater number of users through public sharing and newsfeed views. These posts may represent the greatest demands of the public.

Within the total of analyzed posts, eight were considered to be viral outliers in comparison to other posts within each case (Table 4), including:

- World Bank and UN-Habitat both experienced two posts each that this research identified as viral outliers.
- Unilever was found to have four posts as viral.
- World Business Council for Sustainable Development did not have any posts that could be considered viral which may be partially attributed to its sporadic periods of inactivity.

The trends in these viral Facebook posts have been identified across the case studies and a summary table (Table 3) shows the following relationships within the content:

- The first trend in the viral posts relates to calls for participation, and empowerment, for example a post calling for the public to engage with an online discussion.
- The next set of viral posts do not contain the specific words of engagement and participation, but ask for the public to submit personal stories or ideas about improving social or environmental issues. These can be interpreted as calls for engagement.
- The final trend in the viral posts represents a related but slightly different pattern of engagement. In these posts, rather than calling for input or empowerment, the engagement is seen through acknowledgment of community members. It personalizes and thanks regular people for enabling the organizations to conduct their international development activities.

Table 3. Summary of viral Facebook posts (originally posted by the organizations and turned viral by the public)

Viral Post	Institution	Post Key Words	Popularity*	Trend
1	World Bank	'Empowering citizens'/ '…participate in decision-making process'	2429L/11C/24S	Empowerment Participation
2	UN-Habitat	'…participatory and empowering'	198L/1C/136S	Empowerment Participation
3	World Bank	'…wants to know what you…'/'…leave a comment or post a photo telling us what you…'	741L/12C/2S	Call for participation
4	Unilever	'Have an idea for change? Enter it…'	729L/5C/3S	Call for participation
5	Unilever	'Have a great idea of your own? Enter your big ideas at…'	15095L/21C/511S	Call for participation
6	Unilever	'Do you have a flow of great ideas? Share them with us…'	1580L/35C/32S	Call for participation
7	UN-Habitat	'Thank you to the city of Medellin and all its inhabitants…'	256L/10C/69S	Acknowledgement
8	Unilever	'…big thank you… to our 174,000 amazing employees…'	2546L/156C/222S	Acknowledgement

* L=Likes C=Comments S=Shares

Stage Two

Step two of the study was designed to verify the trends observed in stage one; and to see how the dynamics identified across the social media accounts of the four case study organizations - using Facebook data - in 2014 compares to what is happening in 2017 - using Twitter data. The results are illustrated in Figures 3 and 4. A comparison of the two figures shows the supply and demand ratio based on the presence/occurrence of the three major themes of social, environmental, and economic within the Twitter posts, and the level of reaction that they received form the public (engagement statistics). The occurrence graph (Figure 3) represents the percentage of tweets that relate to each major theme by each organization. The popularity chart (Figure 4) was calculated by summing the number of likes, and retweets of each tweet; and then graphing the median of all summations separated by major theme. Average scores provided less accuracy than medians, as they were prone to distortion from viral posts.

First, the patterns observed within each organizations' activities on the social media (Figure 3) seem to have changed towards being more balanced (see Figure 1 for comparison). To be specific, there is an increase of environmental and social posts across all case studies. Interestingly economic posts are not the highest priority for any of the four case study organizations (unlike what was observed in 2014). This is an interesting development, considering that our earlier round of investigation – based on Facebook data - had portrayed social and then environmental posts as the more popular ones – compared to the economic focused posts.

Figure 3. Comparison of case studies' major theme occurrence (via Twitter)

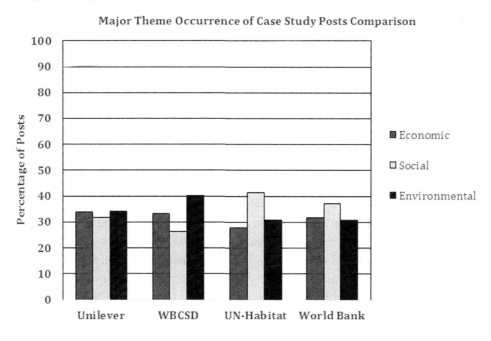

Figure 4. Comparison of case studies' major theme popularity (via Twitter)

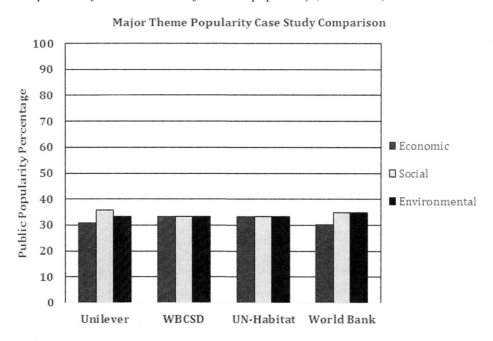

Second, the public engagement data (Figure 4) also shows an increased level of balance in reaction to social, environmental, and economic tweets. There is almost perfect balanced reaction to social, environmental, and economic tweets on UN-Habitat and WBCSD accounts. World Bank and Unilever show just less than perfect balanced reaction with slightly stronger public engagement with their environmental and social posts.

Moreover, examining viral posts reveals a tangential aspect of public demand. These are tweets which attracted enourmous attention from the public and received a large number of likes, and retweets that exceed the average counts for each Twitter acount. Viral posts reach a greater number of users through public sharing (retweets). These posts may represent the greatest demands of the public.

Within the total of analyzed posts, seven were considered to be viral outliers in comparison to other tweets within each case (Table 4), including:

- World Bank has the biggest followers' base among the four case studeis. We have identified two tweets as viral outliers; as the level of public enagement with them was far bigger than other tweets on the organization's account.
- Unilever and UN-Habitat both found to have two tweets as viral. The size of public engagement (the total number of likes and retweets for each viral post) differs across the two companies' accounts which is an indication of different level of social media engagement for the two companies.
- World Business Council for Sustainable Development did not have any tweets that could be considered viral which may be attributed to the fact that it has the smallest follower base on the Twitter among the four cases.

The trends in these viral Twitter posts have been identified across the case studies and a summary table (Table 4) of the viral tweets shows interesting patterns. First, none of the viral tweets has an explicit economic focus. This is quite similar to what was observed in the stage one of the study (focusing on the Facebook data). Second, the identified viral posts all focus on bigger picture social and environmental issues (climate change, and refugee crisis for example). Earlier Facebook investigation in stage one also showed an extraordinary level of public response when betterment of major environmental and social issues was the core of a social media post made by the organizations.

Table 4. Summary of viral Twitter posts (originally posted by the organizations and turned viral by the public)

Viral Post	Institution	Post Key Words	Popularity*	Trend
1	World Bank	Climate change is undeniable; solutions	18102	Environmental Management – Environmental
2	UN-Habitat	Happy Canada Day	13425	Community Building -Social
3	World Bank	Human progress; world betterment	9450	Equality - Social
4	UN-Habitat	Don't stop the refugees; stop the wars that produce them.	8537	Equality - Social
5	World Bank	World's forests; stop deforestation	4752	Resource Management- Environmental
6	Unilever	sustainability goals; growth	2622	Sustainable Urban Planning- Environmental
7	Unilever	young entrepreneurs; world-changing idea	2471	Empowerment – Social

* likes + retweets

DISCUSSION

Our two stage study shows interesting transformation in the dynamic relationship between the four case study organizations in one hand, and the public in the other hand in the short period of 2014-2017. In order to elaborate the transformation observed, we offer the lessons learned in each stage separately before offering the overall learning:

Learning From Stage One

When comparing the relationship between case study organizations' major post themes and public popularity responses, it was found that individual case studies generally favoured one major theme more strongly than the others. In response to this, popularity graph (Figure 2) showed public reaction was relatively balanced across the three major themes of social, environmental, and economic. This trend was evident in all case studies. The conclusion that began to surface was that the public users' level of support was not necessarily dictated by what the institutions posted about. It also showed a demand from the public that is conducive to the balanced triple bottom line for sustainability and showed a public demand for more sustainable information, and potentially outcomes, in development and manufacturing.

It was also noted that the social theme was generally the least common major theme across case study posts, but it received a phenomenal increase in relative popularity across all the case studies except WB-SCD which was incalculable due to the low number of social posts. Such a pattern was also corroborated when the viral posts were examined. Emotive and personal connection is one possible explanation why social posts, especially those relating to community empowerment and acknowledgement, were strongly supported. A study by Swani et al. (2013) on the quantitative public popularity of different corporate posts found a trend in which using emotional content in posts generated more likes. This, however, does not completely explain the pattern in our study, as many other emotional posts of both environmental and economic themes were present, but were not as popular. It should be noted that not all social posts were strongly supported, but the trends indicate a generally high distinction between occurrence of social themed posts and their popularity rate.

The World Urban Forum by UN-Habitat is an example of an online public involvement post that received viral proportions of attention. The World Urban Forum is hosted biennially in different locations as an international discussion of the greatest issues facing urban settlements, and is attended by, but not restricted to, government bodies, community groups, professionals, academics, and researchers (UN Habitat, 2014). The forum also has an educational exhibition open to the public and many of the forum's submissions are shared through social media. Turner-Lee (2010) suggested that with the growing technological innovation around the globe, new forms of social media and online platforms could be designed to make virtual public participation a practical revolution whilst being supplemented with strategies to provide internet access and a more equitable engagement process than traditional physical engagement. As technologies advance and become more widely available, planners and development institutions can take advantage of these opportunities and improve delocalized community engagement practices.

Lessons From Stage Two

Our analysis based on the 2017 Twitter data shows a move towards balance. This move is evident when looking at four case study organizations' tweets; and also the reaction received from the public. Interestingly, compared to 2014, organizations seem to have an increased number of social and environmental posts. Yet again, the level of balance observed in public reaction to posts exceeds the one in organizations' posts. Similar to 2014, this could still be interpreted as a sign for public push for a balanced approach to the triple bottom line of sustainability (economic, environmental, and social) in development, planning and manufacturing; a sign that the public is still ahead of what organizations are offering in terms of balanced approach.

The trend observed in viral posts are, however, different and may help better understand the direction of public push. Similar to what was seen in 2014, no economic post has gone viral. However, there seems to be an equal representation of environmental and social tweets among viral posts. This shows an increased attention to environmental issues (such as climate change and deforestation) in comparison to the pattern observed in 2014. In summary, public engagement with social and environmental tweets on the four case study organizations' accounts are far bigger than the level of attraction for economic posts.

Overall Lessons Learned

Comparative analysis of trends observed on the social media accounts of the four case study organizations in stages one and two of the study suggests that the gap between public demand and what organizations are offering in terms of promoting sustainability might be decreasing. This bold observation is based on the move towards balanced offering across the three major themes of economic, social, and environmental on the social media platforms of all case studies. While the level of balance reported in the public engagement (Figure 4) is still ahead of the balance observed in the organizations' posting (Figure 3); the difference is definitely smaller than what observed in 2014 (see Figure 1 and 2).

The golden question, however, is 'What does this mean? '. Is there a real shift across the case study organizations towards sustainability and sustainable practice? Or have they just got better at playing the game? Unfortunately, our study cannot answer this golden question, as far more detail analysis of their practice on the ground – and not just across social media – is needed. Having said this, the change observed in the social media performance of the case studies suggests that the big international organizations have been paying attention and reacting to public. This per se might be an outcome which shows the potential of social media to gain attention of big players.

In a sense, the trend observed in stages one and two of this study may pertain to the growing use of social media as new avenues to instigate bottom-up community engagement. There is growing research on community groups who share information and coordinate via Facebook and Twitter. A growing number of studies (Afzalan & Evans-Cowley, 2015; Evans-Cowley, 2010, 2012) found a significant number of planning-related groups on Facebook and Twitter – many of which were organized to oppose specific developments or plans. Social media has also been recognized as a platform that engages a more targeted youthful audience (Park, N., Kee, K. F., & Valenzuela, S., 2009). There is, however, conflicting information on whether this online subscription to a cause, translates to physical participation.

It is difficult to explain how, why, and if civic and public involvement over social media platforms can be generated into real life actions. However, recent major events have been researched as bottom-up revolutions through social media, such as the Arab Spring Twitter movement, in which four world leaders were ultimately removed from their positions (Bala, 2014). On this severe level of involvement, social media are concluded to have played a major and phenomenal role in facilitation. However, on a less dramatic level, a survey found that administrators of planning issue Facebook groups reported that community members did join the groups, but little physical action resulted (Evans-Cowley, 2010). This suggests that social media may influence large scale, even globally significant issues, more easily than small local issues. This is related to the low rates of participation in traditional engagement techniques. A study by Vogel et al. (2014) found that in local governments, the highest participation rate of residents was 19%, while the majority of local governments recorded comparatively low participation rates.

Research (Boulianne, 2009; Earl & Kimport, 2011; Quan-Haase, A., Wellman, B., Witte, J. C., & Hampton, K. N., 2002) over the last decade or so argues that the internet could supplement engagement but does not necessarily increase level of participation. This, however, could be due to the inequality and inaccessibility issues of traditional community engagement, as it requires extensive commitments from people in time and relocating to be physically present at meetings (Mandarano, L., Meenar, M., & Steins, C., 2010). Nevertheless, social media and the internet have challenged much of the geographical restrictions associated with obtaining local information - as citizens who are not located in close proximity could have access to development and planning information and join the local community.

SIGNIFICANCE OF FINDINGS

Our findings have contributed to the field of research in several ways. Firstly, the chapter has utilised a methodology process and combination that can contribute to more efficient and meaningful social media research. Secondly, the research suggests a role for global citizens to take part – via the social media- in demanding sustainable practice well beyond the geographical borders of local developments and projects. And finally, it has identified potential links between social media and public engagement in the virtual sphere to pursue more sustainable development outcomes. This should be of interest to both planners and policy makers.

The chapter – within the limitations of a comparative case study research - has investigated international development sustainability demands on Facebook and Twitter, and identified that the public push could be a driving factor for increasing organisational sustainability – at least on their social media platforms. This study has also looked at the types of information that the public Facebook and Twitter users seem to respond to and engage with, around the topic of international development. This could be further explored by examining a greater sample of posts, over an extended period of time; and also a questionnaire submitted to the public may strengthen the findings of this research.

The scope could also be scaled down to see if the findings also fit at national, state, or regional levels of impacts. Conducting this research using varied scopes can have the advantage of being able to follow similar research methods. Upon reflection of the research methods and processes, they have allowed the researchers to quickly navigate and analyse the complicated mountain of information sent over Facebook and Twitter. The grounded theory approach – used in stage one - was in particular a key to unlocking a directed and meaningful pattern in the highly variable data. This then guided the structure of investigation in stage two.

Finally, global online public engagement could help planners to alleviate the issues around the traditional engagement and exclusionary issues. A tangential line of research analysing participation and methods in the new online engagement forums will be invaluable to planners. Future research needs also link to the 'corporate social responsibility' and 'corporate sustainability' (Fernando, 2012; Montiel, 2008; Svensson & Wagner, 2010; Willard, 2009) frameworks; in order to actively involve international organizations in the fight for sustainability across the world.

CONCLUSION

This chapter aimed to explore the social media's potential to improve public involvement and sustainable practices on an international scale across planning and development projects. It was based on a multiple case study analysis, by comparing the supply of online information from development and manufacturing organizations, and the public response to this information.

The findings of this research provide insights into the sustainability and consultation demand-supply relationship on social media. The research suggests that such relationship is driven by the public users. Although the development institutions do not necessarily drive sustainability, there is evidence that they are responding to the public demand for sustainability. Nevertheless, this study warns against the danger of green washing in the online domain, and is yet hopeful that the two-sided conversation in the social media provides an opportunity to hold the international organizations accountable; and reduce (and not eliminate) their chance of promoting sustainability hoaxes. This optimistic – and yet pragmatic- view is in line with the previous research (Bowen & Aragon-Correa, 2014; Jacquet, 2015; Lyon & Montgomery, 2013) which suggests public pressure - in the form of public shaming via social media – can challenge corporations and even governments to change policies and behaviors that are detrimental to the environment.

The fundamental premise of this chapter, which targets the role of social media in public engagement with planning and development projects, has been previously discussed in the literature (Afzalan & Evans-Cowley, 2015; Evans-Cowley, 2010, 2012). But previous studies generally took the approach of discovering whether subscriptions to e-planning and development opposing groups, can lead to physical participation. Results were mixed, and it has been more commonly agreed upon that traditional engagement is supplemented by social media activity, but not increased. However, this chapter relates to public involvement from a different angle. It acknowledges the issues with clicktivism and then explores Facebook and Twitter not as just platforms for information sharing and community organization, but for actual online engagement. This extension could potentially offer an alternative venue to address the traditional low engagement rates and accessibility issues. This could simultaneously provide a space for the virtual citizens of the world – regardless of their physical location – to voice their demands for increase in the sustainability of international development.

The framework developed in this research is still in its infancy. In any future attempt to further develop such a framework, the unfolding limits of social media need to be accounted for. It may offer an application to the planning profession via e-planning, which could result in an alternative form of public engagement through social media. This alternative form of public engagement could go beyond the limiting borders of each local community, and assess planning and development projects for their broader environmental impacts on an international platform.

With social media becoming an ever-more influential factor in the operations of international development, and the behaviors of the public, there is a need to further researching and trialing the practical applications of this in the planning profession. Regardless of country, geographical influence level, public institution, or private, research into the potentials of social media in e-planning should be taken up as a unique opportunity to create more equitable and encompassing planning and development outcomes.

REFERENCES

Afzalan, N., & Evans-Cowley, J. (2015). Planning and Social Media: Facebook for Planning at the Neighbourhood Scale. *Planning Practice and Research*, *30*(3), 270–285. doi:10.1080/02697459.2015.1052943

Alizadeh, T. (2017). An investigation of IBM Smarter City Challenge: What do participating cities want? *Cities (London, England)*, *63*, 70–80. doi:10.1016/j.cities.2016.12.009

Alizadeh, T., Tomerini, D., & Colbran, S. (2016). Teaching Planning Studios: An Online Assessment Task to Enhance the First Year Experience. *Journal of Planning Education and Research*. doi:10.1177/0739456X16647162

Aras, G., & Crowther, D. (2009). Corporate Sustainability Reporting: A Study in Disingenuity? *Journal of Business Ethics*, *87*(S1), 279–288. doi:10.100710551-008-9806-0

Aras, G., & Crowther, D. (2009). Making sustainable development sustainable. *Management Decision*, *47*(6), 975–988. doi:10.1108/00251740910966686

Bala, M. (2014). Civic engagement in the age of online social networks. *Contemporary Readings in Law and Social Justice*, *6*(1), 767–774.

Barker, M. S., Barker, D. L., Bormann, N. F., & Neher, K. E. (2008). *Social Media Marketing: A Strategic Approach*. South-western Cengage Learning.

Batrinca, B., & Treleaven, P. C. (2015). Social media analytics: A survey of techniques, tools and platforms. *AI & Society*, *30*(1), 89–116. doi:10.100700146-014-0549-4

Best, P., Manktelow, R., & Tylor, B. (2014). Online communication, social media and adolescent wellbeing: A systematic narrative review. *Children and Youth Services Review*, *41*, 27–36. doi:10.1016/j.childyouth.2014.03.001

Boulianne, S. (2009). Does Internet Use Affect Engagement? A Meta-Analysis of Research. *Political Communication*, *26*(2), 193–211. doi:10.1080/10584600902854363

Bowen, F., & Aragon-Correa, J. A. (2014). Greenwashing in Corporate Environmentalism Research and Practice: The Importance of What We Say and Do. *Organization & Environment*, *27*(2), 107–112. doi:10.1177/1086026614537078

Brundtland, G. H. (1987). *Our Common Future: Report of the World Commission on Environment and Development*. Oxford, UK: Oxford University.

Carr, C. T., & Hayes, R. A. (2015). Social Media: Defining, Developing, and Divining. *Atlantic Journal of Communication*, *23*(1), 46–65. doi:10.1080/15456870.2015.972282

Cerro Santamaria, G. (Ed.). (2013). *Urban megaprojects: a worldwide view*. Bingley, UK: Emerald Group Publishing Limited. doi:10.1108/S1047-0042(2013)13

Charmaz, K. (2006). *Constructing Grounded Theory: A Practical Guide Through Qualitative Analysis.* London: Sage Publications.

Comunello, F., & Anzera, G. (2012). Will the revolution be tweeted? A conceptual framework for understanding the social media and the Arab Spring. *Journal of Islam and Christian–Muslim Relations, 23*(4), 453–470. doi:10.1080/09596410.2012.712435

Corbin, J., & Holt, N. (2005). Grounded theory. In B. Somekh & C. Lewin (Eds.), *Research Methods in the Social Sciences.* London: Sage Publications.

Corbin, J., & Strauss, A. (2014). *Basics of qualitative research: Grounded theory procedures and techniques.* London: Sage.

Crane, A., & Matten, D. (2016). *Business ethics: Managing corporate citizenship and sustainability in the age of globalization.* Oxford, UK: Oxford University.

Cvijikj, I. P., & Michahelles, F. (2013). Online engagement factors on Facebook brand pages. *Social Network Analysis and Mining, 3*(4), 843–861. doi:10.100713278-013-0098-8

Denskus, T., & Papan, A. S. (2013). Reflexive engagements: The international development blogging evolution and its challenges. *Development in Practice, 23*(4), 455–467. doi:10.1080/09614524.2013.790940

Duro, J. A. (2012). On the automatic application of inequality indexes in the analysis of the international distribution of environmental indicators. *Ecological Economics, 76*, 1–7. doi:10.1016/j.ecolecon.2011.12.019

Dyllick, T., & Hockerts, K. (2002). Beyond the business case for corporate sustainability. *Business Strategy and the Environment, 11*(2), 130–141. doi:10.1002/bse.323

Earl, J., & Kimport, K. (2011). *Digitally Enabled Social Change: Activism in the Internet Age.* Cambridge, MA: MIT Press. doi:10.7551/mitpress/9780262015103.001.0001

Effing, R., & Spil, T. A. M. (2016). The social strategy cone: Towards a framework for evaluating social media strategies. *International Journal of Information Management, 36*(1), 1–8. doi:10.1016/j.ijinfomgt.2015.07.009

Ellison, N. B., Steinfield, C., & Lampe, C. (2007). The benefits of Facebook "friends": Social capital and college students' use of online social network sites. *Journal of Computer-Mediated Communication, 12*(4), 1143–1168. doi:10.1111/j.1083-6101.2007.00367.x

Evans-Cowley, J. (2010). Planning in the age of Facebook: The role of social networking in planning processes. *GeoJournal, 75*(5), 407–420. doi:10.100710708-010-9388-0

Evans-Cowley, J. (2012). There's an App for That: Mobile Applications for Urban Planning. *International Journal of E-Planning Research, 1*(2), 79–87. doi:10.4018/ijepr.2012040105

Facebook. (2014). *Page Post Metrics.* Retrieved 12 May, 2015, from https://www.facebook.com/help/336143376466063/

Facebook. (2015). *Negative Feedback*. Retrieved 12 May, 2015, from https://www.facebook.com/help/401280783409819

Fernando, R. (2012). Sustainable globalization and implications for strategic corporate and national sustainability. *Corporate Governance, 12*(4), 579–589. doi:10.1108/14720701211267883

Ferrara, E., Varol, O., Davis, C., Menczer, F., & Flammini, A. (2016). The rise of social bots. *Communications of the ACM, 59*(7), 96–104. doi:10.1145/2818717

Fieseler, C., & Fleck, M. (2013). The pursuit of empowerment through social media: Structural social capital dynamics in CSR-blogging. *Journal of Business Ethics, 118*(4), 759–775. doi:10.100710551-013-1959-9

Gautier, A., & Pache, A.-C. (2015). Research on Corporate Philanthropy: A Review and Assessment. *Journal of Business Ethics, 126*(3), 343–369. doi:10.100710551-013-1969-7

Hack, R. (2013). The Google fiber project. *Journal of Computing Sciences in Colleges Archive, 28*(5), 140-140.

Hanson, J., & Hogea, A. (2012). The Internet as the public sphere: Deliberative democracy and civic engagement. In A. Manoharan & M. Holzer (Eds.), *E-Governance and Civic Engagement: Factors and Determinants of E-Democracy* (pp. 467–486). Hershey, PA: IGI Global. doi:10.4018/978-1-61350-083-5.ch023

Howard, P. N., & Parks, M. (2012). Social Media and Political Change: Capacity, Constraint, and Consequence. *Journal of Communication, 62*(2), 359–362. doi:10.1111/j.1460-2466.2012.01626.x

Huang, S., & Hsu, W. (2003). Materials flow analysis and emergy evaluation of Taipei's urban construction. *Landscape and Urban Planning, 63*(2), 61–74. doi:10.1016/S0169-2046(02)00152-4

Jacquet, J. (2015). *Is Shame Necessary?: New Uses for an Old Tool*. New York: Pantheon Books.

Jansen, B. J., Zhang, J. M., Sobel, K., & Chowdury, A. (2009). Twitter power: Tweets as electronic word of mouth. *Journal of the American Society for Information Science and Technology, 60*(11), 2169–2188. doi:10.1002/asi.21149

Juris, J. (2012). Reflections on #Occupy Everywhere: Social media, public space, and emerging logics of aggregation. *Journal of American Ethnological Society, 39*(2), 259–279.

Kavada, A. (2015). Creating the collective: Social media, the Occupy Movement and its constitution as a collective actor. *Information Communication and Society, 18*(8), 872–886. doi:10.1080/1369118X.2015.1043318

Khan, G. F. (2017). Social Media Analytics. *Social Media for Government*, 93-118.

Kitchin, R. (2015). Making sense of smart cities: Addressing present shortcomings. *Cambridge Journal of Regions, Economy and Society, 8*(1), 131–136. doi:10.1093/cjres/rsu027

Klausen, J. (2015). Tweeting the Jihad: Social Media Networks of Western Foreign Fighters in Syria and Iraq. *Studies in Conflict and Terrorism, 38*(1), 1–22. doi:10.1080/1057610X.2014.974948

LaRiviere, K., Snider, J., Stromberg, A., & O'Meara, K. (2012). Protest: Critical lessons of using digital media for social change. *About Campus: Enriching the Student Learning Experience*, *17*, 10–17. doi:10.1002/abc.21081

Linders, D. (2012). From e-government to we-government: Defining a typology for citizen coproduction in the age of social media. *Government Information Quarterly*, *29*(4), 446–454. doi:10.1016/j.giq.2012.06.003

Lyon, T. P., & Montgomery, A. W. (2013). Tweetjacked: The Impact of Social Media on Corporate Greenwash. *Journal of Business Ethics*, *118*(4), 747–757. doi:10.100710551-013-1958-x

Maireder, A., & Schwarzenegger, C. (2012). A movement of connected individuals. *Information Communication and Society*, *15*(2), 171–195. doi:10.1080/1369118X.2011.589908

Mandarano, L., Meenar, M., & Steins, C. (2010). Building social capital in the digital age of civic engagement. *Journal of Planning Literature*, *25*(2), 123–135. doi:10.1177/0885412210394102

Marsden, C. (2000). The new corpotate citizenship of big business: Part of the solution to sustainability? *Business and Society Review*, *105*(1), 9–25. doi:10.1111/0045-3609.00062

Matejek, S., & Gossling, T. (2014). Beyond legitimacy: A case study in BP's "green lashing. *Journal of Business Ethics*, *120*(4), 571–584. doi:10.100710551-013-2006-6

McCafferty, D. (2011). Activism vs. slacktivism. *Communications of the ACM*, *54*(12), 17–19. doi:10.1145/2043174.2043182

McNeill, D. (2015). Global firms and smart technologies: IBM and the reduction of cities. *Transactions of the Institute of British Geographers*, *40*(4), 562–574. doi:10.1111/tran.12098

Milanovic, B. (2011). *Worlds apart: Measuring international and global inequality*. Princeton, NJ: Princeton University Press. doi:10.1515/9781400840816

Minton, E., Lee, C., Orth, U., Chung-Hyun, K., & Lynn, K. (2012). Sustainable marketing and social media: A cross-country analysis of motives for sustainable behaviors. *Journal of Advertising*, *41*(4), 69–84. doi:10.1080/00913367.2012.10672458

Mithas, S., Costello, T., & Tafti, A. (2011). Social networking in the enterprise. *IT Professional Magazine*, *13*(4), 16–17. doi:10.1109/MITP.2011.69

Montiel, I. (2008). Corporate social responsibility and corporate sustainability: Separate pasts, common futures. *Organization & Environment*, *21*(3), 245–269. doi:10.1177/1086026608321329

Park, N., Kee, K. F., & Valenzuela, S. (2009). Being immersed in social networking environment: Facebook groups, uses and gratifications, and social outcomes. *Cyberpsychology & Behavior*, *12*(6), 729–733. doi:10.1089/cpb.2009.0003 PMID:19619037

Paroutis, S., Bennett, M., & Heracleous, L. (2014). A strategic view on smart city technology: The case of IBM Smarter Cities during a recession. *Technological Forecasting and Social Change*, *89*, 262–272. doi:10.1016/j.techfore.2013.08.041

Picazo-Vela, S., Gutiérrez-Martínez, I., & Luna-Reyes, L. F. (2012). Understanding risks, benefits, and strategic alternatives of social media applications in the public sector. *Government Information Quarterly*, *29*(4), 504–511. doi:10.1016/j.giq.2012.07.002

Quan-Haase, A., Wellman, B., Witte, J. C., & Hampton, K. N. (2002). Capitalizing on the Net: Social contact, civic engagement, and sense of community. In B. Wellman & C. Haythornthwaite (Eds.), *The Internet in everyday life*. Oxford, UK: Blackwell. doi:10.1002/9780470774298.ch10

Scott, K., & Liew, T. (2012). Social networking as a development tool: A critical reflection. *Urban Studies (Edinburgh, Scotland)*, *49*(12), 2751–2767. doi:10.1177/0042098011435279

Shav-Ami, A. (2013). Social protest: The Israeli case. Journal of Enterprising Communities. *People and Places in the Global Economy*, *7*(4), 373–382.

SparkNotes. (2014). *International Organizations*. Retrieved 4 Feb, 2015, from http://www.sparknotes.com/us-government-and-politics/political-science/international-politics/section4.rhtml

Stubbs, W., & Cocklin, C. (2008). Conceptualizing a "Sustainability Business Model". *Organization & Environment*, *21*(2), 103–127. doi:10.1177/1086026608318042

Suddaby, R. (2006). From the Editors: What Grounded Theory is Not. Academy of Management Journal, 49(4), 633-642.

Svensson, G., & Wagner, B. (2010). Transformative business sustainability: Multi-layer model and network of e-footprint sources. *European Business Review*, *23*(4), 334–352. doi:10.1108/09555341111145735

Swani, K., Milne, G., & Brown, B. P. (2013). Spreading the word through Likes on Facebook: Evalutating the message strategy effectiveness of Fortune 500 companies. *Journal of Research in Interactive Marketing*, *7*(4), 269–294. doi:10.1108/JRIM-05-2013-0026

Tapscott, D., & Williams, A. D. (2006). *Wikinomics: How Mass Collaboration Changes Everything*. New York: Penguin.

Turner-Lee, N. (2010). The challenge of increasing civic engagement in the digital age. *Federal Communications Law Journal*, *63*(1), 19–32.

UN Habitat. (2014). *The World Urban Forum*. Retrieved 2 March, 2015, from http://wuf7.unhabitat.org/theworldurbanforum

Vitak, J., Zube, P., Smock, A., Carr, C. T., Ellison, N., & Lampe, C. (2011). It's complicated: Facebook users' political participation in the 2008 election. *Cyberpsychology, Behavior, and Social Networking*, *14*(3), 107–114. doi:10.1089/cyber.2009.0226 PMID:20649449

Vogel, R., Moulder, R., & Huggins, M. (2014). The extent of public participation. *Public Management*, *96*(2), 6–10.

Walther, J. B., & Jang, J. (2012). Communication processes in particapatory websites. *Computer-Mediated Communication*, *18*(1), 2–15. doi:10.1111/j.1083-6101.2012.01592.x

Waters, R. D., Burnett, E., Lamm, A., & Lucas, J. (2009). Engaging Stakeholders through Social Networking: How nonprofit organizations are using Facebook. *Public Relations Review*, *35*(2), 102–106. doi:10.1016/j.pubrev.2009.01.006

Wellman, B., Haase, A. Q., Witte, J., & Hampton, K. (2001). Does the Internet increase, decrease, or supplement social capital?: Social networks, participation, and community commitment. *The American Behavioral Scientist*, *45*(3), 436–455. doi:10.1177/00027640121957286

Willard, T. (2009). Social Networking and Governance for Sustainable Development. Winnipeg, Canada: International Institute for Sustainable Development (IISD).

Willems, L., & Alizadeh, T. (2015). Social Media for Public Involvement and Sustainability in International Planning and Development. *International Journal of E-Planning Research*, *4*(4), 1–17. doi:10.4018/ijepr.2015100101

This research was previously published in New Approaches, Methods, and Tools in Urban E-Planning; pages 310-342, copyright year 2018 by Engineering Science Reference (an imprint of IGI Global).

Chapter 2
Let´s Talk SMAC:
The Status of Business Today

Cathrine Linnes
Østfold University College, Norway

ABSTRACT

Social Mobile Analytics and Cloud – SMAC the new abbreviation that every business leader is thinking off. It is also part of everyone's lives these days. SMAC technologies are creating enormous opportunities across industries while the consumer willingly gives up personal information. Cloud technologies have made it possible to collect and store such large amounts of data. While each of these four technologies are able to enhance the business on its own, using these four technologies together as a stack has changed the way businesses are looking to maximize their customer base, enhance brand value and off course, increase company profit. For example, SMAC has forced businesses leaders to make analytics part of their marketing strategy and business operation as a whole.

INTRODUCTION

Social, mobile, analytics, and cloud (SMAC) is among the hottest developments in IT enterprise architecture. Its foremost goal is to get closer to the consumer by exploiting these four technologies (Shelton, 2013). There are three business units that are particularly suited for applying the principle of SMAC: business products, business processes, and business models (Chen et al., 2012). Use of all four SMAC principles to these business units goes beyond simply being competitive–these tools allow for a business to become a disruptive force in their respective market segment (Ackx, 2014).

Products become personalized through the application of social media (Dewan & Jena, 2014). When linked with a mobile platform, the architecture enables collection of who, what, where, when, and even why the product is being used - as opposed to the traditional transaction data normally available to non-SMAC products (i.e., who bought which product, from where and when as opposed to who used which product where, when, and why). The cloud is conceivably the most viable procedure through which to direct these types of data for further analytics. This analysis provides deeper insights that help steer the decisions of business leaders.

DOI: 10.4018/978-1-7998-9020-1.ch002

A product that is integrated with social, mobile, analytics, and cloud is also a product that provides a significantly improved customer experience that is more capable of self-service and is more in line with the times. Consumers expect a certain type of convenience and service therefore SMAC has gained such a position in business today. Business methods that are implemented in the cloud and on social platforms gain an efficiency with which it is hard to compete traditionally (Dewan & Jena, 2014). Social and cloud architecture enables the IT raw materials behind the process to be scaled out - that is, adding less expensive hardware, as opposed to scaling up, which means replacing hardware with larger, more high-priced specifications. This allows the business to outlay funds on an as-needed basis. The addition of mobile technologies facilitates collaboration and knowledge sharing from anywhere, anytime. Storing the data (and metadata) behind SMAC-enabled business processes facilitates an easier analysis that allows for data driven decision-making. Besides, a corporate method that is driven by SMAC is better situated to have its mundane tasks automated, and to be more agile and adaptable. Note that in this case, the customer to be closer to is in fact the employee. An enterprise can also base the model of an entire line of business on providing a SMAC technology infrastructure to others (Dewan & Jena, 2014). For example, a traditional software product can be reshaped and offered as a service product in the form of a platform. Interestingly, the best way to provide a SMAC infrastructure is through tools that are themselves SMAC-enabled. This will result in long term growth for the organization and reduce costs, streamline inefficiencies, and improve quality. In fact, even a divided industry can become unified and sustainable again through the utilization of these principles (Thecka, 2014). Ultimately, the SMAC places the small and medium enterprises at the same level with larger organizations.

The objective of this chapter is to provide an overview of SMAC. The importance of implementing SMAC in a business to remain competitive in the future will be emphasized. The different technologies will be introduced, and the benefits and opportunities of SMAC trends will be pointed out. The solution and recommendation, future research directions, and conclusion follow this section.

BACKGROUND

There has been a tremendous push from the U.S. government for schools, universities, businesses, and government agencies to focus on technology, innovation, and effective usage of data. In October 2014, former White House CIO Theresa Payton asked, "Will SMAC hit organizations in the face?" This question should be on the minds of any leader who handles data to meet the demands of his or her job, or for that sake any human being. SMAC is identified as the new set of building blocks for organizations looking ahead to take advantage of internal and external data resources. Theresa Payton warned that implementing SMAC is not a quick shift in mindset or simple investment of hardware and software. It takes time and effort to achieve each pillar of SMAC. Interestingly, the implementation boom of the chief data officer role in the past two years has correlated to how organizations listened to this question, realized they needed to react, and made the changes necessary to realize the benefits (Payton, 2014). One such organization that processes large amounts of data is the United States Government, and President Obama made this clear on June 17, 2014: at TechShop (TechShop is a vibrant, innovative community that provides access to instruction, tools, software and space to its members).

The federal government possesses incredible amounts of data ... Essentially, all the weather apps that you have on your phone are all based on data that the government collected. (Obama, 2014)

Less than a year later, the White House hired a professional to manage the amounts of data. Dr. DJ Patil was named the first "deputy chief technology officer for data policy and chief data scientist, making him the first-ever national data scientist" in February 2015 (Smith, 2015). Throughout the United States, organizations are also following the trend of creating chief data officer (CDO) roles. One such city is San Francisco, where Joy Bonaguro was named their first chief data officer in March 2014 (Shueh, 2014). On June 8, 2016 over 96 CDOs and senior level data leaders from North America gathered in Washington D.C.to examine the role of CDOs to better serve the American people and exploit the power of technology and innovation (Bowater, 2016).

Government: Social Application

Social media have provided a platform where the world can use a digital voice to share their concerns and opinions they have at will. Recent data supplied by the Pew Research Center show that the growth of social media has slowed down but the level of user engagement has increased (Duggan et al., 2015). Some interesting facts presented by Duggan et al. (2015) were 52% of online adults use two or more social media sites, 56% of adults older than 65 years of age use Facebook, 53% of adults 18-29 years of age use Instagram, 50% of those with a college degree use LinkedIn, and 42% of women use Pinterest. For instance, the city of San Francisco is concerned about data coming from social media and so are many other city and county officials as well as corporations. Goals set by the city of San Francisco consists of growing and broadening communication and engagement activities and provide mechanisms to elicit and track feedback and knowledge from data users (Bonaguro, 2015). The city of San Francisco currently monitors 33 Facebook accounts, 39 Twitter accounts, and 16 YouTube accounts (Carver, 2013). As one can see, this is quite a bit to keep track of. SMAC helps bring the government closer to its people; however, the use of social media sites requires monitoring and frequent response to be beneficial.

Government: Mobile Application

To detect whether a corporation or government is serious about mobile technologies, simply navigate to its website using a mobile web browser. When navigating to the national award- winning website Hawaii. gov, a web portal spearheaded by former State of Hawaii CIO Sonny Bhagowalia the user is presented with a page that is designed with responsive design in mind. In responsive layout, the page responds to changes in the browser size that go beyond the width scaling of a liquid layout, such as a normal desktop computer (Connolly & Hoar, 2015).

According to Meunier (2015), 82% of Google webmasters claim they use responsive design. However, Meunier states that the percentage fluctuates quite a bit when surveying various webmaster groups. When Meunier analyzed the top tier web sites only 11.8% of these sites used responsive web design. A similar study was conducted in 2013 by Brian Klais of Pure Oxygen Lab, who reported that only 11% of websites were responsive (Klais, 2013). Responsive sites are a must these days to remain competitive and retain users. They certainly give the user a better experience.

Government: Analytics Application

A privately traded company that might want to track its sales exclusively using analytics, the data found at DataSF are to be shared publicly for anyone who wishes to use them. The same goes for data found on other government websites. The Hawaii Open Data Initiative in conjunction with Socrata is a site used to share government data with its citizens. Burt Lum has been extremely active on the open data initiative in Hawaii, which has benefited the public tremendously. The open data initiative has led to many folks getting involved and it has resulted in new ways of presenting' data. An exciting result of DataSF is its Data Academy, the goal of which is to aid data analysts citywide explore, refine, and enhance their skills in data analysis and visualization (DataSF, n.d.). Courses within Data Academy cover everything from analysis, information design, mapping, data management, data visualization and data science. The offering is quite complete and it is certainly one of the better governmental sites. For citizens of San Francisco, links to courses provided by local educational institutions are available (DataSF, n.d.).

Government: Cloud Application

Socrata is the global leader in software solutions that are designed exclusively for digital government and supports the governments open data initiative (Empson, 2012). Socrata's cloud-based, Software as a Service (SaaS) solutions, supported by the Socrata Open Data Network and Socrata Partner Ecosystem, deliver unprecedented data-driven innovation and cost-savings for hundreds of public sector leaders and millions of their constituents around the globe (Socrata, 2016). Further, Socrata provides an astonishing 264 published datasets that are available to the public to use at will (Socrata, 2016). The government gives the public insight to what goes on at the local or federal level. Citizens can freely use the data, analyze it, and find new ways of displaying the data, and the government is embracing the partnership with the general public, who can assist the government in displaying its data. As an example, the former State of Hawaii CIO Sonny Bhagowalia and former Deputy Director at OMIT Randy Baldemor reached out to the author and her class of students at Hawaii Pacific University to build a prototype to help display State of Hawaii´s data stored in Socrata. This was a fabulous opportunity for the class to learn more about the government and its operations and to work closely with a great group of state people. The prototype was very well received and was showcased around the state to aid the open data initiative (Linnes et al., 2013). Sonny Bhagowalia and Randy Baldemor are true visionaries and leaders and they have done a tremendous job establishing a comprehensive framework and plan to transform government in Hawaii to improve business processes, modernize the information technology infrastructure and increase transparency and accountability. It has been an honor to collaborate with them both on various projects over last 4 years.

OVERVIEW AND IMPACT OF SMAC TECHNOLOGIES

The IT industry stands at the edge of the most significant revolution in 20 years since client-server architecture and web tier platforms. The merging of social, mobile, analytics and cloud has generated a substantial change in the value that enterprise applications can provide to businesses (Mohapatra, Parisa & Banerjee, 2014).

In January of 2014 it was reported that mobile devices accounted for 55% of the Internet usage in the United States; apps made up 47% of the Internet traffic, and the remaining 8% came from mobile browsers (O´Toole, 2014). Data show that 87% of millennials always have their smartphone by their side, day and night. In addition, 78% of millennials spend over 2 hours a day using their smartphones, while 68% of millennials consider their smartphone to be a personal device (Choen, 2015). According to Cisco (2014), the number of devices that are connected to IP networks will actually be three times bigger than the actual population by 2017. This exponential growth will pose new challenges for data centers, existing information infrastructures, and corporations. As such, within the SMAC area, IT departments will need to supply an infrastructure layer that is capable of dealing with vast amounts of data streaming as well as making informative and intelligent decisions. Gartner predicted that 10% of computers will be learning and not processing by 2017 (Cooney, 2013). Further, according to the National Association of Software and Services Companies (NASSCOM), an additional 10% will be spent on IT to deploy mobile solutions before 2020. This mobility market could be worth $140-150 billion on a worldwide basis (Lawton, 2015). To remain competitive, it is important that corporations incorporate SMAC.

Social

In June 2015, Facebook had an average of 968 million daily and 1.59 billion monthly active users (Facebook, 2015; SocialTimes, 2015). Other popular social networking tools are LinkedIn, Instagram, WhatsApp and Twitter. LinkedIn had 400 million members in 2015 compared to 37 million in 2009 (Statista, 2016b). There were 400 million active users on Instagram in 2015, up from 90 million in 2013 (Statistica, 2016d). WhatsApp is approaching 1 billion active users, up from 200 million in 2013 (Statistica, 2016f). Twitter has 320 million active users every month compared to 30 million in 2010. It is projected to have 111.6 million users by 2019, which will equal 40.7% of the U.S. population (Statistica, 2016e). Many of the social media sites allow cross-posting, which helps organizations and government agencies to reach unlimited numbers of individuals while still achieving one to one contact (Hendricks, 2013). The worldwide magnitude of social media is astonishing.

The broad usage of social media has altered and will continue to change businesses and governments, which are faced with new challenges in terms of reaching and interacting with customers to remain competitive (Rouse, 2014). Social media's exponential growth has not bypassed companies. Many have realized the growth potential for their businesses by paying Facebook to acquire detailed profiles of consumers, so they can then pinpoint likely customers for their products or services. This is common practice of other providers as well. Customer interaction used to mean giving a discount on a customer's birthday, now it means giving a discount on a friend's birthday with recommendations of what that friend would like based on his or her Facebook profile. It has transitioned from an intimate relationship to a borderline intrusive relationship; however, customers are more than willing to give up their privacy for the added perks, discounts, enjoyments and benefits of a personalized shopping experience (Surdak, 2014). Some consumers might not be aware of the trail of information they leave behind every time they visit a website or use a coupon at a store. These organizations are tracking information and running an experiment on us all.

In May 2015, an e-commerce vendor TOMS Shoes used Instagram to help meet its goal to donate a pair of shoes for every pair sold. The campaign resulted in the donation of 296,243 pairs of shoes. TOMS Shoes is active in giving back to the community and those in need (Martin, 2015; TOMS, 2016). A successful campaign that was launched through social media was the Share-a-Coke campaign in the United States. The campaign increased U.S. sales by 11% from prior years as a result of the endorsement from teens via Facebook, Instagram, Twitter, and Tumblr. Another effective campaign were Share Your Ears – with Make A Wish Foundation and Disney where each social media post unlocked a $5 donation from Disney to the Make a Wish Foundation (Gallegos, 2016). Of course there are many more. In cases where budget is limited, social media has the potential to bring marketing creativity to life (Fulgoni, 2015). It is almost impossible to run a business without social media.

On the contrary, consumers have become more empowered than ever. Social media gives consumers a global platform from which to share immediate reviews of experiences with companies and the rest of the world. It has been suggested that the speed at which reviews are posted following a negative experience can be measured in seconds. The social norm is for social media users to bare their souls on any and all issues, and they expect the same from the companies on which they spend their money. Companies must follow suit and bare their souls on social media, especially if they fail in the delivery of their services (Surdak, 2014). To better understand, if 10 people one respects all of a sudden follow the same Twitter account, one should not ignore the signs. Social media is so powerful and the influence people can have on a business is tremendous.

Moreover, large corporations have employees in place whose duty is to go through social data and find emerging clues and patterns and respond to accusations. Vendors like DataSift a leader in human intelligence are going through what people talk about, what they are interested in, what they are looking forward to, as well as identifying the basic family demographics of social network users (Hassell, 2015).

Mobile

The explosion of mobile computing can be evidenced by the 2.27 trillion text messages sent between Americans in 2012 alone. This resulted in mobile data traffic growth of more than 100% that same year, totaling 1.1 billion GB of data (Surdak, 2014). In 2015 people sent 8.3 billion text messages. This is approximately 23 billion messages per day (Teckst, 2015). These numbers support the statistics showing that smartphones connect to the Internet more often than computers do just because users carry their smart devices with them all time. These devices can do pretty much everything a computer can do; they just come with a smaller screen. Companies have realized the power of mobile devices and the potential for consumer personalization and convenience that these technologies can offer. For example, the savviest companies identify when the customer needs to only enter numbers into a form on their website. To accommodate this, a small numeric keypad will appear on the screen as opposed to the unnecessary QWERTY keypad. Mobile users appreciate this added touch.

Mobile computing has grown beyond mobile versions of websites to include applications. Companies allow customers to download their app, usually for free, so their customers have immediate access to the most pertinent company information and opportunities for purchasing and service. Repeat customers have the convenient option of clicking an icon (app) on their device as opposed to having to do a web search for the company website and navigating through countless webpages. In 2012 Apple announced that it had reached 25 billion app downloads, and this number is expected to reach 268.69 billion in 2017 (Statista, 2016c; Surdak, 2014). Moreover, there are 2 million available apps to choose from on the Apple app Store today, and the number of apps and downloads keeps increasing (Statista, 2016a). Such apps provide traveler and commuter services, point of sale, stock trading, emergency medical care, law enforcement, package delivery, education, and insurance (Helal, 2002). For example, FedEx, USPS, and UPS utilize mobile computing to send updates on package tracking, banks send fraud alerts or account balance updates, and hospitals send appointment reminders through text messaging or app notifications.

Nearly 90% of the Facebook users and approximately 80% of the Twitter users are using mobile devices to generate news. According to Rouse (2014), a competitive advantage arises only due to the fact, that all four technologies are used jointly but the mobile trend is more than cellphones connected to the Internet. There are also many technologies such as different kinds of sensors, that are used in mobile devices. Radio-frequency identification (RFID) tags can be attached to cash, clothing, and possessions, or implanted in human beings and pets, and the possibility of reading personally linked information without consent has started to raise serious privacy concerns. Another example is driverless cars or electric vehicles like Tesla, which are able to create more data (e.g. speed, acceleration) in addition to location information. Therefore, continued increasing number of devices will create more data, and that in turn will lead to automatic data exploitation.

Mobile devices make it faster and easier to connect with anyone at any time; they are designed to foster social interactions (PricewaterhouseCoopers, hereafter PwC, 2015). Mobile devices are the cornerstone of how new business is being built. With them, users continue with their personal or business interactions by connecting to various wireless signals and near-field communication (NFC) devices (Hassell, 2015). The spread of affordable 3G, 4G, 4G LTE, and the upcoming 5G networks is driving the growth of mobile apps, and the industry is shifting from the PC/laptop to mobile devices. There are 4.61 billion mobile subscribers globally, with a projection of 5.07 billion subscribers in 2019 (Statista, 2016). Each generation is supposedly faster, more secure, and more reliable. The reliability factor is of course the hardest obstacle to overcome.

Analytics

Social analytics is defined as the process of collecting, measuring, analyzing and interpreting the results of interactions and associations among people topics and ideas. Social analytics is viewed as an umbrella term that includes a number of specialized analysis techniques, such as social filtering, social network analysis, social channel analysis, sentiment analysis and social media analytics (Rozwell, Sallam & Sussin, 2013). The prevalence of social media creates an enormous amount of unstructured data, or data that are not organized in a pre-defined manner. Social media analytics is the mechanism by which such data are analyzed. The results of these analyses often show an underlined relationship between entities. These relationships are normally unnoticed or unseen by the naked eye. As a communal form social media is often public facing.

Social media moves quicker than the speed of business, and it is the number one item on any CEO´s list. An overall strategy must be applied that brings both value and purpose. For example, an Indian food manufacturer leveraged social analytics to identify its brand and product shortcomings in order to make brand and product improvements. By making changes and improvements based upon this insight, the company was able to decrease negative comments by 42% (Sussin, Rozwell & Sallam, 2015). This strategy improved the overall reception of the product, which resulted in a financial windfall. At the minimum this process was able to divert potential loss of sales. More importantly, it improved upon something, that could not be bought: the reputation of the company.

In 2015, more than 30% of analytics projects will deliver insights based on structured and unstructured data (Rozwell, Sallam, & Sussin, 2013). Social media is the clear leader of unstructured data. Whether from a desktop, laptop, tablet, or mobile phone, data are input into social media. The unstructured data arrive in the form of comments, blogs, tweets, or instant messages. This is a bidirectional communication between creators and consumers. Creators are able to reach an abundance of potential clients while consumers are able to voice their opinions and make more informed decisions (Leskovec, 2011). Ultimately, social media analytics will be used as a tool to augment decision-making. The costs of these tools fluctuates. In a recent study it was suggested that the financial responsibility of running social media analytics would begin at $18,000 a year and could exceed six-figures per year (Sussin, Rozwell & Sallam, 2013). Not everyone who does social media analytics has such an expansive budget. There are alternatives that are significantly cheaper or even free. The open source alternatives are robust; however, there is the old adages that you get what you pay for. Buyers beware.

Analytics is the discovery and communication of meaningful patterns in data. These enable organizations to mine public, organizational, and workforce data to generate insights and enable better, faster decision-making and new ways of doing business (PwC, 2015). Billions of gigabytes of data are generated by companies and individuals each year. Companies that analyze and gain insights from such data can emerge as leaders (KPMG, 2013). In fact, 93% of United States executives believe their companies are losing revenue by not leveraging available data (Neistat, 2013). Companies cannot just collect and store information; they must do something with the data to remain in power.

In 2013, organizations worldwide spent $31 billion on Big Data, and the spending is predicted to reach $114 billion in 2018 (Capgemini Consulting, 2014). Analytics can assist companies to understand how people interact with other people, goods, and media. The online blogging service Twitter was launched in 2006. Users can follow other users to become subscribers. Status updates also known as tweets are posted, and followers can read these posts. According to Asur and Huberman (2010), social media data can be used to predict events. The two researchers conducted an interesting study where they analyzed 2.89 million tweets (status posts) from 1.2 million Twitter users and extracted keywords for 24 block buster movies. They showed that a movie with a small average rate of tweets per hour (e.g., 10) will be pulled from theatres in a few weeks. On the other hand, a movie will trigger an enormous splash if it has a large rate of tweets per hour (e.g., over 1000). More precisely, they showed that rate of tweets could be used to predict box office sales of movies with a high accuracy (Liu, 2014). Therefore, user data created with social networks, such as Twitter can be used to predict movie revenue. These are extremely powerful tools that should not be ignored. Network analysis is also powerful in preventing crime and predicting election results.

Cloud

Companies such as Google, Amazon, Microsoft, and FDC Servers saw the business potential in buying server space and reselling it to small and medium-sized companies as cloud services. Take for example FDC Servers, which currently has 13 data centers, over 10,000 customers, and 10 Tbps Internet backbone, and reports 99.995% reliability (FDC Servers, 2016). This brings flexibility, cost effectiveness, and efficiency to businesses purchasing the company's services. Company leaders will then be able to focus on what they are good at and will not necessary need to become IT experts. If a company was just starting out, instead of spending millions on hardware, software, brick-and-mortar storefronts, and IT personnel, it could simply purchase cloud space for thousands of dollars and test its business plan and growth potential on the Internet. In 2013, the annual data center traffic amounted to approximately 3.1 zettabytes (1 zettabyte is equal to 1 billion terabytes), and it will increase to 8.6 zettabytes by the end of 2018 (CISCO, 2014). The rise is caused by new technologies; such as cloud services. Famous applications, such as Google Drive, Amazon Cloud Drive, Dropbox, and iCloud are used in everyday life to share files and provide easy access to the user. There are different reasons why cloud services are becoming more and more important. A compound annual growth rate (CAGR) of 32% was expected for global cloud traffic from 2013 to 2018, according to a technical report of CISCO. Further, in 2015, around 1.387 billion people were expected to use personal cloud storage, and this number was expected to increase to around 2 billion users by 2018 (CISCO, 2014).

Cloud computing offers the flexibility to tailor a company's data needs based on its number of users or take it a step further by adjusting to peak shopping seasons (Surdak, 2014). This pay- per-use framework cuts costs and demands fewer personnel to manage servers. Since cloud space is considered a rental space, creating no asset, it is referred to as an operational expenditure. In other words, it can be subtracted from profits. Additional benefits of cloud computing are abundant. Companies can access applications anywhere on any device, receive software and platform upgrades from the service provider, outsource the headache of IT, increase employee collaboration on projects through the use of Dropbox, iCloud and Google Drive. It is even suggested that cloud computing has lent to an increase in telecommuting and subsequently a reduction in travel and environmental impact, as suggested by the fact that 8% of the UK workforce worked from home in 2005 (William, 2010). The company itself cannot compete with cloud providers, companies like Amazon or FDC Servers mentioned above can customize a new server in no time and they provide excellent security monitoring services.

Abhishek Mehta, a digital marketing evangelist for Google, called today's extremely fast- paced and competitive technology industry the next industrial revolution in suggested that the massive amount of data circulating the digital world will replace raw materials, and that manufacturing factories will be swapped for data factories (Minelli et al., 2013). Then, it will become an absolute necessity for companies to utilize the modern raw material, data, to gain a competitive advantage in today's business environment. According to a study published on cloudcomputing-news.net, as of 2015, 89% of the Fortune 500 companies had changed since 1955. The Fortune 500 list is now increasingly being replaced by the Digital 500 companies. Needless to say, the general public could make a good guess which companies lead this list. By July 2015, Google, Facebook, Amazon, Apple, and Netflix were among the six companies that produced more than half of the NASDAQ market that accounts to $664 billion (Moyse, 2015). These companies are also companies that are responsible for generating the massive amount of data we see today. Netflix alone has reached 81 million subscribers, and 42% of its customer base is outside of the United States (Popper, 2016).

One study found that 89% of the business leaders were convinced that Big Data would have a revolutionary impact on business processes. In this study, 83% of the companies had implemented Big Data projects to earn a competitive advantage in their industries. In addition, Wikibon forecast tells us that by 2025, the global Big Data market will reach $122 billion in revenue (Moyse, 2015). It is important to note that the explosion of Big Data was made possible by the advent of cloud computing. As both technologies continue to grow, more and more people will understand the power of cloud computing. According to a survey by Forbes.com in 2015, 93% of the surveyed organizations were using cloud applications or experimenting with it. The enterprises with a hybrid cloud strategy in 2015 increased by nearly 10% from the previous year, from 74% to 82%. Also, 88% of the organizations were utilizing the public cloud, whereas 63% were utilizing a private cloud (Kepes, 2015).

Certain organizations say that cloud storage is proving to be more flexible and efficient for storing and accessing Big Data (Yasuhiro, 2012). In addition, all scientists are encouraged to place their data on the cloud for easy access, and the Big Query by Google offers the simplicity to make it possible (Dobre & Xhafa, 2014). According to Chandran, Cloud storage is a smart answer to the challenge facing Big Data in terms of efficiency, scalability, and cost as well as providing reliability and concurrent access. Consequently, many CEOs are putting effort into identifying the types of data and workloads transferrable to the cloud as they realize their potential insights (Chandran, 2015). This is backed up by the belief of some of the big players in the industry that the return on investment is great in embracing the cloud (Minelli et al., 2013). Another advantage is that users do not have to estimate the hardware capacity or resources for the future because the cloud structure easily scales up or down, when the need changes. Hassan (2011) also pointed out, that cloud services allow companies to better respond to market fluctuations. The opportunity for large-scale parallel processing appeared with the emergence of cloud computing. This is useful for complex computations or time-consuming tasks. A cloud service provider has one or more data centers that can be accessed by users. Only a credit card is needed to get on-demand access to 100,000+ computers distributed throughout the world (Foster et al., 2008). A similar improvement in speed and agility for organizations was pointed out by Amazon Web Services (2016). The time that is, needed to build new infrastructure for data center or to extend it decreased to just a few hours or minutes. In fact, it is only a few clicks away, and users can access it anytime.

There are also several drawbacks that are inevitable with the extensive use of Big Data and cloud services. High-speed Internet connections are necessary for cloud computing, especially when enormous data sets are used. The downtime problem of servers is another challenge. No cloud service provider claims to have permanent uptime. Apple's iCloud service suffered a seven-hour outage in June 2015, which, in turn, affected 11 of the company´s cloud-based services. Approximately 40% of all iCloud users were unable to use the service at that time (Kobialka, 2015). Regarding security, when we deal with data, especially when it is stored centrally on cloud servers, users should keep in mind that all information is accessible from anywhere on the Internet. Computer hackers can get access to every text-message and to phone calls of users, and they can steal sensitive data, such as credit card information, and use it to make money. An even simpler way to hack in is through user passwords to access the cloud, a specific computer software or just a cell phone. According to Cloud Security (2012), passwords such as, "123456" or "password" are very common. Okyle (2015) also mentioned, that 3 out of 4 consumers use duplicate passwords, and many of them have not changed their passwords for 5 or even 10 years. With this knowledge, many users can improve security easily. Cloud computing has an immense potential and can change Internet and user habits. We should be aware, that security and privacy issues should be taken into account, especially when sensitive data are used. The increasing demand of cloud services can also improve security standards. Overall, this summary has shown that advantages are able to outweigh the disadvantages.

SOLUTIONS AND RECOMMENDATIONS

The integration of SMAC requires businesses and governments to create clear policies and guidelines for its organization to be successful. Furthermore, management tools that can automate the business process need to be in place. Organizations need to ask several questions before implementing any social media technologies into their operations.

First, what is the purpose of the social media account, and what is the organization trying to accomplish? Is the purpose aligned with the company goals? It is very important that the social media accounts are aligned with the business´s goals. They need to be part of trying to drive the business in a certain direction. For example, it is important to use some time to try to find a proper username when setting up a Twitter account.

Second, who will be responsible for the account? If organizations have a Twitter account, it is important that they post something every day. You see many organizational leaders who create an account and then it is forget about it. Also, when you have a Facebook account, it is important to monitor the conversation. If customers are complaining about the service or products, try to rectify the situation and show them that you care.

Third, it is also important to decide what type of information should be posted. This will help the employees to focus on the strategic plan of the business. Having a communication plan in place might be a good idea, and if the organization is planning to be collecting feedback, strategize around this.

Forth, how will organizations secure their social media account online? This is public face of the organization, so important measures need to be in place.

Netflix is a great example of a corporation that has empowered SMAC. Customers can either log in with their username and password or opt to use their Facebook credentials to begin streaming a movie. It might be convenient but they are of course giving away some privacy. On the website itself, customers can provide social feedback by rating the movie they just watched. Customers may also write a review or share what they have watched with friends on Facebook or Twitter. Netflix stores this information in the cloud, which allows the company to analyze its customers in detail and provide one-on-one marketing. This should be the ultimate goal of every organization.

FUTURE RESEARCH DIRECTIONS

Gartner, Inc. forecasts that 6.4 billion connected things will be in use worldwide in 2016, up 30% from 2015, and number will reach 20.8 billion by 2020. It is estimated that in 2016, 5.5 million new things will get connected every day (Gartner, 2015b). All of these sensors and devices are producing an enormous amount of data and this is commonly referred to as the Internet of Things (IoT). McKinsey & Company (2015) estimated a potential economic impact of as much as $11.1 trillion per year in 2025 for IoT applications. As IoT continues to evolve, it will lead to more robust data analytics.

An opportunity for the analysis of Big Data in a variety of applications is predictive maintenance. Previously, sensors were used to build and run a machine, and that changed the manufacturing process from manual to automatic production. But manufacturers of wearables, computers, equipment, or clothing can improve the efficiency of their machines even more. According to McKinsey & Company (2015), manufacturers that implement analytic software in their daily operations as well as sensors can reduce downtime by 50%. Real-time monitoring of equipment, such as with sensors or other parts of a machine, can help to reduce downtime before the quality of products diminishes. The result is, that a technical service will not only depend on technicians (implying their skills to observe damages) or maintenance plans (which can be imperfect). This can change the maintenance model from repair and replace to predict and prevent (McKinsey & Company, 2015).

Another trend that one can see is analytics being used in the health care industry. Once in a while patients die in the hospital because they get the wrong medication or the wrong diagnosis is put in place. According to the report "To Err Is Human: Building a Safer Health System," it is estimated that these preventable blunders cost between $17 billion and $29 billion (Institute of Medicine, 1999). In 2008 preventable medical errors were reported to cost 19.5 billion in the United States alone (Andel, Davidow, Hollander & Moreno, 2012). In 2014 a survey of health information technology (IT) leaders found that the U.S. healthcare system could save a total of $23.4 billion in 2016 by implementing SMAC. This is a 11% saving from social media, 16% from mobile, 21% from analytics, and 20% from cloud (Deloitte, 2016). On can clearly see that monitoring of people's health can create a financial benefit to society and health providers. Technologies such as smart pills or nanobots could be available in the near future to reduce the errors. The previously mentioned devices can send information via wireless connections, accelerating medical findings. Unnecessary surgeries can be reduced or omitted. The result is a reduction of working hours and costs. According to Casado and Younas (2014), remote monitoring could create around $1.1 trillion a year in savings. In addition, when there is a drug shortage or when faced with counterfeit drugs, or perhaps misplaced equipment mobile analytics and cloud technologies can aid health providers to make their supply chains more data driven, efficient and secure (Deloitte, 2016).

Beside humans, one could also monitor other areas, such as cities, countries or the entire word for that sake. An important and fast-developing research topic is analytical chemistry (e.g., to monitor air pollution). It is reported that a 35% increase of emissions from human activities expressed as carbon dioxide equivalents from 1990 to 2010 totaled nearly 46 billion metric tons (United States Environmental Protection Agency, 2014). Moreover, other cities around the globe, such as Chinese megacities suffer (visible) smog, which also is caused by air pollution. This visible pollution also affects the Earth's climate, forcing governments to limit emissions of greenhouse gases. The Kyoto Protocol is an example of an international treaty to reduce these emissions worldwide. But a drawback is that major polluters- including China, India and the United States-"... will not ratify any treaty that will commit them legally to reduce CO_2 emissions" (United Nations, 2014). Environmental pollution is a major concern both today and in the future. Not only should governments be conscientious, but companies should try to reduce waste that causes pollution. In fact, every human being should have this goal, because we only have one planet to live on.

Some of the major trends in 2015 include advanced analytics, Big Data and the IoT. The Gartner (2015a) Hype Cycle for Emerging Technologies provides a cross-industry perspective on technologies and emerging trends for the future. Another realm, for example, is autonomous vehicles, which are an omnipresent technology in the car industry.

CONCLUSION

Cloud technology is a way to maximize the effectiveness of shared resources. Different types of cloud computing are available to users. There are public clouds, private cloud services, and a mix of both, namely hybrid clouds. An example is the Apache Hadoop product, which was invented for distributed processing and storage. The financial aspect, caused by higher economies of scale, is a main reason for the cloud's success. Therefore, wider ranges of companies are able to use Big Data analytics. According to Hardiman (2013), cloud computing is available for companies of all sizes. Moreover, users can make use of the parallel processing to accelerate computations and calculations. In fact, only a credit card is needed to get on-demand access to 100,000+ computers distributed throughout the world (Foster et al., 2008).

Security and privacy issues should be taken into account, especially when sensitive data are used. The main concern about the cloud can be, that it is easy for criminals to get a lot of information with little effort. When criminals get access to a data warehouse where all the user information is saved, it is much more efficient for them because they only access one data warehouse but get information from several cloud users. There are also risks companies might not think of when using cloud services. According to Hughes (2014), companies cannot see what measures cloud service providers use to secure their data.

Social media tools cover similar opportunities as mobile and cloud computing. Eventually, an increasing number of connected devices and likewise the demand of SMAC technologies can improve these security standards. Overall, the advantages of these tools outweigh the disadvantages. Cloud computing is a network-based service, served by virtual hardware that runs on one or more real machines. Virtual servers do not physically exist and can therefore be easily relocated and scaled up or down, potentially running in a private or public cloud. "The cloud" maximizes the effectiveness of shared resources and increases flexibility and agility in deploying and maintaining enterprise technology (PwC, 2015). Microsoft is using Hadoop in the cloud to make learning available for data scientists so they can filter through data and have the service itself suggest comparisons, predictions, and key points (Hassell, 2015). The positive feedback on SMAC are coming from CEOs and top-performing companies where 86% of US CEOs think that it is important that they themselves champion the use of digital technologies. They are tapping into social networks. In fact, 29% of top-performing companies gather ideas for technology innovation through employee idea marketplaces (PwC, 2015). There are also some less-than- positive effects. The enterprises that are making the most sustained progress with SMAC and a services-enabled future all have great training programs in place. According to Cognizant (2013), "We need to recognize that SMAC and emerging alternative IT delivery vehicles are like 'free puppies.' They are cheap and cute on the front end, but they require funding, health checks, care and support over time." Furthermore, only 13% of organizations have achieved full-scale production for their Big Data implementations, and 60% of senior executives believe that Big Data will disrupt their industry within the next three years (Capgemini Consulting, 2014). According to Deloitte (2016) 50% of IT and technology, 46% if tele-communications, 35% of entertainment, media, and publishing, 34% of automotive, 34 of professional service, 31% of transportation and tourism, but only 22% of education, 16% of government to mention a few sectors are claiming their company is digitally maturing. There is still room for improvements.

Though individuals are enjoying less energy consumption at their homes as they are shying away from PCs, and businesses are moving away from mainframes and towards the cloud, there is still a cost of such business. That cost goes to the huge data centers that provide the source for cloud computing and Big Data collection. According to Berl et al., (2010) Amazon.com reported that expenses related to the cost and operation of its servers account for 53% of the total budget, while energy-related costs amount to 42% of the total. Given the increase in cloud computing, today massive facilities are needed to house servers. Some of these facilities are the size of warehouses, consuming large amounts of energy, and use diesel generators. As a result, major data centers not only consume large amounts of energy but also now emit significant amounts of greenhouse gases. In 2012, Apple's carbon footprint was 30.9 million metric tons, while Facebook's carbon footprint was 384,000 thousand metric tons (Story, 2014). As much as we are saving energy in our homes and business, the carbon footprint is very high in the centralized data centers. CEO's must continue to prepare themselves for the abundance of information they can obtain through SMAC. Every enterprise will use at least one technology of SMAC, and the majority will strive to implement all four, something we can already appreciate. The bottom line is that the four SMAC technologies go hand in hand. SMAC technologies cannot be ignored by organizations. They have changed the way organizations must operate in years to come. IT does not matter whether a corporation is large or small; it is important that organizations pay attention to the upcoming changes and try to implement the technologies into their strategic plans.

REFERENCES

Ackx, S. (2014). Emerging Technologies, Disrupt or be Disrupted. In ISSE 2014 Securing Electronic Business Processes (pp. 177-187). Springer Fachmedien Wiesbaden.

Amazon Web Services. (2016). *What is Cloud Computing?* Retrieved January 31, 2016, from https://aws.amazon.com/what-is-cloud-computing/

Andel, C., Davidow, S. L., Hollander, M., & Moreno, D. A. (2012). The economics of health care quality and medical errors. *Journal of Health Care Finance, 39*(1), 39–50. PMID:23155743

Asur, S., & Huberman, B. A. (2010). *Predicting the future with social media.* HP Labs. Retrieved January 31, 2016, from http://www.hpl.hp.com/research/scl/papers/ socialmedia/socialmedia.pdf

Berl, A. (2010). *Energy-Efficient Cloud Computing.* Retrieved January 31, 2016 from: https://www.researchgate.net/publication/46116227_Energy-Efficient_Cloud_Computing

Bonaguro, J. (2015). *Data in San Francisco: Meeting supply, spurring demand* (FY2015-16). Retrieved January 31, 2016, from https://docs.google.com/document/d/1mqunsT9wXRt-mBbOmY3WcEJmsWSp-MOISotZ1WHZ1_IU/edit?usp=embed_facebook

Bowater, J. (2016). *Welcome to the Chief Data Officer Forum, Government.* Retrieved February 10, 2016, from http://www.chiefdataofficergovernment.com

Capgemini Consulting. (2014). *Cracking the Data Conundrum: How Successful Companies Make Big Data Operational.* Retrieved February 10, 2016, from http://www.datascienceassn.org/sites/default/files/Cracking%20the%20Data%20Conundrum%20-%20How%20Successful%20Companies%20Make%20Big%20Data%20Operational.pdf

Carver, S. (2013). *How the City of San Francisco uses Social Media to Connect with Citizens.* Retrieved February 10, 2016, from http://www.exacttarget.com/blog/how-the-city-of-san-francisco-uses-social-media/

Casado, R., & Younas, M. (2014). Emerging trends and technologies in big data processing. *Concurrency and Computation, 27*(8), 2078–2209. doi:10.1002/cpe.3398

Chen, H., Chiang, R. H., & Storey, V. C. (2012). Business Intelligence and Analytics: From Big Data to Big Impact. *Management Information Systems Quarterly, 36*(4), 1165–1188.

Choen, H. (2015). *2015 Mobile Marketing – 19 Research Charts.* Retrieved February 10, 2016, from http://heidicohen.com/2015-mobile-marketing/

CISCO. (2014). *Cisco Global Cloud Index: Forecast and Methodology, 2013–2018.* Retrieved February 10, 2016, from https://www.terena.org/mail-archives/storage/pdfVVqL9tLHLH.pdf

Cloud Security. (2012). *What security lessons can be learned from LinkedIn?* Retrieved February 10, 2016, from http://www.cloudcomputing-news.net/news/2012/jun/18/security-lessons-learned-from-linkedin/

Cognizant. (2013). Keep on Smacking: Taking Social, Mobile, Analytics and Cloud to the Bottom Line. *Cognizanti, 6*(1). Retrieved February 10, 2016, from: https://www.cognizant.com/InsightsWhitepapers/Cognizanti-Journal-XaaS-Code-Halos-SMAC-and-the-Future-of-Work.pdf

Connolly, R., & Hoar, R. (2015). *Fundamentals of Web Development.* Boston: Pearson. Retrieved March 5, 2016, from: https://scanlibs.com/fundamentals-of-web-development/

Cooney, M. (2013). *Gartner: Top 10 future strategic IT predictions.* Retrieved March 5, 2016, from http://www.networkworld.com/article/2225521/malware-cybercrime/gartner--top-10-future-strategic-it-predictions.html

Data, S. F. (n.d.). *About.* Retrieved March 5, 2016, from http://datasf.org/about/

Deloitte. (2016). *SMAC: Better together Improving health care efficiency with social, mobile, analytics, and cloud technologies.* Retrieved September 28, 2016, from https://www2.deloitte.com/content/dam/Deloitte/us/Documents/life-sciences-health-care/us-lshc-smac-better-together.pdf

Dewan, B., & Jena, S. R. (2014, December). The State-Of-The-Art of Social, Mobility, Analytics and Cloud Computing an Empirical Analysis. In *High Performance Computing and Applications (ICHPCA), 2014 International Conference on* (pp. 1-6). IEEE.

Duggan, M., Ellison, N. B., Lampe, C., Lenhart, A., & Madden, M. (2015). *Social Media Update 2014.* Retrieved March 5, 2016, from http://www.pewinternet.org/files/2015/01/PI_SocialMediaUpdate20144.pdf

Empson, R. (2012). *Clouds & APIs: Mayor Lee Unveils The San Francisco Open Data Cloud.* Retrieved March 5, 2016, from http://techcrunch.com/2012/03/09/san-francisco-open-data/

Facebook. (2015). *Our Mission.* Retrieved March 5, 2016, from http://newsroom.fb.com/company-info/

FDC Servers. (2016). *The Bandwidth Authority.* Retrieved September 27, 2016, from https://fdcservers.net

Foster, I., Zhao, Y., Raicu, I., & Lu, S. (2008). *Cloud Computing and Grid Computing 360-Degree Compared.* Retrieved March 5, 2016, from https://arxiv.org/pdf/0901.0131.pdf

Fulgoni, G. M. (2015). How Brands Using Social Media Ignite Marketing and Drive Growth. *Journal of Advertising Research*, 235–236.

Gallegos, J. A. (2016, April). *The Best Social Media Campaigns of 2016.* Retrieved September 28, 2016, from http://www.tintup.com/blog/the-best-social-media-campaigns-of-2016-so-far/

Gartner. (2015a). *Gartner's 2015 Hype Cycle for Emerging Technologies Identifies the Computing Innovations That Organizations Should Monitor.* Retrieved March 5, 2016 from http://www.gartner.com/newsroom/id/3114217

Gartner. (2015b). *Gartner Says 6.4 Billion Connected "Things" Will Be in Use in 2016, Up 30 Percent From 2015.* Retrieved March 5, 2016 from http://www.gartner.com/newsroom/ id/3165317

Hardiman, N. (2013). *Cloud computing and the rise of big data.* Retrieved March 5, 2016, from http://www.techrepublic.com/blog/the-enterprise-cloud/cloud-computing-and-the-rise-of-big-data/

Hassan, Q. F. (2011). *Demystifying cloud computing.* Retrieved March 5, 2016, from http://static1.1.sqspcdn.com/static/f/702523/10181434/1294788395300/201101-Hassan.pdf

Hassell, J. (2015, May 4). *Talking SMAC: Revisiting social, mobile, analytics and cloud.* Retrieved September 26, 2016 from http://www.cio.com/article/2918194/cloud-computing/taking-smac-revisiting-social-mobile-analytics-and-cloud.html

Helal, A. (2002). *Anytime, Anywhere Computing: Mobile Computing Concepts and Technology*. New York, NY: The Springer International Series in Engineering and Computer Science.

Hendricks, D. (2013). *Complete History of Social Media: Then and Now*. Retrieved March 5, 2016, from http://smallbiztrends.com/2013/05/the-complete-history-of-social-media-infographic.html

Hughes, J. (2014). *Data breaches in the cloud: Who's responsible?* Retrieved March 5, 2016, from http://www.govtech.com/security/Data-Breaches-in-the-Cloud-Whos-Responsible.html

Institute of Medicine. (1999). *To err is human: Building a safer health system*. Retrieved March 5, 2016, from https://www.nationalacademies.org/hmd/~/media/ Files/Report% 20Files/ 1999/To-Err-is Human/ To%20Err%20is%20Human%201999%20% 20report%20brief.pdf

Kepes, B. (2015). *New Stats from the State of Cloud Report*. Retrieved March 5, 2016, from http://www.forbes.com/sites/benkepes/2015/03/04/new-stats-from-the-state-of-cloud-report/

Klais, B. (2013, June). *Research: Two-Thirds of the Fortune 100 are not Mobile-Optimized for Google*. Retrieved September 26, 2016, from http://pureoxygenlabs.com/research-two-thirds-of-the-fortune-100-are-not-mobile-optimized-for-google/

Kobialka, D. (2015). *7 Worst Cloud Outages of 2015 (So Far)*. Retrieved March 5, 2016, from http://talk-incloud.com/cloud-computing/06172015/7-worst-cloud-outages-2015-so-far#slide-0-field_images-46431

KPMG. (2013). *The SMAC Code Embracing new technologies for future business*. Retrieved April 10, 2016, from https://www.kpmg.com/IN/en/IssuesAndInsights/ ArticlesPublications/ Documents/The-SMAC-code-Embracing-new-technologies-for-future-business.pdf

Lawton, R. (2015). *SMAC – Social, Mobile, Analytics, Cloud: A Guide*. Retrieved March 20, 2016, from http://www.arrkgroup.com/thought-leadership/smac-social-mobile-analytics-cloud-a-guide/

Leskovec, J. (2011). *Social Media Analytics: Tracking, Modeling and Predicting the Flow of Information through Networks*. Retrieved March 10, 2016, from https://pdfs.semanticscholar.org/7ec6/c63dc0b-12cb7e00122ffe08daf1cbd28cba9.pdf

Linnes, C., Viwatmanitsakul, B., Ladegaard, M., Cheng, F., Alamran, S., & Befus, N. ... Tabor, R. (2013). *Welcome to Open Data for Hawaii*. Retrieved March 10, 2016, from http://data.hpu.edu/index.html

Liu, H. (2014). *How to Mine Social Media*. Retrieved March 10, 2016, from http://theinstitute.ieee.org/ieee-roundup/members/achievements/how-to-mine-social-media

Martin, J. A. (2015). *11 most memorable social media marketing successes of 2015*. Retrieved March 10, 2016 from http://www.cio.com/article/2988313/social-networking/11-most-memorable- social-media-marketing-successes-of-2015.html#slide4

McKinsey & Company. (2015). *The Internet of Things: Mapping the Value Beyond the Hype (Tech. Rep.)*. Mc Kinsey Global Institute.

Meunier, B. (2015, January). *82% Of Sites Use Responsive Web Design In 2015? Try 11.8%?* Retrieved September 26, 2016 from http://marketingland.com/82-sites-use-responsive-web-design-2015-try-11-8-114050

Minelli, M., Chambers, M., & Dhiraj, A. (2013). *Big Data Technology. Big Data, Big Analytics: Emerging Business Intelligence and Analytic Trends for Today's Businesses*. Hoboken, NJ: John Wiley & Sons. doi:10.1002/9781118562260

Mohapatra, B., Parisa, V., & Banerjce, J. (2014). *The Value of Big Data Analytics to the Business* (Vol. 5). ISACA Journal.

Moyse, I. (2015). *Big data, Cloud, Mobility, and Why IT Needs to Move at the Speed of Business*. Retrieved March 15, 2016, from http://www.cloudcomputing-news.net/news/2015/aug/25/big-data-cloud-mobility-and-why-it-needs-move-speed-business

Neistat, M. (2013). *What is the 3rd Platform and How Will It Affect Business?* Retrieved March 15, 2016, from https://technologyfirst.org/magazine-articles/124-may-2013/843-mark-neistat-us-signal-company.html

O'Toole, J. (2014). *Mobile apps overtake PC Internet usage in U.S.* Retrieved March 5, 2016, from http://money.cnn.com/2014/02/28/technology/mobile/mobile-apps-internet/

Obama, B. (2014). *Remarks by the President in Q&A with TechShop Workers*. Presented at the Address at TechShop, Pittsburgh, PA. Retrieved March 11, 2016, from https://www.whitehouse.gov/the-press-office/2014/06/17/remarks-president-qa-techshop-workers

Okyle, C. (2015). *Password statistics: The bad, the worse and the ugly (infographic)*. Retrieved March 11, 2016, from http://www.entrepreneur.com/article/246902

Payton, T. (2014). *Will SMAC Hit You in the Face?* Retrieved March, 15, 2016, from http://www.fortalicesolutions.com/blog/2014/10/27/will-smac-hit-you-in-the-face/

Popper, B. (2016, April). *Netflix passes 81 million subscribers, but predicts slower growth ahead*. Retrieved September 27, 2016, from http://www.theverge.com/2016/4/18/11454362/netflix-q1-2016-earnings-81-million-subscribers

PricewaterhouseCoopers. (2015). *The connected workforce is talking SMAC. Are you ready?* Retrieved March 10, 2016, from: https://www.pwc.com/us/en/people-management/publications/assets/connected-workforce.pdf

Rouse, M. (2014). *SMAC (social, mobile, analytics and cloud) definition*. Retrieved March 10, 2016, from http://searchcio.techtarget.com/definition/SMAC-social-mobile-analytics-and-cloud

Rozwell, C., Sallam, L, R., & Sussin, J. (2013, September 27). *Who's who in Social Analytics*. Gartner.

Shelton, T. (2013). Appendix: PwC thought leadership on social, mobile, analytics, cloud (SMAC). Business Models for the Social Mobile Cloud: Transform Your Business Using Social Media. In *Mobile Internet, and Cloud Computing*, (pp. 165-216). Retrieved March 10, 2016, from http://adnanalhashmi.weebly.com/uploads/2/3/7/6/23764062/business_models_for_the_social_mobile_cloud.pdf

Shueh, J. (2014). *San Francisco Announces Chief Data Officer Joy Bonaguro*. Retrieved February 5, 2016, from http://www.govtech.com/data/San-Francisco-Announces-Chief-Data-Officer-Joy-Bonaguro.html

Smith, M. (2015, February). *The White House Names Dr. DJ Patil as the First U.S. Chief Data Scientist*. Retrieved September 26, 2016, from https://www.whitehouse.gov/blog/2015/02/18/white-house-names-dr-dj-patil-first-us-chief-data-scientist

SocialTimes. (2016). *Here's How Many People Are on Facebook, Instagram, Twitter and Other Big Social Networks*. Retrieved September 5, 2016 from http://www.adweek.com/socialtimes/heres-how-many-people-are-on-facebook-instagram-twitter-other-big-social-networks/637205

Socrata. (2016). *Unleashing the Power of Government Data to Improve Society*. Retrieved September 26, 2016, from http://www.socrata.com/company-info/

Statista. (2016a). *Number of apps available in the leading App stores as of June 2016*. Retrieved September 26, 2016, from https://www.statista.com/statistics/276623/number-of-apps-available-in-leading-app-stores/

Statista. (2016b). *Numbers of LinkedIn members from 1st quarter 2009 to 2nd quarter 2016 (in millions)*. Retrieved 26 September 2016 from, https://www.statista.com/ statistics/ 274050/ quarterly-numbers-of-linkedin-members/

Statista. (2016c). *Number of mobile app downloads worldwide from 2009 to 2017 (in millions)*. Retrieved September 26, 2016, from https://www.statista.com/statistics/266488/forecast-of-mobile-app-downloads/

Statista. (2016d). *Number of monthly active Instagram users from January 2013 to June 2016 (in millions)*. Retrieved September 26, 2016 from, https://www.statista.com/statistics/ 253577/number-of-monthly-active-instagram-users/

Statista. (2016e). *Number of monthly active Twitter users worldwide from 1st quarter 2010 to 2nd quarter 2016 (in millions)*. Retrieved 26 September, 2016 from https://www.statista.com/statistics/282087/number-of-monthly-active-twitter-users/

Statista. (2016f). *Number of monthly active WhatsApp users worldwide from April 2013 to February 2016 (in millions)*. Retrieved 26 September, 2016 from https://www.statista.com/ statistics/260819/number-of-monthly-active-whatsapp-users/

Surdak, C. (2014). *Data Crush: How the Information Tidal Wave Is Driving New Business Opportunities*. New York: AMACOM.

Sussin, J., Rozwell, C., & Sallam, L, R. (2015, March 12). *Technology Overview for Social Analytics Applications*. Gartner.

Teckst. (2015). *19 Texg Messaging Stats That Will Blow Your Mind*. Retrieved September 25, 2016, from https://teckst.com/19-text-messaging-stats-that-will-blow-your-mind/

Thecka, S. (2014, May). Transforming fragmented industry into sustainable businesses with SMAC technologies. In *IST-Africa Conference Proceedings* (pp. 1-9). IEEE. 10.1109/ISTAFRICA.2014.6880615

Toms Shoes. (2016). *About TOMS*. Retrieved September 27, 2016, from http://www.toms.com/about-toms#companyInfo

United Nations. (2014). *Status of Ratifications of the Kyoto Protocol*. Retrieved September 25, 2016, from http://unfccc.int/kyoto_protocol/status_of_ratification/items/2613.php

United States Environmental Protection Agency. (2014). *Climate Change Indicators in the United States*. Retrieved September 25, 2016, from: https://www3.epa.gov/climatechange/ pdfs/climateindicators-full-2014.pdf

William, M. (2010). *A Quick Start Guide to Cloud Computing: Moving Your Business Into the Cloud. New Tools for Business*. London: Kogan Page.

Yasuhiro, T. (2012). Tiering and Prioritizing Big Storage -In-House and in the Cloud. *Document News, 30*(1), 2–4.

KEY TERMS AND DEFINITIONS

Carbon Footprint: The amount of carbon dioxide and other carbon compounds emitted due to the consumption of fossil fuels by a particular person, group, etc.

CO2 Emission: Carbon dioxide (CO_2) is a colorless, odorless and non-poisonous gas formed by combustion of carbon and in the respiration of living organisms and is considered a greenhouse gas. Emissions means the release of greenhouse gases and/or their precursors into the atmosphere over a specified area and period of time.

Data Warehouse: An electronic storage that holds large amounts of information for a business.

Internet of Things: (IoT) A computing concept that describes how everyday physical objects will be connected to the Internet and be able to identify themselves to other devices.

Mobile Platform: A mobile platform is also described as an operating system. Example mobile platforms are Windows, BlackBerry, and OS X.

SaaS: A software distribution model where applications are hosted by a vendor or service provider and made available to customers over the Internet.

SMAC: Social, mobile, analytics and cloud is the concept that four technologies are currently changing business.

Socrata: A cloud-based solution, where government and organizations can put their data online for the public to see and use.

Chapter 3
Social Media as a Communication Channel

Yigit Yurder
Istanbul University, Turkey

Buket Akdol
Istanbul University, Turkey

ABSTRACT

In digital world, people spend most of their time on social media. Social media has gone beyond being just an online communication platform. It has become a channel that users prefer to other online platforms, such as websites, blogs, forums to get information about various businesses, events, and individuals. With Industry 4.0, all devices are connected to online platform, smart devices get more place in daily life. Instead of accessing information through individual applications, consumers prefer to obtain information from the company's social media pages and/or the company's internal and external customers' shared content. The purpose of the chapter is to indicate the importance of social media use, for organizations to interact effectively with all stakeholders, and to explain the benefits of social media usage of organizations in terms of different functions with examples from best cases and results of empirical researches.

INTRODUCTION

Today, the use of social media for organizations is no longer an option. With Industry 4.0, companies are trying to take advantage of information technologies to maximize profitability and productivity. Besides this, use of social media has increased in recent years and that made companies to show their presence on social media platforms. Social media is becoming a major source of excessive information for companies (Yilmaz et al.,2017).

Social media is also an effective tool of communication to establish social interaction within the organization and to maintain relations with outside parties. Communicating through both internal and external social media platforms has many benefits such as competitive advantage, corporate reputation and positive job attitudes.

DOI: 10.4018/978-1-7998-9020-1.ch003

The mobile devices and social media are part of Industry 4.0 since the manufacturing environment is leading to real-time transparency, which will make production control, and management processes more flexible (Bauer et al., 2015). Although this "digital transformation" might seem challenging for the companies, many companies have already started their change process since they developed interactive websites, improved customer service.(Berman, 2012). However, big companies use mobile analytics and social media to change customer loyalty, internal communication and even their business models (Westerman and McAfee, 2012).

In this chapter the concepts of social media, social media marketing and enterprise social media are defined, the benefits and importance of social media usage for organization are indicated and, the role of social media as a communication channel for 21st century organizations are explained via cases and findings of empirical researches.

BACKGROUND

In the basic sense, social media is defined as any web site including user-generated content. Such as social networking sites (Facebook, Myspace), creative works sharing sites (Youtube, Instagram, Soundcloud), business networking sites (Linkedin), collaborative websites (Wikipedia), e-commerce communities (Ebay, Amazon), podcasts and open source software communities (Linux, R), social media can take many forms. In all these forms of social media, individuals can share their own content and make comments on other individuals' contents. Establishment of social networking sites such as Myspace and Facebook has changed the concept of "Social media" and made a contribution to importance it has today (Kaplan and Haenlein, 2010).

There are many reasons of using social media sites. Smith and Kidder indicated most cited two reasons of social media usage as: a sense of community and a sense of identity. According to Social Capital Theory people can benefit from strong and weak connections with others. Creating and extending a user's community, a network of relationships, provide common shared values and norms. In terms of business world such networks could help individuals to meet influential people and to find job connections (Smith & Kidder, 2010: 492). According to Social Identity Theory, at the growing stages people need to explore and expose their social identity. Also a positive sense of identity is important for self-esteem. It provides a feeling of belonging to a larger group. Especially for young people social media makes it possible to introduce an identity by posting photos, blogging, listing hobbies, sharing common interest with the community they want to belong (Smith & Kidder, 2010: 492). According to Zhao et al (2008) Facebook users check their profile to see their hoped-for possible selves. According to Liu (2007) there are two types of identities: the differentiation profiles and the self-enhancing profiles. The differentiation profiles represent people who want to be unique and different from others. On the other side the self-enhancing profiles, which are majority, represent people who want to be popular and similar to others.

The development of social media completely changed the way companies communicate with their employees and customers. There is a clear transition from traditional media channels to social media. Comparing these two media types, social media has two-way conversation, open system, brand and user generated contents. Also in social media, the most important actors are users and influencers, the language is informal and every user can involve actively. But in traditional media, one-way conversation is used like broadcasting your message to as many people as you could afford then sit and wait. In contrast to social media, there is professional content, formal language, passive involvement and the leading actors are celebrities.

Social media is increasingly integrated in organizational practices as a communication tool not only among customers but also among employees, shareholders, competitors, suppliers and consumers. In other words, social media is an important communication tool to develop effective interaction between the organization and all stakeholders. Jurgen et al (2016) indicated that primary stakeholders (e.g., customers, suppliers, creditors, employees) traditionally are perceived as more powerful and urgent groups than secondary stakeholders (e.g., the general public, communities, activist groups). This approach makes companies tend to consider more the concerns of primary stakeholders than the concerns of secondary stakeholders. But in digital era the asymmetry of influence between primary and secondary stakeholder groups tend to decrease. Today companies have social media as an effective tool to governance secondary stakeholders as slickly as primary stakeholders.

Researchers have indicated that there are several significant changes to organizational practice as a result of increasing usage of social media. Some of these changes are listed below (Haefliger et al., 2011; Hu & Winstad, 2008; Von Krogh, 2012, Smith & Kidder, 2010):

- Managers could benefit from the cost advantages of social media and personalization of the target group at the social media in order to lead and influence online communities that the organizations have engaged in.
- The competitive advantage and the structure of organizations are more challenged and varied since stakeholder interaction and especially consumer interaction is adjusted to social media. From this perspective social media could be interpreted as a strategic tool, which mediates the relationship between organization and stakeholders.
- Communication among internal and external stakeholders via social media may facilitate appropriate creation of value.
- Firms want to increase sales by using agents on social networks for viral marketing, brand communities, ads in social networks that can direct the consumers' online shopping sites even ads that allow the customers to shop inside social networks. According to Business Insider Social Commerce 2017 Report, social media is becoming rapidly the most influential tool in consumers' purchase decisions .
- More and more organization are utilizing social media as an innovative recruitment tool or a talent pool rather than announcing the vacant positions via traditional media channels.

The following headings present examples and empirical researches on the benefits and the drawback of social media usage in terms of different aspects of business functions. We have specifically focused on internal and external environment and stakeholders of companies. Marketing, sales, brand communities, and consumer relations headings have been formed in order to evaluate the impact of social media usage on external stakeholders. On the other hand,enterprise social media, human resources, and job attitudes headings have been formed to evaluate the impact of social media usage on internal stakeholders. Business performance heading focuses both on internal and external stakeholders.

SOCIAL MEDIA AS A COMMUNICATION TOOL FOR ORGANIZATIONS

Social Media Marketing

Marketing in social media requires more inspiring and attractive content to draw the attention of consumers. Compared to traditional media, social media can be quite challenging because it needs to maintain the consumer interest otherwise their attention will turn elsewhere (Peters K. et al., 2013). Peters K. et al. (2013) also state that the momentum of social media and the enormous amounts of data being created across platforms will make organizations *"feel the need for a central content hub that serves all channels on all relevant topics in almost real-time"* (2013, p. 295).

According to Kabani (2012) we need to give the definitions of social media and marketing separately before explaining social media marketing:

- Marketing: Creating a value, promoting a product or service to increase sales
- Social media: Mobile/online platforms where people connect and communicate

So, simply the social media marketing represents use of all social networks for marketing, creating value, public relations and customer relationship management (Barker et al., 2013). Today's common tools, social media applications and sites such as Facebook, Twitter and Instagram created new challenges and opportunities for companies to enhance communication with current customers and to collaborate in new channels with both current and potential customers (Culnan et al., 2010). As a result, most of the companies are adopting social media to increase customer loyalty and retention, brand awareness, customer satisfaction (He et al., 2013; Kietzmann et al., 2011), and to learn from customers (Saravanakumar and Lakshmi, 2012), to amplify public relations and to reduce customer acquisition costs (Tuten and Solomon, 2017). If we classify simpler, usual actions performed with social media applications, this classification contain branding, sales and customer relations (Culnan et al., 2010). For an example, like many accommodation chains, Starwood Hotels, have been benefiting from the opportunities of social media to stay connected and to get feedback from customers in recent years, they also help potential customers to make their travel decision (Reddy and Dula, 2010; Müller,2011).

Social Media and Brand Communities

Marketers are enthusiastic to create and organize brand communities (McAlexander et al., 2002; Schau et al., 2009). Brand communities include cluster of relationship and connections among people who love a brand (Muniz and O'Guinn, 2001). With the help of learning how brand communities work, companies can observe customer perceptions of brand, new products and competitors; companies also can increase their chances to attract and work together closely with loyal customers of the brand (McAlexander et al., 2002; Franke and Shah, 2003). Being close to loyal customers allows companies to discover how the influencer members make evaluations and acts (Muniz and Schau, 2005), and also allows them to observe rapidly diffusing information among consumers (Jin et al., 2009).

Combining the brand communities and social media communities leads to a concept that can be called "virtual brand community" or online brand communities (Laroche et al., 2012). Social networking sites such as Twitter, Facebook, Instagram allow users to discuss about different issues and topics freely. People register for these sites and other such sites and use text, photographs and videos to keep in touch with their friends, make new ones, exchange experiences, play games, gossip, exchange intellectual knowledge, trade, fall in love, and brainstorm (Lenhart and Madden, 2007; Laroche et al., 2012). Compared to social media, traditional media users consume the content passively. In contrast, social media community members create content through active participation in virtual brand communities. This active structure forms the character of the community and users' influences on each other (Bagozzi and Dholakia, 2002).

As it can be seen in the previous studies, companies can have different objectives and motives behind using social media and creating virtual communities. For example, Chase Cards used social media and mostly influencers to create a new millennial cult brand. On the other hand, Pepsi refresh project targeted millennials and challenged them to refresh and renew their world.

In August 2016, Chase Card Services of JPMorgan Chase, had launched the Chase Sapphire card and the card exceeded the 12 month sales target in 2 weeks. The most important detail was more than half of the new customers were under 35 years old. The reason that drove the social media and the word of mouth was the 100.000 points sign-on bonus. The size of bonus had been drawn the attention of famous bloggers such as Brian Kelly, CEO and founder of The Points Guy, who claimed that "the most appealing card ever".

At launch, Sapphire team knew that the millennial consumers were consuming media differently, rather than traditional media, they preferred media platforms and influencers. So the marketing team approached differently; they engaged relevant influencers, models, and designers such as Nigel Barker, Kelly Wearstler and Chrisy Teigen. They shared their unique experiences through different social media and these contents reached millions of millennial followers. Fueled by proper usage of social media channels and online forums, news spread quickly and the card reached its annual customer target in two weeks after launch. More than half of these consumers were millennials and they were proudly posting photographs with their new Chase Sapphire cards on Facebook, Twitter and Instagram. Some were uploading "unboxing" videos to Youtube. In the end, Chase created a cult millennial brand and build a brand community with the power of social media (Santana et al., 2017).

For the first time in 20 years, Pepsi announced that they would not run advertising for their brands during the Super Bowl in 2010. Contrary to expectations, the company decided to use 20 million dollars, this was the typical Super Bowl budget, for another marketing program. The Pepsi Refresh Project allowed consumers generate ideas to "refresh" their communities. Most voted ideas were awarded with grants. Grants ranging from 5.000 to 250.000 dollars would be awarded to ideas in six categories such as education, the planet, health, neighborhoods, arts & culture and food & shelter. To target the millennial audience, ideas (or projects) would be posted on socials media platforms and the voting would take place on these platforms. Consumers voted for ideas on Facebook and were encouraged to 'like' Pepsi Refresh project page to generate publicity. Before long, 4 to 5 million individuals were visiting the web site of Pepsi Refresh and half of the visitors registered on the site to share their ideas to win grants and coupons. After 2 months, Pepsi earned additional 300.000 friends on Facebook and project was generating 1000 tweets a day. Before the project, Pepsi was behind Coke in Facebook followers with 225.000 fans to 3.5 million. As a result of the project, 3 million Facebook and 53.000 Twitter followers were added and created a strong community.

Social Media and Sales

After witnessing the power of the social media tools at the consumer community level, most of the marketers decided to embrace the ability to use these tools to spread their message to consumers (Andzulis et al., 2012). Big firms such as Ford and P&G planned to cut their advertisement budgets because social media can be more efficient than the traditional media that usually eats the lion's share of the firms' marketing budget (Edwards, 2012). There were many areas of the firms that have been changed by social media impact but the sales function had the potential of being the most significantly changing function by the technology and social media advancements; and it has changed dramatically.

E-commerce is becoming an important tool therefore, trendsetting companies are focusing on unique characteristics of social media. The "likes" in Facebook, Twitter or watching "story" in Instagram is not the most important activity (Anderson et al., 2012). In the present, we are on a phase that went beyond simple communication and influencing. To be more precise, firms want to increase sales by using agents on social networks for viral marketing, brand communities, ads in social networks that can direct the consumers online shopping sites even ads that allow the customers to shop inside social networks. According to Business Insider Social Commerce 2017 Report, social media is rapidly becoming the most influential tool in consumers' purchase decisions. As a matter of fact, the top 500 retailers earned an estimated 6,5 billion dollars from social shopping in 2017, up %24 from 2016 (Business Insider Social Commerce Report, 2017). In addition to report's results, social media is a large part of discovering products and research phase of the consumers' shopping experience. With more and more retailers offer quick access to their sites via social media pages and accounts and purchasable content become popular, it's inevitable that social media will play an even larger role in online commerce.

As it can be seen in Decathlon and Ford Fiesta cases, firms can use agents in social media to create buzz and make sales such as Ford Fiesta Movement or use social media to create awareness and canalize the users to online shopping site to increase online sales like Decathlon did in China. Decathlon, a large multinational French manufacturer and retailer of sporting goods with more than 400 stores operating in Europe and Asia, planned to establish its official Chinese online shopping website in 2011. After reviewing online markets and competitors, they began to take notice of the competitors' (Nike, Adidas and local companies Li-Ning and Anta) aggressive strategies to increase online sales. After that the executives decided to monitor Decathlon's current online marketing status and they deduced that while effort had been made to launch a website for online shopping, there had been no additional efforts made to attract customers to it. Therefore, the head of e-commerce department classified some of the most popular social media sites in China (Geng, 2011). Decathlon decided to try a forum site that has a real atmosphere and mentality to build a social community. They soon identified bbs.8264.com, a website about introducing outdoor activity knowledge, creating outdoor awareness and providing tips about outdoor activities. The members of community can share travel experiences, tips and photos therefore the interaction on this platform make the community grow continuously. Decathlon advertised strategically on the webpage which had the highest community member and least competition. These ads helped to create brand awareness successfully and directed consumers to online shopping site. Finally, Decathlon created an official account on China's important micro-blogging site Sina Weibo and had attracted thousands of followers in a short period. The firm used this platform to announce news and to launch discount contests. The micro blogging site move seemed to create some word of mouth and was shared by the followers. The increasing strength of micro-blogging granted the firm to reach immense number of social media users. After only 3 months, Decathlon generated exemplary brand awareness for its online shopping site with the help of social media mostly (Geng, 2011).

Ford Motor Company, initiated an ambitious new marketing campaign. Usually, the industry uses traditional channel advertising just a few months before the new car goes on sale. Ford Fiesta Movement(FFM), the new campaign's name, started nearly 1 year before the actual car was unveiled and went on sale. The objectives of FFM campaign were like any other typical marketing campaign for a new product: informing the target market segments and building awareness for the new product though, there were many challenges like building awareness for a car that had not been in North America for decades, being in a competitive segment and reaching target customers, young drivers in their 20s, who use traditional media less and less every day. The marketing team gave free Ford Fiestas to a carefully selected very small group. The 100 Ford Fiesta agents were asked to share their experiences on Youtube andTwitter no matter how negative they might be. After the campaign results were impressive. Agents had posted on Youtube, Flickr and Twitter about Fiesta and it created buzz virally. The video on Youtube generated 6.5 million views and the firm reported that 50.000 consumers had expressed their intention to buy Fiesta; 10.000 cars were sold in the first 6 days and %97 of these had not even driven a Ford before.

Social Media and Consumer Relations

The main difference between marketing public relations and the other types of marketing communications is the mediators that spread the message. Marketing Public relations is about creating buzz by drawing attentions of mediators like mass media, social media or the people who voluntarily spread a message about a company to their followers or audience (Papasolomou and Melanthiou, 2012). The unique difference of marketing public relations is putting another party in the communication process than the marketer therefore the message receiver creates a different dimension on his or her mind which can be both threat and opportunity.

Social media users, they can also be called non-media mediators, can either be a professional or a simple consumer who admires a brand or a company. Marketers using 'non-media mediators' expect them to influence their friends, family, professional and social groups through generated content in social media (Voight,2007). However, this also means that the marketers will lose control over the message since mediators usually do not simply deliver the messages but they also change them. As mediators use social media to connect with their followers around the world, companies have a great opportunity; to influence their mediators so that they can generate good publicity (Papasolomou and Melanthiou, 2012). Yet, social media creates an environment that encourages the individuals to generate bad publicity as well as good publicity freely. Example for bad publicity, in 2009 Domino's Pizza had been placed into a difficult situation. A video of two employees of Domino's had been posted online on Youtube. In the video which had gone viral, the employee sticks cheese up his nose before placing it onbread, sneezes on a pizza and boxes it for delivery. The other employee recording the video was heard laughing during the video and commenting, "in about 5 minutes, these foods will be sent to delivery and somebody will eat them." The video was shared in Facebook and Twitter and, as a result, had more than 1 million views (Bigus, 2011). Following the incident, Domino's fired the two employees and posted a video of them apologizing from the customers After two weeks, the buzz about the videos has subsided and customers were speaking more positively about the chain. According to the Vice president Tim McIntyre, it was due to the company reaching out directly to social networks. More examples can be given like this situation, such as in 2016 Daimler Trucks and Buses' chief executive officer in China lost his temper over a parking space and Gartner, the CEO, used pepper spray and one of the bystander got injured. The story went viral, at no time Chinese social media, also newspapers and TV connected this negative situation to Daimler brand and most of them asked people to boycott Mercedes cars. This parking space quarrel not only resulted in social media outrage but also share price of Daimler dropped from 65,69 euros to 61,90 in 10 days (Messner and Yoon, 2018). For the good publicity example, Pepsi Refresh Project was designed to create buzz, celebrities such as Kevin Bacon and Demi Moore participated in a part of the project and this was announced for the first time in The Today Show. Facebook page of the project featured an exclusive chance to watch Pepsi Refresh Everything through Great Ideas brainstorm live. College students and executives of Pepsi Co. discussed ideas that would make positive impact to the world.

Enterprise Social Media

In organizational context social media has been used in two ways: internal and external. Most of the researches are focused on social media as a communication tool with external stakeholders such as customer, vendors, suppliers, competitors, and consumers. Running social media campaign, managing pages or blogs and microblogging in popular social media platforms are some examples of these attempts. Internal communication and social interaction via social media within the organization is less commonly studied field, which is more focused on enterprise social media platforms. Enterprise social media is defined as (Leonardi et. al. 2013):

''Web-based platforms that allow workers to:
- *communicate messages with specific coworkers or broadcast messages to everyone in the organization;*
- *explicitly indicate or implicitly reveal particular coworkers as communication partners;*
- *post, edit, and sort text and files linked to themselves or others; and*
- *view the messages, connections, text, and files communicated, posted, edited and sorted by anyone else in the organization at any time of their choosing.''*

Social media usage as a communication tool among employees is also improving in last decades. Organizations not only encourage their employees to use public social media platforms but also invest special social media platforms inside the company. These kinds of specific internal social media platforms are called enterprise social media. Organization as a sociotechnical system requires both communication about work-related issues and social interactions. Enterprise social media basically refers to web-based platforms used inside an organization to support internal interactions within employees. Most of the enterprise social media platforms allow users to send messages to coworkers, indicate the work team, post, edit and sort common shared work files, opening chat rooms or social groups etc. The difference of enterprise social media from public social media platforms is there is not a chance to communicate with outside parties like, customers, vendors, and competitor. Enterprise social media is also different from other internal communications technologies. Because it gives opportunity to distinguish work related and social conversations among users (Leonardi et al, 2013; Maqbel & Nah, 2017).

There are scientific researches on how enterprise social media affects productivity, workplace integration, positive emotions and attitudes, knowledge share and management performance, and overall job performance (Maqbel & Nah, 2017). For example, Best Buy uses a web-based platform called Connect to let employees have a voice. Connect collecting all tweets, feeds, blogs in to centralize location. It is possible to reach an employee and ask technical questions and experiences with Connect (https://www. stayonsearch.com/best-buy-using-social-media-to-connect-with-customers, online December 28, 2018). Dell also has EnterpriseEfficiency.com for Information Technology executives to discuss and post about their experience about work (http://i.dell.com/sites/content/business/solutions/power/en/Documents/ ps1q11-20110266-socialmedia.pdf, online December 28, 2018)

Although companies like, Best Buy and Dell, have succeeded in using enterprise social media to accomplish significant targets, such as reducing their costs, increasing revenues or stimulating innovation; many other companies failed to see beneficial outcomes of their enterprise social media platform or faced problems of communication based on posts of employees on that platforms. Huy and Shipilov claimed that a successful enterprise social media usage should support the development of emotional capital, which can be defined as '*the aggregate feelings of goodwill toward a company and the way it operates*' (Huy & Shipilov, 2012; 74). Emotional capital represents emotional based assets that the company has developed over time among their employees and executives. The findings of Huy and Shipilov research suggest that using social media to develop emotional capital among employees can improve information flow, collaboration among employees, increase motivation and decrease personal turnover. Unfortunately, some organizations that focus on getting work related information or formal community building processes instead of developing emotional capital, could fail to get benefits of enterprise social media (Huy & Shipilov, 2012; 73-74). For example, in 2016 at a software company called Fresh to Table's, executives fired an office manager after reviewing her conversations with some of other employees, who had been promoted recently, on the internal social media platform called Slack. The CEO and HR vice president figured out that the office manager was spending considerable time on Slack by humiliating other employees, talking about the times when they ran off work and, chatting on other questionable topics (Mukunda & Holtom, 2017).

Another example, Huy and Shipilov mentioned a technology company (writers keep confidential the identity of the firm) that invest an enterprise social media platform and hired some developers to build the tool. By this tool it is possible to send email, microblogging, creating groups etc. The company made participation to enterprise social media platform as a part of employees' performance review. As a result, nobody use the tool voluntary and executives couldn't get tangible outcomes from the initiative (Huy & Shipilov, 2012; 74-75).

In contrast Tupperware invest in an interactive motivational webcast called The Tupperware Radio Show, and become one of the significant cost drivers and example of morale in a direct sales industry. It's not because forcing employees to use that tools but because understanding of the importance of developing positive emotions through enterprise social media platforms (Huy & Shipilov, 2012; 75).

Social Media and Human Resources

Social media is not only for organizations to share information with shareholders, but also individuals as employees or job applicants are sharing information about themselves at social media. It is very easy to check many information via Googling or searching the name of person on social media. Employers commonly use social networking sites to obtain information for purposes of recruiting and assessing job applicants. Social media is an effective tool to gain information but employers have to be careful to use the information gained from social media. Because those information could bring bias, unethical or illegal practices based on violation of special life or individual's right to privacy. For instance, the lifestyle presented by the employee on social media may not be compatible with her social identity at work.

Things that an individual share with her close social environment, such as drinking, cheating, boasting, may not be consistent with the desirable characteristics (such as being responsible, being mature, etc.) of social identity at work. Comparing the social identity showed at social media with preferred criteria of recruiting, promoting, performance evaluating, an employee or job applicant may be exposed negative bias, attitudes or assessments due to their post in social media. Smith and Kidder (2010) suggest organizations to develop guidelines and policies about the use of social media in application and evaluation processes. (Smith & Kidder, 2010: 491-493)

More and more organizations are utilizing social media as an innovative recruitment tool or a talent pool. Furthermore some organizations like accounting firm Ernst&Young use social media with intention to attract young graduates. There are also lots of special online hiring tools and social media websites like LinkedIn. The question needs to be answered is how or under what circumstances employers or even managers should use social networking sites as a means of evaluating job candidates or current employees (Bizze 2018: 30-31; Smith & Kidder, 2010: 494). For example, a non-profit organization at New York rejected an applicant since his Facebook profile shows that he has extreme romantic exploits and interest in violent movies. Company assessed him as a weak fit for the position (Smith & Kidder, 2010: 494). Another example is a company refused a 19 years old internship candidate because she was holding a bottle of vodka in her Facebook profile photo (Stone, 2006)

There is a little legal limitation to prevent employee to monitor their employers' social media accounts. (Smith & Tabak, 2009: 34-46) It is an arguable topic if it is also a privacy problem and, seems to be unethical monitoring people without their permission in an area outside of office space. On the other hand some of the employees may have consequences that could cause damage to the organization, and even the employer may even consider firing the employee. Downcity Motors case could be an example. Downcity Motors, which owned BMW, Range Rover, and Mercedes-Benz dealerships in Charlotte, North Carolina, is a small business and the owners of the company (Dell and Susanna) had been working in this family business for three generations. They had been called from the BMW headquarters and had been told one of their prized salesperson, Kenton, wrote something about the launch they had. The customer had implied that they need to keep a tighter rein on their staff. After hearing that, Susannah checked Kenton's Facebook wall and read: "So thrilled that Downcity went 'all out' for the most important Mercedes launch in years. Nothing says luxury like plastic tablecloths and soda pop." Kenton had posted a photo of a soda can with the Downcity Motors sign looming in the background. In Susannah's opinion, they needed to fire him because Kenton had shared similar negative posts on his Facebook account although he had been warned him before. He said that he was just sharing his work experiences with his friends and family (Watson & Lopiano, 2016). Another example is the two employees of Domino's Pizza who posted a video that one of them sticks cheese up his nose. In this case Domino's posted a video of employees and apologized from customers and also fired those two employees (Bigus, 2011)

Although there are examples of organizations which fires employees because of their inappropriate posts at social media, it is still possible to benefit from the use of social media. Determining the policies about social media usage can guide employees in terms of forbidden behaviors and posts of their work experience at social media. In order to make social media policy effective, it is also important to focus on how well employees understand their employers' policy about social media. O'Connor et al conducted an exploratory research about how young adult employees behave according to their knowledge about the social media policy of the company they work. They obtained data from 166 employed under-graduates of a university at United States. *'Only 31% of participants indicated their company had a social media policy; 34% indicated that their company did not have a social media policy; and 35% reported that they did not know if their company had a social media policy.'* Obviously employees seem to be not clear about organization's social media policy. O'Connor et al. recommend a clarification of the social media policies and trainigs on social media policies (O'Connor et al., 2016: 206-209).

Social Media and Job Attitudes

Its indicated that the effect of social media usage on many different job attitudes and behaviors such as organizational engagement, organizational identification, intrinsic work motivation, proactive work behavior, withdrawal and turnover.

Withdrawal and Turnover

There are many companies support their employees to use of social media sites like Facebook to interact with coworkers to improve coordination. Bizze (2018: 26-27) conducted a research with a sample of 277 employees of a Canadian healthcare institution, about the intention of social media use (for work or for leisure) in workplace and, found that *'employees who use Facebook to facilitate work in the organization have a 50% higher interest in other organizations on social media'*. Apparently there are paradoxically the risks of employee withdrawal intention and personnel turnover. In order to use social media as an innovative recruitment tool, Bizze mentioned some recommendations such as publishing professional content, setting social media referrals, tagging employees, sponsoring recruitment campaigns and events, publishing employee content, opening social media groups and conducting social media analysis (Bizze, 2018: 31)

Organizational Engagement

Private social media activities of employees not only contain risks but also opportunities for the company. Because a company or brand is presented through private social media posts of employees as well as the posts of official social media pages. Employees mostly are free to share brand or industry related posts or comments according to policies of the corporate companies. But the context should be consistent with brand value. Some of companies -such as: L'oreal, cosmetic company; Patagonia Inc., outdoor clothing and gear company; Societe Generale, financial service company and; Pernod Ricard, wine producer- expect their employees become a 'brand ambassador' in order to reflect organizational culture and attract customer or job candidates. But researches show that many employees, especially younger ones don't follow their companies at Facebook, Twitter, LinkedIn or Instagram. Companies tend to evaluate that situation as a lack of organizational engagement (Cervellon & Lirio, 2017).

Intrinsic Work Motivation and Proactive Work Behavior

Bizzi claimed that 'if the job of individuals requires high formal interactions, the relationship between social media use and blogging with coworkers is stronger'. He also indicated that blogging with outsiders (individuals who do not work for the organization) negatively related to intrinsic work motivation and proactive work behavior. But blogging with coworkers positively related to intrinsic work motivation and proactive work behavior. (Bizzi, 2017: 1-28)

Social Capital and Organizational Identification

Sias and Duncan (2018) found a positive correlation between the level of employee interaction with their company's Facebook page and, organizational identification level of employees. Also they indicated there is a partially mediated effect of social capital outcomes on the relationship between employee – company Facebook page interaction and organizational identification. As an overall result, writers suggested that social media activities of company are enhancing employee organization relationship by improving social capital and organizational identification among employees (Sias & Duncan, 2018).

Social Media and Business Performance

Paniagua and Sapena (2014) conduct a research to test the effect of social media usage on business performance. Results show that 'followers' and 'likes' affect business performance (stock prices of publicly traded companies) positively. This effect occur only after the social media account reach a critical mass of followers. Authors also claimed that Twitter is a more powerful tool to enhance business performance than Facebook. (Paniagua & Sapena, 2014)

As it is described in Daimler case, the CEO's scandal went viral on social media and in a short time that had affected the company negatively. Share prices of Daimler dropped by approximately 5 euros in 10 days despite the positive atmosphere in automobile industry.

In April 2017, United Airlines one of the biggest airlines in the world, found itself in a scandal. On the day of incident, the airline company realized that they overbooked the flight and needed four passengers to leave the plane. The company offered 800 dollars as compensation. Finding no takers however, the company decided to chose four passengers randomly to disembark. When one of the four passengers refused to leave the plane, an officer dragged him out of the plane by using force and left him bruised and bloodied. Comments and videos by other passengers on the plane went viral on social media draw attention all around the world. The passenger, David Dao, who is Chinese, claimed that his ethnicity made him the target. Within 48 hours, United Airlines' stock dropped an estimated 255 million dollars in market value. The company experienced a dramatic drop in its reputation. One of the largest investors of the company, Warren Bufett, stated that the company had made a suicidal mistake in managing the incident.

Culnan et al estimated social media as a tool to create 'virtual customer environment' which, shapes the common interests of the customers virtually. In order to gain value by virtual customer environment organizations need to incorporate community engagement (Culnan & Zubillaga, 2010). As stated in the Pepsi example above, instead of using traditional media tools such as advertising on Super Bowl, the company prefers to focus on virtual customer environment. As a result of focusing on Pepsi Refresh Project, the company created a strong community engagement with thousands of Twitter followers and millions of Facebook friends were added in a short time.

CONCLUSION

As it was argued by examples and empirical findings, communication with stakeholders via social media could benefit to all functions (marketing, operations, finance, human resources, research and development, corporate communication etc.). Some of those benefits we can summarize in this chapter are:

- The development of social media completely changed the way companies communicate with their employees and customers. There is a clear transition from traditional media channels to social media.
- Firms want to increase sales by using agents on social networks for viral marketing, brand communities, ads in social networks that can direct the
- Social media is also a tool, which, facilitates creation of value and improve work performance. It has been stated that using popular social media platforms or enterprise social media platforms affect emotions and job attitudes, employee creativity, workplace integration, effective knowledge management system, consumer relations and reputations.

But researches also pointed out some negative impact or risks of both internal and external social media usage. As the contents in social media that reach masses around the world, social media can create an environment that encourages the individuals to generate bad publicity as well as good publicity freely. There is a discussion among professionals and scientists about the negative and positive aspects of social media usage and, researchers suggest formal guides and clearly stated policies about social media usage in order to maintain the benefits.

Social media is a cultural shift, not an operational one so the emergence of social media has created a new normal for the organizational and marketing communications with all the stakeholders. In the future, with the integration of the digital tools like wearable technologies and human body, social media communication and contents will evolve in many different forms and become the new normal. In terms of management, businesses need to re-decide on the formal and informal forms of communication and what arrangements they will make. On the other hand, from the marketing perspective, the importance of developing new marketing strategies and methods to make the most effective use of these new communication channels should be investigated.

REFERENCES

Anderson, M., Sims, J., Price, J., & Brusa, J. (2011). Turning "Like" to "Buy" social media emerges as a commerce channel. *Booz & Company Inc*, *2*(1), 102–128.

Bagozzi, R., & Dholakia, U. (2002). Intentional social action in virtual communities. *Journal of Interactive Marketing*, *16*(2), 2–21. doi:10.1002/dir.10006

Barker, M., Barker, D., Bormann, N., & Neher, K. (2013). *Social Media Marketing, A Strategic Approach*. Cengage Learning International Offices.

Bauer, W., Hämmerle, M., Schlund, S., & Vocke, C. (2015). Transforming to a hyper-connected society and economy–towards an "Industry 4.0". *Procedia Manufacturing*, *3*, 417–424. doi:10.1016/j.promfg.2015.07.200

Berman, S. J. (2012). Digital Transformation: Opportunities to Create New Business Models. *Strategy and Leadership*, *40*(2), 16–24. doi:10.1108/10878571211209314

Bigus, P. (2011). *Domino's Pizza, Ivey Business School Case study*. Harvard Business Publishing.

Bizzi, L. (2017). Should HR managers allow employees to use social media at work? Behavioral and motivational outcomes of employee blogging. *International Journal of Human Resource Management*, 1–28. doi:10.1080/09585192.2017.1402359

Bizzi, L. (2018). The hidden problem of Facebook and social media at work: What if employees start searching for other jobs? *Business Horizons*, *61*(1), 23–33. doi:10.1016/j.bushor.2017.09.002

Cervellon, M., & Lirio, P. (2017). When Employee Don't 'Like' Their Employers On Social Media. *MIT Sloan Management Review*. Retrieved from https://sloanreview.mit.edu/article/when-employees-dont-like-their-employers-on-social-media/

Culnan, M. J., McHugh, P. J., & Zubillaga, J. I. (2010). How large US companies can use Twitter and other social media to gain business value. *MIS Quarterly Executive*, *9*(4).

Edwards, J. (2012). P&G to Lay Off 1,600 After Discovering It's Free to Advertise on Facebook. *Business Insider*. Available at http://articles.businessinsider. com/2012-01 30/news/31004736_1_advertising-digitalmedia- procter-gamble/

Franke, N., & Shah, S. K. (2003). How communities support innovative activities: An exploration of assistance and sharing among end-users. *Research Policy*, *32*(1), 157–178. doi:10.1016/S0048-7333(02)00006-9

Geng, G. (2011). *Decathlon China: Using Social Media to Penetrate the Internet Market, Ivey Business School Case study*. Harvard Business Publishing.

Gillin, P. (2007). *The new influencers: A marketer's guide to the new social media*. Sanger, CA: Quill Driver Books.

Haefliger, S., Monteiro, E., Foray, D., & Von Krogh, G. (2011). Social software and strategy. *Long Range Planning*, *44*(5-6), 297–316. doi:10.1016/j.lrp.2011.08.001

How Best Buy Uses Social Media to Connect with Customers. (n.d.). Retrieved from https://www.stayonsearch.com/best-buy-using-social-media-to-connect-with-customers

Hu, T., & Windstad, G. W. (2018). *Social media use in organizations: exploring the emergence of a new practice: a case study on institutionalization* (Master's thesis).

Huy, Q., & Shipilov, A. (2012). The key to social media success within organizations. *MIT Sloan Management Review*, *54*(1), 73.

Jin, X. L., Cheung, C. M. K., Lee, M. K. O., & Chen, H. P. (2009). How to keep members using the information in a computer-supported social network. *Computers in Human Behavior*, *25*(5), 1172–1181. doi:10.1016/j.chb.2009.04.008

Jurgens, M., Berthon, P., Edelman, L., & Pitt, L. (2016). Social media revolutions: The influence of secondary stakeholders. *Business Horizons*, *59*(2), 129–136. doi:10.1016/j.bushor.2015.11.010

Kabani, S. H. (2013). *The zen of Social Media Marketing: An Easier Way To Build Credibility, Generate Buzz, And Increase Revenue*. Dallas, TX: BenBella Books, Inc.

Kaplan, A. M., & Haenlein, M. (2010). Users of the world, unite! The challenges and opportunities of Social Media. *Business Horizons, 53*(1), 59–68. doi:10.1016/j.bushor.2009.09.003

Laroche, M., Habibi, M. R., Richard, M. O., & Sankaranarayanan, R. (2012). The effects of social media based brand communities on brand community markers, value creation practices, brand trust and brand loyalty. *Computers in Human Behavior, 28*(5), 1755–1767. doi:10.1016/j.chb.2012.04.016

Lenhart, A., & Madden, M. (2007). *Social networking websites and teens: An overview*. PEW Internet and American Life Project.

Leonardi, P. M., Huysman, M., & Steinfield, C. (2013). Enterprise social media: Definition, history, and prospects for the study of social technologies in organizations. *Journal of Computer-Mediated Communication, 19*(1), 1–19. doi:10.1111/jcc4.12029

Liu, H. (2007). Social network profiles as taste performances. *Journal of Computer-Mediated Communication, 13*(1), 252–275. doi:10.1111/j.1083-6101.2007.00395.x

McAlexander, J. H., Schouten, J. W., & Koenig, H. F. (2002). Building brand community. *Journal of Marketing, 66*(1), 38–54. doi:10.1509/jmkg.66.1.38.18451

Messner, W., & Yoon, H. J. (2018). *Daimler China: Facing a Media Firestorm, Ivey Business School Case study*. Harvard Business Publishing.

Moqbel, M., & Nah, F. F. H. (2017). Enterprise social media use and impact on performance: The role of workplace integration and positive emotions. *AIS Transactions on Human-Computer Interaction, 9*(4), 261–280. doi:10.17705/1thci.00098

Mukunda, G., & Holtom, C.B., (2017). Fresh To Table. *Harvard Business School Brief Case*, 917-541.

Muniz, A. Jr, & Schau, H. J. (2005). Religiosity in the abandoned Apple Newton Brand Community. *The Journal of Consumer Research, 31*(4), 737–747. doi:10.1086/426607

Muniz, M. A. Jr, & O'Guinn, C. T. (2001). Brand community. *The Journal of Consumer Research, 27*(4), 412–432. doi:10.1086/319618

Norton, M. I., & Avery, J. (2013). *The Pepsi Refresh Project: A Thirst for Change*. Harvard Business Publishing.

O'Connor, K. W., Schmidt, G. B., & Drouin, M. (2016). Helping workers understand and follow social media policies. *Business Horizons, 59*(2), 205–211. doi:10.1016/j.bushor.2015.11.005

Paniagua, J., & Sapena, J. (2014). Business performance and social media: Love or hate? *Business Horizons, 57*(6), 719–728. doi:10.1016/j.bushor.2014.07.005

Papasolomou, I., & Melanthiou, Y. (2012). Social media: Marketing public relations' new best friend. *Journal of Promotion Management, 18*(3), 319–328. doi:10.1080/10496491.2012.696458

Peters, K., Chen, Y., Kaplan, A. M., Ognibeni, B., & Pauwels, K. (2013). Social Media Metrics - A Framework and Guidelines for Managing Social Media. *Journal of Interactive Marketing, 27*(4), 281–298. doi:10.1016/j.intmar.2013.09.007

Puri, S., Kashyap, K. D., & Singh, G. (2018). *Unidet Airlines' service-recovery challenge after reputation meltdown*. Ivey Business School, Harvard Business Publishing.

Santana, S., Avery, J., & Snively, C. (2017). *Chase Sapphire: Creating a Millenial Cult Brand*. Harvard Business Publishing.

Schau, J. H., Muniz, M. A. Jr, & Arnould, J. E. (2009). How brand community practices create value. *Journal of Marketing*, *73*(5), 30–51. doi:10.1509/jmkg.73.5.30

Sias, P. M., & Duncan, K. L. (2018). Not Just for Customers Anymore: Organization Facebook, Employee Social Capital, and Organizational Identification. *International Journal of Business Communication*.

Smith, W. P., & Kidder, D. L. (2010). You've been tagged!(Then again, maybe not): Employers and Facebook. *Business Horizons*, *53*(5), 491–499. doi:10.1016/j.bushor.2010.04.004

Smith, W. P., & Tabak, F. (2009). Monitoring employee e-mails: Is there any room for privacy? *The Academy of Management Perspectives*, *23*(4), 33–48. doi:10.5465/amp.23.4.33

Stephen, A. T. (2013). *Ford Fiesta Movement, INSEAD case study*. Harvard Business Publishing.

Stone, B. (2006). Web of Risks; Students Adore Social-Networking Sites like Facebook, but Indiscreet Postings Can Mean Really Big Trouble. *Newsweek*. Retrieved from https://www.questia.com/magazine/1G1-149563559/web-of-risks-students-adore-social-networking-sites

Tuten, T. L., & Solomon, M. R. (2017). Social media marketing. *Sage (Atlanta, Ga.)*.

Voight, J. (2007). The new brand ambassadors. *Ad Week*. Retrieved from http://www.adweek.com/aw/content_display/news/strategy/e3i9ec32f006d17a91cccd2559f612b0f42

Von Krogh, G. (2012). How does social software change knowledge management? Toward a strategic research agenda. *The Journal of Strategic Information Systems*, *21*(2), 154–164. doi:10.1016/j.jsis.2012.04.003

Watson, M. A., & Lopiano, G. R. (2016). *Should We He Be Fired For That Facebook Post?* Retrieved from https://hbr.org/2016/03/case-study-should-he-be-fired-for-that-facebook-post

Westerman, G., & McAfee, A. (2012). *The Digital Advantage: How Digital Leaders Outperform Their Peers in Every Industry*. Academic Press.

Yilmaz, İ. G., Aygün, D., & Tanrikulu, Z. (2017). Social Media's Perspective on Industry 4.0: A Twitter Analysis. *Social Networking*, *6*(04), 251–261. doi:10.4236n.2017.64017

Zhao, S., Grasmuck, S., & Martin, J. (2008). Identity construction on Facebook: Digital empowerment in anchored relationships. *Computers in Human Behavior*, *24*(5), 1816–1836. doi:10.1016/j.chb.2008.02.012

Zhao, S., Grasmuck, S., & Martin, J. (n.d.). *How to engage in social media: A Dell perspective*. Retrieved from http://i.dell.com/sites/content/business/solutions/power/en/Documents/ps1q11-20110266-socialmedia.pdf

KEY TERMS AND DEFINITIONS

Social Media: Social media is defined as any web site including user generated content. With social networking sites (Facebook, Myspace), creativity works sharing sites (YouTube, Instagram, Soundcloud), business networking sites (LinkedIn), collaborative websites (Wikipedia), commerce communities (eBay, Amazon), podcasts and open source software communities (Linux, R), social media can take many forms.

Social Media Marketing: Represents use of all social networks for marketing, creating value, public relations, and customer relationship management.

Enterprise Social Media: Web-based platforms used inside an organization to support internal interactions within employees. Most of the enterprise social media platforms allow users to send messages to coworkers, indicate the work team, post, edit and sort common shared work files, opening chat rooms, or social groups, etc.

This research was previously published in Business Management and Communication Perspectives in Industry 4.0; pages 115-131, copyright year 2020 by Business Science Reference (an imprint of IGI Global).

Chapter 4
Understanding e–WOM Evolution in Social Media With Network Analysis

Fatih Pinarbasi
ⓘ https://orcid.org/0000-0001-9005-0324
Istanbul Medipol University, Turkey

ABSTRACT

Today's consumer is in constant interaction with the environment thanks to social media and technology. Consumers who communicate more with each other have pushed businesses to take action on this issue. In this study, network analysis will be processed by marketing approach. Previous studies focus on different aspects of network analysis while examining methodological details. There are a few integrated studies regarding to network analysis from marketing perspective. This study aims to fill this research gap with integrated approach combining marketing scenarios with network analysis methods and social media data. Study consists of two main parts: theoretical background and methodology sections. Theoretical background includes electronic word of mouth, social media and customer networks, network analysis parts. Methodology section includes four different cases regarding to network analysis, social media, and web. Businesses corporating network analysis to their marketing decision-making process can improve their marketing knowledge regarding to changing marketing environment.

INTRODUCTION

Today's business world is witnessing many changes with technological developments and widespread use of the Internet. Internet and social media play an important role in the lives of today's consumers. According to Global Digital Report (We Are Social and Hootsuite, 2019), our world has 7.676 billion people population while penetration rate for internet users is 57% (4.388 billion people) and penetration rate for active social media users is 45% (3.484 billion people). These high rates signal importance of social media for consumers' lives. Today's consumers living in social circles affect each other. Nielsen

DOI: 10.4018/978-1-7998-9020-1.ch004

report (Nielsen, 2015) indicates that 83% of respondents completely or somewhat trust recommendations of friends or family. This reflects importance of word of mouth in consumers' lives.

Worf of mouth concept simply means interaction and effect of people to other people in social circles. As people use digital technologies, electronic word of mouth concept becomes popular in marketing research. Network analysis is one of methodologies for social media sensemaking which helps to marketing decision making regarding to electronic word of mouth. It simply refers to evaluation of networks which means multiple structures of actors in mathematically and graphically way.

Previous studies employ network analysis with different contexts for word of mouth concept. Hambrick and Pegoraro (2014) use network analysis for examining the 2014 Olympic Games and related communities. In another study Yan et al. (2018) employs network analysis for sport context, 2017 UEFA Champions League Final. On the other hand, Iacobucci et al. (1996) use network analysis for marketing context, brand switch behaviour. Several studies have used network analysis for different contexts, but there is lack of integrity for business or marketing concept. This study aims to fill this gap by providing integrative network analysis cases for different marketing cases, especially for e-wom concept.

The phenomenon of study refers to network analysis of social structures related to electronic word of mouth markets. Network analysis will be used for examining different scenarios regarding to market and these scenarios will refer to different levels of research questions. The research questions of study include;

- How can network analysis be helpful for marketing management decision making?
- How can network analysis help to micro and macro level examination of markets?
- How can structures related to social networks like community, group of nodes be detected employing network analysis?
- How can time dimension be usedtogetherwith network analysis?

The study mainly uses R programming language (R Core Team, 2013), several R code packages and Gephi Software (Bastian et al., 2009). Network analysis is not limited to R programming language, as there are many alternative programming languages and softwares for network analysis. But then R programming language is a good alternative with different available code packages like sna(Butts, 2010), igraph (Csardi&Nepusz, 2006),influenceR (Simon & Aditya, 2015), keyplayer (An & Liu, 2016) for different network analysis methodologies.

Cheung and Thadani (2012) examine impact of e-wom communication and conclude that majority of e-wom studies they examine are related to online consumer review sites, as the other types of e-wom are related to online discussion forums, blogs, social networking sites and online brand/shopping sites. In addition, the contexts which electronic word of mouth are studied on refer to Twitter (Jansen et al., 2009), movies (Liu, 2006), music albums (Morales-Arroyo & Pandey, 2010), hospitality (Ladhari& Michaud, 2015; Tsao et al., 2015;Viglia et al., 2016). The scope of e-wom concept has a wide range, scope of study is limited to social media context for this study.

The study has a theoretical background which is the center of e-wom. In the study, where social media is determined as the study area within the scope of E-wom, there are two parts as theoretical and application. In the theoretical part, e-wom concept will be mentioned and then social media and consumer networks will be explained. Following these two topics, theoretical knowledge related to the subject of network analysis will be covered. In the second part of the study, the subject of network analysis will be explained in an integrated way with marketing scenarios. Following these two main sections, there will be sections of solutions and recommendations, future research directions and conclusions.

LITERATURE REVIEW

Electronic Word of Mouth

People live in society and share their opinions and feelings from early times. The roots of word of mouth can go back to ancient times which exchange happens without money. People always tend to share what they like or not related to things. The nature of communication between individuals, groups or societies is always focus of researchers for different science areas including sociology, anthropology and business.

Electronic word of mouth communication refers to any positive or negative statements made by potential, existing or former customers, related to product or company. These statements are available for people and institutions with internet (Hennig-Thurau et al., 2004). Transition from traditional word of mouth to e-wom is mostly related to web 2.0 concept. Cormode (2008) examines difference between web 1.0 and web 2.0 concept and concludes some differences. Author concludes that Web 2.0 sites has users as first class entities in their systems, there is an ability for forming connections between users, there are many forms for posting and other technical details. Web 2.0 popularity empowers consumers to influence other consumers through many platforms (Cheung & Thadani, 2012).

The reason and form of electronic word of mouth is important for marketing decision making. Reason of consumers' expression can signal marketing insights. Hennig-Tharau et al. (2004) conclude primary antecedents of e-wom behaviour as consumers' desire for social interaction, concern for others, desire for economic incentives and potential to enhance their own-self worth. Social interaction and concern for other antecedents are focus of this study as they are related to social network structure of consumers.

People share their ideas, complaints or likings with internet mediums for their networks. The flow of information has several consequences regarding to products or services. Purchase and purchase intention is one of consequences regarding to e-wom. Chevalier and Mayzlin (2006) study Amazon.com and Barnesandnoble.com review data and conclude that improvement of book reviews leads to increase in relative sales at that site. This conclusion reflects the purchase consequence of electronic wom. In addition to main consequence of e-wom, Cheung and Thadani (2012) propose an integrative framework for e-wom communication. This framework includes stimuli variables (argument quality, valence, sidedness and volume), receivers' variables (involvement, prior knowledge), communicatiors' variables (source credibility and attribution), contextual factor (platform) and lastly responses variables (information usefulness, ewom credibility, attitude, ewom adoption, purchase intention and purchase). The variety of variables in framework reflects complex nature of e-wom concept. This study aims to focus on networks related factors and dynamic nature of communication.

Since evaluating consumers recognition regarding to e-wom concept is crucial for marketing decision making and it includes several insights of consumers, there are some questions rising; How people search for information in pre-purchase stage? Which information channels are more effective for different segments of consumers? How the information flow through channels? Next section continues with social media platforms and consumer side of word mouth concept. Social media and consumer networks are related concepts for electronic word of mouth in recent years, therefore it will complete understanding of main concept, before methodology part of this study.

Social Media and Customer Networks

Social network services are defined as individual web page which enables online, human-relationship building as collects useful information and shares it with specific/unspecific people (Kwon & Wen, 2010). On the business side, according to Mangold and Faulds (2009), social media is a hybrid tool of promotion mix which combines traditional integrated marketing communication tools with highly magnified form of word of mouth. The combination includes two segments; first one refers to talking of companies with customers, second one refers to talking of consumers to another. Therefore, marketing decision making must consider both segments for marketing decision making.

Ngai et al. (2015) conclude a framework for social media research and include concepts and variables as antecedents, mediators, moderators and outcomes. Antecedents include social factors (social influence, social capital and others, user attributes (user perception, user experience, user personality and organizational attributes (customer orientation and marketing orientation). On the other hand, outcomes include personal context (user intention and user behavior) and organizational context (brand equity, customer relationship). The scope of this study focuses social factors rather than outcomes of social media applications. Social factors are included as antecedents, mediators and moderators in Ngai et al.(2015)'s model.

Consumer behavior related to social media and electronic word of mouth includes sharing and forwarding information to others. Severity and form of flow is affected by social ties. Brown and Reingen (1987) examine social ties and classic word of mouth with micro and macro levels. They conclude that strong and homophilous ties are more likely to be activated for information flow in micro level. On the other hand, weak ties have important bridging roles for macro level. Wirtz and Chew (2002) study tie strength concept with incentives, deal proneness and satisfaction concepts in electronic word of mouth behavior context. They conclude that tie strength is an important variable for explaining e-wom behavior. Peng et al. (2018) examine content sharing behavior on social media with network overlap context. They conclude that sharing behavior is related to have common followees, followers and mutual followers.

One of the important concepts in social media and consumer networks context is viral marketing which is related to diffusion of content on social media or internet. Viral marketing refers to electronic word-of-mouth by which some forms of marketing messages flows exponentially often through social media applications (Kaplan &Haenlein, 2011).Dobele et al. (2007) study viral marketing concept in terms of emotions. They find that viral messages must contain surprising element in order to be effective, but surprising element does not guarantee success, as it must be combined with other emotions. Concepts like content marketing and inbound marketing focus on content side of viral marketing and have questions including which content types become more popular, which content types are more likely to be shared through networks. This study focuses on network side of viral marketing and examine flow of information and network structure, rather than content element.

Next section of study includes methodological part of research aim which refers to network analysis. Network analysis studies network structure and flow of information regarding to social media or electronic word of mouth. Next section includes details for case part of study.

Network Analysis

Network analysis methodology simply means examining actors in a network structure by mathematically and graphically. Oliviera and Gama (2012) defines social network as set of social entities with patterns of relationships and interactions between them. The entities can be people, groups or organizations. The scope of network includes nodes as actors in network, ties as connections between actors, medium and large size groups as communities. Therefore it can be summarized as nodes, ties and communities are some of main elements of network structure.The process regarding to network examination is related to social network analysis. Oliveira and Gama (2012) trace back origins of social network analysis to Moreno (1951)'s sociometric approach. This approach includes sociograms, the charts which individuals are represented as nodes and relationships between individuals are represented as lines. This dual structure mostly helps understanding basic structure of networks.

First topic related to network analysis in this study refers to actor side. According to Wasserman (1994), actor refers to *discrete individuals, corporates or social collective units.* How actors in networks behave for e-wom is a crucial topic for marketing decision making. Individualist or collectivist people, introvert or extravert nature and many other characteristics affect how people act in networks. Selden and Goodie (2018) review researches regarding to five factor model personality traits and network structure topic. They included many conclusions regarding to personality traits and networks. For example, they conclude that extraverts tend to seek connections more, on the other hand agreeable people receive connections. Marketing decision making can describe or segment customers in their networks, then re-evaluate marketing plan for better decision making.

Second topic in network analysis refers to connections between actors. The strength of a social tie is combination of amount of time, the intimacy, the emotional intensity and reciprocal services characterizing tie (Granovetter, 1977). Brown and Reingen (1987) study wom referral behaviour with network analysis, while they specifically emphasize on social ties. They approach wom referral behavior with micro and macro level and demonstrate roles of strong and weak ties. Weak ties are found as bridging function for spreading of information through network in macro level, while strong and homophilous ties are found more activated for flow of information in micro level. This phenomenon must be controlled for electronic word of mouth concept, since it has own characteristics for communication. Steffes and Burgee (2009) study on social ties online word of mouth concepts and collect data from 482 college students. They conclude that students who obtain information regarding to professor from online, use that source equal influential as their own experiences for their decisions. They also conclude that information from e-wom forum is more influential than speaking with friends (wom). Therefore e-wom has own characteristics for traditional network analysis.

Third topic in network analysis refers to density of network. Network density simply refers to mean strength of connections between units in network (Marsden, 1990). Grund (2012) studies network structure in soccer team context with passes data between players. Author concludes that increased time performance is linked to increase in network density and increase in network centralization leads to decrease in team performance.

Fourth topic in network analysis refers to macro scope of networks. Takhteyev et al. (2012) study on social ties on Twitter network and examine influence of geographic distance, national boundaries and frequency of air travel on formation of social ties. They conclude that 39% share of ties is within the same metropolitan region. The best predictor for ties is found as number of flights between parties and for non-local ties, Twitter ties are affected by distance, border and language differences.

Fifth topic in network analysis refers to scope and contexts of methodology. Oliviera and Gama (2012) identify common tasks of social network analysis as;

- identification of most influential, central, prestigous actors,
- employing statistical measures,
- detection of hubs and authorities,
- employing link analysis algorithms,
- employing community detection techniques to discover communities.

Business studies related to network analysis contain several contexts including; tourism (Shih, 2006; Leung et al., 2012), e-wom (Vilpponen et al., 2006), leadership (Meuser et al., 2016) and brand associations (Wang &Horng, 2016). On the other hand non-business studies includes network analysis/social network analysis with several contexts like disaster (Kim &Hastak, 2018; Kim et al., 2018), education (Lee & Bonk, 2016) and sport (Clemente et al., 2015). One of the use of network analysis refers to literature review and bibliometric analyses. This usage includes several different research areas including; green supply chain management (Fahimnia et al., 2015), internet of things (Mishra et al., 2016) and supply chain finance (Xu et al., 2018).

Following general structure of network and network analysis, there are some important topics for further evaluation of network analysis. These refer to i) weighting degree of actors, ii) similarities of actors, iii)time dimension and iv) flow of information.

Weighted Actors or Equal Actors?

Evaluation of two-sided networks mostly rely on equal sized relationships, however some network structures require weighted constructs for better decision making. Examining actors in complex network could lead researcher to consider which actors are more important or influential. This decision makes connections between actors/nodes changed, as the relations are affected the importance degree of source or receiver. Kim et al. (2018) examine this phenomenon with biomedical context while they study topic evolutions with weighed value (citation influence).

Similarity of Actors in Network

Segmenting actors in networks is important issue in consumer networks as they have useful insights for further marketing decisions. The simple ways of segmenting actors in network refer to evaluation of actor groups regarding to relationships (clusters). However, complex networks can signal about hidden similarities. Alfraidi et al. (2015) examine publications and their similarities regarding to citation/reference relationship, they measure similarity with number of paths and length of each path.

Dimension of Time for Networks

Changing nature of networks have important insights for marketing decision making when it is employed for strategic decision making. Besides static evaluation of networks, including time dimension to networks can help decision making understanding evolution of networks. For example, Prabhakaran et al. (2018) examine scientific literature of Nanotechnology for Engineering and employ a variable named "Flow Vergence" to evaluate paradigm shifts.

Flow of Information

Beyond the general structure of networks, for example clusters and influential actors, the flow of information in social network is one of important issues for marketing decision making. Type and speed of information flow can signal about market and guide for other marketing decisions like advertising and promotion. Himelboim et al. (2017) study information flow in Twitter context and identify six structures of information flow. These structures are divided, undivided, clustered, fragmented, clustered, in and out hub-and-spoke networks. Observing information diffusion over time provides identifying important nodes for expanding company's existing network (Church et al., 2015). Therefore flow of information must be examined, in addition to general network structure.

Network Analysis Methodologic Definitions

Network analysis simply starts with "graphs", which are defined by Freeman (1978) as structures consist of set of points and set of lines/edges which connect points. Points (nodes) and edges (lines between points) are main network elements. Degree of point is another term in network analysis refers to the number of other points which specific point adjacent to (Freeman, 1978). Freeman (1978) concludes that degree-based measure is suggested for concern related to communication activity, while measure-based upon betweenness is suggested for interest in control of communication and measure-based upon closeness is related to concern with independence or efficiency.

Next section of study examines network analysis with cases for better understanding.

SAMPLE CASES ABOUT EVALUATING WORD OF MOUTH NETWORKS

Theoretical background of network analysis will be supported with real life cases in this section of study. The road map for network analysis methodology is summarized as 4 main steps in Figure 1. This roadmap starts with defining target for network analysis and continues with obtaining data related to target network. Following obtaining of network information, several network metrics can be implemented regarding to company's targets. In this stage companies may focus on; i) general structure of network, ii) communities in network, iii) key/local influencers, iv) trending subjects which network talks about. Results of network analysis is reported at last stage of road map.

Figure 1. Road Map for Network Analysis

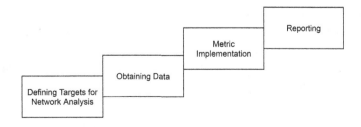

Methodology: This study uses GEPHI software (Bastian et al., 2009) for methodology and also employs Twitter API (Twitter, 2019) and plugin named "TwitterStreamingImporter" (Totet, 2019) for collecting data from Twitter. Graphical representation of network uses Force Atlas 2 algorithm (Jacomy et al., 2014) which is a force-directed layout. As Jacomy et al. (2014) implies regarding to this algorithm;

Nodes repulse each other like charged particles, while edges attract their nodes, like springs. These forces create a movement that converges to a balanced state. This final configuration is expected to help the interpretation of the data.

Next section starts with first case which refers to detection of overall structure of a network. This overall detection signal general information regarding to network and helps to further steps of examination regarding to community detection and influencer evaluation.

Case 1: Detection of Network Structure of Specific Theme in Social Media

Scenario 1: A tourism company is preparing for sports organizations in London. While the company has past information regarding to customers, marketing decision making team wants to prepare a plan for evaluating market on social media. The outcome of scenario includes insights for advertisement team, these insights can guide targeted advertising studies.

The steps for scenario 1;
Defining actors and relationships (nodes and edges) -> Listing local actors for analysis -> Defining centrality metric for campaign -> Analyzing network for centrality measurement -> Reporting segments and structure
First two steps in workflow refers to preparing stage, as they include defining and obtaining information needed for scenario. In third step, marketing team must decide which centrality metric to use for their campaign. Fourth step processes networks regarding to centrality metrics defined and segmentation of network is finished.

Data Collection: Twitter API (Twitter, 2019) and Gephi plugin "TwitterStreamingImporter" (Totet, 2019) is used for data collection regarding to hashtag "#LondonOlympics" at 28.04.2019. London Olympics event is trend topic at 28th April. Data structure in this network refers to directed network which means that each node is connected to other node with a connection.

A network created with 10121 nodes and 15870 edges. Force Atlas 2 algorithm (Jacomy et al., 2014) with 179 iteration is used for graphical representation. Figure 2 shows that there are one cluster of main segments and one additional cluster far away from center. Large and small clusters near center shows that there are users interact with each other and a centered structure. This overall graph can signal; i) main structure of network, ii) clusters near center, iii) niche node areas. The holistic approach in this scenario can guide marketing decision making for evaluating marketing environment better. Density/Cohesion of structure can signal for different marketing insights, therefore marketing decision making must examine overall structure of network firstly.

Figure 2. Overal Structure of Network for Case 1

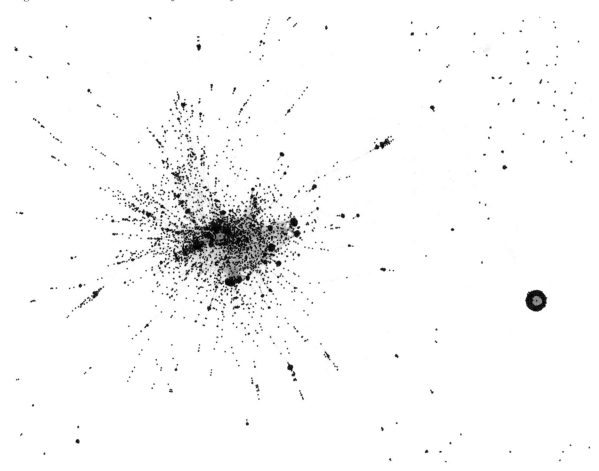

Case 2: Detection of Key Influencers in Networks for Markets

Scenario 2: A travel agency wants to identify local influencers and information flow regarding to them. While general structure of network is already examined, the agency wants to examine it further by detecting influencer and information flow structure. The outcomes of this scenario will be used for influencer marketing studies. Competitive position of the travel agency refers to challenger position in market, therefore detecting right influencers would lead company to competitive advantage.

The steps for scenario 2;

Detection of communities in network -> Detection of segments -> Decision of centrality measurement -> Detection of local influencers -> Evaluation of connections regarding to influencers -> Evaluation of information flow through connections.

Obtained data from first case is used for this case. Degree metric is implemented in Gephi (Bastian et al., 2009) and the size of nodes are corrected to centrality scores, therefore bigger circles refer to bigger centrality score. Force Atlas 2 algorithm (Jacomy et al., 2014) is implemented with 118 iterations.

Figure 3. Degree-Based Measured Network for Case 2

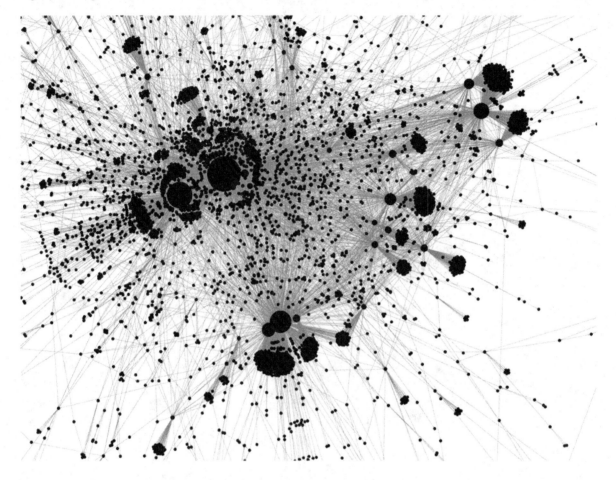

Figure 3 shows network for case 2 regarding to degree-based measurement. Bigger circles near center of figure refers to bigger degree actors in this network. It is also a bigger circle far away from center in this network (it is not included in Figure 3). The bigger circles in this case can be helpful for detecting local and macro influencers in network since they have more connections. Marketing decision making can detect influencer in overall network first, then prepare a communication or promotion plan including reaching these influencers before mass communication.

Detection of influencer has also insights for macro market conditions. The markets with different segments of communities and local influencers can be complex structures for evaluating. Determination of which influencers have most effect on which groups can be crucial for marketing planning.

Case 3: Evaluation Hashtags' Network

Third case focuses on market instead of actors while it examines what networks discusses about. A marketing campaign decision maker can start with evaluation of overall network and detecting of influential actors. But it is not a complete solution for holistic network approach. Determination of main topics and related topics regarding to main topics is crucial for marketing message planning. In this case, the network structure of hashtags in Twitter is examined. One main hashtag is selected for data collection and related hashtags are obtained for evaluation.

Steps for Case 3;
Detection of general hashtags related to industry -> Detection of main hashtag -> Obtaining of data -> Implementation of network analysis -> Reporting

Data Collection: Twitter Stream API (Twitter, 2019) is used with GEPHI software (Bastian et al., 2009) and its plugin named "TwitterStreamingImporter" (Totet, 2019). Hashtag "#celtics" is selected from Worldwide Trend Topics at 28th April 2019. Modularity function of Gephi (Gephi, 2018) is used in software for detecting communities of hashtags. Modularity function uses Blondel et al. (2008)'s algorithm for evaluating of communities. Force Atlas alhorithm (Jacomy et al., 2014) is also implemented for graphical representation.

Figure 4. Hashtag Network for Case 3

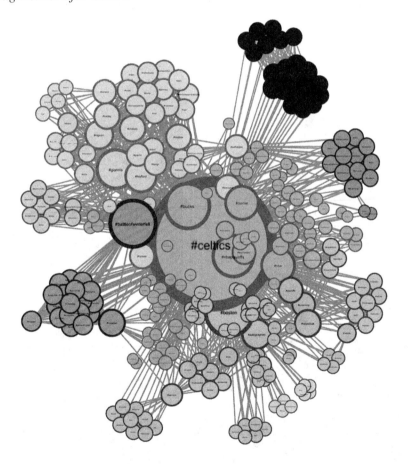

Hashtags are segmented through different colors in Figure 4 and sizes of nodes are adjusted according to degrees of nodes. For example purple nodes contain some of NBA related hashtags.

This segmentation can advise marketing management about electronic word of mouth environment. Understanding what consumers talks online can be helpful for promotion management. It is also suggested to examine outside clusters since they can signal related or unrelated hashtags. Related hashtags can be used for advertising or promotion campaigns, while unrelated hashtags can be used for spam detection.

Case 4: Network of Restaurant Cuisines

Unlike the traditional node-edge structure, a network analysis will be made on the cuisines in the restaurant. This case may be useful in guiding a company with an idea of entering the market by opening a new restaurant at a specific location.

Steps for Case 4;
    Determination of targeted geographic area -> Determination of criteria for selecting restaurants -> Obtaining data -> Implementing network analysis -> Reporting of networks
    Data collection: Data in this case study is used from a Kaggle data set named "Zomato Restaurants Data" (Mehta, 2018). The dataset includes information about different restaurants from several cities.

Figure 5. Cuisine Network for Case 4

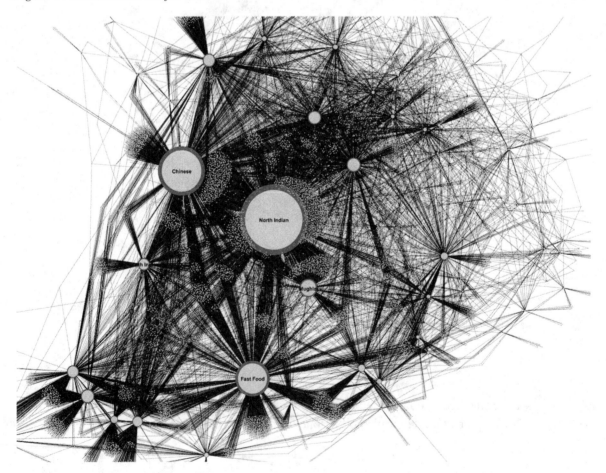

Figure 5 includes that there are several main clusters for cuisines in targeted area. North Indian, Chinese, Fast Food, Mughlai and South Indian are main clusters. This cluster structure signals about most popular cuisine in selected market. Beyond general structure of network, there are some minor nodes/small clusters outside center. These minor nodes can be niche market for new market entry. Therefore both conclusions can be helpful regarding to target of market actor.

This "object" approach has a cluster analysis nature and can be helpful for several marketing targets. For example clustering categories of customer complaints can show most popular and least popular customer complaints, as well as categories with bridging roles.

SOLUTIONS AND RECOMMENDATIONS

Network analysis is one of ideal statistic methodologies for social science due to its roots for social network theory. People (consumers in our study context) often communicate and exchange ideas through word of mouth or internet-based technologies which refer to electronic word of mouth. The harmony of methodology with theory helps marketing decision making about evaluating social media environment. In addition to e-wom concept, the service industry mostly depends on people factor as people (or personnel) reflect image of company to consumers and the experience of service consumption varies from person to person. Thus, evaluation of person related factors with network analysis approach could be a decision making solution.

Recommendations for business world includes strategic approach for network analysis regarding to customer and market analysis. Considering how network analysis can help to marketing plan of company would be a good starting point. The integration of network analysis with other marketing methodologies including sentiment analysis, digital advertising tools and social media marketing would be next step. Second recommendation about network analysis and its implementation refers to sub-concepts of network analysis including community detection, flow of information. These sub-concepts can be useful for specific marketing cases. Context-based differences make sub-concepts necessary for marketing decision making. Third recommendation refers to evaluation of different social media channels and their potentials for marketing plans. Each social media channel has its own characteristics, therefore it can help to marketing decision making.

FUTURE RESEARCH DIRECTIONS

Social media concept has crucial potential for business. According to Global Digital Report (We Are Social & Hootsuite, 2019) active social media users have increased 9% (+218 million) between January 2018 and January 2019. It is obvious that social media will be focused areas of marketing management in following years.

Future research directions of this study consist of three parts; context and industry-based researches, detail researches, researches with time dimension. First part refers examining network analysis with different contexts and industries since the variety of contexts and industries affect network structures. The community detection cases are example for this part. Hospitality industry would have a large network but small communities, on the other hand training/education industry would have large network with large communities. The industry focused approach can be more accurate for marketing researches. Second part refers to extending network analysis concepts for further research. Continuing to general network structure examination with community detection could be next research. Community detection can continue with flow of information research. Thus, next steps for further researches can refer to details. Last part refers to time dimension for researches. Networks have dynamic nature, thus adding time dimension can be helpful for marketing decision making. For example, a network structure of hospitality industry can evolve differently from launch of new branch to holiday season. Therefore, marketing decision making must examine how network structure over time. Existence of new communities, spreading of e-wom messages can signal about market environment. These three directions can be employed as one by one or integrated together for further cases.

CONCLUSION

Traditional word of mouth concept still has crucial role for marketing management decision making, in form of electronic word of mouth, social media and review websites. As people live in groups and society, digital "social" worlds would still continue in similar forms regarding to social structures. People exchange, consume and transfer ideas to each other and companies can make use of these insights. Forms of people's communication have been changed in recent years and will continue to change in future but need of observation of market and consumers will still exist. Therefore, strategic planning must be employed regardless of variety of communication.

Second conclusion regarding to e-wom concept refers to network analysis methodology and its potential for marketing decision making. Social media applications and two-way communications type makes network analysis useful for marketing management. Several methodology options including community detection, key influencer detection, time-based change evaluation, anomaly detection (Savage et al., 2014) can help for different marketing scenarios.

Third conclusion refers to degree of markets which network analysis evaluate for marketing. Micro and macro levels differ and offer different types of insights for e-wom management. Types of social ties (strong or weak), groups of nodes and flow of information have different insights for micro and macro level. Evaluation of levels and transitions with time would be useful for marketing. Dynamic nature of networks makes it necessary to take time dimension into consideration, therefore detailed approach can be useful.

REFERENCES

Alfraidi, H., Lee, W. S., & Sankoff, D. (2015, July). Literature visualization and similarity measurement based on citation relations. In *2015 19th International Conference on Information Visualisation* (pp. 217-222). IEEE. 10.1109/iV.2015.47

An & Liu. (2016). *keyplayer: Locating Key Players in Social Networks*. R package version 1.0.3. Retrieved from https://CRAN.R-project.org/package=keyplayer

Bastian, M., Heymann, S., & Jacomy, M. (2009, March). Gephi: an open source software for exploring and manipulating networks. *Third international AAAI conference on weblogs and social media.*

Blondel, V. D., Guillaume, J. L., Lambiotte, R., & Lefebvre, E. (2008). Fast unfolding of communities in large networks. *Journal of Statistical Mechanics*, *2008*(10), P10008. doi:10.1088/1742-5468/2008/10/P10008

Brown, J. J., & Reingen, P. H. (1987). Social ties and word-of-mouth referral behavior. *The Journal of Consumer Research*, *14*(3), 350–362. doi:10.1086/209118

Carter, T. B. (2016). *sna: Tools for Social Network Analysis*. R package version 2.4. Retrieved from https://CRAN.R-project.org/package=sna

Cheung, C. M., & Thadani, D. R. (2012). The impact of electronic word-of-mouth communication: A literature analysis and integrative model. *Decision Support Systems*, *54*(1), 461–470. doi:10.1016/j.dss.2012.06.008

Chevalier, J. A., & Mayzlin, D. (2006). The effect of word of mouth on sales: Online book reviews. *JMR, Journal of Marketing Research*, *43*(3), 345–354. doi:10.1509/jmkr.43.3.345

Church, E. M., Iyer, L. S., & Zhao, X. (2015). Using interest graphs to predict rich-media diffusion in content-based online social networks. *Information Systems Management*, *32*(3), 210–219. doi:10.1080/10580530.2015.1044340

Clemente, F. M., Martins, F. M. L., Kalamaras, D., Wong, P. D., & Mendes, R. S. (2015). General network analysis of national soccer teams in FIFA World Cup 2014. *International Journal of Performance Analysis in Sport*, *15*(1), 80–96. doi:10.1080/24748668.2015.11868778

Cormode, G., & Krishnamurthy, B. (2008). Key differences between Web 1.0 and Web 2.0. *First Monday*, *13*(6). doi:10.5210/fm.v13i6.2125

Csardi, G., & Nepusz, T. (2006). The igraph software package for complex network research, InterJournal. *Complex Systems*, *1695*. Retrieved from http://igraph.org

Dobele, A., Lindgreen, A., Beverland, M., Vanhamme, J., & Van Wijk, R. (2007). Why pass on viral messages? Because they connect emotionally. *Business Horizons*, *50*(4), 291–304. doi:10.1016/j.bushor.2007.01.004

Fahimnia, B., Sarkis, J., & Davarzani, H. (2015). Green supply chain management: A review and bibliometric analysis. *International Journal of Production Economics*, *162*, 101–114. doi:10.1016/j.ijpe.2015.01.003

Freeman, L. C. (1978). Centrality in social networks conceptual clarification. *Social Networks*, *1*(3), 215–239. doi:10.1016/0378-8733(78)90021-7

Gephi. (2018). *Modularity*. Retrieved from https://github.com/gephi/gephi/wiki/Modularity

Granovetter, M. S. (1977). The strength of weak ties. In *Social networks* (pp. 347–367). Academic Press. doi:10.1016/B978-0-12-442450-0.50025-0

Grund, T. U. (2012). Network structure and team performance: The case of English Premier League soccer teams. *Social Networks*, *34*(4), 682–690. doi:10.1016/j.socnet.2012.08.004

Hambrick, M. E., & Pegoraro, A. (2014). Social Sochi: Using social network analysis to investigate electronic word-of-mouth transmitted through social media communities. *International Journal of Sport Management and Marketing, 15*(3-4), 120–140. doi:10.1504/IJSMM.2014.072005

Hennig-Thurau, T., Gwinner, K. P., Walsh, G., & Gremler, D. D. (2004). Electronic word-of-mouth via consumer-opinion platforms: What motivates consumers to articulate themselves on the internet? *Journal of Interactive Marketing, 18*(1), 38–52. doi:10.1002/dir.10073

Himelboim, I., Smith, M. A., Rainie, L., Shneiderman, B., & Espina, C. (2017). Classifying Twitter topic-networks using social network analysis. *Social Media+ Society, 3*(1).

Iacobucci, D., Henderson, G., Marcati, A., & Chang, J. (1996). Network analyses of brand switching behavior. *International Journal of Research in Marketing, 13*(5), 415–429. doi:10.1016/S0167-8116(96)00022-5

Jacobs & Khanna. (2015). *influenceR: Software Tools to Quantify Structural Importance of Nodes in a Network*. R package version 0.1.0. Retrieved from https://CRAN.R-project.org/package=influenceR

Jacomy, M., Venturini, T., Heymann, S., & Bastian, M. (2014). ForceAtlas2, a continuous graph layout algorithm for handy network visualization designed for the Gephi software. *PLoS One, 9*(6), e98679. doi:10.1371/journal.pone.0098679 PMID:24914678

Jansen, B. J., Zhang, M., Sobel, K., & Chowdury, A. (2009). Twitter power: Tweets as electronic word of mouth. *Journal of the American Society for Information Science and Technology, 60*(11), 2169–2188. doi:10.1002/asi.21149

Kaplan, A. M., & Haenlein, M. (2011). Two hearts in three-quarter time: How to waltz the social media/viral marketing dance. *Business Horizons, 54*(3), 253–263. doi:10.1016/j.bushor.2011.01.006

Kim, J., Bae, J., & Hastak, M. (2018). Emergency information diffusion on online social media during storm Cindy in US. *International Journal of Information Management, 40*, 153–165. doi:10.1016/j.ijinfomgt.2018.02.003

Kim, J., & Hastak, M. (2018). Social network analysis: Characteristics of online social networks after a disaster. *International Journal of Information Management, 38*(1), 86–96. doi:10.1016/j.ijinfomgt.2017.08.003

Kim, M., Baek, I., & Song, M. (2018). Topic diffusion analysis of a weighted citation network in biomedical literature. *Journal of the Association for Information Science and Technology, 69*(2), 329–342. doi:10.1002/asi.23960

Kwon, O., & Wen, Y. (2010). An empirical study of the factors affecting social network service use. *Computers in Human Behavior, 26*(2), 254–263. doi:10.1016/j.chb.2009.04.011

Ladhari, R., & Michaud, M. (2015). eWOM effects on hotel booking intentions, attitudes, trust, and website perceptions. *International Journal of Hospitality Management, 46*, 36–45. doi:10.1016/j.ijhm.2015.01.010

Lee, J., & Bonk, C. J. (2016). Social network analysis of peer relationships and online interactions in a blended class using blogs. *The Internet and Higher Education, 28*, 35–44. doi:10.1016/j.iheduc.2015.09.001

Leung, X. Y., Wang, F., Wu, B., Bai, B., Stahura, K. A., & Xie, Z. (2012). A social network analysis of overseas tourist movement patterns in Beijing: The impact of the Olympic Games. *International Journal of Tourism Research, 14*(5), 469–484. doi:10.1002/jtr.876

Liu, Y. (2006). Word of mouth for movies: Its dynamics and impact on box office revenue. *Journal of Marketing, 70*(3), 74–89. doi:10.1509/jmkg.70.3.074

Mangold, W. G., & Faulds, D. J. (2009). Social media: The new hybrid element of the promotion mix. *Business Horizons, 52*(4), 357–365. doi:10.1016/j.bushor.2009.03.002

Marsden, P. V. (1990). Network data and measurement. *Annual Review of Sociology, 16*(1), 435–463. doi:10.1146/annurev.so.16.080190.002251

Mehta, S. (2018). *Zomato Restaurants Data. Analyzing the best restaurants of the major cities.* Retrieved from https://www.kaggle.com/shrutimehta/zomato-restaurants-data/

Meuser, J. D., Gardner, W. L., Dinh, J. E., Hu, J., Liden, R. C., & Lord, R. G. (2016). A network analysis of leadership theory: The infancy of integration. *Journal of Management, 42*(5), 1374–1403. doi:10.1177/0149206316647099

Mishra, D., Gunasekaran, A., Childe, S. J., Papadopoulos, T., Dubey, R., & Wamba, S. (2016). Vision, applications and future challenges of Internet of Things: A bibliometric study of the recent literature. *Industrial Management & Data Systems, 116*(7), 1331–1355. doi:10.1108/IMDS-11-2015-0478

Morales-Arroyo, M., & Pandey, T. (2010, June). Identification of critical eWOM dimensions for music albums. In *2010 IEEE International Conference on Management of Innovation & Technology* (pp. 1230-1235). IEEE. 10.1109/ICMIT.2010.5492860

Moreno, J. L. (1953). *Who Shall Survive?* New York: Beacon House.

Ngai, E. W., Tao, S. S., & Moon, K. K. (2015). Social media research: Theories, constructs, and conceptual frameworks. *International Journal of Information Management, 35*(1), 33–44. doi:10.1016/j.ijinfomgt.2014.09.004

Nielsen. (2015). *Nielsen Global Trust in Advertising Survey.* Retrieved from https://www.nielsen.com/content/dam/nielsenglobal/apac/docs/reports/2015/nielsen-global-trust-in-advertising-report-september-2015.pdf

Oliveira, M., & Gama, J. (2012). An overview of social network analysis. *Wiley Interdisciplinary Reviews. Data Mining and Knowledge Discovery, 2*(2), 99–115. doi:10.1002/widm.1048

Peng, J., Agarwal, A., Hosanagar, K., & Iyengar, R. (2018). Network overlap and content sharing on social media platforms. *JMR, Journal of Marketing Research, 55*(4), 571–585. doi:10.1509/jmr.14.0643

Prabhakaran, T., Lathabai, H. H., George, S., & Changat, M. (2018). Towards prediction of paradigm shifts from scientific literature. *Scientometrics, 117*(3), 1611–1644. doi:10.100711192-018-2931-3

R Core Team. (2013). *R: A language and environment for statistical computing.* R Foundation for Statistical Computing. Retrieved from http://www.R-project.org/

Savage, D., Zhang, X., Yu, X., Chou, P., & Wang, Q. (2014). Anomaly detection in online social networks. *Social Networks*, *39*, 62–70. doi:10.1016/j.socnet.2014.05.002

Selden, M., & Goodie, A. S. (2018). Review of the effects of Five Factor Model personality traits on network structures and perceptions of structure. *Social Networks*, *52*, 81–99. doi:10.1016/j.socnet.2017.05.007

Shih, H. Y. (2006). Network characteristics of drive tourism destinations: An application of network analysis in tourism. *Tourism Management*, *27*(5), 1029–1039. doi:10.1016/j.tourman.2005.08.002

Steffes, E. M., & Burgee, L. E. (2009). Social ties and online word of mouth. *Internet Research*, *19*(1), 42–59. doi:10.1108/10662240910927812

Takhteyev, Y., Gruzd, A., & Wellman, B. (2012). Geography of Twitter networks. *Social Networks*, *34*(1), 73–81. doi:10.1016/j.socnet.2011.05.006

Totet, M. (2019). *TwitterStreamingImporter*. Retrieved from https://gephi.org/plugins/#/plugin/twitter-streaming-importer

Tsao, W. C., Hsieh, M. T., Shih, L. W., & Lin, T. M. (2015). Compliance with eWOM: The influence of hotel reviews on booking intention from the perspective of consumer conformity. *International Journal of Hospitality Management*, *46*, 99–111. doi:10.1016/j.ijhm.2015.01.008

Twitter. (2019). *Docs - Twitter API*. Retrieved from https://developer.twitter.com/en/docs.html

Viglia, G., Minazzi, R., & Buhalis, D. (2016). The influence of e-word-of-mouth on hotel occupancy rate. *International Journal of Contemporary Hospitality Management*, *28*(9), 2035–2051. doi:10.1108/IJCHM-05-2015-0238

Vilpponen, A., Winter, S., & Sundqvist, S. (2006). Electronic word-of-mouth in online environments: Exploring referral networks structure and adoption behavior. *Journal of Interactive Advertising*, *6*(2), 8–77. doi:10.1080/15252019.2006.10722120

Wang, H. J., & Horng, S. C. (2016). Exploring green brand associations through a network analysis approach. *Psychology and Marketing*, *33*(1), 20–35. doi:10.1002/mar.20854

Wasserman, S., & Faust, K. (1994). *Social network analysis: Methods and applications* (Vol. 8). Cambridge university press. doi:10.1017/CBO9780511815478

We Are Social & Hootsuite. (2019). *Global Digital Report*. Retrieved from https://wearesocial.com/global-digital-report-2019

Wirtz, J., & Chew, P. (2002). The effects of incentives, deal proneness, satisfaction and tie strength on word-of-mouth behaviour. *International Journal of Service Industry Management*, *13*(2), 141–162. doi:10.1108/09564230210425340

Xu, X., Chen, X., Jia, F., Brown, S., Gong, Y., & Xu, Y. (2018). Supply chain finance: A systematic literature review and bibliometric analysis. *International Journal of Production Economics*, *204*, 160–173. doi:10.1016/j.ijpe.2018.08.003

Yan, G., Watanabe, N. M., Shapiro, S. L., Naraine, M. L., & Hull, K. (2018). Unfolding the Twitter scene of the 2017 UEFA Champions League Final: Social media networks and power dynamics. *European Sport Management Quarterly*, 1–18. doi:10.1080/16184742.2018.1517272

ADDITIONAL READING

Bastian, M., Heymann, S., & Jacomy, M. (2009, March). Gephi: an open source software for exploring and manipulating networks. *Third international AAAI conference on weblogs and social media.*

Batagelj, V., & Mrvar, A. (1998). Pajek-program for large network analysis. *Connections*, *21*(2), 47–57.

Borgatti, S. P., Mehra, A., Brass, D. J., &Labianca, G. (2009). Network analysis in the social sciences. *Science, 323*(5916), 892-895.

Butts, C. T. (2008). Social network analysis with sna. *Journal of Statistical Software*, *24*(6), 1–51. doi:10.18637/jss.v024.i06 PMID:18612375

Csardi, G., & Nepusz, T. (2006). The igraph software package for complex network research. InterJournal. *Complex Systems*, *1695*(5), 1–9.

Granovetter, M. S. (1977). The strength of weak ties. In *Social networks* (pp. 347–367). Academic Press. doi:10.1016/B978-0-12-442450-0.50025-0

Jacomy, M., Venturini, T., Heymann, S., & Bastian, M. (2014). ForceAtlas2, a continuous graph layout algorithm for handy network visualization designed for the Gephi software. *PLoS One*, *9*(6), e98679. doi:10.1371/journal.pone.0098679 PMID:24914678

Scott, J. (1988). Social network analysis. *Sociology*, *22*(1), 109–127. doi:10.1177/0038038588022001007

Wasserman, S., & Faust, K. (1994). *Social network analysis: Methods and applications* (Vol. 8). Cambridge university press. doi:10.1017/CBO9780511815478

KEY TERMS AND DEFINITIONS

Electronic Word of Mouth: Using technological channels forf word of mouth activities.
Network Analysis: The statistical and graphical analysis of network structures.
Social Media: Web platform which users exchange ideas, expressions, feelings to each other.
Word of Mouth: The activity of exchanging ideas of people through groups or networks.

This research was previously published in Exploring the Power of Electronic Word-of-Mouth in the Services Industry; pages 69-87, copyright year 2020 by Business Science Reference (an imprint of IGI Global).

Chapter 5
A Literature Review of Social Media for Marketing:
Social Media Use in B2C and B2B Contexts

Bahtışen Kavak
 https://orcid.org/0000-0002-5252-5410
Hacettepe University, Turkey

Neslişah Özdemir
 https://orcid.org/0000-0003-2380-6149
Kastamonu University, Turkey

Gülay Erol-Boyacı
 https://orcid.org/0000-0002-8123-3011
Başkent University, Turkey

ABSTRACT

Digital economy has become a priority for companies and countries since consumer profile and consumption habits have greatly changed. Companies have begun to transfer the services they offer to the Internet. Also, a digital economy creates networks amongst individuals, communities, companies, and markets. With digitalization, not only have consumers' profiles changed, but marketing tools have changed as well. Social media marketing (SMM) is the product of this trend and is marketing through social media channels (SMCs). Therefore, this chapter examines social media use within business-to-consumer (B2C) and business-to-business (B2B) contexts. Moreover, the authors focus on the differences of SMCs adoption in B2C and B2B contexts.

DOI: 10.4018/978-1-7998-9020-1.ch005

INTRODUCTION

The use of social media has expanded in recent years. Social media is a term that academics and professionals use to describe this media. One of the basic definitions of social media is "sites where users actively participate to determine what is popular" ("SEMPO," 2017), and another definition is "a platform for interaction and networking" (Eisenberg, 2008). Social media is beginning to be considered as an important marketing tool in digital economies for companies. The use of social media is assumed to make changes in the ways *business-to-consumer* (B2C) and *business-to-business* (B2B) marketers communicate, interact, consume, and create within and outside the company (Vize & Sherrett, 2017, p. 46).

This chapter aims to provide a literature review of social media for marketing. The main objective of marketing is to reach consumers and influence their purchasing behaviors. As social media is an effective tool to reach audiences and promote products or services, companies give value to Social Media Marketing (SMM). SMM is used for the purpose of brand awareness, developing brand image, increasing communication efficiency, improving customer relationships, and to stimulate sales. However, the purposes of SMM have to be evaluated in terms of the customer life cycle process.

The social media literature gives special emphasis to consumers in the B2C context (Michaelidou, Siamagka, & Christodoulides, 2011). In other words, researchers have focused more on the user side rather than on the companies' views (Jussila, 2015, p. 3). B2C companies are aware of the importance of social media and desire to reach consumers by using social media channels (SMCs). They use social media to attract new customers, develop relationships, and increase awareness. Moreover, they enhance interaction with consumers through SMCs. In contrast, until recently, B2B organizations believed that social media use was only beneficial in a B2C context (Jussila, Kärkkäinen, & Aramo-Immonen, 2014) and perceived SMCs to be inadequate for their industry. Nevertheless, B2B has begun to realize the importance of social media in today's marketing environment. For instance, the Content Marketing Institute (CMI, 2018) put forth that 92% of B2B marketers support using SMCs (e.g., LinkedIn, Twitter, etc.) more than using traditional tools such as trade shows, direct mail, and catalogues.

While trying to adopt social media, B2B companies have different purposes. First, companies desire to scan market trends and evaluate changing customer attitudes. Moreover, demonstrating products and providing training to business partners via social media are important to them. In addition to this, employee recruitment and retention are the leading motives for using SMCs (Vize & Sherrett, 2017, p. 50). Therefore, the use of SMCs as marketing tools has increased. Some B2B brands have their own original content and others have YouTube pages. They publish special content for SMCs on sites such as Facebook, Twitter, and LinkedIn, and share the videos produced via YouTube with users.

Since market characteristics are different from one another, the usage of SMCs also differs within B2C and B2B contexts. While some empirical studies do explore the differences in SMC usage between B2C and B2B contexts, this topic is limited in much of the literature (Moore, Hopkins, & Raymond, 2013; Swani, Brown, & Milne, 2014; Iankova, Davies, Archer-Brown, Marder, & Yau, 2018).

This chapter, therefore, aims to focus on the differences between SMC usage within B2B and B2C contexts. For this reason, this chapter includes background information, definitions and classification of social media, a definition and the purposes of SMM, and social media usage in B2C and B2B environments. Finally, solutions and recommendations, future research directions, and conclusion are also provided.

BACKGROUND

The concept of social media is one of the biggest changes since the industrial revolution (Smith & Zook, 2011, p. 9). The foundation of social media today is based on many of the popular social media sites introduced in the 1990s (Figure 1).

To have a better understanding of the modern communication environment, evolution of social media history is significant. In this regard, Figure 1 demonstrates examples for the timeline of SMCs in chronological order. In the 1990s, the earliest form of SMCs, such as Craigslist, Black Planet, and Blogger, were developed (Flanigan & Obermier, 2016) to provide online services based on sharing information and stories. After 2000, SMCs were advanced and Wikipedia, LinkedIn, MySpace, Facebook, YouTube, and so on were born (Funk, 2011, p. 8). These new channels enabled people to not only share stories or ideas, but also to meet and contact one another. Today, multiple users can communicate in real time, share pictures, videos, and any kind of document through SMCs.

Figure 1. Examples for timeline of SMCs
Source: (Funk, 2011, p. 9; Flanigan & Obermier, 2016)

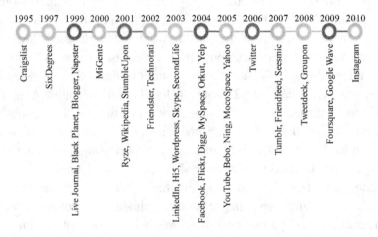

Table 1 shows some statistical indicators about active social media user rates in five regions. As it is shown in Table 1, during the 2016, the total number of Internet users has increased 10% (354 Million); meanwhile the total number of active social media users has increased 21% (482 Million). When it is examined, the regional data, in all the five regions (Africa, Americas, Asia-Pacific, Europe, Middle East), both the Internet and social media user rates have increased.

Social media, one of the basic tools of digital marketing, brings innovations in terms of the relationship between businesses and customers. While customers are the same, their buying behaviors and opportunities have changed as traditional advertising channels, such as TV commercials, billboards, and radio (Smedescu, 2013) have been expanded through the availability of new informational and shopping sites on the Internet. There is less dependence on traditional communication channels in this era. Hence, businesses use social media and shape the marketplace in terms of new communication approaches (Constantinides, 2014).

Table 1. A few statistical indicators of Internet and active social media users for different regions

	Population	Internet Users*	Active Social Media Users*
Total	7,476 Billion	3.773 Billion *(+10%)* *(+354 Million)*	2.789 Billion *(+21%)* *(+482 Million)*
Africa	1.231 Million	362 Million *(+4%)* *(+13 Million)*	170 Million *(+32%)* *(+42 Million)*
America	1.006 Million	718 Million *(+8%)* *(+53 Million)*	599 Million *(+17%)* *(+88 Million)*
Asia Pacific	4.153 Billion	1.909 Billion *(+15%)* *(+247 Million)*	1.514 Billion *(+25%)* *(+303 Million)*
Europe	839 Million	637 Million *(+3%)* *(+21 Million)*	412 Million *(+ 5%)* *(+ 20 Million)*
Middle East	246 Million	147 Million *(+15%)* *(+19 Million)*	93 Million *(+47%)* *(+30 Million)*

*Data shown in parentheses are based on annual change between 01.01.2016 and 01.01.2017.

**Note: Data was retrieved from "We Are Social January Report" (2017).

The use of social media within marketing contexts contributes to businesses in various ways. First, social media contributes to companies engaged in market research. Automated data collection and evaluation of profiles, links, and shares in social media provide market researchers with the opportunity to evaluate market segmentation, monitor consumer behavior, market positions of products, and offer new product development information. Furthermore, social media provides more personalized resolutions to their customers with regard to any problems or concerns with products (Al Khalili, 2018). In addition to this, through the mutual communication provided in SMCs, customers, or potential customers, obtain information about the culture and products of companies, and as a result of this communication, companies obtain feedback by learning the expectations of their customers and their thoughts about the company or their products (Hacıhasanoglu, 2017).

Social media utilization in digital economies is a contemporary issue. In order to determine social media use in digital economies, the organizations classify their markets, such as B2C and B2B. In B2C, customers are ordinary people who want to know other customer reviews and receive special treatment. However, in B2B, companies are seeking direct contact and special offers (AlSuwaidan & Ykhlef, 2016). When compared to B2C markets, there are fewer customers in B2B markets, and the social networks that exist between business partners are important in terms of providing strong cooperation. Therefore, social media use between B2C and B2B markets differ in terms of market features.

While studies on the usage of social media in B2C is widespread, studies focusing on the extent of social media adoption by B2B companies has been limited in the literature. Michaelidou, Siamagka, and Christodoulides (2011) are among the initial researchers who explored SMEs in B2B contexts, their social networking practices, and the measurement of effectiveness of social networking sites. They found that B2B SMEs used social networking sites to accomplish brand objectives and attract new customers. Brennan and Croft (2012) investigated B2B technology companies to determine their social media usage. They found that social media leaders in B2B markets used SMCs to position themselves as opinion leaders, to ensure a market-driven role, and to maintain relationship with third parties.

Research that focuses on the differences between usage of social media between B2C and B2B is limited. Moore, Hopkins, and Raymond (2013) and Swani, Brown, and Milne (2014) investigated the usage differences between these two contexts, but only for social media posts, especially on Twitter and Facebook. Moreover, Iankova, Davies, Archer-Brown, Marder, and Yau (2018) examined the differences in the ways that B2B and B2C businesses used social media, as well as mixed B2B/B2C and B2B2C business models, and perceived significant differences. Therefore, this chapter highlights social media usage in B2C and B2B contexts, especially in terms of differences of trends in usage.

SOCIAL MEDIA

In this next section, the authors have examined social media in terms of two titles: definition of social media and classification of SMCs.

Definition of Social Media

In a broad perspective, social media is "any web presence where users can add their own content, but do not have control over the website in the same way as they would their own website" (Charlesworth, 2015, p. 150). From a similar point of view, social media is defined as, "The production, consumption, and exchange of information through online social interactions and platforms" ("MARKETO," 2010, p. 5).

Moreover, social media is also referred as Web 2.0, which is based on word-of-mouth and information sharing (Barefoot & Szabo, 2010, p. 4). There are different definitions from this perspective:

- Social media is a group of internet-based applications that build on the ideological and technological foundations of Web 2.0 and that allow the creation and exchange of user-generated content (Kaplan & Haenlein, 2010).
- Web 2.0 presents businesses with new challenges, but also new opportunities for getting and staying in touch with their markets, learning about the needs and opinions of their customers, as well as interacting with customers in a direct and personalized way (Tapscott & Williams, 2008, p. 20).

Some academics and professionals use the term "Web 2.0" to define social media. Based on the Web 2.0 definitions, Table 2 provides details that show what Web 2.0 is and how it is different from Web 1.0.

Table 2. Differences between web 1.0 and web 2.0

Web 1.0 was about…	Web 2.0 is about…
• Reading • Advertising • Lectures • Websites • Professionals • Companies • Owning	• Writing • Word-of-Mouth • Conversations • Web Services • Amateurs • Communities • Sharing

Source: (Barefoot & Szabo, 2010, p. 4)

As seen in Table 2, Web 1.0 offers one-way communications, whereas Web 2.0 offers two-way communications. In Web 1.0, people can only read the contents and cannot share their opinions or feelings. However, in Web 2.0, it is possible to write and share opinions. So, Web 2.0 allows people to have conversations via the Internet from wherever they are.

Therefore, social media could be described as Internet-based applications that enable sharing and exchange of information, ideas, interests, and creation of virtual networks and communities. Social media is a new way of sharing and accessing user-generated information in a simple, instant, and bilateral way. It provides users with personal information, videos, photos, and other contents easily transmitted through the virtual environment.

In general, people primarily use social media for searching for entertainment, travel, food, and shopping, or for obtaining information about products and brands ("MARKETO," 2016, p. 10). Charlesworth (2015, p. 155) suggested that social media users are driven by the following:

- The need to socialize is one of the main reasons. People want to be in touch with their friends and have a social network.
- There is a need for self-expression. Expression of personality, emotions, or ideas, through SMCs is easier today when compared to the past.
- People want to find others who have similar tastes and interests. Some SMCs are designed to build networks.
- Contrary to the traditional word-of-mouth, SMCs provide access to unlimited information about any brand or product.
- The desire to search for a job, to find cheaper goods or services, and to find free software products are examples of some of the financial advantages served by social media.

It can be concluded that people have a variety of motives that include socialization, self-expression, networking, accessing information, and utilizing financial advantages while using social media.

Classification of Social Media Channels (SMCs)

SMCs are user-friendly, cost effective, scalable Internet and mobile-based technologies. With these technologies it is possible to share user-generated contents (Fischer & Reuber, 2011). In the literature, there are different classifications for SMCs. One of the classifications made by Kaplan and Haenlein (2010) is based on social presence and media richness (low, medium, high) and self-presentation and self-disclosure (low, high). According to Kaplan and Haenlein (2010), there are six different social media classes: 1). Collaborative projects (e.g., Wikipedia); 2). Content communities (e.g., YouTube); 3). Virtual game worlds (e.g., World of Warcraft); 4). Blogs; 5). Social networking sites (e.g., Facebook); and 6). Virtual social worlds (e.g., Second Life).

When SMCs are evaluated in terms of social presence and media richness, blogs and collaborative projects have the lowest scores. Because they are text based, they include simple exchanges. Social networking sites and content communities are in the medium part, according to social presence and media richness since they often provide visual and video sharing. The highest part consists of virtual social worlds and virtual game worlds that provide to users with face-to-face interaction in a visual environment.

On the other hand, those SMCs can be classified with regards to self-presentation and self-disclosure. Since collaborative projects concentrate on particular content, blogs provide higher self-presentation and self-disclosure. Social networking sites score higher than content communities in terms of self-presentation and self-disclosure, as content communities focus on specific content. Virtual social worlds allow for more self-disclosure and self-presentation than virtual game worlds that have hard rules that push users to act in a precise way (Kaplan & Haenlein, 2010). Furthermore, Zimmerman and Ng (2017, p. 25) categorizes SMCs into six types (Figure 2).

Figure 2. Classification of SMCs
Source: (Zimmerman & Ng, 2017, p. 25)

Social Content-Sharing	Social-Networking	Social-Bookmarking	Social Geolocations and Meetings	Community Building	Social News
• Blogs and content-posting sites • Images • Video • Audio	• Full networks • Short message networks • Professional networks • Specialty networks	• Recommendation services • Social-shopping services • Other bookmarking services.	• Foursquare • Meetups • Other GPS (Global Positioning System) applications	• Community-Building sites • Wikis • Review sites	• Digg • Reddit • Other news sites

As shown in Figure 2, SMCs consist of social content sharing, social networking, social-bookmarking, social geolocations and meetings, community building, and social news channels (Zimmerman & Ng, 2017, p. 25).

- **Social Content-sharing Channels:** These services provide posting and commenting on text, videos, photos, and podcasts. They include blogs and content-posting sites (e.g. WordPress, Blogger, Medium, and Tumblr); video (e.g. YouTube, Vimeo, Vine.co); images (e.g. Flickr, Instagram, Snapchat, SlideShare, Pinterest); and podcasts (e.g. Podbean, BlogTalkRadio).
- **Social-networking Channels:** These channels facilitate the exchange of personal information such as messages, photos to friends and family, and also offer services in terms of business. Social-networking channels consist of full networks (e.g. Facebook, Google Plus); short message networks (e.g. Twitter); professional networks (e.g. LinkedIn); and specialty networks (e.g. Q&A network Quora).
- **Social-bookmarking Channels:** These channels provide users with the opportunity to store, organize, and search Internet pages. Social-bookmarking channels include recommendation services (e.g. StumbleUpon, Delicious), social-shopping services (e.g. Wanelo, ThisNext), and other bookmarking services.
- **Social Geolocation and Meeting Channels:** These channels bring people together in actual space and include Foursquare, Meetups, and other GPS (Global Positioning System) applications.
- **Community-building Channels:** These channels include many comments and material sharing sites. Especially, forums and massage boards, which are good examples of these channels. They include community building sites (e.g. Ning); Wikis (e.g. Wikipedia) and review sites (e.g. TripAdvisor, Yelp).
- **Social News Channels:** A social news website involves user-posted stories. They include Digg, Reddit and other news sites.

While there are different classifications of SMCs, this chapter reviews SMCs in terms of social content sharing and social networking channels. Today, the top five social media networking platforms used by marketers in terms of unique monthly visitors are: Facebook, YouTube, Twitter, Instagram, and LinkedIn ("Most Popular Networking Sites," 2017). Therefore, those channels will be identified in detail.

Facebook is a social networking site launched in 2004. At first, Facebook was a social network for Harvard students. Today, it has more than 300 million active users from 170 countries (Reece, 2010, p. 246). People can get connected with their friends easily around the world thanks to Facebook. LinkedIn is the world's largest proficient network site with more than 175 million members worldwide (Funk, 2011, p. 48).

Twitter, launched in 2006, is based in San Francisco and can be immediately translated from English to 16 other languages. Thus, it can be easily used by people all over the world (Coles, 2015, p. 82). Twitter includes 140 characters and initially was created for college kids somewhat like Facebook, but its popularity is growing very fast.

YouTube was born in 2005. It is a global video-sharing site owned by Google (Coles, 2015, p. 202). With over 600 videos being uploaded to YouTube every 60 seconds, this means that online videos have become much more popular (Odden, 2012, p. 144). People share videos on YouTube and it clicked and spread around the world in a very short while.

Instagram, with nearly 100 million users, provides people with the ability to share photos from their smartphones. It is the largest mobile, social network, and is owned by Facebook (Schaffer, 2013, p. 43). Moreover, it is one of the growing social networks focused on visual communications (Charlesworth, 2015, p. 193).

Popular SMCs used by marketers are important statistical indicator to differentiate the channels from each other. For instance, Figure 3 shows some of commonly used SMCs and changes of usage in over a two-year period (2016-2017) as a percentage.

Figure 3. Examples for commonly used channels
Note: Data was retrieved from "Social Media Marketing Industry Report (SCRIBD)," 2017.

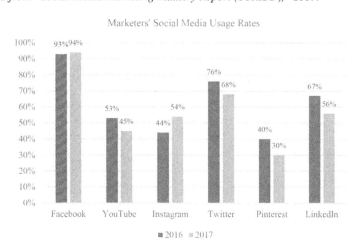

According to Figure 3, in 2017, marketers' usage rates of Facebook rose from 93% to 94%, meanwhile Instagram jumped from 44% to 54%. The other four channels' usage rates declined in 2017. YouTube and Twitter dropped 8%. Pinterest and LinkedIn declined 10% and 11%, respectively. Each product, or even B2B propositions, would be provided over the Internet and retailers would find "creative ways to overcome customer expectations" (Falls & Deckers, 2012, p. 14). For this reason, marketing managers should decide which SMCs to use according to their business context (Funk, 2011, p. 50). For instance, Figure 4 shows some types of SMCs and their usage rates among Inc. 500 companies between 2013 and 2016. During the four-year period, Instagram usage rate rose tremendously while Facebook usage rate fluctuated negatively. This dramatic change may be interpreted as consumer's preferences having changed and marketers monitoring their movements to reach consumers through the best channel. LinkedIn and Twitter usage rates increased in 2014 compared to 2013, but it was nearly stable during the next two years. Another remarkable negative fluctuation is seen in the Google Plus usage rate. When it is examined, it is possible to say that the usage rates of Pinterest and YouTube have tended to decrease.

Figure 4. Examples of SMCs usage rates among Inc. 500 companies in US
Note: Data was retrieved from Barnes & Daubitz, 2017.

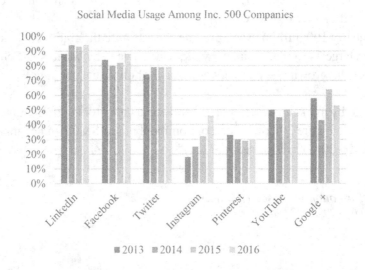

Figure 5. An example of the number of active users (in millions) of some popular channels
Note: Data was retrieved from "We Are Social January Report" (2017).

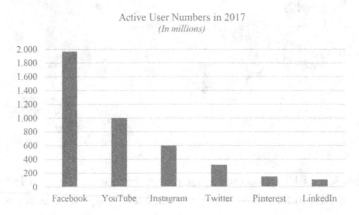

Total active social media user numbers show the importance of social media. Active users of some popular channels are changing over the years. For instance, Figure 5 shows some of the popular SMCs' active user numbers worldwide in 2017.

As seen in Figure 5, some SMCs are more popular than others, and Facebook was the leading SMC worldwide in 2017. That is the reason why marketers should examine which SMCs are more popular year by year.

SOCIAL MEDIA MARKETING (SMM)

Definition of SMM

SMM is considered marketing through SMCs (Smedescu, 2013). It is defined as the use of SMCs for promoting a company and its products. Since SMCs increase the viability on the digital platforms, SMM use these channels. SMM is a term that is related to relationship marketing in terms of giving importance to making connections with the consumers instead of selling (Cicek & Eren-Erdogmuş, 2013). It facilitates companies building communications channels with their customers, marketing their products, and enhancing customer loyalty. In order to manage communication with customers, it requires effort and attention (Saravanakumar & SuganthaLakshmi, 2012).

Therefore, SMM can be described as an accurate digital marketing method that promotes products of a company, increases brand awareness, customer loyalty, and creates potential customers through SMCs for the business.

SMM is assumed to be a set of combined tools and actions that an organization expects to not only accomplish its marketing goals, but also to satisfy the needs of its target market using SMCs (Ananda, Hernández-García & Lamberti, 2016). Companies tend to use SMM to provide information about their products and also interact with their consumers to establish relationships. Moreover, SMM are the marketing strategies adopted by companies to become part of the online networking of consumers (Deepa & Deshmukh, 2013). On the other hand, SMM as a marketing strategy should not be seen only as providing effective communication through SMCs. SMM itself is too complex to be managed. In this direction, Felix, Rauschnabel, and Hinsch (2017) assert a strategic framework for SMM and identify four dimensions of it. These dimensions are SMM scope, SMM culture, SMM structures, and SMM governance. SMM scope explores whether companies use SMM primarily as a real tool for communicating with one or more stakeholders or for extensive (both internal and external) cooperation.

SMM culture allocates between conservatism and modernism. Conservatism is determined in terms of a traditional approach to SMM. On the other hand, modernism is represented by an open and flexible SMM culture. SMM structures refer to the organization and departmentalization of SMM tasks. Hierarchies and networks are important terms for the SMM structure. According to hierarchic structure, there is a SMM assignee in contrast to networks, which show an organizational structure where all employees are accountable for SMM. The last strategic dimension of SMM is SMM governance. This dimension represents how the company sets rules and guidelines and how SMM responsibilities are reviewed within the company. In this way, identifying SMM strategies for businesses contributes to accomplishing SMM purposes. The authors evaluate these purposes in detail.

Purposes of SMM

The purposes of SMM include increasing sales and brand awareness, developing brand image, reducing marketing costs, and composing traffic to online platforms (Felix, Rauschnabel, & Hinsch, 2017). Of these, most marketers value social media most for branding (Ashley & Tuten, 2015). SMM has also a direct impact on product sales, brand recognition, and existing in the sector.

Both B2C and B2B companies use SMM to increase communication efficiency, improve customer relationships, build brands, and stimulate sales (Karjaluoto, Ulkuniemi, & Mustonen, 2015). SMM offers various advantages to companies through SMCs. For example attracting new customers and enhancing the customer interaction already established are one of the advantages (Pradiptarini, 2011). SMM is not only a product promotion area, but also an area where companies can show the sensitivity of their brands, the community view, the company philosophy, and customer sensitivity.

Channels that come to mind for SMM are Facebook, Twitter, Instagram, YouTube, Google Plus, Pinterest, and LinkedIn. Although active campaigns and advertising activities can be organized in all of these channels, it is undoubtedly important to choose the right channels appropriate to the nature of the products provided. For instance, Instagram is considered to be the suitable channel among photo sharing platforms. While it is more appropriate for a textile company to give more importance to this channel by taking advantage of Instagram's practical and photo-based feature, it is more accurately for a game company to focus on YouTube, which is much more preferred by children.

The role of social media in marketing should be explained with the customer's point of view in mind. Customers go through the customer life cycle process that consists of six stages (Figure 6).

Figure 6. Customer life cycle
Source: ("MARKETO," 2016, p. 17)

As it is observed in Figure 6, the first stage of the customer life cycle is awareness. The aim of this stage is to increase brand awareness, capture the interest of audiences, and ensure that they reach the right channels with relevant, personalized messages.

Engagement is the second stage. People, who are willing to buy, are interested in the company. In this stage, businesses listen to the potential customers and then engage them. Using beneficial context would be crucial to maintain a connection with audiences. In other words, this stage is for pushing audiences to purchase by using social media. According to the Global Web Index (2018), more than one-third of users are looking for brands in social media—they are already using them to engage with brands they like.

The third stage in the customer life cycle is purchase. In the purchasing stage, buyers are ready to purchase from the company. Monitoring the purchase process would be useful to understand and control buyers.

Loyalty/retention is the fourth stage. After the purchasing stage, businesses want to build long-term relationships with their customers by establishing trust. For businesses, it is possible only by using social media effectively to respond to customers for any problems and listening to their issues about services.

Growth is the next stage in customer life cycle. This stage shows that selling is not the end of marketing. Businesses must create value by understanding the current customer needs by segmenting them in terms of using different SMCs.

The last stage of customer life cycle is advocacy. The purpose of this stage is to encourage customers to become brand advocates and to provide an excellent customer experience to recommend the brand to friends and family. Since brand advocates are also the social media audiences of businesses, using SMCs, such as Twitter or Facebook, to provide connection with them is important.

Considering these six stages of the customer life cycle, it can be asserted that identifying purposes of each stage in the customer life cycle is crucial for businesses to ensure long-term relationships with their customers. That is why B2C and B2B organizations should decide which social media platforms to choose at every stage of the customer life cycle (Funk, 2011, p. 50).

Social media usage in the marketing context has been a crucial issue. Therefore, the authors also evaluated social media usage for B2B and B2C contexts.

Social Media for B2C

Social media is a tool for creating awareness, persuasion, and accomplishment of marketing objectives in B2C businesses. Many B2C organizations, such as Ford, KLM, ING, NS, and T-Mobile, are already actively using social media for their marketing strategies (Busscher, 2013). For instance, Ford's social media strategy includes using different SMCs such as Facebook, Twitter, and YouTube. Ford users are encouraged to share their experiences on these channels.

Social media usage as a marketing channel in B2C businesses has expanded because businesses can reach their customers to engage them for brand conversations. While SMCs are used in B2B contexts to target professionals, B2C practitioners use SMCs to connect with the general public (Iankova, Davies, Archer-Brown, Marder, & Yau, 2018). Moreover, they add value to the interaction with individual consumers, enabling businesses to engage in one-on-one dialogue with their customers (Moore, Hopkins, & Raymond, 2013). Social media provides B2C companies to contact consumers directly with much lower costs for interaction than traditional communication tools.

B2C companies use SMCs for increasing brand awareness, loyalty, and sales. Moreover, attracting new customers and cultivating relationships are also among their objectives for using SMCs (Swani, Brown, & Milne, 2014). Since consumers perceive the information obtained from social media as being more trustworthy than from other sources (Foux, 2006), B2C marketers desire to use SMCs.

From the B2C point of view, marketers are more focused on Facebook, YouTube, and Instagram (Stelzner, 2016). Thus, these channels need to be considered in terms of B2C marketing.

Facebook

Facebook proposes that marketers reach to highly segmented customers and provide a platform to actively engage with their customers (Charlesworth, 2015, p. 151). Building communities by users and advertising for customers by businesses contribute to Facebook's rapid growth. At first, new users had some hesitation about the site besides being too intrusive, but, in the long run, they became addicted to it (Funk, 2011, p. 48). The research completed by Saravanakumar and SuganthaLakshmi (2012), emphasized that 77% of consumers interacted with brands on Facebook by reading the messages and updates about them. In addition to this, 56% of consumers recommend a brand to their friends after becoming a fan of a brand on Facebook. It shows that Facebook is an influencing tool for customers. For instance, Table 4 supports the importance of Facebook for B2C marketing. It shows the most popular product brands on Facebook for April 2019 in terms of fans in millions.

Figure 7. Examples of product brands with the most Facebook fans as of April 2019 (in millions)
Source: ("STATISTA," 2019)

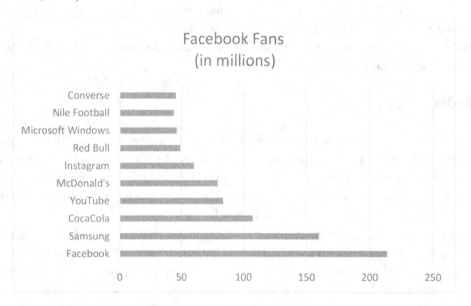

According to data in Figure 7, Facebook for Every Phone is the most popular page on Facebook with 213 million fans. Coca-Cola and Samsung are the following popular pages on Facebook with respectively 159 million and 107 million fans. Other product brands are showed in order with respect to number of their fans. Since Facebook is a popular social network, it might be accepted as a crucial marketing tool to reach target audiences for marketers. Thus, companies should consider using Facebook when formulating their B2C marketing strategies as an effective tool to reach new and existing customers. With regard to a B2C perspective for using Facebook to reach customers, GENOGRAFİ provides a good example in Turkey (Figure 8).

Figure 8. Distribution of GENOGRAFI's fans on Facebook
Note: Figure was retrieved from www.socialbakers.com based on GENOGRAFI's fans on June 1, 2017.

GENOGRAFI is a personal genetic analysis service that allows you to get detailed information about your DNA and how it can affect your life. Genetic analysis is an interesting issue and it needs to be explained to people by using communication channels to elucidate. Therefore, GENOGRAFI tries to provide awareness to its target audience by using SMCs. Figure 8 shows the distribution of GENOGRAFI's Facebook fans all over the world. Most of the company's Facebook followers are from Turkey. As a result of Facebook advertisements, the number of fans are increasing and expanding into new countries such as the United States, Sweden, Germany, and the United Kingdom.

YouTube

Another important tool for B2C marketing is YouTube. YouTube is becoming an important part among SMCs since as viral marketing is becoming more popular. YouTube is a blessing to visual brands, comprising big fashion, entertainment, music, sports, and lifestyle brands (Funk, 2011, p. 50). From B2B to B2C, whether a small business or large, videos in YouTube are effective for all markets and types of customers (Odden, 2012, p. 144). The cost of making a YouTube video is low. Thus, businesses can use YouTube to create greater brand awareness, product advertising, retail promotion, product support, and direct sales (Miller, 2011, p. 11). For instance, they can display advertisements or provide information about a company's products or services for their target customers.

When businesses use YouTube to share video that has customer centric titles, customers can easily find the business content. Subscribers and views are the terms used to determine the impacts of business. For instance, number of views can show the impact of a brand. Companies can use YouTube for giving information or advice about using their products.

Instagram

From the B2C perspective, consumer brands use Instagram to showcase their products and provide a connection with audiences in terms of posts, contests, and giveaways ("MARKETO," 2016, p. 9). Businesses can use Instagram by putting pictures of their brand's products. For instance, customers can follow the brand Instagram page and obtain information about product features and price. Moreover, they can also order the product of the brand. Besides being a platform to reach the target market in terms of brands, events can use Instagram to reach their audiences. For instance, events, such as weddings or birthdays, can share photos on Instagram to promote the company.

Instagram offers an advantage for businesses in terms of creating advertising to reach only the targeted market. By collaborating with Facebook (a database of Facebook contains user's interests), consumers are well known, and with this method, accurate and relevant messages are communicated to the users.

Beyond any doubt, Instagram is the most visual SMC. Companies can create images depending on their industry. For instance, a clothing brand can share images of various styles with their prices. They can also use celebrities to post their images. To conclude, Instagram can be used not only as part of content marketing, but also as a social media strategy to reach specific audiences. Using relevant content that is attractive, informative, and memorable, along with a company's products or services will gain the attention of a large audience.

Social Media for B2B

Using social media for B2B marketing strategies provides companies with a way to create content on SMCs to find, attract, and inform potential customers and suppliers (Batum & Ersoy, 2016). Since companies place special emphasis on the value of relationship networks' for buyers and sellers, they adopt social media to increase buyer engagement and develop customer relationships (Swani, Brown, & Milne, 2014).

B2B organizations also utilize social media to identify new business opportunities and for product development, to enhance relationships with customers, and to improve collaboration, both inside and between organizations (Jussila, Kärkkäinen & Aramo-Immonen, 2014). What is more, social media for B2B provides a variety of marketing applications, such as content marketing, market research, and business networking. For instance, thanks to content marketing, B2B companies can deliver business-related content to customers via social media to be an effective center in the network (Brennan & Croft, 2012). Employee recruitment and retention also constitutes their usage purposes. Moreover, B2B companies adopt SMCs to demonstrate products and provide training to business partners (Vize & Sherrett, 2017, p. 50).

According to Kho (2008), in contrast to B2C users, better-designed social media tools can provide more benefits for B2B users. It is proven that SMCs that facilitate more personalized interactions between buyers and suppliers can improve corporate credibility and build better relationship between both. SMCs can be used for communication with suppliers and customers within a B2B context (Busscher, 2013). The top five SMCs, analyzed in terms of B2B usage are: LinkedIn, Facebook, Twitter, Instagram, and YouTube.

LinkedIn

The purpose of using LinkedIn is to create networks, establish new business connections, and to become aware of innovations. People can learn about a company by following its profile on LinkedIn. Besides this, business experts, communities, associations, and companies can successfully use LinkedIn to obtain information (Reece, 2010, p. 245). LinkedIn also ensures a form of self-promotion and career networking (Tuten, 2008, p. 24). It means people who are interested in a company have a chance to learn more about it by following its LinkedIn page, which will also show any job positions available with the company.

Moreover, it is a professional platform that employees can use not only for promoting their company brand, but also to promote their personal brand.

Building relationships with suppliers and customers is an important issue in B2B marketing. Businesses aim to provide trustworthy relations with their partners. According to Shih (2009, p. 124), B2B companies can use LinkedIn to communicate with their customers and suppliers, and to build relationships and trust. Moreover, they can easily define possible partners with regards to B2B selling.

Despite Facebook and MySpace being favored and having bigger networks, LinkedIn is more suitable for businesses to use as a platform for their marketing (Reece, 2010, p. 245; Zahay, 2015, p. 80). Thus, when marketing to businesses, a company or individual should choose LinkedIn as a platform.

In Turkey, GENOMİZE uses LinkedIn to inform its audiences about the company, declares new job opportunities and views how you are connected with employees. Moreover, GENOMİZE identifies its profession such as Biotechnology, Genomics, Software, RNA-seq, DNA-Seq, Data Management to connect with other businesses in terms of B2B.

Facebook

Facebook is as a viable option for SMM for B2B. Companies can reach current and future customers and potential employees thanks to using Facebook. Therefore, there are some ways for B2B companies to use Facebook efficiently. First of all, companies can use images on their Facebook page to create attention in their news feed. They can share company news, such as showing the company's success. Moreover, if a company shares pictures of employees enjoying their work, it will provide insight to other people about the company's culture and business relations. Companies also share interesting images or inspiring content to attract audiences. Facebook also enables businesses to communicate with their fans through videos. For example, if a company wants to provide training programs for business owners, it can promote this on Facebook through videos. Sharing the company's story is another way in terms of a B2B perspective. "ThrowbackThursday" is a popular word in social media jargon, so companies share their history by telling stories and posting images. Thanks to this, audiences can adopt and feel more connected to a company.

Advertising on Facebook is another way for B2B companies to use this SMC. Companies can easily reach business owners needing their product thanks to Facebook advertisements. To conclude, companies can reach their target audiences using these popular SMCs. They can also identify which media provides them with the best responses from their fans and followers.

From the B2B perspective, in Turkey, GENOMİZE, a young, dynamic, biotechnology initiative that is academically rooted that specializes in the production and analysis of genomic data uses Facebook actively to reach customers and businesses. Initially, customers obtain information about the company thanks to Facebook following its main page about health issues in terms of genomic data. GENOMİZE declares that if you are a business that provides genetic diagnosis, you can use SEQ. Moreover, if you want to apply genome analysis to yourself, GENOMİZE suggests taking a more detailed look at GENO-GRAFI. For GENOMİZE, Facebook is an efficient channel to reach targeted audiences and provide awareness in terms of B2B marketing.

Twitter

People prefer using Twitter for answering the question, "What are you doing?" (Reece, 2010, p. 247) or "What is happening?" (Coles, 2015, p. 82). It can be about a person's action, such as eating something, or business news. By using this platform, people share information about whatever they want, such as other people, companies, or products. Moreover, since Twitter is an effective marketing tool, marketers use its short message format to communicate with their target market (Charlesworth, 2015, p. 167). You can send messages to your followers directly. By following conversations of Twitter, hash tags, or tendency to your keywords, you can easily describe potent people in your industry or market. Thus, it is deduced that Twitter is an effective marketing channel—especially for B2B—for introducing your industry and building brand and customer loyalty. It provides companies with the ability to connect to potential dealers and future customers.

Since Twitter is an essential tool for B2B companies, there are some techniques for Twitter suitably use. First, employees of the company can use Twitter to stay up-to-date and follow the news about an industry. Moreover, companies post links to their latest acquisitions and product news on Twitter. Therefore, other companies interested in the company products can obtain information by following Twitter's news feeds. Companies can also read comments about their products and see competitor's opinions. The most important thing for companies is to optimize their business page with the right brand awareness creation and messaging.

Instagram

Instagram is a notable channel for B2B. Businesses can use Instagram to share attractive offers and funny visuals. Moreover, photographs of events and offices take part in Instagram to give information about businesses. Hashtags special for a company brand or industry are keywords of the business. Using hash tags on company posts provides the ability to reach the target market. For instance, a company can highlight what their products do by creating stunning visuals. Moreover, a company can combine videos and images to make its content interesting on Instagram.

Instagram has two strengths in terms of B2B. These are brand awareness and community. After providing brand awareness, companies build community. By building communities, companies can reach their target market. Instagram also has a story feature. Companies use this feature to take advantage of people's influence in marketing. Moreover, a company can use its leader's message on Instagram, such as building relationships and being the easiest company to do business with. What is more, Instagram can be used to showcase a company's culture. Companies can also display their creativity and expertise. For instance, a company in a creative industry can use Instagram's attractive visuals to gain clients.

YouTube

YouTube is an efficient channel for B2B in terms of sharing videos and providing a channel for companies to reach their target audiences. For instance, a company can create a business channel on YouTube and it would be a free advertising. On YouTube's business channel page is also the home page of the business. Therefore, it is essential to customize the page in terms of design and business content to be suitable as a marketing strategy. Businesses can reach this home page and online videos to obtain information about the business content.

There are some crucial points for B2B companies to know to be able to use YouTube successfully. First of all, videos on the business channel page should be relevant and beneficial for target customers. For this reason, companies should be clear on their purpose for using YouTube. It can be to gain more followers or customers. On the other hand, making the company visible in the search engines or providing customer loyalty might be a company's goals.

Another point regarding YouTube in terms of B2B companies is product demonstrations, conferences, events, and expert advice. Actually, companies should explain the reasons why other companies are doing business with them. Moreover, promoting videos on YouTube is an important point. Using the right description and tags for their videos will make them more accessible. Companies can also use YouTube Analytics to monitor the performance of their channel and videos. Thanks to this, they obtain information about the demographics of their followers and number of views. By using this data, they can formulate marketing strategies to reach their target audiences.

SOLUTIONS AND RECOMMENDATIONS

Usage of social media has become an indispensable part of everyday life. In today's business world, companies consider social media an important component to gain competitive advantage and high performance (Siamagka, Christodoulides, Michaelidou, & Valvi, 2015). Therefore, whether for B2B or B2C marketers, using SMCs becomes an important part for their marketing strategies.

There are some recommendations for B2C and B2B companies in terms of using social media. Defining the goal of using social media is important. Moreover, companies have to analyze their target markets well to understand the needs and interests of potential customers.

As previously mentioned, according to statistical indicators of some years, the total number of Internet users has increased 10% (354 million), meanwhile the total number of active social media users has increased 21% in one year. In other words, marketing practitioners who have not begun to use social media effectively will be left behind in the competition.

Due to the differences in peoples' reasons for participating in social media, SMC variations are designed to answer those different needs. This is one of the reasons that some SMCs become more popular than others. However, being a phenomenon for SMC does not last forever. Year after year, the number of individuals and businesses that use SMCs varies. Therefore, marketing managers should monitor their targeted consumer's online behaviors.

FUTURE RESEARCH DIRECTIONS

This chapter highlights that both B2C and B2B marketers are aware of the power of social media in the framework of their marketing strategy in the digital economy. The digital economy has transformed the marketing strategies of companies. Despite B2C companies often using SMCs as a part of their marketing tactics, adopting social media for B2B companies is a new issue. B2B companies have some hesitations regarding using social media. Actually, they do not know how to use SMCs efficiently. Therefore, researchers might provide guidelines to B2B marketers, so they might be able to begin to include SMCs in their marketing plans and implement their marketing strategies on behalf of social media.

Future studies might also focus on SMM barriers within B2B contexts. In other words, the literature could more clearly explore and define the difficulties for B2B marketers face in using SMCs in their integrated communication strategies, and also how B2B marketers might overcome these barriers.

CONCLUSION

This chapter shows that social media has become an important component when formulating marketing strategies in today's digital economy. Since statistical indicators based on the Internet user rates and active social media user rates all over the world show that traditional marketing communication tools are not enough to reach the consumers, marketers begin to give more importance to SMM, thus traditional marketing tools are being replaced by SMCs.

SMM can be described as an accurate, digital marketing method that promotes the products or services of a company, increases brand awareness, and creates customer loyalty. Because of social media's significant role in marketing, SMM has become a crucial marketing strategy for businesses. As a marketing strategy, SMM itself includes four different dimensions. These four dimensions are: 1). SMM scope; 2). SMM culture; 3). SMM structures; and 4). SMM governance (Felix, Rauschnabel, & Hinsch, 2017). To achieve the purposes of SMM, these four dimensions have to be taken in consideration. The purpose of SMM consists of developing brand awareness and brand image, reducing marketing costs, and inspiring users to post or share contents.

SMM is expressed as the whole of marketing efforts in order to not leave the customer alone during the customer life cycle stages through the use of SMCs. SMCs provide support to the customer's decision journey and aim to increase the number of customers that will progress to additional stages. For instance, in a B2B context, people who are interested in a company have a chance to learn about that company by following its LinkedIn pages, which enables the user to gain an awareness of the field of the business and the products of this company. Using LinkedIn captures the interest of audiences and results in greater awareness. After providing usable content to maintain a connection with audiences in the engagement stage, buyers become ready to purchase from the company. In this stage, using another SMC, such as YouTube to demonstrate and give detailed information about products of the company in which customers are interested, it pushes the customers to purchase the service or product. After the purchasing stage, companies want to cultivate long-term relationships with their customers to achieve loyalty. Their aim is to instantly respond to positive and negative comments through SMCs, such as Twitter and Facebook. During the last stage, advocacy, customers are expected to recommend the company to others. The usage of Twitter and Facebook to maintain the communication is important during this stage. To conclude, the customer life cycle provides a significant framework for B2B and B2C marketers to identify which SMCs are most effective for their specific business.

Social media is the output of the increased usage of the Internet for marketing practices and it had become more interesting for the marketing activities of both B2C and B2B contexts (Constantinides & Fountain, 2008). Due to the different structures of B2B and B2C markets, social media usage in these markets is dissimilar (Iankova, Davies, Archer-Brown, Marder, & Yau, 2018). B2B companies prefer using social media to create demand and build networks through their business partners. In other words, B2B social media interactions are heavily focused on relationships, which should be beneficial for all parties. On the other hand, B2C companies aim to provide interaction with existing and potential customers, share their content, marketing, and advertising campaigns through SMCs.

SMCs provide important opportunities for businesses to conduct marketing communication activities. It is revealed that SMCs are different from one another in terms of their forms of communication. To begin with, Facebook is good at building customer relationships. Secondly, Twitter has an ability to spread messages about a brand or a company to the target customers. Furthermore, Instagram is a channel that enables the sharing of images. In addition, YouTube is known for its ability to share videos. Lastly, LinkedIn is a means of networking with business partners all over the world. According to Charlesworth (2015, p. 195), Facebook and LinkedIn are considered to be social networking sites, while YouTube, Twitter, and Instagram are seen as social sharing sites.

This chapter also considers that SMCs usages are different in B2C and B2B contexts. According to the literature review, which includes trends in usage, B2C marketers are mostly focused on Facebook, YouTube, and Instagram, while LinkedIn is more preferred by B2B marketers (Reece, 2010, p. 245; Zahay, 2015, p. 80). The reason behind the difference is the goal of LinkedIn. LinkedIn is a professional social networking platform, enabling people in the business world to communicate and exchange information with others and wherein one can engage with business decision makers (Schaffer, 2013, p. 43). In the light of all this information, it can be concluded that the purpose of using social media and the adoption of SMCs differ in terms of B2C and B2B businesses.

REFERENCES

Al Khalili, M. (2018). *Barriers impacting social media marketing in industrial B2B* (Unpublished doctoral dissertation, Robert Morris University, Pennsylvania).

AlSuwaidan, L., & Ykhlef, M. (2016). Toward information diffusion model for viral marketing in business. *Int. J. Adv. Comput. Sci. Appl, 7*(2), 637–646.

Ananda, A. S., Hernández-García, Á., & Lamberti, L. (2016). N-REL: A comprehensive framework of social media marketing strategic actions for marketing organizations. *Journal of Innovation & Knowledge, 1*(3), 170–180. doi:10.1016/j.jik.2016.01.003

Ashley, C., & Tuten, T. (2015). Creative strategies in social media marketing: An exploratory study of branded social content and consumer engagement. *Psychology and Marketing, 32*(1), 15–27. doi:10.1002/mar.20761

Barefoot, D., & Szabo, J. (2010). *Friends with benefits: A social media marketing handbook.* San Francisco, CA: No Starch Press.

Barnes, N. G., & Daubitz, C. (2017, February). *The 2017 Inc 500 and social media: time for reevaluation?* University of Massachusetts Dartmouth Center for Marketing Research. Retrieved from http://www.umassd.edu/cmr/

Batum, T., & Ersoy, N. (2016). The use of social media in B2B marketing communications: An explatory study on Turkish companies. *Afyon Kocatepe Üniversitesi İktisadi ve İdari Bilimler Fakültesi Dergisi, 18*(2), 139–151.

Brennan, R., & Croft, R. (2012). The use of social media in B2B marketing and branding: An exploratory study. *Journal of Customer Behaviour, 11*(2), 101–115. doi:10.1362/147539212X13420906144552

Busscher, N. M. (2013). *Social media: Their role as marketing tools in B2B marketing* (Bachelor's Thesis, University of Twente).

Charlesworth, A. (2015). *An introduction to social media marketing.* New York, NY: Routledge.

Cicek, M., & Eren-Erdogmus, I. (2013). Social media marketing: Exploring the user typology in Turkey. *International Journal of Technology Marketing, 8*(3), 254–271. doi:10.1504/IJTMKT.2013.055343

Coles, L. (2015). *Marketing with social media: 10 easy steps to success for business.* Australia: John Wiley & Sons.

Constantinides, E. (2014). Foundations of social media marketing. *Procedia: Social and Behavioral Sciences, 148,* 40–57. doi:10.1016/j.sbspro.2014.07.016

Constantinides, E. & Fountain, S. J. (2008). Web 2.0: Conceptual foundations and marketing issues. *Journal of direct, data and digital marketing practice, 9*(3), 231-244.

Content Marketing Institute (CMI). (2018). *Benchmarks, budgets, and trends: North America.* Retrieved from https://contentmarketinginstitute.com/wpcontent/uploads/2017/09/2018

Deepa, N., & Deshmukh, S. (2013). Social media marketing: The next generation of business engagement. *International Journal of Management Research and Reviews, 3*(2), 2461.

Eisenberg, B. (2008, Nov. 7). *Understanding and aligning the value of social media.* Retrieved from www.clickz.com

Falls, J., & Deckers, E. (2012). *No bullshit social media: The all-business, no-hype guide to social media marketing.* United States of America: Pearson Education.

Felix, R., Rauschnabel, P. A., & Hinsch, C. (2017). Elements of strategic social media marketing: A holistic framework. *Journal of Business Research, 70,* 118–126. doi:10.1016/j.jbusres.2016.05.001

Fischer, E., & Reuber, A. R. (2011). Social interaction via new social media: (How) can interactions on Twitter affect effectual thinking and behavior? *Journal of Business Venturing, 26*(1), 1–18. doi:10.1016/j.jbusvent.2010.09.002

Flanigan, R. L., & Obermier, T. R. (2016). An assessment of the use of social media in the industrial distribution business-to-business market sector. *The Journal of Technology Studies, 42*(1), 18–28. doi:10.21061/jots.v42i1.a.2

Foux, G. (2006). Consumer-generated media: Get your customers involved. *Brand Strategy, 8*(202), 38–39.

Funk, T. (2011). *Social media playbook for business: Reaching your online community with Twitter, Facebook, LinkedIn, and more:* Santa Barbara, CA: ABC- Clio, LLC.

Global Web Index. (2018). *Global web index's flagship report on the latest trends in social media.* Retrieved from https://www.globalwebindex.com/hubfs/Downloads/Social-H2-2018-report.pdf

Hacıhasanoglu, B. (2017). *Sosyal Medyada Pazarlama Stratejilerinin Oluşturulması ve Telekomünikasyon Sektörüne İlişkin Bir Uygulama* (Unpublished Master's Thesis, Istanbul Commerce University, Turkey).

Iankova, S., Davies, I., Archer-Brown, C., Marder, B., & Yau, A. (2018). A comparison of social media marketing between B2B, B2C and mixed business models. *Industrial Marketing Management*. doi:10.1016/j.indmarman.2018.01.001

Jussila, J. (2015). *Social media in business-to-business companies' innovation*. Tampere, Finland: Tampere University of Technology.

Jussila, J. J., Kärkkäinen, H., & Aramo-Immonen, H. (2014). Social media utilization in business-to-business relationships of technology industry firms. *Computers in Human Behavior, 30*, 606–613. doi:10.1016/j.chb.2013.07.047

Kaplan, A. M., & Haenlein, M. (2010). Users of the world, unite! The challenges and opportunities of social media. *Business Horizons, 53*(1), 59–68. doi:10.1016/j.bushor.2009.09.003

Karjaluoto, H., Ulkuniemi, P., & Mustonen, N. (2015). The role of digital channels in industrial marketing communications. *Journal of Business and Industrial Marketing, 30*(6), 703–710. doi:10.1108/JBIM-04-2013-0092

Kho, N. D. (2008). B2B gets social media. *EContent (Wilton, Conn.), 31*(3), 26–30.

MARKETO. (2010). *The definitive guide to B2B social media*. Retrieved from http://designdamage.com/wp-content/uploads/2009/04/The-Definitive-Guide-to-B2B-SM.pdf

MARKETO. (2016). *The definitive guide to social media marketing*. Retrieved from http://www.workforcelink.com/library/The-Definitive-Guide-to-Social-Media-Marketing-Marketo.pdf

Michaelidou, N., Siamagka, N. T., & Christodoulides, G. (2011). Usage, barriers and measurement of social media marketing: An exploratory investigation of small and medium B2B brands. *Industrial Marketing Management, 40*(7), 1153–1159. doi:10.1016/j.indmarman.2011.09.009

Miller, M. R. (2011). *YouTube for business: Online video marketing for any business*. USA: Que Publishing.

Moore, J. N., Hopkins, C. D., & Raymond, M. A. (2013). Utilization of relationship-oriented social media in the selling process: A comparison of consumer (B2C) and industrial (B2B) salespeople. *Journal of Internet Commerce, 12*(1), 48–75. doi:10.1080/15332861.2013.763694

Most Popular Social Networking Sites. Top 15 Rank Report (2017). Retrieved from http://www.ebizmba.com/articles/social-networking-websites

Odden, L. (2012). *Optimize: How to attract and engage more customers by integrating SEO, social media, and content marketing*. Hoboken, NJ: John Wiley & Sons.

Pradiptarini, C. (2011). Social media marketing: Measuring its effectiveness and identifying the target market. *UW-L Journal of Undergraduate Research, 14*, 45–76.

Reece, M. (2010). *Real-time marketing for business growth: How to use social media, measure marketing, and create a culture of execution*. Upper Saddle River, NJ: Pearson Education.

ReportW. A. S. J. (2017). Retrieved from https://wearesocial.com/special-reports/digital-in-2017-global-overview

Saravanakumar, M., & Sugantha Lakshmi, T. (2012). Social media marketing. *Life Science Journal*, *9*(4), 4444–4451.

Schaffer, N. (2013). *Maximize your social: A one-stop guide to building a social media strategy for marketing and business success*. Hoboken, NJ: John Wiley & Sons.

SEMPO. (2017, May 26). *Search engine marketing professional organization glossary*. Retrieved from http://www.sempo.org/ ?page=glossary

Shih, C. (2009). *The Facebook era: Tapping online social networks to build better products, reach new audiences, and well more stuff*. Boston, MA: Pearson Education.

Siamagka, N. T., Christodoulides, G., Michaelidou, N., & Valvi, A. (2015). Determinants of social media adoption by B2B organizations. *Industrial Marketing Management, 51*, 89–99. doi:10.1016/j.indmarman.2015.05.005

Smedescu, D. A. (2013). Social media marketing tools. *Romanian Journal of Marketing, 4*, 23–30.

Smith, P. R., & Zook, Z. (2011). *Marketing communications: Integrating offline and online with social media*. London, UK: Kogan Page Ltd.

Social Media Marketing Industry Report (SCRIBD). (2017). Retrieved from https://tr.scribd.com/ =document/348447903/2017-Social-Media-Marketing-IndustryReport? secret_password=kpsZVgcH wVfmvTHez7rH#download&from_embed

STATISTA. (2019). Product brands with the most Facebook fans as of April 2019 (in millions). Retrieved from https://www.statista.com/statistics/265657/leading-product-brands-with-the-most-fans-on-facebook/

Stelzner, M. A. (2016). *Social media marketing industry report: How marketers are using social media to grow their businesses, online social media examiner*. Retrieved from SocialMediaMarketing Industry Report2016.pdf.

Swani, K., Brown, B. P., & Milne, G. R. (2014). Should tweets differ for B2B and B2C? An analysis of fortune 500 companies' Twitter communications. *Industrial Marketing Management, 43*(5), 873–881. doi:10.1016/j.indmarman.2014.04.012

Tapscott, D., & Williams, A. D. (2008). *WIKINOMICS: How mass collaboration changes everything*. New York, NY: Penguin Group.

Tuten, T. L. (2008). *Advertising 2.0: Social media marketing in a Web 2.0 world: Social media marketing in a Web 2.0 world*. United States of America: Praeger Publishers.

Vize, R., & Sherrett, M. (2017). Social media marketing for B2B: From information to decision to retention. In B. Rishi, & S. Bandyopadhyay (Eds.), *Contemporary issues in social media marketing* (pp. 46–59). New York: Routledge. doi:10.4324/9781315563312-4

Zahay, D. (2015). *Digital marketing management: A handbook for the current (or Future) CEO*. New York: Business Expert Press.

Zimmerman, J., & Ng, D. (2017). *Social media marketing all-in-one for dummies*. Hoboken, NJ: John Wiley & Sons.

ADDITIONAL READING

Agnihotri, R., Dingus, R., Hu, M. Y., & Krush, M. T. (2016). Social media: Influencing customer satisfaction in B2B sales. *Industrial Marketing Management*, *53*, 172–180. doi:10.1016/j.indmarman.2015.09.003

Bailyn, E. (2012). *Outsmarting social media*. Indianapolis, Indiana: Que Publishing.

Baird, C. H., & Parasnis, G. (2011). From social media to social CRM: Reinventing the customer relationship. *Strategy and Leadership*, *39*(6), 27–34. doi:10.1108/10878571111176600

Funk, T. (2013). *Advanced social media marketing: How to lead, launch, and manage a successful social media program*. New York: Apress. doi:10.1007/978-1-4302-4408-0

Järvinen, J., Tollinen, A., Karjaluoto, H., & Jayawardhena, C. (2012). Digital and social media marketing usage in B2B industrial section. *Marketing Management Journal*, *22*(2), 102–117.

Kim, A. J., & Ko, E. (2012). Do social media marketing activities enhance customer equity? An empirical study of luxury fashion brand. *Journal of Business Research*, *65*(10), 1480–1486. doi:10.1016/j.jbusres.2011.10.014

Mangold, W. G., & Faulds, D. J. (2009). Social media: The new hybrid element of the promotion mix. *Business Horizons*, *52*(4), 357–365. doi:10.1016/j.bushor.2009.03.002

Wang, W. Y., Pauleen, D. J., & Zhang, T. (2016). How social media applications affect B2B communication and improve business performance in SMEs. *Industrial Marketing Management*, *54*, 4–14. doi:10.1016/j.indmarman.2015.12.004

KEY TERMS AND DEFINITIONS

Business to Business (B2B): A concept where business is handled between companies rather than companies and individual customers.

Business to Consumer (B2C): A concept describes the commercial relationship conducted by companies directly with consumers.

Customer Lifecycle: A term used to determine the process a customer goes through when considering, buying, using, and maintaining loyalty to a product or service.

Social Media: Websites and applications consist of platforms where individuals or organizations can create, share, and exchange information with people and build online relationships, and communities.

Social Media Channel (SMC): A platform is classified according to the social presence or media richness and answers some kind of consumer needs.

Social Media Marketing (SMM): Part of Internet marketing that is marketing through SMCs.

Web 1.0: The first stage in the WWW, which only offers people one-way communication such as reading the contents.

Web 2.0: The second stage in the WWW, which offers people two-way communication such as showing their opinions or feelings.

This research was previously published in Managing Social Media Practices in the Digital Economy; pages 67-96, copyright year 2020 by Business Science Reference (an imprint of IGI Global).

Chapter 6
Use and Misuse of Technology in Marketing:
Cases from India

Sabeeha Fatma

Amity University, Lucknow, India

ABSTRACT

This article describes how the recent breakthrough in information technology has changed in day-to-day life. The smart phone rules the minds and hearts of a major chunk of the population. Internet has become a basic requirement of many a people. Although technology has affected all functional area of business, marketing is feeling the heat even more. The leap in the information technology replaced mass marketing with one-to-one marketing. Customer relationship, knowledge management, database marketing became the buzz words during 1990s. Search services, biometrics and smart cards, enhanced computational speed, M-commerce, and GPS tracking have changed the way marketing is done. However, technology is often misused by marketers to lure customers on wrong premises. Marketers may at times misuse technology for their vested interest. The article discusses the various cases where technology has been misused by the marketers. The article explores the technological innovations in marketing and the potential misuse of technology with special focus on cases from India.

INTRODUCTION

Gone are the days when brands used to market products merely by placing their advertisements in newspapers or broadcasting them over radio and television. While the traditional marketing tools like billboards and door to door selling still have relevance, focus has shifted towards online marketing. Technology has changed the way customers shopped as well as the way marketers lured them. Internet today has become an indispensable part of our lives as the ultimate source of information and communication. This has made it one of the most happening advertisement platforms. Although technology has opened a number of avenues for marketers, it has raised certain concerns about the authenticity of technology

DOI: 10.4018/978-1-7998-9020-1.ch006

based marketing activities. Many times marketers tend to cross the fine borderline and intrude into the privacy of customers. The paper discusses how technology can at times be misused by marketers and goes against the notion of marketing ethics.

ETHICS

Since the inception of the earth it has been the fittest who had survived. Survival knows no right and wrong. Survival knows no boundaries or limits. Man can surpass any limit in his struggle for survival. But, mere survival is not the aim of the human race. Darwin propounded the theory of survival of the fittest considering man to be just another species of animal kingdom. It is not just survival which a human thrives for, exploration of the unknown is what attracts humans, and it is this quest which pushes him on the path of evolution. Man evolves into human, with myriad values, beliefs, perceptions and attitudes. With evolution comes complications, and there arises a need for a code of conduct, in the absence of which there would be utter confusion. Thus, the concept of ethics originates. Ethics or in other words the do's and don'ts' of society, guides an individual in his pursuit of self-actualization. The word 'ethics' has its origin in a Greek word 'ethos' which means customs followed in a society. Ethics is the course of action that a person should take rather than what he actually does. In the words of Rabindra Nath Tagore, "one of the commonest concerns about ethics revolves around the theme of honesty – not necessarily monetary, but intellectual as well. He says, "And upon this wealth of goodness where honesty is not valued for being the best policy, but it can afford to go against all policies – man's ethics are founded. The clear hint here is that policy can, and often is, time serving, manipulative, cunning, opaque and contaminated with partiality or prejudice. A principle on the other hand is a more universal, transparent and durable guideline" (Chakraborty, 2005). The advocates of profit maximization would argue that business organization is there for earning profits rather than bothering itself with complicated issues of ethics. Despite these moral appreciations, there is a strong tradition in business that insists that business should not be concerned with ethics. As Milton Friedman, a vociferous proponent of this position has put it: "The social responsibility of business is to its shareholders… The business of business is business…" (Friedman, 1970).The argument is myopic, short term measurable indices are preferred over long term immeasurable gains. Long term growth requires honesty, trust, integrity and credibility. Ethics is also defined as "a study of moral standards whose explicit purpose is to determine as far as possible whether a given moral standard (or moral judgment based on that standard) is more or less correct" (Velasquez, 2007). There is definition of ethics from stakeholder's point of view as well. According to this definition the stakeholder is defined as anyone who has a claim or stake in a firm and a successful firm rewards all of its stakeholders. To achieve it, the firm would have to adopt policies which are an optimal balance of interest and ethics. Since the notion of right and wrong, or ethics in other words, come in the way of interest of some of its stakeholders, few managers misrepresent ethics as a cost or a hurdle, rather than a revenue generator (Fernando, 2011).

TECHNOETHICS

Ethics in technology is a sub-field of ethics that addresses the ethical questions specific to the Technology Age. Some prominent works of philosopher Hans Jonas are devoted to ethics of technology. The subject has also been explored, following the work of Mario Bunge, under the term technoethics. Technoethics (TE) is an interdisciplinary research area concerned with all moral and ethical aspects of technology in society. It draws on theories and methods from multiple knowledge domains (such as communications, social sciences, information studies, technology studies, applied ethics, and philosophy) to provide insights on ethical dimensions of technological systems and practices for advancing a technological society.

Marketing Ethics

The term ethics has been defined by a number of researchers in various ways. Runes (1964), Taylor (1975), Barry (1979), DeGeorge (1982) and Beauchamp and Bowie (1983), have explained ethics as morals. Vitell (1986) defined marketing ethics as "an inquiry into the nature and grounds of moral judgments, standards, and rules of conduct relating to marketing decisions and marketing situations." Ethical marketing is defined as "practices that emphasize transparent, trustworthy, and responsible personal and organizational marketing policies and actions that exhibit integrity as well as fairness to consumers and other stakeholders" (Murphy, Laczniak, Bowie and Klein, 2005). Although it is legally binding for marketers to follow ethical marketing practices, it is fruitful for them as well as it increases the credibility of brands and lead to a positive customer perception about the brand.

However, marketing and ethics often tend to oppose one another. Marketing basically aims at customer satisfaction and therefore customer forms the basis of all marketing activities. The bottomline is to deliver a happy and satisfied customer. In the words of Peter Drucker, "…the aim of marketing is to know and understand the customer so well that the product or service fits him and sells itself. Ideally marketing should result in a customer who is ready to buy." Marketers sometimes become myopic in order to accomplish their target and tend to indulge in unethical practices (Bellizzi and Hasty, 2003; Gellert and Schalk, 2012). Mascarenhas (1995) pointed out that higher level marketing executives many a times followed unethical practices and proposed ten propositions that guided marketing executives to adhere to ethical practices not only as a legal prerequisite but as a strategy to build a positive image in the eyes of the consumers and thereby increase market share as well.

Houston (1986) stressed that the raison d'etre of any business is earning profit. Therefore, a marketer would think of the society at large only to the extent that it helps him in earning more profits, however if his concern for the society starts hampering his business, he would definitely forgo societal concern for profits Cressey & Moore, 1983.

Houston (1986) argues that:

Few if any … organisations come into being through altruism; that is, organisations do not come into being to achieve the goals of a nonmember constituency. Instead, it is the set of objectives defined by the membership that guide the organisation… The initiators of a commercial venture do so to satisfy their own needs… (Houston, 1986).

USE OF TECHNOLOGY IN MARKETING

The recent breakthroughs and progress in the field of technology has changed the way the world functions. New media technologies have become a day to day habit and are now an "intrinsic part of contemporary life" (Church et al. 2010, p. 264). We have undergone a rapid and radical transformation in practically every sphere of life. The smart phone rules the minds and hearts of a major chunk of the population. Internet has become a basic requirement of many a people. Technology has become "a basis for future social behaviour" (Venkatesh and Vitalari 1985, p. 3). Technology is bringing a tremendous change in marketing practices as well. It is being extensively used for targeting new customers and engaging with existing customers. Use of technology in marketing increases the reach of marketing programs to a great extent and brings impressive decline in costs (Shugan, 2004).

Shugan 2003 identified search services, biometrics and smart cards, enhanced computational speed, M-commerce, and GPS tracking as the few technologies that have brought a lot of changes in marketing within a short span of time and are likely to stay for long.

Search Services

According to the five-stage model of consumer-buying-behavior-process, consumer buying decision involves five steps: Problem/need recognition, information search, evaluation of alternatives to meet this need, purchase decision and post-purchase behavior (Engel, Blackwell and Kollat, 1968). Second step in the model is that of information search which in today's time is facilitated by internet to a large extent (Moon, 2004). The Internet offers a wide array of search services for finding any information sought by a person regarding a product or a service. Search engines can influence the consumer buying decision by making available information about a product/ service, helping customer to narrow down the options and facilitating the final purchase. Internet is being extensively used by marketers as it provides them a wider platform, decrease the search cost for consumers, enhances the marketing efficiency of the program by targeting the right set of customers with right set of products/services (Bakos, 1997).

Biometrics and Smart Cards

In computer security, biometrics refers to authentication techniques that rely on measurable physical characteristics that can be automatically checked. There are several types of biometric identification schemes:

- face: the analysis of facial characteristics
- fingerprint: the analysis of an individual's unique fingerprints
- hand geometry: the analysis of the shape of the hand and the length of the fingers
- retina: the analysis of the capillary vessels located at the back of the eye
- iris: the analysis of the colored ring that surrounds the eye's pupil
- signature: the analysis of the way a person signs his name.
- vein: the analysis of pattern of veins in the back if the hand and the wrist
- voice: the analysis of the tone, pitch, cadence and frequency of a person's voice.

Although the technology is in its introduction stage, marketers believe that biometrics will play a significant role in future, especially in electronic commerce.

India's national ID program called Aadhaar provides a good example of potential of biometrics for various purposes. It is a biometrics-based digital identity, instantly verifiable online at the point of service (PoS), at anytime, anywhere, in a paperless way. It is designed to enable government agencies to deliver retail public service securely based on biometric data (fingerprint, iris scan and face photo), along with demographic data (name, age, gender, address, parent/ spouse name, mobile phone number) of a person. The data is transmitted in encrypted form over internet for authentication, aiming to free it from limitations of physical presence of a person at a given place. Thus, it can be used for casting vote from anywhere, availing social security benefits from anywhere such as procuring PDS ration from any shop.

Smart cards are credit card-sized cards that contain chips with individual information. Smart card is being extensively used for its wide application. It is used as identification device for GSM digital mobile phones where it identifies and bills the use. In the banking sector smart cards are used as credit, debit or stored value cards. Retailers employ smart cards for customer loyalty programs and electronic coupons where it is used to store customer related information and a history of his past purchases. Health care professionals use smart cards to store and access information about a patient's history when needed. Thus, it can be said that smart card has tremendous potential as marketing device (Sweta, 2015).

Enhanced Computational Speed

According to a report, *"Big data: Changing the way businesses compete and operate"* published by Ernst and Young, the key success factor for companies would be the availability of relevant information at the right time. With technology becoming better and more sophisticated with every passing day, time to collect information and analyze it is decreasing exponentially. It fastens the analysis of traditional databases and enables marketers to improve their targeting strategies. Computation speed also allows to make changes in one's offering as per the changing demands as well as allowing more complex offerings (e.g., bundled offers like combo offers in eateries, quantity discounts like buy two get one free offers, forward sales like reduced price for advanced booking of air tickets, etc.). Interactive marketing has taken altogether new dimensions with increased computational speed. Interactive marketing allows two-way communications between a buyer and a seller for example, e-mail, online ads that can be clicked through, and e-commerce web sites. Interactive marketing techniques include a response mechanism that allows consumers to respond directly to a communication and potentially make a purchase.

M-Commerce and GPS Tracking

Mobile commerce is the use of various information and communication technologies that allow the exchange of information on the go. It is facilitated by a number of devices and technologies like mobile communication devices, wireless Internet (Wi-Fi), personal digital assistants (PDA), global positioning system (GPS), etc. With availability of better infrastructure, penetration of smartphones and introduction of cost effective technology enabled m-commerce is likely to increase in India (Deshmukh, Deshmukh and Thampi, 2013).

With declining prices of GPS devices, the application of the technology is going to increase in coming days. GPS technology has many applications in marketing like monitoring the movement of consignments, determination of the optimal route to a particular destination (e.g. the GPS device fitted in cabs), locating products and services (e.g. hotels, hospitals, shopping malls etc. may be located by customers).

Misuse of Technology

Technology has empowered organizations to a great extent. Marketers with the help of technology are exploring new possibilities like data mining, target marketing and one-to-one marketing (Wirtz, Lwin and Williams, 2007). Technology has led to increase in marketing efficiency as well, by providing cost effective solutions to customer service and loyalty programs (Lovelock and Wirtz, 2006). So far, so good. But there is a flip side also to this otherwise sparkling success story. There is growing concern over security of data and information and its potential misuse (Gauzente and Ranchhod, 2001).

On reviewing the literature, it emerged that the major ways in which technology has been misused by marketers are data theft, invasion of customers' privacy, mass marketing fraud, and ambush marketing. It was also found that in some cases customers have misused technology for their vested interests.

Data Theft

Data theft is the act of extracting computer-based information from an individual or an organization wherein neither the prior permission for doing so was sought nor the real intention and purpose was revealed. Data theft is becoming a big problem for individual computer users and business firms.

Data is a valuable asset. Business thrives on data. The economy practically runs on data. It is therefore very important to ensure the authenticity and security of data.

Cases have been reported where companies have lured employees of their competitors to get access to their customer databases as well as other valuable information. One such case was reported in Arhan Technologies, an Indian firm based in city of Pune. Arhan Technologies was a firm that markets engineering products and deals with a number of Japanese manufacturers looking for business in India. It had been marketing products of a Japanese company, Endo Kogyo. Arhan Technologies has made one of its accomplished employee Mr.Kalmegh incharge of the project. In July 2011, Kalmegh suddenly quit his job and left Arhan Technologies without serving a notice period. Despite quitting, he changed passwords of the company's e-mail addresses and also took a pen drive containing crucial business information with him. On February 24, 2012, Kalmegh signed a settlement agreement in which he said that he would stop using the company's e-mail addresses. But Kalmegh joined Endo Kogyo India, and shortly after Endo Kyogo, Japan parted ways with Arhan Technologies. However, Kalmegh continued to use Arhan's e-mails, accessing its data for expanding business of Endo Kogyo,India. Kalmegh also began to contact clients of Arhan Technologies and lure them towards Endo Kyogo, India. Arhan Technologies then filed a police complaint under the Information Technology Act. The local police found that Arhan had suffered a loss of Rs 60 lakh following the data theft and filed a charge sheet against Kalmegh. The state IT authority ordered the Japanese engineering company's Indian arm, Endo Kyogo, India to pay Arhan Technologies Rs 40 lakh for stealing the latter's confidential data, including e-mails, and indulging in business malpractice to attract competitor's customers.

The easy accessibility of internet connection in Wi-Fi enabled public places, penetration of smartphones and growing trend of availing practically every service online, makes the data even more vulnerable. The US hotel chain Hyatt International reported in 2015 that 20 of its hotels in India were affected by malware that was secretly installed in a hotel's IT system using its free WiFi to steal information from guests using the network. The free WiFi in public places may cause not only the personal information of the individuals to be stolen but also provide access to the IT systems of the companies they may be working with.

INVASION OF CUSTOMER PRIVACY

The right to privacy is recognized as a fundamental right under the Constitution of India. It is guaranteed under the right to freedom (Article 19) and the right to life (Article 21) of the Constitution. The Supreme Court, in dealing with the question on the right to privacy, observed, that the right to privacy is implicit in the right to life and liberty guaranteed to the citizens of the country by Article 21. It is a 'right to be left alone.' "A citizen has a right to safeguard the privacy of his own, his family, marriage, procreation, motherhood, child-bearing and education among other matters." The publication of any of the aforesaid personal information without the consent of the person, whether accurate or inaccurate and 'whether laudatory or critical' would be in violation of the right to privacy of the person and liable for damages.

The notion "right to be left alone" was first used by Louis Brandies, an American Supreme Court Justice in 1890. However. it is difficult to define and identify what is private and what is not (Gavison, 1984). In the USA, "privacy" is used to include everything from anonymity, to control over personal information, and to limiting government intrusions into the home. In Europe, the term more commonly used is "data protection," and is used synonymously worldwide (Wirtz, Lwin and Williams, 2007)

Internationally the right to privacy has been protected in a number of conventions. For instance, the Universal Declaration of Human Rights, 1948 (UDHR) under Article 12 provides that:

No one shall be subjected to arbitrary interference with his privacy, family, home or correspondence, or to attacks upon his honor and reputation. Everyone has the right to the protection of the law against such interference or attacks.

Researchers have worked in the field of consumer privacy and there are quite a few research papers concentrating on studying consumer attitudes towards privacy in different contexts. Researchers tried to find out in their research work the extent to which a customer may agree to allow a marketer to invade his privacy for availing benefits (e.g. soup making company may give a pack of soup free for tasting and telling his opinion about the new flavor of soup). Thus the customer may allow invasion of his privacy to some extent, but the dilemma is how to measure that extent (Culnan, 1993; Milne and Gordon, 1993). Researchers have studied the issues pertaining to privacy invasion from various perspectives, especially business and managerial (Bloom et al., 1994; Cespedes and Smith, 1993, Nash, 1993). Mostly, the subject was studied from legal and ethical point of view (Caudill and Murphy, 2000), and recommended governments mechanism and policies to ensure privacy of its citizens (Clarke, 1999; Pincus and Johns, 1997; Reidenberg, 1996).

An apt example of invasion of privacy is the much talked about case that caused sensation in India. The case involved the union minister who was shopping at the leading ethnic apparel brand's outlet on April 3, 2015. She spotted a CCTV camera pointing towards the change room while she was trying a dress.

Another case of privacy invasion was reported wherein a car rental company, Ola was accused of leaking personal details like mobile numbers, locations of users via SMS. A Chennai based user named Swapnil Midha claimed that Ola leaked the information of 100 customers to her via SMS. According to her, Ola was forwarding her confirmation messages when other customers made a booking in Bangalore and that inside the messages she found mobile numbers, names and addresses. Ola confessed that there has been a manual error on the entry of a driver's device number in their system, because of which the personal details of the customers were getting leaked. The incident raises concerns about the way private data was being handled by Ola.

Mass Marketing Frauds

The term "mass-marketing fraud" refers generally to any type of fraud scheme that uses one or more mass-communication techniques and technologies – such as the Internet, telephones, the mail, and even mass meetings in person -- to present fraudulent solicitations to numbers of prospective victims, to conduct fraudulent transactions with victims, or to transmit the proceeds of the fraud to financial institutions or to others connected with the scheme.

One such mass marketing fraud was a get-rich-quick scheme with Singapore-based SpeakAsia Online Limited (SAOL). The company had asked investors or "panelists" to fill in online survey forms every week to earn Rs 52,000 a year. To sign up, they said, you had to 'invest' Rs 11,000 annually; you would recover that cost in less than three months, they promised. SAOL promised additional commissions if you enrolled more members. In reality, the consumer surveys had no end-user; SAOL had no business-linked revenue stream. 2.4 million Indians fell prey to SAOL's scheme, only to be duped later after the promoters disappeared with their booty. The scam was a Rs 2,200 crore online marketing fraud.

Ambush Marketing

The word "ambush" as used in the expression ambush marketing, means "an attack from a hidden position" and is derived from the old French verb *embuschier*, having the meaning "to place in a wood." The term "ambush marketing" was coined by marketing strategist Jerry Welsh, while he was working as the manager of global marketing efforts for the American Express Company in the 1980s.

Marketers are adhering to ambush marketing for reaching out to children via internet. They use multimedia games, online quizzes and cellphone apps to connect with young customers. Children share messages through social networking sites and unknowingly become the marketers of these brands. Advertisements on internet engage children in a way they cannot on television, where they have to adhere to commercial time. The ads on internet are not subjected to parental control. Therefore, marketers can easily bypass parents. There are many studies which link junk-food marketing and poor diet among children.

Similarly, alcohol companies have been conveniently using social media to target young urban population with direct and surrogate advertisements of their products. Researchers have identified exposure to alcohol marketing as one of the potential factors that may lead to underage alcohol consumption (Lim, Vos, Flaxman, Danaei, Shibuya, Adair-Rohani, et al., 2010). There is a constant increase in promotion of alcohol through social media- India has witnessed 10-15 percent growth each year in the last two decades (Das, Balakrishnan, Vasudevan, 2006). One of the major reasons contributing to increase in consumption of alcohol is increase in marketing activities by the alcohol industry. In India there is restriction on direct advertisement of alcohol through traditional media consisting of print, audio-visual media. However, social media is free from any such restriction. Alcohol companies taking advantage of this legal loophole are misusing social media for marketing of alcohol (Shaikh, Pathak,and Kapilashrami, 2015).

Misuse of Technology by Customers

Customers at times may misuse technology for their vested interests (Chu and Kim, 2011) the customers may threaten companies by using social media platforms and posting their comments leading to defamation of brands which they do not find up to their mark (Chu and Kim, 2011). Although customers may not post a negative comment to intentionally smear a brand, there are internet communities who do so to serve their own purposes such as damaging the image of an organization (Smith, 2009). They know the magnitude of damage that their negative comments can bring to a brand (Agichtein et al., 2008). Sometimes customers may seek favor from companies to post positive things about them on their blogs, facebook pages or company's website.

CONCLUSION

Marketers may gain a lot with the use of technology especially in a developing country like India. Technological advancements like GPS, smart cards, biometrics, fast computational speed can be a boon in supply chain management, distribution and logistics, product planning and development, demand management and other areas. However, the potential risk of misuse or abuse of technology in the form of cyber frauds, invasion of privacy and data theft may hamper the overall enthusiasm. Technology must be safeguarded from people who may use it for their vested interests. Technological advancements should be employed to gain long term sustainable development rather than attainment of short term, materialistic profit. Researchers should find ways for protecting technology against its misuse as well as policy makers should frame rules and regulations to avoid any chance of misuse of technology at any end.

REFERENCES

Agichtein, E., Castillo, C., Donato, D., Gionis, A., & Mishne, G. (2008). Finding high-quality content in social media. In *Proceeding of the 2008 International Conference on Web Search and Data Mining* (pp. 183-194).

Babor, T. (2010). Alcohol: No ordinary commodity- Research and Public Policy. Oxford, UK: Oxford University Press.

Bakos, J. Y. (1997). Reducing Buyer Search Costs: Implications for Electronic Marketplaces. *Management Science*, *43*(12), 12. doi:10.1287/mnsc.43.12.1676

Barry, V. (1979). *Moral Issues in Business* (pp. 39–70). New York: Wadsworth Publishing Co.

Beauchamp, T. L. (1983). Ethical Theory and Business (2nd ed.). Englewood cliffs, NJ: Prentice Hall, Inc.

Bellizzi, J. A., & Hasty, R. W. (2003). Supervising unethical sales force behavior: how strong is the tendency to treat top sales performers leniently? *Journal of Business Ethics*, *43*(4), 337–351. doi:10.1023/A:1023045617076

Chakraborty, S. K. (2005). Ethics: Light from the Golden Quartet. *Journal of Human Values*, *11*(1), 1–8. doi:10.1177/097168580401100101

Chu, S., & Kim, Y. (2011). Determinants of consumer engagement in electronic word-of-mouth (eWOM) in social networking sites. *International Journal of Advertising*, *30*(1), 47–75. doi:10.2501/IJA-30-1-047-075

Collins, D. (2006). Seven Moral Levees: Preventing Ethical Breaches. *Leadership Excellence*, *23*(2), 18.

Cressey, D. R., & Moore, C. A. (1983). Managerial values and corporate codes of ethics. *California Management Review*, *25*(Summer), 53–77. doi:10.2307/41165032

Das, S. K., Balakrishnan, V., & Vasudevan, D. M. (2006). Alcohol: Its health and social impact in India. *The National Medical Journal of India*, *19*, 94–99. PMID:16756199

DeGeorge, R. R. (1982). *Business Ethics* (2nd ed.). New York: Macmillan Publishing.

Deshmukh, S. P., Deshmukh, P., & Thampi, G. T. (2013). Transformation from E-commerce to M-commerce in Indian Context. *International Journal of Computer Science Issues*, *10*(4).

Drucker, P. (1973). *Management: Tasks, Responsibilities, Practises* (pp. 64–65). New York: Harper and Row.

EY. (2014). Big data: changing the way businesses operate. Retrieved from http://www.ey.com/Publication/vwLUAssets/EY_-_/$FILE/EY-Insights-on-GRC-Big-data.pdf

Fernando, A. C. (2011). *Business Ethics: An Indian Perspective* (5th ed.). New Delhi: Pearson Education in South Asia.

Friedman, M. (1970). The social responsibility of business is to increase its profits. *New York Times Magazine*, *32-33*, 122-124.

Gauzente, C., & Ranchhod, A. (2001). Ethical marketing for competitive advantage on the internet. *Academy of Marketing Science Review*, *1*(10).

Gellert, F., & Schalk, R. (2012). Age related: Attitudes the influence on relationships and performance at work. *Journal of Health Organization and Management*, *26*(1), g98–g117. doi:10.1108/14777261211211115 PMID:22524101

Houston, F. S. (1986). The marketing concept: What it is and what it is not. *Journal of Marketing*, *50*(April), 81–87. doi:10.2307/1251602

Kollat, D. T., Roger, B. D., & Engel, J. F. (1972), The Current Status of Consumer Behavior Research: Developments During the 1968-1972 Period. In M. Venkatesan (Eds.), SV - Proceedings of the Third Annual Conference of the Association for Consumer Research (pp. 576-585). Chicago, IL: Association for Consumer Research.

Lim, S. S., Vos, T., Flaxman, A. D., Danaei, G., Shibuya, K., Adair-Rohani, H., ... Ezzati, M. (2010). A comparative risk assessment of burden of disease and injury attributable to 67 risk factors and risk factor clusters in 21 regions, 1990-2010: A systematic analysis for the Global Burden of Disease Study 2010. *Lancet*, *380*(9859), 2224–2260. doi:10.1016/S0140-6736(12)61766-8 PMID:23245609

Lovelock, C., & Wirtz, J. (2006). *Services Marketing – People, Technology, Strategy* (6th ed.). Upper Saddle River, NJ: Prentice-Hall.

Moon, B. J. (2004). Consumer adoption of the internet as an information search and product purchase channel: Some research hypotheses'. *International Journal of Internet Marketing and Advertising*, *1*(1), 104–118. doi:10.1504/IJIMA.2004.003692

Murphy, P. E., Laczniak, G. R., Bowie, N. E., & Klein, T. A. (2005). *Ethical Marketing*. Upper Saddle River, NJ: Pearson Prentice-Hall.

Runes, D. D. (1964). Dictionary of Philosophy, Patterson: Litdefields, Adams & Co.

Shaikh, Z. A., Pathak, R., & Kapilashrami, M. C. (2015). Misuse of social media marketing by alcohol companies. *Journal of Mental Health and Human Behaviour*, *20*(1), 22–27. doi:10.4103/0971-8990.164805

Sharp, F. C., & Fox, P. G. (1937). *Business Ethics*. New York: D. Appleton-Century Company.

Smith, T. (2009). The social media revolution. *International Journal of Market Research*, *51*(4), 599–561. doi:10.2501/S1470785309200773

Sweta. (2015). Smart Card and Its Application. *International Journal of Advanced Research in Computer Science and Software Engineering*, *5*(7).

Taylor, P. W. (1975). *Principles of Ethics: An Introduction*. Encino, California: Dickerson Publishing Co., Inc.

Velaquez, M. G. (2007). *Business Ethics: Concepts and Cases* (6th ed.). Delhi: Pearson Education. Retrieved from http://zeenews.india.com/news/nation/aadhaar-scheme-does-not-violate-fundamental-rights-says-uidai_884850.html

Vitell, S., Jr. (1986). *Marketing Ethics: Conceptual and Empirical Foundations of a Positive Theory of Decision Making in Marketing Situations Having Ethical Content*. Unpublished dissertation, Texas Tech University, US.

Wirtz, J., Lwin, M. O., & Williams, J. D. (2007). Causes and consequences of consumer on-line privacy concern. *International Journal of Service Industry Management*, *18*(4), 326–348. doi:10.1108/09564230710778128

This research was previously published in the International Journal of Technoethics (IJT), 9(1); pages 27-36, copyright year 2018 by IGI Publishing (an imprint of IGI Global).

Chapter 7
Facebook as Marketing Tools for Organizations:
Knowledge Management Analysis

Siti Farzana Izzati Jaman
Universiti Brunei Darussalam, Brunei

Muhammad Anshari
https://orcid.org/0000-0002-8160-6682
Universiti Brunei Darussalam, Brunei

ABSTRACT

Facebook has become widely known around the globe. This chapter applies marketing techniques to Facebook. The concern of using Facebook for both users and marketers is also elaborated in this study. Scenarios will help marketers to comprehend how knowledge management tools like plan-do-check-act (PDCA) and root cause analysis (RCA) are used in Facebook marketing. Other than the concern risk, the chapter presents the importance of using Facebook as well as the implication of these technique for future research.

INTRODUCTION

In the year 2003, people began to grow more comfortable by interacting with one another through social network sites (SNSs) (Treadaway & Smith, 2010, p. 7). The usage of SNSs become more beneficial when large number of users communicate (Anshari & Lim, 2017) and shared information amongst themselves. Boyd and Ellison (2010) distinguish social network as web-based services that enable users to; create a public or semi-public profile within restricted boundary of system, integrate with a list of other users that they share connection with and examine and traverse the users list of connections and those created by others within the system.

Nevertheless, SNSs not only allow users to interact and share information but also to assist users to extend beyond their own personal network. In case of organisation such as businesses, it allows them

DOI: 10.4018/978-1-7998-9020-1.ch007

to tap into consumer behaviour with little amount of risk in financial investment (Stokes, 2010, p. 189; Anshari et al., 2016). Marketers for instance can obtain benefit from using this social network. Social network helps them to interact with customers and conveniently open up a new way to reach the potential customers. Indeed, to stand out and compete with other competitors, the presence of businesses within Facebook has become necessary.

Ever since Facebook was founded in 2004, it aggressively emerged into one of the world's dominant SNSs surpassing more than 1.1 billion active daily users by 2016 (Facebook, 2018). Thus, making them promising for target marketing audience rather than old traditional tactic of marketing to approach the customers (Noyes, 2018; Anshari & Alas, 2015). The previous method employed by marketers such as e-mail promotion, telemarketing and other type of approaches to distribute the information concerning to business products and services might still be effective (Tiago & Veríssimo, 2014). But these days to maintain long-term customer relationship, it is important to include web-based strategy. Facebook for instance have continue to revolve and its trends has gain more popularity among the digital marketers and organisations (Landicho, 2017). Facebook site enable users to develop their own personal profile and obtain opportunity to discover insights of others 'lifestyle and interests (Acar & Polonsky, 2007; Ahad, Anshari, & Razzaq, 2017). With Facebook as powerful portal for organisation and business to spread information about their products and services, the focus has been shifted from developing specific individual relationships to reaching the current and potential customers.

Nevertheless, the research on the social media particularly in Facebook marketing trends are quite minimal. Therefore, this paper will the theory of mantras and the modern risk management, the current practices of Facebook marketing tools exist, the scenario as well as their benefits alongside with critical success factors and risks concerns. Meanwhile the literature review will critically analyse the existing studies on social media and Facebook. Further suggestion on how organisations use Facebook as social marketing tool will be discussed in this study.

WEB 2.0 AND SOCIAL NETWORKS

The new advancement of technology has transformed the usage of internet into more social interactive environment (Allen, 2017). By facilitating the web 2.0 individuals able to communicate and develop online content easier (Lai & Turban, 2008; Montalvo, 2016). With the rise of SNS globally, people more incline to be more engaged in the sites (Mueller et al., 2011). Senecal and Nantel (2004) stated that by using the web 2.0 users especially customers able to gain access different knowledge and enlightenment provided by other customers' reviews and suggestions. Surrounded the web 2.0 there is a development of platforms that connect people together through social network. The ability for them to produce and share the online content with other users within social media and able to architect the success by participating in the community (Meadows-Klue, 2008; White, 2016). With the current situation, organisation especially marketers trying their best to utilise the usage of web 2.0 to bring benefits for their organisation.

Even though many scholars have debated on the topic of social networks and many theories have been developed on how SNS act as marketing tool for marketers, but the academic studies merely focus on social network as a whole. The work publishes earlier circulated on social media such as Twitter, Myspace, Facebook and others packed into one study (Charnigo & Barnett-Ellis, 2007). Chen et al. (2011) mention social media allows business to be more attractive and communicative. A possible platform where customers able to interact and become more familiar with each other may enhance the likelihood the source of trust. Bear in mind that there is a slight different between social network and social media. Social media often referred to the formation of online communities where the main intention is to interact, share and exchange information with one another (Buss & Strauss, 2009; Hiremath, & Kenchakkanavar, 2016). Meanwhile social network is namely status update, posts, video, links, pages in the websites (Eley & Tilley, 2009). As being mentioned above, this paper will explore on how organisation use Facebook as marketing tool while in the same time considered risk associated with it.

Facebook as Marketing Tool

Distinct from other social media, Facebook data is quite reliable and useful to comprehend customer's patterns and behaviours (Casteleyn, Mottart, & Rutten, 2009). From looking through the Facebook site, users action can be distinguished from the *news feed* at the right end corner of the sites where *top stories* and *most recent* can be viewed by the users. Nevertheless, let's face the reality, users can create their own profile base on whatever they wish to do but it is not necessary the users would provide a valid and accurate information about themselves (Doyle, 2007; Palmer & Koenig-Lewis, 2009; Treadaway & Smith, 2010). For instance, an individual would create different name rather than using his or her real name and manipulate his or her profile details and status in Facebook. Nevertheless Casteleyn et al. (2009) pointed out that by using Facebook, marketers may able to obtain valuable information from the users' profile, post and preferences. After all, not everyone uses Facebook to create a different version of them. Other most likely use Facebook to find the common interest and preferences of other individual users. Hence, by understanding the customers (users) preferences, it will help marketers to plan ahead and target their market segmentation. In the same time position themselves one step forward against their competitors (Acar & Polonsky, 2007; Treadaway & Smith, 2010). The next section, we will further highlight the approach that can be useful for the marketers when targeting customers in Facebook.

ASEAN Digital Marketplace

ASEAN countries are no exception from this case and can be more highly at risk than the other countries. There are cases where many physical stores have to close down due to the increase in the number of people purchasing goods and products from the digital market. Half of the ASEAN countries received more than 50% Internet penetration with Singapore as the country with the highest percentage of Internet penetration, while Myanmar is at the last position, with its 13% internet penetration. The same statistic also shows that Indonesia has the most internet users, where there are 88 million internet users. However, the internet penetration for this country falls below 50% as the number of the internet users are relatively low compared to the population in the country, which is 258.7 million people. Brunei, with only 0.3 million internet users, is the country with the least number of internet users, but, Brunei is right behind Singapore, making it the second country with the highest percentage of internet penetration (Sen, Attravar, & Jaiswal (2016). By 2017, it is expected of ASEAN to expand its market size up to 25%, making ASEAN one of the digital market leads, together with China. By 2018, every ASEAN country is predicted to have above 50% of internet penetration. This increase is expected to continue over years, and the advancement of the internet penetration will contribute a raise of at least In addition to this, if new industries are established and mobile workers' productivity is increased, ASEAN may have a total of about $5,000 to $5,600 GDP for its digital market economy (Maria et al., 2017). Based on this, it is safe to say that ASEAN countries have high potential in becoming countries with strong digital developments.

PROBLEM SOLVING TOOL

Plan, Do, Check and Act (PDCA)

In the early of 1950s, Edward Deming organised seminars with manager in Japan. During that time Deming Wheel (Cycle) was introduced to discuss on the concern of stability interface surrounded on studies, design, production and sales to ensure a better-quality improvement in product and services and to gain customer trust (Lodgaard, Gamme, & Aasland, 2012). The Deming Cycle which also called PDCA Cycle is a continuous apprehended and improved model that capture 4 repetitive cycles; Plan, Do, Check (Study) and Act (iSixSigma, 2018). It is founded that PDCA often practices by organisation around the world to enhance their main competitive advantageous and endless issues on solving methods (Gidey et al., 2014). Indeed, to be able to capture competitive advantageous organisation first must exceed the customers' demands and specification. In order to do so companies try to compete with one another to establish latest research and innovation (Katz, 2004). Undoubtedly, customers will not prefer to buy waste products and services as neither value and benefit bring give advantage to them (Gidey et al., 2014). Hence, organisation should devise a method to ensure there is unnecessary processes include and try their best to enhance the additional value to obtain better quality products and services. This is where the Deming Cycle play important role. The solution eliminates or minimal the amount of original wastes and errors (Marrs & Mundt, 2007). Conforming this situation, Cole (2002) discuss the activities of Deming Cycle as the main key to attract the customer attention. Below the Table 1 shows the content of Deming Cycle (PDCA Cycle).

Table 1. Significant characters of 4 stages in PDCA cycle

1. Plan • Gather suitable team members • Collect all available data • Explore customers' needs & demands • Identify the process circulate the queries/problems • Find out the cause of the root • Design an action plan • Develop the plan	2. Do • Execute the improvement • Gather suitable & valid data • Measure the progress • Documented the result
3. Check/Study • Write the summary & analyse the data • Evaluate the result relates to target & compare • Review if there are only errors/issues • Documented the lesson learned • Define any existing issues/unintended costs/abnormal cost	4. Act • Standardise the required improvement • Formulate the best approach • Communicate the result broadly & efficiently • Find out the next improvement (if necessarily)

(Adapted from Cole, 2012)

Root Cause Analysis (RCA)

When a negative event occurs, Root Cause Analysis (RCA) will be used to identify the causal agents (Senders, 2004). RCA is considered as a guide to correct the roots causes by focusing on the symptoms of the problem (Vliet, 2010). Basically, RCA reflected in the 'new moment' as compare to Failure Mode and Effect Analysis (FMEA) in solving the problems or issues. In order to take a corrective measure 5 identifiable steps are being used in the process (MindTools, 2018). As being illustrate in Figure 1, 5 steps are significant in finding the cause of the problem.

Figure 1. 5 steps in RCA
(Adapted from MindTools, 2018)

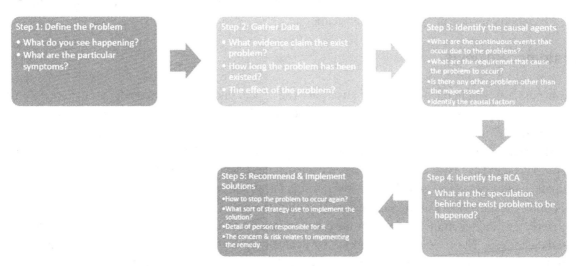

Nevertheless, there are better RCA technique that can be used to search for the root cause of the problem (Mulder, 2012). One of the technique will be using the 5 Why Analysis developed by Sakichi Toyoda (Vliet, 2014). By using 5 Whys Analysis, it may help to avoid people to focus only on the common assumption and classic cause of the problems (Mulder, 2012). The common assumption of the problems may consist of lack of time, not appealing and shortage of workforce. Although these factors might be considered as causes however 5 Whys help to determine the particular origins that may be responsible behind the problem. An example of RCA using F Whys will be discussed in the case scenario later to enhance further understanding on this topic.

METHODOLOGY

In nature, this study contains element of exploratory research and use secondary data to support the degree of Facebook act as marketing tools for organisations. To analyse the utilisation of marketing tool, the researchers decides to choose Facebook as the area of the study. Prior to recent research Facebook is selected due to its strong presence and engagement of organisations especially the companies in exploiting Facebook as part of their marketing efforts. As being highlighted on the first section, Facebook is a dominant SNS that surpass billions of active users (Facebook, 2018). The study focuses on executing mostly base on secondary data to help with the research.

DISCUSSION

As web 2.0 acts as catalyst for customers to seek authenticity and sense of belonging, organisations try to capture these customers attention. It is important to take note that customer involvement is a key towards marketing approach (Park et al., 2007). In this case marketers need to take notes on the *customer reviews* and their *recommendations* in the Facebook. After discussing these two parts, a following section on how Facebook is being used as marketing tool, case scenario on PDCA and RCA and the benefits of using Facebook marketing will be further deliberate.

Customer Reviews

Nambisan (2002) mentioned that for organisation to be appear visible in social media, a customer review is substantial. Organisation must encourage their customers to give them rating and reviews through social media (Bronner & De Hoog, 2010) One of the good example will be a local company in Brunei named Escape Square Brunei. Escape Square Brunei is one of the problem-solving game where customers (players) need to find a way to escape and solve the puzzle (Escape Square Brunei, 2018). The company instigate their customers to give them review through Facebook ad Instagram in exchange the customers will obtain certain amount of discount before they play the game. By doing so, it encourages customers to give review and recommendations for the company products and services. Thus, attracting more potential customers. These views are supported by Ridings and Gefen (2004) that potential customers are more likely attracted towards other users' reviews and recommendations. Eventually the interaction in social media help to gain the customers trust and reduce the risk for the customers to encounter frauds and danger as they rely on the genuine reviews and recommendations from their friends.

Recommendations From Other Users

Based on the relevant literature reviews, online social communities and SNS provides social supports to other users (Ballantine & Stephenson, 2011). For instance, by using Facebook users can simply search the name of products or company that individual intended to seek for. The Facebook search then direct the users to *the post, pages, group/communities, rating and recommendation* relates to the search. In a research made by Hajli (2014), the advancement of the web 2.0 along with social media have created tremendous impact to the customers. In this circumstance, customers act as support value in the social media platform as they volunteer to share the online content about the company's products and services in Facebook. Consequently, attract new potential clients and establish trust amongst the users as users are willing to share with the public about their purchase experiences.

Dominant Facebook Tools to Support Marketing Tools

Based on the Table 2 shown below, the Facebook method are adapted from the previous scholar articles on 'The implication of Facebook Marketing for Organisation' from Central Queensland University. The TABLE is an improve proposed version that may help to assist the marketers in achieving their target in using Facebook marketing.

Table 2. Step to achieve marketing target in Facebook

Common Facebook Tools	How to Attract the Customers?
1. Facebook Profile	Well develop profile of organisation can create authentic & project audience the organisation vision/ mission statement clearly
2. Facebook Group	To retain/attract more customers, the name of the group, topic of interest and image is vitally important (Ramsaran-Fowdar, & Fowdar, 2013).
3. Facebook Business Page	A great approach to grow the brand identity and product (Marrs, 2013).
4. Organise Events	By using Facebook, organisations able to promote their upcoming events, articles, blogs, etc.
5. Sponsored ads and Stories	Capitalise the Word-of-Mouth by promoting advertisement and stories that link to the users' behaviour or friend's like.

6. Facebook Live	• A new latest trend of Facebook towards customer engagement & sharing (Dudharejia, 2017)
	• Provide a sneak peek to customer in several ways:
	  o Hosting evens
	  o Customer post purchase experience
	  o Sneak peek on latest product or services

7. Chatbots	Organisation use chatbots to interact with their customers through Facebook messenger (Dudharejia, 2017).

Concerns and Risks Allied With Marketing in Facebook

Indeed, trust issue is often associate with social media such as Facebook. A sense of fear that Facebook may reveals the users' peculiarity and intervene their privacy whenever they share online information amongst their friends and larger community might endanger these anxious users (Eley & Tilley, 2009). It remains questionable on how much Facebook able to gather information about the users and tailor the advertisement to their taste and preferences (Poh, 2018). Nevertheless, certain studies suggest users that own social media are perceived risk compare to those who do not have one (Fogel & Nehmad, 2009). They fully aware of the risk associate with social media but they consider themselves as risk takers. Even though Facebook might share their information with the third parties such as organisations, but they feel comfortable to have their common interest share with others.

Nonetheless, bot many Facebook users use their Facebook to check sponsored stories or advertisement. A study conducted by Palmer and Koenig-Lewis (2009) revealed that people use Facebook to socialise and tend to ignore the ads whenever they log into the Facebook. Although it is not surprise that Facebook may help to reduce the marketing cost incur in every month for organisation. But the question is, is it worthy to invest in Facebook to increase the organisation profit? If yes, is there any proper technique that may help fix a problem for marketers and help them plan ahead to make marketing efforts. In this situation we will be exploring two scenarios by using PDCA and RCA to help the marketers.

Scenario I: Applying PDCA on Viral Marketing

How to dissect the consumers' minds seems to be the main concern for marketers these days. Therefore, by using Deming Cycle, the study will intend to use the Rayport Virus Marketing and further divided them into 4 steps in achieving viral marketing in Facebook.

Step 1: Plan

First step to understand the problems face by the organisation when using the viral marketing. One of the way is to collect the data through obtaining response and feedbacks from the customers who use the Facebook. Since reactions and response to online sharing in Facebook grow faster compare to using traditional marketing approach, it helps the organisation to comprehend the patterns and behaviours of their consumer quickly than before. For example, a company want to find out the most "Viral Post" or type of popular food brand that engage successfully with their customers through Facebook. So, the plan should be;

What are the most popular and friendly post about food brands found in Facebook? How they able to capture/engage with customers? How did they response to their customers post on Facebook Page/Business?

Hence, the data will be gathered from the dominant users of food sectors or industry in Facebook and in this stage plans and strategy will be set up in order to successfully viral the products/ services and rise the brand of the organisation.

Step 2: Do

A being stated by Rayport (1996), "What's up-front is free; payment comes later". In other words, if you want to be profitable you must be willingly to invest certain amount of money and effort to your company first before bearing those fruits. In this case, to pioneer the viral marketing, marketers need to execute the plan that can help their organisation to promote in Facebook Page/Business. For instance, the organisation decides to use 'Facebook Live' to provide sneak peek on the latest promotion of its products. By executing this plan, the marketer can monitor the result and find out how *many reviews, like* and *share* the company able to obtain by using the Facebook Live. For the second step, the question ask for this scenario will be;

What type of promotional method can be used on our Facebook Page/Business? Would it be successful to have our customer involve more in our Facebook Page/Business?

Step 3: Check

After that, marketer need to let the user carry out the messages to online community posts. From here the customers evaluation will be observe and taken into account. Customer evaluation often bring either positive or negative impact on the brand evaluation (Chevalier & Goolsbee, 2002). By looking through the circumstances, marketer will check whether the plan he executes i.e. using Facebook Live will delivered a particular message intends for the current and potential customers. Therefore, the question applies for the third stage;

By using the XX promotional tool, does it create better impact to the brand and deliver specific messages? If yes, does the message deliver is well received by the customers?

Step 4: Act

If organisations want their customers to be committed to their brands, the organisations need to make customers feel welcome and make the brand be part of their identity (Duboff 1986; Plummer, 1985). Ki and Hon (2007) state people will be more appreciative towards organisations that maintain friendly and reliable customer relationship strategies. This can be done by targeting different market segment with different strategies. By using the current scenario, if marketer products and services aim at different market segment (i.e. youngsters). Then particular technique must be use to reach the target market segment. Although capturing the attention of particular market segment can be tricky, but it may help to increase the number of potential customer if the technique use is the appropriate one. Hence in this situation, marketers need to understand:

Does the current method lead to enhancement of brand loyalty. Does it require another approach that may help to comprehend the requirement of the customers?

Scenario II: 5 Whys for Negative Image of Brand in the Social Media

In case of RCA analysis, we will explore a scenario of a recent establish company and use 5 Whys of RCA to find the origin of the problems and provide solution to minimal the issue in the future.

A company uses Facebook to generate campaign on its new latest release products and services. Since the company is a new establish business, the marketers aim to enhance their brand popularity in short amount of time. However, considering the company is quite new, the marketers and campaign managers are not acquaintance with digital marketing. In fact, in the company only the owner has previous experience in handling this matter. When the company first launch its products and brand, it is unsuccessful and the company gain a lot of critics by the Facebook users. Hence to solve these issues, 5 Whys will be used to identify the causes:

1. Why the problem occurs?
   Reason: Fail to launch their first campaign successfully
2. Why?
   Cause: Because the marketers and campaign manager lack of experience
3. Why?
   Cause: Because the marketers and campaign manager are not familiar with digital marketing and no proper guidance given to them.
4. Why?
   Cause: The company is recently established and the person who has the experience (owner) is not available to help them.

5.   Why?

Root Cause: The owner is busy and do not give any specific guidance on how to do digital marketing though Facebook.

To solve this situation, owner should appoint a person who is familiar with digital marketing especially a person that acquaintance with Facebook marketing. The owner need to ensure that the content of the campaign advertisement do not generate any negative impact to any users. Research and proper guidance must be done before launching any advertisement in Facebook. By identifying the cause of the problem, it helps the marketers to formulate better plan and try their best to make further improvement.

Advantages of Using Facebook Marketing

Facebook continue to dominant the world of social media and metamorphize into world number 1 sites to connect and share online (Marrs, 2013). Edelman (2007) claims that customers are moving towards social network and spend most of their time accompany with viral and online marketing. This is considered as 'win-win situation' for both customers and organisation. Customers regard the usage of social media as the current trend while organisation take this opportunity to cut their marketing expense as it is very costly to use traditional methods. Indeed, with the current volatile economic circumstance, organisations are trying to look for better opportunity to minimise their spending (Ramsaran-Fowdar, & Fowdar, 2013). They see the usage of SNS is one of the way to penetrate their business to the global market, in the same time reduce their costs of expenditure

Secondly, Facebook can be treated as one of the viral marketing method. Viral marketing refers to marketing approach that influence users to share the marketing massages to other sites/users, thus create exponential growth and influence the messages to be appear visible in SNS (Rouse & Kiwak, 2017). This viral marketing efforts can be treated a modern marketing of word of mouth. Trusov, Bucklin and Pauwels (2009) believed that word of mouth from family, friends and others have strong influence over customer purchase experience. . In addition, it is proven by recent studies that word of mouth is one of the crucial elements in influencing customers behaviours.

Thirdly, in accordance to Ramsaran-Fowdar and Fowdar, (2013), Facebook is an absolute epitome towards telemarketing and marketing research institute. This probably due to following reasons:

- People do not have to dial the call centres to seek for data and information
- No need to hire people to collect market survey data as the marketers able to do so by using Facebook analytics
- Facebook provides quick response and answer to any marketing enquiries within short-term frame.

CONCLUSION

The advantage for organisation to use the marketing tools can be seen from above, but Facebook users simply can ignore the advertisement and any flooding information share to them. The Facebook platform circulates on the trust and shares. Every organisation must learn not to violate the users' privacy and follows the rules regulate when doing marketing activities or else opt to be "unlike" or critics in the Facebook. It is not only learning on how to enhance brand popularity, organisation need to keep up to date with the current trends and tailor to customer taste. This is why marketers of the organisation need to understand, it is not all about the organisation only but how they able to deliver and interact the message clearly to these customers in Facebook. Yet, the sequel is barely unfolded, the journey is just the beginning. For organisation especially the marketers, understanding the approach towards utilising marketing tool in Facebook is not restricted to social media only. Any particular strategy to ensure the flow of process within organisation is smooth and less error also need to be considered. Furthermore, relying on Facebook marketing is one of the good strategy but it requires skills and experience in using the tools in the same time understand who the customers are quite important. Finally, social media has helped to gain the customers trust and reduce the risk for the customers to encounter frauds and danger as they rely on the genuine reviews and recommendations from their friends.

REFERENCES

Acar, A. S., & Polonsky, M. (2007). Online social networks and insights into marketing communications. *Journal of Internet Commerce*, 6(4), 55–72. doi:10.1080/15332860802086227

Ahad, A. D., Anshari, M., & Razzaq, A. (2017). Domestication of Smartphones among Adolescents in Brunei Darussalam, *Journal of Cyber Behavior. Psychology and Learning*, 7(4), 26–39. doi:10.4018/IJCBPL.2017100103

Allen, M. (2017). Web 2.0: An argument against convergence. In *Media Convergence and Deconvergence* (pp. 177–196). Cham: Palgrave Macmillan. doi:10.1007/978-3-319-51289-1_9

Anshari, M., & Alas, Y. (2015). Smartphones Habits, Necessities, and Big Data Challenges. *Journal of High Technology Management Research*, 26(2), 177-185. DOI: . doi:10.1016/j.hitech.2015.09.005

Anshari, M., Alas, Y., Hardaker, G., Jaidin, J. H., Smith, M., & Ahad, A. D. (2016). Smartphone habit and behaviour in Brunei: Personalization, gender, and generation gap. *Computers in Human Behavior*, 64, 719–727. doi:10.1016/j.chb.2016.07.063

Anshari, M., & Lim, S. A. (2017). E-Government with Big Data Enabled through Smartphone for Public Services: Possibilities and Challenges. *International Journal of Public Administration*, 40(13), 1143–1158. doi:10.1080/01900692.2016.1242619

Ballantine, P. W., & Stephenson, R. J. (2011). Help me, I'm fat! Social support in online weight loss networks. *Journal of Consumer Behaviour*, 10(6), 332–337. doi:10.1002/cb.374

Buss, A., & Strauss, N. (2009). *Online communities handbook: Building your business and brand on the Web*. Berkeley, CA: New Riders.

Boyd, D., & Ellison, N. (2010). Social network sites: Definition, history, and scholarship. *IEEE Engineering Management Review*, 3(38), 16–31. doi:10.1109/EMR.2010.5559139

Bronner, F., & De Hoog, R. (2010). Consumer-generated versus marketer-generated websites in consumer decision making. *International Journal of Market Research*, 52(2), 231–248. doi:10.2501/S1470785309201193

Casteleyn, J., Mottart, A., & Rutten, K. (2009). How to use data from Facebook in your market research. *International Journal of Market Research, 51*(4), 439–447. doi:10.2501/S1470785309200669

Charnigo, L., & Barnett-Ellis, P. (2007). Checking out Facebook. com: The impact of a digital trend on academic libraries. *Information Technology and Libraries, 26*(1), 23. doi:10.6017/ital.v26i1.3286

Chevalier, J., & Goolsbee, A. (2003). Measuring prices and price competition online: Amazon. com and BarnesandNoble. com. *Quantitative Marketing and Economics, 1*(2), 203–222. doi:10.1023/A:1024634613982

Chen, Y., Fay, S., & Wang, Q. (2011). The role of marketing in social media: How online consumer reviews evolve. *Journal of Interactive Marketing, 25*(2), 85–94. doi:10.1016/j.intmar.2011.01.003

Cole, R. E. (2002). From continuous improvement to continuous innovation. *Total Quality Management, 13*(8), 1051–1056. doi:10.1080/09544120200000001

Doyle, S. (2007). The role of social networks in marketing. *Journal of Database Marketing & Customer Strategy Management, 15*(1), 60–64. doi:10.1057/palgrave.dbm.3250070

Duboff, R. S. (1986). Brands, like people, have personalities. *Marketing News, 20*(1), 8.

Dudharejia, M. (2017). *8 reasons Facebook will beat all other digital marketing channels this year.* Retrieved March 11, 2018, from https://www.entrepreneur.com/article/286441

Edelman, D. C. (2007). From the periphery to the core: As online strategy becomes overall strategy, marketing organizations and agencies will never be the same. *Journal of Advertising Research, 47*(2), 130–134. doi:10.2501/S0021849907070146

Eley, B., & Tilley, S. (2009). *Online marketing inside out.* Collingwood, Vic.: SitePoint.

Facebook. (2018). *Facebook pages for marketing your business.* Retrieved February 9, 2018, from https://www.facebook.com/business/products/pages#

Fogel, J., & Nehmad, E. (2009). Internet social network communities: Risk taking, trust, and privacy concerns. *Computers in Human Behavior, 25*(1), 153–160.

Escape Square Brunei. (2018). *About Escape Square Brunei.* Retrieved March 11, 2018, from https://www.facebook.com/pg/escapesquarebn/about/?ref=page_internal

Gidey, E., Jilcha, K., Beshah, B., & Kitaw, D. (2014). The plan-do-check-act cycle of value addition. *Industrial Engineering & Management, 3*(124), 2169–0316.

Hajli, M. N. (2014). A study of the impact of social media on consumers. *International Journal of Market Research, 56*(3), 387–404. doi:10.2501/IJMR-2014-025

Hiremath, B. K., & Kenchakkanavar, A. Y. (2016). An alteration of the web 1.0, web 2.0 and web 3.0: a comparative study. *Imperial Journal of Interdisciplinary Research, 2*(4).

iSixSigma. (2018). *Deming Cycle, PDCA, iSixSigma.* Retrieved from https://www.isixsigma.com/dictionary/deming-cycle-pdca/

Katz, R. (2004). *The human side of managing technological innovation: A collection of readings.* New York: Oxford University Press.

Ki, E. J., & Hon, L. C. (2007). Testing the linkages among the organization–public relationship and attitude and behavioral intentions. *Journal of Public Relations Research, 19*(1), 1–23.

Lai, L. S., & Turban, E. (2008). Groups formation and operations in the Web 2.0 environment and social networks. *Group Decision and Negotiation, 17*(5), 387–402. doi:10.100710726-008-9113-2

Landicho, J. (2017). *Facebook marketing trends for 2018.* Retrieved from https://learn.infusionsoft.com/marketing/social-media/2018-facebook-trends

Lodgaard, E., Gamme, I., & Aasland, K. E. (2012, September). Success factors for PDCA as continuous improvement method in product development. In *IFIP International Conference on Advances in Production Management Systems* (pp. 645-652). Springer.

Maria, R. S., Urata, S., & Intal, J. P. S. (2017). *The ASEAN Economic Community Into 2025 and Beyond.* Academic Press.

Marrs, F. O., & Mundt, B. M. (2007). Handbook of industrial engineering: Technology and operations management (3rd ed.). Academic Press. doi:10.1002/9780470172339.ch2

Marrs, M. (2013, April 15). *7 ways to market your business on Facebook.* Retrieved March 11, 2018, from https://www.wordstream.com/blog/ws/2013/04/15/facebook-marketing

Meadows-Klue, D. (2008). Opinion piece: Falling in Love 2.0: Relationship marketing for the Facebook generation. *Journal of Direct. Data and Digital Marketing Practice, 9*(3), 245–250. doi:10.1057/palgrave.dddmp.4350103

Milne, G. R., Rohm, A., & Bahl, S. (2009). If It's Legal, Is It Acceptable? *Journal of Advertising, 38*(4), 107–122. doi:10.2753/JOA0091-3367380408

MindTools. (2018). *Root Cause Analysis: Tracing a problem to its origins.* Retrieved March 12, 2018, from https://www.mindtools.com/pages/article/newTMC_80.htm

Montalvo, R. E. (2016). Social media management. *International Journal of Management & Information Systems (Online), 20*(2), 45.

Mueller, J., Hutter, K., Fueller, J., & Matzler, K. (2011). Virtual worlds as knowledge management platform–a practice-perspective. *Information Systems Journal, 21*(6), 479–501. doi:10.1111/j.1365-2575.2010.00366.x

Mulder, P. (2012). *5 Whys analysis.* Retrieved March 12, 2018, from ToolsHero: https://www.toolshero.com/problem-solving/5-whys-analysis/

Nambisan, S. (2002). Designing virtual customer environments for new product development: Toward a theory. *Academy of Management Review, 27*(3), 392–413. doi:10.5465/amr.2002.7389914

Noyes, D. (2018). *Top 20 Facebook statistics.* Retrieved February 9, 2018, from https://zephoria.com/top-15-valuable-facebook-statistics/

Palmer, A., & Koenig-Lewis, N. (2009). An experiential, social network-based approach to direct marketing. *Direct Marketing: An International Journal, 3*(3), 162–176. doi:10.1108/17505930910985116

Park, D. H., Lee, J., & Han, I. (2007). The effect of on-line consumer reviews on consumer purchasing intention: The moderating role of involvement. *International Journal of Electronic Commerce, 11*(4), 125–148. doi:10.2753/JEC1086-4415110405

Plummer, J. T. (1985). How personality makes a difference. *Journal of Advertising Research, 24*(6), 27–31.

Poh, M. (2018). *Facebook & your privacy: Why it matters.* Retrieved from https://www.hongkiat.com/blog/facebook-privacy-matters/

Ramsaran-Fowdar, R. R., & Fowdar, S. (2013). The implications of Facebook marketing for organizations. *Contemporary Management Research, 9*(1), 73–84. doi:10.7903/cmr.9710

Rayport, J. (1996). The virus of marketing. *Fast Company, 6*, 68.

Ridings, C. M., & Gefen, D. (2004). Virtual community attraction: Why people hang out online. *Journal of Computer-Mediated Communication, 10*(1).

Rouse, M., & Kiwak, K. (2017). *What is viral marketing?* Retrieved March 10, 2018, from http://searchsalesforce.techtarget.com/definition/viral-marketing

Sen, A., Attravar, A., & Jaiswal, R. (2016). *Internet: E-commerce in ASEAN-Taking Off.* Retrieved from https://www.jefferies.com/CMSFiles/Jefferies.com/files/Insights/EcommerceinASEAN.pdf

Senders, J. W. (2004). FMEA and RCA: The mantras; of modern risk management. *BMJ Quality & Safety, 13*(4), 249–250. doi:10.1136/qshc.2004.010868 PMID:15289625

Senecal, S., & Nantel, J. (2004). The influence of online product recommendations on consumers' online choices. *Journal of Retailing, 80*(2), 159–169. doi:10.1016/j.jretai.2004.04.001

Stokes, R. (2010). Social media. In *EMarketing: The essential guide to online marketing* (p. 189). Washington, D.C.: Saylor Academy.

Tiago, M. T. P. M. B., & Veríssimo, J. M. C. (2014). Digital marketing and social media: Why bother? *Business Horizons, 57*(6), 703–708. doi:10.1016/j.bushor.2014.07.002

Treadaway, C., & Smith, M. (2010). *Facebook marketing: An hour a day.* Indianapolis, IN: Wiley Publishing Incorporation.

Trusov, M., Bucklin, R. E., & Pauwels, K. (2009). Effects of word-of-mouth versus traditional marketing: Findings from an internet social networking site. *Journal of Marketing, 73*(5), 90–102. doi:10.1509/jmkg.73.5.90

Vliet, V. V. (2010). *Root Cause Analysis (RCA)*. Retrieved March 12, 2018, from ToolsHero: https://www.toolshero.com/problem-solving/root-cause-analysis-rca/

Vliet, V. V. (2014). *Sakichi Toyoda*. Retrieved March 12, 2018, from ToolsHero: https://www.toolshero.com/toolsheroes/sakichi-toyoda/

White, C. M. (2016). *Social media, crisis communication, and emergency management: Leveraging Web 2.0 technologies*. CRC Press.

This research was previously published in Dynamic Perspectives on Globalization and Sustainable Business in Asia; pages 92-105, copyright year 2019 by Business Science Reference (an imprint of IGI Global).

Chapter 8

More Cost–Effective but Confusing Advertising Options:
Digital Marketing Opportunities Changing Daily

Kenneth E. Harvey

Xiamen University Malaysia, Malaysia

ABSTRACT

Since 2006, American newspapers have lost nearly two-thirds of their advertising revenue, and a similar tipping point has now hit broadcast and cable television. In 2016, digital advertising expenditures in the U.S. surpassed TV advertising for the first time, and by 2021, digital is expected to surpass all traditional forms of advertising combined. Traditional advertising is dying, and the battle between the digital competitors is heating up, leading to diverse and rapidly changing advertising opportunities. And yet, marketing executives say they are confused and frustrated by all the changes. This chapter documents the new and continuing trends that are reshaping the advertising landscape.

INTRODUCTION

In 2011 eMarketer published a Media Mismatch report, showing that Americans were spending only about 5% of their media time reading newspapers, but newspapers were still collecting nearly 17% of all advertising revenues. At the same time, Americans were spending about 8% of their media time on mobile devices, yet mobile advertising revenues were miniscule – 0.5% of all ad expenditures and barely visible on eMarketer's chart. I told my media management and advertising students, "Watch what happens over the next few years. Advertising always follows the audience, as illustrated in Figure 1. It may take a while, but it will happen. In a free market, opportunities like this act like a vacuum, sucking in innovation and investment." At the time, almost all mobile advertising took the form of SMS messaging, but since then companies like Google, Twitter and Facebook have adapted their advertising to take advantage of multimedia content and the increasing mobile audience, while newspaper ad revenues have

DOI: 10.4018/978-1-7998-9020-1.ch008

continued to fall precipitately. An eMarketer table published in 2014 suggests that even in 2011 their calculations of the time spent with newspapers was exaggerated or perhaps skewed by excluding some "other" types of media advertising (eMarketer, 2011; eMarketer, 2014). Revised data for 2009-2014 showed that time spent with newspapers dropped from 3.1% in 2010 to 1.6% in 2014 while time spent on mobile (non-voice) soared from 3.7% in 2010 to 23.3% in 2014. Subsequently, in 2016 U.S. newspapers lost another 8% of their circulation – the 28th consecutive year of decline, and advertising revenues that fell 8% in 2015 fell an estimated 10% in 2016, now totaling only about one-third of what the industry was accumulating before it hit its tipping point in 2005 (Barthel, 2017).

Figure 1. Disparity between media audience and media ad share. This figure shows statistics from alternating years for the three media types for which audience share and ad share have fluctuated the most. The Print media include newspapers, magazines, directories and signage.
Sources: Several eMarketer studies (2011, 2014, 2017a, 2017b, 2017c)

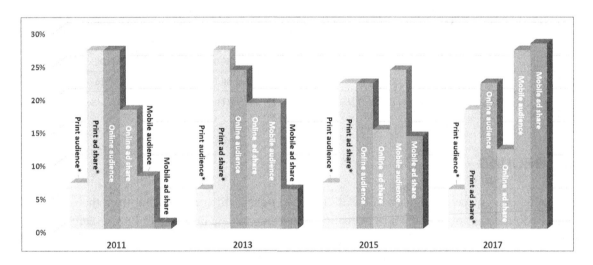

In 2015 I reviewed data from several studies related to cable and broadcast television and concluded that TV was then coming to its tipping point – almost exactly 10 years after American newspapers had hit their tipping point – but the TV market had just not yet adjusted (Harvey, 2016). Data are increasingly supporting that conclusion.

In 2017 Americans will have spent almost exactly 12 hours of every day tuned in to some kind of media, but the traditional media -- TV, radio, newspapers and magazines – absorb less of Americans' time and attention now than do the digital media (5:28 traditional vs. 5:53 digital), according to eMarketer (2017a). Nonetheless, digital still lags behind in advertising revenues, with an estimated 41% -- \$83 billion of the \$205 billion estimated for all U.S. ad expenditures (eMarketer, 2017b). And mobile advertising has climbed from that miniscule 0.5% in 2011 to 28.5% of all ad expenditures. While the time Americans spent with digital surpassed that of traditional media in 2017, digital ad expenditures in America are not projected to exceed that of the combined traditional advertising until 2021.

Besides the decline of audience among traditional media, the cost of digital advertising per hour of adult exposure is a fraction of the cost of traditional media, as shown in Table 1, providing further incentive for marketers to move more advertising online. The cost of digital advertising is less than 1/8 the cost of print advertising per audience member, and about half the cost of TV. Mobile is the cheapest of all the advertising media.

In this chapter we will review the rapidly changing marketing landscape and the new opportunities and challenges that organizations face in developing and implementing new advertising strategies.

Table 1. U.S. Major Media Ad Cost Per Hour Spent with Each Medium Per Adult, 2010-2014

CATEGORY	MEDIUM	2010	2011	2012	2013	2014
PRINT	All	$0.53	$0.56	$0.62	$0.70	$0.83
	Magazines	$0.53	$0.58	$0.62	$0.70	$0.83
	Newspapers	$0.53	$0.55	$0.59	$0.67	$0.82
TV	Broadcast & cable	$0.16	$0.15	$0.16	$0.17	$0.17
RADIO*	Broadcast only	$0.11	$0.11	$0.11	$0.12	$0.13
DIGITAL	All	$0.10	$0.10	$0.09	$0.09	$0.10
	Online**	$0.11	$0.12	$0.13	$0.13	$0.12
	Mobile	$0.02	$0.02	$0.03	$0.05	$0.07
TOTAL		**$0.17**	**$0.16**	**$0.16**	**$0.16**	**$0.16**

Note: Ages 18+; *Excludes off-air radio and digital; **Time spent online includes all non-mobile Internet activities. Source: eMarketer, April 2014

BACKGROUND

The hope that newspapers and television stations could transfer their advertising from their traditional formats to digital has not turned out to be reality. According to data provided to Pew researchers newspapers', digital advertising has recently begun increasing significantly to $4.6 billion in 2015 and to $5.2 billion in 2016, but the digital increases fell far short of offsetting the continuing decline of print advertising. Thus, total ad sales – print and digital -- declined from $22 billion in 2014 to $20 billion in 2015 and to $18 billion in 2016. The newspapers' disappearing ad revenues seemingly moved directly over to new media giants, such as Google, whose ad revenues since 2004 grew by about $75 billion (Statista, 2017). Local TV stations have fared better than their newspaper counterparts, with over-the-air ad revenues falling from $22.4 billion in 2004 to an estimated $19.8 in 2017 while increasing their digital ad revenue by about $1.1 billion – about 5% of their total (Pew, 2017). But if TV has reached its tipping point in America, station owners in 10 years may look back at 2017 and wished they had sold while revenues were relatively stable. Indeed, nearly 300 local stations were sold for a total of $9.7 billion in 2013 and 171 were sold for $5 billion in 2014. During the previous 15 years, only the sale of stations in 2006 surpassed those of 2013. (Pew, 2015, p. 51). Those high sales prices were not due to advertising sales but rather to the growth of cable retransmission fees – what stations are paid for having their programming carried on local cable networks (Pew, 2014, p. 6-7). Those were projected to grow from about $3.5 billion in 2013 to $9 billion in 2020. But what happens if both the TV and cable audiences shrink and begin moving in mass online. Then TV stations would find themselves in the same situation as newspapers. Will that happen?

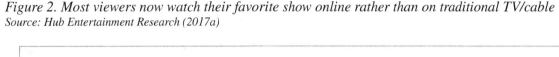

Figure 2. Most viewers now watch their favorite show online rather than on traditional TV/cable
Source: Hub Entertainment Research (2017a)

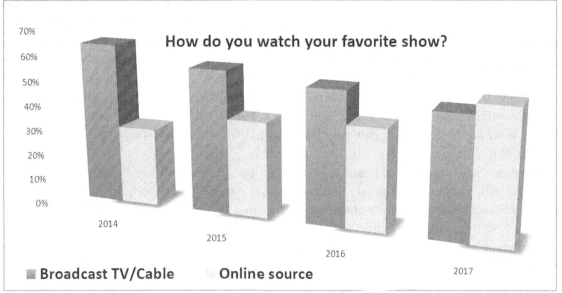

Hub Entertainment Research (2017a, p. 9) survey responses from 2,214 consumers showed that 52% now turn to online or mobile media to watch their favorite entertainment – a sharp increase from 31% three years earlier. Preferred viewing on live TV, VOD and DVR has dropped from 64% in 2014 to 48% in 2017 as seen in Figure 2. In 2017 68% of all survey respondents subscribed to at least one of the top three streaming video providers – Netflix, Amazon or Hulu – and more than half of the subscribers (36%) subscribed to more than one of the services (p. 5). It's also important to know who's getting the "buzz." Of those whose favorite show is online, 40% learned about it via word of mouth, and only 22% from advertising. Those viewing their favorite show on TV learned about it 51% of the time from advertising and only 26% by word of mouth (p. 11). Crimson Hexagon (2017, p. 33-36) reviewed more than one trillion social media posts, finding and analyzing 1,089,793 conversations about "cord-cutting," and those conversations have more than quadrupled since 2013. The report noted that the conversations are gradually turning into action. In the latest Nielsen data Crimson Hexagon analyzed, in the one year between the fourth quarter of 2015 and the third quarter of 2016, the pay-TV households in America declined by 1.8 million while the number of households using only over-the-air broadcast TV and Internet-streamed content increased by 2.5 million – now making up about 20% of the U.S. adult population. And a survey with 1,129 respondents conducted by Blueshift (2015, p. 2-4) found that 10.2% were very or extremely likely to cancel their cable within the next 6 months, and an additional 29.5% were moderately or slightly likely to do so. So a total of nearly 40% were at least considering that possibility.

Hub also noted in their report that 2017 will be a record year for the production of scripted series. And respondents indicate that TV networks are losing their brand value. Forty percent said that network brands have little impact on which shows they watch now, and nearly a quarter of the respondents gave network brand the lowest possible importance in their ranking (p. 35). This may be in part caused by the record increase in programming options. In 2016 there were a record 325 scripted series, and as of

August 2017 there were already 342 (p. 3). Of 79 series yet to be aired, 22% were scheduled for streaming video and 18% for broadcast, premium cable and basic cable (p. 4).

In a separate survey with 1,806 responding consumers, Hub (2017b) found that pay TV (cable, satellite, etc.) is still the "default provider" of entertainment – the one that they turn to first and the one they would disconnect last. Even among those with broadband Internet, 86% still subscribe to pay TV (p. 6). But the percentage who subscribe to any of the Big 3 online providers is climbing – Netflix climbing from 57% to 61% between 2016 and 2017, Amazon from 24% to 36%, Hulu from 13% to 22%, and those subscribing to all three simultaneously from 6% to 14% (p. 10). When asked if they had to drop all but one service, which would they keep, 36% said live TV, but 33% said Netflix (p. 14). Among viewers under 35, however, Netflix was highly preferred over live TV – 41% to 24% (p. 15), suggesting that supporters of live TV are a dying breed.

While most technology-related trends begin in America and spread slowly around the world, that is not the case with mobile. While mobile first caught on in America, its importance in the lives of consumers is greater in many other parts of the world. In many villages, for example, mobile was their first and only access to broadband. Technology has skipped a generation in such locations, and consumers there may never have fixed-wire broadband. Smartphones and mobile broadband is also much cheaper even where fixed-wire broadband is available. In Malaysia, for example, mobile broadband is available for as little as $7 a month (USD). That makes it accessible to a much larger portion of the population in the developing world. Thus an Accenture study (2017) found even more startling results than Hub when they asked 26,000 internet users around the world what was their favorite platform on which to watch TV shows. In 2016 52% said they still preferred watching shows on television, but in 2017 that number collapsed to just 23%. Meanwhile, desktop and laptop viewing of TV shows increased from 32% to 42%, and smartphone viewing preference rose from 10% to 13%, bringing the preference for digital devices to 55% in 2017, compared to only 23% for TV.

All of these data combine to make eMarketer's projection that pay TV will only decline by 10% in America by 2021 extremely conservative. And that is the basis for its projection that TV advertising will slow but will actually continue to grow through 2021 in dollar value, even as it falls as a percentage of all advertising spending (eMarketer, 2017c).

Such is the nature of this uncertain and rapidly changing media landscape. Newspapers' future in America appears very dim, and newspapers in other parts of the world can anticipate the same ultimate fate. The video audience will also almost certainly continue to move online until local TV joins local newspapers in an almost certain fatal struggle to survive. What does that mean for advertising? Advertising will follow the audience after a short adjustment period. Just as it happened with newspapers, TV's portion of all U.S. advertising is falling, projections are being adjusted downward, and yet those projections may still be too high, based on the snowballing effect seen after newspapers passed their tipping point. The eMarketer study (2017c) has reduced their projections downward but still projects that the decline as a portion of overall ad spending will be less than one percentage point per year through 2021, from 35% of all U.S. advertising in 2017 to 29% in 2021. A major reason why that may still be too optimistic for TV is the vacuum effect we saw in comparing mobile and newspaper usage in 2011. As the usage of Internet and mobile entertainment rises and viewership of TV declines, innovation and investment will be sucked increasingly into the marketplace to take advantage of the new opportunities. This is already happening. Netflix, for example, announced in 2017 that it had contracted for $15.7 billion in new original programming, including $6 billion in 2017 and most of the rest anticipated for 2018 (LaMonica, 2017). Up-and-coming TV competitors Facebook and Apple each committed $1 billion to original programming in 2018 (Etherington, 2017). Disney announced it would enter the competition in 2019 (LaMonica, 2017), and Dish Network has launched its own streaming video service, Sling TV. Such networks as HBO and ESPN are making standalone subscription services available, allowing users to access their programming without a cable subscription. Hulu and YouTube are now delivering live TV channels at reasonable prices — including sports programming (eMarketer, 2017c). And sports leagues like the National Basketball Association and the National Football League have made online streaming available. Changes in the competitive marketplace like these make trend lines much more difficult to forecast.

RAPIDLY CHANGING NATURE OF DIGITAL ADVERTISING

As advertisers move online, they encounter a strange and ever-evolving marketing environment that is challenging even for the largest corporations to navigate. In a global survey of B2B marketing executives, Forrester Research and the Business Marketing Association (Ramos, 2013, p. 2-4) found that 97% of the executives are doing new tasks for which they were not hired nor trained. Many felt as if they were "navigating chaos," with more than one-third feeling "overwhelmed" by the new challenges. While 60% of the executives were looking for younger, more tech-savvy employees to help, 47% said they had failed to find qualified applicants. Despite floundering in their efforts, 75% said their organizations are asking them to provide greater input on corporate strategy and giving them a greater voice in executive decision-making. If this is happening to the big companies, how will the smaller companies handle the transition? Many of them have yet to venture very far into this chaos.

In 2016 digital surpassed TV as the top American advertising medium, achieving 38% of all ad spending, compared with 35.8% for TV. And that difference is expected to grow rapidly over the coming years, reaching a 45% to 32.9% advantage in 2020 (Urban, 2017, p. 6).

For the newbies in digital advertising, there are distinct advantages, even for local advertisers. Many do not understand that they can buy pay-per-click (PPC) advertising that will only be seen by consumers in their own market area – as local as a single zip code in America. Once their local consumers click their ad, they are immediately sent to the company's website. Ideally the advertiser has created a special landing page related to the small PPC ad and entices the prospective buyer to review all the company's products and services at a PPC cost of perhaps 30 cents per prospect. Depending on the nature of that company, however, there is a great variety of advertising options, of which the small PPC display ad is only one. A video ad may be more powerful and appropriate, or instead of the video ad, the video can be the center of focus on a website landing page where prospects end up once they click on that small PPC ad. If the company decides to use Facebook, it may find "native advertising" to be more fruitful. Native advertising on Facebook is called "sponsored' advertising, and it appears within the timeline of demographically selected prospects. It should be made to look as much as the surrounding organic postings as possible – but perhaps even more enticing. There are many different opportunities with online and mobile advertising, even for local advertisers, but to be successful, advertisers need to develop or hire people with appropriate skills. Here are some of the strongest tools in online marketing.

Video Advertising

With enhanced average bandwidth, improved server software, and the rapid overall growth of mobile devices, the number of online videos viewed in America in June 2012 skyrocketed by 550% over the previous year -- from 6 billion to 33 billion (xStream, 2013), and by August 2014 the number of videos viewed per month worldwide surpassed 300 billion (Nguyen, 2014). Those numbers are now being dwarfed just by YouTube, Facebook and SnapChat, which have 22 billion of their videos viewed every day – over 660 billion per month just on those three channels (Schroeder, 2016). Other social media are also pushing video – some entertainment, some personal and some paid advertising disguised as organic content. About 82% of Twitter users watch videos on that medium. Periscope users have created more than 200 million broadcasts.

Mobile provided impetus to this video revolution because it rapidly increased the number of Internet devices capable of broadband viewing of video. Video was also among the easiest content to convert from PC to mobile, whereas many websites are still not mobile friendly. And video was preferred content for the younger generations that are most mobile. Now more than half of all online video content is viewed on mobile, including 90% of Twitter videos (Insivia, 2017; Lister, 2017).

About 1.3 billion people watch videos on YouTube – one-third of all internet users worldwide. While many YouTube videos are short, their average length is still longer than those typically viewed on Facebook and Snapchat. So while fewer videos are viewed daily on YouTube than on Facebook and Snapchat, their average length is greater, adding up to more than 500 million hours of view time daily – greater than either of their top competitors. YouTube reaches more 18- to 49-year-olds than any cable network in America, but it can be navigated in 76 languages, and 80% of its views are from outside the U.S. Facebook, on the other hand, has about 500 million users on its social site daily, and together they watch an average of 8 billion videos daily. The various platforms count "video views" in different ways, however, and Facebook controversially has videos starting automatically as users approach them in the timeline and has been counting them as a video view after only 3 seconds. Studies show that 85% of Facebook videos are "viewed" without the user ever turning on the audio. It can be readily seen that many of the videos now use subtitles to address that trend. (eMarketer, 2017f; FortuneLords, 2017; Insivia, 2017; Lister, 2017).

Projections are that video will account for 74% of all online traffic in 2017. The explosion of video views has also spurred the increase in video advertising. eMarketer (2017f) projected an increase in video advertising of 24% in 2017 and a further increase of about 75% by 2021, as illustrated in Figure 3. Based on trends we are analyzing, that forecast again seems to be rather conservative. Whether video ads are inserted into YouTube entertainment videos, posted on Facebook timelines as native ads, embedded into emails, or used within a company's website, between 90-95% of marketing executives believe video is the most powerful form of online advertising (Aberdeen, 2014) just as TV has been the most powerful of the traditional advertising media. HubSpot co-founder and CEO Brian Halligan declared in his keynote address at INBOUND 2016 that social media and video make the perfect marriage for advertisers and that half of all content created by marketing teams in 2017 should be video (Vidyard, 2016).

Figure 3. U.S. digital video ad spending estimates, 2017-2021
Source: eMarketer (2017f)

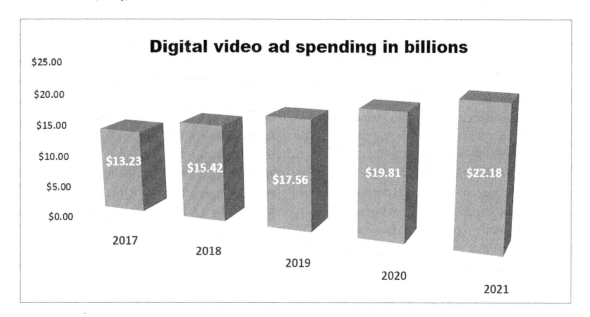

The 2017 Video in Business Benchmark Report prepared by Vidyard (2016) was based on 500+ businesses using the Vidyard video platform, augmented by analysis of 600 million video streams over a 12-month period. Consequently, when it reports that the average business has produced 293 marketing videos and that 85% of the businesses have hired internal staff to produce them, that cannot be understood to represent all businesses – just those using their video platform. However, their report is of value in understanding how businesses that have actively undertaken video campaigning are doing so. For example, knowing what kinds of video Vidyard's diverse clientele were creating is valuable: 59% "explainer videos," 51% product feature videos, 45% how to or educational videos, 44% customer testimonials, 37% thought leader interviews, 32% talking head style videos, 29% live action videos, 28% pre-recorded demos, 23% live streaming, and 20% cultural content (p. 18). And it is valuable to know how they distributed the videos, including: 78% on their own websites, 72% in social media, 49% on landing pages on their websites, 36% in emails, and 25% in sales conversations. Once a company invests in producing a video, it frequently uses that video in different platforms (p. 19). It is also useful to know that the average length of their clients' videos was 8 minutes, but it depended on the video's purpose. A majority (56%) of the videos were less than 2 minutes long, and 73% were under 4 minutes. Only 7% were in the 7- to 20-minute range, but then 12% were apparently of a webinar type that exceeded 20 minutes (p. 21). Regardless of the length of the video, there is a significant drop-off of engagement (about 31%) in the first 10% of the video, but the top performers do retain 77% engagement to the end. Top performing short videos under 90 seconds achieved 99% engagement, and, on the other end of the spectrum, top performing videos over 30 minutes still had a 43% retention rate. There is a major drop-off in the last 10% of the long videos, which may reflect wrap-up content, such as a Q&A period (p. 27). Although it takes more effort if not automated, videos that are personalized with the recipient's name, the company name, or other unique content enjoy much higher average retention. Instead of losing 31%

of their viewers in the first 10% of the video, they lose only 19%, and, on average, they retain 50% of their audience all the way to the end, compared to 37% for the average marketing video (p. 31).

More indicative of advertisers as a whole was a survey by the Social Media Examiner with 5,700 online marketers responding (Stelzner, 2017). About 75% of these marketers wanted to increase their use of video advertising, but 74% of them felt that they needed more training. These numbers were almost identical to how they responded in 2015, but apparently they did not follow through, since only 57% said they were using video advertising in 2017 -- the same percentage as two years earlier. Instead of video, they had increased their use of other visuals from 71% to 85% during that period of time. While the portion of advertisers able to undertake significant video advertising was limited, some 28% of respondents were also proceeding with the a rapidly increasing tactic of live video.

Social media postings with video have far more reach than those featuring photos and other graphics, according to an analysis of 670,000 posts on 4,445 different brand pages by the social marketing agency SocialBakers (Ross, 2015). Perhaps because they lack the expertise to develop good video, companies still use photos and graphics most frequently to attract the attention of their fans, but the study showed that graphics are the least effective type of posting in achieving reader response. On Facebook, the average organic reach was 8.7% for videos posts, 5.8% for status posts, 5.3% for links including video links, and only 3.7% for photos. Thus, video achieved 137% more promotion than photos and graphics.

Aware that video is the fastest-growing format on the Internet, social networks such as Facebook, Instagram and Twitter quickly made changes to help them compete with YouTube and Vimeo for a bigger share of consumers' attention and the resulting advertising (Mixpo, 2015). Facebook's changes in 2014 allowed it to double its desktop video views and overtake YouTube, according to comScore. In January 2014 Facebook's audience averaged 71% as many views as YouTube's audience, but by February 2015 the Facebook audience was viewing 55% more videos than YouTube's. And Facebook claimed that desktop views were only 10% of their total video views -- that most views are by mobile devices. Mixpo surveyed 125 advertising agencies and predicted that by catering more to both mobile and to video-based posts and ads, Facebook would become the top video advertising medium in 2015. In 2014 about 78% of those surveyed had run video campaigns on YouTube, compared to 63% on Facebook. But in 2015 that was predicted to reverse, with 87% planning a campaign on Facebook versus 82% for YouTube, followed by Twitter, Instagram and LinkedIn.

In eMarketer's Cross-Platform Video Trends Roundup (2015b), advertisers already using online video expressed strong feelings about it for the following reasons:

- 77% because it has superior targeting and is more measurable than TV.
- 61% because it provides higher ROI than TV.
- 54% because it is maturing and becoming a viable competitor to TV.
- 42% because online/mobile video ads are increasingly being viewed as equivalent to TV.

Of U.S. digital video viewers polled, 83% said product demonstrations are helpful, 77% said product overview videos are helpful, 59% said videos showing how a product is made are helpful, 56% said customer testimonials are helpful, and 49% said even "about the company" videos are helpful (eMarketer, 2015a, p. 7).

Marketo (2015) also reviewed the benefits of video marketing, based on a variety of research findings by it and other organizations (p. 3):

- Video achieves greater engagement. It cites research that 65% of viewers watch more than three-fourths of each video consumed – much higher than text-based content.
- Video achieves higher conversion rates, according to 70% of marketers, and 85% greater product purchase intent.
- Video boosts the effectiveness of other content that surrounds it.
- Adding video to email increases click-through rates by 100%-200%.
- Adding video to the front page of a website increases the chance of a first-page Google search by 5300%.
- Adding video to a landing page increases conversion by 80%.
- And adding video to social media mix enhances audience engagement by 1000%.

Native Advertising

Native advertising grew by 74% between the first quarter of 2016 and the first quarter of 2017 (Fulgoni, Pettit & Lipsman, 2017). "Native ads — or ads that take on the look and feel of the content surrounding them — are taking over digital advertising," says Business Insider (Boland, 2016). Basing its projections on data from the Interactive Advertising Bureau (IAB), PwC and HIS, a BI Intelligence report estimates that native ads will make up 74% of all U.S. digital display ad revenue by 2021. They are also growing in popularity worldwide, predicted to reach $59 billion in sales in 2018 (Politt, 2017).

Fulgoni, et al. (2017, p. 1) describe in some detail how native advertising is being used:

Native-advertising units especially are prevalent on social media platforms, with Facebook's sponsored posts, Twitter's promoted Tweets, and Pinterest's promoted pins among the most notable. Many nonsocial-platform digital publishers also are making native advertising and branded content core to their monetization strategy. Traditional news outlets, such as The New York Times, The Wall Street Journal, and The Washington Post all have developed their own branded-content studios to aid in the creation of this content. The Times' branded-content effort has been so successful that in 2015 it accounted for 18% of the company's digital revenue.

To date, most of the academic publications about native advertising and closely related branded content have focused on the legal and ethical issues that face especially the traditional news media selling such advertising (e.g. these academic articles in the top journals listed on the first page of a Google Scholar search: Conill, 2016; Carlson, 2015; Manic, 2015; Wojdynski & Evans, 2016; Wojdynski, 2016).

By far the fastest growth of native advertising is in social media where native ads embedded into a news feed is barely distinguished from organic posts. Many of these categories of advertising overlap. For example, native advertising can take the form of a video, but it can also be a written story content, multimedia story or an infographic. Whatever the form, they have been shown to be extremely effective, thus accounting for their rapid growth. Business Insider predicted in 2015 that online native advertising would increase from $4.7 billion in 2013 and $7.9 billion in 2014 to $21 billion by 2018, but one year later it had to drastically revise its estimates, projecting that it would hit $21 billion a year earlier, $25 billion by 2018, and $35 billion by 2021 (Boland, 2016). Facebook's rapid growth in 2014 was in part due to its change in policy that allowed native video advertising. With that change, Facebook overtook YouTube and became, temporarily, the No. 1 medium for video viewership. Its total video views on desktop computers went from 4.9 billion in January 2014 to 9.6 billion in February 2015 (Mixpo, 2015, pp. 3-5).

This is a growing revenue stream for both traditional and new media. It may be a new trend, but it is not a new idea. I used it successfully as newspaper political advertising in 1974, and it was an important component of the doubling of my newspaper's ad revenue a year later when I bought my first newspaper. But such venerable newspapers as the *New York Times*, the *Washington Post* and the *Wall Street Journal* originally opposed the idea of paid ads being confused as news stories. Desperate times led to desperate measures, however, and now some of those same newspapers even assign journalists to write native advertising stories for clients. Some organizations that have expressed ongoing concern now express hope that some traditional media might be able to use it to survive which otherwise might not (Pew, 2014, p. 3-4). Indeed, already 90% of the ad revenue for The Daily Beast news site is native advertising, 75% of the advertising for The Atlantic, and 50% of the Slate advertising (Contently, 2017).

Such content is typically labeled "Paid advertisement" in very small print in newspapers. Facebook and other online media sell native ads within users' timelines or news feeds with the small one-word label of "Sponsored." A survey by Contently, in conjunction with The Tow-Knight Center for Entrepreneurial Journalism at CUNY, found that 77% of 1,212 respondents had failed to identify native advertising as paid content and 54% had felt deceived by native advertising (Contently, 2017). Contently suggests that media need to make it clearer what native advertising is or that there may be a major backlash by consumers or government agencies. Fulgoni, Pettit and Lipsman (2017, p. 1) are comScore executives rather than academics, and they argue that branded content is adequately transparent and a lot different than advertorials from decades past, but academics and others continue to lump them together. "Continued confusion on the definition and transparency of branded content only exacerbates matters, which the Interactive Advertising Bureau says detracts from 'higher-level discussions such as effectiveness and disclosure,'" the executives say. And, indeed, there is little academic research supporting the use of native advertising in an increasingly effective manner.

Social Media Marketing

Since Obama's successful Internet-driven campaign in 2008, social media have continued to grow and diversify – and become a primary tool for marketers. Responses by 5,700 online marketers to a Social Media Examiner survey suggest that this trend has still not peaked (Stelzner, 2015 & 2017). In 2017 92% of the respondents said social media was important to their business, however only 38% were certain that they could measure its return on investment (ROI) – a lower percentage than in years past. Facebook was being used by 94% of the marketers, Twitter by 68%, LinkedIn by 56%, Instagram by 54%, YouTube by 45%, Pinterest by 30% and Snapchat by 7% (p. 19). This represents a lot of change in just the past two years, when Twitter and YouTube were much higher; Instagram, Pinterest and Snapchat hardly used; and since when Google+ has fallen from third place to off the list. The marketers ranked them in a different order as to their most important medium: 62% ranked Facebook No. 1 (up 10 percentage points from 2015), 16% LinkedIn (down 5 points), 9% Twitter (down 4 points) and 4% YouTube, with Instagram jumping over YouTube at 7% and Pinterest sneaking up at 2% (p.25). Until 2017 B2B marketers ranked LinkedIn No. 1 over Facebook, but in 2017 B2B marketers favored Facebook 43% to 37%. While Facebook remained strongly in first place for marketers overall, many expressed concern about its dwindling effectiveness. Forty-two percent agreed that Facebook is effective, that was down 4 percentage points from 2015. Most believe it is either ineffective (18%) or are uncertain (40%). And when asked if their news feed exposure has decreased because of changes in Facebook's algorithm, 53% said it had and 42% were unsure. (p. 10-11). Despite their doubts about measuring social media ROI, 88% said the use of social media increases their exposure, 78% that it increases web traffic, 69% that it develops loyal fans, 66% that it provides marketplace insight, 66% that it generates leads, 57% that it improves thought leadership, 53% that it grows business partnerships, and 52% that it improves sales (p. 14).

According to the Social Media Examiner survey, about 93% regularly paid for Facebook ads in 2017, up from 84% in 2015; 24% for Instagram ads, up from just 4%; 16% for LinkedIn ads, down from 18% in 2015; 15% for Twitter ads, down from 17%; 11% for YouTube ads, down from 12%; 3% for Pinterest ads, down from 4%; and 1% for Snapchat ads, which did not make the list in 2015 (p. 35). Advertising projections for 2018 raise lots of questions, with 15% of the marketers not planning to use Facebook and 3% planning to decrease Facebook advertising. This could mean that some marketers have simply not created a plan for 2018, or it could mean that Facebook support is fading very quickly. If the projections are accurate, Instagram will jump from 24% to as much as 55% usage in 2017; LinkedIn from 16% to as much as 46%; Twitter from 15% to as much as 46%; YouTube from 11% to as much as 44%; Pinterest from just 3% to between 16-29%; and Snapchat from 1% to between 11-21% (p. 36). These major changes raise questions as to whether respondents had really solidified their 2018 plans, whether Facebook is essentially facing an insurrection, or whether an "increase" in advertising with the other social media might only mean some minor experimentation, with no major budget shift. This is something to watch very carefully.

According to the same survey, visuals have increased substantially in their use by marketers over the past two years, from 71% to 85%, but, despite video's perceived importance and increased usage, the percentage of individual marketers using video has remained at 57%. However, "live video" is a new category and was used by 28% of the marketers in 2017 -- a lot for being such a relatively new tool. The use of blogs has declined slightly from 70% to 66%, and podcasting may offer an opportunity for some practitioners since only 8% now use it (p. 39). Marketers want to increase their marketing tools, perhaps requiring training in some cases (p. 41-44). Most planned to increase their use of videos (75%), visuals (73%), blogging (65%), live video (61%) and podcasting (26%). As in 2015, the tool they most want to use more is video and it's probably no coincidence that it is the tool for which they still feel they most need additional training (74%). Video training is followed by that new related tool -- live video (69%), then by visuals (65%), blogging 63%) and podcasting (45%). Marketers also feel the need to learn more about emerging technologies, such as Facebook Messenger and similar apps (74%), virtual reality and 360 video (61%) and the use of artificial intelligence and bots (59%).

Perhaps because of frequent changes made by the heavily competing social media, the number of marketers expressing the need for more social media training has risen significantly over the past two years: from 68% to 80% for Facebook, from 49% to 71% for Instagram, from 56% to 65% for YouTube, from 62% to 63% for LinkedIn, from 58% to 61% for Twitter, unchanged at 48% for Pinterest, and, with the biggest increase, from 19% to 42% for Snapchat (p. 33). Marketers can use social media as a free PR service or can pay for advertising, such as pay per click (PPC) ads and increasingly popular "native ads" that mimic free postings. Most of the marketers also wanted to know more about the advertising opportunities with the different social media, which also suggests some confusion because of the frequent and recent changes. Even though the vast majority of the marketers already use Facebook ads, for example, 84% feel they need to know more about their advertising options. In addition, 64% want to know more about Instagram ads, 57% about YouTube ads, 56% about LinkedIn ads, 55% about Twitter ads, 41% about Pinterest ads, and 33% about Snapchat ads.

Social media are regularly improving ad management, tracking, testing, targeting and creation tools. For example, after Facebook put increased emphasis on mobile in 2015, its advertising revenues jumped 46% over the same time in 2014, with mobile accounting for 73% of its total ad sales (Heine, 2015). Facebook and Twitter are now favored by many marketers over YouTube because they collect more data from their users, which allows advertisers to better target their ads. And they are then able to re-target those ads across all devices. Those media also provide more behavioral data, which facilitates more "lookalike modeling" – the selection of targeted ad viewers similar to previously responding consumers. "When you have that much known information tied to analytics and an ad server, you can start doing messaging in a way no one's ever done before. That's marketing nirvana. Facebook is different from every other media company because they actually know who you are. We will see this whole business go to another level because of this kind of knowledge that's about actual people. It's about real behavior," said Jonathan Nelson, CEO of Omnicom Digital (Sloane, 2014).

Independently developed software is also available to facilitate online marketing. For example, Ad-Espresso's Facebook Ads Compass conducts in-depth analysis of ad campaigns, and the Hootsuite ads program allows small advertisers to use a type of programmatic advertising -- automatically generating native ads based on previous organic posts, and automatically selecting, targeting and bidding on ad space (Kim, 2015). But to take advantage of these marketing opportunities requires enhanced training and skills.

INDUSTRY VS. ACADEMIC RESEARCH

eMarketer, one of the top communications industry research organizations, projected in 2010 that annual U.S. spending on mobile marketing would increase by 37% annually between 2008 and 2013, reaching $1.56 billion in 2013 (Okazaki, 2012). That prediction seemed generous at the time but now looks silly in hindsight. Just in 2012 mobile advertising expenditures skyrocketed by about 120% to $8.8 billion, and in 2013 that total doubled again (105%) to almost $18 billion (eMarketer, 2014). By 2017 mobile accounted for 70% of all digital advertising in the U.S. (eMarketer, 2017d). In 2010 researchers were still inclined to think of mobile as a phenomenon mostly impacting the developed nations like the U.S., but by 2016 global advertising on mobile hit $80 billion, $105 billion in 2017, and is projected to hit $215 billion by 2021 (Chen, 2017; Molla, 2017). If a company with a large staff of specialists and major resources cannot come close to predicting the future of the dynamic digital ecosystem, how can individual academics?

Chinese academic researchers Gao and Zang (2014) compiled a series of hypotheses based on about two dozen previous academic studies on the effectiveness of SMS ads and tested them as a group, employing questions used in the previously published studies. Their hypotheses were compiled and tested as a group. Support was found for these six concepts, which could be valuable in real-world application.

1. Prior attitudes of consumers toward mobile advertising affect their response to mobile advertising.
2. Irritation factors in mobile advertising have a negative effect on mobile advertising.
3. Entertainment qualities improve users' attitudes toward mobile advertising.
4. Credible, useful information leads to more positive attitudes toward mobile advertising.
5. Personalization of messages leads to more positive attitudes toward mobile advertising.
6. Providing incentives improves consumer attitudes toward mobile advertising.

While the study confirmed Gao and Zang's study and the many studies on which theirs was based, there were two problems. First, by the time it was published, SMS advertising was of little interest to most advertisers, and, second, to the degree that it was still used, especially with new GPS-triggered geo-targeted advertising, these concepts were already well understood and applied in the real world. This exemplifies the challenges for academics doing research in the field of digital marketing.

Another example of how academia lags being industry research is with the rapid ascension of native advertising as the No. 1 strategic approach for online marketing. Native advertising became increasingly popular as marketers realized how effective free inbound or content marketing was. Attracting consumers to an organization's website with interesting social media posts and offers of free e-books, webinars, fremiums, games, etc., organizations were able to collect contact information with which to initiate an online relationship with potential customers. According to an Adobe survey (2015, p. 7) with 6,000 executives responding, it became the most exciting digital marketing opportunity of 2014. And, indeed, for the plurality of marketing organizations, inbound marketing became the No. 1 source of leads (HubSpot, 2014, p. 29). And yet Feng and Ots (2015) found "as a rising phenomenon, content marketing is a relatively unexplored area for academic research." With the success of inbound marketing, organizations began wondering how they could most effectively expand the target market beyond what they might achieve with free social media. With prodding from the marketers, both traditional and new media recognized the potential for native advertising that mimics its surrounding organic content. Its ascent has been meteoric to such an extent that industry researchers, including Business Insider (Boland, 2016), say it is now the No. 1 online advertising strategy and will be used in 74% of all U.S. digital display advertising by 2021. With such an explosive new trend in marketing, there should be a plethora of academic research now, right? On the first three pages of a Google Scholar search for "native advertising" in December of 2017, all of the academic publications we found focused on related ethical and legal issues, especially with the sale of native advertising by traditional and online news media, in which native advertising is frequently mistaken as real news. There was not a single academic article specifically about the effectiveness and best practices of native advertising. Non-academics Fulgoni and Lipsman, executives at comScore, had an article in the Journal of Advertising Research (2014) about the transformation of social media advertising in the Era of Mobile, but only spent two paragraphs mentioning the importance of native advertising in that transformation. Finally on Page 4 of the Google Scholar search there was an article in the Journal of Brand Strategy (Basney, 2014) that was essentially a case study of how IBM had used a blend of content marketing and native advertising "to reposition the brand from its legacy perception as 'the copier company' to its current business as a global provider of business process services and solutions." Batra and Keller (2016) produced a thorough 23-page analysis of Integrated Marketing Communications-related research from traditional to digital channels, comparing years of research that might or might not still have relevance and proceeding through what they considered the most relevant research from the Digital Age. During this process they highlighted "six key online communication options that are receiving increased research attention" (p. 126-7). These included search ads, display ads, websites, email, social media and mobile, as well as how these and traditional marketing could be "mixed and matched." But in all this analysis, it only made the vaguest references to this powerful and popular form of advertising, and seemed to refer to it erroneously when they wrote of the value of "helpful and inspiring native content on websites and blogs" (p. 135). Since brand-generated content on their own website or in their own blog would not be considered native advertising, this seems to be just a confusing use of the term at a time when native advertising is dominating the industry. But, more importantly, they seemed oblivious to this fact.

On the other hand, industry research, while massive in total amount, is relatively superficial in methodology and results. Indeed, the reliability and validity of their research could be seriously questioned by academic researchers. Similar studies within the industry are not coming out with results that show high reliability in the academic world but "close enough" for those in industry. Validity seeks assurance that researchers are measuring what they intend to measure and reaching conclusions adequately supported by their findings. Industry could also use a lot of expert support in validating their research. Because much of the industry research is survey based, for example, it is easy to mistake correlation for causation. In comparing successful websites with less effective websites, for example, industry researchers find such correlations as that B2C websites with more than 1,000 pages of content achieve, on average, 3,500% more traffic than websites with fewer than 50 pages (HubSpot, 2014). But if a company added 1,000 pages of content to its website, would it automatically achieve 3,500% more traffic or anything close to that? I have actually tried it on my experimental http://IEI-TV.net website, and the extra pages had little impact at all. What other advantages might marketers with an advanced website enjoy that might be totally unrelated to the number of website pages? Perhaps a lot more employees, more brick-and-mortar stores, larger paid advertising budgets, etc. As with many correlations that can be found in industry research, more sophisticated research would be required to prove causation.

There is a need for more skilled social scientists to work with industry if they can gain industry support and access to industry resources and data. Former HubSpot social media scientist Dan Zarrella, for example, went beyond the superficial research so common in the industry and used experiments and content analysis on a more scientific basis to better identify how the most successful social media marketers were succeeding. He found, even before native advertising was allowed on most social media sites, that social media content and social media advertising strongly supported each other. In analyzing the organic search traffic to the HubSpot website, Zarrella (2013) found a positive correlation of higher organic search rates with paid search tactics and pay-per-click advertising, along with such unpaid tactics as email campaigns. He found during times when they were sending out information about new ebooks or webinars available to people in their database, they were also the subject of more organic searches on Google. So, the more active a company is in its PPC and emailing programs, the more likely visitors will independently search for more information and, ultimately, decide to visit the company website. Two possible causes of this are (1) that people receiving non-organic prompts are also more likely to have questions of their own for which they go to a search engine for answers, and (2) that there may be a two-step opinion leader process in effect, as has been found with traditional media. In other words, when opinion leaders (aka in social media as evangelists) are prompted by an organization, they are also more likely to prompt their opinion followers online or offline.

An example of academics conducting research beyond the capability of most industry researchers was a study by Lee, Hosanagar and Nair (2015). The Carnegie-Mellon researchers content-coded more than 106,000 Facebook messages posted by 782 companies. Using both Amazon Mechanical Turk and Natural Language Processing algorithms, they examined the association of social media marketing content with such user engagement data as likes, comments, shares and click-throughs. They found that company-generated content that reflects brand personality, such as humor and emotion, achieved much greater engagement than directly informative content about special deals and promotions. But they did find positive results when personality and informational messages were blended. This, of course, can provide advertisers with some valuable directions in conducting content engineering.

Another positive example of academic research that helps answer a major industry question is a study by Draganska, Hartmann and Stanglein (2014). They noted that many advertisers are hesitant to shift a major proportion of their advertising to the Internet because they had not been convinced that online video advertising was as cost-effective as TV commercials. Analyzing 20 campaigns from a variety of industries and employing brand-building metrics that marketers commonly use and trust, the study demonstrated that Internet ads were as cost-effective as TV once the researchers used a pretest to control for preexisting brand knowledge. Since these advertisers were using more TV advertising, naturally TV viewers had higher brand recall before the advertising campaigns even began. Once that was taken into account, the results were statistically indistinguishable. These are important results for industry to understand as TV declines and online video increases. To conduct this study, the authors clearly required significant cooperation by the advertisers involved. This could lead to more cooperative research between academia and industry.

As sociologists and psychologists initiated scientific studies of mass communication in the 1930s, they began with the assumption that the media had a powerful direct and sometimes controlling influence on their audience – the so-called direct effects or mass society theory. The theory was a grand theory that original researchers thought could explain all aspects of the media phenomenon (Hanson, 2009, p. 80-81). They quickly found it could not. Lazarfeld's People's Choice Study, conducted in 1940, demonstrated that citizens were not voting a certain way because a politician inundated the radio waves and newspapers with his persuasive messages. Many voters were influenced more by interpersonal relationships and by specific opinion leaders (Lazarsfeld, Berelson & Gaudet, 1944). Subsequently, the two-step or multi-step flow theory of communication was developed by Paul Lazarsfeld and Elihu Katz (Katz & Lazarfeld, 1955; Katz, 1957). That also was not comprehensive enough, so additional communication theories have been developed over the decades. Media sometimes change attitudes rather than opinions and knowledge sets, so Carl Hovland led the way in developing the attitude change theory and related theories of dissonance, selective exposure, selective perception and selective retention (Hovland, Harvey & Sherif, 1957). Later theory introduced the idea that media don't just use their audience, but the audience also uses the media. Thus, the uses and gratifications theory was developed (Papacharissi, 2009). But psychological researchers countered with the social cognitive theory, relating to how audience members copy or model behaviors they see in the media through imitation and identification (Baran, 2006, pp. 420-431). With the rapid changes in business practices, technology and marketing in today's digital economy, the push-pull theory that innovation is most likely to be adopted when a need and a means to resolve that need are simultaneously recognized has been helpful (Poe, 2011).

These general theories of communication have also been adapted more specifically to advertising, along with related models and strategies. Selective perception, for example, causes consumers to focus on some stimuli and ignore other stimuli. Why? Advertising researchers explore perceptual screens of both physiological nature (the five senses) and of psychological nature (such innate factors as personality and instinctive human needs and such learned factors as self-concept, attitudes, past experiences and lifestyle). If advertising messages can get past the perceptual screens, then cognition can occur in the form of learning and persuasion. Cognition theory considers the processes of memory, thinking and rational application of knowledge, while conditioning theory (aka, stimulus-response theory) explores how an advertising stimulus causes a need arousal, leading to a behavioral response (e.g., the purchase of a product), leading to either a satisfied or unsatisfied need and a subsequent response – a different response if unsatisfied and a repeat response if satisfied. These theories have led to exploration of the different kinds of needs, such as Maslow's hierarchy of needs: physiological, safety, social, esteem and self-actualization, and the matching of products and services with appropriate advertising messages to match the perceived needs. Also explored more thoroughly is the impact of opinion leaders within the family, society and personalized reference groups on consumers' decision-making. Models such as AI DA (Attention-Interest-Desire-Action) have been developed to help guide these concepts in actual application. And, finally, precise advertising strategies and tactics have been explored in advertising research (Arens, 2002, pp. 139-159).

All of these theories, models, strategies and tactics need to be re-examined in light of the new marketing ecosystem. For example, even the early two-step or multi-step flow theory of communication by Lazarsfeld and Katz needs to be re-examined in light of how messages can spread so quickly and easily from person to person in creating what is now called viralization. Academic researchers Wu, Hu and Zhang (2013) conducted a simulation study in an effort to discover key elements to viral advertising in social networks, but the factors they explored were very limited because they had to be elements they could easily quantify and control. Viral information flow is not the same as general information diffusion, on which their research was based. Wu et al. correctly noted the viral advertising is a new and relatively young research topic in the era of Web 2.0, but they still founded their research on old diffusion studies that fail to fully take into account some elements of rapid viral action seen on the Internet today. One of the earliest explorations of viral action was when Haroldsen and Harvey (1979) studied the first documented case of "shocking good news." Until then diffusion studies of "good news," such as the launch of Explorer I and the announcement of Alaskan statehood, never reached more than 49% of the studied population in the first day, and in most studies of "good news," the largest portion of respondents heard the news from the media. In contrast, the shocking news of John F. Kennedy's assassination reached 100% of the surveyed population in the first day, and over half heard the news from friends, family or even strangers. The shocking news ignited the interpersonal network very much as strong viral messages sweep through social media today. The 1979 study successfully demonstrated that "shocking good news" could do likewise even before the Worldwide Web was developed, but this phenomenon is seen on a regular basis now that social media expedite interpersonal communication as never before.

Within the marketing industry today, professionals frequently use the word "shocking" when they describe the kinds of videos and other messages that organically achieve strong viral action in social media, but they, as Wu et al, find it very difficult to quantify viral factors in a way that creates any kind of reliable formula. While Zarrella (2013) studied such elements as specific word usage in viral headlines, time of day messages are initiated, etc., Wu et al were trying to determine how many people to select to optimally initiate a viral message at minimal cost. They were asking, essentially, what proportion of a group would need to receive the initial advertisement before they could expect it to spread by itself to most of the remaining portion of the group. They referred to that number as "the tipping point," as previously described by Gladwell (2000) and referred to in this chapter. They also discussed how to select people for this group but with little clarity and no specific recommendations useful in actual practice. Their suggestion that simultaneous mass media advertising enhances the viral action also needs more clarification and research. It seems difficult to employ their research without considering the message content and the degree to which the message content itself will initiate viral action, as discussed even in the 1979 "shocking good news" research.

Online advertising also dictates a total rethinking of how ads are designed. A small PPC (pay per click) ad on Facebook has little in common with a full-page newspaper or magazine ad. Ads in traditional publications are most frequently portrait-shape and can be quite large in their dimensions, whereas most online display ads are very small -- frequently less than 1.5 inches per side and square in layout. A print ad typically has four primary parts – a visual to attract attention, a headline to help develop interest, body copy to develop a desire and to issue a call to action, and logo to achieve brand recognition/credibility and to provide essential contact information. Most of these traditional elements are missing from most online ads. Many online display ads lack space for body copy, but a visual and headline may attract enough attention and interest to get consumers to click the hyperlinked ad for more information. The hyperlinked headline and graphic then take the consumer to the organization's website landing page, where all the traditional advertising elements are typically employed to achieve the desired action. The established theories may stand up under this new scrutiny, but how they are applied is definitely changing. And their application continues to change rapidly.

One element that is always of value in marketing, no matter the platform, is creativity. Of course, that makes advertising as much an art as a science, but even within the artistic side of advertising, science can give marketing professionals some direction and guidance. Thus, research such as that conducted by Reinartz and Saffert (2013) should be perceived of value by professionals even as technology and innovation changes the marketing ecosystem. That creativity is of value is certainly not a new concept for professionals. Ogilvy & Mather Germany's chief creative officer, Stephan Vogel, says, "Nothing is more efficient than creative advertising. Creative advertising is more memorable, longer lasting, works with less media spending, and builds a fan community…faster." But Reinartz and Saffert decided to put that premise to the test to see if creative ads actually lead to better results and to see if certain elements of creativity could be isolated and analyzed. They used a communications psychology tool to measure perceived creativity in five different dimensions (originality, flexibility, elaboration, synthesis, and artistic value), then applied it in the study of 437 TV ad campaigns related to 90 different brands and a wide range of products. Their research did confirm what professionals already new … that creativity works. However, they also found that different dimensions of creativity work better than others, that some combinations of dimensions work better than others, and that focusing on the wrong dimension can undermine the effectiveness of a campaign. The researchers are fine-tuning their analytical instruments, believing that they can dramatically improve marketers' ability to predict the effectiveness of creative ads and, consequently, achieve greater success.

Businesses all over the world are competing to gain the edge in a volatile marketplace, putting out new studies every week. And even they cannot keep up with all the changes occurring in the current marketing environment. They are shooting at a moving target. Online advertising media are regularly changing their strategies, their technologies and their offerings. Just one weekly post in late 2017 by the Social Media Examiner (Duffy, 2017) reported about two dozen changes that had just been made or were soon to be made by major social media. Each change requires retraining of an organization's marketing staff, and, of course, even recent research is suddenly outdated. As noted previously (Ramos, 2013; Stelzner, 2017), the vast majority of full-time marketers were already feeling overwhelmed, having difficulty keeping up with all of the changes and wanted additional training on how to use existing social media tools. And suddenly there were more. If full-time marketing professionals cannot keep up with the changes, and numerous industry consulting organizations are already producing hundreds of studies every year to try to analyze the effects of such changes and to suggest new tools and strategies to implement them, where do academic researchers fit in? In the fall of 2016, as I was wrapping up the last of seven chapters of a book that I was co-authoring, I realized that the chapters completed four or five months earlier were already out of date, and the book was not released for purchase for another 9 months. Similarly, academic studies frequently take one to two years to complete research and to achieve journal publication. The focus for academics in a field like this cannot be on such details unless they are working closely with industry and on the broader issues. Industry researchers base their insights primarily on surveys of marketers and consumers to whom they have much easier access than do most academics. There are also some content analysis studies being performed within the industry, especially to identify best practices. Perhaps there are opportunities for experimental research by academics, but it would need to focus on enduring issues and, if possible, on predictive overriding theories similar to what Harvard Professor Clayton Christensen has achieved with his disruptive innovation theories. Indeed, his theories of how major monopolies or oligopolies can be disrupted or overcome by small startup enterprises have turned many previously accepted business principles upside down and are very usable in the context of the modern media and marketing ecosystem (Bower & Christensen, 1995; Christensen, 2014; Christensen, 2016). As Christensen explains, many powerful businesses have faced a similar dilemma as are the powerful media conglomerates of choosing between:

1. Achieving the greatest revenue possible from current customers (primarily advertisers and subscribers, in this case), or
2. Implementing disruptive innovation that would have the effect of providing cheaper opportunities that would diminish profits from current customers with no certainty that those profits would be replaced with income from new customers.

Companies are going out of business or seeing their business greatly diminish because Option 1 is the obvious choice for them to make while the small startup company has nothing to lose and much to gain by pursuing disruptive innovation. Despite warnings by people like Professor Jeff Jarvis years ago that newspapers should stop printing and start reinventing themselves while they still had money in the bank and strong brands, they could not do it. Despite warnings that they needed to begin collaborating and using their joint resources to create an online medium that could compete effectively against Facebook and other online media that are, from their perspective, stealing their advertising (Harvey, 2016), they could not do that, either. Thus major media conglomerates like McClatchy are now reporting huge losses ($34 million in 2016) and trying to sound optimistic about minor digital gains that come nowhere close to offsetting their losses (McClatchy, 2017). Ironically, many media and society textbooks still devote large sections discussing the dangers to society of fewer and fewer conglomerates controlling more and more traditional media, and yet at the same time many academics and practitioners share concerns about what happens to the watchdog function of news media as the traditional media sink into pools of red ink, staffs are cut, and significant investment of resources into investigative reporting becomes unprofitable. Indeed, there have been proposals in America for the government to provide grants to prop up the investigative efforts of newspapers owned by the conglomerates. In the midst of this crisis, the business of media could be one area of research where sociology- and psychology-oriented communication researchers have rarely ventured.

FUTURE RESEARCH DIRECTIONS

There are many subjects to explore concerning digital advertising. Here are a few:

- **Message Viralization:** Never before have marketing messages had such an opportunity to viralize and spread to large numbers of people spontaneously – sometimes at no cost to the advertiser. The multi-step flow theory of communication serves as a foundation for new research into how to identify and use opinion leaders to viralize online messages. Current advertisers, for example, are looking into how micro-influencers (people with about 10,000 social media followers) and middle influencers with up to 250,000 followers can promote their brands. These cost a lot less than celebrities, and brands are finding that they can be more cost-effective. Advertisers are already experimenting with this strategy, but current "best practices" is to use video and to let the influencers speak from their heart, helping the resulting native ads to come across as truly authentic, despite the fact that influencers are being paid for their services (eMarketer, 2017e). Professionals frequently suggest that initiating a strong viral action is as much an art as a science, and, similar to a Hollywood movie producer, an advertiser might have to invest in numerous efforts before achieving blockbuster success in a large network like YouTube, even employing strategies acknowledged as "best practices" to achieve the shock, excitement, passion or other responses that could significantly increase the number of viewer shares. Nevertheless, further research into the artistic elements that help achieve viralization are certainly warranted in trying to approach a more scientific strategy.

- **Exploring and Teaching Social Media Marketing:** In this rapidly changing industry, one thing that has remained consistent over the years has been the feeling expressed by most of the marketers that they need to learn more about how to use social media, to create excellent content, and to use the most effective technical tools (Stelzner, 2017). While social media marketing became a marketer's "must" after Barrack Obama's first campaign, 9 years later more than 90% of 5,700 online marketers responding to the Social Media Examiner survey still felt they had lots of unanswered questions (Stelzner, 2017, p. 6). The biggest problem, the study suggests, is lack of clarity in how to use the social media tools. But a related problem is certainly the speed with which social media marketing is changing. All of the major social media introduced new tools and tactics within the past year. New tools and tactics demand new research and new training for marketers. The key questions raised by the online marketers in 2017 were almost identical to those expressed two years earlier. They include:
    - 93% wanted to know what social tactics are most effective.
    - 91% wanted to know the best ways to engage their audience with social media.
    - 89% wanted to know how to best measure ROI with social media marketing.
    - 87% wanted to know what are the best ways to use paid social media.
    - 87% wanted to know which are the best tools for managing social media marketing.

With such a high percentage of professionals feeling lost within the world of online marketing, there are clearly questions to be explored and better outreach to be provided.

- **Explore Video:** With video spearheading the rapid growth of online and mobile marketing, and seemingly destined to dominate all marketing worldwide, there is still much to learn as to what conditions, tools and strategies achieve the greatest success online. Enhancements in training, technology, bandwidth, accessibility, strategies, opportunities and investments will foster even more growth and utilization of digital video advertising. Integrated use of such technologies as virtual reality, 3D projection systems, voice-operated operating systems, surface computing, e-paper, geo-targeting, internet of things, artificial intelligence, and cloud-based personalization engines could all enhance the video experience for both advertisers and consumers. There is also an opportunity to explore how video advertising can be used most effectively in the mobile environment, when embedded as commercials within entertainment videos, used as standalone marketing tools, developed as inbound marketing content, or launched in social media as potential viral videos. There are ongoing and developing issues related to the death of traditional media and the rapid transfiguration of new media, and some of the most important of those issues revolve around video technologies, applications and strategies. What will be the impact and the opportunities of this new tipping point?
- **Explore How Different Digital Media Affect the Message:** The eMarketer Video Trends Roundup (2015b, p.4) cited experimental research suggesting that the digital medium is the message in the sense of how much attention viewers pay to digital video ads on different platforms. High attention was achieved by 64% of the smartphone viewers, 54% of the tablet viewers and 52% of the PC viewers. What causes the difference in focus between advertising viewers using these different devices? How reliable is this experimentation, and what other psychological differences might be detected in how digital consumers respond to the different digital media?
- **Explore 'Time-Spent' Predictive Research:** With Figure 1 we discussed the great disparity in the time spent with newspapers and mobile devices in 2010, compared with how much advertising was being devoted to them. People were spending only about 5% of their media time with newspapers, but newspapers were receiving almost 17% of the advertising revenue. People were spending more time (8%) with mobile content, on the other hand, but mobile only garnered a miniscule 0.5% of advertising revenues. I saw that as a predictive tool and directed my students to look for adjustments more proportional to the degree of audience attention each medium was marketing. While time spent with different media certainly provides some predictive capability, as we subsequently saw, it took several years for advertising to make the adjustment. The same thing is now happening with video advertising. In 2013 U.S. adults spent 7.3% of their media time watching online video, but video ad spending was only 2.4%. In 2014, 9.2% of media time was spent on video with only 3.5% of ad share. And in 2015 the projection was for 10.9% of the time spent on media to be online video but with only 4.4% of the ad share (eMarketer, 2015a, p. 4). We predicted in 2015 that both video consumption and video advertising were at a tipping point and that we would see dramatic increases (Harvey and Auter, 2016, p. 352-354, 369-372, 375). We advised newspapers in 2015 (Harvey, 2016, p. 190) that they should get in front of this trend and begin promoting video advertising on their websites. Subsequently, in the two years since we made these predictions, video advertising has skyrocketed 67% and is projected to maintain its rapid growth for the next few years (eMarketer, 2017g, and Figure 5). Indeed, eMarketer may still

be too conservative in their projections. Watching these massive adjustments, we ask, "Can this time-spent quantitative tool be fine-tuned and become even more predictive as to the timing and degree of future adjustments when so many elements within the marketing field are qualitative in nature? Can a formula be created to more accurately predict how long it takes for advertising to catch up with such audience shifts?

- **Exploring Potential Disruptive Innovation in the Communications Industry:** Clayton Christensen notes that his Disruptive Innovation theories recognize that while many disruptive innovations have a technology component, they are not typically the technology, per se. They are the application of innovation in a way that targets an inadequately served consumer mass with a product or service previously not available to them at an affordable price or without some other barrier, such as required training, clarity of usage, etc., that has previously prevented them from participating. Nonetheless, where technology innovations abound, as they do in the communications industry, there are abundant opportunities to explore how the technologies might be applied as a disruptive innovation. Marketing executives have expressed an interest in learning more about some of these, such as artificial intelligence, virtual reality, internet of things and drone video. Others could include e-paper, 3-D projections, surface computing. Even something as common as a smart tablet could become the disruptive innovation with a few adaptations and strategic applications. For example, let's say a high-circulation newspaper such as the New York Times decided that it was time to turn off the presses before its circulation, advertising and brand diminished too much more. Christensen's theories suggest that their executives would find it very difficult to do that, so it might be a new competitor applying this strategy instead. But let's imagine that the Times was losing money and Times executives saw no clear-cut avenue to rectify their situation without drastic action. Then they might apply disruptive innovation against Facebook and Google. They could develop their own smart pad with one-button access to their online newspaper, another button for their own online TV channel, another for their own education channel, another for their own online library of books and magazines, another for their own mobile phone service, and another for their own search engine browser. Then they announce that they are going all digital on a specific date and offer their subscribers their customized smart pad free of charge in exchange for a 4-year subscription contract (perhaps with or without the phone/internet service). Currently the Times' printing and distribution expenses are so high that eliminating them would more than pay for the smart pad in one year. After that, the subscription fee would be all profit. If they could get just half of their subscribers to accept the offer, they would have those four years to convince them that the new package of services was worth the subscription price they were continuing to pay. And with "just" perhaps a reduced 500,000 paid subscribers, they would be able to get many of their current advertisers to make the transition from print to digital, as well. Indeed, with a new format of interactive, multimedia social news, education and entertainment, they might build their subscriber base even bigger than it was before and compete with Facebook and YouTube for both audience and advertising. In similar fashion, there are opportunities for the traditional media to turn the tables and become the disruptors of the digital giants. This is the greatest period of innovation in human history, and academic researchers in the field of communications could explore possibilities for applying Dr. Christensen's theories. The key is in recognizing that it is not new technology that directly causes disruption, it is the innovative application of the technology in which academics could play a part (Bower & Christensen, 1995; Christensen, 2014; Christensen, 2016).

CONCLUSION

This chapter is designed first and foremost to raise readers' understanding of the rapidly changing marketing ecosystem. The fact that so many marketing executives feel overwhelmed by the rapid and ongoing changes, cannot find employees to hire who have the new skills required in the industry, and are crying out for more training for themselves to help them adapt to these new challenges suggests that universities are not fulfilling these needs. Thus, this chapter may be a beginning point for some. It is also obvious from the myriad of studies being completed within the industry and the specific survey of over 5,000 marketing executives by the Social Media Examiner (Stelzner, 2017) that they have major questions that they still want answered by a more credible voice. The challenge, as noted, is how rapidly everything is changing month by month, which suggests that academics will need to address the larger, overriding questions and build a network of theory to support their efforts. But this also provides an opportunity for outreach – perhaps a multimedia e-journal offering a faster turnaround time for articles with training videos and with content aimed at communication executives as its primary market. In a field renown for a wide gap between the concerns and interests of academia and industry (Manweller & Harvey, 2013, p. 257), a new era of cooperation could be achieved.

REFERENCES

Aberdeen Group. (2014). *Analyzing the ROI of video advertising.* Retrieved from http://go.brightcove. com/bc-aberdeen-analyzing-roi-b

Accenture. (2017). *Winning experiences in the new video world (infographic summary).* Retrieved from https://www.accenture.com/us-en/_acnmedia/PDF-50/Accenture-Winning-Experiences-Infographic.pdf

Advertiser Perceptions. (2015). *As the industry continues heavy shift to programmatic buying, disconnects grow between buyers and sellers, agencies and marketers.* Retrieved from http://www.advertiser-perceptions.com/blog

Arens, W. F. (2002). *Contemporary Advertising.* New York: McGraw-Hill Companies Inc.

Baran, S. (2006). *Introduction to mass communication: Media literacy and culture.* New York: McGraw-Hill.

Barthel, M. (2017). *Despite subscription surges for largest U.S. newspapers, circulation and revenue fall for industry overall.* Retrieved from http://www.pewresearch.org/fact-tank/2017/06/01/circulation-and-revenue-fall-for-newspaper-industry/

Bartosz, W., Wojdynski, B. W., & Evans, N. J. (2016). Going native: Effects of disclosure position and language on the recognition and evaluation of online native advertising. *Journal of Advertising*, *45*(2), 157–168. doi:10.1080/00913367.2015.1115380

Basney, B. (2014). Brands as publishers: Using content and paid media to fuel a brand transformation. *Journal of Brand Strategy*, *3*(2), 101–110.

Batra, R., & Keller, K. L. (2016). Integrating marketing communications: New findings, new lessons, and new ideas. *Journal of Marketing*, *80*(6), 122–145. doi:10.1509/jm.15.0419

Blueshift Research. (2015). *June 2015 Trends tracker report.* Retrieved from https://smaudience.surveymonkey.com/download-trends-tracker-report-june-2015.html?utm_source=email&recent=email&program=Q2_15_June_Trends-Tracker_Wrap-Up&source=email&utm_campaign=trends-tracker&utm_content=trends-tracker-june-2015&mkt_tok=3RkMMJWWfF9wsRoiu6vJZKXonjHpfsX66e4vW6C1lMI%2F0ER3fOvrPUfGjI4FTcFiI%2BSLDwEYGJlv6SgFSrbFMaJy2LgJWBb0TD7slJfbfYRPf6Ba2Jwwrfg%3D

Boland, M. (2016). *Native ads will drive 74% of all ad revenue by 2021.* Retrieved from http://www.businessinsider.com/the-native-ad-report-forecasts-2016-5?r=US&IR=T&IR=T

Bower, J., & Christensen, C. (1995). Disruptive technologies: Catching the wave. *Harvard Business Review.* Retrieved from https://hbr.org/1995/01/disruptive-technologies-catchingthe-wave

Brightcove. (2015). *The hero's guide to video marketing.* Retrieved from http://go.brightcove.com/brightcove-video-hero-guide?cid=70114000002QvKv&pid=70114000002Qu9G

Carson, M. (2015). When news sites go native: Redefining the advertising–editorial divide in response to native advertising. *Journalism, 16*(7), 849–865. doi:10.1177/1464884914545441

Chen, Y. (2017). *The state of mobile advertising.* Retrieved from https://digiday.com/marketing/state-mobile-advertising/

Christensen, C. M. (2014). Disruptive innovation. In *Encyclopedia of human-computer interaction* (2nd ed.). Retrieved from https://www.interactiondesign.org/encyclopedia/disruptive_innovation.html

Christensen, C. M. (2016). *Talks at Google: Where does growth come from?* Retrieved from https://youtu.be/rHdS_4GsKmg

Conill, R. F. (2016). Camouflaging church as state: An exploratory study of journalism's native advertising. *Journalism Studies, 17*(7), 904–914. doi:10.1080/1461670X.2016.1165138

Contently. (2017). *Fixing native advertising: What consumers want from brands, publishers, and the FTC.* Retrieved from https://contently.com/strategist/2016/12/08/native-advertising-study/

Crimson Hexagon. (2017). *U.S. consumer trends report.* Retrieved from http://pages.crimsonhexagon.com/rs/284-XQB-702/images/US-Trends-Full-Report.pdf

Draganska, M., Hartmann, W., & Stanglein, G. (2014). Internet versus television advertising: A Brand-building comparison. *JMR, Journal of Marketing Research, 51*(5), 578–590. doi:10.1509/jmr.13.0124

Duffy, G. (2017). *Twitter expands character count to 280, Snapchat upcoming redesign and algorithm.* Retrieved from https://www.socialmediaexaminer.com/twitter-expands-character-count-to-280-snapchat-upcoming-redesign-and-algorithm/?utm_source=Newsletter&utm_medium=NewsletterIssue&utm_campaign=New&omhide=true

eMarketer. (2011). *Ad dollars still not following online and mobile usage.* Retrieved from http://www.emarketer.com/Article/Ad-Dollars-Still-Not-Following-Online-Mobile-Usage/1008311

eMarketer. (2014). *Despite time spent, mobile still lacks for ad spend in the US.* Retrieved 20 Feb. 2015 from http://www.emarketer.com/Article/Despite-Time-Spent-Mobile-Still-Lacks-Ad-Spend-US/1010788 eMarketer. (2015a). *Mobile video roundup.* Retrieved from http://www.emarketer.com/articles/roundups

eMarketer. (2015b). *Cross-platform video trends roundup.* Retrieved from https://www.emarketer.com/public_media/docs/eMarketer_Cross_Platform_Video_Trends_Roundup.pdf

eMarketer. (2017a). *eMarketer lowers US TV ad spend estimate as cord-cutting accelerates.* Retrieved from https://www.emarketer.com/Article/eMarketer-Lowers-US-TV-Ad-Spend-Estimate-Cord-Cutting-Accelerates/1016463?ecid=NL1001

eMarketer. (2017b). *US ad spending: eMarketer's updated estimates and forecast for 2017.* Retrieved from https://www.emarketer.com/Report/US-Ad-Spending-eMarketers-Updated-Estimates-Forecast-2017/2002134

eMarketer. (2017c). *eMarketer updates us time spent with media figures.* Retrieved from https://www.emarketer.com/Article/eMarketer-Updates-US-Time-Spent-with-Media-Figures/1016587

eMarketer. (2017d). *StatPack: US omnichannel retail.* Retrieved from https://www.emarketer.com/public_media/docs/eMarketer_US_Omnichannel_Retail_StatPack_2017_1.pdf

eMarketer. (2017e). *Influencer marketing roundup 2017.* Retrieved from https://www.emarketer.com/public_media/docs/eMarketer_Roundup_Influencer_Marketing_2017_5.pdf

eMarketer. (2017f). *Measuring the effectiveness of video ad campaigns.* Retrieved from https://www.emarketer.com/Article/Measuring-Effectiveness-of-Video-Ad-Campaigns/1016706

eMarketer. (2017g). *Measuring the effectiveness of video ad campaigns.* Retrieved from https://www.emarketer.com/Article/Measure-of-Video-Ad-Spending-Shows-Sharp-Increase/1015793

Etherington, D. (2017). *Facebook plans to spend up to $1B on original shows in 2018.* Retrieved from https://techcrunch.com/2017/09/08/facebook-plans-to-spend-up-to-1b-on-original-shows-in-2018/

Fortuneloards. (2017). *36 mind blowing YouTube facts, figures and statistics – 2017.* Retrieved from https://fortunelords.com/youtube-statistics/

Fulgoni, G., & Lipsman, A. (2014). Numbers, please: Digital game changers: How social media will help usher in the era of mobile and multi-platform campaign-effectiveness measurement. *Journal of Advertising Research, 54*(1), 11–16. doi:10.2501/JAR-54-1-011-016

Gao, S., & Zang, Z. (2014). An empirical examination of users' adoption of mobile advertising in China. *Information Development, 32*(2), 203–215. doi:10.1177/0266666914550113

Gladwell, M. (2000). *The tipping point: How little things can make a big difference.* New York: Little, Brown and Company.

Hanson, R. (2009). *Mass Communication: Living in a Media World.* Washington, DC: CQ Press.

Haroldsen, E., & Harvey, K. (1979). The diffusion of shocking good news. *The Journalism Quarterly, 56*(4), 771–775. doi:10.1177/107769907905600409

Harvey, K. (2016). Local news and mobile: Major tipping points. In X. Xu (Ed.), *Handbook of Research on Human Social Interaction in the Age of Mobile Devices* (pp. 171–199). Hershey, PA: IGI Global. doi:10.4018/978-1-5225-0469-6.ch009

Harvey, K., & Auter, P. (2016). Advertising and mobile: More than a platform shift. In X. Xu (Ed.), *Handbook of Research on Human Social Interaction in the Age of Mobile Devices* (pp. 352–385). Hershey, PA: IGI Global. doi:10.4018/978-1-5225-0469-6.ch015

Heine, C. (2015). Facebook's Q1 ad revenue increased 46 percent to $3.3 billion. *AdWeek*. Retrieved from http://www.adweek.com/news/technology/facebooks-q1-ad-revenue-increased-46-percent-33-billion-164234

Hovland, C. I., Harvey, O. J., & Sherif, M. (1957). Assimilation and contrast effects in reactions to communication and attitude change. *Journal of Abnormal and Social Psychology*, 55(2), 244–252. doi:10.1037/h0048480 PMID:13474895

Hub Entertainment Research. (2017a). *Conquering content: What factors decide what content viewers find, choose and watch* (free company excerpt). Retrieved from http://hubresearchllc.com/reports/

Hub Entertainment Research. (2017b). *Decoding the default*. Retrieved from http://hubresearchllc.com/reports/

HubSpot. (2014). *State of Inbound 2014*. Retrieved from http://offers.hubspot.com/2014-state-of-inbound

HubSpot. (2015). *Marketing benchmarks from 7000+ businesses*. Retrieved from https://offers.hubspot.com/marketing-benchmarks-from-7000-businesses

Insivia. (2017). *27 Video stats for 2017*. Retrieved from http://www.insivia.com/27-video-stats-2017/

Jarvis, J. (2009). *Newspapers in Decline?* Video presented on the CBC (Canadian) TV network. Retrieved from https://youtu.be/YjUeJH4mdF4

Johnson, L. (2017). *Why 86% of brands plan to take part of their programmatic spend in-house*. Retrieved from http://www.adweek.com/digital/why-86-of-brands-plan-to-take-part-of-their-programmatic-spend-in-house/

Katz, E. (1957). The two-step flow of communication: An up-to-date report on a hypothesis. *Public Opinion Quarterly*, 21(1), 61–78. doi:10.1086/266687

Katz, E., & Lazarsfeld, P. F. (1955). *Personal influence: The part played by people in the flow of mass communications*. New York, NY: The Free Press.

Kim, L. (2015). *5 Facebook advertising tools that save time and improve your ROI*. Retrieved from https://www.socialmediaexaminer.com/5-facebook-advertising-tools/

LaMonica, P. R. (2017). *CNN money: Netflix plans to spend nearly $16 billion on content*. Retrieved from http://money.cnn.com/2017/08/14/investing/netflix-disney-content-costs/index.html

Lazarsfeld, P. F., Berelson, B., & Gaudet, H. (1944). *The people's choice: how the voter makes up his mind in a presidential campaign*. New York, NY: Columbia University Press.

Lee, D., Hosanagar, K., & Nair, H. S. (2015). *Advertising content and consumer engagement on social media: Evidence from Facebook.* A working paper by researchers at Tepper School of Business, Carnegie-Mellon University.

Lister, M. (2017). 37 Staggering video marketing statistics for 2017. *WordStream.* Retrieved from http://www.wordstream.com/blog/ws/2017/03/08/video-marketing-statistics

Manic, M. (2015). The rise of native advertising. *Bulletin of the Transilvania.*, *8*(1), 53–58.

Manweller, M., & Harvey, K. (2013). Do political reporters need to be political scientists? *Journal of Political Science Education, 9*(3), 255–272. doi:10.1080/15512169.2013.796232

Marketo. (2015). *How to use video content and marketing automation.* Retrieved from http://www.marketo.com/ebooks/how-to-use-video-content-and-marketing-automation-to-better-engage-qualify-and-convert-your-buyers/

McClatchy. (2017). *2016 annual report.* Retrieved from http://investors.mcclatchy.com/phoenix.zhtml?c=87841&p=irol-reportsannual

Mixpo. (2015). *The state of video advertising.* Retrieved from http://marketing.mixpo.com/acton/fs/blocks/showLandingPage/a/2062/p/p-00b4/t/page/fm/0

Molla, R. (2017). *Mobile is driving most ad spending growth worldwide.* Retrieved from https://www.recode.net/2017/9/14/16294450/mobile-ad-spending-growth-worldwide

Nguyen, J. (2014). *Online video consumption in APAC and Total Video.* Retrieved from http://www.comscore.com/Insights/Presentations-and-Whitepapers/(offset)/10/?cs_edgescape_cc=KZ

Okazaki, S. (2012). Teaching mobile advertising in advertising theory. In S. Rodgers & E. Thorson (Eds.), *Advertising Theory* (pp. 373–387). New York: Routledge.

Papacharissi, Z. (2009). Uses and gratifications. In D. Stacks & M. Salwen (Eds.), *An Integrated Approach to Communication Theory and Research* (p. 137). New York: Routledge.

Pew Research Center. (2014). *The revenue picture for American journalism, and how it is changing.* Retrieved http://www.journalism.org/files/2014/03/Revnue-Picture-for-American-Journalism.pdf

Pew Research Center. (2017). *Local TV news fact sheet.* Retrieved from http://www.journalism.org/fact-sheet/local-tv-news/

Poe, M. T. (2011). *A history of communications.* New York: Cambridge University Press.

Ramos, L. (2013). *The B2B CMO role is expanding: Evolve of move on.* Retrieved from http://solutions.forrester.com/Global/FileLib/Reports/B2B_CMOs_Must_Evolve_Or_Move_On.pdf

Reinartz, W., & Saffert, P. (2013, June). Creativity in advertising: When it works and when it doesn't. *Harvard Business Review*, 107–112. Retrieved from https://hbr.org/2013/06/creativity-in-advertising-when-it-works-and-when-it-doesnt

Ross, P. (2015). *Native Facebook videos get more reach than any other type of post.* Retrieved from http://www.socialbakers.com/blog/2367-native-facebook-videos-get-more-reach-than-any-other-type-of-post

Schroeder, P. (2016). *37 video marketing statistics you need to know for 2017*. Retrieved from http://www.rendrfx.com/video-marketing-statistics

Sloane, G. (2014). Facebook's new people-based ad technology is 'marketing nirvana'. Pepsi and Intel are early testers as social net unleashes data. *Adweek*. Retrieved from http://www.adweek.com/news/technology/facebooks-new-people-based-ad-technology-marketing-nirvana-160438

Statista. (2017). *Google's ad revenue from 2001 to 2016 (in billion U.S. dollars)*. Retrieved from https://www.statista.com/statistics/266249/advertising-revenue-of-google/

Stelzner, M. (2015). *2015 social media marketing industry report*. Retrieved from https://www.social-mediaexaminer.com/social-media-marketing-industry-report-2015/

Stelzner, M. (2017). *2017 social media marketing industry report*. Retrieved from https://www.social-mediaexaminer.com/report/

Urban, R. (2016). *The Marketer's map to the digital goldmine*. Retrieved from http://convert.bounceexchange.com/rs/445-fjv-353/images/bx-marketers-map-digital-goldmine.pdf

Vidyard. (2017). *2017 Video in business benchmark report*. Retrieved from http://awesome.vidyard.com/rs/273-EQL-130/images/Video-in-Business-Benchmark-Report-2017.pdf

Wojdynski, B. W. (2016). The deceptiveness of sponsored news articles: How readers recognize and perceive native advertising. *Journalism Studies*, *17*(7), 904–914.

Wojdynski, B. W., & Evans, N. J. (2016). Going native: Effects of disclosure position and language on the recognition and evaluation of online native advertising. *Journal of Advertising*, *45*(2), 157–168. doi:10.1080/00913367.2015.1115380

Wu, J., Hu, B., & Zhang, Y. (2013). Maximizing the performance of advertisements diffusion: A simulation study of the dynamics of viral advertising in social networks. Simulation. *Transactions of the Society for Modeling and Simulation International*, *89*(8), 921–934. doi:10.1177/0037549713481683

Zarrella, D. (2013). *The science of marketing: When to tweet, what to post, how to blog, and other proven strategies*. Hoboken, NJ: John Wiley & Sons.

KEY TERMS AND DEFINITIONS

Inbound Marketing: Promotional tools such as social media postings, blogs, white papers, ebooks, webinars, videos, and freemiums that earn the attention of prospective customers, make the brand easy to find, and draw prospects to the organization's website.

Native Advertising: Any advertising—online or offline—designed to blend in with the non-advertising content around it. Online, it relates particularly to social media, but is paid advertising that mimics organic postings but are indicated as "sponsored." As such, advertisers can have them placed in the news feed of potential customers meeting their criteria.

Omnichannel or Cross-Channel Marketing: Relates closely to personalized marketing because marketing messages are not fully personalized until they can follow the customer or prospective customer across different social, programming, advertising, or technical channels. To do so, this also requires the use of a system to gather and organize data and provide real-time access.

Personalization: As related to marketing, it is the increased use of big data to personalize marketing messages to prospective customers. It may be in the form of personalized email, videos, shopping basket recommendations, customer service, etc.

Programmatic Advertising: An approach to advertising using technology to pursue low-cost advertising opportunities all over the web and contract and fill those advertising opportunities through a technologically automated process.

This research was previously published in Diverse Methods in Customer Relationship Marketing and Management; pages 109-136, copyright year 2018 by Business Science Reference (an imprint of IGI Global).

Chapter 9
Social Media and Social Identity in the Millennial Generation

Guida Helal
American University of Beirut, Lebanon

Wilson Ozuem
University of Cumbria, UK

ABSTRACT

The active presence of fashion brands online serves as a channel for customers to connect with brands for different intentions. This connection acts as an outlet customers employ in furthering social identity through brand associations. Brand perceptions are accordingly formed among consumers based on the promised functional and symbolic benefits consumption of that brand guarantees. Social media has assumed an integral role in fostering brand-customer relationships that ultimately augment social identity. The following chapter examines the role social media has played on brand perceptions in the fashion apparel and accessories industry from a social identity theory perspective. The chapter focuses on theoretical implications and managerial implications. The concluding section offers some significant roles that social media and social identity may play in keeping up with the design and development of marketing communications programs.

INTRODUCTION

Marketing logics and developments have comparably and effectively progressed over the years to parallel the whirlwind innovations that primarily define the fashion industry. The dynamic nature of marketing means fashion companies are relentlessly on guard for the next groundbreaking development (Jayachandran, Gimeno & Varadarajan, 1999; Lusch, 2007; Vargo & Lusch, 2004; Webster, 1992). One case of a sought after phenomenon that has dramatically revolutionised today's society, is the technological Millennial approach to communication. Traditional marketing has gradually lost bearing, as the rigid likes of one-way communication is superseded by active two-way interchange (Houman Andersen, 2001; Ozuem, Howell, & Lancaster, 2008). The shift in communication has consequently encouraged worldwide organisations

DOI: 10.4018/978-1-7998-9020-1.ch009

to assume the likes of Internet technologies along with their varied manifestations, such as social media, as an outlet allowing brands to produce content for followers (Evans, 2012; Hoffman & Novak, 1996; Zarrella, 2009). An abundance of literature has consequently surfaced examining the evolution social media has enthused in routine life (Fischer & Reuber, 2011; Hanna, Rohm & Crittenden, 2011; Hoffman & Fodor, 2016; Huy & Shipilov, 2012; Kaplan & Haenlein, 2010; Kietzmann, Hermkens, McCarthy, & Silvestre, 2011; Michaelidou, Siamagka, & Christodoulides, 2011). Further studies have explored the application of social media within a brand's marketing strategy (Luo, Zhang, & Duan, 2013; Naylor, Lamberton & West, 2012; Simmons, 2008; Tuten & Solomon, 2014).

Kim and Ko (2012) addressed the promising relationship between social media marketing and resultant customer equity among luxury fashion brands. The study aimed to demonstrate †he success luxury fashion brands gain from employing social media marketing activities including entertainment, interaction, or word of mouth. Based on the findings, the study concluded that the use of social media is directly correlated with subsequent enhanced purchase intentions and customer equity within the luxury fashion industry. However, the study paid limited attention to a demographic age that is familiar with social media and able to produce pertinent feedback that enhances the accuracy of research results. An analysis conducted by a statistic portal, Statista, on the worldwide daily usage of social media found that the highest degree of daily social media usage in 2016 was held by global users aged 25 to 34 years old (Statista, 2016). A more recent study revealed the highest time consumption of visual activities on social networking sites such as Facebook and Instagram to be among ages 16-34 years, while preceding generations demonstrated fewer percentages of average time spent participating in such activities (Statista, 2017). The Millennial generation outruns other age groups as the leading social media user. Albeit the current extensive literature investigating social media, few studies have examined the use of social media in the fashion industry, particularly on the Millennial generation.

Social media is a development of the World Wide Web that began gaining ground between the late 1990's and early 2000's, establishing worldwide prominence by the late 2000's (Dewing, 2010). Yet before delving into the profound significance social media has exerted globally, the course of events leading up to its inception are considered

The initiation of the World Wide Web began in the early 1990's upon Tim Berners-Lee linking hypertext technology to the Internet. This allowed for one common worldwide foundation to be formed, whereby networked communication was born (Van Dijck, 2013). The consequent evolution of Web 2.0 brought about social media. Web 2.0 is described as consisting of two features that help define it, and these are *microcontent* and *social media*. *Microcontent* comprises of pieces of content that express a primary idea. Such pieces cover much less information than websites and may take the form of blog posts, comments, or small images. These are designed for easy upload, reuse, and stimulating participation. The second feature of Web 2.0, *social media* or *social software*, consists of platforms organized around the framework of connecting people to one another. The *microcontent* produced by multiple users creates a page of shared interests different users can access to bond with one another (Alexander & Levine, 2008). In time, the growth of Web 2.0 prompted the birth of two-way communication platforms and the flow of user-generated content, which is today identified as social media (Arora, 2014; Fuchs, 2014; Gillies & Cailliau, 2000; O'Reilly, 2005).

A study conducted by Statista further affirms the significance social media has gained across the fashion industry (Statista, 2016). This study emphasizes the sheer 'clout' that virtual channels have when it comes to the fashion domain through the integration of social media throughout London Fashion Week. The show is a highly anticipated bi-annual fashion trading weeklong event, and in 2014, it generated over half a million mentions on social media. The majority of these mentions emerged over Instagram. Reports show that user access to fashion brands online is set to reach over one billion users by the year 2020 (Statista, 2016). Additional analyses identified social media as the most commonly used source by Millennials for updates on high-end fashion (Statista, 2017). These figures demonstrate the on-going unification social media has brought about within the fashion world, as more brands race towards social networking sites to attain followers. Online channels offer fashion brands further leeway for original content contribution that facilitates for an intimate connection with Millennials. The social platform cultivates brand-customer relationships, as brands strive to publicly evoke customer loyalty, and customers, in turn, are receptive to demonstrate brand association and acquire the promised relationship equity such brands are perceived to offer (Lemon, Rust, & Zeithaml, 2001; Kim & Ko, 2012; Vogel, Evanschitzky, & Ramaseshan, 2008).

Drawing on social identity, this study investigates the application of social media in advancing online brand communities and relationship equity that consumers chase in enforcing social identity. Social identity theory holds that individuals seek to allocate themselves or others according to social categories (Tajfel & Turner, 1985). Individuals trail the groups that guarantee positive recognition and ultimately enhance the self through association (Ashforth & Mael, 1989; Hogg & Terry, 2000). Numerous studies have explored the tendency of customers to identify with particular brands in forming a desired social identity (Arnett, German, & Hunt, 2003; Bhattacharya & Sen, 2003; Lam, Ahearne, Hu, & Schillewaert, 2010). Consumption can be a significant attribute within an individual's journey to build an identity for his/her own self, as well as for others (Elliot & Wattanasuwan, 1998; Kleine, Kleine, & Kernan, 1993). The consumption of popular culture has been recognized as a paramount contributor to the attainment of social status or social placement for individuals. Fashion, a major segment of present pop culture, has manifested into a prominent facilitator of social enhancement (Barron, 2012). Fashion brands are pursued by consumers with the intention of embracing individuality that, in fact, complies with a universal standard of social classification. People seek to individually speak, behave, or dress in a manner that is perceptible and significant, but that simultaneously resides within putative group norms. A consumer is placed amid two forces, the individual/psychological influence of personal opinions and preferences, and the public/social weight of uniform beliefs and attitudes (Burke, 2006; Carlson, Suter, & Brown, 2008; Nowak, Szamrej and Latané, 1990).

Customers are enticed by a brand's online presence as a means of furthering social identity through brand association, and ultimately this can shape brand perceptions among customers through promised functional and symbolic benefits. Social media embodies the leading channel for casual interactions that develop brand-customer relationships and enrich social identity. Consumer touch points have accordingly been reinvented to accommodate for more than physical exchanges. Rather, brand-customer interaction has ensued beyond the point of sale and into a virtual realm of open interchange (Edelman, 2010; Fromm & Garton, 2013) that has become second nature to the Millennial generation. This study supplements present available research on social media in numerous ways. There exists abundant literature examining the implementation of social media means as marketing tools, however current literature does not account for Millennial presence in investigating the influence social media exerts on brand perceptions in the fashion industry. In exploring the impact social media holds as a marketing instrument, consequent outcomes from this study develop literature concerning the impact of social media on the Millennial age, and this cohort's dependence on social identity in further connecting with brands. This research provides a footing for fashion brands to develop in future research, which might look at how social media accounts can be appropriately handled in targeting consumers. The findings in this study uncovers the imprint social media has provoked on Millennial brand perceptions in the fashion industry.

BACKGROUND

The fashion industry comprises of various sectors from apparel and accessories, perfumes and cosmetics to watches and jewellery. This vast industry has been globally valued at 3 trillion US dollars (approx. 2.4 trillion pounds) with a compound annual growth rate of 2 percent. Positive market figures are anticipated to resume with industry growth projected across major regions such as China, Europe, USA and India, to name a few (Statista, 2016). Sales growth in the fashion industry have noticeably materialised across regions such as Asia Pacific and Europe, with anticipated global fashion industry growth to reach 4.5 percent in 2018 (Statista, 2017). As the fashion world engages a wide scope of sectors, this study focuses on the use of social media among the Millennial generation exclusively within the apparel and accessories sector.

In a study conducted by Deloitte on the global fashion and luxury market in 2016, the apparel and accessories sector demonstrated more than 80% of revenues recorded in the industry for years 2014 and 2015. Consequently, the expected market trends for 2016 demonstrated a 59% increase in the apparel and accessories sector worldwide (Deloitte, 2016). These figures can be expected to materialize among top billionaire players such as Zara (Inditex), LVMH, and H&M, among others (Statista, 2016). Multinational fast-fashion retailer Zara (Inditex) revealed a 10% climb within nine months of fiscal 2017 as the group persisted with its' effective tactic of globally locating flagship stores around peak shopping strips. Inditex complemented its highly visible brick-and-mortar stores with an integrated online-offline model offering same-day delivery and next-day delivery in certain markets (Inditex, 2017). Major competitor, H&M, was ranked one of the world's largest retail companies in 2016 with a 4 percent sales growth in the financial year of 2017. The company acknowledges the prominence of complementing the industry shift moving into 2018, through digital and offline integration of customer interaction and purchase points (H&M, 2017). Parent luxury fashion company LVMH (Moët Hennessy Louis Vuitton) has likewise asserted its place in the fashion industry boasting a revenue growth of 13% in 2017 compared to the previous year. LVMH's *Fashion and Leather Goods* sector exhibited optimistic figures across all luxury brands citing Louis Vuitton's innovative operation as a strong contributor to performance (LVMH, 2018). In an exhaustive forecast titled *The State of Fashion 2018,* conducted by Mckinsey & Company and The Business of Fashion, the report demonstrates an evolving shift in consumer behaviour as online platforms gain primary grounds as points of consumer exposure to brands. Revenue growth is subsequently projected to witness 2-3x increase online in 2018 versus 2015 as consumers push to personalise experiences through online channels and global mobile payment transactions surge (BOF & McKinsey & Co., 2018).

Social media has empowered the fashion industry with the free-flow of content shared between brands and consumers worldwide. Brands are able to penetrate international markets through the likes of Facebook, Instagram and fashion blogs that document the latest runways, campaigns and trends to an active audience. Brand followers likewise share their own content among brands and consumers. This two-way interchange and freedom in exchanging content has allowed brands and customers to connect, customers to express affiliation to brands, and online fashion communities to develop. Such a platform of communication enables vast brand exposure and awareness among worldwide social media users. H&M was recorded to have an average of over 10 million Instagram engagements consisting of likes, retweets and comments across over a one month period, signifying the scope of market saturation a single social media platform is capable of achieving (Statista, 2016).Luxury brands Chanel, Louis Vuitton and Christian Dior were placed in the top most influential luxury brands on social media worldwide as of October 2016 (Statista, 2016). The implementation of social media as a promotional technique has served as a gateway to market prominence as brands are given the opportunity to reach global customers on an intimate level. Consumers are drawn to online platforms to connect with brands in a more unique experience that may contribute to a brand's exclusivity and authenticity.

As affirmed by Van Dijck (2013), upon the initial development of social media, "participatory culture was the buzzword that connoted the Web's potential to nurture connections, build communities, and advance democracy." (Van Dijck, 2013, p.4). Such universal engagement has propelled the immense growth of social media into worldwide cultures. A study by Statista (2018) reveals the enormity social media holds as a defining phenomenon of the present time through a global infiltration of approximately 2 billion active social media users. Instagram, a photo-based application and social networking site, solely yielded a 21% global reach merely one year after its launch in 2013; and reached a record in 2018 of over 800 million monthly active users (Statista, 2018). Social media has infiltrated a generation of devoted users comprising of the Millennial age, as more than 85% of 18-29 years olds use online social platforms (Smith & Anderson, 2018). Fashion leaders Zara and H&M have prevailed among the Millennial age group (Forbes, 2012); a technological age that has grown to embody social media as a key communication portal. By utilizing social media as a major delivery approach, such brands are able to considerably impress their weight within the Millennial market.

MILLENNIAL GENERATION

The Millennial Generation is defined as a demographic cohort born between the early 1980s and the early 2000s. This generation differs remarkably from previous groups, as the Millennial perception of communication is that it is conveniently available and instant, therefore obstacles such as time or geography do not impinge upon the presence of technology (Strauss & Howe, 1991; Lingelbach, Patino, & Pitta, 2012; Rainer & Rainer, 2011). Global boundaries are diminishing as the use of the Internet empowers the Millennial age as a consumer group defined by homogeneous behaviour (Moore, 2012). Millennials worldwide are able to relate through identical behaviour and consumption patterns due to the network of mass media. The innate existence of the Internet has altered their way of interaction and characterised them as *digital natives* (Hershatter & Epstein, 2010; Prensky, 2001). The Millennial generation is the first cohort to entirely absorb social media as the leading source of communication within an era that values public and conspicuous behaviour (Bennett, Matson & Kervin, 2008; Bakewell & Mitchell, 2003; Paulin, Ferguson, Jost & Fallu, 2014). Twenge (2006) and Twenge, Campbell and Freeman (2012) interestingly describe the generation as both "Generation We", concerned with public and environmental obligations, and "Generation Me", stemming from the significance placed on materialistic behaviour and preserving image. Social media offers the platform to express activities, consumption and lifestyles that accentuate the *"me"* quality Millennials seek to achieve.

This cohort has wholly integrated social media into daily activities including the use of such interactive portals to connect to brands (Moore, 2012; Nowak, Thach & Olsen, 2006). Marketers recognise the reliance Millennials place on social media to connect with peers and brands in acquiring relevant information from such networks (Eastman, Iyer & Thomas, 2012; Eastman & Liu, 2012; Hewlett, Sherbin

& Sumberg, 2009). The notion of remaining connected to real-time occurrences is an underlying motivation for Millennials to seek social media, and brands to consequently use interactive technologies to directly reach Millennials (Engel, Bell, Meier & Rumpel, 2011; Fiore, Kim & Lee, 2005; Valentine & Powers, 2013). Recurring brand-customer contact bears the potential to evolve into emotional interaction through trust, loyalty and commitment that advances brand equity (Nowak, Thach & Olsen), symbolically influencing Millennial perceptions of brands. The relevance of social media is only expected to grow with continuing consumer dependence on the network to which it caters, and newfound proficiency amongst brands in delivering a unified message worldwide is also set to evolve (Stephen & Galak, 2010; Mangold & Faulds, 2009; Prensky, 2001). Such characteristics justify the worth of social media as a phenomenon that merits exploration.

CONTEXT AND FOUNDATION

Social media has shrewdly manoeuvred its way into people's lives over the past decade. While it may have commenced with the prime intention of socially linking people together, it later developed and was described using broader definitions spanning from connecting individuals to connecting industries. The extensive exploration of this communication portal through numerous studies has generated multiple definitions, all of which tend to highlight a parallel overview: social media comprises of Internet-centred platforms that enable and promote a free flow of user-generated information (Kaplan & Haenlein, 2010; Safko, 2012; Kietzmann, Hermkens, McCarthy, & Silvestre, 2011; Hanna, Rohm, & Crittenden, 2011; Luo, Zhang, & Duan, 2013; Ngai, Tao, & Moon, 2015; Stokinger, & Ozuem, 2015).

Kaplan and Haenlein (2010) define social media as a "group of Internet-based applications that build on the ideological and technological foundations of Web 2.0, and allow the creation and exchange of user generated content." (Kaplan & Haenlein, 2010, p.61). This, much celebrated, definition has prevailed in acknowledging the key role of social media in facilitating the movement of content across a shared floor. Safko (2012) outlines a comparable explanation whilst emphasizing the efficiency social media facilitates in allowing human interactions and relationships to develop. Social media has cultivated an environment driven by an open exchange between networks of users. Ngai, Tao and Moon (2015) recognize the capacity of social media networks to form relationships, but they also discuss the potential of networks to influence career prospects. Building on this progression of explanations, social media can be defined as an evolving phenomenon that continues to mature across society.

Mayfield (2008) describes five characteristics of social media which are 1) *participation* that stimulates sharing 2) *openness,* which eliminates barriers and enables free-flow of information 3) *conversation* generated from the public stream of content shared 4) *community* that develops from open interactions, and 5) *connectedness*, which describes the network created between users. Kietzmann et al. (2011) have likewise categorized social media into seven similar functional blocks and these are 1) *identity,* that considers the degree to which a user is willing to reveal his/her identity 2) *conversation*, which considers the level of communication between users 3) *sharing,* which is the degree of content circulating between users 4) *presence,* which refers to the access given to display available users 5) *relationships* reflect the extent of users relating to one another 6) *reputation* considers the degree to which users can identify their stance within settings, and finally 7) *groups* refers to the ability to form or belong to a community. The functional blocks social media are built on create its flexibility in producing an open environment that consolidates worldwide users and progresses relationships.

Before proceeding to the next section, it is imperative to address the connotation of social media with regards to social networking sites. While social media and social networking sites are frequently used interchangeably, the two terms hold separate meanings. Social media generally concerns collective construction and the circulation of media on a large scale, which can include countless applications and services such as social networking sites, wikis, or podcasts, to name a few (Collin, Rahilly, Richardson, & Third, 2011; Dewing, 2010; Weinberg & Pehlivan, 2011). Social networking sites are web-based services, which are a part of social media and which are crafted for sharing media between networks of users (Collin, Rahilly, Richardson, & Third, 2011). Boyd and Ellison (2008) define social network sites as, "web-based services that allow individuals to 1) construct a public or semi-public profile within a bounded system 2) articulate a list of other users with whom they share a connection, and 3) view and traverse their list of connections and those made by others within the system." (Boyd & Ellison, 2008, p.211). Social networking sites comprise of websites such as Facebook, Instagram or Twitter that characteristically require users to primarily register on the website and create a network, after which content can be shared with networks of connections. The virtually interactive platforms that social media create have induced a shift in the web towards a more people-driven community, whereby regular users influence the content produced (Berthon, Pitt, Planger, & Shapiro, 2012; O'Reilly & Battelle, 2009; Smith, 2009). Account holders now have the liberty of broadcasting (receiving) any message on a global scale with the click of a button. This self-expression encourages a dynamic and democratic setting through which users feel more inclined to engage and share their own opinions (Susarla, Oh, & Tan, 2012). This study focuses on exploring how social media has influenced Millennial brand perceptions through different marketing methods.

Social Media as a Marketing Tool

Social media has progressively emerged on marketing agendas as an influential promotional tool within business operations (Fischer & Reuber, 2011; Luo, Zhang & Duan, 2013; Mangold & Faulds, 2009). This communication portal has compelled organizations to combine different marketing strategies, such as outbound marketing (dispensing promotional messages) with inbound marketing (receiving consumer messages through social media), to achieve an optimized balance of promotion (Smith & Zook, 2011). The viral chatter and ample exposure social media incites, cues brands to capitalize on potential networks as part of founding strong brand-customer relationships within brand communities, while amassing critical customer feedback (Chiu, Hsu, & Wang, 2006; Enders, Hungenberg, Denker, & Mauch, 2008). Brands benefit from eliciting social ties with customers that evoke an exchange of resources, such as trust between users, and facilitate a shared vision for companies that extend beyond overpowered geographic distances and broken organization-customer barriers (Ngai, Tao, & Moon, 2015; Heinonen, 2011; Tsai & Ghoshal, 1998).

Certain axioms are applied in designing attractive platforms for consumers when implementing social media within organizational marketing strategies. These axioms allow companies to reflect on each nation's local economic, political, and cultural stance in communicating with users on social media, while also maintaining consistency of content produced at a global level (Berthon, Pitt, Planger, & Shapiro, 2012; Hinz, Skiera, Barrot, & Becker, 2011). Brands form a universal norm of social network activities that produce memorable content worldwide customers pertain to. Corresponding touch-points are employed to connect with customers throughout the day and ultimately ensure incessant brand awareness (Ashley & Tuten, 2015; Tsimonis & Dimitriadis, 2014).

Viral Marketing and E-WOM

Stealth marketing has permeated industries via engagement of practises, such as viral marketing, that tactfully and subtly promote brands (Kaikati & Kaikati, 2004; Martin & Smith, 2008; Roy & Chattopadhyay, 2010; Ozuem, Borrelli & Lancaster, 2017). Viral marketing is defined as, "the process of getting customers to pass along a company's marketing message to friends, family, and colleagues." (Laudon & Traver, 2015, p.381). The unreserved, free flow quality supporting social media instigates web circulation. One form of viral marketing that has predominantly flourished offline, as an eminent promotional technique is word-of-mouth (Katz & Lazarsfeld, 1955). Word-of-mouth (WOM) has been defined as the exchange of information on a particular subject among consumers (Arndt, 1967; Kaplan & Haenlein, 2011; Stern, 1994).

Buttle (1998) describes WOM according to five characteristics; *valence, focus, timing, solicitation* and *intervention. Valence* considers the positive or negative force WOM may impress on receivers with regards to a brand. According to a study by File et al. (1994), WOM can be appropriately managed to produce a desired effect among customers. The second characteristic Buttle (1998) addresses is the *focus,* which the brand adopts in influencing customers through the management of WOM. *Timing* refers to the use of WOM as a pre-purchase or post-purchase evaluation amongst consumers. *Solicitation* discusses the potential of customers to accept WOM and this may be influenced by the *intervention* of spokespeople, or celebrities hired by the brand. In most cases, WOM is assumed to occur naturally among customers who share brand experiences, and this consequently creates trails of chatter that diffuse across multiple receivers (Anderson, 1998; Bone, 1995; Herr, Kardes, & Kim, 1991; v. Wangenheim & Bayon, 2004). However, brands have managed to exert their own influence over handling WOM, particularly through virtual outlets (Biyalogorsky, Gerstner, & Libai, 2001; Godes & Mayzlin, 2009; Mayzlin, 2006).

A movement of shoppers probing for broader brand reviews and scrutiny has summoned for the progression of traditional WOM to online channels as electronic Word-Of-Mouth (eWOM), consequently unveiling copious volumes of user inputs (Cheung & Thadani, 2012; Chu & Kim, 2011; Trusov, Bucklin, & Pauwels, 2009). Being mindful that while virtual interchange cannot suffice as the sole vehicle to contact in place of conventional offline communication, it bears the competence to act as an adjunct to evolving consumer behaviour (Kozinets, 1999).

Chevalier and Mayzlin (2006) undertook a study to evaluate customer dependence on eWOM. This study compared sales of the same products from different websites. The results demonstrated a discrepancy between the businesses in terms of sales of the same products generated, as the website with more positive feedback submitted on those products generated more sales. Positive eWOM exhibits the capability of shaping customer purchase decisions. However, Schlosser (2005) demonstrates that negative reviews also significantly influence buyer behaviour by discouraging potential customers whilst swaying current customers that have a positive stance towards the brand. You, Vadakkepatt & Joshi (2015) draw on varied factors that may affect the reception of eWOM. The study underlines the potency of eWOM to be dependent on the motivation of the sender. EWOM is accordingly categorised into *organic,* material that an eWOM sender innately chooses to share, or *incentivised eWOM,* material that is induced by the promise of company incentives (You, Vadakkepatt & Joshi, 2015). The latter may not be perceived as genuine or trustworthy.

Electronic word of mouth enables an accumulation of customer feedback that evidently adds to the image of a brand, and shapes a customer's screening process (Baker, Donthu & Kumar, 2016; Chakravarti & Janiszewski, 2003; Dellarocas, 2006; Dhar & Chang, 2009; Trusov, Bucklin, & Pauwels, 2009).

Consumers have gradually come to refer to and rely on eWOM to make purchase decisions. Typically, the consumer decision process involves different stages, beginning with *need recognition, information search, evaluation of alternatives, purchase,* and *post-purchase evaluation* (Solomon, 2012; Liang & Huang, 1998). De Valck, van Bruggen, & Wierenga (2009) conducted a study to explore the influence of virtual communities on the consumer decision processes. The findings reveal that substantial virtual interactions weighed on a number of the phases involved within the decision process; largely the first three stages and the final stage of the process through the retrieval, supply, and discussion of information. This study accentuates the development in decision-making as the profusion of information online contributes to customers' retrieval of choices for needs recognition, information search, alternative evaluation, and encourages supply of experiences in the post purchase stages.

Brand Communities and E-WOM

The accessibility of sharing content online has expedited eWOM's wide reception among Millennials and empowered the upswing of online communities and brand-customer relationships (Gruen, Osmonbekov, & Czaplewski, 2006; Taken Smith, 2012; Veloutsou and McAlonan, 2012). Social media interactions have developed into a trialogue of communication between brands and customers, and among customers as online communities are formed through back and forth user exchanges (Hung & Li, 2007; Mangold & Faulds, 2009; Miller, Fabian, & Lin, 2008). This trialogue is further matured as companies cultivate brand communities to enrich brand-customer relationships and offer customers a platform to bond with one another, eliciting a sense of belonging (Robards & Bennett, 2011; Veloustou & Moutinho, 2009). A tribe of followers is consequently founded based on shared behaviours or preferences around a particular brand (Cova & Cova, 2001).

Muniz and O'Guinn (2001) define brand community as, "a specialized, non-geographically bound community, based on a structured set of social relationships among admirers of a brand." (Muniz & O'Guinn, 2001, p.412). Consumers are gathered under one umbrella of brand devotees irrespective of geographic distances.

According to (Schau, Muniz, & Arnould, 2009), brand community can be categorized into four value-creating activities,

1.   Social networking, which centres on building and maintaining relationships within the brand community.
2.   Impression management, that involves managing a positive brand image both within and past the brand community.
3.   Community engagement, which ensures continuous interaction among members and brand.
4.   Brand use, whereby the brand regularly shares guidance for greater utilization of the product.

The population of brand communities on social media has granted companies a leverage of brand impressions that can be crafted and communicated across global networks. A triad of interchange between brand-customer and customer-customer has advanced to produce an unrestricted environment for continuous engagement, relationship growth and, in the long run, customer loyalty (Fischer, Bristor, & Gainer, 1996; Luo, Zhang, & Duan, 2013; Muniz & O'Guinn, 2001; Sheth & Parvatiyar, 1995). Amid the instant communication of social media, brand-customer interaction is escalated as more frequent engagement propels satisfaction, trust and commitment among followers (Jang, Olfman, Ko, Koh, &

Kim 2008; Kim, Choi, Qualls, & Han, 2008; Wirtz et al., 2013). Consistent brand-customer interchange further impels brands to reinforce the brand image among consumers, and evidently create an attractive environment that drives purchase intentions (Adjei, Noble, & Noble, 2009; Lipsman, Mudd, Rich, & Bruich, 2012).

Brand-customer interactions via social media are openly displayed for the entire brand community to see. Brands are even more so compelled to heed and preserve positive customer experiences and customer engagement (Dessart, Veloutsou, & Thomas, 2015; Gu and Ye, 2014; Ozuem, Howell & Lancaster, 2016a). According to Gummerus et al. (2012), a study was conducted on customer engagement with a company Facebook profile. The findings of the study showed that members of online brand communities were predominantly drawn to connect with a brand to seek help or express approval. Brands benefit from creating inviting environments that encourage customers to reach out when given the chance.

Fournier and Lee (2009) identify the development of brand societies as competitive business strategies engineered to produce pools of admirers that sustain stronger brands. This band of followers takes on the role of a buffer, whereby every individual openly demonstrates support for his/her community. An interactive community facilitates the strength of brand impressions beyond the place of purchase into a society of individuals that, in turn, act as ambassadors in further extending the brand name (Dobele et al., 2007; McAlexander, Schouten, & Koenig, 2002). Online brand community members are exposed to large-scale global networks that embody diverse demographics, thus enlisting worldwide users under a common union of social integration. Relationships are formed across worldwide customers that have diverse backgrounds, but share a similar devotion, or following towards a particular brand, and who institute a strong community solely based on that devotion (Brown, Broderick, & Lee, 2007; Jones, 1998). A study on the correlation between the presence of online brand communities and consequent customer purchase frequency demonstrated a parallel link of the variables (Wu, Huang, Zhao & Hua, 2015). Wu, Huang, Zhao & Hua (2015) revealed positive outcomes for brands involved in online communities regardless of the degree of online participation by customers.

Reference Groups

The degree of influence customer interactions are capable of exerting on receivers depends on the credibility and expertise of the sender (Gilly, Graham, Wolfinbarger, & Yale, 1998; Sweeney, Soutar, & Mazzarol, 2008). Messages produced by opinion leaders, or reference groups hold higher appeal and exert greater influence on consumer brand judgments (Flynn, Goldsmith, & Eastman, 1996; Senecal & Nantel, 2004). A reference group is defined as, "that group in which the actor aspires to gain or maintain acceptance: hence, a group whose claims are paramount in situations requiring choice." (Shibutani, 1955, p.563). Shibutani (1955) portrays the modern world as consisting of mass societies that have been segregated into communities of social groups run by different communication systems, ultimately identified as reference groups. Such social groups have today been utilized in the marketing realm as a means of influencing consumers by assigning more than just a functional use for products. Such products are instead assigned a symbolic significance (Ekinci et al., 2011; Englis & Solomon, 1995; Escalas & Bettman, 2005; Levy, 1959). Hogg et al. (2009) comparably highlight the significance the social environment imposes on consumption through consumers' symbolic interaction with brands that they perceive and interpret to be embraced or rejected within different social groups. The symbolic value a brand is believed to deliver, weighs heavily on consumption behaviour.

Reference groups may be normative in the sense that family members, friends and peers influence one another through direct interactions. They may be comparative when, for example, public figures set benchmarks that individuals aspire to (Carmeli & Schaubroeck, 2007; Childers & Rao, 1992; Kelley, 1952; Li & Su, 2007). Marketers have long used the exploitation of the demographic, psychographic and cultural characteristics of public figures as a tactic of reference groups (McCracken, 1989; Escalas & Bettman, 2003; Amaldoss & Jain, 2008; Choi & Rifon, 2012; Seno & Lukas, 2007; Ozuem & Tan, 2014). The aspirations of consumers to achieve the perfect self and to belong within a specific social group further drive their idolization of celebrity figures (Amos, Holmes, & Strutton, 2008; Atkin & Block, 1983; Choi & Rifon, 2012). Association with such figures brings them one step closer to achieving their lifestyle objectives. A study conducted on the impact of celebrities using social media to endorse a brand found that the greater the following a celebrity had, the bigger the resulting product exposure and buying intention towards that brand (Jin & Phua, 2014). Social media users are drawn to, and follow brands that reflect the people those users strive to be and emulate through overt consumption of brands. Customers become more committed to virtual communities that not only assist in product research, but more importantly they become attached to communities that enhance their social needs (Dholakia, Bagozzi, & Pearo, 2004; Pentina, Prybutok, & Zhang, 2008).

Within the presence of brand communities, the consumption of brands surpasses their functional use. Brand acquisition becomes symbolic as social gratification is experienced and emotional fulfilment is achieved from the brand (Cova, 1997). Self identification, group identification and involvement in a brand community add to the emotional attachment customers foster for brands. The more emotional feelings are elicited, the greater the prospect that customers will maintain a relationship with the brand (Hwang & Kandampully, 2012). Social media further intensifies customer immersion as the brand assumes a customer-centric approach to generating value within a community built on the principal notion of active engagement with customers (Huy & Shipilov, 2012; Sashi, 2012).

SOCIAL IDENTITY THEORY AND SOCIAL MEDIA

Social media has granted individuals a large platform in relaying identities (Bagozzi & Dholakia, 2002; Bargh & McKenna, 2004; Dholakia, Bagozzi, & Pearo, 2004; Hogg & Reid, 2006; Pentina, Prybutok, & Zhang, 2008; Hennig-Thurau, Gwinner, Walsh & Gremler, 2004; Kane, Alavi, Labianca, & Borgatti, 2014; Schivinski & Dabrowski, 2016; Veletsianos, 2013). By route of social media and subsequent online brand communities, current and aspirational customers are emboldened in voicing affiliation with a brand and consequently augmenting self-presentation. Consumers seek to rely on brands, among the public network of social networking sites, to enhance the self. Customer engagement is consequently heightened and relationships are formed within brand communities as such interchanges promise customers the symbolic benefit of social placement (Algesheimer, Dholakia, & Herrmann, 2005; Ma & Agarwal, 2007; Ren et al., 2012; Zhu & Chen, 2015). Individuals are more compelled to express affiliation with a brand that empowers them to climb the ladder of social enhancement.

Social identification of the self is comprised of two identities, personal and social. Personal identity refers to an identification of personal characteristics; whereas social identity considers a collective identification of the group that the individual belongs to (Luhtanen & Crocker, 1992; Nowak, Szamrej, & Latané, 1990; Onorato & Turner, 2004). Individuals seek to enhance both identities by embracing behaviour that accentuates their individuality; however, individualism that is socially commended.

Customers pursue brands that convey personal attributes, while maintaining societal compliance over a public scale. Drawing on Onorato and Turner's (2004) study to investigate the weight individuals place on either identity, their findings revealed that greater importance is placed on social identity, since personal identity has more of a context-driven, variable nature. Individuals altered their behaviours according to societal standards, especially within circumstances involving high salience. Conspicuous situations influenced individuals to assert behaviour that complied with the salient identity.

Social media is a prime example of a public setting that may exert such social influence. The consolidated global network of users, under a common platform of user-generated content, encourages individuals to express any personal opinion or preference. However, personal identity is shared under the premise that it parallels the salient identity held by the public (Clement & Krueger, 2002; Haslem, Oakes, Reynolds, & Turner, 1999; Hogg & Turner, 1987; Kietzmann, Hermkens, McCarthy, & Silvestre, 2011). Individuals adopt social media as a platform to enforce social inclusion by expressing identical behaviour among the desired social group.

Turner, Oakes, Haslem, & McGarty (1994) describe social identity theory as, "self-categories that define the individual in terms of his or her shared similarities with members of certain social categories in contrast to other social categories." (Turner, Oakes, Haslem, & McGarty, 1994, p.454). Social categories are used as a means of social classification or identification. Individuals form definitions of themselves based on the characteristics of the groups they follow (Hogg & Abrams, 1988; Hogg, Terry, & White, 1995). The self-definition formed by an individual arises from the social categories he/she pursues. Individuals identify themselves with groups of similar social categories that grant them a sense of social consensus from being affiliated with that group (Jenkins, 2008; Tajfel & Turner, 1985; Trepte, 2008). Such social consensus ensures a sense of belonging, and reinforces self-identity. Individuals chase social identification within groups to establish prominent inclusion that is socially recognized (Ashforth & Mael, 1989; Hogg & Terry, 2000). Social identification foments value among individuals as affiliation with the desired group stimulates public perception, and inflates an individual's identity.

Bearden and Etzel (1982) demonstrated a connection between social influence and subsequent consumption behaviour in a study that explored influences between public-private consumption and luxury-necessity dimensions. The findings revealed a significant influence of social reference on the public consumption of luxury products. Motivation for consuming certain products may be elicited through functional values; however noneconomic values are also drawn from investing in the purchases of a particular brand (Arnett, German, & Hunt, 2003; Kleine, Kleine, & Kernan, 1993; Laverie, Kleine III, & Kleine, 2002). Brands are built on foundations of an image and personality that is communicated to the public through brand equity (Aaker, 1996; Keller, 2012). The image of a brand is associated with the brand community it has manifested, and with particular consumers that fit into particular social collectives. Customers seeking to identify with certain groups or consequent statuses may resort to brands and brand communities to advance personal image based on brand equity (Argo, Dahl, & Manchanda, 2005; Gurau, 2012; O'Cass & McEwen, 2004; Bearden & Etzel, 1982). For instance, individuals may adopt pronounced fashion or luxury brands in depicting a level of wealth and establishing identification with a certain socio-economic status.

The desire to establish social consensus among a particular social group drives individuals to exploit brand association across a public platform, like social media. Online brand communities retain a vital presence for consumer assertion of affiliation. Interestingly, brand-customer connections are strengthened as consumers publicly identify with brands in pursuit of building a self-identity based on what that brand represents (Bhattacharya & Sen, 2003; Escalas & Bettman, 2005). Customers form distinct relations with brands through their personal pursuit of gaining the desired social identity.

SOCIAL MEDIA PLATFORMS

Social media constitutes of various Internet-based services enabling audiences to partake in user-generated online interactions; such services range from blogs, wikis, and social networking sites, among others (Campbell, Pitt, Parent & Berthon, 2011, Dewing, 2010; Weinberg & Pehlivan, 2011). Social networking sites especially gained prominence amid recent generations, particularly empowering consumers' open exchange within a formerly restricted market (Bernoff & Li, 2008; Bolton et al., 2013; Dutta, 2010; Hansen, Dunne, & Shneiderman, 2010). The likes of Facebook, Twitter, Instagram, Snapchat as well as blogs have assumed a platform role that has permitted the free-flow of user-generated information among consumers, but also the interchange between companies and customers. While Facebook and Twitter have amassed pronounced success, this study will focus on the surge visual social networking sites such as Instagram, Snapchat and lifestyle blogs have gained in the fashion industry.

Instagram

Social networking sites have created and accelerated dynamic communication settings in which users interchange globally within seconds. This has compelled marketers to adapt accordingly via the utilization of such platforms to promote corresponding brands. One noteworthy social networking site, Instagram, has ensured its mark in generating significant influence, and it has caught the attention of marketers worldwide (Holmes, 2015; Miles, 2014; Kerpen, 2015; Richards, 2015; Macarthy, 2013). Instagram began in 2012 as an easy, direct photo-sharing application, later expanded into a website, allowing universal users to connect through pictures. Almost overnight, Facebook had acquired the application, and Instagram boasted the adoption of over six million users within a six-month period (Holmes, 2015; Miles, 2014). Its simple purpose and layout demonstrated vast success as the mere sharing of photos birthed a fascination for communicating with appealing visuals that ultimately spoke louder than words.

As the name indicates, Instagram revolves around the notion of capturing an 'instant', and sharing it. Unlike Facebook or Twitter, the central theme employs visuals rather than words, aside from the caption or *hashtag*[1], which is part of the post. In addition, through the use of a *hashtag*, the image is shared beyond a constricted line-up of followers (Miles, 2014). The publicity one shared post is capable of accumulating within moments not only underlines the clout the social networking site carries, but also highlights the speed of communication the world has embraced. Marketers have thus assumed their place in such platforms to remain relevant among customers (Kerpen, 2015; Richards, 2015; Macarthy, 2013). Considering the immediacy of Instagram, brands from consequent dynamic industries have found their presence within this progressive portal an effective match in relaying fleeting messages. A study on the influence marketers may expect through Instagram demonstrated the significance a brand successfully exerts on consumers upon employing an active Instagram account with many followers (Veriman, Cauberghe & Hudders, 2017).

Snapchat

One prominent fast-growing social network is Snapchat. Similar to Instagram, Snapchat primarily employs the use of visuals. Founded in 2011, the social networking site was built on the notion of communication via ephemeral photos and videos that last between a timeframe of a few seconds to 24 hours after being posted, to engage its' users in real-time interaction (Snap Inc., 2018). As of the fourth quarter of 2017, Snapchat was reported to have over 185 million active users worldwide on a daily basis, predominantly between the millennial ages of 18 and 24 years old (Statista, 2018). While the social media company is relatively novel to marketers in most industries, the fashion and lifestyle industry holds a leading presence on Snapchat as of late 2017 (Statista, 2018). In a study on the impact of brand presence via Snapchat on college students, Sashittal, DeMar & Jassawalla (2016) produced a figure highlighting the relationship between a brand's use of Snapchat and subsequent brand perception among college students. The results demonstrated greater familiarity linked with brands on Snapchat that ultimately led to intimate brand-customer relationships and emotional association. The higher the brand was placed on an intimacy axis (proportional to its' presence on Snapchat), the more superior that brand's social status was perceived to be (Sashittal, DeMar & Jassawalla, 2016). Another exploratory analysis of brand use of Snapchat demonstrated immense potential for marketers to reach millennials through the spontaneous nature of storytelling and posts on Snapchat (Gomen, Alvarado, Bernabe & Melendez, 2017). As Snapchat is in the midst of being deciphered by marketers, this study indicates significant prospective brand resonance among users if Snapchat is coherently utilised within a brand's marketing communication practice.

An industry that has especially revelled in the use of Instagram and on a successive path in Snapchat is the fashion industry. The nature of immediate and relatively momentary crazes that swarm social networking sites before receding behind the next craze is proportional to the unceasing evolvement the fashion industry is known for. Fashion brand marketers are able to apply this instant marketing tool as a means of promoting ever-changing fashion trends while receiving immediate feedback (Gomen, Alvarado, Bernabe & Melendez, 2017; Kim & Ko, 2012; Sashittal, DeMar & Jassawalla, 2016; Wolny & Mueller, 2013). A brand profits from painting the exact image it wishes to depict on a more intimate level with customers. Instagram and Snapchat serve as channels for brands to interact with, amid key prevailing moments in pop culture to remain relevant among the consuming masses.

Blogs

Apart from operating their own social networking sites and using reference groups, brands have taken the approach of liaising with bloggers to further influence customers (Colliander & Dahlen, 2011). Weblogs or blogs began as dated virtual writing tools for personal use before expanding into globally influential social networking sites run by bloggers of various demographic and geographic backgrounds. Blogs are outlets for any potential bloggers to document life activities, share opinions and feelings and also create relationships with readers in a community (Hsu & Lin, 2008; Kumar, Novak, & Tomkins, 2004; Nardi, Schiano, Gumbrecht, & Swartz, 2004; McKenna & Pole, 2008; Singh, Veron-Jackson, & Cullinane, 2008). This further shapes social identity as readers shadow such blogs as part of an attempt to obtain belonging within a group or community (Dholakia, Bagozzi, & Pearo, 2004; Farrell & Drezner, 2008).

The blog environment of free flowing information within a friendly setting has uniquely captured the attention of marketers to further promote brands as the open nature of blogs, similar to other social media platforms, has minimized the power a brand has over its own reputation (Simmons, 2008). Devoted followers are indirectly fed brand promotions via third parties they occasionally refer to for general advice.

The additional buzz of a brand generated through supplementary websites such as bloggers boosts visibility and allows for further perceptions of brands through eWOM (Weinberg, 2009; Huang, Shen, Lin, & Chang, 2007). Evidently, as users more frequently visit blogs for reference, bloggers gain prominence among users (Colliander & Dahlen, 2011; Rettberg, 2008). Para-social interaction involves the fantasy of having a relationship with a media personality (Horton & Wohl, 1956). While the theory of para-social interaction initially originated from media personalities seen on television or heard on the radio, the following para-social relationship a viewer establishes on television can be paralleled to the relationship a computer-mediated user forms with a brand spokesperson or blogger on social media. Repeated encounters drive customers to develop a strong bond of trust and association with media figures (Ballantine & Martin, 2005; Hoerner, 1999). According to Escalas & Bettman (2017) in a study on consumers' use of celebrities to find belonging, consumers expressed belonging by affiliating to particular brands endorsed by celebrities they established a one-sided (para-social) relationship with. Another study administered on the degree of influence an online personality inflicts on readers indicated that eWOM is received with more credibility and effectiveness when delivered by a particular brand or website representative (Thorson & Rodgers, 2006). Bloggers develop into instrumental reference groups as the pin-up example of trending actions. As consumers develop social identification in which people identify themselves with social groups, consumer behaviour is assessed by brands and reference groups that allow for ideal placement of personal social identity according to model group norms (Langner, Hennigs, & Wiedmann, 2013; Liu & Hu, 2012; Van Knippenberg et al., 2004).

SOCIAL MEDIA ADDED VALUE ON BRANDS

Brand salience is considerably elevated through social media, as one mention of a brand is expected to travel across a global network of receivers. Brand communities accordingly flourish to accommodate wider customer engagement and commitment that progressively fosters into brand loyalty (Chaudhuri & Holbrook, 2001; Chauhun & Pillai, 2013). Companies advancing into a customer-centric environment of users stimulating substantial content require an adjustment of brand promotion that accentuates brand-customer interchange. Considering the paramount importance of brand and customer interactions on social media, managing customers has become an increasingly crucial asset, which is managed comparably to other company assets (Blattberg, Getz, & Thomas, 2001; Da Silva & Alwi, 2008; Hollebeek, Glynn, & Brodie, 2014; Malthouse et al., 2013; Sashi, 2012). The widespread interchange facilitated through social media develops brand perceptions and brand equity that is communicated to all customers alike across prevalent platforms (Keller, 2009; Naylor, Lamberton, & West, 2012). Worldwide users receive the same brand messages that ensure identical brand presentation across all audiences.

Brand equity represents the incremental value that a brand name adds to the product (Feldwick, 1996; Park & Srinivasan, 1994; Rangaswamy, Burke, & Oliva, 1993). Keller (1993) further elaborates on this explanation in noting that "a brand is said to have positive (negative) customer-based brand equity if consumers react more (less) favourably to the product, price, promotion, or distribution of the brand than they do to the same marketing mix element when it is attributed to a fictitiously named or unnamed version of the product or service." (Keller, 1993, p.8). A brand has succeeded in establishing strong brand equity once it exerts a profound impact on a customer that a similar marketing mix approach under a different brand name did not have.

Keller (2001) describes four building blocks that make up customer-based brand equity. These blocks are achieved in sequence and begin with *brand identity*, established through creating *brand salience*. *Brand salience* is described as the brand awareness customers have, and the degree to which they are able to identify a brand. The second block is *brand meaning,* which involves the perspective image customers have towards a brand or brand image. *Brand meaning* includes *brand performance;* the functional aspect of the product belonging to the brand, and *brand imagery* focuses on more of a symbolic approach to how the customer is fulfilled mentally, emotionally or socially. This may include aspects that consider the demographic and psychographic characteristics of a typical customer, the channel through which the brand is sold, the history and personality of the brand and the overall the manner in which the brand is portrayed to customers.

The third block is *brand responses* that refer to *judgments,* in terms of quality or advantage a brand holds, and *feelings,* in terms of the favourability felt from consuming or being associated with the brand. The fourth and final block is *brand relationships*, which considers *brand resonance* and the degree of commitment, loyalty, or engagement a customer may build with a brand (Keller, 2001). The relationship a customer establishes with a brand involves a series of steps from the point at which a customer primarily becomes aware of a brand to when he/she benefits from it functionally or symbolically, and creates a perception of it. It also extends to the moment at which the customer forms feelings towards a brand, and interacts with it well enough to form a connection.

Aaker (1996) identified a similar method to determine brand equity called The Brand Equity Ten. This proposes four classifications to denote how the customer perceives a brand, and a fifth classification, which measures market behaviour. The first category is labelled *loyalty* and comprises of how much a customer is willing to pay for a brand and consequently how fulfilling the experience of consuming the brand was for the customer. The second category, *perceived quality/leadership*, involves what the customer believes will be achieved in terms of functionality and, more importantly, recognition from investing in the brand. The third set is called *association/differentiation*, which involves key factors that distinguish the brand from other brands within the same industry. The next set considers *value,* and this is mainly centred on notions of what the brand physically offers in return for the price paid. This category also considers *brand personality* and how the customer deems the brand by defining the typical customer. Finally, this measure comprises of *organizational association* that focuses on the credibility and reliability of the company. Lastly the *awareness* set reflects on the extent to which a brand is recognized, remembered and truly considered in the market (Aaker, 1996). This brand equity measurement attempts to pinpoint how a customer primarily assesses a brand, according to different categories, before proceeding to consumption.

After the initial awareness stage of a brand, a perception of the potential advantages of using that brand is drawn from the brand image, before an acquisition is made following customer recognition and evaluations of producing brand equity (Aaker, 1991; Biel, 1993; Kirmani & Zeithaml, 2013; Bong Na, Marshall, & Keller, 1999; Ozuem, Howell & Lancaster, 2016b). Lemon et al. (2001) consider customer equity to be at the heart of any effective business strategy that ensures long-term success. Customer equity is driven by value, brand and relationship equity. Value equity comprises of the price, quality, and convenience of consuming a brand. It also refers generally to how a customer evaluates a brand depending on the perception of what is forgone in exchange for the value of the brand. Brand equity is believed to entice, serve as a reminder of the brand, as well as construct customer attitudes towards the brand. Finally, relationship equity ascertains the emotional bond and the prospect that a customer returns to the brand. Relationship equity may be strengthened by how the brand has promised to enhance social identity through consumption (Lemon et al., 2001). The foundation of brand equity is considered through the potential social media exhibits in generating brand awareness. Moreover, whether by conceptualizing the brand through an ideal customer or considering the possible personality that brand personifies (Hoeffler & Keller, 2002; Brakus et al., 2009; Valette-Florence et al., 2011), the brand image that is drawn from a customer's outlook is the chief reflection that embodies brand perceptions in this study.

Social media retains a reach that extends beyond brand communities to touch on prospective customers. The potential of online platforms drives companies to follow suit in the adoption of social media as a vital portal to communicating brand messages (Tiago & Verissimo, 2014). The widespread chatter social media is capable of steering induces awareness and enriches brand knowledge among potential customers (Barwise & Meehan, 2010; Hoffman & Fodor, 2010; Weinberg & Pehlivan, 2011). Wider brand recognition through exposure triggers reassurance among customers as the presumed risk of interacting with, and purchasing from the brand is reduced (Huang, Schrank, & Dubinsky, 2004). Brand awareness assumes the role of a foundation and paves the way to the development of brand equity. Thus, a brand lacking in awareness is subsequently bereft of equity, as it holds no value among consumers (Hakela, Svensson, & Vincze, 2012; Kumar & Mirchandani, 2012). Exposing a brand through multiple platforms, amid the interactive global interchange of social media, manifests brand awareness that underpins the development of a brand's equity. Once a brand has attained initial attention, the ensuing step comprises of delivering an identifiable brand image that an audience can grasp, relate to, and retain for later use. Park et al. (1986) identified three stages in managing a brand image commencing with the *introduction stage,* during which a brand establishes its image and positioning in the market. This allows it to distinctly communicate itself to customers. The second stage, the *elaboration stage,* centres on developing and augmenting the brand image to create value that is superior to, and provides an edge over competitors. Finally, the *fortification stage,* aims to build a consistent image fit to sheltering all subsequent products produced under the following solitary image of a brand. Companies may have succeeded in accentuating brand images through offline outlets; however the advent of presence and communication through social media has pushed brands to evolve brand promotion in accordance with online channels.

Aaker and Joachimsthaler, (2000) describe brand identity as "a set of brand associations that the brand strategist aspires to create or maintain. These associations imply a promise to customers from the organization members." (Aaker & Joachimsthaler, 2000, p.45). Brand identity represents the core that remains consistent to the company and customers throughout a brand's evolvement into new domains such as social media; and hence it acts as the connection between brand and customer (Aaker, 2004; Ghodeswar, 2008). However, the core that forms brand identity consists of exclusive brand associations. The brand image entails a series of associations of a brand carried in the memory of a customer. Brand association begins with brand awareness as certain brand nodes are initially realized and, with repeated exposure, more information is assembled around the brand (Keller, 1993). Based on the following accumulation, customers construct a meaning around the brand.

Social media allows a brand to translucently communicate its own identity through direct communication while offering transparency to its followers via communal interaction, and subsequent customer profiles. It is in the marketers' hands to generate and maintain brand associations that leave a positive impression and distinguish the consequent brand from competitors (Aaker & Keller, 1990; Pitta & Katsanis, 1995; Andzulis, Panagopoulos, & Rapp, 2012; Bolton et al., 2013; Huang & Sarigollu, 2012; Kaplan & Haenlein, 2011; Vermeulen & Seegers, 2008). Another study has shown that such virtual presence exposes brands to a greater chance of expression and richer brand associations, impacting brand evaluations and purchase intentions (Naylor, Lamberton, & West, 2012). Brand-mapping techniques have been constructed to assist companies in identifying the associations customers hold of the brand (John et al., 2006). Brands may apply such techniques in generally evaluating where it is positioned in customers' minds.

As social media depicts the brand on a larger scale, brands must remain mindful that exposure and engagement stretches beyond committed customers to a wider audience (Kozinets et al., 2010; Singh & Sonnenburg, 2012) thus appropriate brand presentation and association is exceedingly crucial to users that are less familiar with the brand. Organizations have succeeded in leveraging social media as a means of accentuating brand associations, and evidently brand perceptions, through the publicity of spokespeople and celebrity endorsers (Cornwell, Roy, & Steinard, 2001; Cornwell, Weeks, & Roy, 2005). The use of influential reference groups creates brand associations that are retained in customers' minds and are evidently associated with the attainment of social consensus. The greater prominence brand associations are able to exert, the greater chance a brand can expect to have in achieving strong brand equity and a competitive edge (Cheng-Hsui Chen, 2001). Another association of brand image that influences perceptions is brand personality. Brand personality has been defined as, "the set of human characteristics associated with a brand." (Aaker, 1997, p.347). As part of digesting a brand, consumers tend to anthropomorphize brands in an attempt to further relate to the label on a humanly level and to better envision and grasp an identity. This also helps them to evaluate the brand in terms of a status enhancer and social group admission (Maehle, Otner, & Supphellen, 2011; Plummer, 2000; Wee, 2004). As a brand establishes an image with human traits constituting a personality, and as it depicts this through boundless platforms via social media, a global consumer perception is drawn (Parker, 2009) that brands are significantly able to manipulate through the widespread communication of social media. Consumer preference further grows as the brand becomes easily identifiable and distinguished and as the symbolic values the brand personality imbues allows customers to extract it from a market of competitors (Biel, 1993; Freling & Forbes, 2005). The subsequent surge of preference in a particular brand emanates loyalty and induces emotion towards that brand. Brands are continually in pursuit of expanding interactions with consumers, beyond the point of purchase, into grounds of connection and emotional brand-customer bonding (Malar et al., 2011; Whan Park et al., 2010; Gobe, 2010). Fashion brands have assumed increasingly active roles on Instagram through posts that communicate the latest trends, campaigns and collaborations that feed into the ultimate fantasy of the brand. This approach has enticed customers as communication transpires past the product into a deeper and more authentic feature of the people, time and effort devoted to creating the outcome of the brand customers see. Brands have thus produced a more intimate nature in reaching and relating to customers. Emotional branding, as such, takes on an angle of richer interchange that inspires and manifests into a relationship with customers (Thompson, Rindfleisch, & Arsel, 2006; Roberts, 2006). The overall emotion-stimulating brand experience further evokes contentment and loyalty (Brakus, Schmitt, & Zarantonello, 2009; Sung & Kim, 2010). According to a study performed on potential influencers of brand equity, the method in which a brand communicates itself coupled with consumer interference, through their own input and promotion, enhances brand equity (Valette-Florence et al., 2011). Social media is thus applied as a complement to a brand's strategy in building a presence and image among viewers.

MANAGERIAL IMPLICATIONS AND RECOMMENDATIONS

The outcome of this paper is that it offers an insight into a relatively unexplored area of how social media influences brand perceptions in the fashion industry, particularly among Millennials (Colliander & Dahlen, 2011; Gensler et al., 2013; Kim & Ko, 2012; Moore, 2012; Singh & Sonnenburg, 2012; Taken Smith, 2012). The results suggest there is much for the fashion industry to be optimistic about in reaching customers through social media by identifying a relationship between social media and social identity in influencing brand perceptions. Millennials (today's main users of social media) express social identity through brand affiliation on social media, depending on that brand's social status.

Brands benefit from the use of social networking sites such as Instagram or Snapchat as dynamic platforms to maintain relevance in real-time events. The consistent brand presence allows for powerful resonance as the brand asserts its' existence in consumers' social world. Brands supplement awareness and image through marketing efforts produced on social media (Godey et al., 2016). Instagram, for example, can be used to entice customers, develop relationships and to draw them to the website or, more conventionally, to stores. Lifestyle bloggers, for instance, use Snapchat and Instagram stories to document authentic day-to-day associations to fashion brands through fashion weeks, promotional events, or product endorsements that assist both brand and blogger in preserving social status among audiences. The fashion industry would benefit from employing social networking sites in promoting never-ending new collections, seasons, runways, and campaigns that define the fashion businesses. Finally, the findings from this study can be used to initiate future research based on a larger sample.

The conception of social media induced a shift in brand-customer dynamic causing consumers to possess more power (Hanna, Rohm, & Crittenden, 2011; Kaplan & Haenlein, 2010; Ngai, Tao and Moon, 2015; Ozuem, Howell & Lancaster, 2008). Brands have transferred communication to the virtual realm in being active pursuers of customers. This study presents a richer understanding of how social media has developed in the fashion industry. Industries are moving at a quicker pace and the fashion sector has become the frontrunner in generating a rapid turnover of ever-changing trends to feed the relentless demand of consumerism. The findings of this research demonstrate the significance of social media as a marketing tool in remaining relevant within the modern world, as traditional methods can no longer sustain such power. This study contributes to the existing literature on marketing to the technologically savvy generation of Millennials (Kilian, Hennigs and Langner, 2012; Moore, 2012; Taken Smith, 2011). This age has grown with the presence of technology and resorts to social media for regular interaction. Brands may find social media beneficial for communicating with such customers in real-time. However, Millennials use offline channels as well, and view social media as a complement to traditional brand outlets. Companies should be mindful of creating an online presence that is in keeping with a brand identity. Brands should reconsider handling social media as a separate entity. Rather, social media should be integrated as a key aspect of a marketing strategy. The content produced through social networking sites represents the brand DNA aligned to fit the entire personality of the brand. This study highlights the importance of integrating online channels into business operations when employing social media as a marketing tool among Millennial ages.

This research contributes to the literature on the application of social identity theory within virtual platforms (Bagozzi & Dholakia, 2002; Ozuem, Thomas & Lancaster, 2016; Dholakia, Bagozzi, & Pearo, 2004; Hogg & Reid, 2006; Pentina, Prybutok, & Zhang, 2008). This study acknowledges the motivations behind the use of social media by consumers for social benefits. Social media extends beyond providing a common portal between brands and customers. Rather it acts as a platform for the two to further relationships. Continuous interaction manifests into a society of casual triad interchange that facilitates belonging, and establishes the symbolic benefits of brand association. This study demonstrates that individuals enjoy the pursuit of specific brands to express their sense of belonging to a social group or status. Connecting with a brand becomes a vital facet to satisfy the personal needs of inclusion within a society, but additionally, to flaunt that association to others. Social media provides the public podium of expressing affiliation and fulfilling social identity through brand communities. Brands can profit from offering customers such non-economic values.

REFERENCES

Aaker, D. (1991). *Managing Brand Equity: Capitalizing on the Value of a Brand Name*. New York: Free Press.

Aaker, D. (1996). Measuring Brand Equity Across Products and Markets. *California Management Review, 38*(3), 102–120. doi:10.2307/41165845

Aaker, D. (2004). Leveraging the Corporate Brand. *California Management Review, 46*(3), 6–18. doi:10.1177/000812560404600301

Aaker, D., & Joachimsthaler, E. (2000). *Brand leadership*. New York: Free Press.

Aaker, D., & Keller, K. (1990). Consumer Evaluations of Brand Extensions. *Journal of Marketing, 54*(1), 27–41. doi:10.2307/1252171

Aaker, J. (1997). Dimensions of Brand Personality. *JMR, Journal of Marketing Research, 34*(3), 347. doi:10.2307/3151897

Adjei, M., Noble, S., & Noble, C. (2009). The influence of C2C communications in online brand communities on customer purchase behavior. *Journal of the Academy of Marketing Science, 38*(5), 634–653. doi:10.100711747-009-0178-5

Alexander, B., & Levine, A. (2008). *Web 2.0 Storytelling Emergence of a New Game*. EDUCAUSE Review.

Algesheimer, R., Dholakia, U., & Herrmann, A. (2005). The Social Influence of Brand Community: Evidence from European Car Clubs. *Journal of Marketing, 69*(3), 19–34. doi:10.1509/jmkg.69.3.19.66363

Amaldoss, W., & Jain, S. (2008). Research Note —Trading Up: A Strategic Analysis of Reference Group Effects. *Marketing Science, 27*(5), 932–942. doi:10.1287/mksc.1070.0350

Anderson, E. (1998). Customer Satisfaction and Word of Mouth. *Journal of Service Research, 1*(1), 5–17. doi:10.1177/109467059800100102

Andzulis, J., Panagopoulos, N., & Rapp, A. (2012). A Review of Social Media and Implications for the Sales Process. *Journal of Personal Selling & Sales Management, 32*(3), 305–316. doi:10.2753/PSS0885-3134320302

Argo, J., Dahl, D., & Manchanda, R. (2005). The Influence of a Mere Social Presence in a Retail Context. *The Journal of Consumer Research, 32*(2), 207–212. doi:10.1086/432230

Arndt, J. (1967). Role of Product-Related Conversations in the Diffusion of a New Product. *JMR, Journal of Marketing Research*, *4*(3), 291–297. doi:10.1177/002224376700400308

Arnett, D., German, S., & Hunt, S. (2003). The Identity Salience Model of Relationship Marketing Success: The Case of Nonprofit Marketing. *Journal of Marketing*, *67*(2), 89–105. doi:10.1509/jmkg.67.2.89.18614

Arora, P. (2014). *The Leisure Commons*. New York: Routledge.

Ashforth, B., & Mael, F. (1989). Social Identity Theory and the Organization. *Academy of Management Review*, *14*(1), 20–39. doi:10.5465/amr.1989.4278999

Ashley, C., & Tuten, T. (2015). Creative Strategies in Social Media Marketing: An Exploratory Study of Branded Social Content and Consumer Engagement. *Psychology and Marketing*, *32*(1), 15–27. doi:10.1002/mar.20761

Atkin, C., & Block, M. (1983). Effectiveness of Celebrity Endorsers. *Journal of Advertising Research*, *23*(1), 57–61.

Bagozzi, R., & Dholakia, U. (2002). Intentional social action in virtual communities. *Journal of Interactive Marketing*, *16*(2), 2–21. doi:10.1002/dir.10006

Baker, A., Donthu, N., & Kumar, V. (2016). Investigating How Word-of-Mouth Conversations About Brands Influence Purchase and Retransmission Intentions. *JMR, Journal of Marketing Research*, *53*(2), 225–239. doi:10.1509/jmr.14.0099

Bakewell, C., & Mitchell, V. (2003). Generation Y female consumer decision-making styles. *International Journal of Retail & Distribution Management*, *31*(2), 95–106. doi:10.1108/09590550310461994

Ballantine, P., & Martin, B. (2005). Forming Parasocial Relationships in Online Communities. *Advances in Consumer Research. Association for Consumer Research (U. S.)*, *32*, 197–201.

Bargh, J., & McKenna, K. (2004). The Internet and Social Life. *Annual Review of Psychology*, *55*(1), 573–590. doi:10.1146/annurev.psych.55.090902.141922 PMID:14744227

Barron, L. (2012). *Social theory in popular culture*. Basingstoke, UK: Palgrave Macmillan.

Barwise, P., & Meehan, S. (2010, December). The One Thing You Must Get Right When Building a Brand. *Harvard Business Review*.

Bearden, W., & Etzel, M. (1982). Reference Group Influence on Product and Brand Purchase Decisions. *The Journal of Consumer Research*, *9*(2), 183–194. doi:10.1086/208911

Bennett, S., Maton, K., & Kervin, L. (2008). The 'digital natives' debate: A critical review of the evidence. *British Journal of Educational Technology*, *39*(5), 775–786. doi:10.1111/j.1467-8535.2007.00793.x

Bernoff, J., & Li, C. (2008). Harnessing the power of the oh-so-social web. *Sloan Management Review*, *49*(3), 36–42.

Berthon, P., Pitt, L., Plangger, K., & Shapiro, D. (2012). Marketing meets Web 2.0, social media, and creative consumers: Implications for international marketing strategy. *Business Horizons*, *55*(3), 261–271. doi:10.1016/j.bushor.2012.01.007

Bhattacharya, C., & Sen, S. (2003). Consumer-Company Identification: A Framework for Understanding Consumers' Relationships with Companies. *Journal of Marketing*, *67*(2), 76–88. doi:10.1509/jmkg.67.2.76.18609

Biel, A. (1993). Converting image into equity in the book. In D. Aaker & A. Biel (Eds.), *Brand equity and advertising: Advertising's role in building strong brands* (1st ed.; pp. 67–82). New York: Psychology Press.

Biyalogorsky, E., Gerstner, E., & Libai, B. (2001). Customer Referral Management: Optimal Reward Programs. *Marketing Science*, *20*(1), 82–95. doi:10.1287/mksc.20.1.82.10195

Blattberg, R., Getz, G., & Thomas, J. (2001). *Customer Equity: Building and Managing Relationships as Valuable Assets*. Boston: Harvard Business School Press.

BOF & McKinsey&Co. (2018*). The State of Fashion 2018*. Retrieved from https://cdn.businessoffashion.com/reports/The_State_of_Fashion_2018_v2.pdf

Bolton, R., Parasuraman, A., Hoefnagels, A., Migchels, N., Kabadayi, S., Gruber, T., ... Solnet, D. (2013). Understanding Generation Y and their use of social media: A review and research agenda. *Journal of Service Management*, *24*(3), 245–267. doi:10.1108/09564231311326987

Bone, P. (1995). Word-of-mouth effects on short-term and long-term product judgments. *Journal of Business Research*, *32*(3), 213–223. doi:10.1016/0148-2963(94)00047-I

Bong Na, W., Marshall, R., & Lane Keller, K. (1999). Measuring brand power: Validating a model for optimizing brand equity. *Journal of Product and Brand Management*, *8*(3), 170–184. doi:10.1108/10610429910272439

Boyd, D., & Ellison, N. (2008). Social network sites: Definition, history, and scholarship. *Journal of Computer-Mediated Communication*, *13*(1), 211.

Brakus, J., Schmitt, B., & Zarantonello, L. (2009). Brand Experience: What Is It? How Is It Measured? Does It Affect Loyalty? *Journal of Marketing*, *73*(3), 52–68. doi:10.1509/jmkg.73.3.52

Brown, J., Broderick, A., & Lee, N. (2007). Word of mouth communication within online communities: Conceptualizing the online social network. *Journal of Interactive Marketing*, *21*(3), 2–20. doi:10.1002/dir.20082

Burke, P. (2006). *Contemporary social psychological theories*. Stanford, CA: Stanford Social Sciences.

Buttle, F. (1998). Word of mouth: Understanding and managing referral marketing. *Journal of Strategic Marketing*, *6*(3), 241–254. doi:10.1080/096525498346658

Campbell, C., Pitt, L., Parent, M., & Berthon, P. (2011). Understanding Consumer Conversations Around Ads in a Web 2.0 World. *Journal of Advertising*, *40*(1), 87–102. doi:10.2753/JOA0091-3367400106

Carlson, B., Suter, T., & Brown, T. (2008). Social versus psychological brand community: The role of psychological sense of brand community. *Journal of Business Research*, *61*(4), 284–291. doi:10.1016/j.jbusres.2007.06.022

Carmeli, A., & Schaubroeck, J. (2007). The influence of leaders' and other referents' normative expectations on individual involvement in creative work. *The Leadership Quarterly*, *18*(1), 35–48. doi:10.1016/j. leaqua.2006.11.001

Chakravarti, A., & Janiszewski, C. (2003). The Influence of Macro-Level Motives on Consideration Set Composition in Novel Purchase Situations. *The Journal of Consumer Research*, *30*(2), 244–258. doi:10.1086/376803

Chaudhuri, A., & Holbrook, M. (2001). The Chain of Effects from Brand Trust and Brand Affect to Brand Performance: The Role of Brand Loyalty. *Journal of Marketing*, *65*(2), 81–93. doi:10.1509/ jmkg.65.2.81.18255

Chauhan, K., & Pillai, A. (2013). Role of content strategy in social media brand communities: A case of higher education institutes in India. *Journal of Product and Brand Management*, *22*(1), 40–51. doi:10.1108/10610421311298687

Cheng-Hsui Chen, A. (2001). Using free association to examine the relationship between the characteristics of brand associations and brand equity. *Journal of Product and Brand Management*, *10*(7), 439–451. doi:10.1108/10610420110410559

Cheung, C., & Thadani, D. (2012). The impact of electronic word-of-mouth communication: A literature analysis and integrative model. *Decision Support Systems*, *54*(1), 461–470. doi:10.1016/j.dss.2012.06.008

Chevalier, J., & Mayzlin, D. (2006). The Effect of Word of Mouth on Sales: Online Book Reviews. *JMR, Journal of Marketing Research*, *43*(3), 345–354. doi:10.1509/jmkr.43.3.345

Childers, T., & Rao, A. (1992). The Influence of Familial and Peer-Based Reference Groups on Consumer Decisions. *The Journal of Consumer Research*, *19*(2), 198–211. doi:10.1086/209296

Chiu, C., Hsu, M., & Wang, E. (2006). Understanding knowledge sharing in virtual communities: An integration of social capital and social cognitive theories. *Decision Support Systems*, *42*(3), 1872–1888. doi:10.1016/j.dss.2006.04.001

Choi, S., & Rifon, N. (2012). It Is a Match: The Impact of Congruence between Celebrity Image and Consumer Ideal Self on Endorsement Effectiveness. *Psychology and Marketing*, *29*(9), 639–650. doi:10.1002/mar.20550

Chu, S., & Kim, Y. (2011). Determinants of consumer engagement in electronic word-of-mouth (eWOM) in social networking sites. *International Journal of Advertising*, *30*(1), 47–75. doi:10.2501/IJA-30-1-047-075

Clement, R., & Krueger, J. (2002). Social Categorization Moderates Social Projection. *Journal of Experimental Social Psychology*, *38*(3), 219–231. doi:10.1006/jesp.2001.1503

Colliander, J., & Dahlén, M. (2011). Following the Fashionable Friend: The Power of Social Media. *Journal of Advertising Research*, *51*(1), 313–320. doi:10.2501/JAR-51-1-313-320

Collin, P., Rahilly, K., Richardson, I., & Third, A. (2011). *The Benefits of Social Networking Services. Research Report*. Melbourne: Cooperative Research Centre for Young People.

Cornwell, T., Roy, D., & Steinard, E. II. (2001). Exploring Managers' Perceptions of the Impact of Sponsorship on Brand Equity. *Journal of Advertising, 30*(2), 41–51. doi:10.1080/00913367.2001.10673636

Cornwell, T., Weeks, C., & Roy, D. (2005). Sponsorship-linked Marketing: Opening the Black Box. *Journal of Advertising, 34*(2), 21–42. doi:10.1080/00913367.2005.10639194

Cova, B. (1997). Community and consumption. *European Journal of Marketing, 31*(3/4), 297–316. doi:10.1108/03090569710162380

Cova, B., & Cova, V. (2001). Tribal aspects of postmodern consumption research: The case of French in-line roller skaters. *Journal of Consumer Behaviour, 1*(1), 67–76. doi:10.1002/cb.54

Da Silva, R., & Alwi, S. (2008). Online brand attributes and online corporate brand images. *European Journal of Marketing, 42*(9/10), 1039–1058. doi:10.1108/03090560810891136

de Valck, K., van Bruggen, G., & Wierenga, B. (2009). Virtual communities: A marketing perspective. *Decision Support Systems, 47*(3), 185–203. doi:10.1016/j.dss.2009.02.008

De Veirman, M., Cauberghe, V., & Hudders, L. (2017). Marketing through Instagram influencers: The impact of number of followers and product divergence on brand attitude. *International Journal of Advertising, 36*(5), 798–828. doi:10.1080/02650487.2017.1348035

Dellarocas, C. (2006). Strategic Manipulation of Internet Opinion Forums: Implications for Consumers and Firms. *Management Science, 52*(10), 1577–1593. doi:10.1287/mnsc.1060.0567

Deloitte. (2016). *Global Fashion & Luxury Market. Private Equity and Investors Survey 2016*. Author.

Dessart, L., Veloutsou, C., & Thomas, A. (2015). Consumer engagement in online brand communities: A social media perspective. *Journal of Product and Brand Management, 24*(1), 28–42. doi:10.1108/JPBM-06-2014-0635

Dewing, M. (2010). *Social Media: An Introduction*. Ottawa: Library of Parliament.

Dhar, V., & Chang, E. (2009). Does Chatter Matter? The Impact of User-Generated Content on Music Sales. *Journal of Interactive Marketing, 23*(4), 300–307. doi:10.1016/j.intmar.2009.07.004

Dholakia, U., Bagozzi, R., & Pearo, L. (2004). A social influence model of consumer participation in network- and small-group-based virtual communities. *International Journal of Research in Marketing, 21*(3), 241–263. doi:10.1016/j.ijresmar.2003.12.004

Dobele, A., Lindgreen, A., Beverland, M., Vanhamme, J., & van Wijk, R. (2007). Why pass on viral messages? Because they connect emotionally. *Business Horizons, 50*(4), 291–304. doi:10.1016/j.bushor.2007.01.004

Duggan, M., Ellison, N., Lampe, C., Lenhart, A., & Madden, M. (2015). Demographics of Key Social Networking Platforms. *PewResearch Center*. Retrieved from http://www.pewinternet.org/2015/01/09/demographics-of-key-social-networking-platforms-2/

Dutta, S. (2010, November). What's Your Personal Social Media Strategy? *Harvard Business Review*, 1–5. PMID:21049685

Eastman, J., Iyer, R., & Thomas, S. (2013). The Impact of Status Consumption on Shopping Style: An Exploratory Look at the Millennial Generation. *The Marketing Management Journal, 23*(1), 57–73.

Eastman, J., & Liu, J. (2012). The impact of generational cohorts on status consumption: An exploratory look at generational cohort and demographics on status consumption. *Journal of Consumer Marketing, 29*(2), 93–102. doi:10.1108/07363761211206348

Economic Times. (2016). *Zara Key Statistics: A detailed report on how Zara is using social media.* Retrieved from http://retail.economictimes.indiatimes.com/social-analytics/Fashion/Zara/494

Edelman, D. (2010). Branding in the digital age: You're spending your money in all the wrong places. *Harvard Business Review*, (88), 62–69.

Ekinci, Y., Sirakaya-Turk, E., & Preciado, S. (2011). Symbolic consumption of tourism destination brands. *Journal of Business Research, 66*(6), 711–718. doi:10.1016/j.jbusres.2011.09.008

Elliott, R., & Wattanasuwan, K. (1998). Brands as Symbolic Resources for the Construction of Identity. *International Journal of Advertising, 17*(2), 131–144. doi:10.1080/02650487.1998.11104712

Enders, A., Hungenberg, H., Denker, H., & Mauch, S. (2008). The long tail of social networking. *European Management Journal, 26*(3), 199–211. doi:10.1016/j.emj.2008.02.002

Engel, C., Bell, R., Meier, R., & Rumpel, J. (2011). Young consumers in the new marketing ecosystem: An analysis of their usage of interactive technologies. *Academy of Marketing Studies Journal, 15*(2), 23–44.

Englis, B., & Solomon, M. (1995). To Be and Not to Be: Lifestyle Imagery, Reference Groups, and The Clustering of America. *Journal of Advertising, 24*(1), 13–28. doi:10.1080/00913367.1995.10673465

Escalas, J., & Bettman, J. (2003). You Are What They Eat: The Influence of Reference Groups on Consumers' Connections to Brands. *Journal of Consumer Psychology, 13*(3), 339–348. doi:10.1207/S15327663JCP1303_14

Escalas, J., & Bettman, J. (2005). Self-Construal, Reference Groups, and Brand Meaning. *The Journal of Consumer Research, 32*(3), 378–389. doi:10.1086/497549

Escalas, J., & Bettman, J. (2017). Connecting With Celebrities: How Consumers Appropriate Celebrity Meanings for a Sense of Belonging. *Journal of Advertising, 46*(2), 297–308. doi:10.1080/00913367.2016.1274925

Evans, D. (2012). *Social Media Marketing: An Hour a Day* (2nd ed.). Indianapolis: John Wiley & Sons Publishing, Inc.

Farrell, H., & Drezner, D. (2008). The power and politics of blogs. *Public Choice, 134*(1-2), 15–30. doi:10.100711127-007-9198-1

Feldwick, P. (1996). Do we really need 'Brand Equity'? *Journal of Brand Management, 4*(1), 9–28. doi:10.1057/bm.1996.23

Fiore, A., Kim, J., & Lee, H. (2005). Effect of image interactivity technology on consumer responses toward the online retailer. *Journal of Interactive Marketing, 19*(3), 38–53. doi:10.1002/dir.20042

Fischer, E., Bristor, J., & Gainer, B. (1996). Creating or escaping community? An exploratory study of Internet consumers' behaviors. *Advances in Consumer Research. Association for Consumer Research (U. S.), 23,* 178–182.

Fischer, E., & Reuber, A. (2011). Social interaction via new social media: (How) can interactions on Twitter affect effectual thinking and behavior? *Journal of Business Venturing, 26*(1), 1–18. doi:10.1016/j.jbusvent.2010.09.002

Flynn, L., Goldsmith, R., & Eastman, J. (1996). Opinion Leaders and Opinion Seekers: Two New Measurement Scales. *Journal of the Academy of Marketing Science, 24*(2), 137–147. doi:10.1177/0092070396242004

Forbes. (2012). *The Future Of Fashion Retailing -- The H&M Approach (Part 3 of 3).* Retrieved from http://www.forbes.com/sites/gregpetro/2012/11/05/the-future-of-fashion-retailing-the-hm-approach-part-3-of-3/#49f3d33d6dbf

Forbes. (2015). *H&M Has Largest Audience On Social Media, Latest Data From Sprinklr Shows.* Retrieved from http://www.forbes.com/sites/fionabriggs/2015/12/22/hm-has-largest-audience-on-social-media-latest-data-from-sprinklr-shows/#4ce692054ac0

Forbes. (2016). *The World's Most Valuable Brands.* Retrieved from http://www.forbes.com/powerful-brands/list/#tab:rank_header:oneYearValueChange_industry:Retail

Fournier, S., & Lee, L. (2009, April). Getting Brand Communities Right. *Harvard Business Review,* 2–8.

Freling, T., & Forbes, L. (2005). An empirical analysis of the brand personality effect. *Journal of Product and Brand Management, 14*(7), 404–413. doi:10.1108/10610420510633350

Fromm, J., & Garton, C. (2013). *Marketing to Millennials.* Barkley, Inc.

Fuchs, C. (2014). *Social Media: A Critical Introduction.* London: Sage Publications, Ltd.

Gensler, S., Völckner, F., Liu-Thompkins, Y., & Wiertz, C. (2013). Managing Brands in the Social Media Environment. *Journal of Interactive Marketing, 27*(4), 242–256. doi:10.1016/j.intmar.2013.09.004

Ghodeswar, B. (2008). Building brand identity in competitive markets: A conceptual model. *Journal of Product and Brand Management, 17*(1), 4–12. doi:10.1108/10610420810856468

Gillies, J., & Cailliau, R. (2000). *How the Web was born.* Oxford, UK: Oxford University Press.

Gilly, M., Graham, J., Wolfinbarger, M., & Yale, L. (1998). A Dyadic Study of Interpersonal Information Search. *Journal of the Academy of Marketing Science, 26*(2), 83–100. doi:10.1177/0092070398262001

Gobé, M. (2010). *Emotional Branding* (2nd ed.). New York: Allworth Press.

Godes, D., & Mayzlin, D. (2009). Firm-Created Word-of-Mouth Communication: Evidence from a Field Test. *Marketing Science, 28*(4), 721–739. doi:10.1287/mksc.1080.0444

Godey, B., Manthiou, A., Pederzoli, D., Rokka, J., Aiello, G., Donvito, R., & Singh, R. (2016). Social media marketing efforts of luxury brands: Influence on brand equity and consumer behavior. *Journal of Business Research, 69*(12), 5833–5841. doi:10.1016/j.jbusres.2016.04.181

Gomez, L., Alvarado, Y., Bernabe, K., & Melendez, L. (2017). Snapchat As An Influential Tool For Marketing Communication: An Exploratory Analysis Of Brands Usage. In *2017 Academy of Marketing Science Annual Conference*. Coronado, CA: 2017 Academy of Marketing Science Annual Conference.

Grucn, T., Osmonbekov, T., & Czaplewski, A. (2006). eWOM: The impact of customer-to-customer online know-how exchange on customer value and loyalty. *Journal of Business Research*, *59*(4), 449–456. doi:10.1016/j.jbusres.2005.10.004

Gu, B., & Ye, Q. (2014). First Step in Social Media: Measuring the Influence of Online Management Responses on Customer Satisfaction. *Production and Operations Management*, *23*(4), 570–582. doi:10.1111/poms.12043

Gummerus, J., Liljander, V., Weman, E., & Pihlström, M. (2012). Customer engagement in a Facebook brand community. *Management Research Review*, *35*(9), 857–877. doi:10.1108/01409171211256578

Gurău, C. (2012). A life-stage analysis of consumer loyalty profile: Comparing Generation X and Millennial consumers. *Journal of Consumer Marketing*, *29*(2), 103–113. doi:10.1108/07363761211206357

Hakala, U., Svensson, J., & Vincze, Z. (2012). Consumer-based brand equity and top-of-mind awareness: A cross-country analysis. *Journal of Product and Brand Management*, *21*(6), 439–451. doi:10.1108/10610421211264928

Hanna, R., Rohm, A., & Crittenden, V. (2011). We're all connected: The power of the social media ecosystem. *Business Horizons*, *54*(3), 265–273. doi:10.1016/j.bushor.2011.01.007

Hansen, D., Dunne, C., & Shneiderman, B. (2010). *Analyzing Social Media Networks with NodeXL*. HCIL University of Maryland.

Haslam, S., Oakes, P., Reynolds, K., & Turner, J. (1999). Social Identity Salience and the Emergence of Stereotype Consensus. *Personality and Social Psychology Bulletin*, *25*(7), 809–818. doi:10.1177/0146167299025007004

Heinonen, K. (2011). Consumer activity in social media: Managerial approaches to consumers' social media behavior. *Journal of Consumer Behaviour*, *10*(6), 356–364. doi:10.1002/cb.376

Hennig-Thurau, T., Gwinner, K., Walsh, G., & Gremler, D. (2004). Electronic word-of-mouth via consumer-opinion platforms: What motivates consumers to articulate themselves on the Internet? *Journal of Interactive Marketing*, *18*(1), 38–52. doi:10.1002/dir.10073

Herr, P., Kardes, F., & Kim, J. (1991). Effects of Word-of-Mouth and Product-Attribute Information on Persuasion: An Accessibility-Diagnosticity Perspective. *The Journal of Consumer Research*, *17*(4), 454–462. doi:10.1086/208570

Hershatter, A., & Epstein, M. (2010). Millennials and the World of Work: An Organization and Management Perspective. *Journal of Business and Psychology*, *25*(2), 211–223. doi:10.100710869-010-9160-y

Hewlet, S., Sherbin, L., & Sumberg, K. (2009, July). How Gen Y & Boomers Will Reshape Your Agenda. *Harvard Business Review*.

Hinz, O., Skiera, B., Barrot, C., & Becker, J. (2011). Seeding Strategies for Viral Marketing: An Empirical Comparison. *Journal of Marketing*, *75*(6), 55–71. doi:10.1509/jm.10.0088

H&M. (2017). *The H&M Group's sales development for the full-year 2017 including the fourth quarter 2017*. Retrieved from https://about.hm.com/en/media/news/financial-reports/2017/12/2765961.html

Hoeffler, S., & Keller, K. (2002). Building Brand Equity Through Corporate Societal Marketing. *Journal of Public Policy & Marketing*, *21*(1), 78–89. doi:10.1509/jppm.21.1.78.17600

Hoerner, J. (1999). Scaling The Web: A Parasocial Interaction Scale for World Wide Web Sites. In D. Schumann & E. Thorson (Eds.), *Advertising and the World Wide Web* (1st ed.; pp. 135–147). Mahwah, NJ: Lawrence Erlbaum Associates.

Hoffman, D., & Fodor, M. (2016). Can you measure the ROI of your social media marketing? *Sloan Management Review*, *52*(1), 41–49.

Hoffman, D., & Novak, T. (1996). Marketing in Hypermedia Computer-Mediated Environments: Conceptual Foundations. *Journal of Marketing*, *60*(3), 50–68. doi:10.2307/1251841

Hogg, M., & Abrams, D. (1988). *Social identifications*. London: Routledge.

Hogg, M., Banister, E., & Stephenson, C. (2009). Mapping symbolic (anti-) consumption. *Journal of Business Research*, *62*(2), 148–159. doi:10.1016/j.jbusres.2008.01.022

Hogg, M., & Reid, S. (2006). Social Identity, Self-Categorization, and the Communication of Group Norms. *Communication Theory*, *16*(1), 7–30. doi:10.1111/j.1468-2885.2006.00003.x

Hogg, M., & Terry, D. (2000). Social Identity and Self-Categorization Processes in Organizational Contexts. *Academy of Management Review*, *25*(1), 121–140. doi:10.5465/amr.2000.2791606

Hogg, M., Terry, D., & White, K. (1995). A Tale of Two Theories: A Critical Comparison of Identity Theory with Social Identity Theory. *Social Psychology Quarterly*, *58*(4), 255–269. doi:10.2307/2787127

Hogg, M., & Turner, J. (1987). Intergroup behaviour, self-stereotyping and the salience of social categories. *British Journal of Social Psychology*, *26*(4), 325–340. doi:10.1111/j.2044-8309.1987.tb00795.x

Hollebeek, L., Glynn, M., & Brodie, R. (2014). Consumer Brand Engagement in Social Media: Conceptualization, Scale Development and Validation. *Journal of Interactive Marketing*, *28*(2), 149–165. doi:10.1016/j.intmar.2013.12.002

Holmes, J. (2015). *Instagram black book*. Lexington, KY: Academic Press.

Horton, D., & Wohl, R. (1956). Mass Communication and Parasocial Interaction: Observations on Intimacy at a Distance. *Psychiatry*, *19*(3), 215–229. doi:10.1080/00332747.1956.11023049 PMID:13359569

Houman Andersen, P. (2001). Relationship development and marketing communication: An integrative model. *Journal of Business and Industrial Marketing*, *16*(3), 167–183. doi:10.1108/08858620110389786

Hsu, C., & Lin, J. (2008). Acceptance of blog usage: The roles of technology acceptance, social influence and knowledge sharing motivation. *Information & Management*, *45*(1), 65–74. doi:10.1016/j.im.2007.11.001

Huang, C., Shen, Y., Lin, H., & Chang, S. (2007). Bloggers' Motivations and Behaviors: A Model. *Journal of Advertising Research, 47*(4), 472–484. doi:10.2501/S0021849907070493

Huang, R., & Sarigöllü, E. (2012). How brand awareness relates to market outcome, brand equity, and the marketing mix. *Journal of Business Research, 65*(1), 92–99. doi:10.1016/j.jbusres.2011.02.003

Huang, W., Schrank, H., & Dubinsky, A. (2004). Effect of brand name on consumers' risk perceptions of online shopping. *Journal of Consumer Behaviour, 4*(1), 40–50. doi:10.1002/cb.156

Hung, K., & Li, S. (2007). The Influence of eWOM on Virtual Consumer Communities: Social Capital, Consumer Learning, and Behavioral Outcomes. *Journal of Advertising Research, 47*(4), 485–495. doi:10.2501/S002184990707050X

Huy, Q., & Shipilov, A. (2012). The key to social media success within organisations. *Sloan Management Review, 54*(1), 73–81.

Hwang, J., & Kandampully, J. (2012). The role of emotional aspects in younger consumer-brand relationships. *Journal of Product and Brand Management, 21*(2), 98–108. doi:10.1108/10610421211215517

Inditex. (2017). *Inditex's net sales climb 10% to €17. 96 billion in the first nine months of fiscal 2017.* Retrieved from https://www.inditex.com/article?articleId=541893&title=Inditex's+net+sales+climb+10%25+to+€17.96+billion

Jang, H., Olfman, L., Ko, I., Koh, J., & Kim, K. (2008). The Influence of On-Line Brand Community Characteristics on Community Commitment and Brand Loyalty. *International Journal of Electronic Commerce, 12*(3), 57–80. doi:10.2753/JEC1086-4415120304

Jayachandran, S., Gimeno, J., & Varadarajan, P. (1999). The Theory of Multimarket Competition: A Synthesis and Implications for Marketing Strategy. *Journal of Marketing, 63*(3), 49–66. doi:10.2307/1251775

Jenkins, R. (2008). *Social identity (Key Ideas)* (3rd ed.). London: Routledge.

Jin, S., & Phua, J. (2014). Following Celebrities' Tweets About Brands: The Impact of Twitter-Based Electronic Word-of-Mouth on Consumers' Source Credibility Perception, Buying Intention, and Social Identification With Celebrities. *Journal of Advertising, 43*(2), 181–195. doi:10.1080/00913367.2013.827606

John, D., Loken, B., Kim, K., & Monga, A. (2006). Brand Concept Maps: A Methodology for Identifying Brand Association Networks. *JMR, Journal of Marketing Research, 43*(4), 549–563. doi:10.1509/jmkr.43.4.549

Jones, S. (1998). Information, Internet and community: Notes toward an understanding of community in the information age. In S. Jones (Ed.), *Cybersocierty 2.0: Revisiting computer-mediated communication and community* (2nd ed.; pp. 1–34). London: Sage Publications. doi:10.4135/9781452243689.n1

Kaikati, A., & Kaikati, J. (2004). Stealth Marketing: How to Reach Consumers Surreptitiously. *California Management Review, 46*(4), 6–22. doi:10.2307/41166272

Kane, G., Alavi, M., Labianca, G., & Borgatti, S. (2014). What's Different About Social Media Networks? A Framework and Research Agenda. *Management Information Systems Quarterly, 38*(1), 274–304. doi:10.25300/MISQ/2014/38.1.13

Kaplan, A., & Haenlein, M. (2010). Users of the world, unite! The challenges and opportunities of Social Media. *Business Horizons, 53*(1), 59–68. doi:10.1016/j.bushor.2009.09.003

Kaplan, A., & Haenlein, M. (2011). Two hearts in three-quarter time: How to waltz the social media/ viral marketing dance. *Business Horizons, 54*(3), 253–263. doi:10.1016/j.bushor.2011.01.006

Katz, E., & Lazarsfeld, P. (1955). *Personal influence.* Glencoe, IL: Free Press.

Keller, K. (1993). Conceptualizing, Measuring, and Managing Customer-Based Brand Equity. *Journal of Marketing, 57*(1), 8. doi:10.1177/002224299305700101

Keller, K. (2001). *Building a Customer-Based Brand Equity: A Blueprint for Creating Strong Brands.* Marketing Science Institute.

Keller, K. (2009). Building strong brands in a modern marketing communications environment. *Journal of Marketing Communications, 15*(2-3), 139–155. doi:10.1080/13527260902757530

Keller, K. (2012). *Strategic brand management* (4th ed.). Upper Saddle River, N.J.: Prentice Hall.

Kelley, H. (1952). Two functions of reference groups. In G. Swanson, T. Newcomb, & E. Hartley (Eds.), *Society for the psychological study of social issues, readings in social psychology* (1st ed.; pp. 410–414). New York: Holt.

Kietzmann, J., Hermkens, K., McCarthy, I., & Silvestre, B. (2011). Social media? Get serious! Understanding the functional building blocks of social media. *Business Horizons, 54*(3), 241–251. doi:10.1016/j. bushor.2011.01.005

Kilian, T., Hennigs, N., & Langner, S. (2012). Do Millennials read books or blogs? Introducing a media usage typology of the Internet generation. *Journal of Consumer Marketing, 29*(2), 114–124. doi:10.1108/07363761211206366

Kim, A., & Ko, E. (2012). Do social media marketing activities enhance customer equity? An empirical study of luxury fashion brand. *Journal of Business Research, 65*(10), 1480–1486. doi:10.1016/j. jbusres.2011.10.014

Kim, J., Choi, J., Qualls, W., & Han, K. (2008). It takes a marketplace community to raise brand commitment: The role of online communities. *Journal of Marketing Management, 24*(3-4), 409–431. doi:10.1362/026725708X306167

Kirmani, A., & Zeithaml, V. (1993). Advertising, perceived quality, and brand image. In D. Aaker & A. Biel (Eds.), *Brand Equity & Advertising: Advertising's Role in Building Strong Brands* (1st ed.; pp. 143–162). Hilldale, NJ: Lawrence Erlbaum Associates.

Kleine, R. III, Kleine, S., & Kernan, J. (1993). Mundane Consumption and the Self: A Social-Identity Perspective. *Journal of Consumer Psychology, 2*(3), 209–235. doi:10.1016/S1057-7408(08)80015-0

Kozinets, R. (1999). E-tribalized marketing?: The strategic implications of virtual communities of consumption. *European Management Journal, 17*(3), 252–264. doi:10.1016/S0263-2373(99)00004-3

Kozinets, R., de Valck, K., Wojnicki, A., & Wilner, S. (2010). Networked Narratives: Understanding Word-of-Mouth Marketing in Online Communities. *Journal of Marketing, 74*(2), 71–89. doi:10.1509/jmkg.74.2.71

Kumar, R., Novak, J., Raghavan, P., & Tomkins, A. (2004). Structure and evolution of blogspace. *Communications of the ACM, 47*(12), 35–39. doi:10.1145/1035134.1035162

Kumar, V., & Mirchandani, R. (2012). Increasing the ROI of social media marketing. *Sloan Management Review, 54*(1), 55–61.

Lam, S., Ahearne, M., Hu, Y., & Schillewaert, N. (2010). Resistance to Brand Switching When a Radically New Brand Is Introduced: A Social Identity Theory Perspective. *Journal of Marketing, 74*(6), 128–146. doi:10.1509/jmkg.74.6.128

Langner, S., Hennigs, N., & Wiedmann, K. (2013). Social persuasion: Targeting social identities through social influencers. *Journal of Consumer Marketing, 30*(1), 31–49. doi:10.1108/07363761311290821

Laudon, K., & Traver, C. (2015). *E-commerce*. Boston: Addison Wesley.

Laverie, D., Kleine, R. III, & Kleine, S. (2002). Reexamination and Extension of Kleine, Kleine, and Kernan's Social Identity Model of Mundane Consumption: The Mediating Role of the Appraisal Process. *The Journal of Consumer Research, 28*(4), 659–669. doi:10.1086/338208

Lemon, K., Rust, R., & Zeithaml, V. (2001). What drives customer equity. *Marketing Management, 10*(1), 20–25.

Levy, S. (1959). Symbols for Sale. *Harvard Business Review*, (37), 117–124.

Li, J., & Su, C. (2007). How face influences consumption. *International Journal of Market Research, 49*(2), 237–246. doi:10.1177/147078530704900207

Liang, T., & Huang, J. (1998). An empirical study on consumer acceptance of products in electronic markets: A transaction cost model. *Decision Support Systems, 24*(1), 29–43. doi:10.1016/S0167-9236(98)00061-X

Lingelbach, D., Patino, A., & Pitta, D. (2012). The emergence of marketing in Millennial new ventures. *Journal of Consumer Marketing, 29*(2), 136–145. doi:10.1108/07363761211206384

Lipsman, A., Mudd, G., Rich, M., & Bruich, S. (2012). The Power of "Like": How Brands Reach (and Influence) Fans through Social-Media Marketing. *Journal of Advertising Research, 52*(1), 40–52. doi:10.2501/JAR-52-1-040-052

Liu, X., & Hu, J. (2012). Adolescent Evaluations of Brand Extensions: The Influence of Reference Group. *Psychology and Marketing, 29*(2), 98–106. doi:10.1002/mar.20507

Luhtanen, R., & Crocker, J. (1992). A Collective Self-Esteem Scale: Self-Evaluation of One's Social Identity. *Personality and Social Psychology Bulletin, 18*(3), 302–318. doi:10.1177/0146167292183006

Luo, X., Zhang, J., & Duan, W. (2013). Social Media and Firm Equity Value. *Information Systems Research*, *24*(1), 146–163. doi:10.1287/isre.1120.0462

Lusch, R. (2007). Marketing's Evolving Identity: Defining Our Future. *Journal of Public Policy & Marketing*, *26*(2), 261–268. doi:10.1509/jppm.26.2.261

LVMH. (2016). *Interim Financial Report Six-Month Period Ended June 30, 2016*. Retrieved from https://r.lvmh-static.com/uploads/2016/06/lvmh-2016-first-half-financial-report.pdf

LVMH. (2018). *LVMH 2017 record results*. Retrieved from https://r.lvmh-static.com/uploads/2018/01/lvmhannualresults2017va.pdf

Ma, M., & Agarwal, R. (2007). Through a Glass Darkly: Information Technology Design, Identity Verification, and Knowledge Contribution in Online Communities. *Information Systems Research*, *18*(1), 42–67. doi:10.1287/isre.1070.0113

Macarthy, A. (2013). *500 Social Media Marketing Tips: Essential Advice, Hints and Strategy for Business*. Charlotte, NC: CreateSpace Independent Publishing Platform.

Maehle, N., Otnes, C., & Supphellen, M. (2011). Consumers' perceptions of the dimensions of brand personality. *Journal of Consumer Behaviour*, *10*(5), 290–303. doi:10.1002/cb.355

Malär, L., Krohmer, H., Hoyer, W., & Nyffenegger, B. (2011). Emotional Brand Attachment and Brand Personality: The Relative Importance of the Actual and the Ideal Self. *Journal of Marketing*, *75*(4), 35–52. doi:10.1509/jmkg.75.4.35

Malthouse, E., Haenlein, M., Skiera, B., Wege, E., & Zhang, M. (2013). Managing Customer Relationships in the Social Media Era: Introducing the Social CRM House. *Journal of Interactive Marketing*, *27*(4), 270–280. doi:10.1016/j.intmar.2013.09.008

Mangold, W., & Faulds, D. (2009). Social media: The new hybrid element of the promotion mix. *Business Horizons*, *52*(4), 357–365. doi:10.1016/j.bushor.2009.03.002

Martin, K., & Smith, N. (2008). Commercializing Social Interaction: The Ethics of Stealth Marketing. *Journal of Public Policy & Marketing*, *27*(1), 45–56. doi:10.1509/jppm.27.1.45

Mayzlin, D. (2006). Promotional Chat on the Internet. *Marketing Science*, *25*(2), 155–163. doi:10.1287/mksc.1050.0137

McAlexander, J., Schouten, J., & Koenig, H. (2002). Building Brand Community. *Journal of Marketing*, *66*(1), 38–54. doi:10.1509/jmkg.66.1.38.18451

McCracken, G. (1989). Who is the Celebrity Endorser? Cultural Foundations of the Endorsement Process. *The Journal of Consumer Research*, *16*(3), 310–321. doi:10.1086/209217

McKenna, L., & Pole, A. (2008). What do bloggers do: An average day on an average political blog. *Public Choice*, *134*(1-2), 97–108. doi:10.100711127-007-9203-8

Michaelidou, N., Siamagka, N., & Christodoulides, G. (2011). Usage, barriers and measurement of social media marketing: An exploratory investigation of small and medium B2B brands. *Industrial Marketing Management*, *40*(7), 1153–1159. doi:10.1016/j.indmarman.2011.09.009

Miles, J. (2014). *Instagram power.* McGraw Hill.

Miller, K., Fabian, F., & Lin, S. (2009). Strategies for online communities. *Strategic Management Journal, 30*(3), 305–322. doi:10.1002mj.735

Moore, M. (2012). Interactive media usage among millennial consumers. *Journal of Consumer Marketing, 29*(6), 436–444. doi:10.1108/07363761211259241

Muniz, A. Jr, & O'Guinn, T. (2001). Brand Community. *The Journal of Consumer Research, 27*(4), 412–432. doi:10.1086/319618

Muniz, A. Jr, & O'Guinn, T. (2016). Brand Community. *The Journal of Consumer Research, 27*(4), 412–432. doi:10.1086/319618

Nardi, B., Schiano, D., Gumbrecht, M., & Swartz, L. (2004). Why we blog. *Communications of the ACM, 47*(12), 41–46. doi:10.1145/1035134.1035163

Naylor, R., Lamberton, C., & West, P. (2012). Beyond the "Like" Button: The Impact of Mere Virtual Presence on Brand Evaluations and Purchase Intentions in Social Media Settings. *Journal of Marketing, 76*(6), 105–120. doi:10.1509/jm.11.0105

Ngai, E., Tao, S., & Moon, K. (2015). Social media research: Theories, constructs, and conceptual frameworks. *International Journal of Information Management, 35*(1), 33–44. doi:10.1016/j.ijinfomgt.2014.09.004

Nowak, A., Szamrej, J., & Latané, B. (1990). From private attitude to public opinion: A dynamic theory of social impact. *Psychological Review, 97*(3), 362–376. doi:10.1037/0033-295X.97.3.362

Nowak, L., Thach, L., & Olsen, J. (2006). Wowing the millennials: Creating brand equity in the wine industry. *Journal of Product and Brand Management, 15*(5), 316–323. doi:10.1108/10610420610685712

O'Cass, A., & McEwen, H. (2004). Exploring consumer status and conspicuous consumption. *Journal of Consumer Behaviour, 4*(1), 25–39. doi:10.1002/cb.155

O'Reilly, T. (2005). *Web 2.0: Compact Definition?* Retrieved from http://radar.oreilly.com/2005/10/web-20-compact-definition.html

O'Reilly, T., & Battelle, J. (2009). *Web Squared: Web 2.0 Five Years On.* O'Reilly Media, Inc.

Onorato, R., & Turner, J. (2004). Fluidity in the self-concept: The shift from personal to social identity. *European Journal of Social Psychology, 34*(3), 257–278. doi:10.1002/ejsp.195

Ozuem, W., Borrelli, M., & Lancaster, G. (2017). Leveraging the co-evolution of offline and online video games: An empirical study. *Journal of Strategic Marketing, 24*(1), 75–97. doi:10.1080/0965254X.2015.1076883

Ozuem, W., Howell, K., & Lancaster, G. (2008). Communicating in the new interactive marketspace. *European Journal of Marketing, 42*(9/10), 1059–1083. doi:10.1108/03090560810891145

Ozuem, W., Howell, K., & Lancaster, G. (2016a). An exploration of consumers' response to online service recovery initiatives. *International Journal of Market Research, 59*(1), 97–115.

Ozuem, W., Howell, K., & Lancaster, G. (2016b). Understanding technologically induced customer services in the Nigerian banking sector: The Internet as a post-modern phenomenon. *International Journal of Information Technology and Management, 15*(3), 272–290. doi:10.1504/IJITM.2016.077349

Ozuem, W., & Tan, K. (2014). Reconciling Social Media with Luxury Fashion Brands: An exploratory study. In L. Aiello (Ed.), *Management of Cultural Products: E-Relationship Marketing and Accessibility Perspective*. Hershey, PA: IGI Publications.

Ozuem, W., Thomas, T., & Lancaster, G. (2016). The Influence of customer loyalty on small island economies: An empirical and exploratory study. *Journal of Strategic Marketing, 24*(6), 447–469. doi:1 0.1080/0965254X.2015.1011205

Park, C., Jaworski, B., & MacInnis, D. (1986). Strategic Brand Concept-Image Management. *Journal of Marketing, 50*(4), 135–145. doi:10.1177/002224298605000401

Park, C., & Srinivasan, V. (1994). A Survey-Based Method for Measuring and Understanding Brand Equity and Its Extendibility. *JMR, Journal of Marketing Research, 31*(2), 271–278. doi:10.2307/3152199

Parker, B. (2009). A comparison of brand personality and brand user-imagery congruence. *Journal of Consumer Marketing, 26*(3), 175–184. doi:10.1108/07363760910954118

Paulin, M. J., Ferguson, R., Jost, N., & Fallu, J. (2014). Motivating millennials to engage in charitable causes through social media. *Journal of Service Management, 25*(3), 334–348. doi:10.1108/JOSM-05-2013-0122

Pentina, I., Prybutok, V., & Zhang, X. (2008). The role of virtual communities as shopping reference groups. *Journal of Electronic Commerce Research, 9*(2), 114–136.

PewResearch. (2014). *Social Media Use by Age Group Over Time*. Retrieved 29 September, from http://www.pewinternet.org/data-trend/social-media/social-media-use-by-age-group/

Pitta, D., & Katsanis, L. (1995). Understanding brand equity for successful brand extension. *Journal of Consumer Marketing, 12*(4), 51–64. doi:10.1108/07363769510095306

Plummer, J. (2000). How Personality Makes a Difference. *Journal of Advertising Research, 40*(6), 79–83. doi:10.2501/JAR-40-6-79-83

Prensky, M. (2001). Digital Natives, Digital Immigrants Part 1. *On the Horizon, 9*(5), 1–6. doi:10.1108/10748120110424816

Rainer, T., & Rainer, J. (2011). *The Millennials: Connecting to America's Largest Generation*. Nashville, TN: B & H Pub. Group.

Rangaswamy, A., Burke, R., & Oliva, T. (1993). Brand equity and the extendibility of brand names. *International Journal of Research in Marketing, 10*(1), 61–75. doi:10.1016/0167-8116(93)90034-V

Ren, Y., Harper, M., Drenner, S., Terveen, L., Kiesler, S., Riedl, J., & Kraut, R. (2012). Building member attachment in online communities: Applying theories of group identity and interpersonal bonds. *Management Information Systems Quarterly, 36*(3), 841–864. doi:10.2307/41703483

Rettberg, J. (2008). *Blogging: Digital Media and Society Series*. Cambridge, UK: Polity.

Richards, M. (2015). *Social Media: Dominating Strategies for Social Media Marketing*. CreateSpace Independent Publishing Platform.

Riedinger, D. (2015). *Likeable Social Media, Revised and Expanded* (2nd ed.). McGraw-Hill.

Robards, B., & Bennett, A. (2011). MyTribe: Post-subcultural Manifestations of Belonging on Social Network Sites. *Sociology*, *45*(2), 303–317. doi:10.1177/0038038510394025

Roberts, K. (2006). *Lovemarks: The future beyond brands* (2nd ed.). New York: PowerHouse Books.

Roy, A., & Chattopadhyay, S. (2010). Stealth marketing as a strategy. *Business Horizons*, *53*(1), 69–79. doi:10.1016/j.bushor.2009.09.004

Safko, L. (2012). *The social media bible: Tactics, tools, and strategies for business success*. Hoboken, NJ: John Wiley & Sons.

Sashi, C. (2012). Customer engagement, buyer-seller relationships, and social media. *Management Decision*, *50*(2), 253–272. doi:10.1108/00251741211203551

Sashittal, H., DeMar, M., & Jassawalla, A. (2016). Building acquaintance brands via Snapchat for the college student market. *Business Horizons*, *59*(2), 193–204. doi:10.1016/j.bushor.2015.11.004

Schau, H., Muñiz, A. Jr, & Arnould, E. (2009). How Brand Community Practices Create Value. *Journal of Marketing*, *73*(5), 30–51. doi:10.1509/jmkg.73.5.30

Schivinski, B., & Dabrowski, D. (2016). The effect of social media communication on consumer perceptions of brands. *Journal of Marketing Communications*, *22*(2), 189–214. doi:10.1080/13527266.2013.871323

Schlosser, A. (2005). Posting versus Lurking: Communicating in a Multiple Audience Context. *The Journal of Consumer Research*, *32*(2), 260–265. doi:10.1086/432235

Senecal, S., & Nantel, J. (2004). The influence of online product recommendations on consumers' online choices. *Journal of Retailing*, *80*(2), 159–169. doi:10.1016/j.jretai.2004.04.001

Seno, D., & Lukas, B. (2007). Exploring the relationship between celebrity endorser effects and advertising effectiveness. *European Journal of Marketing*, *41*(1/2), 121–134. doi:10.1108/03090560710718148

Sheth, J., & Parvatlyar, A. (1995). Relationship Marketing in Consumer Markets: Antecedents and Consequences. *Journal of the Academy of Marketing Science*, *23*(4), 255–271. doi:10.1177/009207039502300405

Shibutani, T. (1955). Reference Groups as Perspectives. *American Journal of Sociology*, *60*(6), 562–569. doi:10.1086/221630

Simmons, G. (2008). Marketing to postmodern consumers: Introducing the internet chameleon. *European Journal of Marketing*, *42*(3/4), 299–310. doi:10.1108/03090560810852940

Singh, S., & Sonnenburg, S. (2012). Brand Performances in Social Media. *Journal of Interactive Marketing*, *26*(4), 189–197. doi:10.1016/j.intmar.2012.04.001

Singh, T., Veron-Jackson, L., & Cullinane, J. (2008). Blogging: A new play in your marketing game plan. *Business Horizons*, *51*(4), 281–292. doi:10.1016/j.bushor.2008.02.002

Smith, A., & Anderson, M. (2018). *Social Media Use in 2018*. PewResearch Center. Retrieved from http://assets.pewresearch.org/wp-content/uploads/sites/14/2018/03/01105133/PI_2018.03.01_Social-Media_FINAL.pdf

Smith, K. (2011). Digital marketing strategies that Millennials find appealing, motivating, or just annoying. *Journal of Strategic Marketing, 19*(6), 489–499. doi:10.1080/0965254X.2011.581383

Smith, P., & Zook, Z. (2011). *Marketing Communications* (5th ed.). London: Kogan Page.

Smith, T. (2009). The social media revolution. *International Journal of Market Research, 51*(4), 559–561. doi:10.2501/S1470785309200773

Snap Inc. (2018). Retrieved from https://www.snap.com/en-US/

Solomon, M. (2012). *Consumer behavior* (10th ed.). Pearson Education Limited.

Statista. (2016a). London Fashion Week: Social Buzz 2014. Social Media & User-Generated Content. *Statista - The Statistic Portal*. Retrieved 18 January 2016, from http://www.statista.com/statistics/315224/social-media-mentions-london-fashion-week/

Statista. (2016b). *Leading luxury brands ranked by number of Instagram followers as of October 2016 (in millions)*. Retrieved 29 September 2016, from https://www.statista.com/statistics/483753/leading-luxury-brands-instagram-followers/

Statista. (2016c). *Daily time spent on social networking by internet users worldwide as of 2nd quarter 2016, by age group (in minutes)*. Retrieved 5 March 2018, from https://www.statista.com/statistics/613456/daily-social-media-usage-worldwide-age/

Statista. (2016d). *Global apparel market size projections from 2012 to 2025, by region (in billion U.S. dollars)*. Retrieved 29 September 2016, from https://www.statista.com/statistics/279757/apparel-market-size-projections-by-region/

Statista. (2016e). *Brand value of the leading 10 apparel brands worldwide in 2016 (in million U.S. dollars)*. Retrieved 29 September 2016, from https://www.statista.com/statistics/267931/brand-value-of-the-leading-10-apparel-brands-worldwide/

Statista. (2016f). *Sales of the H&M Group from 2008 to 2015, by country (in million U.S. dollars)*. Retrieved 29 September 2016, from https://www.statista.com/statistics/252187/sales-of-the-hundm-group-by-country/

Statista. (2016g). *Leading luxury brands ranked by number of Instagram followers as of October 2016 (in millions)*. Retrieved 29 September 2016, from https://www.statista.com/statistics/483753/leading-luxury-brands-instagram-followers/

Statista. (2016h). *Leading high street fashion labels ranked by Instagram user engagement as of May 2016*. Retrieved 6 March 2018, from https://www.statista.com/statistics/677609/high-street-fashion-labels-instagram-engagement/

Statista. (2017a). *Daily time spent on social media by social video viewers worldwide as of 2ⁿᵈ quarter 2017, by age group.* Retrieved 5 March 2018, from https://www.statista.com/statistics/267138/social-media-usage-per-day-global-social-video-users-age/

Statista. (2017b). *Sources used by Millennials to hear about the latest high-end fashion or luxury item trends worldwide in 2017.* Retrieved 5 March 2018, from https://www.statista.com/statistics/441758/sources-for-hearing-about-new-luxury-brands-worldwide/

Statista. (2017c). *Worldwide forecasted sales growth in the fashion industry in 2018, by region.* Retrieved 6 March 2018, from https://www.statista.com/statistics/802943/fashion-industry-sales-growth-worldwide-by-region/

Statista. (2018a). *Most famous social network sites worldwide as of January 2018, ranked by number of active users (in millions).* Retrieved 6 March 2018, from https://www.statista.com/statistics/272014/global-social-networks-ranked-by-number-of-users/

Statista. (2018b). *Number of daily active Snapchat users from 1ˢᵗ quarter 2017 to 4ᵗʰ quarter 2017 (in millions).* Retrieved 27 March 2018, from https://www.statista.com/statistics/545967/snapchat-app-dau/

Stephen, A., & Galak, J. (2010). The Complementary Roles of Traditional and Social Media in Driving Marketing Performance. *INSEAD Working Papers Collections*, *2010*(97).

Stern, B. (1994). A Revised Communication Model for Advertising: Multiple Dimensions of the Source, the Message, and the Recipient. *Journal of Advertising*, *23*(2), 5–15. doi:10.1080/00913367.1994.10673438

Stokinger, E., & Ozuem, W. (2015). Social media and customer retention in the luxury fashion sector. In G. Bowen & W. Ozuem (Eds.), *Computer-mediated marketing strategies: social media and online brand communities*. Hershey, PA: IGI. doi:10.4018/978-1-4666-6595-8.ch009

Strauss, W., & Howe, N. (1991). *Generations: The History of America's Future*. New York: Morrow.

Sung, Y., & Kim, J. (2010). Effects of brand personality on brand trust and brand affect. *Psychology and Marketing*, *27*(7), 639–661. doi:10.1002/mar.20349

Susarla, A., Oh, J., & Tan, Y. (2012). Social Networks and the Diffusion of User-Generated Content: Evidence from YouTube. *Information Systems Research*, *23*(1), 23–41. doi:10.1287/isre.1100.0339

Sweeney, J., Soutar, G., & Mazzarol, T. (2008). Factors influencing word of mouth effectiveness: Receiver perspectives. *European Journal of Marketing*, *42*(3/4), 344–364. doi:10.1108/03090560810852977

Tajfel, H., & Turner, J. (1985). The Social Identity Theory of Intergroup Behaviour. In S. Worchel & W. Austen (Eds.), *Psychology of intergroup relations* (2nd ed.; pp. 7–24). Chicago: Nelson-Hall.

Taken Smith, K. (2012). Longitudinal study of digital marketing strategies targeting Millennials. *Journal of Consumer Marketing*, *29*(2), 86–92. doi:10.1108/07363761211206339

Thompson, C., Rindfleisch, A., & Arsel, Z. (2006). Emotional Branding and the Strategic Value of the Doppelgänger Brand Image. *Journal of Marketing*, *70*(1), 50–64. doi:10.1509/jmkg.2006.70.1.50

Thorson, K., & Rodgers, S. (2006). Relationships Between Blogs as EWOM and Interactivity, Perceived Interactivity, and Parasocial Interaction. *Journal of Interactive Advertising*, *6*(2), 5–44. doi:10.1080/15 252019.2006.10722117

Tiago, M., & Veríssimo, J. (2014). Digital marketing and social media: Why bother? *Business Horizons*, *57*(6), 703–708. doi:10.1016/j.bushor.2014.07.002

Trepte, S. (2008). Social Identity Theory. In J. Bryant & P. Vorderer (Eds.), *Psychology of Entertainment* (2nd ed.; pp. 255–271). New York: Routledge.

Trusov, M., Bucklin, R., & Pauwels, K. (2009). Effects of Word-of-Mouth Versus Traditional Marketing: Findings from an Internet Social Networking Site. *Journal of Marketing*, *73*(5), 90–102. doi:10.1509/ jmkg.73.5.90

Tsai, W., & Ghoshal, S. (1998). Social capital and value creation: The role of intrafirm networks. *Academy of Management Journal*, *41*(4), 464–476.

Tsimonis, G., & Dimitriadis, S. (2014). Brand strategies in social media. *Marketing Intelligence & Planning*, *32*(3), 328–344. doi:10.1108/MIP-04-2013-0056

Turner, J., Oakes, P., Haslam, S., & McGarty, C. (1994). Self and Collective: Cognition and Social Context. *Personality and Social Psychology Bulletin*, *20*(5), 454–463. doi:10.1177/0146167294205002

Tuten, T., & Solomon, M. (2014). *Social Media Marketing* (2nd ed.). Boston: Pearson.

Twenge, J. (2006). *Generation Me: Why today's young Americans are more confident, assertive, entitled- -and more miserable than ever before*. New York: Free Press.

Twenge, J., Campbell, W., & Freeman, E. (2012). Generational differences in young adults' life goals, concern for others, and civic orientation, 1966–2009. *Journal of Personality and Social Psychology*, *102*(5), 1045–1062. doi:10.1037/a0027408 PMID:22390226

Valentine, D., & Powers, T. (2013). Generation Y values and lifestyle segments. *Journal of Consumer Marketing*, *30*(7), 597–606. doi:10.1108/JCM-07-2013-0650

Valette-Florence, P., Guizani, H., & Merunka, D. (2011). The impact of brand personality and sales promotions on brand equity. *Journal of Business Research*, *64*(1), 24–28. doi:10.1016/j.jbusres.2009.09.015

Van Dijck, J. (2013). *The culture of connectivity*. Oxford, UK: Oxford University Press. doi:10.1093/ac prof:oso/9780199970773.001.0001

van Knippenberg, D., van Knippenberg, B., De Cremer, D., & Hogg, M. (2004). Leadership, self, and identity: A review and research agenda. *The Leadership Quarterly*, *15*(6), 825–856. doi:10.1016/j. leaqua.2004.09.002

Vargo, S., & Lusch, R. (2004). Evolving to a New Dominant Logic for Marketing. *Journal of Marketing*, *68*(1), 1–17. doi:10.1509/jmkg.68.1.1.24036

Veletsianos, G. (2013). Open practices and identity: Evidence from researchers and educators' social media participation. *British Journal of Educational Technology*, *44*(4), 639–651. doi:10.1111/bjet.12052

Veloutsou, C., & Moutinho, L. (2009). Brand relationships through brand reputation and brand tribalism. *Journal of Business Research, 62*(3), 314–322. doi:10.1016/j.jbusres.2008.05.010

Vermeulen, I., & Seegers, D. (2009). Tried and tested: The impact of online hotel reviews on consumer consideration. *Tourism Management, 30*(1), 123–127. doi:10.1016/j.tourman.2008.04.008

Vogel, V., Evanschitzky, H., & Ramaseshan, B. (2008). Customer Equity Drivers and Future Sales. *Journal of Marketing, 72*(6), 98–108. doi:10.1509/jmkg.72.6.98

v. Wangenheim, F., & Bayón, T. (2004). The effect of word of mouth on services switching. *European Journal of Marketing, 38*(9/10), 1173–1185. doi:10.1108/03090560410548924

Webster, F. (1992). The Changing Role of Marketing in the Corporation. *Journal of Marketing, 56*(4), 1–17. doi:10.2307/1251983

Wee, T. (2004). Extending human personality to brands: The stability factor. *Journal of Brand Management, 11*(4), 317–330. doi:10.1057/palgrave.bm.2540176

Weinberg, B., & Pehlivan, E. (2011). Social spending: Managing the social media mix. *Business Horizons, 54*(3), 275–282. doi:10.1016/j.bushor.2011.01.008

Weinberg, T. (2009). *The New Community Rules: Marketing on the Social Web*. Sebastopol, CA: O'Reilly Media, Inc.

Whan Park, C., MacInnis, D., Priester, J., Eisingerich, A., & Iacobucci, D. (2010). Brand Attachment and Brand Attitude Strength: Conceptual and Empirical Differentiation of Two Critical Brand Equity Drivers. *Journal of Marketing, 74*(6), 1–17. doi:10.1509/jmkg.74.6.1

Wirtz, J., den Ambtman, A., Bloemer, J., Horváth, C., Ramaseshan, B., van de Klundert, J., ... Kandampully, J. (2013). Managing brands and customer engagement in online brand communities. *Journal of Service Management, 24*(3), 223–224. doi:10.1108/09564231311326978

Wolny, J., & Mueller, C. (2013). Analysis of fashion consumers' motives to engage in electronic word-of-mouth communication through social media platforms. *Journal of Marketing Management, 29*(5-6), 562–583. doi:10.1080/0267257X.2013.778324

WSJ. (2016). *H&M Hennes & Mauritz AB Series B*. Retrieved from http://quotes.wsj.com/SE/XSTO/HMB/financials

Wu, J., Huang, L., Zhao, J., & Hua, Z. (2015). The deeper, the better? Effect of online brand community activity on customer purchase frequency. *Information & Management, 52*(7), 813–823. doi:10.1016/j.im.2015.06.001

You, Y., Vadakkepatt, G., & Joshi, A. (2015). A Meta-Analysis of Electronic Word-of-Mouth Elasticity. *Journal of Marketing, 79*(2), 1–39. doi:10.1509/jm.14.0169

Zarrella, D. (2009). *The Social Media Marketing Book*. Sebastopol, CA: O'Reilly Media, Inc.

Zhu, Y., & Chen, H. (2015). Social media and human need satisfaction: Implications for social media marketing. *Business Horizons, 58*(3), 335–345. doi:10.1016/j.bushor.2015.01.006

KEY TERMS AND DEFINITIONS

Brand Associations: Brand associations are the main factors that differentiate one brand from another.

Brand Equity: Brand equity is the value of a brand based on the consumer's perception of that brand in his/her mind.

Brand Perceptions: Brand perceptions are consumers' perceptions of the potential advantages, disadvantages or overall image portrayed from consuming a certain brand.

E-WOM: E-WOM involves the online exchange of information about a product among customers.

Fashion Industry: The fashion industry comprises a global enterprise that involves the production, retail, and consumption of clothing.

Millennial Generation: The millennial generation is a demographic cohort born between the early 1980s and the early 2000s and raised in a technological age where communication has become globally boundless.

Social Identity Theory: Social identity theory considers how individuals may classify themselves or others according to certain social categories.

Social Media: Social media comprises internet-centered platforms that enable and promote a free flow of user-generated information.

ENDNOTE

[1]   A *hashtag* acts as a form of categorization so that any user searching a topic will be exposed to a considerable volume of images (Miles, 2014).

Section 2

Development and Design Methodologies

Chapter 10
An Absorptive Capacity Perspective of Organizational Learning Through Social Media:
Evidence From the Ghanaian Fashion Industry

Richard Boateng
https://orcid.org/0000-0002-9995-3340
University of Ghana, Ghana

Edna Owusu-Bempah
University of Ghana, Ghana

Eric Ansong
https://orcid.org/0000-0002-0262-3485
University of Ghana, Ghana

ABSTRACT

The Absorptive Capacity Theory was used as the theoretical lens for this study to help analyze how organizations absorb new knowledge using social media tools and applications. A survey of fashion designers and employees numbering 196 was carried out in 55 fashion firms whereas two fashion firms were used in a case study. Data analysis was performed using the Structural Equation Modelling. The findings from the study suggest that Ghanaian fashion designers do not intensively use social media to assimilate knowledge but rather to acquire, transform and exploit knowledge. The popular social media applications include; Facebook, Twitter, and Instagram. Facebook, for instance, is used on a daily basis by most Ghanaian fashion designers. Fashion designers use social media to acquire, transform and exploit knowledge through research, interaction, communication, and marketing with suppliers, customers, and other fashion designers. Future research can extend this work by looking at organizational learning and social media use in a different industry.

DOI: 10.4018/978-1-7998-9020-1.ch010

INTRODUCTION

Organizational learning is necessary for the successful operation of organizations. Businesses thrive on information and this information accumulates forming a knowledge base. Such knowledge can be acquired both internally and externally and must be managed properly to achieve organizational set goals and objectives (Karkoulian, Messarra & McCarthy, 2013). Therefore, it can be argued that communities that have mechanisms that create and connect relationships between individuals to work collectively for common goals is an organization (Boateng et al., 2009). According to Nonaka, Toyama and Konno (1998), critical among these mechanisms are those that result in sharing information and make the cognitive map of individuals, as employees, accessible for the greater good; thus, creating collective knowledge. Organizations learn and create knowledge through dynamic interactions between employees. Organizations have long recognized knowledge management (KM) as an important business strategy (Hull, Coombs & Peltu, 2000). A 2001 United States Government Accountability Office (GAO) report indicated that a substantial portion of the federal workforce would become eligible to retire or will retire over the next five to 10 years, and hence workforce planning is critical to ensure that agencies have sufficient and appropriate staff to account for these retirements. Usually, when people leave an organization, they take a wealth of knowledge about their jobs with them. Consequently, Lien, Hung, Yang and Li (2006) posits that firms have to pay particular attention to the enhancement of their learning patterns. One of the ways through which organizations can learn is through the use of social media tools or applications to acquire and also disseminate information both internally and externally (O'Reilly, 2005).

Quite a number of organizations have been asking what they can use social media for. Current literature demonstrates a dominance on social media and marketing (Hanna, 2011). On the other hand, in IS literature, social media has been studied from the perspectives of social media and text mining; social media and crisis management; and social media and organizational learning.

One very important area of study regarding social media is social media and text mining. He et al. (2013) carried out an in-depth case study, which applies text mining to analyse unstructured text content on Facebook and Twitter sites of the three largest pizza chains: Pizza Hut, Domino's Pizza and Papa John's Pizza. Results from the text mining and social media competitive analysis show that these pizza chains actively engaged their customers in social media. They suggested future research focus on finding innovative ways to turn businesses' social media fans from "like" to "buy". For example, pizzerias will have to provide consumers easy ways to purchase pizzas using social media from "selecting pizza, adding their selections to shopping carts, and completing purchases through payment with credit cards and points". Rickman and Cosenza (2007) have also examined the theoretical/conceptual development and application of weblog-text mining to fashion forecasting in general and street fashion trending in particular. They postulate that future research should look at semantic and image mining of the web as the next frontiers of data mining and trend spotting. According to Kaiser and Bodendorf (2012), combining text mining and social network analysis enables the study of opinion formation and yields encouraging results. They analysed opinion formation based on consumer dialogs in online forum.

Another area, which has also been studied is social media and organizational learning. A study by Bochenek and Blili (2013) looked at four companies of different sizes, different scopes of operation, and different industries. They found that all the companies learn socially and use social media to strengthen the organization and build business benefits through using social media as a marketing tool and having a strategic framework that makes the company active on social media. Their learning patterns (the learning process and the learning aggregation in social media) are, however, different. It shows that social media is beyond being a tool. They propose that future research should study a larger sample of companies in order to see the learning patterns and profiles of strategic management of social media at the statistically important level. A collaborative setting based on social media principles enables the sharing of different insights on current topic, and therefore adds value to an outcome by enriching information (Vuori & Okkonen, 2012). Chua and Banerjee (2013) analysed the extent to which the use of social media can support customer knowledge management (CKM) in organizations relying on a traditional bricks-and-mortar business model. From their findings, social media is not a tool exclusive to online businesses. It can be a potential game-changer in supporting CKM efforts even for traditional businesses.

Most of these research works on learning processes of organizations were carried out in developed countries (Vuori & Okkonen, 2012; Chua & Banerjee, 2013), little has been carried out in developing countries (Grabski, 2009), specifically Ghana. Moreover, there have been arguably no studies on organizational learning through social media using the Absorptive Capacity Theory as its theoretical lens, ascertaining the need for this study. Also, the most apparent gap in the use of methods was the lack of studies using the mixed-method approach. The qualitative studies tend to dominate this area of study.

Diverse studies have been carried out relating to social media as discussed above. However, this research would do an analysis of how organizations using social media and to understand the knowledge absorption process using the Absorptive Capacity Theory (ACT), which will serve as the theoretical lens for this research. To achieve the research purpose, the following objectives are outlined:

1. To describe the forms of learning for firms in the fashion industry;
2. To describe the sources of learning for firms in the fashion industry; and
3. To explain how social media supports learning in the fashion industry.

The first section is therefore the introduction to this paper. The second section also presents a review of literature pertaining to organizational learning and social media including the research framework that was adopted for this study. The constructs and variables of the framework are explained followed by how they were measured. The third section presents the study setting by providing a brief overview of the Ghanaian fashion industry studying specifically Vlisco and Nallem Clothing. The fifth section describes the research methodology adopted, which includes research design, data collection procedure and development of data collection instruments. The sixth section discusses the data collected from the field and is analysed using Structural Equation Modelling (SEM) and qualitative analysis. The last section presents a summary of the key findings, and contributions made to the study of organizational learning through social media in the Ghanaian fashion industry. Implications for practice and recommendations for future research are also mentioned in this section.

LITERATURE REVIEW

This section comprises of a brief overview of absorption or learning, the social media and learning as well as the research framework for the study which is Absorptive Capacity Theory.

Learning Through Web 2.0

Through knowledge sharing and interaction with people there may be an emerging opportunity for organizations to adapt Web 2.0 for learning. The need to learn and the learning process in organizations are addressed by this opportunity. Web 2.0 can be considered as a learning enabler that allows people to access their knowledge and share with others. Individuals who use Web 2.0 applications are able to create knowledge more efficiently than the conventional methods because of their collaboration properties. It is through this collaboration that knowledge can be shared at the two levels; individual and collective. At the organizational level, knowledge assets must be made accessible by the tools that enable learning (Dixon, 1994; 2000); Web 2.0 facilitates this. The idea is to make internal knowledge visible and to access external sources of new knowledge through 'boundary spanning' (Pawlosky et al., 2001).

For the purpose of this study, social media will include Instant Messaging tools (WhatsApp), Content Management tools (YouTube, Blogger), and social media tools (Facebook, Twitter). Some of these tools are under Web 2.0 technologies.

Absorption/Learning and Social Media

The process of acquiring knowledge is termed learning (Cook & Yanow, 1993). Learning can occur at two levels; the individual and the organizational levels. Employees within an organization can acquire knowledge to facilitate their specific business roles; however, to achieve organizational goals such knowledge must be diffused to other parts of the organization (Hong, 1999). Organizational learning implies knowledge acquisition by members across the organization and the diffusion of lessons learnt by individuals to other parts of the organization to enhance collective understanding, adaptation and easy response to change (Dodgson, 1993).

Arguably, not all learning leads to adaptation. Similarly, not all learning at the individual level generates into learning at the organizational level. Learning occurs in a more limited form and in a less significant way in some organizations. Such learning does not lead to a reassessment of values and adaptation.

There are different types and methods of learning. Argyris and Schön (1978) postulate three types of learning that happen within an organization, namely: single loop-learning; double-loop learning; and deutro-learning. Single-loop learning happens when an organization identifies an error and undertakes corrective measures without questioning or transforming its current policy. Double-loop learning also occurs when the error detected which has to be corrected requires alteration of the organization's underlying policies, norms and objectives. Basic assumptions are re-tested in the quest to understand the problem faced. With deutro-learning, members develop new strategies after they have learnt about previous context of learning and have understood the reasons behind the ability and inability to learn in previous context. According to Dodgson (1993), Organisational learning starts with double-loop learning. Very few organizations are effective with double-loop and deutro-learning; however, most of them tend to do well with single-loop learning.

Social media tends to enhance collaboration within an organization. Social media is certainly in the public eye at the moment. For instance, 2013 statistics from Alexa.com depicts that social media is ranked the 2nd top website out of the top 500 websites worldwide. Today, Facebook is the largest social network in the world with more than 5000 active users of whom 50% log in on a daily basis. It is not surprising therefore, that marketers are devising ways to use Facebook to reach their target audience. In our working lives, an aspect where collaboration plays an important role is the aspect of learning. A greater proportion of what individuals in an organization learn comes through mutual problem-solving and the sharing of experiences. However, Shepherd (2011) is of the view that some people do not benefit from working within the same four walls hence making face-to-face interactions difficult to come by and limiting the opportunities for collaboration in the past. Social media has the potential to maximize collaborative learning, not just now and then but on a continuous basis, and not just when and where it suits others, but at a time and place of your own choice.

There are diverse ways in which social media (Shepherd, 2011) can be used to facilitate workplace learning. Firstly, in order to enrich longer formal programmes, such as professional and postgraduate qualifications and management development programmes, social media can be used as a vehicle for group collaboration that is on-going. Many firms are already reaping benefits from using forums to share ideas and discuss issues, blogs as learning journals, and wikis as a focus for group collaborative projects, not to mention use of podcasts and videos as a means for sharing research. Another example is the use of online communities of practice to share new ideas and debate issues. Those in more of a hurry might now use micro-blogging services such as Twitter and Yammer to quickly update peers on new developments (Pawlosky, 2001). Learning largely takes place on-demand, at the point when it is needed most. Organizations can do their best to satisfy the needs of employees for on-demand information but they will scarcely be able to exhaust it all on a top-down basis. Members of an organization can use social networks to find sources of expertise or offer their own expertise to others; they can also diffuse their own home-made learning content, using whatever medium is best suited to the job and their talents.

Learning at work is as much about ''learning from'' as it is ''learning to''. We learn through our own experiences and the experiences of those around us, but only if we make a deliberate attempt to reflect. Here is where blogging can play a valuable role. This discipline will not be for everybody, but for those that really engage with the medium the opportunities for learning exceed all others. Writing a blog post to capture an idea or review an experience forces you to reflect and clarify your thoughts. It greatly amplifies the possibility that the experience will be a lasting one – in other words, you will have learnt something (Pham, 2011).

Learning and Social Media Models

According to Cook and Yanow (1993) the process of acquiring knowledge is termed as learning. Boateng et al. (2009) used the SECI model to study Web 2.0 and organizational learning. The SECI model (Nonaka & Takeuchi, 1995) looks at knowledge conversion in four modes: socialization, externalization, combination and internalization. The emphasis of this model is knowledge conversion. This study will not lay emphasis on knowledge conversion but the absorptive capacity of firms.

Linke and Zerfass (2012) used the Social Media Governance framework to study online communication management. The emphasis of this framework is social media governance, which involves the formal or informal frameworks, which regulate the actions of the members of an organization within the social web. The framework looks at the following: regulatory frameworks for social media; skills for social media: strategies for social media PR; and activities in social media PR. This is not what this study seeks to do.

Finally, the Theory of Performance Feedback was used by Schwab (2007) to study performance feedback with the goal of identifying principles that will promote a more integrated understanding of learning during the execution of innovative practices and contribute to the development of more fine-grained multilevel models of organizational learning.

Absorptive Capacity Theory (ACT)

Absorptive Capacity Theory inspects the degree to which a firm can perceive the estimation of new outside data, acclimatize it, and apply it toward attaining to organizational objectives (Cohen & Levinthal, 1989; 1990). The theory expects that retaining new learning can help a firm get to be more inventive and adaptable and accomplish larger amounts of execution than it would without engrossing new information. The theory additionally expects that organizations that have higher capacities for retaining new learning will have a game changer over firms with lower capacities. The theory expects that firms oblige an information base to have the capacity to assimilate and utilize new learning. Keeping in mind the end goal to perceive, acclimatize, and utilize new information, firms must have a learning base that is moderately like the new learning that is being transformed. Most hierarchical developments originate from acquiring thoughts from other individuals, as opposed to through imagining them (March & Simon, 1958). There are two components that will influence an association's impetuses to obtain new information: (1) the amount of learning accessible to retain and endeavour; and (2) the trouble and expenses included in engrossing that new learning. An organization's capacity to discover and utilize new information relies on the absorptive limit of its workers. In any case, an association's absorptive limit is not simply the total of its individuals' absorptive limits. Associations rely upon proficient people to survey and assess the potential positives and negatives of new learning. These individuals can serve as "guards" who can avoid or encourage the ingestion of new learning

Zahra and George (2002) re-conceptualized part of the theory. They took the steps of recognizing the value of new knowledge and assimilating and applying it, and created four capabilities or dimensions: (1) acquisition; (2) assimilation; (3) transformation; and (4) exploitation. (They refer to acquisition and assimilation as "potential" absorptive capacity; transformation and exploitation as "realized" absorptive capacity.) Murovec and Prodan (2009) showed that there can be two sorts of absorptive limit: demand-pull and science-push. Demand-pull alludes to new learning obtained from business sources (for instance, clients, rivalry, and suppliers). Science-push alludes to new learning obtained from exploration and exploratory sources (such as books, diaries, meetings, exchange shows, and other scholastic sources).

Justifying the Use of Absorptive Capacity Theory (ACT)

Primarily most of the studies on organizational learning and social media used theoretical frameworks in their studies. For instance, Roblek et al. (2013) used the Social Media Value Added Model to study the role of social media in enhancing organizational change and value creation in knowledge-based industries. However, this research study will use the Absorptive Capacity Theory (ACT) as its theoretical lens.

In addition, the literature reviewed on organizational learning and social media uses several research frameworks, arguably, none of these studies have used the Absorptive Capacity Theory (ACT) as its theoretical lens. Chua and Banerjee (2013) used a Customer Knowledge Management Framework in their study. Vuori (2012) used the Resource-based View (RBV) to study Web 2.0 and social media use. Similarly, Bartlett-Bragg (2009) used the Social Learning Network Approach in studying social learning networks. None of these studies stated used the Absorptive Capacity Theory (ACT). This reinforces the need to use ACT as the theoretical lens to study organizational learning and social media from a different theoretical view.

Lastly, the absorptive capacity theory emphasizes a firm's recognition of new external information, assimilating that information, and applying that information with the aim of attaining organizational goals (Cohen & Levinthal, 1989; 1990). Social media is external to an organization hence using this theory is suitable for this study. Wagner et al. (2014) in their study used the SECI model to study knowledge creation, which can be both internal and external as well as across different sources. This study however is using social media as its sole external source of knowledge to the industry under study to measure the impact of social media use on organizational learning.

Figure 1. The conceptual framework
Adapted from Zahra and George (2002).

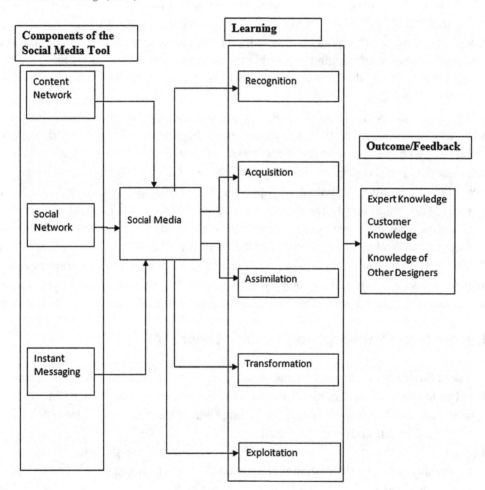

This framework as shown in Figure 1 will help to answer the research question of "what are the sources of knowledge for firms in the Ghanaian fashion industry". According to ACT, the sources of knowledge for an organization are four, which can be categorized into internal and external sources. The internal sources consist of the following;

1. The firm conducts its own research and development (R&D).
2. The firm derives new knowledge from its own current manufacturing operations.
3. The firm borrows new knowledge from other organizations or other sources.
4. The firm purchases new knowledge, such as through buying new equipment, hiring new knowledgeable people, or paying a consultant to train individuals in the use of a new method.

In addition, the framework will help to answer the question: "what are the forms of knowledge for firms in the Ghanaian fashion industry"? According to Murovec and Prodan (2009), there are two kinds of absorptive capacity:

1. Demand-pull; and
2. Science-push.

Demand-pull alludes to new knowledge acquired from market or business sources (for example, customers, competition i.e. from other fashion designers, experts and suppliers). Science-push alludes to new learning derived from exploration and scientific sources (such as books, journals, conferences, trade shows, and other scholarly sources).

Furthermore, the conceptual framework will help to answer the question: "How do social media support organizational learning in fashion firms in Ghana?" And the sub-questions:

1. What are the types of social media often used by firms in the Ghanaian fashion industry?
2. Which of the two types of social media (social network or content network) better enhances PACAP (Potential Absorptive Capacity); and which of the two better enhances RACAP (Realized Absorptive Capacity)?

HYPOTHESIS DEVELOPMENT

Social Media and Absorptive Capacity

The relationship between network structure and absorptive capacity has been addressed by previous studies (Tsai, 2001; Van Gilsing et al., 2008), but without reference to the organization of networking behaviour. In a study by Peltola (2014), social network literature was used to hypothesize on the organization of networking behaviour and its relation with absorption of external knowledge. In a study about networking behaviour of hospitals, Goes and Park (1997) established that the type and degree of ties affect the ability of the firm to integrate and assimilate external knowledge. Frequency of contact, as one of the indicators of strong ties (Granovetter 1982; Krackhardt 1992), is considered an important relational trait, which enables transfer of especially complex knowledge and information entailed in innovation (Krackhardt 1992; Uzzi 1997; Hansen 1999; Reagans & McEvily 2003; Van Gilsing & Nooteboom 2005; Nooteboom et al., 2007). At the same time, a wide network range (Reagans & McEvily 2003) is important to gain new external knowledge. An individual with a widespread network of connections across multiple pools of knowledge and expertise bridges holes between people and is exposed to more diverse knowledge (Reagans & McEvily, 2003).

Boateng et al. (2009) is of the view that the Internet has introduced the next level of collaboration to the doorsteps of organizations, and it is termed 'Web 2.0' (which includes social media). According to them, arguably little academic research has so far been conducted on the implications of this new approach for the domain of organizational learning.

Social media is a very effective networking structure. For fashion designers, interaction with different types of actors (customers, fashion bloggers, other fashion designers, suppliers etc.) may be important for accumulation of relevant information and knowledge to realize different types of goals and profitability. This is being made possible through the social media. Frequent contact with customers and other actors through social media, for instance Facebook, will enable the dissemination of complex knowledge and information (Nooteboom et al., 2007). Social media tools, applications and web applications are key to enhancing the use of social media to learn.

Reagans and McEvily (2003) conclude that an individual surrounded by a diverse network could transfer knowledge across a structural hole, even when the connection is weak. Apparently, transferring knowledge and maintaining a diverse network are related, as experience with one of the two helps to achieve the other. Debatably, fashion designers engaged in more frequent networking with a wider range of knowledge sources are more likely to experience a rich exchange of knowledge and in this way, are more skilled in recognizing and approaching specific actors for the acquisition of the knowledge that they need. Frequency of interaction and information exchange increases the amount of information the fashion designers accumulate, which contributes to a better ability to identify and understand the pieces of knowledge that are relevant for their own firms and profitability. As the higher level of inter-action increases the likelihood of (tacit and explicit) knowledge recognition, transfer and assimilation (Dhanaraj et al. 2004), it is expected that:

H1: The use of social media by fashion designers has a positive relationship with the recognition capacity of knowledge by these fashion designers.

H2: The use of social media by fashion designers has a positive relationship with the acquisition capacity of knowledge by these fashion designers.

H3: The use of social media by fashion designers has a positive relationship with the assimilation capacity of knowledge by these fashion designers.

Recognition and Acquisition Capacity

The acquisition capacity of fashion designers can be demonstrated in the ability of fashion designers to identify knowledge and the need of that knowledge through frequency of contact with the prevailing social media tools, applications or web applications. According to Zahra and George (2002), the recognition capacity of knowledge implies "recognizing the need for new knowledge". Recognizing the need for new knowledge results in the collection of that knowledge.

H4: The recognition capacity of fashion designers has a positive relationship with their acquisition capacity.

Acquisition and Assimilation Capacity

Acquisition capacity of the fashion designers can be reflected by more skills in collecting knowledge about developments in the sector through discussions with business partners, fashion bloggers and customers through social media: for instance, getting feedback from customers on preferred styles (helping to know fashion trends) and also acquiring information on market competition and using that knowledge to meet customer specifications, make changes to their business (styles, designs and marketing strategies), and detect new possibilities so as to attain the organizational goal of profitability.

Consequently, fashion designers' acquisition capacity is expected to have a positive relationship with their assimilation capacity.

H5: The recognition capacity of fashion designers has a positive relationship with their acquisition capacity.

Assimilation and Transformation Capacity

Fashion designers who are more skilled in the recognition of changes in technical possibilities and who are always among the first to detect changes in fashion trends and changes in market competition are said to have a better ability to analyse, process, interpret and understand external knowledge and information (assimilation capacity). Fashion designers with higher assimilation capacity are also expected to be more skilful in assessing the relevancy of new information and knowledge for their own firms. Greater ability to understand new possibilities and opportunities is expected to result in more skill in recognizing the usefulness of new and external knowledge for profitability of their own firms and a greater capacity to translate new information and knowledge into changes and adaptations. Accordingly, it is hypothesized:

H6: The assimilation capacity of fashion designers has a positive relationship with their transformation capacity.

Transformation and Exploitation Capacity

It is expected that the capacity to transform and apply knowledge to one's own firm has a positive relationship related to exploitation capacity. Skill in assessing the relevancy and usability of new information for profitability on one's own firm, plus the capacity and ability to translate market trends into adaptations in the firm, is expected to result in the ability to make an additional step. The latter is related to exploitation of knowledge. Firms with high transformation capacity are expected to be more skilful in transposing the information into profitable changes and adaptations on the firm. Fashion designers who translate new knowledge into actual adaptations usually also have an idea about how the adaptation will contribute to increased profit. Therefore, it is expected that:

H7: The transformation capacity of fashion designers has a positive relationship with their exploitation capacity.

The hypotheses discussed are captured in the conceptual framework as shown in Figure 2.

Figure 2. The conceptual framework and hypothesis
Adapted from Zahra and George (2002).

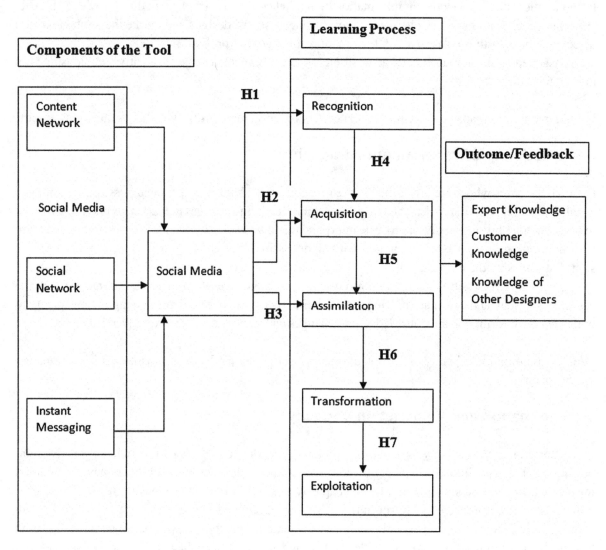

METHODOLOGY

This section highlights the methodology adopted for the study. It consists of research paradigm, research design, research approach, sample size, data collection method, data analysis techniques, ethical considerations, research limitations and challenges.

This study was undertaken from the perspective of realism. The realism paradigm provides the information systems researcher with both elements of positivism and constructivism (Healy & Perry, 2000). While positivism concerns a single, concrete reality and constructivism multiple realities, realism enables the IS researcher to acquire multiple perceptions about a single, mind-independent reality (Bisman, 2002). This study in extending the use of realism in IS research, gains the opportunity of obtaining detailed answers to the question of the impact social media has on organizational learning – thus analysing from the perspective of the Absorptive Capacity Theory (ACT). Realism recognizes that perceptions have certain plasticity (Churchland, 1979) and that there are differences between reality and people's perceptions of reality (Bisman, 2002), rather than being supposedly value-free, as in positive research, or value-laden as in interpretive research (Lincoln & Guba, 1985). The researcher therefore adopted both quantitative and qualitative methods for this research.

The type of mixed method approach used was the sequential explanatory strategy. The quantitative method was used before the qualitative method. In this approach, quantitative data are collected and analysed first and the results used to inform the subsequent qualitative phase. This explains why this strategy is considered explanatory.

Conducting the Survey

According to Castillo (2009), samples are drawn because it will be impractical to investigate all members of a target population. Sampling is a process of selecting research participants (Creswell, 2009). To arrive at the sample or target population for this study, data collection was therefore scheduled in two stages consisting of a pilot study, which took place from 1st May, 2014 to 5th May, 2014; and a main study which took place from 6th May 2014 to 12th May, 2014. In the pilot study, data (questionnaires) were collected across five different Ghanaian fashion firms. The firms selected were obtained from the internet. The criteria for selection were related to the researcher's theoretical concepts, namely:

- Learning organizations
- Fashion firms which learn though the social media

After the pilot survey, fifty (50) organizations were added to the sample size to continue with the actual data collection.

Table 1. Questionnaire development

Hypothesis	Factors	No. of Questions
H1: The use of social media by fashion designers has a positive relationship with their recognition capacity **H4:** The recognition capacity of fashion designers has a positive relationship with their acquisition capacity	Recognition Capacity	2
H2: The use of social media by fashion designers has a positive relationship with their acquisition capacity. **H5:** The acquisition capacity of fashion designers has a positive relationship with their assimilation capacity	Acquisition Capacity	3
H3: The use of social media by fashion designers has a positive relationship with their assimilation capacity.	Assimilation Capacity	3
H6: The assimilation capacity of fashion designers has a positive relationship with their transformation capacity	Transformation Capacity	3
H7: The transformation capacity of fashion designers has a positive relationship with their exploitation capacity	Exploitation Capacity	3

Source: Author's Construct.

Questionnaire Development

The questionnaires for the survey were designed to meet the purpose of the research and to answer the research questions. The researcher administered the questionnaires among the 55 fashion firms used for the study. The Table 1 shows how the researcher designed the survey questionnaires.

Data Collection

Data was collected among the 55 fashion houses in Ghana on a purposive as well as snowballing basis. The questionnaires were left with the organizations to complete after which they called the researcher to fetch them. In all, 196 completed questionnaires were returned.

Selecting Case Organization

At the end of the survey data collection, only two organizations; Aya Morrison and Inka Accessories gave access to the researchers for a case study and had sufficient experience to enable such a detailed analysis of Organisational Learning through social media. The selected companies had been in operation for over 5 years and were actively involved in using social media for Organisational Learning. Evidence of their use of social media for Organisational Learning was authenticated through documents and interviews with CEOs and the responses of employees to the questionnaires administered to them. The firm also assured its commitment to the case study.

Questions Used and Data Collection

The primary data collection method employed was semi-structured interviews. The researcher interviewed the fashion designers and Chief Executive officers (CEO) of the case firms with regard to the issue being discussed. For Aya Morrison Fashion firm, the CEO was the person the researcher interviewed for the case study. She has a Bachelor of Arts degree. For Inka Accessories, the CEO who holds a Bachelor of Science degree was interviewed. The interview for Aya Morrison Fashion firm was conducted on 12th June, 2014 at the office of the CEO with the aim of determining the impact of social media on the organization's learning ability and the profitability of the organization. The interview for Inka Accessories was carried out on 14th June, 2014 via telephone. The CEOs were interviewed to obtain a wider view of the ideal situation of learning in a typical Ghanaian fashion firm and they were indeed able to account largely for the impact of social media on their learning potential as a business. The interviews were taped and transcribed, with copies of transcribed interviews returned to the interviewees to check and resolve any discrepancies.

Realism encourages the use of multiple data collection methods to enhance triangulation of perspectives and know the single reality and people's perception of the reality. The researcher further observed the CEOs, brand managers and other employees of these firms to find out their perception on the use of social media in organizational learning. Secondary data sources included documentary materials of the organization's history, industry reports and verified online information.

Mode of Analysis

The survey questionnaires were coded and entered into the IBM SPSS Amos software (version 22) in order to run the analysis. The data set was screened and cleaned. This was done to rectify mistakes that occurred during data entering. Three techniques were used, namely: Confirmatory Factor Analysis to analyse the factors of the Absorptive Capacity Theory (ACT) to understand how social media supports organizational learning; Excel was used to analyse the forms and sources of knowledge and to analyse the tools and applications to verify those which are frequently used by fashion designers, and to discover those applications which have an effect on the Potential Absorptive Capacity (PACAP); and crosstabs were used to test the hypothesis whereas the Structural Equation Modelling was used to confirm the factors of the Absorptive Capacity Theory (ACT) and to as well test the fitness of the model using Pclose.

RESEARCH ANALYSIS AND DISCUSSION

This section presents the results of the study and is organized into two main sections: background of the sample and examination of the hypotheses. To examine the hypotheses, descriptive statistics of cross tabulations were used to test the hypothesized model of social media facilitating organizational learning and identify important relations between the variables (Recognition, Acquisition, Assimilation, Transformation and Exploitation) of interest. PACAP means Potential Absorptive Capacity which encapsulates Recognition, Assimilation and Acquisition of knowledge whereas RACAP implies Realized Absorptive Capacity which captures Transformation and Exploitation Capacity. Confirmatory factor analysis was used to confirm the factors in the hypothesized model. Descriptive statistics were used to explain the forms and sources of knowledge and the tools and applications predominantly used in the Ghanaian fashion industry.

Background of the Study

One hundred and ninety-six (196) respondents participated in this study. The participants' backgrounds, i.e., age, level of completed education and the number of workers in the organization, the number of years the company has been in existence and the company's turnover are shown in Table 2.

Frequency Distribution

The frequency analysis shown below answer the following research questions:

1. What are the forms of learning for firms in the Ghanaian fashion industry?
2. What are the sources of learning for firms in the Ghanaian fashion industry?
3. How does social media support organizational learning in fashion firms in Ghana?

Table 2. Frequency table of demographic variables

Category	Variables	*f*	Percent
Age	Less than 18	4	2.0
	18-25	90	45.9
	26-30	88	44.9
	31-35	14	7.1
	Total	196	100
Education	Senior High	67	34.2
	Diploma	16	8.2
	Bachelor's Degree	96	49.0
	Master's Degree	14	7.1
	Professional Certificate	3	1.5
	Total	196	100
Years of company's existence	1-5	81	41.3
	6-10	32	16.3
	11-15	55	28.1
	Over 20 years	28	14.3
	Total	196	100
Turnover	Less than 3,000	20	10.2
	3000- 10,000	114	58.2
	100,000 or more	62	31.6
	Total	196	100

Source: Field survey, 2014.

Forms of Learning for Firms in the Fashion Industry

Demand-Pull Form of Learning

The respondents were asked to indicate the extent to which they communicate and interact with others (customers, fashion bloggers, other fashion designers) to acquire knowledge through social media. The results of the analysis showed that 11.2% (n= 22) of respondents indicated they have a neutral stance on the usage of social media for communication and interaction with others. Whereas, 32.7% (n= 64) of respondents indicated that they intensively use social media to communicate and interact with others through social media to acquire knowledge. Acquiring knowledge through others demonstrates the form of knowledge termed demand-pull postulated from the Absorptive Capacity Theory (ACT). This answers an aspect of a research question raised for this study: "what are the forms of knowledge which aid learning in fashion firms in Ghana?"

Finding 1: Most fashion firms use social media to communicate with others (who could be customers, suppliers, fashion bloggers, fashion enthusiasts etc.) very intensively to acquire knowledge

In addition, respondents were asked to indicate the extent to which they make use of social media knowledge and information for marketing (communication). The data analysis also showed that, 48.5% (n= 95) of respondents intensively use the social media, knowledge and information for marketing; 32.1% (n=63) of respondents semi-intensively use the social media, knowledge and information for marketing; whereas 19.4% (n=38) of respondents use the knowledge and information for marketing. Knowledge acquired from market sources such as marketing can be classified under the demand-pull form of knowledge. Further answering the research question: "what are the forms of knowledge which aid learning in fashion firms in Ghana?"

Finding 2: Most fashion designers in Ghana intensively use social media to acquire knowledge from market sources through marketing.

Respondents also indicated the extent to which they used of social media knowledge and information for designing (generative purposes). From the analysis, 52.6% (n= 103) of the respondents intensively use social media knowledge and information for designing; 35.2% (n=69) of respondents semi-intensively use social media knowledge and information for designing; whereas 12.2% (n=24) of respondents use the knowledge and information very intensively for designing. Knowledge acquired from market sources such as competition and suppliers as well as customers can be used for designing which falls under the demand-pull form of knowledge, also answering the research question: "what are the forms of knowledge which aid learning in fashion firms in Ghana?"

Finding 3: Most fashion designers in Ghana intensively use knowledge from social media for designing

Science-Push Form of Learning

The respondents indicated the extent to which they prevented all employees voluntarily transmitting useful scientific and technological knowledge acquired to others. The data analysis showed that most fashion firms in Ghana do not prevent their employees from disseminating useful scientific information to other employees or even to customers. This knowledge falls into the category of science-push knowledge as defined by ACT, also answering the research question: "what are the forms of knowledge which aid learning in fashion firms in Ghana?"

Finding 4: Most fashion designers in Ghana do not prevent their employees from transmitting useful scientific and technological knowledge.

Sources of Learning (Knowledge) for Firms in the Fashion Industry

Internal Source of Knowledge

The extent at which the respondents coordinated and integrated all phases of the Research and Development process with its interrelations with the functional tasks of production, marketing and translated external information into adaptations were also analysed. Deductions from the analysis indicated that most fashion firms in Ghana use social media to carry out research intensively and the knowledge (new styles, new designs and new fashion trends) is adapted by these fashion houses into new designs. Knowledge of this form is acquired internally through R&D; answering the research question: "what are the sources of knowledge which aid learning in fashion firms in Ghana?"

Finding 5: Most fashion firms in Ghana use social media to carry out research intensively and the knowledge (new styles, new designs and new fashion trends) is adapted by these fashion houses into new design.

External Source of Knowledge

The analysis of data indicated that 7, 54.6% (n= 107) of respondents "strongly agree" that they translate external information into new business applications; 41.8% (n=82) of respondents "agree" that they translate external information into new business applications; whereas 3.6% (n=7) of respondents have a neutral stance on translating external information into new business applications. External information according to ACT could either be borrowed knowledge or purchased knowledge. Hence, fashion designers either borrow or purchase external knowledge and translate them into new business applications (new marketing strategies, new designs etc.); also, answering the research question: "what are the sources of knowledge which aid learning in fashion firms in Ghana?"

Finding 6: Fashion designers either borrow or purchase external knowledge and translate them into new business applications (new marketing strategies, new designs etc.).

Both External and Internal Source of Knowledge

Respondents indicated how they make use of social media knowledge and information for interaction. According to ACT, knowledge could be obtained both internally and externally and the analysis showed that fashion firms in Ghana obtain knowledge or disseminate knowledge through interaction with customers or suppliers through social media (for instance; Facebook, Blogger); further answering the research question: "what are the sources of knowledge which aid learning in fashion firms in Ghana?"

Finding 7: Fashion firms in Ghana obtain knowledge or disseminate knowledge through interaction with customers or suppliers through social media (for instance; Facebook, Blogger).

Social Media as Tools and in Usage

Application of Social Media

Respondents indicated the extent to which they normally use social media applications to identify knowledge and the data analysis showed that communicative, interactive and generative social media applications are mostly used by fashion firms in Ghana to recognize new knowledge, and the tools and web applications under these applications can be classified as social networks. Hence, social networks are mostly used for acquiring new knowledge. Recognition capacity forms a part of PACAP, hence it can be concluded that the type of social media that supports PACAP the most are social networks, thus, answering the research question: "How do social media support organizational learning in fashion firms in Ghana?" and the sub-questions:

1. What are the types of social media often used by firms in the fashion industry?
2. Which of the two types of social media (social network and content network) greatly enhance PACAP (Potential Absorptive Capacity) and which of the two greatly enhance RACAP (Realized Absorptive Capacity)?

    Finding 8: Social networks are mostly used for acquiring new knowledge. Recognition capacity forms a part of PACAP, hence it can be concluded that the type of social media that supports PACAP the most are social networks.

Social Media as Tools for Assimilation

The analysis of data shows that Facebook, YouTube, Myspace, Twitter, Podcasts and Flickr are the social media tools very intensively used by fashion firms to acquire knowledge. These web applications can be classified under social network type of social media web application. And these web applications are those mostly used to acquire knowledge. Hence, it can be concluded that social networks support PACAP since acquisition capacity is an aspect of PACAP. This further answers the research question: "How do social media support organizational learning in fashion firms in Ghana?"

Finding 9: Social networks support PACAP since acquisition capacity is an aspect of PACAP.

Confirmation of Factors

Discussion of Factors of Absorptive Capacity

This section is in two parts: the measurement model will be completely assessed to find out the factors which are significant from the conceptual model and which fit the measurement model; as well as a summary of the hypotheses which were accepted and rejected respectively.

The factors of ACT according to Zahra and George's (2002) re-conceptualizing of part of the ACT theory, thus including the step of recognizing the value of new knowledge are these four capabilities or dimensions: (1) acquisition; (2) assimilation; (3) transformation; and (4) exploitation. However, based on the critique of Turodan and Dorova (2007), the step of recognizing the value of new knowledge is included in this study. The following are therefore the constructs that measure ACT for the purpose of this study:

1. Recognition Capacity
2. Acquisition Capacity
3. Assimilation Capacity
4. Transformation Capacity
5. Exploitation Capacity

The Figure 3 has factor loadings, which measure the four capabilities of the Absorptive Capacity Theory (ACT). From the measurement, some first order latent variables have factor loading below the recommended threshold of 0.70. Consequently, those variables were dropped resulting in a final measurement model, which shows the factors which truly measure the absorptive capacity of fashion designers in the Ghanaian fashion industry.

Figure 3. Initial measurement model
Source: Field Data.

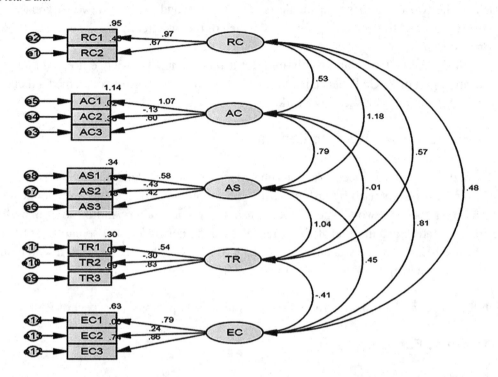

Assessment of the Overall Measurement Model

Some first order latent variables that had factor loading below the recommended threshold of 0.70 were deleted at the validation stage of the measurement model. The variables which were dropped include; AC2 (from the Acquisition Capacity Factor), AS1, AS2, AS3 (from the Assimilation Capacity Factor), TR2 (from the Transformation Capacity Factor), and EC2 (from the Exploitation Capacity Factor). The Assimilation Capacity Factor was dropped completely. After the problematic factors were deleted from the initial constructs, there was a regeneration of the measurement model with just eight first order latent variables; and there was much improvement in the results as compared to the initial measurement model. Standardized factor loadings above the threshold were recorded for all the eight first order latent variables. Then, the model was fitted as was done earlier with the first model using the goodness of fit indices of absolute, incremental and parsimonious fit measures. The final measurement model is depicted in Figure 4 with the respective factor loadings while Tables 3 and 4 shows the goodness of fit indices and average variable estimation.

The p-value of the final measurement was not significant therefore showing that there is no statistical difference between the factors of the measurement model, implying that the model best fits this study. In terms of the RMSEA, the final model had a value of 0.076, which is less than 0.08 as recommended, therefore, the model fits the dataset. The incremental fit indices obtained in the final measurement model were greater than 0.90 ranging from 0.97 to 0.99 which shows the model fits the data set. Whereas the parsimonious fit indices also recorded values of 0.315 and 0.318 less than the recommended value of greater than 0.50.

The Figure 3 has factor loadings, which measure the four capabilities of the Absorptive Capacity Theory (ACT). From the measurement, some first order latent variables have factor loading below the recommended threshold of 0.70. Consequently, those variables were dropped resulting in a final measurement model, which shows the factors which truly measure the absorptive capacity of fashion designers in the Ghanaian fashion industry.

Assessment of the Overall Measurement Model

Some first order latent variables that had factor loading below the recommended threshold of 0.70 were deleted at the validation stage of the measurement model. The variables which were dropped include; AC2 (from the Acquisition Capacity Factor), AS1, AS2, AS3 (from the Assimilation Capacity Factor), TR2 (from the Transformation Capacity Factor), and EC2 (from the Exploitation Capacity Factor). The Assimilation Capacity Factor was dropped completely. After the problematic factors were deleted from the initial constructs, there was a regeneration of the measurement model with just eight first order latent variables; and there was much improvement in the results as compared to the initial measurement model. Standardized factor loadings above the threshold were recorded for all the eight first order latent variables. Then, the model was fitted as was done earlier with the first model using the goodness of fit indices of absolute, incremental and parsimonious fit measures. The final measurement model is depicted in Figure 4 with the respective factor loadings while Tables 3 and 4 shows the goodness of fit indices and average variable estimation.

The p-value of the final measurement was not significant therefore showing that there is no statistical difference between the factors of the measurement model, implying that the model best fits this study. In terms of the RMSEA, the final model had a value of 0.076, which is less than 0.08 as recommended, therefore, the model fits the dataset. The incremental fit indices obtained in the final measurement model were greater than 0.90 ranging from 0.97 to 0.99 which shows the model fits the data set. Whereas the parsimonious fit indices also recorded values of 0.315 and 0.318 less than the recommended value of greater than 0.50.

Table 3. Goodness-of-fit indices for final measurement model

Goodness-of-Fit Indices	Benchmark	Final Model
Absolute Goodness of Fit Measure		
Chi-square (CMIN) ($x2$)	$P \geq 0.05$	19.011
Chi-square /degree of freedom	≤ 2	2.112
Absolute Badness of Fit Measure		
Root mean Square Error of Approximation (RMSEA)	≤ 0.08	0.076
Incremental Fit Measure		
Comparative Fit Index (CFI)	≥ 0.90	0.989
Incremental fit index (IFI)	≥ 0.90	0.989
Turker-Lewis Index (TLI)	≥ 0.90	0.965
Parsimony Fit Measure		
Parsimony Comparative of Fit index (PCFI)	≥ 0.50	0.318
Parsimony Normed of Fit index (PNFI)	≥ 0.50	0.315

Source: Field Data.

To sum it all, eight latent variables fitted the final measurement model instead of the proposed fourteen in the conceptual model. The factors which critically measure the absorptive capacity of knowledge through social media in the Ghanaian fashion industry are Recognition Capacity, Acquisition Capacity, Transformation Capacity and Exploitation Capacity.

Regarding the test of discriminate validity, the Average Variable Estimate (AVE) recorded by the second order latent variables ranges from 0.53 to 0.79, above the validity threshold of 0.50, which shows an acceptable convergent validity of the measuring scales (Hair et al., 2006). The square of the correlation between a construct and any other factor is higher than the AVE for each latent variable, which indicates adequate discriminant validity between the constructs (Chin, 1998). Table 5 also shows an assessment of the normality test for the study.

Figure 4. Final measurement model
Source: Field Data.

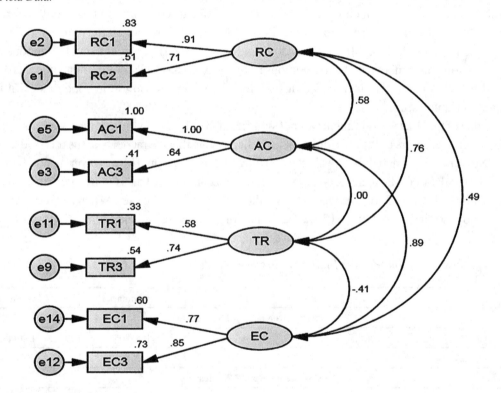

Table 4. Shared variance

Construct	CR	AVE	MSV	ASV	EC	RC	AC	TR
EC	0.796	0.661	0.797	0.380	0.813			
RC	0.875	0.791	0.726	0.407	0.469	0.890		
AC	0.816	0.698	0.797	0.358	0.893	0.524	0.835	
TR	0.669	0.530	0.726	0.283	-0.348	0.852	0.052	0.728

Source: Analysis output.

Table 5. Assessment of normality

Variable	Min	Max	Skew	c.r.	Kurtosis	c.r.
Q26	3.000	5.000	-.628	-3.591	-.622	-1.777
Q28	3.000	5.000	-.563	-3.216	-.657	-1.879
Q23	3.000	5.000	-.588	-3.358	-.770	-2.199
Q25	3.000	5.000	-.391	-2.233	-.691	-1.976
Q15	3.000	5.000	-.855	-4.886	-.486	-1.389
Q17	1.000	5.000	-1.580	-9.029	4.729	13.513
Q12	4.000	5.000	-1.063	-6.077	-.870	-2.485
Q13	4.000	5.000	-2.166	-12.380	2.691	7.691
Multivariate					17.105	9.466

Source: Analysis Output .

Summary of Hypotheses Confirmation

The Table 6 shows the confirmation of the hypothesis.

Table 6. Hypothesis confirmation of cross tabulation

Hypothesis	p-Value	Support for Model
Social Media & Recognition Capacity	0.612	H1: Rejected
Social Media & Acquisition Capacity	0.000	H2: Supported
Social Media & Assimilation Capacity	0.787	H3: Rejected
Social Media & PACAP	0.030	H4: Supported
Recognition Capacity & Acquisition Capacity	0.000	H5: Supported
Acquisition Capacity & Assimilation Capacity	0.000	H6: Supported
Assimilation Capacity & Transformation Capacity	0.000	H7: Supported
Transformation Capacity& Exploitation Capacity	0.000	H8: Supported

Source: Analysis Output.

DISCUSSION OF FINDINGS

Social media is an asset for firms who use it in absorbing knowledge. From the findings, most fashion designers use the documentative Applications to recognize knowledge and those who use the communicative Applications to assimilate knowledge are in the majority. YouTube, for instance, is mostly used by fashion designers to acquire knowledge.

From literature, research has concentrated on communicative applications of Web 2.0 technologies not concentrating on other applications such as the documentative which this study has been able to cover (Vuori & Okkonen, 2012; Chua & Banerjee, 2013). Statistics from Alexa.com depicts that traffic on social media sites especially Facebook is on the rise. Other findings from this study confirm this assertion that social media usage is on the rise. According to the findings of this study, most fashion firms in Ghana use social media intensively on a daily basis to acquire knowledge.

From the analysis of findings, it can be argued that fashion designers do not intensively use social media to assimilate knowledge as proposed by Zahra and George (2007). Thus, assimilation of knowledge when absorbing new knowledge does not play an inevitable role in the fashion firms absorption new external knowledge.

Most fashion firms use social media to communicate with their customers, suppliers, fashion bloggers, and fashion enthusiasts. This they do very intensively to acquire knowledge. The knowledge they acquire through these means may include but not limited to fashion trends, consumer taste and preferences, existing prices, orders from customers, supplier lists, comments and suggestions among others.

There is also a positive relationship between the Transformation Capacity and the Exploitation Capacity of fashion firms in Ghana. Thus, knowledge acquired when transformed is mostly used by these fashion firms to develop new ideas and designs.

The findings further suggest that most Fashion designers in Ghana use social media to research and acquire knowledge which informs future designs. However, they do not prevent their employees from using social media to transmit scientific and technological knowledge.

In addition, the findings suggest that, these fashion designers acquire knowledge from both internal (among employees), for instance through WhatsApp and external sources (from suppliers, customers, fashion enthusiasts and other fashion designers), through for instance, Facebook, Twitter, Instagram, WhatsApp among others. From the case studies, it can also be deduced that ideas for designs can be derived from social media. Another source of ideas for designs could be the designer's own mind as well as inspiration from nature.

Hong et al. (2013) studied blogs as a tool for learning which seems to be unpopular among fashion designers in Ghana. However, some Ghanaian fashion designers use blogs to communicate internally (with employees) as well as externally (with customers and suppliers). Trending ideas are communicated by designers through this social media platform.

Findings from this study also depicts that WhatsApp technology which falls under the instant messaging category of the social media tool is also used mostly by fashion designers for internal communication and sharing of design patents but not through other social media platforms like Facebook to avoid theft of designs. However, social media applications such as Facebook is an ideal application for marketing.

Some popular social media web applications include Facebook and YouTube, which has also been studied by most researchers (Vuori & Okkonen, 2012; He et al., 2013; Bochenek & Blili, 2013; Chua & Banerjee, 2013). Twitter is also popular among Fashion designers. Facebook is popular for marketing and publicity.

From the findings of the study, WhatsApp is the emerging Web 2.0 technology that is gaining popularity and dominance among fashion designers in Ghana today. The assertion is that it is convenient and easily accessible.

Arguably, the findings of the study also suggest that Facebook is popular among Ghanaian fashion designers for the reasons of its wider network coverage, accessibility and convenience of use. This finding is corroborated by Vuori and Okkonen (2012) who carried out a study on social media and discovered Facebook as one of the popular social media applications.

CONCLUSION AND RECOMMENDATIONS

This study examined the use of social media for organizational learning in the Ghanaian fashion industry. To this end, these research questions were formulated:

1. What are the forms of learning for firms in the Ghanaian fashion industry?
2. What are the sources of learning for firms in the Ghanaian fashion industry?
3. How does social media support organizational learning in fashion firms in Ghana?

Absorptive Capacity Theory (ACT) therefore appropriately helped answer these research questions. The constructs of the ACT were ideal for gathering the needed information on fashion designers and their usage of social media to absorb knowledge. Knowledge on recognition, acquisition, assimilation, transformation and exploitation of new external knowledge among Ghanaian fashion designers is thereby attained.

Summary of the Research Findings

The findings of the study are in three divisions: first, the findings on the forms of knowledge that aid learning in the Ghanaian fashion industry; second, the sources of knowledge that aid learning in the Ghanaian fashion industry; and third, how social media supports organizational learning in the Ghanaian fashion industry.

Nature of Absorptive Capacity

It was discovered that most fashion firms in Ghana use social media to communicate with others (who could be customers, suppliers, fashion bloggers, fashion enthusiasts etc.) very intensively to acquire knowledge. They also use social media to market designs as well as to acquire knowledge to create new designs. Acquiring knowledge through others or through market sources demonstrates the form of knowledge termed demand-pull postulated from the Absorptive Capacity Theory (ACT).

Interestingly, most fashion designers in Ghana do not prevent their employees from transmitting useful scientific and technological knowledge, which falls under a form of knowledge termed as science-push. The forms of knowledge for fashion firms in Ghana can therefore be classified as demand-pull and science-push as postulated by ACT.

Another finding was that the sources of knowledge predominantly used by fashion designers were both internal sources and external sources. The internal source predominantly being through research since most fashion firms in Ghana use social media to carry out research intensively and the knowledge (new styles, new designs, and new fashion trends) is adapted by these fashion houses into new designs. The external sources of knowledge on the other hand were customarily borrowed or purchased knowledge. Fashion designers either borrow or purchase external knowledge and translate them into new business applications (new marketing strategies, new designs etc.). This knowledge is disseminated to others (customers, suppliers) both internally and externally by means of social media.

Moreover, it was revealed that social networks are mostly used for acquiring new knowledge. Recognition capacity forms a part of PACAP; hence, it can be concluded that the type of social media that supports PACAP the most are social networks. Facebook, YouTube, Myspace, Twitter, Podcasts and

Flickr are social media tools that are used very intensively by fashion firms to acquire knowledge. These web applications can be classified under social network type of social media web applications and these web applications are mostly used to acquire knowledge. Hence, it can be concluded that social networks support PACAP since acquisition capacity is an aspect of PACAP.

From the findings of the study, it can be stated that Ghanaian fashion designers also use social media to recognize, acquire, transform and exploit knowledge intensively. They poorly use social media to assimilate knowledge.

Critical Constructs of Absorptive Capacity Theory (ACT)

In order to see the fitness of the conceptual model derived from ACT, with the objective of determining the factors critical to the absorption of knowledge, the Confirmatory Factor Analysis technique under Structural Equation Modelling was used; and cross tabulation was used to test the stipulated hypothesis.

The first conceptual model was built from ACT with 5 factors and 14 variables. The results of the measurement model validation under CFA indicated that Recognition Capacity (RC1), Acquisition Capacity (AC1, AC3), Transformation Capacity (TR1, TR2) and Exploitation Capacity (EC1, EC2) were the factors critical to the absorption of knowledge through social media in the fashion industry of Ghana. Other variables like AS1, AS2 AS3 (Assimilation Capacity factor), TR3 and EC3 were insignificant to the model; hence, were deleted from the final model.

Cross tabulations were used to test and validate the hypotheses proposed regarding the 5 factors of ACT (14 variables) and two (2) of the hypotheses were rejected whereas the rest (7) were accepted. The seven hypotheses supported were H2, H4, H5, H6, H7, H8 and H9 and two rejected were H1 and H3 with a p-value greater than the threshold of 0.05. Overall, the critical factors for measuring absorption of knowledge through social media in the Ghanaian fashion industry are Recognition, Acquisition, Transformation and Exploitation.

Implications of Research

In terms of research, this study will add up to existing studies on fashion designing, social media as well as adding to studies which use the Absorptive Capacity Theory as its theoretical Lens.

In relation to practice, the findings of this study will inform the decision of other firms or fashion designers who are not currently using social media in absorbing knowledge to decide to do so for the purposes of research and ease of communication, effective marketing and publicity both internally and externally and also reap the benefit of cutting down cost.

Regarding policy, policy makers in the fashion industry of Ghana can embrace the idea of social media adoption and usage by Ghanaian fashion houses, by explicitly stating and communicating its benefits to practice and research.

Limitations and Future Research

The study focused on fashion houses within the Greater Accra Region of Ghana; consequently, not covering fashion firms in other parts of Ghana. Thus, future studies should cover other areas of the country to provide a holistic understanding of the use of social media in organizational learning.

REFERENCES

Argyris, C., & Schön, D.A. (1978). Organizational Learning: A Theory of Action Perspective. *Reis, 77*(78/97), 345-348.

Bartlett-Bragg, A. (2009). Reframing practice: Creating social learning networks. *International Journal of Development and Learning in Organizations, 23*(4), 16–20. doi:10.1108/14777280910970747

Boateng, R., Malik, A., & Mbarika, V. (2009). Web 2.0 and Organizational Learning: Conceptualizing the link, Americas Conference on Information Systems. *Proceedings of the Fifteenth Americas Conference on Information Systems*, 1-2.

Bochenek, L., & Blili, S. (2013). Social Media Champions- Drivers and Sophistication Process of Social Media Strategic Management. *Social Media in Strategic Management*, 143-167.

Chua, A. Y., & Banerjee, S. (2013). Customer knowledge management via social media: The case of Starbucks. *Journal of Knowledge Management, 17*(2), 237–249. doi:10.1108/13673271311315196

Cohen, W. M., & Levinthal, D. A. (1989). Innovation and learning: The two faces of R&D. *The Economic Journal, 99*(397), 569–596. doi:10.2307/2233763

Cohen, W. M., & Levinthal, D. A. (1990). Absorptive capacity: A new perspective on learning and innovation. *Administrative Science Quarterly, 35*(1), 128–152. doi:10.2307/2393553

Cook, S. D. N., & Yanow, D. (1993). Culture and Organizational Learning. *Journal of Management Inquiry, 2*(4), 373–390. doi:10.1177/105649269324010

Creswell, J. W. (2009). *Research design: Qualitative Quantitative and Mixed Methods Approaches*. Thousand Oaks, CA: SAGE Publications.

Dixon, N. (1994). *The Organizational Learning Cycle: How We Can Learn Collectively*. London: McGraw-Hill Company.

Dixon, N. (2000). *Common Knowledge: How Companies Thrive by sharing what they know*. Boston: Harvard University Press.

Dodgson, M. (1993). Organizational learning: A review of some literatures. *Organization Studies, 14*(3), 375–394. doi:10.1177/017084069301400303

Grabski, J. (2009). Making fashion in the city: A case study of tailors and designers in Dakar. *Senegal. Fashion Theory, 13*(2), 215–242. doi:10.2752/175174109X414268

Hanna, R., Rohm, A., & Crittenden, V. L. (2011). Were all connected: The power of the social media ecosystem. *Business Horizons, 54*(3), 265–273. doi:10.1016/j.bushor.2011.01.007

Hong, K. S. (2002). Relationships between students and instructional variables with satisfaction and learning from a Web-based course. *The Internet and Higher Education, 5*(3), 267–281. doi:10.1016/S1096-7516(02)00105-7

Hull, R., Coombs, R., & Peltu, M. (2000). Knowledge management practices for innovation: An audit tool for improvement. *International Journal of Technology Management, 20*(5-8), 633–656. doi:10.1504/IJTM.2000.002885

Kaiser, C., & Bodendorf, F. (2012). Mining consumer dialog in online forums. *Internet Research, 22*(3), 275–297. doi:10.1108/10662241211235653

Karkoulian, S., Canaan Messarra, L., & McCarthy, R. (2013). The intriguing art of knowledge management and its relation to learning organizations. *Journal of Knowledge Management, 17*(4), 511–526. doi:10.1108/JKM-03-2013-0102

Lien, B. Y. H., Hung, R. Y. Y., Yang, B., & Li, M. (2006). Is the learning organization a valid concept in the Taiwanese context? *International Journal of Manpower, 27*(2), 189–203. doi:10.1108/01437720610666209

March, J. G., & Simon, H. A. (1958). *Organizations*. Hoboken, NJ: Wiley.

Murovec, N., & Prodan, I. (2009). Absorptive capacity, its determinants, and influence on innovation output: Cross-cultural validation of the structural model. *Technovation, 29*(12), 859–872. doi:10.1016/j.technovation.2009.05.010

Nonaka, I., & Takeuchi, H. (1995). *The Knowledge-creating Company: How Japanese Companies Create the Dynamics of Innovation*. Oxford University Press.

Nonaka, I., Toyama, R., & Konno, N. (1998). Leading Knowledge Creation: A New framework for dynamic Knowledge Management. *Proceedings at the 2nd Annual Knowledge Management Conference*.

Nooteboom, B. (2000). Learning by interaction: absorptive capacity, cognitive distance and governance. *Journal of Management and Governance, 4*(1-2), 69-92.

O'Reilly, T. (2005). *What is Web 2.0?*. O'Reilly Media. Available: http://tinyurl.com/743r5

Pham, M. H. T. (2011). Blog ambition: Fashion, feelings, and the political economy of the digital raced body. *Camera Obscura, 26*(176), 1–37. doi:10.1215/02705346-2010-013

Rickman, T. A., & Cosenza, R. M. (2007). The changing digital dynamics of multichannel marketing: The feasibility of the weblog: text mining approach for fast fashion trending. *Journal of Fashion Marketing and Management, 11*(4), 604–621. doi:10.1108/13612020710824634

Shepherd, C. (2011). Does social media have a place in workplace learning?. *Strategic Direction, 27*(2), 3–4. doi:10.1108/02580541111103882

Vuori, V., & Okkonen, J. (2012). Refining information and knowledge by social media applications: Adding value by insight. *Vine, 42*(1), 117–128. doi:10.1108/03055721211207798

Zahra, S. A., & George, G. (2002). Absorptive capacity: A review, reconceptualization, and extension. *Academy of Management Review, 27*(2), 185–203.

This research was previously published in Evaluating Media Richness in Organizational Learning; pages 49-81, copyright year 2018 by Business Science Reference (an imprint of IGI Global).

Chapter 11
Social Media Data Into Performance Measurement Systems:
Methodologies, Opportunities, and Risks

Deborah Agostino
Politecnico di Milano, Italy

Michela Arnaboldi
Politecnico di Milano, Italy

Giovanni Azzone
Politecnico di Milano, Italy

ABSTRACT

Social media data are spreading widely across the world with a number of public institutions now active on social media. Much attention is being paid to how public institutions can exploit social media, for example, to provide better public services or engage with the general public. Little is, however, known about the potential offered by the data generated through social media, in particular, the possibility of applying social media data formally within a performance measurement system (PMS). The aim of this chapter is to explore how social media data can be integrated into a PMS for a public institution, proposing in this respect a framework of analysis. This framework places the decision-maker at the centre of the cycle and it consists of three main phases: the collection of social media data, the computation of indicators, and the visualization of data.

DOI: 10.4018/978-1-7998-9020-1.ch011

INTRODUCTION

Over the past few years, Performance Measurement Systems (PMSs) used within public administrative bodies have been at the centre of academic and practitioner debates, with the publication of several contributions on how to design, implement and use a PMS to support public institutions in managing, controlling and reporting on their work (Arnaboldi, Lapsley, Steccolini, 2015).

The data that allow the system to work are a core component of a PMS. Financial and non-financial data have traditionally acted as the main sources for the system, enabling financial and non-financial indicators to be elaborated. Typically, these data are highly reliable (since data are certified and sometimes audited) updated less frequently and involve lower volumes. Traditional financial and non-financial data are not immune to problems such as "excessively long publication delays, insufficient coverage of topics of interest, and the top-down process of data creation" (Severo et al., 2016, p. 354).

Latterly, a further type of data has emerged, social media data, fuelling debate on their potential and opportunities. Social media, broadly defined as online platforms based on two-way interaction (Kaplan and Haenlein, 2010), have spread extremely rapidly in recent years, with people posting all the time about anything from anywhere, contributing to the mass generation of social media data.

Two characteristics distinguish social media data from traditional organizational data: social media data are provided by the users, rather than the organization, and in real time, rather than when the organization deems it appropriate. Volumes are consequently higher, more frequent and data must be extracted from social platforms, since they are not readily available within the organization.

Social media data provide a real opportunity for organizations to improve their accountability practices. In this continuous evolving landscape, we have some degree of knowledge on how public authorities use social media. For example, it is widely recognized that public authorities endorse social media for a broad spectrum of purposes that range from citizen involvement and participatory budgeting, to improving the delivery of public services, fraud detection and transparency (Bonsón et al., 2012; Janssen and van den Hoven, 2015). Little, however, is known in terms of how social media data can be used to set in place a PMS, with the final end of enabling public sector accountability internally and externally.

The aim of this chapter is to provide a framework for integrating social media data into a PMS, which is achieved by identifying the main phases of analysis, as well as determining the risks and opportunities within each phase. In view of this, three main questions will be addressed:

- What are the main steps, and associated risks, for extracting and downloading data from social media platforms? This question is connected with the problem of data collection: not all social media platforms allow their data to be freely extracted and, at the same time, the type of data downloaded can vary depending on the search formulae employed.
- How to make sense of social media data? This question is connected to the appropriate Key Performance Indicators (KPIs) that must be identified in order to transform social media conversations into usable information.
- How can social media data be reported? This concerns the problem of bringing social media analysis into the sphere of non-experts.

Methodologically, the proposed framework is the outcome of six years during which the authors were engaged in social media projects alongside a number of public sector bodies and institutions, including municipalities, public museums, theatres and institutions of higher education.

The chapter is organized into three main sections. The first contains the background on the evolution of data for PMSs, with particular attention placed on social media data. The main arguments are then developed, presenting and discussing the framework to assimilate social media data into a PMS, and this framework will, in turn, be organized into three parts that follow the main phases of analysis. The third and final section covers the directions for future research, the recommendations for academics and practitioners, and lastly draws some conclusions.

BACKGROUND: FROM TRADITIONAL DATA TO SOCIAL MEDIA DATA

The aim of this section is to provide the background literature in support of the central theme of this chapter, that of integrating social media data into a PMS. The section is divided into two parts: the first part will discuss how the data feeding a PMS have evolved from traditional financial data to social media data. The second part will present the distinctive features of social media data.

The Evolution of Data to Feed a PMS

Data are of central importance to a PMS and, indeed, a PMS can be defined as: "The regular collection and reporting of information about the efficiency, quality and effectiveness of government programs" (Nyhan & Martin, 1999, p. 348). Data are collected and elaborated into a set of KPIs and then communicated using a reporting system that can take the form of a dashboard or a scorecard. Data so collected, elaborated and communicated can support internal accountability, by being able to provide public sector managers and policy-makers with a series of indicators that can guide them in defining future targets and help them to identify the corrective actions (Behn, 2003). Data can also serve external accountability purposes, since they are available outside the organization to other public entities and the general public (Kloot and Martin, 2000).

The actual elements of a PMS can vary from one organization to another. The KPIs can differ according to the strategic objectives set in place within a given organization and, similarly, the dashboards reporting the results can take different forms. Regardless of the PMS's structure, data are of crucial importance if the system is to function: data feed a PMS system.

Over the years, the data available to the public sector have increased drastically, on the back of the frequency of their collection and the volumes and variety of data gathered. In particular, three main types of data are progressively becoming available to public institutions (see Table 1):

- Financial data, both internal and external;
- Non-financial data, both internal and external;
- Social media data.
- **Financial Data:** Entities in the public sector have traditionally used financial data to account for their actions (Carmeli, 2002). The data come from official financial reports relating to the organization itself or the market. The organization's financial data consist of data from balance sheets, income statements and financial statements. Data referring to the market consists of data from tax payers or the financial market.

Both internal and external financial data are defined to be of low frequency, since the documents from which they are generated are produced on a periodical basis, usually quarterly or annually. The reliability of financial data is high, since the data are retrieved from trustworthy sources and have been validated by the organization and external auditors. Annual reports, for example, must be audited externally to be approved, and data from tax payers are verified periodically. The volume of data produced is relatively low, in part because this occurs with low frequency. Lastly, these data are of a similar type, so variety is low, since they refer to monetary matters and they are often summarized in tables (for example, an annual report template).

●**Non-Financial Data:** These refer to data expressed in numbers, but not in monetary terms. Non-financial data traditionally measure information, such as time, quality, flexibility, social and environmental responsibility. Once again, non-financial data can refer to the organization itself or to the external environment. When non-financial data relate to the organization, they often include information about the quality and length of the administrative processes, and the sustainability of the organization. When data relate, instead, to the external environment, they often refer to aspects such as customer satisfaction regarding a given service. Kaplan and Norton (1992) stressed the importance of non-financial data when introducing their balanced scorecard. The authors criticized traditional financial data for how they have been appraised and utilized in the past, and, to overcome this issue, they suggested adopting non-financial data, more specifically, leading indicators, defined so because of their greater timeliness (compared to financial data). Kaplan and Norton underscored the importance of having a PMS that balances both types of data, prompting a wide clutch of studies covering the application of balanced scorecards in public institutions (Kloot and Martin, 2000; Dimitropoulos Kosmas, Douvis 2017).

Non-financial data are collected more frequently than financial data, since there is no need to wait for consolidated information at the end of a given period. Reliability of such data is medium-high, even though they are not validated by an external auditor, as is the case with financial data. Volumes are higher than for financial data, since the intervals between collecting data can be smaller, for example, months, weeks or days. The variety of the data is low since non-financial data comes in numerical form.

● **Social Media Data:** These have set the trend of the past ten years. Data is produced through the users' conversations and interaction on social media platforms. They have led to a break from financial and non-financial data since, for the first time, data are generated by users during their online conversations with their peers. Social media data are generated at a high frequency, since conversations on social media take place in real time (Kaplan and Haenlein, 2010). It has been estimated that, in one internet minute, people post 3.3 million items on Facebook, send 448,800 tweets and upload 65,972 photos on Instagram (Allen, 2017). The reliability of social media data is very low, a fact that has been often been pointed out by social media opponents, who underline how easy it is to obtain fake or unreliable information without being able to verify it (Graham and Avery, 2013). Everyone can create his/her own social media account, but no one is in charge of checking the reliability of the information provided, or the truth in social media conversations. The high frequency at which social media data are generated is also associated with high volumes of data. This can create problems for organizations in terms of their storage capacity, which is one factor behind the emergence of the cloud as a solution to manage this matter (Kitchin, 2014).

Unlike financial and non-financial data, social media data also come in any garb, since users can post a message or join a discussion (hence text), upload an image, a video or a website link. This variety of formats can create problems in terms of data homogeneity and subsequent analysis.

Table 1. Comparison between financial data, non-financial data and social media data

	Frequency	Reliability	Volume	Variety	Boundaries
Financial data	Low	High	Low	Low	Internal or external
Non-financial data	Medium	Medium-high	Medium	Low	Internal or external
Social media data	High	Low	High	High	Mainly external

Social Media Data Between Proponents and Opponents

It has been generally recognized that social media data can drastically change the way in which organizations in the private, public and non-profit sector all operate:

- "Our increasing ability to produce, collect, store, and analyse vast amounts of data is going to transform our understanding of the political world" (Clark and Golder, 2015, p. 65).
- "One of the key promises of big data tomorrow is the ability - through sheer size and comprehensiveness - to analyse small populations, extreme outcomes, or rare events, that is, the 'tails of the distribution'" (Mergel et al., 2016, p. 931).
- "Though these conversations are predominantly practice driven, organizations are exploring how large-volume data can usefully be deployed to create and capture value for individuals, businesses, communities, and governments" (George et al., 2014, p. 321).
- "Data gathered by social media such as Twitter and Facebook, by content sharing websites such as Flickr and Panoramic, or by participatory platforms such as Wikipedia and OpenStreetMap, seem to provide interesting solutions to the failures of traditional data" (Severo et al., 2016, p. 355).

These quotes underline the new possibilities linked to how public sectors authorities can exploit social media data. Little is, however, known about the possibility of assimilating social media data within a PMS belonging to a public sector entity, and the opportunities and threats linked to this type of data are sparking lively debate. Concentrating on the opportunities offered by social media data, these can refer to three main aspects:

- The possibility for public sector authorities to obtain *detailed knowledge of service users and the general public.* By monitoring social media, they can gain further insights into the public, their habits and their opinions simply from their social media conversations (Khan, 2014; Bonsón et al., 2015; Severo et al., 2016; Reddick et al, 2017). This has led to the emergence of a set of techniques for monitoring social media conversations (Agostino and Sidorova, 2016), as well as engendering new opportunities to establish a closer relationship with the social media users themselves. Moreover, social media data do not merely help in acquiring better knowledge about individual users, with a focus on the present. Some authors have observed that it is possible to use data analytics techniques can be used to predict the likelihood of future events or future actions (George et al., 2014).

- The possibility of gaining *unexpected insights* into the environment, the organization or the general public, a concept often referred to as "data-driven society" (Power, 2015). By listening to social media conversations, data flows from the public to the organization, which, in turn, investigates and analyzes the data without having a specific question in mind. It has been stated, on this point, that "New analytics might present the illusion of automatically discovering insights without asking questions, but the algorithms used most certainly did arise and were tested scientifically for validity and veracity" (Kitchin, 2014, p. 5). While it is true that this approach can provide the means for gleaning new and unexpected insights into a specific phenomenon, the approach itself has been criticized by some other authors for driving actions without any specific questions or knowledge in mind: "Indeed, much of the "promise" of these data has been their "post-theoretical" nature - focusing on the possibilities for discovery within huge and newly accessible data sets without well-developed conceptual foundations that also provide actionable insights for policy makers or public managers" (Mergel et al., 2016)

- The possibility of *gaining insights into the general public without asking them directly*, but rather by monitoring their conversations on social media (Agostino and Arnaboldi, 2016). Usually, organisations needing to collect opinions expressed by service users or the general public must implement customer satisfaction surveys, which is a time-consuming and costly exercise. Conversations analyzed on social media can provide some degree of knowledge about the general public's perception on a matter without questioning people directly.

It is, however, the case that social media data have not been immune to criticism, and threats and various problems have been also pointed out:

- Social media data can be of *low reliability* since no one is in charge of checking them for trustfulness (e.g. Lazer et al., 2014). This occurs at different levels. In first place, social media users can set up fake accounts, because anyone is free to define whatever profile features they wish on a social media account. When searching for a public sector entity on Facebook or Twitter, it is more than likely that the search will return several hits. This can create problems in terms of trusting the data source. In second place, neither the data provided by users on social media nor their conversations are verified or in any way certified, which is the case with traditional data.

- Social media are likely to be of *limited representativeness*. Even though the number of people with a personal internet connection has significantly increased over the years, social media data can only give a restricted representation of the reality. This is compounded by the fact that not all geographical areas are covered by internet, restricting its use for some people. In addition, not everyone uses social media; elderly people are often less keen about using these technologies and these factors could affect the distribution of the social media data, which may not reflect that of the population.

- Social media data can present some *privacy issues*. While social media data improve the transparency of governmental action, there can be issues of privacy when public institutions download and analyze conversations on social media (Janssen and van den Hoven, 2015). This aspect is also associated with the authenticity of the information posted: if you know that your account and your digital traces are monitored, will you be honest and genuine in your social media conversations?

It follows that, while personal data can provide several new insights to support, for example the delivery of better public services, there is also concern about how the data are used for public affair purposes.

Within this complex world of social media data, little is known about how players in the public sector can integrate this new type of data into a PMS. This is important because PMSs continue to play a central role in the private sector, but, at the same time, more resources are now dedicated to managing and using social media (e.g. Bonsón et al., 2015; Severo et al., 2016; Reddick et al, 2017) and, with the continuous evolution in data analysis technology, these public sector entities will find that they are becoming able to manage – and use – the data. Given the background above, this chapter examines how social media data can be brought into a PMS, and therefore utilized, addressing three main research questions:

- What are the main steps, and correlated risks, for extracting and downloading data from social media platforms?
- How can we make sense of social media data?
- How can social media data be represented and reported?

A Reference Framework for Integrating Social Media Data Into a PMS

The process of assembling social media data into a PMS can be represented as a cycle, involving three main phases: the collection of social media data, the elaboration of KPIs and the visualization of the data (see Figure 1). Each of these phases is based upon a common core assumption: the decision-maker is positioned at the centre of the cycle. The decision-maker is responsible for defining how each phase in the cycle is performed, how the analysis is conducted and for what purposes are the data collected. It is worth underlining that there must be a research question or research objective expressed by the decision-maker underpinning the collecting of data and which address an initial issue. This underlying need is of crucial importance for two reasons in particular. Firstly, the idea of a "data-driven" society is misleading. Without having in mind a specific question that needs answering, it is actually quite difficult to define which types of social media data are to be collected and over what period of time, or which key words to use. Secondly, even at the point of choosing the software for social media analytics, public institutions need to come up with a research question. There is, sometimes, the incorrect assumption that social media data flows automatically into organizations. This is not the case, given that, even when the software for analyzing social media data has been selected, the criteria for analysis still need to be set. Depending on how these criteria are defined, the results can vary, in some instances quite significantly. For example, by changing the period of time to be analyzed or by choosing different keywords to download the social media posts, the data retrieved for input to further analyses can be utterly different.

When software is introduced for social media analytics, although the time and skill necessary to perform the internal analyses is reduced, a whole range of new issues appears in terms of price, how well those who will be using the software know it, user-friendliness, training requirements, flexibility of use, installation requirements, security and source code security scans.

Each phase of the cycle will be described in this section, with particular attention regarding the various choices for decision-makers.

Figure 1. Graphical representation of the framework for integrating social media data into a PMS

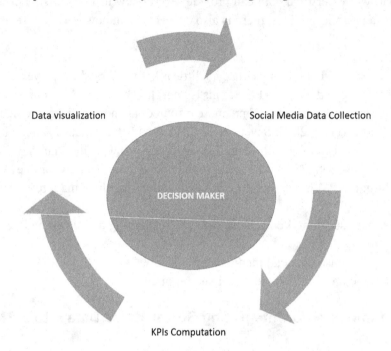

Phase 1: Social Media Data Collection

The first phase of the cycle concerns the collection of social media data, which involves downloading and storing data obtained from social media conversations. This phase is associated with a set of decisions that will affect what can be gained from the social media data in terms of its contribution (see Table 2), as well as the results of the following analysis. These decisions include the following:

- **Frequency of Social Media Data Collection:** As already mentioned in this chapter, a key feature of social media is that data are generated in real time through social media conversations. Real time generation has its own set of decisions about how often social media data are collected: data can be obtained through web crawling in real time, while the conversation is actually taking place, or periodically at predefined times, such as at the end of the day, week or month. In all cases, substantial storage capacity is required, especially when the social media to be analyzed and the social media accounts monitored are many. The frequency of data collection affects the timeliness of the actions: when data are collected in real time, actions can be taken immediately, which is not the case when data are collected periodically. Real-time data collection is used in crisis/disaster management and in politics to monitor voter perception during an election (e.g. Ceron et al., 2014). Periodical data collection is more common when evaluating public services and measuring cultural events (e.g. Chua et al., 2016).
- **Types of Social Media Channels:** Social media is a generic term to describe social platforms based on web 2.0 technology (Kaplan and Haenlein, 2010). Numerous platforms come under the umbrella term of social media, among which are Twitter, Facebook, Instagram, Google +, YouTube and many others. In order to retrieve social media data, one of the first decisions is to

identify the social media sources to be investigated. The choice of sources, either all social media channels or a selection of them, is dependent on the *accessibility* of social media data. While some social media allow data to be downloaded for free, with Twitter being a prime example, others, such as Facebook, do not allow this (although some software tools analyse data on Facebook without the need to download them). Different levels of social media data accessibility can, in some cases, determine the choice.

- **Criteria for Data Collection:** For social media data to be downloaded, the criteria for data collection must also be defined. Data can be downloaded with reference to a set of pre-determined accounts, or data can be downloaded via keywords. When data are downloaded from social media accounts, such as that of the institution for public administration being analyzed, then the insights gleaned relate mainly to the topics posted by the organization itself, together with the ensuing reactions expressed by social media users. When data are, instead, downloaded via keywords, the data collected relate to the general public's perception of whatever subject matter was decided by the decision-maker. For example, in a study conducted by Agostino and Arnaboldi (2016) on a sample of Italian universities, the authors used Twitter to investigate the students' perception of university support services. In their analysis, the authors distinguished between the results obtained through data collected from the university account and the results obtained through keyword searches (which, in that specific case, were the names of the universities concerned). It emerged that more tweets were extrapolated through a keywords search and opinions about services were also more frequent. The decision-maker is once again responsible for determining the criteria to be used in the data collection phase, which are strictly connected to the objective of the investigation. In general terms, when the purpose is to get an understanding of what is said in conversations posted on the official social media account belonging to a public sector entity, it is preferable to go down the route of downloading per account. When, instead, the purpose is mainly related to investigating the general public's perception of some matter, then a keyword search is preferred.

- A further decision concerns the types of data to be extracted. A single social media post contains several pieces of information, even in the 140 characters of a tweet. The information associated to a single post contains the body of the post (i.e. text, video, image or link), the date and time of publication, the language, the number of likes, comments and retweet/shares, where it was posted and by whom – with the author's set of information (gender, DoB, the user's Twitter lists, tweets per month, number of followers, user's location). This list gives a further indication of the potential information that can be retrieved from one single post on social media, and the several insights that can be gleaned when subjected to social media analysis. Two aspects need to be considered when making decisions about the types of data to extract. First, retrieving more information implies more time for downloading and more storage space needed. Second, this decision needs to be optimized for the purposes of the analysis. For example, if the intention is to build a network of all people using the social media account belonging to a public institution, then the authors' details are relevant, while statistics concerning the post or its language and location are probably redundant. If, on the contrary, the purpose is to understand the reach of each social media post and whether the public entity is able to engage with the general public, the statistics for the posts are relevant, while the users' details are not.

Once these decisions are made, data can be downloaded and the data collected can be analyzed.

Table 2. Managerial decisions connected to phase 1 of social media data collection

Decision	Alternatives/Options
Frequency of data collection	Real-time vs periodical
Types of social media channels	All social media platforms vs a sample of social media platforms
Criteria for data collection	Per account vs per keywords
Types of data to be extracted	Data on single post and/or data about the author of the posts

Step 2: Computation of KPIs

The second phase of the cycle concerns the computation of Key Performance Indicators (KPIs). The elaboration of the KPIs is a crucial phase, as this is when the social media data are translated into a source of knowledge to support the decision-maker.

Before elaborating the KPIs, an intermediate data-cleaning step is performed to verify that the downloaded data reflect the initial intentions and, if necessary, the previous data download phase can be refined and re-run. The data-cleaning process requires some manual work. The downloaded data are usually stored in an Excel spreadsheet or in a .csv format, and need to be checked against a sample of the posts. The reliability and consistency of the information can easily be corroborated by reading the posts. If they are and the posts are coherent with the purpose of the analysis, then the KPIs can be computed. If not, the decisions taken in phase one of the data collection must be revised and data collected a second time. For example, Manchester can be the name of the city in England as well as part of the name of a football team (i.e. Manchester United). If the purpose of the analysis is to understand which topics connected to the city of Manchester are generating discussions and the word Manchester is used as a keyword, then all the posts pertinent to the Manchester United football team will also be downloaded. This could lead to problems in analyzing the data, since the data set cannot be trusted. Issues such as these can be managed by inserting stop words into the analysis: by, for example, downloading the posts that include the word "Manchester" but not those that also contain the word "football" or "team" or the names of football players.

Several indicators and techniques have been presented to date concerning the computation of KPIs for social media conversations (see Agostino and Sidorova, 2016 for a review), although only a few have found application in the public sector field. This assembly of techniques and measures can be organized into two main dimensions: KPIs to measure social media conversations and KPIs to measure social media users (see Table 3).

The KPIs measuring social media conversations generally include the following:

- **Reach:** This comprises several different indicators, such as the number of likes, comments, retweets and shares of a post. These are the most common measures, and have found wide-spread application in studies to evaluate the ability of public institutions to inform and engage with the general public. For example, Bonsón et al. (2015) elaborated the metrics of popularity, virality, commitment and engagement for the Facebook pages of local governments in western Europe to gain an understanding about the level of stakeholder engagement associated with the local governments who adopt social media.

Table 3. Key Performance Indicators related to social media data

Dimension of analysis	KPIs
KPIs for social media conversations	• Reach (e.g. number of likes, comments, retweets, shares of a post) • Language • Content • Timing (Date and Time) • Sentiment
KPIs for social media users	• Social media influencer • Centrality of the social media network • Density of the social media network

- **Language:** This is an indicator used to determine the distribution of social media conversations between the different languages appearing in a thread. It can provide valuable information for understanding language distribution in a conversation. For example, in their study, Arnaboldi et al. (2017) used the indicator for the language used in conversations on social media posts, in combination with geo-referenced information for the associated posts, to identify language communities within the city neighbourhoods of Milan. This information, with its insights into multilingualism and the diffusion of cultural communities in the city – which was obtained via this indicator from social media data - was then passed on to municipality officials.

- **Content:** This indicator can be used to analyse the topics of conversations taking place on social media, mainly by counting word frequency. A range of techniques have been developed to identify topics of discussion, which include natural language processing and semantic web approaches (e.g. Shet and Nagarajan, 2009; Bhardwaj et al., 2014). Regardless of the techniques used to compute the indicator, measures about the content of the conversation help to establish what a conversation is about, with the most common words being listed, and this in turn can support the decision-making process. For example, in their study, Reddick et al. (2017) used text mining techniques on Facebook data concerning the local government of San Antonio, in Texas, to understand the public's perception of the city's waste management services, examining how far social media encouraged, and facilitated, public engagement and what lessons the local government learnt from its use of social media.

- **Sentiment:** This relates to a set of indicators used to determine the users' opinion on a certain topic. This elaboration is usually performed in combination with the content analysis of the conversation. The most common words are first identified to understand what social media users are talking about; then the indicators that determine the sentiment of the conversation are elaborated in order to work out the feelings associated to the conversation. This analysis can be useful ex-post to analyze public opinion about a given public service or an event, or the analysis can be in real time to investigate what people are thinking about a topic while discussing it on social media. For example, in their study, Zavattaro et al. (2015) explored the sentiment of tweets to connect the general public's opinion with their level of engagement, finding that positive sentiment is usually linked to a more active level of engagement.

A second cluster of KPIs are used to investigate social media users, in terms of the structure of the network that is being generated through social media conversations. In this case, the investigation is concerned with the identification of social media influencers or the detailed analysis of the centrality or density of the network of social media users. Three main indicators can be identified:

- **Social Media Influencers:** This indicator is used to identify social media users who have a high status within the network generated around a given institution or around a set of keywords. A social media influencer is a social media user with a high number of connections (contacts) on social media, who is trusted by the general public and who can spread social media posts with ease. Whenever an influencer retweets a post, this will immediately reach numerous other users through the influencer's network of connections. Discussions on social media influencers are a recurrent theme in marketing analysis, but are less common in the field of public administration. One of the few exceptions is the study by Antoniadis et al. (2016), who defined a Twitter Authority Index to identify the influence of e-government Twitter accounts. Despite their limited diffusion within the field of public administration, the methods and indicators that identify influencers on social media can recognize the key influencers in the sector, and public sector institutes can manage their social media accounts accordingly.
- **Centrality of the Social Media Network:** These indicators are used to analyse the structure of the network generated through social media conversations, and so identify the social media users that send most posts or those closest to the organization under analysis, as well as the distance between the different users within a social media network. Social network analysis techniques are, in general, used to carry out this analysis (e.g. Chen et al., 2012), where the end aim is to characterize the network of social media users in order learn more about the users themselves. In this respect, the study by Ediger et al. (2010) proposes a graph analysis for social networks that can be used to extract useful information. They suggest using the indicator of betweenness centrality to rank users on the basis of whether they can be positioned between other users, and hence within a conversation.
- **Density of the Social Media Network:** This measure is used to determine the number of connections between the different social media users. High density implies a network where social media users interact intensely with each other while a low density social media network is when social media users have few conversations. Here, also, social network analysis techniques can be used to perform the analysis (e.g. Chen et al., 2012). The managerial relevance of this indicator is associated to the possibility of evaluating how significantly a public sector entity can enhance dialogue with the general public on its social media accounts. For example, in their study, Khan et al. (2014) used social network analysis techniques and, among other things, also computed an indicator of network density to investigate the high or low density of network interaction between South Korean ministries. They found that the network presented a high level of density, which therefore acted as a proxy of the numerous interactions between the South Korean ministries.

At the end of this phase, some level of knowledge has been acquired in terms of content and topics of conversation, as well as structure of the network and the features of social media users.

Step 3: Data Visualization

Data visualization has been defined as the "visual representation of data whereby information [...] has been abstracted in some schematic form with the goal of communicating information clearly and effectively through graphical means" (Batrinca and Treleaven, 2015, p. 90)

At the end of the two previous phases (i.e. download of data and computation of KPIs), social media data have been transformed into a usable set of information. The format in which KPIs are provided is often, however, not easy to access or understand. Think of an Excel spreadsheet with a long list of positive or negative opinions or a long list of key words to highlight topics or, again, a graphical network representation. This can provide useful insights for those who perform the analysis but, for other public sector managers, public officials and the general public, it is not particularly easy to understand. Data visualization is used to transform the computed indicators into dashboards, infographics or other visual tools that can help users to understand the insights generated. With the diffusion of social media, data visualization has become of primary importance, given the scale of data generated and the need to identify a suitable format of communication.

Various data visualization tools are available, which provide different functions, such as multidimensionality, interactivity or give the possibility to drill down for data. Three main data visualization tools are presented here: dashboards, images and interactive maps. It is important to underline that this is not an exhaustive list of all possible tools for data visualization, but it does provide a selection of the ideal types, isolating their main distinctive features. These tools can also be adopted simultaneously and the same analysis can be reported using different visualization tools, according to whom will receive the information.

- **Dashboards:** This tool consists of a module or template, usually divided into different areas. The performance dimensions are represented through a list of indicators and their relative values in each area.

Data are presented on dashboards as numbers, but are separated into different areas so that the performance dimension of reference for the information provided can be understood more readily.

There are two main distinctive features for dashboards: multi-dimensionality and the possibility to drill down to reach the information shown. Dashboards are, by definition, distinguished by multiple dimensions of analysis, since they are a balance of financial, non-financial and social media data. In this respect, they answer the need to integrate insights from social media with evidence obtained from other sources to inform decision-making. The second feature is related to the possibility of drilling down for the data provided. Kaplan and Norton (1996), when introducing the best-known dashboard (i.e. the balanced scorecard) underlined the possibility of creating a cascade down the scorecard, starting from the organizational level and going down to the individual scorecard, thereby ensuring a connection between the organizational strategy and individual actions.

Dashboards as a visualization tool are often easy to implement for use in public administration (Kloot and Martin, 2000; Dimitropoulos et al., 2017). Focusing specifically on a social media dashboard, each social media platform can automatically provide the owner of the social media page with a dashboard to monitor the statistics relating to the proprietary social media page. The predefined social media dashboard can be an easy tool to monitor the statistics for an individual social media account in the public sector.

- **Images:** These are another type of visualization tool and their main feature is to paint a picture of a given situation. Unlike dashboards, where data are visualized as numbers, in images, numbers are generally replaced by pictures.

Images present a given situation in a clear way that is easy to understand, especially when those receiving the information are not keen on numbers. Hence, these tools are mainly the preferred option for external communication purposes or when the person receiving the image is not an analysis expert. While an image gives a message that is immediate, this method does have two basic disadvantages: the detail cannot be caught since there is no numerical value describing the situation; and multi-dimensionality and data integration are difficult to achieve since only a small amount of information can typically be represented.

The visual representation of social media data has found great applications in existing social media studies, since masses of data can be translated into a comprehensible format. For example, in the previously mentioned study on multilingualism within the city of Milan (Arnaboldi et al., 2017) the geo-referenced tweets analyzed were represented visually to highlight the different clusters of languages within the city. Maps and visual maps are particularly useful for combining and integrating spatio-temporal data, increasing the insights that can be gleaned from social media data (Tsou, 2015). The study by Chae et al (2012) is another example in this field, where spatio-temporal data are filtered and zoomed in on a map. The authors used the spatio-temporal location of Twitter data to link posts on Titter to the area and the date/time when the tweet was sent, as a means to provide insights into crisis management (i.e. fires or earthquakes).

- **Interactive Maps:** This is another visualization tool, based mainly on images. Interactive maps offer real time visualization of data with their spatio-temporal location, giving users the possibility of fine-tuning the data shown.

Interactive maps have two main features: interactivity between the person analyzing the information and the person receiving it, and possibility to drill down to the data to be provided, in keeping with the need for visualization. With reference to interactivity, unlike images that plot data at a given moment of time, interactive maps allow users to refine their analysis independently. It is clearly often an advantage if users search for their own perspective of analysis, for example by zooming in on items that interest them the most. At the same time, for interactive maps to be effective, the tools need to be easy to use, since they are managed by the person who receives the information. Looking at the drill-down feature, an interactive map usually allows users to define their own level of analysis. Think, for example, of an interactive city map where the level of analysis can be defined by the user, to take the entire city, a certain neighbourhood or a given street.

Interactive maps have found great favour in open government initiatives to provide the general public with real time visualizations of certain phenomena. For example, the city of Chicago developed an open portal (data.cityofchicago.org) in 2010. The idea of interactive maps is not simply to present data but to exploit its open format and allow the users reading the data to use them again. In the example of the city of Chicago, after the open data portal was published, a group of people set up an independent project based on re-using the published data. Interactive city maps using an open format, where social media data were linked with traditional data and data from sensors, were found to be powerful not only in terms of external accountability, but also for strengthening public engagement (Kassen, 2013).

Every visualization tool has different features and requires different set of skills to produce results. The choice of the most appropriate visualization tool depends on who is receiving the information and the skills available. The lesser the experience in data analysis matters, the simpler the data visualization tool needs to be. In addition, the lack of internal competences concerning social media data management is a factor that forces public institutions to opt for a predefined dashboard.

Recommendation

The previous analysis has highlighted the three main phases to be followed in order to integrate social media data into a PMS for use in public administration. These three phases determine a cycle, and for the cycle to be completed, the centrality of the decision-maker is critical, being in charge of the entire process. At this stage, it is also important to set out several recommendations for public managers and public officials who intend to make use of the above mentioned cycle to introduce social media data into their PMSs:

- **Quality of Social Media Data:** Social media data are generated by users and there is no control over their quality, as instead is the case with financial data. Financial data, traditionally used in the public sector, are audited and certified, a fact that is reassuring for readers, who can therefore trust the data and rely on them being of high quality (although, as we know well, there have been frauds and scandals in connection with financial data). Social media data, by their very definition, cannot be audited, since they are generated by users and any attempt to check the truthfulness would be extremely complex, either in connection with a post or to verify truthfulness of the personal data provided by users (if the data are then used in any user profiling analysis). This means that the quality of the social media data can range from credible to rubbish. Importantly, public sector bodies with the intention of including social media data in their PMSs must be aware of this aspect and introduce techniques to verify the credibility of any posted content. On this point, several authors (Castillo, Mendoza, Poblete, 2011; Shao et al., 2016) have provided techniques and tools for assessing the credibility of social media posts, to avoid the risks associated to fake information.
- **Integration of Social Media Data With Other Sources:** Social media data, even when they fall under the three-phase cycle, do not, on their own, provide knowledge. They have to be combined with other types of data in order to provide evidence and support internal and external accountability: "Whilst Big Data Analytics might provide some insights, it needs to be recognized that they are limited in scope, produce particular kinds of knowledge, and *still need contextualization with respect to other information (emphasis added)*, whether that be existing theory, policy documents, small data studies, or historical records, that can help to make sense of the patterns evident" (Kitchin, 2014, p. 9). This citation stresses the importance of integrating social media data with pre-acquired knowledge of the context under investigation, as well as with traditional financial and non-financial data. Social media data are a powerful source of data for public institutions, but cannot replace traditional financial reports or non-financial analysis. What they can do is provide a new and different perspective on some events. They can also address the shortcoming of low timeliness and missing values that sometimes are the bane of traditional data (Severo et al., 2016)
- **Competences in Social Media Data:** When dealing with social media data for a PMS, a key issue concerns the competences required of the professionals and public officials who are handling these data. These competences are needed both in terms of completing the cycle and of using the

data and indicators obtained. For the cycle to be executed, a level of expertise in social media and data analytics is required. Skills in ICT are generally necessary to download social media data, statistical skills are possibly needed to elaborate the KPIs, as large datasets come into play and some indicators (especially those related to social network analysis) can require advanced statistical expertise. Finally, visual reports may have to be prepared with the help of professionals with skills in data design. This heterogeneous set of skills can be a problem for public institutions given the current climate of financial austerity. These are the reasons why public institutions have set up social media accounts, but do not analyze the data. An alternative solution to developing the previous competences is to purchase software for social media analytics. The offer on the market is relatively broad. It is, however, important to make the further observation that any software still needs a decision-maker at the centre of the process to drive the entire cycle. Moreover, performance and accounting-based competences are required, if the data is actually to be used. In this respect, public accountants and/or public administrators in charge of decision-making must have some knowledge of the distinctive features of social media data and their role in enhancing the decision-making process. The issue of skills leads to a further reflection on the training for public officials needed now and in the future, a point that will be discussed at the end of this section.

- **The Decision-Maker at the Centre and Identification of a Process Owner:** As has been emphasized several times in this chapter, this aspect is of crucial importance. We are mentioning it again here to underline the importance of having a unique owner in charge of the entire process of integrating social media data within a PMS. In several public institutions, there is separation between the person/function responsible for social media management (usually in charge of the communication area), the person/function who deals with public finance and who manages traditional financial data, and the head of each specific service. For the cycle to work properly, a unique process owner must be identified. The process owner has the function of collecting insights from the different technical experts and is in charge of driving the entire cycle to integrate social media data into a PMS. This implies having a good understanding of the problems and questions to be answered, which can be acquired in a number of ways, including by dealing with the heads of the different public services; interacting with the social media manager to understand how social media are used and define the criteria for data collection accordingly; and determining the necessary KPIs on the basis of the initial research question. At this stage, alongside social media data, other types of data can be retrieved, thereby providing a complete overview. Finally, data can be represented graphically using the most appropriate visualization tool, in view of the receiver of the information.

Applicability of the Proposed Framework

While the proposed framework sets out a series of phases to exploit social media data and bring them into a PMS, its greater use within the public sector can be underpinned by two main strategies:

- **Training Current and Future Public Officials:** This can be achieved by designing ad hoc courses to teach social media technologies and the use of social media data as part of the public administration programmes taught at universities. Moreover, ad hoc courses can also be designed for public sector professionals to give them advanced background knowledge on social media data and their role in a PMS. In this last case, action-learning methods can be particularly useful for putting theory into practice. Training of this type can be provided through public sector courses as well as in performance management courses, given the multi-disciplinarity of the topic.

- **Creating Awareness About the Potential of Integrating Social Media Data Within a PMS:** While awareness around social media and social media data in the public sector is high, as clearly seen by the increasing number of practitioner reports on social media in public affairs (Mergel, 2014), creating awareness of the benefits connected to integrating social media data within a PMS can help the model to propagate. This awareness can be achieved by publishing practitioner reports on social media data for PMSs and through workshops targeting practitioners, with the aim of sharing best practice on the use of social media data. European projects could act as a setting for workshops and practitioner reports.

The expected impact of including social media data in a PMS belonging to a public institution is improvement in the management of public services. This is because the information that informs the decision-making process combined – and enriched - with data from the users themselves can lead to more timely information. A typical example is in emergency management, with several examples of the public sector relying on social media data to respond more effectively during emergencies such as hurricanes and earthquakes (Conrado et al., 2016), and the same can be the case in health care, education and public transport. Including social media data into a PMS can produce a real time control system, and offer the real opportunity of improving public service management.

A final remark relates to the pace at which social media and social technologies evolve. The types of social media and their functions are continuously evolving, which makes it difficult to provide knowledge – an indeed insights - that will last into the future. The model we propose is, however, unconnected to any specific technology or to any single feature, but provides an overall method that can be applied to all social media data. This ensures that the approach can be replicated using new technology in the future.

FUTURE RESEARCH DIRECTIONS

In this chapter, we have highlighted the opportunities offered by social media data, providing a framework for social media data to be integrated into a public sector PMS. The framework presented offers some reflections for future research. In particular, three areas of investigation are worth considering in future studies:

- The implementation process of the social media data framework. The proposed framework is organized into three main phases of analysis: the collection of social media data, the computation of KPIs and the visualization of data. The framework was obtained after the authors were engaged over a six-year period in social media projects of public administration. The framework is conceptual in nature, despite being derived from empirical observations. Future research can investigate how this framework is being implemented by the public institutions that intend to integrate social media data into their PMSs. An analysis of the implementation process would allow us to identify any obstacles and the factors that enable the process itself.
- The integration of other types of big data. The entire analysis has been centred on the possibility of including social media data within a PMS. Social media data are, however, only one type of big data – data of high volume, high velocity and high variety (George et al., 2014). The big data

realm also includes data from city sensors, from GPS (Global Positioning Systems) and from medical records. Future investigations can explore how other types of big data can be integrated into the PMS alongside social media data. The decision here to focus particularly on social media data was driven by the wide diffusion of these tools in the public sector.

- The effectiveness of public decisions informed by social media data. Proponents of social media and big data make all sorts of claims about the faster and novel insights provided by social media data (e.g. Clark and Golder, 2015; Mergel et al., 2016; Severo et al., 2016). Despite this, there is limited empirical evidence on if and how public decisions can benefit from the adoption of social media data. Further studies can enter this field by investigating institutes in the public sector that endorse including social media data in their PMSs, paying particular attention to the impact of these data on decision-making processes. It would certainly be interesting to understand whether the decision-making process is faster when social media data come into the equation and what effect do they have on the quality of the decisions taken. If I use social media data, are my decisions better or worse?

CONCLUSION

In this chapter, we have investigated the possibility of integrating social media data within a PMS for public administration. In particular, a reference framework is described here, which identifies three main phases used to gain insights from social media data, by applying them within a PMS. The framework has underlined the importance of going through the three phases of social media data analysis, KPI computation and data visualization, and has emphasized the centrality of the decision-maker. Although some tools of data analytics can offer the illusion of a data-driven society with insights derived directly from social media conversations, in practice, even when implementing software to download, analyse and report on the data, some decisions must still be taken. If these are not carried out by a decision-maker who has a definite question in mind and good knowledge of the context, then the process will revert to the default provided in the software.

The proposed framework offers several insights for both academics and practitioners. At the academic level, this study enriches the current literature on social media in the public sector by providing a new perspective that moves beyond how social media can be used, to concentrate instead on fully exploiting the data derived from social media platforms. This study also highlights how social media data can be of value, offering future directions for research about performance management in public institutes, a research stream defined by the continuous debate on the uses and usefulness of performance measures for public administration purposes (Arnaboldi et al., 2015)

At the practitioner level, this study provides a tangible tool that can guide public managers in how to exploiting social media data within a PMS. The proposed framework details the phases of the analysis, with the main choices associated to the process. It can support the social media managers and/or accountants who will be in charge of gaining value from the social media data accessed and accessible.

REFERENCES

Agostino, D., & Arnaboldi, M. (2017). Social media data used in the measurement of public service effectiveness: Empirical evidence from Twitter in higher education institutions. *Public Policy & Administration*, *32*(4), 296–322. doi:10.1177/0952076716682369

Agostino, D., & Sidorova, Y. (2016). A performance measurement system to quantify the contribution of social media: New requirements for metrics and methods. *Measuring Business Excellence*, *20*(2), 1–21. doi:10.1108/MBE-05-2015-0030

Allen, R. (2017). *What happens online in 60 seconds?* Retrieved April 20, 2017 from http://www.smartinsights.com/internet-marketing-statistics/happens-online-60-seconds/

Antoniadis, K., Zafiropoulos, K., & Vrana, V. (2016). A Method for Assessing the Performance of e-Government Twitter Accounts. *Future Internet*, *8*(2), 12. doi:10.3390/fi8020012

Arnaboldi, M., Brambilla, M., Cassottana, B., Ciuccarelli, P., & Vantini, S. (2017). Urbanscope: A lens to observe language mix in cities. *The American Behavioral Scientist*, *61*(7), 774–793. doi:10.1177/0002764217717562

Arnaboldi, M., Lapsley, I., & Steccolini, I. (2015). Performance Management in the Public Sector: The Ultimate Challenge. *Financial Accountability & Management*, *31*(1), 1–22. doi:10.1111/faam.12049

Batrinca, B., & Treleaven, P. C. (2015). Social media analytics: A survey of techniques, tools and platforms. *AI & Society*, *30*(1), 89–116. doi:10.100700146-014-0549-4

Behn, R. (2003). Why measure performance? Different purposes require different measures. *Public Administration Review*, *63*(5), 586–606. doi:10.1111/1540-6210.00322

Bhardwaj, N., Shukla, A., & Swarnakar, P. (2014). Users' sentiment analysis in social media context using natural language processing. In *Proceedings of the International Conference on Digital Information* (pp. 103-111), Networking, and Wireless Communications (DINWC2014).

Bonsón, E., Royo, S., & Ratkai, M. (2015). Citizens' engagement on local governments' Facebook sites. An empirical analysis: The impact of different media and content types in Western Europe. *Government Information Quarterly*, *32*(1), 52–62. doi:10.1016/j.giq.2014.11.001

Bonsón, E., Torres, L., Royo, S., & Flores, F. (2012). Local e-Government 2.0: Social Media and Corporate Transparency in Municipalities. *Government Information Quarterly*, *29*(2), 123–132. doi:10.1016/j.giq.2011.10.001

Carmeli, A. (2002). A Conceptual and Practical Framework of Measuring Performance of Local Authorities in Financial Terms: Analysing the Case of Israel. *Local Government Studies*, *28*(1), 21–36. doi:10.1080/714004135

Castillo, C., Mendoza, M., & Poblete, B. (2011). Information Credibility on Twitter. In *Proceedings of the 20th International Conference on World Wide Web*, 675-684).

Ceron, A., Curini, L., Iacus, S. M., & Porro, G. (2014). Every tweet counts? How sentiment analysis of social media can improve our knowledge of citizens' political preferences with an application to Italy and France. *New Media & Society*, *16*(2), 340–358. doi:10.1177/1461444813480466

Chae, J., Thom, D., Bosch, H., Jang, Y., Maciejewski, R., Ebert, D. S., & Ertl, T. (2012). Spatiotemporal Social Media Analytics for Abnormal Event Detection and Examination using Seasonal-Trend Decomposition. In *Proceedings of the IEEE Conference on Visual Analytics Science and Technology*. Brighton, UK: IEEE Conference on Visual Analytics Science and Technology. 10.1109/VAST.2012.6400557

Chen, H., Chiang, R. H. L., & Storey, V. C. (2012). Business intelligence and analytics: From big data to big impact. *Management Information Systems Quarterly*, *36*(4), 1165–1188.

Chua, A., Servillo, L., Marcheggiani, E., & Moere, A. V. (2016). Mapping Cilento: Using geotagged social media data to characterize tourist flows in southern Italy. *Tourism Management*, *57*, 295–310. doi:10.1016/j.tourman.2016.06.013

Clark, W. R., & Golder, M. (2015). Big Data, Causal Inference, and Formal Theory: Contradictory Trends in Political Science? *PS, Political Science & Politics*, *48*(1), 65–70. doi:10.1017/S1049096514001759

Conrado, S. P., Neville, K., Woodworth, S., & O'Riordan, S. (2016). Managing social media uncertainty to support the decision making process during Emergencies. *Journal of Decision Systems*, *25*(sup1s1), 171–181. doi:10.1080/12460125.2016.1187396

Cranshaw, J., Schwartz, R., Hong, J. Y., & Sadeh, N. (2012). The Livelihoods Project: Utilizing Social Media to Understand the Dynamics of a City. In *Proceedings of the 6th. International Conference on Weblogs and Social Media* (pp. 58-65), ICWSM'12, AAAI Press.

Dimitropoulos, P., Kosmas, I., & Douvis, I. (2017). Implementing the balanced scorecard in a local government sport organization: Evidence from Greece. *International Journal of Productivity and Performance Management*, *66*(3), 362–379. doi:10.1108/IJPPM-11-2015-0167

Ediger, D., Jiang, K., Riedy, J., Bader, D. A., & Corley, C. (2010). Massive Social Network Analysis: Mining Twitter for Social Good. Paper presented at the International Conference on Parallel Processing (ICPP 2010). 10.1109/ICPP.2010.66

George, G., Haas, M. R., & Pentland, A. (2014). Big Data and Management. *Academy of Management Journal*, *57*(2), 321–326. doi:10.5465/amj.2014.4002

Graham, M., & Avery, E. J. (2013). Government public relations and social media: An analysis of the perceptions and trends of social media use at the local government level. *The Public Relations Journal*, *7*(4), 1–21.

Janssen, M., & van den Hoven, J. (2015). Big and Open Linked Data (BOLD) in Government: A Challenge to Transparency and Privacy? *Government Information Quarterly*, *32*(4), 363–368. doi:10.1016/j.giq.2015.11.007

Kaplan, A., & Haenlein, M. (2010). Users of the world, unite! The challenges and opportunities of social media. *Business Horizons*, *53*(1), 59–68. doi:10.1016/j.bushor.2009.09.003

Kaplan, R. S., & Norton, D. P. (1992). The balanced scorecard measures that drive performance. *Harvard Business Review*, *70*, 71–79. PMID:10119714

Kaplan, R. S., & Norton, D. P. (1996). Using the Balanced Scorecard as a strategic measurement system. *Harvard Business Review*, *74*, 75–85.

Kassen, M. (2013). A promising phenomenon of open data: A case study of the Chicago open data project. *Government Information Quarterly*, *30*(4), 508–513. doi:10.1016/j.giq.2013.05.012

Khan, G. F., Yoon, H. Y., Kim, J., & Park, H. W. (2014). From e-government to social government: Twitter use by Korea's central government. *Online Information Review*, *38*(1), 95–113. doi:10.1108/OIR-09-2012-0162

Kitchin, R. (2014). Big data, new epistemologies and paradigm shifts. *Big Data and Society*, *1*(1), 1–12. doi:10.1177/2053951714528481

Kloot, L., & Martin, J. (2000). Strategic performance management: A balanced approach to performance management issues in local government. *Management Accounting Research*, *11*(2), 231–251. doi:10.1006/mare.2000.0130

Lazer, D., Kennedy, R., King, G., & Vespignani, A. (2014). The parable of Google flu: Traps in big data analysis. *Science*, *343*(6176), 1203–1205. doi:10.1126cience.1248506 PMID:24626916

Mergel, I. (2014). *A Manager's Guide to Assessing Government Social Media Impact. IBM Center for the Business of Government, Report "Using Technology"* Series.

Mergel, I., Rethemeyer, R. K., & Isett, K. (2016). Big data in public affairs. *Public Administration Review*, *76*(6), 928–937. doi:10.1111/puar.12625

Nyhan, R. C., & Martin, L. L. (1999). Comparative performance measurement: A primer on data envelopment analysis. *Public Productivity & Management Review*, *22*(3), 348–364. doi:10.2307/3380708

Power, D. J. (2015). Creating a Data-Driven Global Society. In Reshaping Society through Analytics, Collaboration, and Decision Support. Springer International Publishing Switzerland doi:10.1007/978-3-319-11575-7_3

Reddick, C. G., Chatfield, A. T., & Ojo, A. (2017). A social media text analytics framework for double-loop learning for citizen-centric public services: A case study of a local government Facebook use. *Government Information Quarterly*, *34*(1), 110–125. doi:10.1016/j.giq.2016.11.001

Severo, M., Feredj, A., & Romele, A. (2016). Soft Data and Public Policy: Can Social Media Offer Alternatives to Official Statistics in Urban Policymaking? *Policy and Internet*, *8*(3), 354–372. doi:10.1002/poi3.127

Shao, C., Ciampaglia, G. L., Flammini, A., & Menczer, F. (2016). Hoaxy: A Platform for Tracking Online Misinformation. *Proceedings of the 25th International Conference Companion on World Wide Web (WWW '16)*, 745-750. 10.1145/2872518.2890098

Shet, A., & Nagarajan, M. (2009). Semantics-empowered social computing. *IEEE Internet Computing*, *13*(1), 76–80. doi:10.1109/MIC.2009.21

Tsou, M. H. (2015). Research challenges and opportunities in mapping social media and Big Data. *Cartography and Geographic Information Science, 42*(s1), 70–74. doi:10.1080/15230406.2015.1059251

Zavattaro, S. M., French, P. E., & Mohanty, S. D. (2015). A sentiment analysis of U.S. local government tweets: The connection between tone and citizen involvement. *Government Information Quarterly, 32*(3), 333–34.1. doi:10.1016/j.giq.2015.03.003

KEY TERMS AND DEFINITIONS

Big Data: Data featuring high volume, high variety, high velocity, high veracity, and high value.

Data Collection: The process of retrieving data from different sources and storing them in a unique location for further use.

Data Visualization: The process of translating data into a comprehensive and schematic format.

Key Performance Indicator: An indicator to measure an event.

Performance Measurement System: A tool that collects data, computes indicators, and reports on results.

Social Media: Communication tools based on Web 2.0 features.

Social Media Data: Data generated by users on social media in conversations or from their personal profile.

This research was previously published in the Handbook of Research on Modernization and Accountability in Public Sector Management; pages 254-275, copyright year 2018 by Information Science Reference (an imprint of IGI Global).

Chapter 12
Virtual Communities and Social Networking in Franchising

Ye-Sho Chen
ⓘ https://orcid.org/0000-0002-7459-9891
Louisiana State University, Baton Rouge, USA

ABSTRACT

Franchising has been a popular approach to growing a business. Its popularity continues to increase, as we witness an emergence of a new business model Netchising or Online-to-Offline, combining the Internet for global demand-and-supply, virtual communities, and social networking processes and the international franchising arrangement for local responsiveness. In this article, we show that building up a good "family" relationship between the franchisor and the franchisee is the real essence of franchising, and proven working knowledge is the foundation of the "family" relationship. Specifically, we discuss the process of how to make big data and business analytics meaningful for virtual communities and social networking in franchising. The process consists of business challenges, data foundation, analytics implementation, insights, execution and measurements, distributed knowledge, and innovation.

INTRODUCTION

Franchising has been a popular approach to growing a business globally (Justis & Judd, 2002; U.S. Commercial Service, 2018). Its popularity continues to increase, as we witness an emergence of a new business model, Netchising or O2O (online-to-offline), which is the combination of the Internet for global demand-and-supply, virtual communities, and social networking processes and the international franchising arrangement for local responsiveness (Chen, Justis, & Yang, 2004; Chen, Chen, & Wu, 2005, 2007; Chen & Wu, 2007; Chen, Liu, Zeng, & Azevedo, 2012; Qiang & Wang, 2018). In his best seller, *Business @ the Speed of Thought*, Bill Gates (1999) wrote: "Information Technology and business are becoming inextricably interwoven. I don't think anybody can talk meaningfully about one without talking about the other." (p. 6) Gates' point is quite true when one talks about franchise's use of virtual communities and social networking (Perrigot, Kacker, Basset, and Cliquet, 2012). Thus, to see how virtual

DOI: 10.4018/978-1-7998-9020-1.ch012

communities and social networking can be "meaningfully" used in franchising, one needs to know how franchising really works.

In this paper, we show that building up a good "family" relationship between the franchisor and the franchisee is the real essence of franchising, and proven working knowledge is the foundation of the "family" relationship. Specifically, we use the following seven pillars of business analytics (Laursen & Thorlund, 2010; Isson & Harriott, 2013) to discuss the process of how to make how virtual communities and social networking "meaningful" in franchising: business challenges, data foundation, analytics implementation, insights, execution and measurements, distributed knowledge, and innovation.

BUSINESS CHALLENGES: MANAGING THE FRANCHISOR-FRANCHISEE RELATIONSHIP

Franchising is "a business opportunity by which the owner … grants exclusive rights to an individual for the local distribution ... The individual or business granting the business rights is called the franchisor, and the individual or business granted the right to operate … is called the franchisee." (Justis & Judd, 2002, pp. 1-3) Developing a good "family" relationship between the franchisor and the franchisee is the key business challenge of a successful franchise (Justis & Judd, 2002). Figure 1 describes how such a "family" relationship is built in the franchise business community. In the figure, it shows that the franchise system is operated in the dynamic business environment of global, national, regional, and local communities. The resilience of the business environment is also getting significant attention nowadays (UNISDR, 2018). The "family" relationship is developed through a mutual influencing process of family-centric relationship building enabled by virtual communities and social networking.

Figure 1. Understanding how to manage the franchisor/franchisee relationship

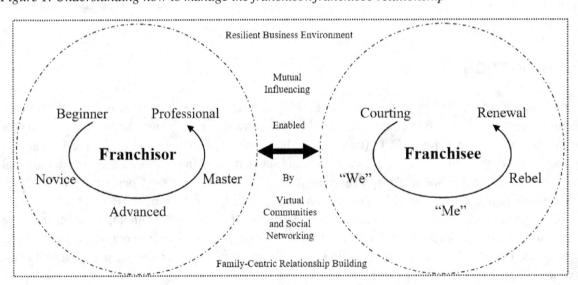

The franchisor's learning process is incrementally developed through five stages (Justis & Judd, 2002): Beginner – learning how to do it; Novice – practicing doing it; Advanced – doing it; Master – teaching others to do it; and Professional – becoming the best that you can be. Once attaining the advanced stages of development, most preceding struggles have been overcome. However, further convoluted and challenging enquiries will arise as the franchise continues expansion. This is especially true once the system reaches the "Professional" stage, where various unpredicted and intricate problems could arise. To capture the learning process, a counter-clockwise round arrow surrounding the franchisor is used to depict the increasing intensity of learning as the franchisor continues to grow.

To understand how the "family" relationship is developed, one needs to know the five phases of franchisee life cycle (Schreuder, Krige, & Parker, 2000): Courting: both the franchisee and the franchisor are eager with the relationship; "We": the relationship starts to deteriorate, but the franchisee still values the relationship; "Me": the franchisee starts to question the reasons for payments related issues with the attitude that the success so far is purely of his/her own work; Rebel: the franchisee starts to challenge the restrictions being placed upon; and Renewal: the franchisee realizes the "win-win" solution is to continue teaming up with the franchisor to grow the system. Similar to the franchisor, a counter-clockwise round arrow surrounding the franchisee is used in Figure 1 to depict the increasing intensity of franchisee life cycle as the franchisee continues learning and growing.

As the franchisee progresses through the life cycle, the "family" relationship gradually develops a mutually influencing process (Justis & Vincent, 2001) as depicted in Figure 1 with a bi-directional arrow: working knowledge, proven abilities of expanding the franchise system profitably; positive attitude, constructive ways of presenting and sharing the working knowledge; good motivation, providing incentives for learning or teaching the working knowledge; positive individual behaviour, understanding and leveraging the strengths of the participants to learn and enhance the working knowledge; and collaborative group behaviour, having the team spirit to find the best way to collect, dissimilate, and manage the hard-earned working knowledge. By going through the processes of learning and influencing, both the franchisor and the franchisee gain the progressive working knowledge in the franchise business community. The franchisor, the franchisee, and the franchise business community in Figure 1 are surrounded with dashed lines, indicating that there is no limit to the learning process.

DATA FOUNDATION: MANGING FRANCHISE BIG DATA

There are many "touchpoints" within the franchise business community where the franchisor and the franchisee can influence each other via virtual communities and social networking. Based on the Customer Service Life Cycle (CSLC) model, Chen, Chong, and Justis (2002) proposed a framework (Table 1) to harness the Internet to develop the big data foundation needed to serve its customers, i.e., franchisees and their customers. Four exemplar types of data are (1) unit operational data: the daily activities at the franchisee units and franchisor headquarters; (2) external benchmarking data: the relationship management activities in the franchise community; (3) external data gathered in the virtual communities and social networking; and (4) business legacy data: the activities that have been working well or gradually adapted since the franchise system came into existence.

Table 1. The Customer-service-life-cycle model in franchising

CSLC	Sub-stages	Example: WSI Internet
Requirements	Understanding How Franchising Works	Internet • WSI Proven Franchise Business Model • WSI Franchise Lifecycle • Master Franchise Opportunities • Virtual Communities and Social Networking
	Investigating Franchise Opportunities	Internet • About WSI • Client Portfolio • Virtual Communities and Social Networking
	Obtaining Franchisee Prospectus	Internet • E-mails • Virtual Communities and Social Networking
	Making the Choice	Internet • Global Franchise Leader • Success Stories • WSI in the News • Virtual Communities and Social Networking
Acquisition	Preparing Business Plan	Internet • Virtual Communities and Social Networking
	Financing the Franchised Business	Internet • Virtual Communities and Social Networking
	Signing the Contract	Internet • Own a WSI Franchise • Virtual Communities and Social Networking
Ownership	Marketing & Promoting the Franchise Products or Services	Internet/Intranet/Extranet • WSI Proven System • Virtual Communities and Social Networking
	Managing the Franchise System	Internet • WSI Community Outreach Intranet • Franchise Training and Support • Serving Franchisee's Customers Extranet
	Building the Relationship between the Franchisor and the Franchisee • The Courting Phase • The "We" Phase • The "Me" Phase • The Rebel Phase • The Renewal Phase	Internet • Virtual Communities and Social Networking Intranet • Knowledge Centre • Training at Headquarters • Newsletter • Meetings • Toll-free Phone Line Extranet • Purchasing Cooperative
Renewal or Retirement	Becoming a Professional Multi-unit Franchisee or Retiring from the Franchise System	More refined and diverse views of the customer information are gathered through Internet, Intranet, and Extranet at the different stages of "touchpoints". This will help the franchise system look into the customer insights (Suther, Burkart, & Cheng, 2013) and better serve the customers.

To tap the full potential of the CSLC framework, more refined and diverse views of the customer information shall be gathered at the different stages of "touchpoints". This will help the franchise system look into the customer insights (Suther, Burkart, & Cheng, 2013) and better serve the customers. A well-designed Internet strategy, often enabled by Application Service Providers (Chen, Ford, Justis, & Chong, 2001), shall empower the franchisor and the franchisees to collect, use, renew, store, retrieve, transmit, and share the organizational data needed to do the collaborative work in the various phases of the CSLC model.

ANALYTICS IMPLEMENTATION: MANAGING FRANCHISE ORGANIZATIONAL INFORMATION

An architecture, adapted from Inmon (1996) and Thomas & McSharry (2015), of big data and business analytics in franchising is shown in Figure 2. The architecture consists of four levels of operational processes: (1) data collection level, holding operational, external, and legacy data collected from the franchise business environment depicted in Figure 1; (2) reconciled data level, holding data warehouse data and meta data; (3) derived data level, containing several data marts derived from the data warehouse based on various franchisee/customer-centered segmentations; and (4) the analytical presentation level, producing various relationship performance indicators with strong data visualization capabilities for decision making via decision support systems (DSS).

To move from the data collection level to the reconciled data level, data integration is needed. It is a very time-consuming process that involves the activities such as recovery, cleansing, extracting, filtering, conditioning, scrubbing, and loading. To move from the reconciled data level to the derived data level, data transformation is needed which involves the activities such as exploration, replication, propagation, summary, aggregate, and metadata. To move from the derived data level to the analytical presentation level, data analysis is needed which involves activities such as online analytical processing (OLAP) and data mining (Chen, Zhang, & Justis, 2005; Chen, Justis, & Chong, 2008).

A typical OLAP analysis consists of pre-defined multi-dimensional queries such as (Chen, Justis, & Watson, 2000): (1) Show the gross margin by product category and by franchise outlets from Thanksgiving to Christmas in the last five years; (2) Which franchise outlets are increasing in sales and which are decreasing? And (3) Which kinds of customers place the same orders on a regular basis at certain franchise outlets? Other OLAP activities include spreadsheet analysis, data visualization, and a variety of statistical data modelling methods. Since the query activities are pre-defined, we call the supporting systems reactive DSS.

Data mining is used to identify context-sensitive patterns of the data residing in the data marts. Typical data mining modelling analysis can be classified into the following three categories: Classification and Prediction, using techniques such as RFM (recency, frequency, and monetary), regression, decision tree, and neural network; Association Rules, using techniques such as market basket analysis, correlation analysis, cross-sell analysis, and link analysis; and Cluster Analysis, using techniques such as partition, hierarchy, outlier, and density analysis. Table 2, adapted from Delmater & Hancock (2001), shows that data mining techniques can be used to help serve franchisees' customers at the different stages of the CSLC model.

Figure 2. Architecture of big data and business analytics in franchising

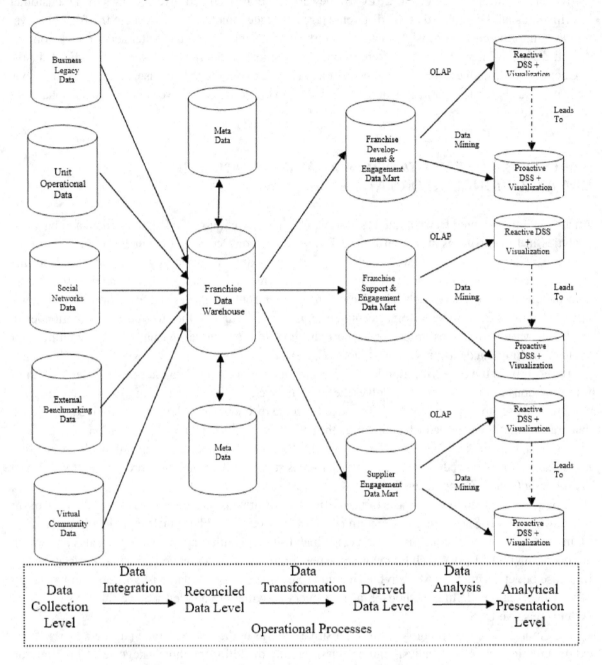

Since the data mining queries and related activities are not pre-defined, we call the supporting systems proactive DSS. A major drawback of proactive data mining is the fact that without vigilant preliminary examination of data characteristics, the mining activities may end in vain (Delmater & Hancock, 2001). In order to achieve higher success rate of data mining, we suggest (on the right side of Figure 2) that OLAP-based queries need to be conducted first. For example, one may find, through daily OLAP queries, that certain segments of customers buy certain products frequently. This pattern may lead to perform thorough and proactive analysis of the customer-product relationship and human resource analytics (Pease, Byerly, & Fitz-enz, 2012). The results may help the company provide legendary services to its clients and generate higher profits.

Table 2. Data mining in franchising using the CSLC approach

CSLC	Explanation	Data Mining (and Techniques Used) for Context-Sensitive Patterns

Requirements	Finding and reaching the customers	• Context-Sensitive Lead Generation
		  • Market Analysis & Segmentation (Classification and Prediction)
		  • Mining Web Site Visitors (Association Rules)
		  • Text Mining Usenet Newsgroups in Virtual Communities and Social Networking (Cluster Analysis)

Acquisition	Selling to the customers	• Context-Sensitive Customer Acquisition Profiling
		  • Customer Segmentation Strategy (Classification and Prediction)
		  • Online Shopping Tracking (Association Rules)
		  • Pricing Strategy (Association Rules)
		  • Customer-centric Selling (Association Rules)
		  • Text Mining Contact E-Mails in Virtual Communities and Social Networking (Cluster Analysis)
		  • Scenario Notification (Association Rules)

Ownership	Satisfying the customers after the sales	• Context-Sensitive Customer Service
		  • Inquiry Routing (Association Rules)
		  • Text Mining E-Mails & Inquiries in Virtual Communities and Social Networking (Cluster Analysis)
		  • Scenario Notification (Association Rules)
		  • Staffing Level Prediction (Classification and Prediction)

Retirement or Renewing	Retaining the customers so that you can continue coming back	• Context-Sensitive Customer Retention
		  • Sharper Customer Focus through Loyalty Program (Classification and Prediction)
		  • Detecting Customer Complaints through Text Mining (Cluster Analysis)
		  • Detecting Inappropriate Customer Services (Cluster Analysis)
		  • Individual Customer Profiles (Classification and Prediction)
		  • Scenario Notification in Virtual Communities and Social Networking (Association Rules)

INSIGHTS: MANAGING FRANCHISE ORGANIZATIONAL WORKING KNOWLEDGE

As mentioned in the discussions of Figure 1, the key for building the franchisor/franchisee "family" relationship is in the franchise organizational mutual influencing and learning enabled by virtual communities and social networking. In addition, there are five vital insights for a successful learning program: knowledge, attitude, motivation, individual behaviour, and group behaviour. Thus, working knowledge is the real foundation of a successful franchise "family" relationship. The working knowledge is structured in many forms of profiles that are embedded in the operational manuals of the franchise business processes. Table 3 gives some examples of those working knowledge profiles with respect to the CSLC business processes associated with the sub-stages in Table 1.

A working knowledge profile is developed when a certain task of the CSLC process is repeated several times with superior results. Consider the Site Profile used at the "Marketing & Promoting the Franchise Products/Services" sub-stage in Table 3. The Site Profile is used to assist the new franchisee locate a top business site. Typically, it is the real estate department at the franchisor headquarters responsible for the profile development. The Site Profile is unremittingly being tested and enhanced. Various OLAP/ Data Mining analytical reports, monitoring the performance of the sites, are generated at the Analytical Presentation Level shown in Figure 2. Based on those reports, the real estate experts and their teams are able to fine-tune the attributes and the parameters within the Site Profile. Most often, the corresponding data collection procedures in the CSLC sub-stage also need to be revised and perfected so that better scorecards can be generated.

Table 3. The CSLC model of working knowledge management in franchising

CSLC Sub-stages	Examples of Working Knowledge Profiles
Understanding How Franchising Works	Lead Generation Profiles Website Visitor Profile
Investigating Franchise Opportunities	Benchmarking Profile Successful Franchisee Profile
Obtaining Franchisee Prospectus	Prospectus Profile
Making the Choice	Competitor Profile
Preparing Business Plan	Business Plan Profile
Financing the Franchised Business	Financing Institute Profile Non-traditional Franchising Profile
Signing the Contract	Franchisee Profile
Marketing & Promoting the Franchise Products or Services	Site Profile Product Profile Virtual Community Profiles
Managing the Franchise System	Support Team Profile Employee Profile Demand-Supply Matching Profile
Building the Relationship between the Franchisor and the Franchisee	Event Management Profile Best Practices Profile
Becoming a Professional Multi-unit Franchisee or Retiring from the Franchise System	Multi-unit Franchisee Profile Social Networking Profile

EXECUTION AND MEASUREMENTS: DEVELOPING A GROWING FRANCHISE

This process of executing and enhancing the working knowledge profiles will achieve its high peak when both the franchisor and the franchisees are arriving at the Professional and Renewal stage of growth. A significant phenomenon of being a Professional franchisor and a Renewal franchisee are their ability to leverage the assets of the hard-earned working knowledge profiles into dynamic capabilities and high-business-value-creation completive-advantage strategies (Chen, Yuan, & Dai, 2004; Chen, Seidman, & Justis, 2005). Business performance tracking, using mobile analytics (Munteanu & Puican, 2012) with effective analytics communication strategies, is very important here. The new products or services coming out of the process of leveraging the working knowledge profiles may transform the franchise business into a more, sometimes surprisingly, profitable enterprise.

The capability of leveraging the assets of franchise working knowledge into profitable products or services is at the heart of a successful franchise. For instance, consider the site selection working knowledge at McDonald's. The Franchise Realty Corporation real estate business, a result of site selection asset leveraging, is the real moneymaking engine at McDonald's. This as can be evidenced from the following speech of Ray Kroc, founder of McDonald's, to the MBA class at the University of Texas at Austin in 1974: "… I 'm not in the hamburger business. My business is real estate." (Kiyosaki, 2000, p.85) In the book McDonald's: Behind the Arches (Love, 1995, p. 152), Ray Kroc commented further: "What converted McDonald's into a money machine had nothing to do with … the popularity of McDonald's hamburgers, French fries, and milk shakes. Rather, McDonald's made its money on real estate …." McDonald's makes money out of real estate by leasing properties from landlords and then subleasing the stores to the franchisees. The Professional franchisees, many of them are multiunit operators, can then focus on expending the business without worrying about finding good locations for the growth. This moneymaking real estate strategy is what separates McDonald's from other fast-food chains.

DISTRIBUTED KNOWLEDGE: FRANCHISE KNOWLEDGE REPOSITORY

Knowledge repository systems, consisting of working knowledge profiles such as the one shown in Table 4 (Chen, Chong, & Justis, 2000; Chen, Hammerstein, & Justis, 2002; Chen, Justis, & Wu, 2008), can be linked into the franchisor headquarters and the franchisee outlets for knowledge sharing and learning. Such a repository has two dimensions. First, there is a working knowledge level for the collaborative team, the franchisee outlet, the franchisor headquarters, and the franchise community. Second, there are user skill levels, including Beginner in the Courting Phase, Novice in the "We"-Phase, Advanced in the "Me"-Phase, Master in the Rebel Phase (since the rebel ones tend to be those who know the system very well and are capable of influencing others to follow them), and Professional in the Renewal Stage of franchisee life cycle. The foundation of the framework is the working knowledge of the five crucial elements—Knowledge, Attitude, Motivation, Individual Behaviour, and Group Behaviour—used by the collaborative team, to effectively influence others in building the franchise "family" relationship. The working knowledge profiles at the franchisee outlet, the franchisor headquarters, and the franchise community can be modularized according to user's level. An Intranet-based curriculum of working knowledge modules can then be designed for the users to learn the working knowledge profiles effectively.

Table 4. Working knowledge repository in franchising

		User Skill Levels				
		Beginner in the Courting Phase: Beginner Guide	Novice in the "We"-Phase: Practicing	Advanced in the "Me"-Phase: Doing	Master in the Rebel Phase: Teaching Others	Professional in the Renewal Stage: Improving and Leveraging
Working Knowledge Levels	Collaborative Team	Culture and Process of Influencing Others for Knowledge Sharing: Knowledge, Attitude, Motivation, Individual Behavior, and Group Behavior				
	Franchisee Outlet	Learning and Training of Working Knowledge Profiles for Running the Franchisee Outlet: Customer Profile, Employee Profile, Product Profile				
	Franchisor Headquarters	Learning and Training of Working Knowledge Profiles for Running the Franchisor Headquarters: Franchisee Profile, Site Profile, Product Profile, Employee Profile, Event Management Profile				
	Franchise Community	Learning and Training of Working Knowledge Profiles for Relationship Management in Virtual Communities and Social Networking: Supplier Profiles, Community Profiles				

INNOVATION BY LEVERAGING FRANCHISE VALUE NETWORKS in VIRTUAL COMMUNITIES AND SOCIAL NETWORKING

The third industrial revolution, combining Internet technology with globalization, produces various new big data and business analytics opportunities for the innovative franchise growth through virtual communities and social networking. For example, value network applications, using business analytics techniques such as social network analysis, can be developed to connect the virtual communities and social networking of Professional franchisees in the world. The goal is to enable the franchise system to venture into new global emerging markets, e.g., China, through international franchising and develop innovative products/services through asset leveraging. This could be done because franchise capabilities, structured in the working knowledge repository shown in Table 4, empower the Professional franchisees to work with the franchisor to continuously improve and leverage the current franchise working knowledge.

An example of value networks of Professional franchisees can be illustrated in Figure 3. There are seven Professional franchisees (A - G) in the figure with four clusters (A-B-C, D, E-F, and G) of value networks. Each Professional franchisee (a dot) has his/her personal value network (arrows pointing out of the dot) tested and built over the years while doing day-to-day problems solving at the franchisee outlet. The value network may include the customers' likes and dislikes, the kind of employees to hire, the competitors' and suppliers' pricing strategies, the social needs in virtual communities and social networking. Each Professional franchisee is surrounded with a circle with dashed lines, meaning there is no limit to the personal value network. In order to solve the problems more effectively, Professional franchisees may share with each other their approaches. Thus, clusters (connected dots) of value network are formed for solving various problems more effectively (Chen, Justis, & Wu, 2006). The big data gathered from the Professional franchisees and networks are connected to the business analytics hub to enhance and strengthen the value networks.

CONCLUSION

Franchising has been popular as a growth strategy for small businesses; it is even more so in today's global and e-commerce world (Chen, Chen, & Wu, 2005) enabled by virtual communities and social networking. The essence of franchising lies in managing the "family" relationship between the franchisor and the franchisee. In this paper we showed big data and business analytics play an important role in growing and nurturing such a "family" relationship. Specifically, we used the seven pillars of business analytics (Isson & Harriott, 2013) to discuss the process of how to make big data and business analytics "meaningful" for virtual communities and social networking in franchising: how franchise big data can be managed effectively using the methodology of Customer Service Life Cycle; how franchise organizational information is deciphered from the customer-centered data using business analytical techniques such as OLAP and data mining; and how the franchise organizational working knowledge is leveraged to grow the franchise system. The ability to continue creating value networks in virtual communities and social networking by leveraging the organizational working knowledge assets based on the good "family" relationship is really what a franchise business is about.

Figure 3. Business analytics hub enhances and strengthens the value networks in virtual communities and social networking

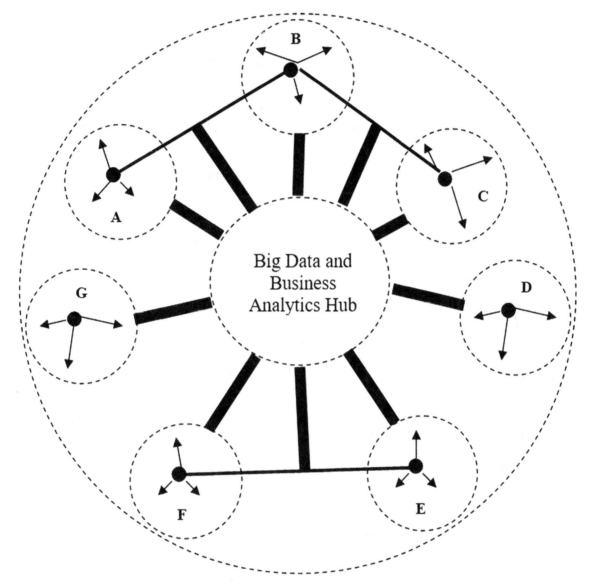

REFERENCES

Chen, Y., Chong, P., & Justis, R. T. (2000, February). Franchising knowledge repository: A structure for learning organizations. *Proceedings of the 14th Annual International Society of Franchising Conference* (pp. 19-20). Academic Press.

Chen, Y., Chong, P. P., & Justis, R. T. (2002). E-business strategy in franchising: A customer-service-life-cycle approach. *Proceedings of the 16th Annual International Society of Franchising Conference* (pp. 8-10). Academic Press.

Chen, Y., Ford, C., Justis, R. T., & Chong, P. (2001, February). Application service providers (ASP) in franchising: Opportunities and issues. *Proceedings of the 15th Annual International Society of Franchising Conference* (pp. 24-25). Academic Press.

Chen, Y., Hammerstein, S., & Justis, R. T. (2002). Knowledge, learning, and capabilities in franchise organizations. *Proceedings of the 3rd European Conference on Organizational Knowledge, Learning, and Capabilities* (pp. 5-6). Academic Press.

Chen, Y., Justis, R., & Watson, E. (2000). Web-enabled data warehousing. In M. Shaw, R. Blanning, T. Strader, & A. Whinston (Eds.), *Handbook of electronic commerce* (pp. 501–520). Springer-Verlag. doi:10.1007/978-3-642-58327-8_24

Chen, Y., Justis, R., & Wu, S. (2006, February). Value networks in franchise organizations: A study in the senior care industry. *Proceedings of the 20th Annual International Society of Franchising Conference* (pp. 24-26). Academic Press.

Chen, Y., Justis, R., & Wu, S. (2008). Skew distributions and the sizes of franchise firms: A study in the senior care industry. *Proceedings of the 22nd Annual International Society of Franchising Conference* (pp. 20-21). Academic Press.

Chen, Y., Justis, R. T., & Yang, H. L. (2004, March). Global e-business, international franchising, and theory of netchising: A research alliance of east and west. *Proceedings of the 18th Annual International Society of Franchising Conference* (pp. 5-7). Academic Press.

Chen, Y., Seidman, W., & Justis, R. (2005). Strategy and docility in franchise organizations. *Proceedings of the 19th Annual International Society of Franchising Conference* (pp. 20-22). Academic Press.

Chen, Y. & Wu, S. (2007). E-business research in franchising (Invited editorial preface). *Information Management, 20*(1/2), 9.

Chen, Y., Yuan, W., & Dai, W. (2004). Strategy and nearly decomposable systems: A study in franchise organizations. *Proceedings of the International Symposium on "IT/IS Issues in Asia-Pacific Region, Co-sponsored by ICIS-2004*. Academic Press.

Chen, Y., Zhang, B., & Justis, R.T. (2005). Data mining in franchise organizations. In *Encyclopaedia of Information Science and Technology* (pp. 714-722). Hershey, PA: IGI Global.

Chen, Y. S., Chen, G., & Wu, S. (2005). Issues and opportunities in e-business research: A Simonian perspective. *International Journal of E-Business Research, 1*(1), 37–53. doi:10.4018/jebr.2005010103

Chen, Y. S., Chen, G., & Wu, S. (2007). A Simonian approach to e-business research: A study in netchising. In E-business innovation and process management (pp. 136–164). Hershey, PA: IGI Global. doi:10.4018/978-1-59904-277-0.ch007

Chen, Y. S., Justis, R., & Chong, P. P. (2002). Franchising and information technology: A framework. In Managing information technology in small business: Challenges and solutions (pp. 118–139). Hershey, PA: IGI Global.

Chen, Y. S., Justis, R., & Chong, P. P. (2004). Data mining in franchise organizations. In Organizational data mining: Leveraging enterprise data resources for optimal performance (pp. 217–229). Hershey, PA: IGI Global. doi:10.4018/978-1-59140-134-6.ch015

Chen, Y. S., Liu, C., Zeng, Q., & Azevedo, R. F. (2012). E-business strategy in franchise relationship management. *International Journal of Strategic Information Technology and Applications, 3*(1), 54–65. doi:10.4018/jsita.2012010104

Delmater, R., & Hancock, M. (2001). *Data mining explained: a manager's guide to customer-centric business intelligence*. Digital press.

Gates, W. (1999). *Business @ the speed of thought*. Warner Books. doi:10.1111/1467-8616.00097

Inmon, W. H. (1996). *Building the data warehouse*. John Wiley & Sons.

Isson, J., & Harriott, J. (2013). *Win with advanced business analytics: Creating business value from your data*. Wiley and SAS Business Series.

Justis, R. T., & Judd, R. J. (2002). *Franchising*. DAME Publishing.

Justis, R. T., & Vincent, W. S. (2001). *Achieving wealth through franchising*. Adams Media Corporation.

Kiyosaki, R. (2000). *Rich dad, poor dad*. Time Warner.

Laursen, G. H. N., & Thorlund, J. (2010). *Business analytics for managers: Taking business intelligence Beyond Reporting*. Wiley.

Love, J. (1995). *McDonald's: behind the arches*. Bantam Books.

Munteanu, A. and Puican, F. (2012). Mobile analytics: Modern decision support systems. *Revista Economica [Applied Informatics in Economy]*, 5, 139-146.

Pease, G., Byerly, B., & Fitz-enz, J. (2012). *Human capital analytics: How to harness the potential of your organization's greatest asset*. Wiley. doi:10.1002/9781119205050

Perrigot, R., Kacker, M., Basset, G., & Cliquet, G. (2012). Antecedents of early adoption and use of social media networks for stakeholder communications: Evidence from franchising. *Journal of Small Business Management, 50*(4), 539–565. doi:10.1111/j.1540-627X.2012.00366.x

Qiang, L. I. and Wang, X. F. (2017). Research on sharing economic business model based on O2O. *DEStech Transactions on Computer Science and Engineering*. Academic Press.

Schreuder, A. N., Krige, L., & Parker, E. (2000). The franchisee lifecycle concept – A new paradigm in managing the franchisee-franchisor relationship. *Proceedings of the 14th annual International Society of Franchising Conference*, San Diego, CA, February 19-20. Academic Press.

Suther, T. Burkart, B., & Cheng, J. (2013). Jack and the big data beanstalk: Capitalizing on a growing marketing opportunity. In J. Liebowitz (Ed.), Big data and business analytics. CRC Press.

Thomas, R., & McSharry, P. (2015). *Big data revolution*. Wiley.

UNISDR. (2018). *Making cities resilient: My city Is getting ready*. Retrieved from https://risingtide.joincca.org/news3

U.S. Commercial Service. (2018). *2018 export resource guide for franchising*. Retrieved from https://2016.export.gov/industry/franchising/index.asp

This research was previously published in the International Journal of Virtual Communities and Social Networking (IJVCSN), 10(4); pages 33-44, copyright year 2018 by IGI Publishing (an imprint of IGI Global).

Chapter 13
Knowledge Management and Social Media in Tourism Industry

Rocco Agrifoglio
University of Naples "Parthenope", Italy

Concetta Metallo
University of Naples "Parthenope", Italy

ABSTRACT

The chapter aims to provide an overview of the role of social media for knowledge management in tourism industry. Respect than traditional tools, the social media penetration within such industry is growing thanks to opportunity for travelers and travel professionals to access critical tourism knowledge everywhere and every time. Prior research has mainly focused on how social media are changing the tourism industry, while it is lacking enough the contribution of these technologies to managing touristic knowledge. This chapter seeks to shed light on how social media support knowledge management, with particular attention to knowledge creation, sharing, and preservation processes, in tourism industry. In particular, while knowledge creation and sharing process have attracted the attention of scholars, knowledge preservation via social media seems be still in its infancy stage.

INTRODUCTION

The chapter aims to provide an overview of the role of social media for knowledge management in tourism industry.

According to Davenport and Prusak (1998, p. 5) knowledge is defined as "a fluid mix of framed experience, values, contextual information, and expert insights that provides a framework for evaluating and incorporating new experiences and information. It originates in and is applied in the minds of knowers". This perspective focuses on the dynamic character of knowledge, that is conceived both as an outcome and a process for "incorporating new experiences and information" (e.g., Tsoukas & Vladimirou, 2001;

DOI: 10.4018/978-1-7998-9020-1.ch013

Nonaka & Takeuchi, 1995). The managerial literature agrees that one of the major problems of knowledge is its exploitation. Often individuals and organizations possess an enormous amount of information, but they are not able to exploit it for getting sustainable competitive advantage. When organizations operating in non-traditional markets and/or information-intensive industry, the management and processing of knowledge are considered even more critical factors for sustainability and organizational survival.

Knowledge management is a process that enables organizations to identify, capture and effectively leverage collective knowledge in an organization (Von Krough, 1999). It consists of various sets of socially enacted "knowledge processes," such as knowledge creation (known as contraction or development), knowledge sharing (known as transfer, distribution or dissemination), and knowledge preservation (known as storage and retrieval). Knowledge management, and the managing of explicit or tacit and individual or collective forms of knowledge, has been investigated by various authors from many countries and disciplines. However, while managerial literature mainly focuses on the process of knowledge management, with the aim of understanding how organizational knowledge can and should be managed effectively, the Information Systems (IS) literature pays more attention to the tools – traditional or Information Technology-assisted (IT-assisted) – for creating, sharing and preserving such knowledge. The IS literature recognized the IT-assisted tools as enablers of knowledge creation, sharing and preservation (e.g., Alavi & Leidner, 2001; Sher & Lee, 2004; Pezzillo Iacono, Martinez, Mangia, & Galdiero, 2012, Agrifoglio, 2015). Respect than traditional tools, IT-assisted tools, and social media in particular, are increasingly providing novel ways of supporting processes of knowledge creation, sharing and preservation within and between organizations.

Social media have been defined as "a group of Internet-based applications that build on the ideological and technological foundations of Web 2.0, and that allow the creation and exchange of user-generated content" (Kaplan & Haenlein, 2010). The literature agrees that social media are a set of the Internet-based applications based on the peer-to-peer communication, which enables the creation, collaboration and exchange of information between organizations, communities and individuals (e.g., Kaplan & Haenlein, 2010). Social media are playing an increasingly important role as information sources for organizations and individuals in various industries, such as tourism. Tourism is an information-intensive industry whereby social media usage was recognized as critical in many aspects and for different levels. In particular, social media enable to exchange information between travellers and industry suppliers (e.g., hotels, transportation sectors, attractions), intermediaries (e.g., travel agents), controllers (e.g., governments and administrative bodies) (Werthner &Klein, 1999). Thanks to social media, the enormous amount of information is now exploitable for improving many aspects of tourism, especially in information search and decision-making behaviours, tourism promotion and in focusing on best practices for interacting with consumers (Zeng & Gerritsen, 2014). More in general, the considerable adoption of social media has extended organizational boundaries of companies operating in tourism industry, changing the way their communicate, collaborate and managing knowledge. For these reasons, growing role of social media in tourism has been increasingly an emerging research topic (e.g., Leung, Law, Van Hoof, & Buhalis, 2013; Zeng & Gerritsen, 2014).

This chapter focuses on the role of social media for knowledge management in tourism industry. In particular, it seeks to shed light on how organizations, destinations and, more in general, tourism sector create, share and preserve tourism knowledge. The structure of the chapter is as follows. Firstly, we introduce the theoretical background on knowledge management (Section 2) and on knowledge management issues in tourism industry (Section 3). Furthermore, we provide an overview of the role of social media in tourism industry (Section 4) and of the main dynamics of knowledge management through social media in tourism industry (Section 5). Finally, we show the summary of the chapter (Section 6).

From Knowledge to Knowledge Management in Organizations

Defining organizational knowledge is not an easy task. Knowledge represents a complex topic because of being abstract, it is difficult to define and quantify. Agreement with Davenport et al. (1998), knowledge tends to be fuzzy in nature and it is usually deeply and closely attached to the individuals who hold it, thus this issue is challenging to define, measure and manage in any organizational settings (Ipe, 2003).

Since the classical Greek era, the history of philosophy has taught us that the pursuit of the meaning of knowledge is a never-ending search (Nonaka, 1994). The research on rationalism advanced by Descartes and other philosophers in the 17th century, as well as subsequent research on empiricism (Locke and others in the 18th century) and interactionism (Kant and others in the 19th century) are some examples. More in general, the Greek philosophers have focused on absolute, static and nonhuman nature of knowledge, which can typically be expressed in propositional structures in formal logic. Overcoming the debates related to the Greek philosophy, more recent research looks at knowledge as a "dynamic human process of justifying personal beliefs as part of an aspiration for the truth" (Nonaka 1994, p. 15). Specifically, according to Nonaka (1994) and Huber (1991), knowledge has been conceived as the specific and justified belief of an individual that is able to increase his/her capacity to take effective action. In this context several factors are necessary in order to take the action, such as physical skills and competencies (e.g., playing football, or handicraft), cognitive/intellectual activity (e.g., problem solving), or both (e.g., in the surgery both manual skills and cognitive elements, that is knowledge of human anatomy and medicine, are required).

Without going into too much detail, it clear that the concept of knowledge has taken on different meanings over time that change depending on the various research fields and the analytical perspectives.

In particular, scholars from the IS field tend to define knowledge mainly making a distinction between knowledge, information, and data. At first, the IS literature does not clearly distinguish the terms knowledge and information, in fact they were sometimes used interchangeably. Consistent with this point of view, information was defined as "that commodity capable of yielding knowledge, and what information a signal carries is what we can learn from it" (Dretske, 1981, p. 44). It is a flow of messages or meanings which might be able to enrich, restructure or change knowledge (Machlup, 1983). Then, Vance (1997) provides a clear distinction between knowledge and information. In his opinion, information is a flow of messages, while knowledge is the result of a process of creation and management by the flow of information, related to the commitment and beliefs of its holder. Also, as suggested by Maglitta (1996), data is raw numbers and facts, instead information is processed data, and knowledge is "information made actionable". In this perspective, the emphasis is on the human action for knowledge and each term is conceptualized considering the differences among them clarifying when information becomes knowledge[1].

Unlike prior research, another interesting perspective looks at the dynamic character of knowledge. It could be defined as "a fluid mix of framed experience, values, contextual information, and expert insights that provides a framework for evaluating and incorporating new experiences and information. It originates in and is applied in the minds of knowers. In organizations, it often becomes embedded not only in documents or repositories but also in organizational routines, processes, practices, and norms" (Davenport & Prusak, 1998, p. 5). In agreement with this point of view, other research, such as

Nonaka (1991) and Nonaka and Takeuchi (1995), looks at dynamic dimension of knowledge, focusing on the interplay between knowledge and action in an organizational settings. Indeed, as Nonaka (1991) pointed out an organization is not merely an information-processing machine, but an entity that creates knowledge through such action and interaction. In this regard, organizational knowledge is could be defined as a 'stock' of knowledge emerging from interaction and stored in rules, procedures, routines, and shared norms of an organization (Walsh & Ungson 1991; Lam 2000). This perspective has been also stressed by other managerial scholars who mainly emphasized the interplays between what people know (knowledge) and what people do (knowing) in organizational settings (e.g., Weick, 1991; Cook & Brown, 1999; Agrifoglio, 2015).

Since defining 'what organizational knowledge is a very complex task, it should be easier to understand 'what constitutes it'. The taxonomy of organizational knowledge was investigated along two dimensions, such as epistemological (explicit and tacit forms of knowledge) and ontological (individual and collective forms of knowledge). With reference to the epistemological dimension, we can distinguish explicit and tacit forms based on the modes of expression of knowledge. Explicit is a kind of knowledge that can be formalized and codified, since it is easy to identify, store, and retrieve (Brown & Duguid, 1998). As Nonaka (1994) stated, it is that form of knowledge codified and communicated by symbolic and natural language, and appears valuable. From a managerial perspective, explicit knowledge can be easily and effectively handled within organizations. Unlike explicit, tacit knowledge refers to knowledge that is largely experience based. Polanyi (1966) defines tacit knowledge as something everyone knows but cannot describe. It referred to know-how, that is, that part of the knowledge that is intuitive, hard to define and to communicate, as well as deeply rooted in action, commitment, and involvement (Nonaka, 1994). Since tacit knowledge cannot be formalized and codified and is often context dependent and personal in nature, it can be developed through access to the sources of knowledge, rather than to the information itself. From a managerial perspective, managing tacit knowledge is a very complicated task, since it is often embodied in people rather than organizations. With reference to the ontological dimension, we can distinguish individual and collective forms based on the locus of knowledge that resides at individual and collective level. Leaving aside the older ontological debate on the subject, and the anthropomorphic view of knowledge in particular, the managerial literature looks at individual form of knowledge as that knowledge created by and inherent in the individual, while collective form of knowledge (well-known as social knowledge) as that knowledge created by and inherent in the collective actions of a group (e.g., Alavi & Leidner 2001).

Knowledge management is largely regarded as a process that enables organizations to identify, capture and effectively leverage collective knowledge (Von Krough 1999; Alavi & Leidner, 2001). As remarked by Agrifoglio (2015, p. 10), knowledge management consists of "various sets of socially enacted 'knowledge processes', such as knowledge creation (known as contraction or development), knowledge sharing (known as transfer, distribution or dissemination), and knowledge preservation (known as storage and retrieval)". In particular, knowledge creation is "the process of making available and amplifying knowledge created by individuals as well as crystallizing and connecting it with an organization's knowledge system" (Nonaka, von Krogh, & Voepel, 2006, p. 1179). It concerns the process of knowledge transformation from an individual to a collective state through dynamic interactions among individuals, organization and environment (Nonaka & Takeuchi, 1995; Nonaka & Toyama, 2002). On the contrary, knowledge sharing is that process whereby organizational knowledge is made available to others. According to Ipe (2003, p. 341), it is a voluntary act through which "knowledge held by an individual is converted into a form that can be understood, absorbed, and used by other individuals". Knowledge preservation, instead, is the process of selection, storage and effective actualization of organizational knowledge (Agrifoglio, 2015). After knowledge has been developed or acquired, it must be carefully preserved in order to avoid memory loss. Preserving knowledge is recognized as one of the most relevant processes of organizational knowledge management. It concerns a process constituted of three phases, such as selection, storage, and actualization. The selection is related to the identification of that organizational knowledge that must be saved because it is usable for a third party in the future. The storage is the second stage of knowledge preservation process. After selecting the organizational knowledge that is worth protecting, storage enables individuals to save it in an effective way and in a suitable form (Romhardt, 1997; Agrifoglio, 2015). Finally, the last stage of preservation process is the actualization of organizational knowledge previously stored. The actualization stage of knowledge preservation consists of making the previously stored organizational knowledge available in acceptable quality for decision-making.

KNOWLEDGE MANAGEMENT IN TOURISM

The creation and use of knowledge to feed innovation and product development was recognized as critical for both organizations and industries. In many economic sectors, such as primary industries, the knowledge, and knowledge creation and sharing processes in particular, has emerged as a topic of growing interest among academics and practitioners because of it was acknowledged as basis for competitive advantage in firms. Unlike other industries, although academic tourism research did not pay sufficient attention to knowledge management approach in the past, the sector is not as competitive as it could be (e.g., Ruhanen & Cooper, 2004; Cooper, 2015). This is true for two reasons. First, the tourism sector is mainly composed of micro and small companies, including family businesses, where often missing that managerial skills that are usually more oriented to knowledge management. Second, tourism organizations are traditionally research averse (Ruhanen & Cooper, 2004). Indeed, although the growth of academic research on knowledge management in tourism sector in the last years, entrepreneurs and practitioners are often not able to look at managing knowledge for tourism enterprises, destinations and governments (Cooper, 2006, 2015). This result once again confirms that the academic research seldom influences working practice.

More in general, although the managerial research in tourism has unquestionably grown in recent years, the presence of the barriers to the implementation of knowledge management in such sector makes this sector as less competitive than other ones (e.g., Grizelj, 2003; Ruhanen & Cooper, 2004; Cooper, 2006, 2015). The remaining part of the paragraph provides a review of the main contributes on knowledge management in tourism. Such contributes agree to recognize the need for tourism organizations, destinations and, more in general, industry to adopt a knowledge management approach to transform tourism research and intellectual property into capabilities for the sector.

Cooper's (2006) research provided one of the first and most important contributes to apply a knowledge management approach for tourism. He proposed a model for tourism aimed at explaining how tourism organizations and destinations managing knowledge, by focusing on the creation, transmission and use processes of tourism knowledge. Cooper's (2006) research has also pointed out the critical role of tacit form of knowledge in tourism due to the difficult of absorptive capacity of micro and small sized enterprises that often are not able to take advantage of business relationships and cooperation. Similarly, other research (e.g., Grizelj, 2003; Ruhanen & Cooper, 2004; Cooper, 2015) also suggested the need of contractual and cooperative forms, such as networks and communities of practice, that ensure the continuity of knowledge transfer and adoption in tourism. There is no doubt that networks are a traditionally suited contexts for generating and sharing knowledge among organizations that belong to them. Destinations as inter-organizational networks are composed of enterprises, governments and other organizations where how learning takes place and knowledge is transferred. In particular, as Cooper (2015, p. 114) suggested, destinations enable to articulate "tacit knowledge at the individual organization level into explicit knowledge, which is transmitted through the wider network of organizations through the usual processes of KM". The tourism academic literature was widely recognized the critical role of social relationships in destinations, as well as the important contribution that these knowledge networks make to knowledge transfer (e.g., Grizelj, 2003; Xiao & Smith, 2010; Cooper, 2015).

Like the destinations, community of practice also contributes to knowledge transfer in tourism, even if with a different degree of effectiveness than other sectors (e.g., Shaw & Williams, 2009; Cooper, 2015). Indeed, people are "members of different communities and also act as 'boundary spanners' across such divides and help knowledge more between these communities" (Shaw & Williams, 2009, p. 329). Also, as Cooper (2015, p. 116) suggested, "a COP differs from a destination is in the fact that a COP depends upon a high degree of trust [..] this notion of trust – or lack of it – that is central to the issues surrounding effective KM in tourism". However, such research has also remarked some criticisms on communities of practice's contribution to knowledge transfer in tourism. Community of practice tends often to be constrained by the shared word view of the members and thus it aids more the knowledge movement rather than new creation.

Furthermore, other research has also investigated the role of other mechanisms, such as the interlocking directorships and the human mobility, in aiding the tacit knowledge transfer in tourism industry (e.g., Shaw & Williams, 2009; Beritelli, Strobl, & Peters, 2013). While the contribution of human mobility was recognized, interlocking directorship leads to obtain divergent results. Indeed, although interlocking directorates are considered as 'boundary spanners' that link across organizations, the use of mechanisms of interlocking directorships with local board members could obtain greater benefits in terms of knowledge acquisition and transfer and, more in general, the development of social capital, than interlocking directorships with non-local board members (Beritelli, Strobl, & Peters, 2013).

SOCIAL MEDIA IN TOURISM INDUSTRY

Tourism is a an information-intensive industry (Sheldon, 1997; Werthner & Klein, 1999), in which the web-based technologies are changing the way in which tourism-related information is created and distributed (Xiang & Gretzel, 2010) as well as the way for planning and consuming travel (Buhalis & Law, 2008). Research on the role of information and communication technologies (ICTs) in the tourism industry is a widely studied topic in literature (Poon, 1993; Buhalis, 1998; Buhalis & Schertler, 1999; Fesenmaier, Klein, & Buhalis, 2000; Buhalis & Licata, 2001). In fact, ICTs have always been an important support for management practices' tourism organizations, especially for allowing information sharing (for example, such as prices and availability) regarding to reservation management (Poon, 1993). Therefore, tourism industry is interesting field for the investigation of the potential offered by new technologies (Lee, 2000). The tourist product consists of information on price, availability, qualitative characteristics and convenience of the single services of the holiday; it cannot be evaluated prior to consumption, as it is intangible. As a consequence, the ability to arouse interest and attract potential consumers is mostly determined by amount of information available, communicated and exchanged for describe and presentation the tourist product. Not surprising that the web-based technologies have found in the tourist industry the first and most popular applications, accompanied by a change that, in parallel, covered the behaviours and attitudes of consumers (Buhalis, 1998; O'Connor, 1999; Smith & Jenner, 1998; Werthner & Klein, 1999; O'Connor & Frew, 2002; Buhalis & Licata, 2001).

In the past few years, there has been considerable growth of the use of Web 2.0 applications in the tourism industry, commonly known as Travel 2.0 (Leung, Law, van Hoof, & Buhalis, 2013). Recently, Travel Weekly has published a study on social media usage in tourism, showing the rise in travelers with social media accounts from 2013 to 2016. Figure 1 shows the travellers with social media accounts from 2013 to 2016.

Figure 1. Rise in Travellers with Social Media Accounts (Tobin, 2016)
Source: Tobin, 2016.

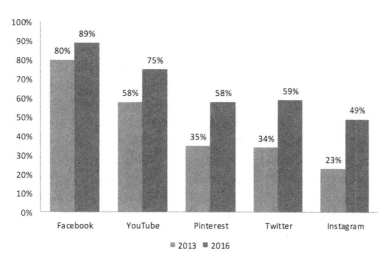

Results show the growth of social media usage, such as Facebook (+8%), YouTube (+23%), Pinterest (+23%), Twitter (+25%), and Instagram (+26%), in tourism in the last 3 years.

More in general, social media have become an important and popular tool for increasing information potentially available to travellers. Virtual context such as, for example, travelblog.org, travelpod.com, blog.realtravel.com, yourtraveljournal.com, worldnomads.com, travelpost.com, represent the specialized blogs that receive information by travellers (Pan, MacLaurin, & Crotts, 2007; Schmallegger & Carson, 2008). Moreover, travel agencies (statravelblogs.com, tui.com) or travel guides (lonelyplanet.com, community.roughguides.com, frommers.com), as well as several countries (on their official destination websites) provide a web space for tourists to share their experiences (Schmallegger & Carson, 2008).

Social Media Usage in Tourism Industry

The Travel Weekly has published the results of a survey based on responses from 1,193 travel agents about the current social media trends for consumers (c) and travel professionals (t). The survey's results have shown that more than 90% of travellers and travel agents have a Facebook account (c=94%; t=94%), while other platforms, such as Twitter (c=76%; t=37%), LinkedIn (c=75%; t=41%) and Instagram (c=74%; t=33%), are less used above all for business reasons. Also, the results shown that the most popular medium used for travel agents is the e-mail (78%), following by social media (67%), agency website (57%), newsletter (28%), and others media (less than 28%). Respect than e-mail, the usage of social media (+3%), agency website (+2%) and newsletter (+1%) is respectively increased from 2015 to 2016. *Source:* http://www.travelweekly.com/IndustrySurvey2016/Social-media

Through social media, people can share travel-related comments, opinions, stories and personal experiences about holidays, as well as can obtain information to support the trip-planning process and to assist in decision-making about destinations, accommodation, restaurants, tours, and attractions (Buhalis & Law, 2008; Xiang & Gretzel, 2010; Hays, Page, & Buhalis, 2013). Moreover, social media users can enrich the shared contents uploading images, audios, and videos, helping to create an objective and reliable information source in travel planning (Kang & Shuett, 2013).

For example, these contributions can elicit review sites, such as Tripadvisor.com, providing reviews and ratings, or online travel communities, such as that of Lonely Planet, to engage consumers in conversations. The recommendations shared on social media applications seem be the main tool for supporting the choice of services of the holiday; travellers rely on other travellers' advice (Hays et al., 2013). In fact, findings of the BrightLocal's Annual Local Consumer Review Survey 2015 has shown that the 92% of consumers read online reviews and about the 40% of consumers form an opinion by reading just 1-3 reviews. For Search Engine Land (2014) the 85% of consumers read up to 10 reviews before they feel that they can trust a business. Research by Deloitte (2015) found that 42% of holidaymakers use review websites and these sites are the most important sources that influenced the booking decisions (59%).

The role and use of social media in tourism and hospitality industry has become an interesting area of inquiry (see for a review Leung, Law, Hoof, & Buhalis, 2013 and Zeng & Gerritsen, 2014), for analysing the effect of social media on travellers' decision-making as well as in tourism operations and management. For example, some scholars investigated the effect of users' shared travel experiences on holiday planning processing (e.g., Di Pietro, Di Virgilio, & Pantano, 2011; Fotis, Buhalis, & Rossides, 2012; Jacobsen & Munar, 2012; Litvin, Goldsmith, & Pan, 2008) showing that people prefer independent travel-related information provided by the individuals who have travelled previously. Other studies deepened the use of social media tools as destination marketing tools (Mariani, Di Felice, & Mura, 2016; Hays et al., 2013; Stankov, Lazic, & Dragicevic, 2010; Xiang & Gretzel, 2010). Overall, for tourism organizations, social media are a challenge to increase their service quality because the use of feedback or negative postings also by travellers should represent an input to improve the efficiency and effectiveness of their processes (Kang & Shuett, 2013). Thus, tourism organizations, considering the consumer perspective in every business decision, would be able to identify new ways for reengineer business models and operations, such as customer service, marketing, networking and knowledge management (Zeng & Gerritsen, 2014).

USING SOCIAL MEDIA FOR KNOWLEDGE MANAGEMENT IN TOURISM INDUSTRY

As information-intensive industry, the management practices' tourism organizations are highly focused on the information exchanges and knowledge transfer because the tourism product is a combination of many different services offered by several actors, resulting in complex and intense interdependence conditions amongst tourism firms (Cooper, 2006). The information and knowledge sharing is fundamental for any coordination and interaction to occur among parties. Particularly, one way in which inter-organizational relationships materialize is through the exchange of information (Czepiel, 1975; Levine & White, 1961), and this is a prerequisite to cooperative inter-organizational activity (Schermerhorn, 1977; Van de Ven & Koening, 1975). Therefore, information sharing, as a set of information flows exchanged between more actors in a collective action, is a prerequisite of cooperation between different organizations.

Many scholars have recognized the knowledge management as an important topic for tourism research (e.g., Yang & Wan, 2004; Cooper, 2006; Hallin & Marnburg, 2008; Sigala & Chalkiti, 2014), deepening knowledge management applications across destination networks (Baggio & Cooper 2010; Scott, Cooper, & Baggio, 2008; Hays et al., 2013) or in the hospitality industry (Hallin & Marnburg 2008; Kyriakidou & Gore, 2005; Yang & Wan, 2004). For example, hotel chains are collections of hotel services organizations, differentiated in physical space, that are linked together into a larger organization. The distance in geographical space among the components of a chain suggests that each hotel affiliated belongs at least to two kinds of networks, the local destination network and the chain network. The linkage with a chain affects its components by giving resources, reputation and market power; moreover, the collection in a chain of organizations of different destinations fosters a transfer of knowledge within the local network (Buonocore & Metallo, 2004). In fact, Baum and Ingram (1997) shown that the value of the experience of a chain to a component depends on the similarity between the environment of the component and the environment of the chain. To the extent the chain has experience in the component's local environment it should result in a significant and valuable transfer of knowledge to component organizations.

ICTs have been regarded as one of the main enablers of knowledge creation and sharing activities (e.g., Sigala & Chalkiti 2014; Skok & Kalmanovitch, 2005; Sher & Lee, 2004). Traditionally, ICT in support of knowledge creation and sharing process in organizations are viewed as applications for (Alavi & Leidner, 2001): the coding and sharing of best practices; the creation of corporate knowledge directories; the creation of knowledge networks.

The ICTs have a crucial role for information exchange between all actors of tourism industry (Werthner & Klein, 1999; Xiang & Gretzel 2010): consumer, suppliers (e.g., hotels, transportation sectors, attractions), intermediaries (e.g., travel agents, tour operators), controllers (e.g., governments and administrative bodies), non-profit organizations (e.g., destination marketing organizations). For example, Ingram and Roberts (2000) described that relationships among managers of Sydney hotels supported by web tools allowed knowledge sharing and the consolidation of many best practices, improving the hotels' performance. In fact, in the hotel industry, the implementation of knowledge management (KM) systems is a very common practice for benefits resulting from hotel chains requirements of an overall quality standard of their geographically dispersed hotels (see for a review Hallin & Marnburg, 2008). Bouncken (2002) described Accor Hotel Group's KM systems, with 3500 hotels worldwide, that has implemented a KM system based on three components: IT-based knowledge accumulation; access to the IT-based knowledge system; and motivation for knowledge use and creation. In tourism destination management, ICTs are tools able to support the integrated offer of facilities and attractions for tourists, facilitating knowledge management in the geographical area.

The Case of the Visittrentino.it

Nowadays, Web 2.0 tools allow people to take an active role in knowledge co-creating and sharing, by contributing and debating content with others through a collaborative approach (e.g., Sigala & Chalkiti, 2012, 2014; Yu, Lu, & Liu, 2010; Wagner & Bolloju, 2005). For example, knowledge sharing in online travel communities occurs when people share travel-related comments, opinions, experiences, and prospective travellers can consult this information, posting questions and interacting with members (Lee, Reid, & Kim, 2014; Arsal, Woosnam, Baldwin, & Backman, 2010; Ip, Lee, & Law, 2010). Moreover, in these communities, the accumulation of knowledge shared by traveller is a particularly important factor for the success of the online travel communities (Hsu et al., 2007; Shen et al., 2010; Qu & Lee, 2011). Munar and Jacobsen (2014) have shown that in social media, tourists share not only knowledge, aspects about holiday attributes (e.g., prices or weather conditions), but typically also tourism experiences defined as an individual's subjective evaluation of events related to his/her tourist activities (Tung & Ritchie, 2011). Travel experiences can be shared through storytelling, artefacts (such as photographs and videos) or both; Noor and colleagues (2005) observed that experience sharing is one form of tacit knowledge sharing. Therefore, social media provide the opportunity for users to share also tacit knowledge that relies on experience and practices (Nezakati et al., 2015).

The Case of the Castagna di Montella IGP

Montella is an small mountain village of less than 10,000 inhabitants located in Campania, a southern region of Italy. The village has always had a vocation for producing chestnuts, cheese and other typical local products thanks to its specific territorial location, climate and the fertility soil. The chestnuts were always considered as extremely important because of they provided food and work to whole generations of rural people in the Montella village and more in general in the Avellino Province. The Montella Chestnut is so highly valued to obtain a certificate of the recognition of the IGP label (Protected Geographical Indication). After harvesting of chestnut that begins in September and October, the inhabitants of Montella organizes the annual festivity (well-known as 'Sagra della Castagna di Montella IGP') of the Montella Chestnut (now in its 34th edition) which has become a famous tourist attraction not only for locals, but also for tourists from the region of Campania. It is a way for promoting the typical local products and for preserving the traditional handcrafted methods that have been handed down from generation to generation. The annual festivity, the chestnut's museum, etc. are some examples of touristic initiatives aimed at promoting and preserving the cultivation techniques and processing of chestnuts. Such touristic destination is also known thanks to Internet web sites and social media, such as Facebook fan page (34a Sagra della Castagna di Montella IGP), which are increasingly used for sharing touristic knowledge. The Facebook fan page (https://www.facebook.com/SagraCastagnaDiMontella/) of the '34a Sagra della Castagna di Montella IGP' has more than 2.800 likes and 1.400 fans are talking about this. It contains information, photos and videos posted by local organizers and tourists on various initiatives organized during the festivity, so representing an important medium for promoting and for preserving the typical local product and for enhancing sustainable tourism. Source: http://www.castagnamontella. it/; https://www.facebook.com/SagraCastagnaDiMontella/.

Buhalis and Licata Hays (2002) suggested that technology applications can encourage the diffusion of the knowledge about typical customs and traditions of a destination, promoting visibility of cultural resources, and supporting relationships between cultural and tourism operators (Jamhawi & Hajahjah, 2016). Therefore, it seems that social media tools could favour the destination sustainability and, thus, to reduce the negative impacts of the tourism growth through the promotion of local events such as markets or festivals that characterize the community culture and the local identity. Local traditions are an important way of preserving the community knowledge and its sustainability. However, many destinations, mainly rural areas, risk the loss of local traditions as well as the abandonment of some professions and as Silberman (2005, p. 12) observed digital technology allows a "quicker and more efficient methods of recording endangered data … to deal with cultural heritage emergencies". Trough social media it is possible the digital storytelling of the tourism experiences or the description of the customs, form of art, social practices, values, lifestyles, or typical products that distinguish local identity of the destination. Preserving cultural heritage appears to be a key factor for supporting tourism development as well as tourism product differentiation (Cuccia & Cellini, 2007).

CONCLUSION AND FUTURE RESEARCH DIRECTIONS

This chapter focused on the role of social media for knowledge management in tourism industry.

Although prior academic literature has mainly deepened the effects of social media on organizations, destinations and, more in general, tourism industry, there is limited research addressing how social media support knowledge management and, in particular the processes of knowledge creation (known as contraction or development), knowledge sharing (known as transfer, distribution or dissemination), and knowledge preservation (known as storage and retrieval). Further research should be addressed to investigate how social media usage influences the processes of creation, sharing and preservation of touristic knowledge.

Furthermore, while the tourism academic literature has paid particular attention to knowledge creation and sharing processes, knowledge preservation issue is still in its infancy stage. Indeed, with reference to knowledge creation and sharing processes, social media tools have been regarded as an important enabler of knowledge creation and sharing activities in destination management and/or hospitality industry, so allowing people to take an active role in knowledge co-creating and sharing trough a collaborative approach (e.g., Baggio & Cooper 2010; Yu, Lu, & Liu, 2010). On the contrary, with reference to knowledge preservation process, there are only few studies that highlight as social media can favour community knowledge and cultural heritage for development tourism product (e.g., Munar & Ooi, 2012; Silberman, 2005). Managerial literature underlined that after knowledge has been developed or acquired, it must be carefully preserved in order to avoid memory loss, emphasizing the process of selection, storage and effective actualization of knowledge. According to these arguments, we think that future research should work along these lines by investigating the use of social media for knowledge preservation in terms of customs, traditions and cultural resources. In this way, organizations and tourism destinations could use social media for preserving history and heritage, which affect the brand marketing and characterizes the place, playing a significant role for destination sustainability and competitiveness.

REFERENCES

Agrifoglio, R. (2015). *Knowledge Preservation Through Community of Practice. Theoretical Issues and Empirical Evidence. Information Systems Series.* Springer. doi:10.1007/978-3-319-22234-9

Alavi, M., & Leidner, D. E. (2001). Review: Knowledge management and knowledge management systems: Conceptual foundations and research issues. *Management Information Systems Quarterly, 25*(1), 107–136. doi:10.2307/3250961

Arsal, I., Woosnam, K. M., Baldwin, E. D., & Backman, S. J. (2010). Residents as Travel Destination Information Providers: An Online Community Perspective. *Journal of Travel Research*, *49*(4), 400–413. doi:10.1177/0047287509346856

Baggio, R., & Cooper, C. (2010). Knowledge transfer in a tourism destination: The effects of a network structure. *Service Industries Journal*, *30*(10), 1757–1771. doi:10.1080/02642060903580649

Baum, J. A. C., & Ingram, P. (1997). Chain affiliation and the failure of Manhattan hotels, 1898-1980. *Administrative Science Quarterly*, *42*(1).

Beritelli, P., Strobl, A., & Peters, M. (2013). Interlocking directorships against community closure: A trade-off for development in tourist destinations. *Tourism Review*, *68*(1), 21–34. doi:10.1108/16605371311310057

Bouncken, R. B. (2002). Knowledge management for quality improvements in hotels. *Journal of Quality Assurance in Hospitality & Tourism*, *3*(3-4), 25–59. doi:10.1300/J162v03n03_03

BrightLocal. (2015). *Local Consumer Review Survey*. Retrieved from https://www.brightlocal.com/learn/local-consumer-review-survey/

Brown, J. S., & Duguid, P. (2000). Mysteries of the region: knowledge dynamics in Silicon Valley. *The Silicon Valley Edge*, 16-45.

Buhalis, D. (1998). Strategic use of information technologies in the tourism industry. *Tourism Management*, *19*(5), 409–421. doi:10.1016/S0261-5177(98)00038-7

Buhalis, D., & Law, R. (2008). Progress in information technology and tourism management: 20 years on and 10 years after the Internet—The state of eTourism research. *Tourism Management*, *29*(4), 609–623. doi:10.1016/j.tourman.2008.01.005

Buhalis, D., & Licata, M. C. (2002). The future eTourism intermediaries. *Tourism Management*, *23*(3), 207–220. doi:10.1016/S0261-5177(01)00085-1

Buhalis, D., & Schertler, W. (1999). Information and Communication Technologies in tourism. *ENTER 99 Conference Proceedings*.

Buonocore, F., & Metallo, C. (2004). Tourist Destination Networks, Relational Competencies and "Relationship Builders"–the Central Role of Information Systems and Human Resource Management. In *Networking and partnerships in destination development and management: Proceedings of the ATLAS annual conference* (pp. 377-398).

Cook, S. D. N., & Brown, J. S. (1999). Bridging Epistemologies: The Generative Dance Between Organizational Knowledge and Organizational Knowing. *Organization Science*, *10*(4), 381–400. doi:10.1287/orsc.10.4.381

Cooper, C. (2006). Knowledge management and tourism. *Annals of Tourism Research*, *33*(1), 47–64. doi:10.1016/j.annals.2005.04.005

Cooper, C. (2015). Managing tourism knowledge. *Tourism Recreation Research*, *40*(1), 107–119. doi:10.1080/02508281.2015.1006418

Cuccia, T., & Cellini, R. (2007). Is cultural heritage really important for tourists? A contingent rating study. *Applied Economics*, *39*(2), 261–271. doi:10.1080/00036840500427981

Czepiel, J. A. (1975). Patterns of interorganizational communications and the diffusion of a major technological innovation in a competitive industrial community. *Academy of Management Journal*, *18*(1), 6–24. doi:10.2307/255621

Davenport, T. H., & Prusak, L. (1998). *Working Knowledge*. Boston: Harvard Business School Press.

Davidavičienė, V., & Raudeliūnienė, J. (2010). ICT in Tacit Knowledge Preservation. In *The 6th International Scientific Conference "Business and Management 2010"* (pp. 822-828).

Deloitte, L. L. P. (2015). *Travel Consumer 2015. Engaging the empowered holidaymaker*. Retrieved from http://www2.deloitte.com/content/dam/Deloitte/uk/Documents/consumer-business/deloitte-uk-travel-consumer-2015.pdf

Di Pietro, L., Di Virgilio, F., & Pantano, E. (2012). Social network for the choice of tourist destination: Attitude and behavioural intention. *Journal of Hospitality and Tourism Technology*, *3*(1), 60–76. doi:10.1108/17579881211206543

Dretske, F. (1981). *Knowledge and the Flow of information*. MIT Press.

Fesenmaier, D., Klein, S., & Buhalis, D. (2000). *Information and Communication Technologies in Tourism*. Vienna: Springer.

Fotis, J., Buhalis, D., & Rossides, N. (2012). *Social media use and impact during the holiday travel planning process*. Springer-Verlag. doi:10.1007/978-3-7091-1142-0_2

Grizelj, F. (2003). Collaborative knowledge management in virtual service companies-approach for tourism destinations. *Tourism*, *51*(4), 371–385.

Hallin, C. A., & Marnburg, E. (2008). Knowledge management in the hospitality industry: A review of empirical research. *Tourism Management*, *29*(2), 366–381. doi:10.1016/j.tourman.2007.02.019

Hays, S., Page, S. J., & Buhalis, D. (2013). Social media as a destination marketing tool: Its use by national tourism organisations. *Current Issues in Tourism*, *16*(3), 211–239. doi:10.1080/13683500.2012.662215

Hsu, M., Ju, T. L., Yen, C., & Chang, C. (2007). Knowledge sharing behavior in virtual communities: The relationship between trust, self-efficacy, and outcome expecta- tions. *International Journal of Human-Computer Studies*, *65*(2), 153–169. doi:10.1016/j.ijhcs.2006.09.003

Huber, G. (1991). Organizational Learning: The Contributing Processes and the Literatures. *Organization Science*, *2*(1), 88–115. doi:10.1287/orsc.2.1.88

Ingram, P., & Roberts, P. W. (2000). Friendships among competitors in the Sydney Hotel Industry1. *American Journal of Sociology*, *106*(2), 387–423. doi:10.1086/316965

Ip, C., Lee, H., & Law, R. (2010). Profiling the users of travel websites for planning and online experience sharing. *Journal of Hospitality & Tourism Research (Washington, D.C.)*, *36*(3), 418–426. doi:10.1177/1096348010388663

Ipe, M. (2003). Knowledge sharing in organizations: A conceptual framework. *Human Resource Development Review*, 2(4), 337–359. doi:10.1177/1534484303257985

Jacobsen, J. K. S., & Munar, A. M. (2012). Tourist information search and destination choice in a digital age. *Tourism Management Perspectives*, *1*, 39–47. doi:10.1016/j.tmp.2011.12.005

Jamhawi, M. M., & Hajahjah, Z. A. (2016). It-Innovation and Technologies Transfer to Heritage Sites: The Case of Madaba, Jordan. *Mediterranean Archaeology and Archaeometry*, *16*(2), 41–46.

Kang, M., & Schuett, M. A. (2013). Determinants of sharing travel experiences in social media. *Journal of Travel & Tourism Marketing*, *30*(1-2), 93–107. doi:10.1080/10548408.2013.751237

Kaplan, A. M., & Haenlein, M. (2010). Users of the world, unite! The challenges and opportunities of Social Media. *Business Horizons*, *53*(1), 59–68. doi:10.1016/j.bushor.2009.09.003

Kyriakidou, O., & Gore, J. (2005). Learning by example: Benchmarking organizational culture in hospitality, tourism and leisure SMEs. *Benchmarking: An International Journal*, *12*(3), 192–206. doi:10.1108/14635770510600320

Lam, A. (2000). Tacit Knowledge, Organizational Learning and Societal Institutions: An Integrated Framework. *Organization Studies*, *21*(3), 487–513. doi:10.1177/0170840600213001

Lee, A. (2000). *Computer reservation systems: an industry of its own. Centre for Asian Business Cases, School of business*. The University of Hong Kong.

Lee, H., Reid, E., & Kim, W. G. (2014). Understanding knowledge sharing in online travel communities: Antecedents and the moderating effects of interaction modes. *Journal of Hospitality & Tourism Research (Washington, D.C.)*, *38*(2), 222–242. doi:10.1177/1096348012451454

Leung, D., Law, R., Van Hoof, H., & Buhalis, D. (2013). Social media in tourism and hospitality: A literature review. *Journal of Travel & Tourism Marketing*, *30*(1-2), 3–22. doi:10.1080/10548408.2013.750919

Levine, S., & White, P. E. (1961). Exchange as a conceptual framework for the study of interorganizational relationships. *Administrative Science Quarterly*, *5*(4), 583–601. doi:10.2307/2390622

Litvin, S. W., Goldsmith, R. E., & Pan, B. (2008). Electronic word-of-mouth in hospitality and tourism management. *Tourism Management*, *29*(3), 458–468. doi:10.1016/j.tourman.2007.05.011

Machlup, F. (1983). *The study of information: Interdisciplinary messages*. Retrieved from http://philpapers.org/rec/MACTSO-9

Maglitta, J. (1996). Smarten up! *Computerworld*, *29*(23), 84–86.

Mariani, M. M., Di Felice, M., & Mura, M. (2016). Facebook as a destination marketing tool: Evidence from Italian regional Destination Management Organizations. *Tourism Management*, *54*, 321–343. doi:10.1016/j.tourman.2015.12.008

Munar, A., & Ooi, C. (2012). *What Social Media Tell Us About The Heritage Experience*. Retrieved from https://www.researchgate.net/profile/can_seng_ooi/publication/265060043_what_social_media_tell_us_about_the_heritage_experience_what_social_media_tell_us_about_the_heritage_experience/links/55faa40c08aeba1d9f369106.pdf

Munar, A. M., & Jacobsen, J. K. S. (2014). Motivations for sharing tourism experiences through social media. *Tourism Management*, *43*, 46–54. doi:10.1016/j.tourman.2014.01.012

Nelson, R. R., & Winter, S. G. (1982). *An Evolutionary Theory of Economic Change*. Cambridge, MA: Belknap Press.

Nezakati, H., Amidi, A., Jusoh, Y. Y., Moghadas, S., Aziz, Y. A., & Sohrabinezhadtalemi, R. (2015). Review of social media potential on knowledge sharing and collaboration in tourism industry. *Procedia: Social and Behavioral Sciences*, *172*, 120–125. doi:10.1016/j.sbspro.2015.01.344

Nonaka, I. (1991). The knowledge-creating company. *Harvard Business Review*, *69*, 96–104.

Nonaka, I. (1994). A Dynamic Theory of Organizational Knowledge Creation. *Organization Science*, *5*(1), 14–37. doi:10.1287/orsc.5.1.14

Nonaka, I., & Konno, N. (1998). The concept of Ba: Building a foundation for knowledge creation. *California Management Review*, *40*(3), 40–55. doi:10.2307/41165942

Nonaka, I., & Takeuchi, H. (1995). *The Knowledge- Creating Company: How Japanese Companies Create the Dynamics of Innovation*. New York: Oxford University Press.

Nonaka, I., & Toyama, R. (2002). A firm as a dialectical being: Towards a dynamic theory of a firm. *Industrial and Corporate Change*, *11*(5), 995–1009. doi:10.1093/icc/11.5.995

Nonaka, I., & Toyama, R. (2003). The knowledge-creating theory revisited: knowledge creation as a synthesizing process. *Knowledge Management Research & Practice, 1*(1), 2-10.

Nonaka, I., von Krogh, G., & Voepel, S. (2006). Organizational knowledge creation theory: Evolutionary paths and future advances. *Organization Studies*, *27*(8), 1179–1208. doi:10.1177/0170840606066312

Noor, N. L. M., Hashim, M., Haron, H., & Aiffin, S. (2005). Community acceptance of knowledge sharing system in the travel and tourism websites: an application of an extension of TAM. *ECIS 2005 Proceedings*, 71.

O'Connor, P. (1999). *Electronic information distribution in tourism and hospitality*. CAB international.

O'Connor, P., & Frew, A. J. (2002). The future of hotel electronic distribution: Expert and industry perspectives. *The Cornell Hotel and Restaurant Administration Quarterly*, *43*(3), 33–45. doi:10.1016/S0010-8804(02)80016-7

Pan, B., MacLaurin, T., & Crotts, J. C. (2007). Travel blogs and their implications for destination marketing. *Journal of Travel Research*, *46*(1), 35–45. doi:10.1177/0047287507302378

Pezzillo Iacono, M., Martinez, M., Mangia, G., & Galdiero, C. (2012). Knowledge creation and inter-organizational relationships: The development of innovation in the railway industry. *Journal of Knowledge Management*, *16*(4), 604–616. doi:10.1108/13673271211246176

Polanyi, M. (1966). *The Tacit Dimension*. New York: Doubleday.

Poon, A. (1993). *Tourism, Technology and Competive Strategies*. Wallingford, UK: CAB International.

Qu, H., & Lee, H. (2011). Travelers social identification and membership behaviors in online travel community. *Tourism Management, 32*(6), 1262–1270. doi:10.1016/j.tourman.2010.12.002

Romhardt, K. (1997). Processes of knowledge preservation: Away from a technology dominated approach. In Proceedings der 21, "Deutschen Jahrestagung für Künstliche Intelligenz", 9.

Ruhanen, L., & Cooper, C. (2004). Applying a knowledge management framework to tourism research. *Tourism Recreation Research, 29*(1), 83–87. doi:10.1080/02508281.2004.11081434

Schermerhorn, J. R. Jr. (1977). Information sharing as an interorganizational activity. *Academy of Management Journal, 20*(1), 148–153. doi:10.2307/255469 PMID:10305920

Schmallegger, D., & Carson, D. (2008). Blogs in tourism: Changing approaches to information exchange. *Journal of Vacation Marketing, 14*(2), 99-110.

Scott, N., Cooper, C., & Baggio, R. (2008). Destination networks: Four Australian cases. *Annals of Tourism Research, 35*(1), 169–188. doi:10.1016/j.annals.2007.07.004

Search Engine Land. (2014). *About Local Consumer Review Survey 2014*. Retrieved from http://searchengineland.com/88-consumers-trust-online-reviews-much-personal-recommendations-195803

Shaw, G., & Williams, A. (2009). Knowledge transfer and management in tourism organisations: An emerging research agenda. *Tourism Management, 30*(3), 325–335. doi:10.1016/j.tourman.2008.02.023

Sheldon, P. (1997). *Tourism Information Technologies*. Oxford, UK: CAB.

Shen, K. N., Yu, A. Y., & Khalifa, M. (2010). Knowledge contribution in virtual communities: Accounting for multiple dimensions of social presence through social identity. *Behaviour & Information Technology, 29*(4), 337–348. doi:10.1080/01449290903156622

Sher, P. J., & Lee, V. C. (2004). Information technology as a facilitator for enhancing dynamic capabilities through knowledge management. *Information & Management, 41*(8), 933–945. doi:10.1016/j.im.2003.06.004

Sigala, M., & Chalkiti, K. (2012). Knowledge management and Web 2.0: preliminary findings from the Greek tourism industry. *Social Media in Travel, Tourism and Hospitality: Theory, Practice and Cases*, 261.

Sigala, M., & Chalkiti, K. (2014). Investigating the exploitation of web 2.0 for knowledge management in the Greek tourism industry: An utilisation–importance analysis. *Computers in Human Behavior, 30*, 800–812. doi:10.1016/j.chb.2013.05.032

Silberman, N. A. (2005). Beyond theme parks and digitized data: what can cultural heritage technologies contribute to the public understanding of the past? *Interdisciplinarity or The Best of Both Worlds: The Grand Challenge for Cultural Heritage Informatics in the 21st Century*. Available at: http://works.bepress.com/neil_silberman/39/

Skok, W., & Kalmanovitch, C. (2005). Evaluating the role and effectiveness of an intranet in facilitating knowledge management: A case study at Surrey County Council. *Information & Management, 42*(5), 731–744. doi:10.1016/j.im.2004.04.008

Smith, C., & Jenner, P. (1998). Tourism and the Internet. *Travel & Tourism Analyst,* (1), 62-81.

Stankov, U., Lazic, L., & Dragicevic, V. (2010). The extent of use of basic Facebook user-generated content by the national tourism organizations in Europe. *European Journal of Tourism Research, 3*(2), 105.

Tobin, R. (2016). Social media: Platform use keeps rising. *Travel Weekly.* Retrieved from http://www.travelweekly.com/ConsumerSurvey2016/Social-media-platform-use-keeps-rising

Tsoukas, H., & Vladimirou, E. (2001). What is organizational knowledge? *Journal of Management Studies, 38*(7), 973–993. doi:10.1111/1467-6486.00268

Tung, V. W. S., & Ritchie, J. B. (2011). Exploring the essence of memorable tourism experiences. *Annals of Tourism Research, 38*(4), 1367–1386. doi:10.1016/j.annals.2011.03.009

Van de Ven, A. H., & Koenig, R. Jr (1975). *Pair-Wise Inter-Agency Relationships: theory and preliminary findings.* Working Paper, Department of Administrative Sciences, Kent State University.

Vance, D. M. (1997). Information, knowledge and wisdom: the epistemic hierarchy and computer-based information system. In B. Perkins & I. Vessey (Eds.), *Proceedings of the Third Americas Conference on Information Systems.* Academic Press.

Von Krogh, G. (1999). *Developing a knowledge-based theory of the firm.* St. Gallen: University of St. Gallen.

Wagner, C., & Bolloju, N. (2005). Supporting knowledge management in organizations with conversational technologies: Discussion forums, weblogs, and wikis. *Journal of Database Management, 16*(2), 1–8.

Walsh, J. P., & Ungson, G. R. (1991). Organizational Memory. *Academy of Management Review, 16*(1), 57–91. doi:10.5465/AMR.1991.4278992

Weick, K. E. (1991). The nontraditional quality of organizational learning. *Organization Science, 2*(1), 116–123. doi:10.1287/orsc.2.1.116

Werthner H., & Klein S. (1999). *Information technology and tourism. A challenging relationship.* Springer Computer Science.

Werthner, H., & Klein, S. (1999). ICT and the changing landscape of global tourism distribution. *Electronic Markets, 9*(4), 256–262. doi:10.1080/101967899358941

Xiang, Z., & Gretzel, U. (2010). Role of social media in online travel information search. *Tourism Management, 31*(2), 179–188. doi:10.1016/j.tourman.2009.02.016

Xiao, H., & Smith, S. L. J. (2010). Professional communication in an applied tourism research community. *Tourism Management, 31*(3), 402–411. doi:10.1016/j.tourman.2009.04.008

Yang, J. T., & Wan, C. S. (2004). Advancing organizational effectiveness and knowledge management implementation. *Tourism Management, 25*(5), 593–601. doi:10.1016/j.tourman.2003.08.002

Yoo, K. H., & Lee, W. (2015). Use of Facebook in the US heritage accommodations sector: An exploratory study. *Journal of Heritage Tourism*, *10*(2), 191–201. doi:10.1080/1743873X.2014.985228

Yu, T. K., Lu, L. C., & Liu, T. F. (2010). Exploring factors that influence knowledge sharing behavior via weblogs. *Computers in Human Behavior*, *26*(1), 32–41. doi:10.1016/j.chb.2009.08.002

Zeng, B., & Gerritsen, R. (2014). What do we know about social media in tourism? A review. *Tourism Management Perspectives*, *10*, 27–36. doi:10.1016/j.tmp.2014.01.001

KEY TERMS AND DEFINITIONS

e-Tourism: The use of Web 2.0 applications in the tourism industry (commonly known also as Travel 2.0).

Knowledge Creation: Is a process that enables organizations to transform knowledge created by individuals from an individual to a collective state.

Knowledge Management: Is a set of socially enacted processes that enable to identify, capture and effectively leverage collective knowledge within an organizational context.

Knowledge Preservation: The process of selection, storage and effective actualization of organizational knowledge.

Knowledge Sharing: Is a process that enables to make available knowledge to others within an organizational context.

Social Media: A set of Web 2.0 applications for creating, organizing, combining, sharing, commenting, and rating user-generated content.

Tourism Destination: Local agglomerations of actors of different nature (tourist firms, local governments, public agencies, cultural organizations, etc.) that cooperate for the development of local tourism product.

Tourism Industry: An information-intensive industry comprised by several activities which need to be combined and assembled, gathering together actors geographically and/or organizationally dispersed such as industry suppliers (e.g., hotels, transportation sectors, attractions), intermediaries (e.g., travel agents), and controllers (e.g., governments and administrative bodies).

ENDNOTE

[1] Contrary to the hierarchical structure of knowledge discussed above, other scholars proposed an inverse perspective in defining knowledge from knowledge to data. From this point of view, knowledge exists before formulating information and measuring data, because of it is a results from a cognitive processing triggered by the inflow of new stimuli (Alavi & Leidner, 2001; Nonaka, von Krogh, & Voelpel, 2009). In this regard, information could be converted to knowledge because processed by people's minds, while knowledge becomes information once it is structured and formally represented through text, graphics, words, or other symbolic forms.

This research was previously published in Social Media for Knowledge Management Applications in Modern Organizations; pages 92-115, copyright year 2018 by Business Science Reference (an imprint of IGI Global).

Chapter 14
A Conceptual Framework to Understand Online Destination Images:
A Research Model Utilizing User–Generated Content Through Twitter

Zeynep A. Gedikoglu

https://orcid.org/0000-0003-1390-2305
Clemson University, USA

Sheila J. Backman
Clemson University, USA

Joseph P. Mazer
Clemson University, USA

Kenneth F. Backman
Clemson University, USA

ABSTRACT

This chapter proposes a new conceptual model to understand the construction of online destination images. This will lead to a more accurate and realistic portrayal of how destination images are created, and allow destination managers (and other stakeholders) to better understand the images promoted, and how these comport with the actual experience of users. The model integrates a sequential and mixed methods approach, enabling a conceptualization of how user generated content (UGC) is utilized to formulate and construct destination images.

DOI: 10.4018/978-1-7998-9020-1.ch014

INTRODUCTION

The construction of image of a destination is vital in tourism marketing. In the early 2000s, Destination Marketing Organizations' (DMO) marketing of the tourism product was the preponderant research medium. Attracting visitors is a major concern for destinations, and the destination image can critically influence a traveler's destination choice (Cai, 2002). Destination marketers use the physical reality, artifacts, architecture, weather, culinary features, and the history to sell a destination to potential tourists. However, an image goes beyond the physical characteristics of a place.

The definition of a destination image (and its constructs) is contested and multi-faceted. Not surprisingly, the tourism literature does not seem to agree upon a universal definition (Martin-Santana et al., 2017). Crompton defines destination image as the sum of beliefs, ideas and impressions a person about a destination (Crompton, 1979). Given the multi-faceted definition, the concept of a destination image depends on how people get informed.

Destination branding has been the core of what marketers have communicated to travelers. However, due to Social Media Platforms, the image of a place is no longer framed by destination marketers. Alternative information sources can market a destination through a collective global outreach where brands are formed by individual, group or official sources. Existing models of the conceptualization of the destination image through studies of tourist perceptions via onsite, mail or phone surveys, focus groups, or interviews are outdated in the context of globalization and technological improvements such as WEB networks. Web technologies make it possible to assess online and global communication data without structured survey questions with pre-tested constructs. Thus, the traditional image-makers, DMOs and tourism promoters, are not the only stakeholders that can construct a destination image. Previous research has shown that destination managers may be active players through creating content and communicating by understanding images communicated by influencers (Chatzigeorgiou, 2017). This chapter presents a new approach to investigate destination images which are communicated by influencers through Twitter. An influencer is a user on social media who has access to a large audience, is mentioned by others and whose posts are re-posted so that can persuade others by virtue of their authenticity and reach. This approach will stimulate better planning for sustainable brand image in tourism practices as an exemplary model for any destination.

User Generated Content (UGC) is any type of shared communicated content that has been created and shared through online platforms by unpaid contributors. The explosion of UGC is a result of WEB and mobile technologies, which provide individuals with unprecedented power to instantaneously add digital traces when performing tasks such as reviewing and documenting travel experience (Lu & Stepchenkova, 2015). Although the term Social Media is difficult to define, a typical definition is an internet-based application that construct user generated content (Blackshaw, 2006). Social media content is produced by consumers and can challenge the content of DMOs (Xiang & Gretzel, 2010).

Perceptions about any destination might shift due to personal experiences or learned knowledge through communication. Social Media (SM) platforms, such a twitter, enables individuals to share personal experiences and/or information much quicker than word-of mouth. To understand the change in people's perceptions towards a destination, this study integrates thematic networks, cognitive and affective components of destination image, time element and sentiment analysis. This chapter offers a sequential mixed methods approach which may be operationalized in future studies. In this chapter, destination image constructs are utilized to understand the current latent variables of destination images. The model visually depicts a destination image through a deductive approach of UGC content.

Qualitative methodologies reveal themes of a destination image from unstructured online communication data and further may be assessed according to the affective and cognitive constructs' properties such as time and sentiment. The objective of this chapter is to propose a new model using social media data to understand online destination images.

The study method proposes to conduct unstructured social media data and sequential mixed methods research design. This model is the first integrated multi-method framework in destination image scholarship. The first part of the chapter provides relevant background about destination image research and adaptation of online data to image studies. The second part of the chapter explains in detail the research model utilizing user generated content through twitter. Each sequential method is explained in detail in the second part. Third part is composed of issues, controversies and problems related to the methodology of the model. The fourth part provides solutions and recommendations for future studies that are going to employ the research model utilizing user generated content through twitter for destination image studies. The fifth part discusses and provides future research directions for the model.

BACKGROUND

Studies of destination images have been the subject of much attention in the academic literature. Tourism researchers have long assumed that the images people have of the world around them significantly influences their travel behavior (Walmsley & Young, 1998). The destination image literature dates to the early 1970s, and consumer marketing research was the initial territory that led scholars' research destination image as a product of tourism service industry. In the academic literature, destination image research has conducted under several alternative names: tourism image, tourist destination image, country image, holiday destination image, brand equity in tourism, destination brand image, destination perceptions, destination branding, and destination marketing.

The earliest phase of tourism studies started with the tourist as the subject and the originator of tourism. Destination image has become a fertile topic since Hunt's research on image as a factor in tourism development (Hunt, 1975). Destination image research was built on the general assumption that images as perceived by individuals have as much to do with a tourism destination's development success as the tangible tourism resources (Hunt, 1975). Image differences between prospective (non-visitors), first-time, and repeat visitors have found that each group is affected by different images such as induced or organic that are communicated to them via tradition channels or tourism promoters (Fakeye & Crompton, 1991). Gunn (1972) suggested that organic image of a destination is formed by print or visual media. An organic image evolves into an induced image with additional information gathered from tourism promoters and organizations. With the decision to travel, a prospective tourist experiences the place herself and forms a complex image in her mind. Previous studies showed that the perceived image of a place is vulnerable to myriad experiences for both visitors and citizens.

Destination image formation is a construction of a mental representation on the basis of information cues selected and delivered by the image formation agents. The image of a place is represented by the consumer's general perception of that place, based on the strong and weak points by which the respective place has made itself known (Roth & Romeo, 1992). Dichter found that image describes not individual traits or qualities, but the total impression an entity makes on others (Dichter, 1985). Telisman defined images of tourism destinations as a crucial component of a destination's tourism product (Telisman, 1989). Telisman stated that a destination image needs to be continuously assessed, as it exists in the minds of potential customers and it is a prerequisite to meaningful marketing strategy and competitive positioning (Telisman, 1989). Gartner looked at attribute measurement and his conclusions were that image does not equate to reality and image studies represent only specific time period (Gartner, 1989). Therefore, online data might reveal up-to-date image perceptions with respect to time. Embacher & Buttle has a global approach to destination image perceptions people hold. They tried to understand it as a perception construct rather than fragmenting it to socio-psychological or psychological factors (Embacher & Buttle, 1989).

Van den Berg, van der Borg, and van der Meer (1995) suggest that tourism managers should engage all available resources without losing sight of the necessity to bring about and communicate a diverse, stable, original, and attractive image to the destination. Online communication platforms are manifestations of social construction and presence for contemporary tourism destinations. These platforms provide relevant data as a representation for researchers and for managers to mold their marketing strategies.

The main concern of researchers is the association of tangible physical components of place perception commonly associated with the destination image (Pearce 1977, 1982; Walmsley & Jenkins, 1992). Echtner & Richie examined the literature in order to understand the unique characteristics of the destination image concept, and developed a measure and framework (Echter & Richie, 1991; Echter & Richie, 1993). Their framework consists of three characteristics; attribute-holistic, functional-psychological, and common-unique, which is then used to measure the destination image (Echter & Richie, 1991). Fakeye & Crompton developed a model in order to understand the components of destination image. Their research described the relationship between induced, organic and complex images that amalgamated experiences to that destination (Fakeye & Crompton, 1991). Walmsley & Young examined the applicability of the local scales of destination image to the international scale. Their results support a common pattern to be used to evaluate destination images at the local and international levels (Walmsley & Young, 1998). The existence of a basic schema to evaluate intangible characteristics of a destination image has been important for future tourism scholarship about destination image.

Chon found that destination image is the most important influence in tourist buyer behavior and satisfaction (Chon, 1990). Building on Chon's analysis, Echtner and Ritchie examined the conceptualization and operationalization of 15 previous destination image studies to find a pattern for future studies (Echtner & Ritchie, 1991). Their 1991 review concluded that researchers still had not successfully operationalized the destination image construct. Echtner and Ritchie also found that researchers held a strong preference for quantitative research techniques (Pike, 2002). Several authors have looked at what visitors know about a destination, the cognitive image, and how visitors emotionally feel about that destination, the affective image (Baloglu & McCleary, 1999b; San Martin & Del Bosque, 2008; Beerli & Martin, 2004). Cognitive components of destination image are an individual's unique knowledge, perceptions and beliefs about the attributes of a destination which are observable, descriptive and measurable. On the other hand, affective components of destination image are an individual's unique emotional interpretation of a destination which is composed of feelings and emotions. In the context of tourism, research empirically indicates that cognitive and affective evaluations directly influence the overall image (Baloglu & McCleary, 1999a, 1999b; Stern & Krakover, 1993). Previous research recognized multidimensionality and complexity (Ryan & Cave, 2005) of the destination image concept and applied different methods for measuring different components (Pezenka, 2016).

The extent to which consumers use an overall or composite image is not yet understood (Dichter, 1985; Stern & Krakover, 1993; Baloglu & McCleary, 1999a). The sources, through which individuals receive information such as promotions and recommendations, have been found to influence destination image (Baloglu and McCleary 1999b). Pike in his analysis of 142 papers from 1973 to 2000 found that in destination image analysis cognitive image attributes are generally generated from previous literature (Pike, 2002). Sometimes, a content analysis of destination guidebooks (or brochures) is also used to generate cognitive image attributes (Di Marino, 2008; Tasci, Gartner, & Cavusgil, 2007; Y. Wang & Fesenmaier, 2007). Affective evaluations, on the other hand, are generally measured using the bipolar scales developed by. Russell and his colleagues (Russell & Pratt, 1980; Stepchenkova & Mills, 2010). Previous research shows that some image components may be universal to all destinations, while others are destination specific (Echtner & Ritchie, 1993). Therefore, a new model may extend understanding of the components and attributes of destination image.

According to Woodside and Lysonski's (1989) destination choice model, marketing variables or information sources influence the formation of perceptions or cognitive evaluations but not the affective component of image (Woodside & Lysonski, 1989). The image and brand of a destination are two different concepts but not mutually exclusive (Munar, 2012), meaning that the brand's existence depends on the image formation (Cai, 2002). Image represents the sum of beliefs, attitudes and impressions that a group has of an object (Nadeau et al., 2008). Previous research has shown that, the destination image evolves organically through word-of-mouth and other communication received about the destination (Gartner, 1986). While numerous studies contributed significantly to the understanding of destination image formation, more recent communication technologies, especially the influence of Social Media, haven't been considered in these frameworks (Kislali, Kavaratzis & Saren, 2016). Social Media is an important means to access information from trusted sources and a vital new platform to share personal experiences. Globalization processes of how potential visitors choose, decide, and behave have enriched options through information communication technologies (ICTs).

Every social networking site has millions of users, and each provides worldwide connectivity. The connections provide, among other things, free advice and free advertising. Social networking sites have revolutionized real time sharing of information. The sharing of personal stories through social networks alter perceptions and influence tourism behaviors. Thus, people interactively co-construct and re-create destination images by digital storytelling verbally and/or visually; sharing their own narratives about tourism destinations through their experiences (Amersdorffer, Bauhuber, & Oellrich, 2012) as well as perceptions and expectations.

Recently, tourism has become the largest industry for online transactions (Mack et al., 2008). The rapid increase in internet usage and Social Media adaptation brings new challenges and opportunities both for tourism destinations and travelers (Schmallegger & Carson, 2008). Social Media has changed the information search and purchase behaviors of all tourism stakeholders (Lo et al., 2011) and ultimately has affected how destination images are formed (Kislali, Kavaratzis, & Saren, 2016). Research has not investigated if destination images may be sustained via incorporating contemporary communication platforms such as Social Media, which are global and instant.

Social Media (SM) is affecting tourists' consumption behavior by facilitating conversations. Social Media websites, representing various forms of UGC such as blogs, virtual communities, wikis, social networks, collaborative tagging, and media files shared on sites like YouTube and Flickr, have gained substantial popularity with online travelers (Gretzel, 2006; Pan, MacLaurin, & Crotts, 2007). UGC is a mixture of fact and opinion which are sentimental impressions on various social media platforms. This is shifting the broadcast medium from one-to-many to a many-to-many model, rooted in conversations between authors, people, and peers (Solis, 2010). Social Media platforms such as YouTube, Twitter and Flickr, play a central role in empowering enhanced levels of interactions among multiple parties (Neuhofer, Buhalis, & Ladkin, 2014).

Social Media marketing leverages specific Social Media platforms (places where people connect and communicate) to promote a product or a service to increase sales (Sotiriadis & Van Zyl, 2013). Tourism companies use Social Media as a platform to apply their marketing strategies and spread their destination images through images and texts. Whatever these companies are communicating is just a fraction of communication data that is produced about a destination on Social Media. Fotis, confirmed the importance of Social Media as a platform for tourism providers and tourist consumers to engage, interact and share experiences (Fotis et al., 2011).

Online/virtual destination image concepts has been researched by few scholars until now such as Govers & Go, 2004; Dwivedi, 2009 and Stepchenkova & Morrison, 2006. With online technologies tourism destination images are becoming increasingly fragmented and ephemeral in nature (Govers et al., 2007). One of the first papers published in Information Technology and Tourism Journal, tried to deconstruct the destination image concept into attribute-based components using structured methodologies (Govers & Go, 2003). The article demonstrated for the first time that the multi-attribute destination image research is inadequate in predicting destination choice behavior. Govers, Go, and Kumar (2007) utilized a qualitative approach to study seven case studies with an online survey; the respondents of the online survey were not current or potential tourists, but anyone who provided an input about a destination.

Dwivedi (2009) researched the use of WEB 2.0 in destination image formation, specifically by exploring India's online image through consumer queries posted on travel message boards. The results of the study showed that consumers are not only perceivers of destination image information, but they actively construct and share their own images via the WEB 2.0 platforms (Dwivedi, 2009). Traditional internet-based travel studies have focused on supply side sources such as tour Websites and government travel websites, while this paper provides a much-needed and different perspective.

Hunter showed that an image is an aggregate online product and it is not entirely in the hands of tourism marketers (Hunter 2013). The first study which compared national tourism organizations' and tourists' perspectives of an online destination image was done by Mak (2017. The study examined perceived and projected online destination images that are manifested in tourist and national tourism organization generated content (Mak, 2017). Findings revealed that tourist generated textual content tended to outperform that of national tourism organizations in reflecting affective destination image attitudes (Farías et al., 2016).

Globalism has affected the tourism industry and how people perceive tourism products. The Internet has fundamentally reshaped how tourism-related information is distributed, and how people plan for and consume travel (Buhalis & Law, 2008). Before the Internet, DMOs controlled the media messages, and they tried to create desired destination images through their marketing campaigns. Generalizations of destination images were prominent within the marketing products of tourism promoters when mass tourism peaked in 1980s. However, today tourism is a very fragmented industry and an information-rich business, which makes it especially receptive for the benefits offered by the WEB 2.0 (Schwartz, 1998). Therefore, destinations compete through images held in the minds of potential tourists (Baloglu & McClearly, 1999a).

Waters's case study demonstrated thematic analysis to be a rigorous and valid means of analyzing tourism texts, particularly where it is recognized that the meaning or significance of the whole may be more than the sum of its parts (Walters, 2016). The most frequent use of thematic analysis in tourism research has been its application to the interpretation of written documents (Walters, 2016). Although not commonly utilized in tourism research, thematic analysis has been applied to big data in various social sciences. In tourism scholarship, several recent examples which utilize thematic analysis in destination image research include analysis of information sources construct and its relevance to destination image formation (Llodra-Riers et al., 2015) and the social construction of tourism online destination images (Hunter, 2016).

Use of social media on the Internet has changed DMOs use social media, especially blogs, as part of their business strategy for each of the five key marketing functions—promotion, product distribution, communication, management, and research above-listed functions (Schmallegger & Carson, 2008). However, authors have not yet sufficiently addressed the stability of a destination image, in predicting destination choice across different tourists and destinations, how to sustain an image through communication actors (Lin, Morais, Kerstetter, & Hou, 2007). A review of the literature shows that there is a gap in research which integrates new communication technologies to destination image research. The destination image critically influences the traveler's destination choice process (Cai, 2002). Therefore, in this chapter a new model is proposed which utilizes data from technologies that have and will have a potent influence on destination image formation. This challenges long-standing assumptions about information-technology image measurement paradigms. The main focus of the proposed model is to deconstruct the image into affective and cognitive components looking at the influencers' communication.

A RESEARCH MODEL UTILIZING USER GENERATED CONTENT THROUGH TWITTER

The objective of this chapter is to explain a research model which relies on unstructured online communication data to understand online destination images. Proof of concept is explored in the case study by looking at how the destination image of the capital of France, Paris, is affected by the terror crisis after the November 2015 terror attacks in Paris (Gedikoglu, 2018). Influencers diffuse information that shapes perceptions in online communication platforms such as twitter. Twitter is possibly the best-known microblogging site and was launched in 2006 (Sotiriadis & Van Zyl, 2015). In a 24-hour period, 140 million active Twitter users send out more than 340 million tweets (Gašpar & Mabić, 2017). Therefore, through Twitter data, it is possible to evade the problem of ensuring a representative sample using the population of all users of Twitter with respect to search query. Therefore, Twitter is chosen as the data collection platform for this study,

The purpose is to ascertain basic and organizing themes about a destination through thematic analysis, and then model a further quantitative analysis framework. This will fill the gap in literature for exploring the Social Media sites as agents and online identities as influencers of cognitive and affective components of destination image. At the same time, it uniquely supports a holistic approach which embraces cognitive and affective factors with a qualitative analysis methodology: thematic network analysis.

Additionally, the sequential approach of the model utilizes the themes generated in thematic analysis to further operationalize the model by a quantitative analysis to understand the relationship between time, sentiments, and cognitive and affective constructs. There is copious research that focuses on analyzing user sentiment towards different products, services or even intangible aspects on Twitter (Mochón & Martínez, 2014). It is important to note that online communication networks such as Twitter are only a tool in analysis, not the analysis itself. However, there is a lack of related work on the analysis of users' feelings towards tourist applications (Fujita & Herrera-Viedma, 2018). Such knowledge could be used as part of a recommendation system for tourism.

This model is the first integrated multi-method framework in destination image scholarship. The first part of the model explores the thematic network of online destination image themes. This fills the gap in literature for exploring Twitter as the platform for influencers as agents of cognitive and affective components of destination image. At the same time, it will present a novel analysis approach to destination image literature by utilizing a qualitative analysis methodology: thematic network analysis. The second part of the model investigates the patterns of change in destination image themes with respect to time and sentiments incurring. Specifically, it will investigate the relationship between online destination image themes, time and sentiments.

The nature of online data can potentially incorporate mixed methods. This model incorporates a mixed methods approach. Classification of the mixed methods design is qualitative methods to develop quantitative variables (Figure 1). The first step in analyzing a destination image through UGC content is to access the social media communication cloud with respect to the destination and particular time period in which the destination image is analyzed. Several studies have accessed online data through Social Studio Software (Boatwright & Mazer, 2019; Gedikoglu, 2018; Jenkins & Mazer, 2018). Social Studio Software is a social media listening software which mines the data from the internet. This allows access to online textual communication data through unobtrusive observation. The data is composed of people's interactive online communication, which are interpersonal, and/or intrapersonal. Data sources, which are Tweets, are public posts (Gašpar & Mabić, 2017). Tweets are driven from people's intended actions and perceptions rather than a prepared answer for a survey question. In other words, this model uses unstructured secondary data, which creates a big data set composed of Tweets.

Figure 1. Sequential mixed methods research design
(Baran, 2016)

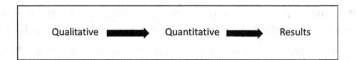

The detection of UGC of influencers is the second step in the model. Today's new type of opinion leaders, influencers, persuade their followers (Martensen et al., 2018). Developing a model of destination image via UGC with important technological and personal characteristics poses a challenge due to the large number of potential constructs. To overcome this challenge, this model utilizes previous findings in literature using three influence measures to ascertain the online influencers: Influence of re-posts (Oh & Nguyen, 2010); the number of followers (indegree) (Creamer, 2011), and the number of mention names (Sameh, 2013). Indegree represents the popularity of a user, how many followers that account has; re-posts represent the content value of one's tweets; and mention names represent the trustability of a user. First, an UGC influencer must have at least 1 follower; second, the posts should have been re-posted at least once in the relative time period; and third, the online name of the influencer should have been mentioned at least once in the big data during the particular time period in which destination image is analyzed.

The third step in the model details a technique for conducting thematic analysis of textual data, presenting a step-by-step guide of the analytic process (Guest et al., 2011). The thematic analysis method employs established, well-known techniques, and presented as thematic networks. Thematic networks are web-like illustrations that summarize the main themes constituting a piece of text (Attride-Stirling, 2001). The thematic networks technique is a robust and highly sensitive tool for the systematization and presentation of qualitative analyses (Attride-Stirling, 2001). Thematic network modelling is the qualitative method this research utilizes to ascertain relevant destination image themes. Thematic analysis is done by inductively coding themes of a destination image for each post. Open coding is utilized to identify the organizing themes. Word counts and word trees retrieve relevant themes and networks. The purpose of the qualitative methodology is to understand the meanings in conversation beyond word counts, and to reveal a network of global, organized and basic themes.

This technique enables a methodical systematization of textual data, facilitates the disclosure of each step in the analytic process; aids the organization of an analysis and its presentation; and allows a sensitive, insightful and rich exploration of a text's overt structures and underlying patterns. It is important that the researcher has a comprehensive understanding of the content of the interaction and has familiarized him/herself with all aspects of the data.

Thematic networks systematize the extraction of: (i) lowest-order premises evident in the text (Basic Themes); (ii) categories of basic themes grouped together to summarize more abstract principles (Organizing Themes); and (iii) super-ordinate themes encapsulating the principal metaphors in the text as a whole (Global Themes). Figure 3 shows the web-like maps depicting the salient themes at each of the three levels, illustrating their relationships (Figure 2). The procedure of thematic networks. Web-like representations do not aim or pretend to discover the beginning of arguments or the end of rationalizations; but simply provide a technique for breaking up text and finding its explicit rationalizations and implicit signification.

Figure 2. A social media model for destination image formation
(Gedikoglu, 2018)

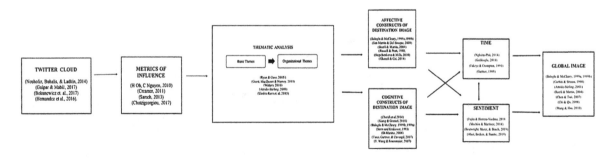

Basic themes are the lowest-order themes that are derived from the textual data. Once familiar with the data, the researcher must then start identifying preliminary codes, which are the data features that appear interesting and meaningful. These codes are more numerous and specific than themes, while indicating the context of the conversation. Basic Themes are simple premises characteristic of the data, and on their own indicate very little about the text or group of texts as a whole. In order for a Basic Theme to make sense beyond its immediate meaning it needs to be read within the context of other Basic Themes.

The next step requires a deeper review of identified themes where the researcher needs to question whether to combine, refine, separate, or discard initial themes. Data within themes should coalesce meaningfully, while there should be clear and identifiable distinctions between themes. This is done over two phases, where the themes need to be checked in relation to the coded extracts (phase 1), and then for the overall data set (phase 2). A thematic 'map' can be generated from this step.

Organizing themes are the clusters of the Basic Themes in similar issues. Relevant data extracts are sorted, combined or split according to overarching themes. The researcher's thought process should allude to the relationship between codes, subthemes, and themes. Clusters summarize the principal assumptions of a group of Basic Themes, so they are more abstract and more revealing than the texts. They are the principles on which a super-ordinate claim is based (Attride-Stirling, 2001). Thus, Organizing Themes simultaneously group the main ideas proposed by several Basic Themes. A group of Organizing Themes then constitutes a Global Theme, which is like a claim in that it is a concluding or final tenet. As such, a Global Theme groups sets of Organizing Themes that together present a position about a reality. A pool of attributes related to each global theme is developed, based on a review of the previously used items in measuring destination image (Beerli & Martin, 2004; Chen & Tsai, 2007; Chi & Qu, 2008; Wang & Hsu, 2010). It must go beyond a mere description of the themes and portray an analysis supported with empirical evidence that addresses the destination image. For example, in the research of Gedikoglu (2018) the thematic analysis revealed four organizing themes around the global theme which is the destination itself (Gedikoglu, 2018).

Figure 3. Structure of a thematic network
(Attride-Stirling, 2001)

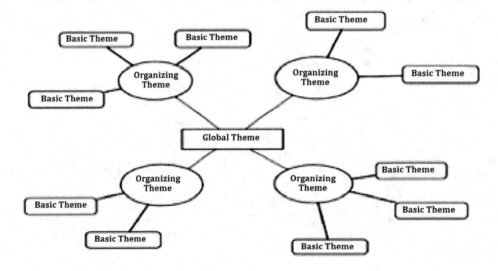

Past research has delineated a number of destination image dimensions and concluded that image is a complex and multifaceted concept (e.g., Beerli & Martin, 2004; Bonn et al., 2005; Lin et al., 2007). The fourth step of the model is to assign affective or cognitive themes. Baloglu and McClearly (1999a) have provided a formation model in which information sources are factors of perceptual/cognitive and affective global destination images. The coding of posts according to cognitive and affective constructs of destination image in line with previous studies is preferred.

The fifth step of the model uses the themes generated in thematic analysis. The purpose of this step is to take the model a step further by quantitative analysis to understand the relationship between time, sentiments towards the cognitive and/or affective themes. Quantitative analysis unfolds the factors of the holistic destination image construct. Destination image is formed over time from a variety of influential information sources (Nghiêm-Phú, 2014). To operationalize this analysis to empirical data, depending on the nature of the data several quantitative methods may be applied to understand the hierarchical relationship and the clusters of factors of online destination images. The main purpose is to understand the relationship between sentiments (Alaei et al., 2019) and time. In this step, hypothesis may be analyzed with SPSS analytical software. The results of F-tests will show the significance of predictors for each hypothesis for any regression model the researcher wants to analyze. For example, results of significance for Null Hypothesis will show the probability of getting negative, neutral and positive sentiments differ for each theme with respect to time.

Global evaluations of image are a function of cognitive and affective constructs of image (Baloglu & McCleary, 1999a). The objective of this research is to evaluate the formation of destination image through a global approach and thus evaluations are deemed necessary in which non-visitors and visitors are included (Cherifi et al., 2014). UGC possesses a global approach to understand destination image. The measurement of destination image in this model involves cognitive and affective evaluations with respect to time and sentiment variables.

ISSUES, CONTROVERSIES, PROBLEMS

Collecting, sampling and analyzing Social Media data for qualitative and/or quantitative research presents several challenges. First, a central issue with methods of data collection have their own limitations. For one thing, the researcher must have the computational skills in order to collect relevant data from Social Media platforms. It is important to note that the specific software such as Social Studio Software is an interphase between Twitter and the researcher, therefore big data gathered from Twitter may influence research questions and bias the selection of relevant search queries.

Social Studio Software was not able to yield an influencer analysis because the analytical tools cannot analyze past data to ascertain influential digital identities. Therefore, for this model previous studies and research were incorporated from the communication sciences literature. Another challenge is that Social Media users are not a homogeneous group, and thus users are hardly a representative group of the entire population. However, taking mixed methods research online produces a more representative sample that improves researchers' ability to generalize overall results. The data collected through Twitter may have an in-built bias toward users who are the most active content contributors, whereas the data say very little about the users who may read their Twitter streams with great interest on a daily basis, but who barely post anything to the stream (Giglietto, Rossi, & Bennato, 2012; Gonzales-Bailon et al., 2013).

Finally, in addition to the methodological limitations and challenges of sampling, generalization and validity, there are ethical implications of researching online data. On Twitter, by the time content is posted, it is by default public. As argued by Markham and Buchanan (2012), ethical issues vary by scope of the research questions. Ethical judgments must be made according to the research questions at hand and entirety of the data. This kind of research acknowledges that public Social Media data may be personal and any empirical research performed by utilizing this model should ensure that it is handled according to the privacy laws.

SOLUTIONS AND RECOMMENDATIONS

Scholars have increasingly recognized the advantages of applying quantitative and qualitative data analysis methods in a single study. A number of destination image studies employed sorting and categorization techniques to identify the frequencies of certain words, concepts, objects, or people, and treated the most frequent ones as variables (or dimensions) of the destination image construct (Echtner & Ritchie, 1993; Dann, 1996; MacKay & Fesenmaier, 1997; Tapachai & Waryszak, 2000; Andsager & Drzewiecka, 2002; Echtner, 2002). Proposed destination image analysis model suggests that portrayals through social media platforms are global depictions of destination image. In other words, online users share their own narratives about tourism through their perceptions and expectations.

Operationalizing the proposed online destination image model will show the change with respect to time and sentiments of organizational themes. A distinct advantage of this model in the tourism literature is the application of thematic network analysis to destination image research using social media data. The approach of utilizing unstructured data is a novel approach. Social media is a continuous, global and instantaneous meeting space for friends and strangers where people share content to social networks by exporting their information, knowledge and experience. A positive aspect of data collected from social media is that people post about issues by their own will and motivation. Therefore, the researcher bias disappears from the data collection stage. Additionally, findings indicate that online WOM communications have a significant impact on attitudes toward visitation, subjective norms, perceived behavioral control, and intention to travel (Jalilvand & Samiei, 2012). To overcome challenges of representation and sampling, this model should use the purposeful sampling technique rather than random sampling to select the Twitter accounts.

This study unites several approaches from the literature to identify online influencers. Informational influence may occur in online travel communities when facts, evidence, and other travel related information is discussed via postings (Arsal, Woosnam, Baldwin, & Backman, 2010). This study defines a new metric to identify online influencers with three influence measures, which provide a better understanding of different roles users play in Social Media platforms.

The contributions to tourism research of this study include: the utilization of social media data in destination image studies; a mixed methods approach to big data analysis, the singular approach to first-time or repeat visitors' perceptions; and expansion of influencers studies in tourism literature. Additionally, there are some unique approaches in this model that are worth to mention such as the use of time and sentiment variables.

In conclusion, the implications of this research go beyond academia. The empirical findings utilizing this model may support professional tourism planning. To develop effective marketing campaigns and promotions this model might be utilized to understand the dynamics in the market and respond to change promptly. This study suggests that future tourism players might be proactive and reactive by understanding online the formation of destination images. Therefore, this model contributes not only to the academic literature, but offers professional tourism players a model that might be applied to future marketing strategic planning.

DISCUSSION AND FUTURE RESEARCH DIRECTIONS

This study will initiate future research, which may extend o understanding of destination image, using social media platforms as mass medium which can influence formation of community opinion. Acceptance of the social media platforms as the new global communication landscape brings new research areas. Traditional media is subjectively selective in setting the agenda about other places. This study suggests that portrayals through a social media platform also create an aggregate image of a place.

This study brings together many unique methods and approaches to destination image research. Future studies may operationalize approaches explained to look at case studies. Research might look at alternative social media platforms other than Twitter. Recently, Social Media has moved towards more visual than social content, e.g., such as Instagram and Snapshot. Even though the methodological approaches to visual analysis are limited, there is a dearth of research using online depictions of destination images. This model might integrate visual data in future studies.

Another orientation may be a comparative analysis of destination images as projected by user generated content (UGC) creators and various travel intermediaries, government sources, and general media. Such a comparison analysis has consistently captured differences in destination images transmitted via various information channels (e.g., Choi, Lehto, & Morrison, 2007; Dwivedi, Yadav, & Patel, 2009; Law & Cheung, 2010); however, it has never utilized UGS content. Comparison of online sources to traditional sources of destination information may provide beneficial implications to tourism literature. Additionally, the literature lacks comparative analysis of online sources with each other.

Previous destination image studies have looked at perceptions of tourists through structured questionnaires. It is important to note that online communication networks such as Twitter, are only a tool, not the analysis itself. Once a thematic network has been constructed, it will then serve as an organizing principle and an illustrative tool in the interpretation of the text, facilitating disclosure for the researcher and understanding for the reader. Therefore, future studies may apply the qualitative methodology of this research in a different context.

CONCLUSION

The main purpose of this chapter is to propose a model to ascertain the destination image themes communicated by influencers on Twitter. Additionally, the model may be used to further investigate relationships between sentiments of themes and time constructs such as seasons or days. Thematic analysis is a useful tool in measuring the multi-dimensional nature of destination image through online textual data. Applying quantitative methods to the results of thematic analysis may further provide insights on online destination image. In sum, this model suggests that social media is a communication data source that reveals standard schemas on the dynamics of destination image for future studies. In conclusion, this model particularly fills the gap in the literature by applying a variety of novel analysis methods and offers a new approach to understanding destination image.

ACKNOWLEDGMENT

This research received no specific grant from any funding agency in the public, commercial, or not-for-profit sectors.

REFERENCES

Alaei, A. R., Becken, S., & Stantic, B. (2019). Sentiment Analysis in Tourism: Capitalizing on Big Data. *Journal of Travel Research*, *58*(2), 175–191. doi:10.1177/0047287517747753

Amersdorffer, D., Bauhuber, F., & Oellrich, J. (2012). The Economic and Cultural Aspects of The Social Web: Implications for The Tourism Industry. *Journal of Vacation Marketing*, *18*(3), 175–184. doi:10.1177/1356766712449364

Andsager, J. L., & Drzewiecka, J. A. (2002). Desirability of Differences in Destinations. *Annals of Tourism Research*, *29*(2), 401–421. doi:10.1016/S0160-7383(01)00064-0

Arsal, I., Woosnam, K. M., Baldwin, E. D., & Backman, S. J. (2010). Residents as Travel Destination Information Providers: An Online Community Perspective. *Journal of Travel Research*, *49*(4), 400–413. doi:10.1177/0047287509346856

Attride-Stirling, J. (2001). Thematic Networks: An Analytic Tool for Qualitative Research. *Qualitative Research*, *1*(3), 385–405. doi:10.1177/146879410100100307

Baloglu, S., & McCleary, K. W. (1999a). A Model of Destination Image Formation. *Annals of Tourism Research*, *26*(4), 868–897. doi:10.1016/S0160-7383(99)00030-4

Baloglu, S., & McCleary, K. W. (1999b). US International Pleasure Travelers' Images of Four Mediterranean Destinations: A Comparison of Visitors and Nonvisitors. *Journal of Travel Research*, *38*(2), 144–152. doi:10.1177/004728759903800207

Baran, M. L. (2016). It Is All in The Design: Creating the Foundations of a Mixed Methods Research Study. In Mixed methods research for improved scientific study (pp. 66-78). Hershey, PA: IGI Global.

Beerli, A., & Martin, J. D. (2004). Factors Influencing Destination Image. *Annals of Tourism Research*, *31*(3), 657–681. doi:10.1016/j.annals.2004.01.010

Berg, L. V. D., Borg, J., & Meer, J. V. (1995). *Urban Tourism: Performance and Strategies in Eight European Cities*. Avebury.

Blackshaw, P., & Nazzaro, M. (2006). Word of Mouth in The Age of The Web-Fortified Consumer. *Consumer-generated media (CGM)*, *101*.

Boatwright, B., Mazer, J. P., & Beach, S. (2019). The 2016 US Presidential Election and Transition Events: A Social Media Volume and Sentiment Analysis. *The Southern Communication Journal*, 1–14.

Bonn, M. A., Joseph, S. M., & Dai, M. (2005). International versus domestic visitors: An examination of destination image perceptions. *Journal of Travel Research*, *43*(3), 294–301. doi:10.1177/0047287504272033

Buhalis, D. (1998). Strategic Use of Information Technologies in The Tourism Industry. *Tourism Management, 19*(5), 409–421. doi:10.1016/S0261-5177(98)00038-7

Buhalis, D., & Law, R. (2008). Progress in Information Technology and Tourism Management: 20 Years on and 10 Years After the Internet—The State of Etourism Research. *Tourism Management, 29*(4), 609–623. doi:10.1016/j.tourman.2008.01.005

Butowski, B. (2011). Tourism-An Academic Discipline. *Tourism (Zagreb), 21*(1-2), 17–24.

Cai, L. A. (2002). Cooperative Branding for Rural Destinations. *Annals of Tourism Research, 29*(3), 720–742. doi:10.1016/S0160-7383(01)00080-9

Chatzigeorgiou, C. (2017). Modelling the Impact of Social Media Influencers on Behavioral Intentions of Millennials: The Case of Tourism in Rural Areas in Greece. *Journal of Tourism. Heritage & Services Marketing, 3*(2), 25–29.

Chen, C. F., & Tsai, D. (2007). How Destination Image and Evaluative Factors Affect Behavioral Intentions? *Tourism Management, 28*(4), 1115–1122. doi:10.1016/j.tourman.2006.07.007

Cherifi, B., Smith, A., Maitland, R., & Stevenson, N. (2014). Destination Images of Non-Visitors. *Annals of Tourism Research, 49*, 190–202. doi:10.1016/j.annals.2014.09.008

Chi, C. G. Q., & Qu, H. (2008). Examining the Structural Relationships of Destination Image, Tourist Satisfaction and Destination Loyalty: An Integrated Approach. *Tourism Management, 29*(4), 624–636. doi:10.1016/j.tourman.2007.06.007

Choi, S., Lehto, X. Y., & Morrison, A. M. (2007). Destination Image Representation on The Web: Content Analysis of Macau Travel Related Websites. *Tourism Management, 28*(1), 118–129. doi:10.1016/j.tourman.2006.03.002

Chon, K. S. (1990). The Role of Destination Image in Tourism: A Review and Discussion. *Tourism Review, 45*(2), 2–9.

Creamer, M. (2011). Your Followers Are No Measure of Your Influence. *Advertising Age, 82*(1), 1–22.

Crompton, J. L. (1979). An Assessment of The Image of Mexico As A Vacation Destination and The Influence of Geographical Location Upon That Image. *Journal of Travel Research, 17*(4), 18–23. doi:10.1177/004728757901700404

Dann, G. M. (1996). Tourists' Images of a Destination-An Alternative Analysis. *Journal of Travel & Tourism Marketing, 5*(1-2), 41–55. doi:10.1300/J073v05n01_04

Di Marino, E. (2008, May). The Strategic Dimension of Destination Image: An Analysis of The French Riviera Image from The Italian Tourists' Perceptions. *Proceedings of the 17th International Tourism and Leisure Symposium* (pp. 17-18). Academic Press.

Dichter, E. (1985). What's in An Image. *Journal of Consumer Marketing, 2*(1), 75–81. doi:10.1108/eb038824

Dwivedi, M. (2009). Online Destination Image of India: A Consumer Based Perspective. *International Journal of Contemporary Hospitality Management, 21*(2), 226–232. doi:10.1108/09596110910935714

Dwivedi, M., Yadav, A., & Raghavjibhai Patel, V. (2009). The Online Destination Image of Goa. *Worldwide Hospitality and Tourism Themes*, *1*(1), 25–39. doi:10.1108/17554210910949869

Echtner, C. M. (2002). The Content of Third World Tourism Marketing: A 4A Approach. *International Journal of Tourism Research*, *4*(6), 413–434. doi:10.1002/jtr.401

Echtner, C. M., & Ritchie, J. B. (1991). The Meaning and Measurement of Destination Image. *Journal of Tourism Studies*, *2*(2), 2–12.

Echtner, C. M., & Ritchie, J. B. (1993). The Measurement of Destination Image: An Empirical Assessment. *Journal of Travel Research*, *31*(4), 3–13. doi:10.1177/004728759303100402

Embacher, J., & Buttle, F. (1989). A Repertory Grid Analysis of Austria's Image as A Summer Vacation Destination. *Journal of Travel Research*, *27*(3), 3–7. doi:10.1177/004728758902700302

Fakeye, P. C., & Crompton, J. L. (1991). Image Differences Between Prospective, First-Time, And Repeat Visitors to The Lower Rio Grande Valley. *Journal of Travel Research*, *30*(2), 10–16. doi:10.1177/004728759103000202

Farías, D. I. H., Patti, V., & Rosso, P. (2016). Irony Detection in Twitter: The Role of Affective Content. *ACM Transactions on Internet Technology*, *16*(3), 19. doi:10.1145/2930663

Fotis, J., Buhalis, D., & Rossides, N. (2011). Social Media Impact on Holiday Travel Planning: The Case of The Russian And the FSU Markets. *International Journal of Online Marketing*, *1*(4), 1–19. doi:10.4018/ijom.2011100101

Fujita, H., & Herrera-Viedma, E. (2018). A Proposal for Sentiment Analysis on Twitter for Tourism-Based Applications. *A Proposal for Sentiment Analysis on Twitter for Tourism-Based Applications*. Academic Press.

Gartner, W. C. (1986). Temporal Influences on Image Change. *Annals of Tourism Research*, *13*(4), 635–644. doi:10.1016/0160-7383(86)90006-X

Gartner, W. C. (1989). Tourism Image: Attribute Measurement of State Tourism Products Using Multidimensional Scaling Techniques. *Journal of Travel Research*, *28*(2), 16–20. doi:10.1177/004728758902800205

Gašpar, D., & Mabić, M. (2017). Strengths and Limitations of Social Media Analytics Tools. In Applying Predictive Analytics Within the Service Sector (pp. 198–219). Hershey, PA: IGI Global. doi:10.4018/978-1-5225-2148-8.ch012

Gedikoglu, Z. A. (2018). Exploring Destination Image Themes on Twitter, Before, During, and After Terror Attacks in Paris: An Application of Agenda Setting Theory.

Giglietto, F., Rossi, L., & Bennato, D. (2012). The Open Laboratory: Limits and Possibilities of Using Facebook, Twitter, And YouTube As A Research Data Source. *Journal of Technology in Human Services*, *30*(3-4), 145–159. doi:10.1080/15228835.2012.743797

González-Bailón, S. (2013). Social Science in The Era of Big Data. *Policy and Internet*, *5*(2), 147–160. doi:10.1002/1944-2866.POI328

Govers, R., & Go, F. M. (2003). Deconstructing Destination Image in The Information Age. *Information Technology & Tourism*, *6*(1), 13–29. doi:10.3727/109830503108751199

Govers, R., & Go, F. M. (2004). Projected Destination Image Online: Website Content Analysis of Pictures and Text. *Information Technology & Tourism*, *7*(2), 73–89. doi:10.3727/1098305054517327

Govers, R., Go, F. M., & Kumar, K. (2007). Promoting Tourism Destination Image. *Journal of Travel Research*, *46*(1), 15–23. doi:10.1177/0047287507302374

Govers, R., Go, F. M., & Kumar, K. (2007). Virtual Destination Image A New Measurement Approach. *Annals of Tourism Research*, *34*(4), 977–997. doi:10.1016/j.annals.2007.06.001

Gretzel, U. (2006). Consumer Generated Content–Trends and Implications for Branding. *Ereview of Tourism Research*, *4*(3), 9–11.

Guest, G., MacQueen, K. M., & Namey, E. E. (2011). *Applied Thematic Analysis*. Sage Publications.

Gunn, C. A. (1972). *Vacationscape: Designing Tourist Regions (Vol. 1.)*. Austin: Bureau of Business Research, University of Texas at Austin.

Hunt, J. D. (1975). Image as A Factor in Tourism Development. *Journal of Travel Research*, *13*(3), 1–7. doi:10.1177/004728757501300301

Hunter, W. C. (2013). China's Chairman Mao: A Visual Analysis of Hunan Province Online Destination Image. *Tourism Management*, *34*, 101–111. doi:10.1016/j.tourman.2012.03.017

Hunter, W. C. (2016). The Social Construction of Tourism Online Destination Image: A Comparative Semiotic Analysis of The Visual Representation of Seoul. *Tourism Management*, *54*, 221–229. doi:10.1016/j.tourman.2015.11.012

Jalilvand, M. R., & Samiei, N. (2012). The Impact of Electronic Word of Mouth on A Tourism Destination Choice: Testing the Theory of Planned Behavior (TPB). *Internet Research: Electronic Networking Applications and Policy*, *22*(5), 591–612. doi:10.1108/10662241211271563

Jenkins, A. S., & Mazer, J. P. (2018). #Notokay: Stories of Sexual Assault in The Midst of the 2016 US Presidential Election. *Qualitative Research Reports in Communication*, *19*(1), 9–17. doi:10.1080/17459435.2017.1404487

Kislali, H., Kavaratzis, M., & Saren, M. (2016). Rethinking Destination Image Formation. *International Journal of Culture, Tourism and Hospitality Research*, *10*(1), 70–80. doi:10.1108/IJCTHR-05-2015-0050

Law, R., & Cheung, S. (2010). The Perceived Destination Image of Hong Kong As Revealed in The Travel Blogs of Mainland Chinese Tourists. *International Journal of Hospitality & Tourism Administration*, *11*(4), 303–327. doi:10.1080/15256480.2010.518521

Leung, D., Law, R., Van Hoof, H., & Buhalis, D. (2013). Social Media in Tourism and Hospitality: A Literature Review. *Journal of Travel & Tourism Marketing*, *30*(1-2), 3–22. doi:10.1080/10548408.2013.750919

Lin, C. H., Morais, D. B., Kerstetter, D. L., & Hou, J. S. (2007). Examining the Role of Cognitive and Affective Image in Predicting Choice Across Natural, Developed, And Theme-Park Destinations. *Journal of Travel Research, 46*(2), 183–194. doi:10.1177/0047287507304049

Lin, C. H., Morais, D. B., Kerstetter, D. L., & Hou, J. S. (2007). Examining the Role of Cognitive and Affective Image in Predicting Choice Across Natural, Developed, And Theme-Park Destinations. *Journal of Travel Research, 46*(2), 183–194. doi:10.1177/0047287507304049

Llodrà-Riera, I., Martínez-Ruiz, M. P., Jiménez-Zarco, A. I., & Izquierdo-Yusta, A. (2015). A Multidimensional Analysis of The Information Sources Construct and Its Relevance for Destination Image Formation. *Tourism Management, 48*, 319–328. doi:10.1016/j.tourman.2014.11.012

Lo, I. S., McKercher, B., Lo, A., Cheung, C., & Law, R. (2011). Tourism and Online Photography. *Tourism Management, 32*(4), 725–731. doi:10.1016/j.tourman.2010.06.001

Lu, W., & Stepchenkova, S. (2015). User-Generated Content as A Research Mode in Tourism and Hospitality Applications: Topics, Methods, And Software. *Journal of Hospitality Marketing & Management, 24*(2), 119–154. doi:10.1080/19368623.2014.907758

MacKay, K. J., & Fesenmaier, D. R. (1997). Pictorial Element of Destination in Image Formation. *Annals of Tourism Research, 24*(3), 537–565. doi:10.1016/S0160-7383(97)00011-X

Mak, A. H. (2017). Online Destination Image: Comparing National Tourism Organization's and Tourists' Perspectives. *Tourism Management, 60*, 280–297. doi:10.1016/j.tourman.2016.12.012

Markham, A., & Buchanan, E. (2012). Ethical Decision-Making and Internet Research: Version 2.0. The Aoir Ethics Working Committee. Retrieved from aoir.org/reports/ethics2.pdf

Martensen, A., Brockenhuus-Schack, S., & Zahid, A. L. (2018). How Citizen Influencers Persuade Their Followers. *Journal of Fashion Marketing and Management: An International Journal, 22*(3), 335–353. doi:10.1108/JFMM-09-2017-0095

Martín-Santana, J. D., Beerli-Palacio, A., & Nazzareno, P. A. (2017). Antecedents and Consequences of Destination Image Gap. *Annals of Tourism Research, 62*, 13–25. doi:10.1016/j.annals.2016.11.001

Mochón, F., & Martínez, O. S. (2014). A first approach to the implicit measurement of happiness in Latin America through the use of social networks. *IJIMAI, 2*(5), 16–22. doi:10.9781/ijimai.2014.252

Munar, A. M. (2012). Social media strategies and destination management. *Scandinavian Journal of Hospitality and Tourism, 12*(2), 101–120. doi:10.1080/15022250.2012.679047

Nadeau, J., Heslop, L., O'Reilly, N., & Luk, P. (2008). Destination in A Country Image Context. *Annals of Tourism Research, 35*(1), 84–106. doi:10.1016/j.annals.2007.06.012

Neuhofer, B., Buhalis, D., & Ladkin, A. (2014). A Typology of Technology-Enhanced Tourism Experiences. *International Journal of Tourism Research, 16*(4), 340–350. doi:10.1002/jtr.1958

Nghiêm-Phú, B. (2014). A Review of Destination Image Studies From 2008 to 2012. *European Journal of Tourism Research, 8*, 35.

Oh, H., & Nguyen, C. (2010). Influence of Retweets.

Pan, B., MacLaurin, T., & Crotts, J. C. (2007). Travel Blogs and The Implications for Destination Marketing. *Journal of Travel Research, 46*(1), 35–45. doi:10.1177/0047287507302378

Pearce, P. L. (1977). Mental souvenirs: A study of tourists and their city maps. *Australian Journal of Psychology, 29*(3), 203–210. doi:10.1080/00049537708255282

Pearce, P. L. (1982). Perceived changes in holiday destinations. *Annals of Tourism Research, 9*(2), 145–164. doi:10.1016/0160-7383(82)90044-5

Pezenka, I. (2016). Paired Comparisons or Sorting? Comparing Web-Based Methods for Collecting Similarity Data for Large Stimulus Sets for Destination Image Positioning. *Journal of Travel Research.*

Pike, S. (2002). Destination Image Analysis—A Review of 142 Papers from 1973 to 2000. *Tourism Management, 23*(5), 541–549. doi:10.1016/S0261-5177(02)00005-5

Roth, M. S., & Romeo, J. B. (1992). Matching Product Category and Country Image Perceptions: A Framework for Managing Country-Of-Origin Effects. *Journal of International Business Studies, 23*(3), 477–497. doi:10.1057/palgrave.jibs.8490276

Russell, J. A., & Pratt, G. (1980). A Description of The Affective Quality Attributed to Environments. *Journal of Personality and Social Psychology, 38*(2), 311–322. doi:10.1037/0022-3514.38.2.311

Ryan, C., & Cave, J. (2005). Structuring Destination Image: A Qualitative Approach. *Journal of Travel Research, 44*(2), 143–150. doi:10.1177/0047287505278991

Sameh, A. (2013). A Twitter Analytic Tool to Measure Opinion, Influence and Trust. *Journal of Industrial and Intelligent Information, 1*(1), 37–45. doi:10.12720/jiii.1.1.37-45

San Martín, H., & Del Bosque, I. A. R. (2008). Exploring the Cognitive–Affective Nature of Destination Image and The Role of Psychological Factors in Its Formation. *Tourism Management, 29*(2), 263–277. doi:10.1016/j.tourman.2007.03.012

Schmallegger, D., & Carson, D. (2008). Blogs in Tourism: Changing Approaches to Information Exchange. *Journal of Vacation Marketing, 14*(2), 99–110. doi:10.1177/1356766707087519

Sotiriadis, M. D., & Van Zyl, C. (2013). Electronic Word-Of-Mouth and Online Reviews in Tourism Services: The Use of Twitter by Tourists. *Electronic Commerce Research, 13*(1), 103–124. doi:10.100710660-013-9108-1

Stepchenkova, S., & Mills, J. E. (2010). Destination Image: A Meta-Analysis Of 2000–2007 Research. *Journal of Hospitality Marketing & Management, 19*(6), 575–609. doi:10.1080/19368623.2010.493071

Stepchenkova, S., & Morrison, A. M. (2006). The Destination Image of Russia: From the Online Induced Perspective. *Tourism Management, 27*(5), 943–956. doi:10.1016/j.tourman.2005.10.021

Stern, E., & Krakover, S. (1993). The Formation of a Composite Urban Image. *Geographical Analysis, 25*(2), 130–146. doi:10.1111/j.1538-4632.1993.tb00285.x

Tapachai, N., & Waryszak, R. (2000). An Examination of The Role of Beneficial Image in Tourist Destination Selection. *Journal of Travel Research, 39*(1), 37–44. doi:10.1177/004728750003900105

Tasci, A. D., Gartner, W. C., & Tamer Cavusgil, S. (2007). Conceptualization and Operationalization of Destination Image. *Journal of Hospitality & Tourism Research (Washington, D.C.)*, *31*(2), 194–223. doi:10.1177/1096348006297290

Telisman-Kosuta, N. (1989). Tourist Destination Image. In *Tourism Marketing and Management Handbook* (pp. 557-561). Academic Press.

Walmsley, D. J., & Jenkins, J. M. (1992). Tourism Cognitive Mapping of Unfamiliar Environments. *Annals of Tourism Research*, *19*(2), 268–286. doi:10.1016/0160-7383(92)90081-Y

Walmsley, D. J., & Young, M. (1998). Evaluative Images and Tourism: The Use of Personal Constructs to Describe the Structure of Destination Images. *Journal of Travel Research*, *36*(3), 65–69. doi:10.1177/004728759803600307

Walters, T. (2016). Using Thematic Analysis in Tourism Research. *Tourism Analysis*, *21*(1), 107–116. doi:10.3727/108354216X14537459509017

Wang, C. Y., & Hsu, M. K. (2010). The Relationships of Destination Image, Satisfaction, And Behavioral Intentions: An Integrated Model. *Journal of Travel & Tourism Marketing*, *27*(8), 829–843. doi:10.108 0/10548408.2010.527249

Wang, Y., & Fesenmaier, D. R. (2007). Collaborative Destination Marketing: A Case Study of Elkhart County, Indiana. *Tourism Management*, *28*(3), 863–875. doi:10.1016/j.tourman.2006.02.007

Woodside, A. G., & Lysonski, S. (1989). A General Model of Traveler Destination Choice. *Journal of Travel Research*, *27*(4), 8–14. doi:10.1177/004728758902700402

Xiang, Z., & Gretzel, U. (2010). Role of Social Media in Online Travel Information Search. *Tourism Management*, *31*(2), 179–188. doi:10.1016/j.tourman.2009.02.016

ADDITIONAL READING

Garay Tamajón, L., & Cànoves Valiente, G. (2017). Barcelona Seen Through the Eyes of TripAdvisor: Actors, Typologies and Components of Destination Image in Social Media Platforms. *Current Issues in Tourism*, *20*(1), 33–37. doi:10.1080/13683500.2015.1073229

Kirilenko, A. P., Stepchenkova, S. O., Kim, H., & Li, X. (2018). Automated Sentiment Analysis in Tourism: Comparison of Approaches. *Journal of Travel Research*, *57*(8), 1012–1025. doi:10.1177/0047287517729757

Kladou, S., & Mavragani, E. (2015). Assessing Destination Image: An Online Marketing Approach and The Case of TripAdvisor. *Journal of Destination Marketing & Management*, *4*(3), 187–193. doi:10.1016/j. jdmm.2015.04.003

Marine-Roig, E., & Anton Clave, S. (2016). Affective Component of The Destination Image: A Computerized Analysis. In *Destination Marketing: An International Perspective* (pp. 49-58). Academic Press.

Marine-Roig, E., & Clavé, S. A. (2016). A Detailed Method for Destination Image Analysis Using User-Generated Content. *Information Technology & Tourism*, *15*(4), 341–364. doi:10.100740558-015-0040-1

Park, S. B., Ok, C. M., & Chae, B. K. (2016). Using Twitter Data for Cruise Tourism Marketing and Research. *Journal of Travel & Tourism Marketing*, *33*(6), 885–898. doi:10.1080/10548408.2015.1071688

Uysal, M., Harrill, R., & Woo, E. (2011). Destination Marketing Research: Issues and Challenges. In *Destination Marketing and Management: Theories and Applications* (pp. 99-112). Academic Press.

Yoon, S., Petrick, J. F., & Backman, S. J. (2017). Twitter Power and Sport-Fan Loyalty: The Moderating Effects of Twitter. *International Journal of Sport Communication*, *10*(2), 153–177. doi:10.1123/IJSC.2017-0010

KEY TERMS AND DEFINITIONS

Affective Components of Destination Image: An individual's unique emotional interpretation of a destination which is composed of feelings and emotions.

Cognitive Components of Destination Image: An individual's unique knowledge, perceptions and beliefs about the individual attributes of a destination which are observable, descriptive and measurable.

Destination Image: The sum of attitudes, experiences, beliefs, ideas and impressions a non-visitor, visitor, or repeat-visitor has of a tourism destination.

Destination Image Formation: A construction of a mental representation on the basis of information cues selected and delivered by the image formation agents.

Influencer: An influencer is a user on social media who has access to a large audience, is mentioned by others and whose 's posts are re-posted so that can persuade others by virtue of their authenticity and reach.

Online/Virtual Destination Image: The sum of attitudes, experiences, beliefs, ideas and impressions a non-visitor, visitor, or repeat-visitor has and has communicated through an online communication platform of a tourism destination.

Sentiment Analysis: The Process of analyzing various sources of unstructured online communication data to mine conversations online and to determine deeper context as they apply to a topic, brand, or theme.

User Generated Content: Any type of shared communicated content that has been created and shared through online platforms by unpaid contributors.

Chapter 15
Maximizing Social Presence to Improve Website Loyalty

Wen-Jang (Kenny) Jih
Middle Tennessee State University, USA

ABSTRACT

Technology plays a crucial role in the development of customer brand loyalty. However, technological user interface often falls short on major important aspects of business interaction, such as context-based exchange of information and opinions. Adding social networking features to the corporate website is an attempt to mitigate this weakness. This chapter investigates the driving forces of website loyalty, an issue of interest to the businesses deploying social networks as a new technological tool for business promotion. Using Facebook as the target of observation, this study evaluates the effects of social presence and social capital on website loyalty. The analysis reveals a positive influence of social presence on all three (structural, relational, and cognitive) dimensions of social capital. Further, both the relational and cognitive dimensions of social capital show positive influence on the website loyalty. These findings have practical implications for company seeking to cultivate brand loyalty via website design and management.

INTRODUCTION

It has been widely accepted that information technology has become a competitive necessity. Companies in virtually all sectors must constantly look for creative ideas to deploy the ubiquitous Internet for some sort of strategic benefits. With the technological capability continuing to advance in all areas, the user-engaging interfaces that facilitate aggressive applications of the technology in pursuit of competitive advantage have allowed even novice users to make Internet-enabled services a critical part of their work and life. Today, it is not any longer a surprise to see people using an information technology to interact with each other without even noticing the existence of the technology at all. The social aspect and the technological aspect of technology utilization are so tightly inter-woven in the usage experience that some researchers have found it appropriate to refer to communication networks as social networks (e.g., Biocca & Harms, 2002; Biocca, et al. 2003). As a result, including social networking capabilities in company websites is becoming more a norm than an exception.

DOI: 10.4018/978-1-7998-9020-1.ch015

Beginning primarily as a Web 2.0 technological service facilitating personal interaction through the Internet about a decade ago, social media has rapidly evolved to become a critical communication channel for organizations communicating with customers and other stakeholders (Kane, et al., 2009). These social media services provide a variety of multimedia features that not only are useful but also easy and convenient for non-technical people to use. Virtually all social networking websites adopt a free usage business model in order to grow the user base. As a result, the ubiquity of social media usage has become one of the major forces that make the Internet an important part of people's daily life. Currently, there are at least twenty social networking services with more than 2.46 billion users collectively worldwide. Facebook, the leading social networking service provider, has more than 1 billion registered accounts and 2.06 active monthly global users as of September 2017 (Statista, 2017). The collective attention these social media have garnered provides a strong foundation for innovative companies to reap a sustainable competitive advantage.

How do these social media websites attract so many users? Is there any theoretical explanation for the success of these social networking services? It would just be a fad and may quickly fade away if it is not much more than a mere random phenomenon. However, these social networking services will likely continue to influence the physical world even at a deeper level if there are sustainable reasons that systematically justify the user's behaviors in using social media. Following this line of reasoning, the purpose of this study is to explore the role of social capital in building users' loyalty to a social networking website. We also look at if the notion of social presence influences users' perception of social capital in the context of social networking service usage. These three constructs - social presence, social capital, and website loyalty - span across several reference fields. Specifically, social presence is a well-researched topic in computer-mediated communication and online education (Tu, 2001; Tu & McIssac, 2002). Social capital has received much attention in such fields as sociology (Lin, 1999; Ellison et al., 2007), online learning (Oztok et al., 2015), organizational knowledge management (Bharati et al., 2015), and organizational study (Adler & Kwon, 2002; Naphapiet & Ghoshal, 1998). Both information systems (Cyr et al., 2007; Kuo & Feng, 2013) and marketing (Lee, Jih &-Fang, 2006) regard user loyalty to website as an important dependent variable. However, both social presence and social capital are relatively new to information systems research (Cyr et al., 2007; Han et al., 2015).

In the next section, we first briefly describe the concept of social presence, social capital and website loyalty. We then discuss our research hypotheses and research model employed in this study. A description of our approach for data collection and data analysis follows. We then present the findings and interpretation. The paper ends with suggestions for business practice as well as for academic research.

Social Presence

Short, Williams & Christie (1976) investigated the notion of social presence in a series of experiments. Many researchers have revisited and enhanced the concept since then. The concept resulted from lab experiments, conducted from the social psychology perspective, to compare various communication media using semantic differential scales. The experiments confirmed the assumption that one should view the notion of social presence as a subjective characteristic of the communication medium. Users perceive difference levels of social presence with different media. Since then, researchers in various academic fields have examined the concept of social presence in order to develop it into a more robust theory. Most of these follow-up works appear in computer-mediated communication (CMC) and online education literature. A relatively smaller number of researches in information systems also involved social presence either as an independent variable or as a dependent variable (e.g., Han et al., 2015; Cyr et al., 2007).

The emphasis of CMC is on building a broader theory of social presence than originally proposed. Biocca, Harms & Burgoon (2003), for example, reviewed and critically commented on existing theories and measures. They also propose a set of criteria and scope conditions to serve as the foundation for a more robust theory and measure of social presence. The ultimate goal is a better understanding of the networked minds theory and measures. A notable contribution of CMC research to the theory of social presence is the clarification that one should view social presence as a stable property of the medium. Rather, it would be more appropriate to treat social presence as a dynamic aspect of the subjective feelings of individuals as interacting with the mediated others. Remesal and Colomina (2013), for example, integrated the concept of social presence into their notion of learning presence.

Social presence has been an important independent variable in education research in various contexts, such as collaborative works and community. According to Oztok et al. (2015), the main stream thinking of social presence research in education has gone through three phases over time. At first, the focus was mainly on properties of media, a position commonly held in social psychology at that time. Then the focus shifted to more on the people and less on the media in the second phase. In the third phase, the focus was on the interactive activities and the development of online learning community. Currently, online education researchers primarily regard social presence as "the degree to which individuals represent themselves and perceive others in mediated environments" (Oztok, 2015. p. 20). Consistent with CMC research, research in online education holds that individuals dynamically reconstruct their sense of social presence when they engage with others within a mediated context (Kehrwald, 2010).

Several researches in information systems and marketing employ social presence in the research model to evaluate its impact on the variables that are significant in the context of website-mediated activities such as e-service and online shopping. An early study conducted by Fulk et al. (1987) defined social presence as the degree to which a communication medium used to process business transaction allows users to experience the other parties involved in the transaction as being psychologically present. Several empirical studies examined the effect of social presence on constructs associated with brand loyalty. Hassanein and Head (2006), for example, found that higher user perceptions of social presence on websites contributed to higher levels of trust placed in the vendor. This finding confirmed the same conclusion of a study conducted by Gefen, Karahanna & Straub (2003). Based on these and other researches, Cyr et al. (2007) conducted a survey research and found that social presence positively contributed to three important success measures of e-service: trust, e-loyalty, and perceived usefulness. It appears that information systems research community is expanding its more traditional set of research variables to incorporate more recent, Web-based system characteristics, such as social presence.

Social Capital

With the wide variety of academic fields addressing the issues from different points of view, the concept of social capital naturally does not have a universally accepted operational definition. A number of definitions of social capital exist in such fields as sociology, communication, education, organizational study, online shopping and information systems. In this section, we discuss the similarities of as well as differences among these definitions, describe the nature of different types of social capital, introduce its distinct dimensions, and provide examples of social capital used as an independent variable or a dependent variable as found in existing research literature.

The definitions found in existing literature are similar in the sense that they all recognize social capital as a form of existing or potential assets that actors may derive from a network, online or offline, of social relations. These assets are desirable resource because they may bring about some forms of social or economic benefits for the members of the relation network. The differences are primarily due to the different levels of inquiry (micro vs. macro), perspectives (external vs. internal) or focuses (dimensions) employed by the research. In the early era, communication and community studies viewed social capital as benefits embedded in the networks of personal relationships that nurture trust and facilitate cooperation and collaboration activities of the community members (Jacobs, 1965). Researchers then applied the concept to broader contexts involving human capital, economic performance of firms, geographical regions, and nations (Nahapiet & Ghoshal, 1998). To accommodate both levels of analysis, Nahapiet and Ghoshal (1998) define social capital as "the sum of the actual and potential resources embedded within, available through, and derived from the network of relationships possessed by an individual or social unit" (p. 243).

The definitions of social capital also vary depending on whether the focus is primarily on external network (bridging) or the social relations within the network (bonding). Fukuyama (1995), for example, focused on the internal structure and defined social capital as "the ability of people to work together for common purposes in groups and organizations" (p. 10). By contrast, Bourdieu and Wacquan, (1992) focused more on the external networks in defining social capital as "the sum of the resources, actual or virtual, that accrue to an individual or a group by virtue of possessing a durable network of more or less institutionalized relationships of mutual acquaintance and recognition" (p. 52). Nahapiet and Ghoshai (1998) noted this subtle distinction of focus and indicated "social capital comprises both the network and the assets that may be mobilized through that network" (p. 243). Some researchers (e.g., Adler & Kwon, 2002) adopted both views in their social capital definitions in the belief that "the distinction between the external and the internal views is, to a large degree, a matter of perspectives and unit of analysis" (p. 21).

What are the core elements of social capital in order to meet members' expectation for the benefits and become practical assets? Lin (1999) answered the question by highlighting three essential features of social capital: embeddedness, accessibility, and use. Social capital represents the "resources embedded in a social structure which are accessed and/or mobilized in purposive actions" (Lin, 1999, p. 35). All three must be present in order for the social capital to exist in a social network.

Discussions of social capital often address distinction between bridging social capital and boding social capital. While bridging social capital comes from relatively loose connections between individuals, bonding social capital is associated with individuals who more tightly relate to each other. Tight connections, or strong ties, often are responsible for providing emotional supports. Loose connections, or weak ties, may bring about economic benefits resulting from sharing of, say, employment information (Coleman, 1988). More recently, a third type of social capital, maintained social capital, was identified by Ellison, Steinfield and Lampe (2007) to represent reestablished existing relationships once lost due to major life changes. An example is the relationship between high school friends reclaimed after several years of disconnection after high school graduation. Their research also suggested that all three types of social capital exist among users of social networking websites such as Facebook.

Social capital is a multi-dimensional construct. Nahapiet and Ghoshal (1998) delineated social capital as consisting of three distinct dimensions: structural, relational, and cognitive. The structural dimension concerns the structural characteristics of the social system and network of relations such as existence and strength of the linkages. A structurally friendly social network allows one to access the network and interact with existing and new friend conveniently. The network also has mechanisms for maintaining and increasing the connections among members. The relational aspect of social capital describes the nature of the relationships between members of the network as well as the history of their interactions. Members have trust for each other and respect regulations that nurture community development. The cognitive dimension of social capital refers to any form of resources that establishes the commonality among the network members in terms of value system and shared understanding of meaning. This dimension is usually the most implicit aspect of social capital, but is observable by the content as well the amount of information and opinions member share with one another. Because of this composite nature, research employing social capital in the research framework must address all three dimensions in order to measure the construct in its entirety. This three-dimension framework of social capital has provided an influential conceptual guidance in a number of previous researches (Bharati et al., 2015; Oztok et al., 2015).

Social capital was either an independent variable or a dependent variable in various researches. Sanchez-Casado et al. (2016), for example, investigated how features of social networking sites affect customer capital (equivalent to social capital by their definition). In Huang et al. (2017) and Bharati et al. (2015), researchers examined the impact of social capital on customers' loyalty to a consumer-to-consumer e-commerce platform and organizational knowledge management initiatives, respectively. Our study investigated the role of social capital both as a dependent variable and as an independent variable.

Whereas social presence often relates to individuals communicating with each other via a computer network, computer network is not an essential element in the social capital theory. Social capital can significantly contribute to service quality in face-to-face service settings (e.g. doctors, financial planning consultants, real estate agents). Social capital and social presence traditional have not been associated with each other in academic inquiry. The web-enabled social networking has brought these two constructs closer together. Oztok et al. (2015), for example, investigated the relationship between social capital and social presence in online learning environments. The research revealed that both bridging and the bonding social capital have significant relationships with social presence. Prompted by these findings, we conducted this research to examine the impact of social presence on social capital in the context of online social networking.

Website Loyalty

Website loyalty (or e–loyalty) refers to customer loyalty to a website for the purpose of online shopping, information acquisition or exchange, learning, or social networking. As one of performance indicators in the Internet-enabled business transactions, website loyalty has received much attention in a wide variety of contexts (Lee et al., 2006). Both the design and the usage of the website may affect users' loyalty to the website. Jih et al. (2010) conducted a questionnaire survey to find a positive effect of website interactivity on online shoppers' loyalty to website using confirmatory factor analysis and structural equation modeling. A research conducted by Cyr et al. (2007) investigate to the role of social presence in establishing the loyalty of shoppers to the website revealed a significant role played by social presence in online shoppers' loyalty to the e-commerce website. Huang et al. (2017) also found that, among other factors, social capital significantly contributed to buyers' loyalty to a consumer-to-consumer platform.

Way before the Internet era, customer loyalty has been a popular construct in marketing research. Customer loyalty is often associated with repeat purchasing. However, as pointed out by Jacoby and Kyner (1973), although loyal customers tend to purchase repetitively, those who purchase repetitively do not necessarily do so out of loyalty, such as what might happen in the scenario of lacking an alternative offering. Customer loyalty usually results from the satisfaction with the product or service received from the seller. This is applicable in the physical economy and even more so in the Internet-enabled, online commerce. In light of the importance of the customer loyalty to a firm's success, researchers have continued to examine the nature of as well as factors affecting customer loyalty. Early views of brand loyalty almost exclusively emphasized the customer behavior of repeat purchase over a period of time (Brown, 1952; Cunningham, 1956; Lipstein, 1959; Kuehn, 1962; Newman & Werbel, 1973; Reynolds & Darden, 1974; Monroe & Guiltinan, 1975). There are also researches that contended that customer loyalty and repeat purchase do not equal (e.g., Dick & Basu, 1994). This latter view suggests that, when examining the impact of customer loyalty on the company marketing performance, one must make a distinction between behavioral and attitudinal aspects of the concept (Chaudhuri & Holbrook, 2001; Jacoby & Kyner, 1973; Lim & Razzaque, 1997; Dick & Basu, 1994). However, for convenience of measurement, most researches still view customer loyalty as a customer's intention to purchase. In the context of online shopping, customers may visit websites just to gather information but purchase offline. For this reason, Cyr et al. (2007) defined e-loyalty as "perceived loyalty toward an online service provider, as opposed to actually loyal behavior, such as repeat visits/purchase (p. 45)." For our study of the social network website, we adopted this prevailing concept of customer loyalty as intention of repeated visits being an appropriate definition.

RESEARCH HYPOTHESES AND RESEARCH MODEL

Since the purpose of our research was to evaluate causal relationships from social presence to social capital and then to users' loyalty to the social networking website, we formulated a research model comprising these three research constructs - social presence, social capital and website loyalty. We used two sets of hypotheses to represent the causal relationships between the research variables that we were to test using empirical data. We discuss the rationale before listing each set of the hypothesis.

When connecting and communicating via a social network website that has a high level of social presence, users may feel a strong sense of others' presence and tend to open up themselves more in the communication process (Gunawardena & Zittle, 1997; Tu & MaIssac, 2002). This deeper level of participation in the social networking activities may influence the perception of all three aspects of social capital, which in turn may influence loyalty to the social networking website. Users participate more in the networking activities when they find the network trustworthy and useful (Cyr et al., 2007). We postulate that, in the context of social networking, social presence has significant impact on the structural, the relational, as well as the cognitive aspects of social capital. This set of hypotheses appears below in the alternative form.

- **H1:** Social presence positively affects social capital in the context of social networking website.
  - **H1a:** Social presence positively affects the structural dimension of social capital.
  - **H1b:** Social presence positively affects the relational dimension of social capital.
  - **H1c:** Social presence positively affects the cognitive dimension of social capital.

Social capital represents the desirable resources, existing and potential, that members can derive from the social network. The perceived value of these assets is a function of the participating members, linkages among members and the size, of the network (structural), the quality of relationships (relational), and shared value and understanding (cognitive) of the social network. User engagement increases when they clearly perceive the value of participation (Zheng et al., 2015). Huang et al. (2017) also found all three dimensions of social capital positively affect a consumer-to-consumer website users' loyalty to the website. We found it logical to postulate the existence of a causal relationship from all three dimensions of social capital to website loyalty in the context of social networking.

- **H2:** Social capital positively affects user loyalty to the social networking website.
  - **H2a:** The structural dimension of social capital positively affects website loyalty.
  - **H2b:** The relational dimension of social capital positively affects website loyalty.
  - **H2c:** The cognitive dimension of social capital positively affects website loyalty.

Figure 1. Research Hypotheses

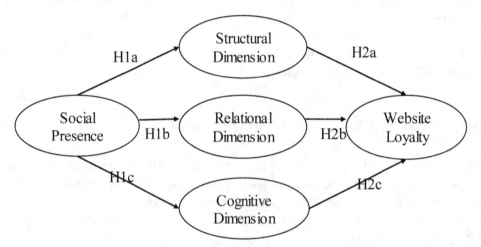

Asian countries and regions embrace the Internet as an important component of their development efforts. As of June 2016, Asia had 55.2% of world population. About 50.2% of this population had access to the Internet. With 48.2% of the adoption rate, Facebook is the leading social networking website among Asian Internet users (Internet World Stats, 2016). Facebook revealed on February 28, 2014 that Taiwan has higher per capita Facebook adoption rate than any other market in the world (Taipeitimes, 2014).

We posted a 5-point Likert-type scale questionnaire on the survey website www.my3q.com to collect Facebook users' perceptional data about social presence, social capital, and website loyalty. Table 1, as presented below, summarize the operational definitions of the research variables in terms of question items. This questionnaire was made available to Facebook users in Taiwan for two months in the Fall 2014 semester for them to respond. The data collection instrument passed reliability and validity assessments (See Table 2 and Table 3).

Table 1. Operational Definitions of Research Variables

Research Variables	Research Constructs	Operational definitions
Social Presence (Short et al. 1976)		The perception of each other's presence.
		1. I can express my emotions through this social media. 2. I do feel the atmosphere of enthusiasm. 3. I feel this website is personable. 4. I feel the sense of friendliness with this media.
Social Capital (Nahapiet & Ghoshal, 1998)	Structural Dimension	The Overall configuration or pattern of linkages between people or units
		1. I can connect with many friends of common interest. 2. No obstacles exist on this website that hinder my interaction with friends. 3. This website allows for meeting new friends through existing friends. 4. This website allows me to access the resource provided by many of my friends.
	Relational Dimension	The degree to which trust, trustworthiness, regulations, sanctions, obligations and expectations are embraced and expected among the members
		5. I am willing to follow the community regulations of this website. 6. I feel obligated to making this website community even better. 7. I identify with the value of this website's existence. 8. Most of my friends are part of this website community.
	Cognitive Dimension	The degree to which the website is perceived to be able to provide shared representations, interpretations, and systems of meaning among participating parties
		9. We have many issues of common interest for our discussion. 10. We share important information with each other through this website. 11. We share our common secrets in this website community. 12. We grow together and share our experience along the way.
Website Loyalty (Chaudhuri & Holbrook, 2001)		The degree to which I consider myself committed to remaining a loyal user of this website
		1. I am emotionally committed to this website and will not easily switch to other social media websites 2. I am going to continue to use this website. 3. I would be glad to recommend this website to my family and friends. 4. I would be happy to recommend this website to other people.

DATA ANALYSIS

During the response period, a total number of 390 users submitted their responses. The screening procedure removed 92 of them deemed significantly incomplete or too casual in responding. The remaining data passed the non-response bias test. The dominant categories of the respondents are female (50.7%), age range of 19-24 (72.1%), students in occupation (61%), college or above in education (60.8%), and 1-3 hours of online time (62%).

We assessed nonresponse bias to ensure the appropriateness of sample data collected through a website questionnaire. We used Pearson χ^2 test to determine if a significant difference exists between early and late respondents with regard to their demographical backgrounds and other personal information. As indicated in Table 2, none of the Pearson χ^2 values is large enough to fail the test, a statistical evidence for lack of significant difference between the two groups.

We evaluated the reliabilities of measurement constructs by Cronbach α value. The Cronbach α value of each of the measurement constructs is greater than 0.8, which is higher than the commonly practiced acceptable level of 0.7. The composite reliabilities (CR) of all constructs are greater than 0.7. The average variance extracted (AVE) values higher than 0.5, evidence of acceptable convergent validity. We evaluated the discriminant validities by the factor loadings, inter-constructs correlation coefficients, and the square roots of AVE (Komiak & Benbasat, 2006). When the square root of AVE is greater than the correlation coefficient between the two constructs under evaluation, the discriminant validity of the constructs is acceptable, which is the case in this study.

Table 2. Result of Pearson χ² test

Personal Information	Pearson χ²	Degrees of Freedom	p-value
Gender	0.057	1	0.811
Age	4.828	4	0.305
Education	3.021	3	0.388
Occupation	1.630	9	0.996
Hours of online time	2.603	3	0.457

Table 3. Reliability and Validity Assessment of Research Variables and Variable Dimensions

Variable and Dimension			Standardized Factor Loading	α	CR	AVE	Social Presence	Social Capital			Website Loyalty
								Structural	Relational	Cognitive	
Social Presence		A1 A2 A3 A4	0.749 0.827 0.783 0.828	0.871	0.875	0.636	*0.797*				
Social Capital	Structural Dimension	B1 B2 B3 B4	0.790 0.804 0.842 0.838	0.889	0.890	0.670	0.678	*0.816*			
	Relational Dimension	B5 B6 B7 B8	0.739 0.722 0.811 0.761	0.843	0.844	0.576	0.514	0.644	*0.759*		
	Cognitive Dimension	B9 B10 B11 B12	0.841 0.810 0.811 0.773	0.884	0.883	0.655	0.561	0.627	0.684	*0.809*	
Website Loyalty		C1 C2 C3 C4	0.735 0.861 0.910 0.878	0.908	0.911	0.720	0.491	0.524	0.667	0.679	*0.849*
Fitness Indices			χ²/df		GFI		AGFI		NFI		CFI
Criteria			<3		>0.9		>0.9		>0.9		>0.9
Index Values			2.062		0.900		0.869		0.924		0.959

FINDINGS

Causal relationships of the three research constructs were evaluated using structural equations modeling (SEM) analysis. Prior to evaluating the model fitness, we examined the error variances, standardized parameter coefficients, and the standard errors to see if it even makes sense to validate the fitness of the theoretical model as a whole. We also looked at the skewness, kurtosis, and multivariate kurtosis coefficient to ensure normal distribution of the sample data. A normally distributed data set has both skewness and kurtosis close to zero. In general, a skewness great than three or kurtosis higher than eight signals concern. All skewness measures of our sample data are less than three and, and all kurtosis measures less than eight. In fact, they are all close to zero, a good evidence to justify the fitness of the theoretical model.

We used an SEM analysis software, AMOS 17.0, to test our research hypotheses. The result of the hypotheses testing, with the standardized structural coefficients and the corresponding t-values indicated in the parentheses, is summarized as follows.

- **H1a:** Social Presence → Social Capital (Structural Dimension) (0.830, 11.629)
- **H1b:** Social Presence → Social Capital (Relational Dimension) (0.718, 9.749)
- **H1c:** Social Presence → Social Capital (Cognitive Dimension) (0.741, 11.427)
- **H2a:** Social Capital (Structural Dimension) → Website Loyalty (-0.050, -0.749)
- **H2b:** Social Capital (Relational Dimension) → Website Loyalty (0.465, 6.806)
- **H2c:** Social Capital (Cognitive Dimension) → Website Loyalty (0.483, 6.620)

These results, along with the model fitness index values (GFI = 0.856, AGFI = 0.828, NFI = 0.895, CFI = 0.930, RMESA = 0.077) support the good fitness of the model (Bentler & Hu, 1995; Chin, 1998; Fornell & Larcker, 1981). All hypotheses except H2a pass the significance test. Social presence positively affects all three dimensions of social capital. Both the relational dimension and the cognitive dimension of social capital positively affect user loyalty to the social network website. However, we did not find enough evidence to support our hypothesis that the structural dimension of social capital significantly affects users' loyalty to the social networking site. This is probably because several other social network sites (e.g., Instagram, WeChat, LINE, and Twitter) also provide similarly appealing network structures. Facebook does not enjoy competitive advantage relative to other social networking platform choices in this respect. The contribution of social capital to website loyalty come from the other two aspects, relational and cognitive dimensions, of social capital.

SUMMARY AND CONCLUSION

Brand loyalty is an important aspect of consumer behavior that prompts repeat purchasing. Loyal customers often provide free word-of-mouth marketing for the company. In a competitive market, brand loyalty may result from meaningful engagement, pleasant shopping experience and satisfied usage experience. Companies must identify all opportunities that hold the potential of leading to favorable customer perception toward their offerings. Maintaining a warm and sociable web interface enables such a friendly round-the-clock interaction with customers.

Figure 2. Result of Model validation
*The symbol ** indicates a significant relationship.*

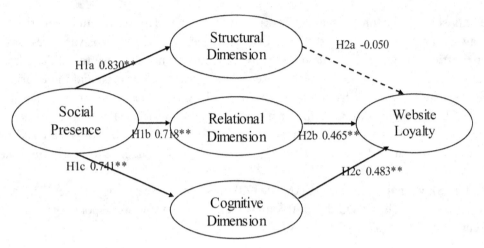

Table 4. Summary of model validation result

Causal Path	Hypothesis	Expected Sign	Theoretical Model	
			Standardized Structural Coefficient	t-value
Social Presence→Social Capital (S)	H1a	+	0.830	11.629**
Social Presence→Social Capital (R)	H1b	+	0.718	9.749**
Social Presence→Social Capital (C)	H1c	+	0.741	11.427**
Social Capital (S)→Website Loyalty	H2a	+	-0.050	-0.749
Social Capital (R)→Website Loyalty	H2b	+	0.465	6.806**
Social Capital (C)→Website Loyalty	H2c	+	0.483	6.620**
Fitness Indices	Critical Values		Fitness Test Result	
GFI	> 0.8		0.856	Good
AGFI	> 0.8		0.828	Good
NFI	> 0.9		0.895	Fair
CFI	> 0.9		0.930	Good
RMSEA	< 0.08		0.077	Good

**P<0.01

Both the notion of social presence and the theory of social capital have received much attention in education and communication studies. The widespread usage of web-enabled social networks also provides opportunities to examine the significance of these theoretical constructs from information systems and online marketing perspectives. Past academic researches either investigated one of the two or explored the impact of social capital on social presence. This research brought together three constructs (social presence, social capital, and website loyalty) in the research model and empirically validated the theoretical model among Facebook users. The sample data collected in Taiwan via a web questionnaire were analyzed using structural equations modeling to explore the causal effects of social presence on social capital, and social capital on website loyalty. The analysis results supported our hypotheses that social presence exhibits a positive impact on all three dimensions of social capital. We also found that both the relational aspect and the cognitive aspect of social capital positively affect website loyalty. However, the causal effect of the structural aspect of social capital on website loyalty was not present. One possibility is that the structural aspect of Facebook was probably not a distinguishing factor that motivated its users to use the website. Other social networking sites are equally appealing to the users in this area. Another possibility is that many Facebook users desired even more structural features than what was currently available. Nevertheless, these findings provided additional empirical evidence supporting the significant role of social presence and social capital in the context of online social networking, a valuable endorsement for companies adding social component to their customer-facing websites to promote active conversation with their customers.

Viewing online interaction as an important area with great potential for companies to nurture customer brand loyalty, this research contributes to the research in social presence, social capital, and online social networking in several days. Our findings shed some light on the roles of social presence and social capital in the online social networking phenomenon. Our result is generally consistent with those of several existing studies that addressed different domains. Specifically, Oztok et al. (2015) a correlation relationship between social capital and social presence in online learning. We found a causal relationship from social presence to social capital. Bharati et al. (2015) found the use of social media affecting structural capital and cognitive capital but only affecting relational capital through structural and cognitive capitals. Their research also discovered that social capital helped promote organizational efforts in knowledge management, an important organizational performance measure. Conducted for a different domain, our research reinforced their findings with regard to the role of social capital as a significant determinant in online interactions. We also found similar conclusion as we relate our findings to those of Sanchez-Casado et al. (2016) and Cyr et al. (2007).

The Internet has become a competitive necessity and, to a certain degree, leveled the playground for business competition. Most businesses, large and small, find it an essential business initiative to establish a presence in the cyber space. What can creative companies do to reap more competitive advantage benefit? The findings of this research have important implications for management practitioners seeking to differentiate their web interactions with customers. An increasing number of company websites now have social component embedded in their websites. The purpose is to develop and nurture online or offline communities to help further company performance (Kane et al., 2009). The positive effect of perceived social presence on social capital suggests the importance of adding interface features that enhance the emotional aspect of online interactions. To accomplish this goal, website managers should pay attention to social presence and treat it as a valuable design consideration. Hassanein and Head (2007) conducted a lab experiment to demonstrate how one can manipulate social presence features to make the e-commerce website more effective by increasing the perceived usefulness, trust and enjoyment of shopping websites. A high degree of social presence nurtures social capital. If website loyalty is an important success indicator for online shopping and other e-commerce activities, increasing social capital through social presence features appears to be a viable strategic initiative. In addition, in order to increase website loyalty, our findings also suggest companies should consider other motivational measures, such as those related to resource investment, to enrich social capital embedded in the organizational social networks (Adler & Kwon, 2002). A particular technological development that is worth experimenting with, in this regard, is artificial intelligence that embodies both domain-specific knowledge and context-sensitive interaction.

The external validity of this research is limited in several ways, however. Readers should apply the findings with caution. Our research data came from Taiwanese users of Facebook based on a web questionnaire. Replicating this research in different settings with regard to social networking platform as well as cultural environment may reduce the influence of platform and culture. Similarly, repeating this research at different points in time also has the benefit of increasing the generalizability of the findings. Despite these limitations, our findings contribute to academic inquiry as well as managerial decision-making by adding more evidence about the significant roles of social presence and social capital in nurturing users' loyalty to online social networks in general and online social networking sites in particular.

REFERENCES

Adler, P. S., & Kwon, S.-W. (2002). Social capital: Prospects for a new concept. *Academy of Management Journal, 27*(1), 17–40.

Bentler, P. M., & Hu, L. T. (1995). Evaluating model fit. Structural Equations Modeling, 76-99.

Bharati, P., Zhang, W., & Chaudhury, A. (2015). Better knowledge with social media? Exploring the roles of social capital and organizational knowledge management. *Journal of Knowledge Management, 19*(3), 456–475. doi:10.1108/JKM-11-2014-0467

Biocca, F., & Harms, C. (2002). Defining and measuring social presence: Contribution to the networked minds theory and measure. *Proceedings of 2002 Telepresence.*

Biocca, F., Harms, C., & Burgoon, J. K. (2003). Toward a new robust theory and measure of social presence: Review and suggested criteria. *Presence (Cambridge, Mass.), 12*(5), 456–480. doi:10.1162/105474603322761270

Bourdieu, P., & Wacquant, I. J. D. (1992). *An invitation to reflexive sociology.* Chicago: University of Chicago Press.

Brown, G. H. (1952). Brand loyalty – fact or fiction? *Advertising Age, 23*, 53–55.

Chaudhuri, A., & Holbrook, M. B. (2001). The chain of effects from brand trust and brand affect to brand performance: The role of brand loyalty. *Journal of Marketing, 65*(2), 81–93. doi:10.1509/jmkg.65.2.81.18255

Chin, W. W. (1998). Issues and opinion on structural equation modeling. *Management Information Systems Quarterly, 22*, 1.

Coleman, J. S. (1988). Social capital in the creation of human capital. *American Journal of Sociology, 94*, S95-S120.

Cunningham, R. M. (1956). Brand-loyalty-what, where, how Much. *Harvard Business Review, 34*(1), 116–128.

Cyr, D., Hassanein, K., Head, M., & Ivanov, A. (2007). The role of social presence in establishing loyalty in e-service environments. *Interacting with Computers, 19*(1), 43–56. doi:10.1016/j.intcom.2006.07.010

Dick, A. S., & Basu, K. (1994). Customer loyalty: Toward an integrated conceptual framework. *Journal of the Academy of Marketing Science*, *22*(2), 99–113. doi:10.1177/0092070394222001

Ellison, N., Steinfield, C., & Lampe, C. (2007). The benefits of Facebook "friends:" Social capital and college students' use of online social network sites. *Journal of Computer-Mediated Communication*, *12*(4), 1143–1168. doi:10.1111/j.1083-6101.2007.00367.x

Fornell, C., & Larcker, D. F. (1981). Evaluating structural equations model with unobservable variables and measurement error. *JMR, Journal of Marketing Research*, *18*(1), 39–50. doi:10.2307/3151312

Fukuyama, F. (1995). *Trust: The social virtues and the creation of prosperity*. New York: Free Press.

Fulk, J., Schmitz, J., & Power, G. G. (1987). A social information processing model of media use in organization. *Communication Research*, *14*(5), 520–552. doi:10.1177/009365087014005005

Gefen, D., Karahanna, E., & Straub, D. W. (2003). Trust and TAM in online shopping: An integrated model. *Management Information Systems Quarterly*, *27*(1), 51–90. doi:10.2307/30036519

Gunawardena, C. N., & Zittle, F. J. (1997). Social presence as a predictor of satisfaction within a computer-mediated conferencing environment. *American Journal of Distance Education*, *11*(3), 8–26. doi:10.1080/08923649709526970

Han, S., Min, J., & Lee, H. (2015). Antecedents of social presence and gratification of social connection needs in SNS: A study of Twitter users and their mobile and non-mobile usage. *International Journal of Information Management*, *35*(4), 459–471. doi:10.1016/j.ijinfomgt.2015.04.004

Hassanein, K., & Head, M. (2006). The impact of infusing social presence in the Web interface: An investigation across different products. *International Journal of Electronic Commerce*, *10*(2), 31–35. doi:10.2753/JEC1086-4415100202

Hassanein, K., & Head, M. (2007). Manipulating perceived social presence through the Web interface and its impact on attitude towards online shopping. *International Journal of Human-Computer Studies*, *65*(8), 689–708. doi:10.1016/j.ijhcs.2006.11.018

Huang, Q., Chen, X., Ou, C. X., Davison, R. M., & Hua, Z. (2017). Understanding buyers' loyalty to a C2C platform: The roles of social capital, satisfaction and perceived effectiveness of e-commerce institutional mechanisms. *Information Systems Journal*, *27*(1), 91–119. doi:10.1111/isj.12079

Internet World Stats. (2016). *Internet Usage in Asia*. Retrieved from http://www.internetworldstats.com/stats3.htm

Jacobs, J. (1965). *The Death and Life of American Cities*. London: Penguin Books.

Jacoby, J., & Kyner, D. B. (1973). Brand loyalty vs. repeat purchasing behavior. *JMR, Journal of Marketing Research*, *10*(1), 1–9. doi:10.2307/3149402

Jih, W. J., Lee, S. F., & Tsai, Y. C. (2010). Effects of website interactivity on e-loyalty: A social exchange perspective. *International Journal of E-Business Journal*, *6*(4), 1–12.

Kane, G., Fichman, R. G., Gallaugher, J., & Glaser, J. (2009). Community relations 2.0. *Harvard Business Review*, *87*(11), 45–50. PMID:19891388

Kehrwald, B. (2010). Being online: Social presence as subjectivity in online learning. *London Review of Education*, 8(1), 39–50. doi:10.1080/14748460903557688

Komiak, S. Y. X., & Benbasat, I. (2006). The effects of personalization and familiarity on trust and adoption of recommendation agents. *Management Information Systems Quarterly*, 30(4), 941–960. doi:10.2307/25148760

Kuehn, A. (1962, March). Consumer brand choice as a learning process. *Journal of Advertising Research*, 2, 10–17.

Kuo, Y. F., & Feng, L. H. (2013). Relationships among community interaction characteristics, perceived benefits, community commitment, and oppositional brand loyalty in online brand communities. *International Journal of Information Management*, 33(6), 948–962. doi:10.1016/j.ijinfomgt.2013.08.005

Lee, S. F., Jih, W. J. K., & Fang, S. R. (2006). Investigating the impact of customer relationship management practices of e-commerce on online customer's web site satisfaction: A model-building approach. *International Journal of E-Business Research*, 2(4), 61–77. doi:10.4018/jebr.2006100104

Lim, K. S., & Razzaque, M. A. (1997). Brand loyalty and situational effects: An interactionist perspective. *Journal of International Consumer Marketing*, 9(4), 95–115. doi:10.1300/J046v09n04_06

Lin, N. (1999). Building a network theory of social capital. *Connections*, 22(1), 28–51.

Lipstein, B. (1959). The dynamics of brand loyalty and brand switching. *Proceedings of the Fifth Annual Conference of the Advertising Research Foundation*, 101-108.

Monroe, K. B., & Guiltinan, J. P. (1975). A path-analytic exploration of retail patronage influences. *The Journal of Consumer Research*, 2(1), 19–28. doi:10.1086/208612

Nahapiet, J., & Ghoshal, S. (1998). Social capital, intellectual capital and the organizational advantage. *Academy of Management Review*, 23(2), 242–266.

Newman, J. W., & Werbel, R. A. (1973). Multivariate analysis of brand loyalty for major household appliances. *JMR, Journal of Marketing Research*, 10(4), 404–409. doi:10.2307/3149388

Oztok, M., Zingaro, D., Makos, A., Brett, C., & Hewitt, J. (2015). Capitalizing on social presence: The relationship between social capital and social presence. *Internet and Higher Education*, 26, 15–24. doi:10.1016/j.iheduc.2015.04.002

Remesal, A., & Colomina, R. (2013). Social presence and online collaborative small group work: A socioconstructivist account. *Computers & Education*, 60(1), 357–367. doi:10.1016/j.compedu.2012.07.009

Reynolds, F. D., & Darden, W. R. (1974). *Constructing Life Style and Psychograghics*. Chicago: AMA.

Sanchez-Casado, N., Cegarra Navarro, J. G., Wensley, A., & Tomaseti-Solano, E. (2016). Social networking sites as a learning tool. *The Learning Organization*, 23(1), 23–42. doi:10.1108/TLO-10-2014-0058

Short, J., Williams, E., & Christie, B. (1976). *The Social Psychology of Telecommunications*. London: John Wiley & Sons, Ltd.

Statista. (2016). *Number of social network users worldwide from 2010 to 2020 (in billions)*. Retrieved from https://www.statista.com/statistics/278414/number-of-worldwide-social-network-users/

Taipeitimes. (2014). Retrieved from www.taipeitimes.com/News/biz/archives/2014/02/28/2003584495

Tu, C.-H. (2001). How Chinese perceive social presence: An examination of interaction in online learning environment. *Educational Media International*, *38*(1), 45–60. doi:10.1080/09523980010021235

Tu, C.-H., & McIsaac, M. S. (2002). An examination of social presence to increase interaction in online classes. *American Journal of Distance Education*, *16*(2), 131–150. doi:10.1207/S15389286AJDE1603_2

Zheng, X., Cheung, C. M. K., Lee, M. K. O., & Liang, L. (2015). Building brand loyalty through user engagement in online brand communities in social networking sites. *Information Technology & People*, *28*(1), 90–106. doi:10.1108/ITP-08-2013-0144

Chapter 16

A Content Marketing Framework to Analyze Customer Engagement on Social Media

Sofia Balio

School of Economics and Management, University of Porto, Portugal

Beatriz Casais

(iD) https://orcid.org/0000-0002-7626-0509

School of Economics and Management, University of Minho, Portugal & IPAM Porto, Portugal

ABSTRACT

Factors influencing customer engagement on Facebook have been extensively analyzed but there are barely evidences if those factors also effect customer engagement on Instagram. A digital analysis was conducted including a content analysis of the post appeals and of the message interactivity as well as multiple linear regressions to explore the influence of the factors mentioned above on customer engagement. It was possible to conclude which factors can be used to increase customer engagement on social media, namely message interactivity and certain post appeals. Different conclusions are withdrawn when comparing Facebook to Instagram, proving empirically that different social networking sites have distinct influence on customer engagement. This chapter is relevant for content and social media strategies and helps brands increase their customer engagement.

INTRODUCTION

Social media has been increasing its presence in our daily lives and therefore it has introduced various opportunities to companies to exploit different ways of improving their business. As so, social media has also been increasing its importance in the business world (Ngai et al., 2015; Phua et al., 2017). The

DOI: 10.4018/978-1-7998-9020-1.ch016

main advantage is the possibility of a two-way communication between companies and customers, encouraging the customer engagement on social media (Malthouse et al., 2016).

It is it vital for companies to understand how they can better interact with their online community and what factors influence the customer engagement. Academic research in this field, despite being common, does not capture the continuous development in terms of metrics, features of social networking sites and new platforms (Coelho et al., 2016; Dessart et al., 2016).

Both Facebook and Instagram are constantly changing and thus the academic field is also in a permanent need to renew its conclusions and results. As so, this study enters the wide range of papers that covered the social networking sites topics, but in a deeper and more concise sub-subject that lacks in terms of academic studies: the customer engagement on Facebook and Instagram.

This study aims to help managers and brands to better analyze their customer engagement, in particular, to understand the influence that certain factors have on the content that brands share with their customers.

Post type, time frame, message interactivity and post appeal were considered as the four types of factors influencing how customers express their engagement through the likes, reactions, comments and shares on Facebook and Instagram. Previous studies have only focused on likes and comments (De Vries et al., 2012; Sabate et al., 2014; Erkan, 2015; Coelho et al., 2016), and therefore, this study will contribute with more in-depth insights by adding the number of reactions and shares as metrics of customer engagement on social media. Additionally, this work will narrow the gap concerning the knowledge about how these factors influence customer engagement on social media platforms beyond Facebook, by extending the analysis to Instagram (Carah & Shaul, 2015).

In summary, this study aims to upgrade the past studies according to the evolution of the social networking sites and to answer the following question:

What factors should be taken into consideration and what is the impact of each one on the customer engagement on Facebook and Instagram?

BACKGROUND

Customer Engagement

One of the key factors of success for business nowadays is the ability to create and maintain long term relationships with customers. This has been a concern and a goal for managers and brands since a long time but the appearance of social media and the evolution of Web 2.0 highlighted the importance of establishing interactions with customers (Malthouse et al., 2016). Thus, customer engagement is a relevant topic for managers across all industries and companies.

Customer engagement presents several advantages for brands since it is seen as a factor that drives better organizational performance, increases sales, profitability and customer loyalty (Bowden, 2009). Gambetti and Graffigna (2010) also argue that customer engagement plays a key role in having a competitive advantage and that due to the change of customers' role in the buying process, companies have to adapt and respond to their new needs (the desire of co-create brand content, interact with other customers and have emotional experiences). Similarly, Verhoef et al. (2010) discuss that the role of customers has changed over the past few years as they have become more active and participate, not only in the buying process but also in activities provided by brands and/or initiated by themselves.

As pointed out by both van Doorn et al. (2010) and Sashi (2012), customer engagement goes beyond the simple act of purchase as customers now are deeply involved with brands. For instance, customers who are engaged and have a relationship with the brand are more likely to give good feedback about their experience with family and friends which generates word-of-mouth about the brand. Consequently, they could become brand advocates that generate value for the brand. Thus, customer engagement isn't static, but instead, is a process of interactions that goes beyond the moment of the purchase (Verhoef et al., 2010).

Nevertheless, customer engagement can also have a negative impact on brands. As stated before, if customers start sharing negative eWOM, for instance, brands will suffer negative publicity and potential customers could be pulled away. Thus, it is crucial for brands to properly manage customer engagement (Hollebeek et al., 2014).

As suggested by previous studies (Cvijikj & Michahelles, 2013; Sabate et al., 2014; Kim & Yang, 2017), users can engage on Facebook through three distinct behaviors: liking, commenting and sharing. Regarding Instagram, the main behaviors of engagement are liking and commenting (Erkan, 2015; Coelho et al., 2016).

Notwithstanding, it is proposed by Kim and Yang (2017) that these behaviors don't have the same weight and don't represent the same level of engagement. Neither for the customers nor for the algorithms of Facebook and Instagram. Consequently, it is relevant to include all of them when studying the costumer engagement on an environment such as social media.

Both social networking sites (SNSs) have an internal algorithm that is in charge of analyzing each post that is made. Based in that analysis, the algorithm then ranks them and decides which posts will appear in the News Feed or Timeline of users. This algorithm is constantly changing and always incorporating new variables, but one of the key criteria is the user interaction which is determined by the number of likes, comments and shares that a post receives. Furthermore, it is thought that a share is equivalent to 2 comments and that each comment is equivalent to 7 likes (Wagner et al., 2017).

In regard to the customer effort, Kim and Yang (2017) also propose that these three behaviors require a different amount of intensity. The like is the behavior that requires the lowest cognitive effort, once that it can be done through a simple click. On the contrary, a comment needs more commitment from the user, since he will have to express himself through words or *emojis*. Sharing represents the highest level of effort. On one hand, when a user shares a post, it will appear both on the News Feed and on his profile, while when someone comments a post, it will only appear in the News Feed and disappear after some time. On the other hand, as the shared post will appear on the profile of the user, it could indicate that it is part of the user's self-presentation. Online users tend to be very careful when it comes to their self-presentation. Therefore, it could indicate that a higher level of effort is required as it may be a strategic and thought behavior.

Reactions are a powerful measure and are a more precise indicator of how users feel about a given content. This is particularly important for brands, once they can get a deep knowledge on how their products are perceived online or how their community feels about their content strategy. This is an indication that indeed reactions are now part of the metrics that should be analyzed and that brands should pay attention to them. As it was suggested by Swani and Milne (2017) it would be interesting to investigate the effect of this new type of interaction on customer engagement on social media. Also, as there are more forms of engagement beyond likes and comments, it is crucial to include and analyze this matter more extensively. However, barely no literature was found on the thematic of establishing this relationship. Most the authors so far still only consider the number of likes and comments as their dependent variables (Sabate et al., 2014; Erkan, 2015; Coelho et al., 2016; Kim & Hull, 2017). More recently, authors such Wagner et al. (2017) and Wang et al. (2017) also incorporate into their conceptual framework the shares as a dependent variable, which, as explained above, is one of the behaviors that users have to engage on SNSs.

Determinants of Customer Engagement on Social Media

In the conceptual framework proposed by De Vries et al. (2012), the brand post popularity was measured through the number of likes and the number of comments. As determinants of it, they suggested that the vividness and interactivity of the brand post should be taken into consideration as well as the position of the post in the brand fan page. Additionally, they argued that the valence of comments could also have an impact on the brand post popularity, as a positive comment could improve the interest of a post. Finally, as the content of a post could be either informational or entertaining, the model also incorporated this dimension.

In respect to the results they found out that in order to increase the number of comments, managers should create highly interactive posts, such as posts with a question to encourage the response of users. However, it was also empirically proven that this type of posts are negatively related to the number of likes. This study made a crucial contribution to the academic field and contributed with important insights for managers but they also pointed out some limitations such as not incorporating other SNSs (De Vries et al., 2012). Sabate et al. (2014) even made a distinction between soft criterion and hard criterion. The first one takes into consideration semantic and interpretation aspect behind the message of the post. On the other hand, hard criterions are the ones that don't require a subjective interpretation and that can be quantified. A group of studies have focused only on soft criterions and have analyzed the effect of such post categories as advertising, fan, events, information and promotion (Coelho et al., 2016) or the post appeals as emotional and utilitarian (Wagner et al., 2017). Another group only analyzed hard criterion by studying the content richness taking into consideration if the post was an image, a video or a link and the time frame depending on the time of publication and the day of the week of publication (Sabate et al., 2014). Some who went deeper, developed their conceptual framework including both soft and hard criterion. For instance, Kim and Yang (2017) studied how different message features could impact the engagement on social media. They argued that both the form (text, photo, audio, video) and message interactivity defined as if the message was response-inviting or not, should be criterions in their framework, for example.

Post Type

Concerning post type, which is a hard criterion, it has been studied by a few authors. The results concerning its impact prove its relevance once that most of the studies show that this category is a significant predictor of the measures of customer engagement (Cvijikj & Michahelles, 2013; Sabate et al., 2014; Kim & Yang, 2017; Swani & Milne, 2017). However, when analyzing the results of these studies, it is also possible to see the variety of different conclusions. For instance, Kim and Yang (2017) showed that photos have a negative impact on the number of comments while Cvijikj and Michahelles (2013) showed the opposite. These specific studies had focus on different industries and companies as the object of study, which may explain the contrary conclusions, among other factors. Nevertheless, this indicates that this kind of study is relevant through the years and the academic research still needs different industries and countries incorporated in the analysis, in order to have more solid results.

In past studies, post type, have been related with the vividness of the posts. Academics argued that vividness represents the richness of the features of a post (De Vries et al., 2012). In other words, this richness is the breadth and depth of a message that stimulates different senses of the user. For instance, when a brand posts an image with contrasting colors or an interesting link to another website, the attractiveness of the post can increase. By stimulating different senses, the different post types can potentially condition the behavior towards the posts which consequently, affects customer engagement (Sabate et al., 2014).

De Vries et al. (2012) suggested that the vividness of each post should be divided into different levels. The low level of vividness was defined as a photo or image, the medium level was an event and the highest level was a video. One could argue that defining different levels of vividness can lead to potential subjective bias, because there is no certainty on how users will perceive it (Sabate et al., 2014).

Time Frame

Previous research has also studied the effect of time on customer engagement, as it is of extreme importance for brands to know when to post on SNSs, as pointed out by the literature (Cvijikj & Michahelles, 2013; Sabate et al., 2014). Academics have studied time frame through mainly, three different perspectives: the first one takes into account either the post is published on weekdays or during the weekend; the second one argues about the influence of the time of publication (hours) and finally, the third one considers the seasonality of the post through the analysis of the different months of the year.

Regardless the different views and results, the consensus among the authors is that, in an environment such Facebook or Instagram, where the News Feed or Timeline is always receiving new content, brands must take into consideration the influence of time on customer engagement (Cvijikj & Michahelles, 2013; Coelho et al., 2016).

The most frequent perspective is the contrast between weekdays and weekends. Wagner et al. (2017) and De Vries et al. (2012) included this as a control variable and Sabate et al. (2014) and Cvijikj and Michahelles (2013) studied it as one of the independent variables of their models. Some studies showed that this variable had no impact while others showed that posts during weekdays had more customer engagement. Moreover, although Sabate et al. (2014) had included both weekdays and time of publication, their model was only able to establish a connection between the time of publication and the number of comments. This indicates that, despite previous efforts, work on this field is still needed.

The second approach was implemented on the work of Sabate et al. (2014) and Cvijikj and Michahelles (2013) who suggested that users were more active on the Internet during peak hours (the period when users were more active on SNS). Contrary to what was expected, on the work of Cvijikj and Michahelles (2013), it was found that posts during peak hours have a negative effect on engagement. The authors state that this probably happens because during peak hours, users want to interact with their friends and not with brands. As a consequence, it is suggested that companies should post during the period with low activity (off peak hours) in order to increase customer engagement.

Coelho et al. (2016) applied the third perspective and studied the seasonality as a control variable. The work included months from January to August and showed that different months implied different behaviors, proving that customer engagement is influenced by the month a post is published. On Facebook, some months had a positive effect while others a negative one. In the case of the number of likes, months such as March, April, May and June had one of the most powerful increases and the number of comments also increased during February, March, April and July. The authors believe that these results could be explained by the existence of a national holidays and the vacation period of the country of the companies surveyed. On Instagram the impact, although not the same for every month, was all positive.

There is a massive amount of content on social media, but not all receive the same engagement. Another key factor is the perceived interactivity that a user have (Kim & Yang, 2017). In other words, the perception that an online user has on the communication that he or she can establish with the brand is decisive to create engagement. This communication should happen in a two-way dialogue, be responsive and controllable (Mollen & Wilson, 2010).

Interactivity

Interactivity has been a topic of interest for the past few years and a lot of definitions and categories were suggested and added to the discussion. Although there is no agreement on the definition, there is a consent about its importance in communication and in the maintenance of relationships (Kim & Yang, 2017). Ariel and Avidar (2015), show that there are three common perspectives about interactivity: it could be seen as a "perception-related variable", as a "process-related variable" or as a "medium characteristic". From their point of view, interactivity is part of the communication process. This is, as interactivity is "an attribute of the process of communication itself", it is present on traditional media as well as in new media platforms. It is acknowledged that new media can facilitate the interactivity but the main predictor of the degree of interactivity will rely on the "process of message transition and reciprocity". Go and Bortree (2017) also believe that social media enables message interactivity by providing several ways in which organizations can communicate with their audience.

In an environment as Facebook and Instagram, where all the organizations have the same opportunities in terms of technological aspects in order to influence interactivity (Kim & Yang, 2017), the perceived interactivity does not depend on technology but on the degree to which brands decide to take actions and use the tools available to engage in a two-way communication (Lee & Park, 2013).

Post Appeal

Post appeal have also received attention from the academic field and its relationship with customer engagement have been suggested as well as tested. The firsts authors trying to study how the message appeal can influence the way consumers are persuaded, focused on two main approaches, that although being different aren't mutually exclusive.

One of the approaches had its focus on the importance of factual information. The other approach had the emotions as the focus and in this case, the content could take advantage of emotions. Brands could try to provoke feelings or emotions associated to the product and people would adjust their buying behavior accordingly, either emotions were positive or negative (Bagozzi et al., 1999).

Academics continued to study and analyzing what kind of appeal, either rational or emotional would be the best, but the question remains controversial. Nevertheless, what has been proven is that, beyond the type, message appeal as a whole has an effect on message perception, which consequently results in an effective communication (Wagner et al., 2017).

Present studies, still utilize this categorization of functional and emotional appeals in order to contribute to the literature (Liu et al., 2017). However, as suggested by Swani et al. (2017) it would be beneficial to go further and to also analyze the categories of emotional and functional appeals such as humor, love, and so on and so forth. This was already attempted by some studies, but it is still at its early stage of analysis.

Wagner et al. (2017) was one of that studies. Through the proposed framework, it was also concluded that the main factor of success on communication is the "overall theme of a post", or as it was posited, the post appeal. As suggested by the authors, post appeal can affect the attitude of a user toward a post, once that every post has a theme and it is perceived by SNSs users. Consequently, depending on the attitude, an action such as liking, commenting or sharing can be generated. Thus, the post appeal constitutes an important factor on the study of customer engagement.

Results from the studies of Wang et al. (2017) and Liu et al. (2017) corroborate that post appeal have a significant effect on social media engagement. The first one only included likes and shares as the metrics of engagement and the second one incorporated likes, comments and shares.

In the work of Wang et al. (2017) the motivation arouse because there was a significant difference between the engagement of the posts. Notwithstanding, the relation of post appeals with engagement has barely been analyzed.

Both studies showed that some themes or topics have a positive effect while others have a negative effect. Additionally, some appeals have a more significant effect than others. What is curious is that, Wang also found out that the most frequent themes are not the ones which create more engagement. This could mean that brands are not defining their strategies taking this important information into consideration and this way they are missing out the full potential of SNSs and customer engagement.

Content Marketing

Nowadays, traditional marketing is not sufficient in order for brands to remain competitive, the paradigm has shifted and strategies must be adjusted. This era is known as the new digital era and content marketing is one of the key factors of success and one of the crucial tools of digital marketing. Consequently, is it important for companies to understand what is this concept about and how to incorporate it in their marketing efforts.

Although its relevance has been growing only in the past decade, the truth is that content marketing was already present in the early nineties. In fact, some business owners were developing their brands through this approach. For instance, André Michelin, launched the Michelin Guide which featured information about how to repair tires and a list of hotels and city maps. This magazine instead of being commercialized was given for free. Other examples exist and the common aspect about them is that, these businessmen were already building brand stories as a way of creating an emotional connection that hopefully would result in the sales of their product or service.

The difference between content marketing and advertising was also established. It is stated that advertising has its focus on sales and motivating purchase whereas content marketing is more about establishing relationships with the customer and using storytelling in order to fortify their brand messaging and positioning.

Moreover, content marketing serves several objectives such as increasing brand awareness, attracting news leads into the business, building relationships with the customer as well as enhancing customer loyalty, among others. Nevertheless, if these advantages for companies aren't trackable and measurable, they would never know when the goal is fulfilled. As a consequence, some metrics are required in order to validate the approach of content marketing. There are four different types of metrics that could be used, namely consumption metrics, sharing metrics (likes, shares, among others), lead and sales metrics

(Holliman & Rowley, 2014). Ahmad et al. (2016) also pointed out that metrics such as liking, *hashtagging*, retweeting, commenting and sharing the content that brands post online are measures for analyzing the effectiveness of content marketing.

Additionally, Ahmad et al. (2016) also stated that social media platforms are useful tools for gathering such measures. If in traditional marketing it was sometimes difficult to measure the impacts of strategies, in the era of digital marketing it is easier to analyze results. It is thanks to the technology of Web 2.0 that brands can follow the outcomes of their marketing efforts, as it is the case of monitoring the customers' behavior through their engagement on social media.

Content plays a crucial role on the marketing world and as emphasized by some studies, having a valuable and relevant content can help driving engagement on social media. On the other hand, engagement itself also helps to increase the effectiveness of content marketing once it is easier to influence costumers' perceptions on a brand or product if they are indeed engaged and paying attention to the content. Otherwise, it is difficult to really accomplish objectives such as establishing relationships with customers and increasing brand awareness.

THE RESEARCH OBJECTIVE

The objective of this study is to provide insights about what should be taken into consideration and its impact when using Facebook and Instagram in order to understand customer engagement. For this purpose, four main categories were inducted: post type, time frame, message interactivity and post appeal to better explain the behaviors of customer engagement on Facebook and Instagram. Two conceptual frameworks are presented due to the differences between the two SNSs, Facebook and Instagram.

Figure 1. Framework to analyze customer engagement on Instagram

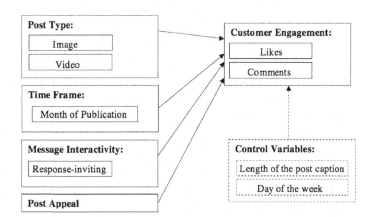

A content analysis of the post appeals and message interactivity and an empirical analysis were conducted. For each dependent variable and for each SNS, multiple OLS linear regressions were estimated. All the dependent variables were transformed using the natural logarithm in order to ensure a normal distribution of the residuals. Additionally, outliers were eliminated if the studentized residual exceeded

-3 or +3. Moreover, in order to improve the explanatory power of the variable *Length of the post caption*, it was transformed by using the natural logarithm. Thus, this study tested six models, four concerning Facebook, namely *LN (Likes +1), LN (Reactions +1), LN (Comments +1)* and *LN (Shares +1)*, and two regarding Instagram, respectively *LN (Likes +1)* and *LN (Comments +1)*.

Figure 2. Framework to analyze customer engagement on Facebook

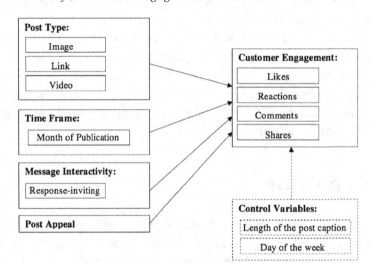

After the data collection of posts from Instagram and Facebook of a company, posts were treated and coded for post type, time frame, message interactivity and post appeal. The first two correspond to hard criterion and enable a pragmatic coding procedure while the other ones require a more subjective analysis as it is natural for soft criterion.

Regarding post type, there were three different and mutually exclusive possibilities: image, link and video. Thus, a post could only be one type and this differentiation was intuitive to code. For the time frame, the coding procedure was also immediate as it is possible to see in the screenshots the date of publication of the post. Consequently, the month of publication was coded for each post.

Message Interactivity investigates the response-inviting aspect of the message of the post. Any message that asks or encourages a response directly will be considered as interactive. Additionally, messages that include questions (excluding rhetorical questions) or actions verbs are examples of what can be considered response-inviting. As suggested by the coding scheme of Kim and Yang (2017), in order to the post be considered as interactive, the message needs to "solicit responses from the public directly".

The posts were also coded for its central appeal as performed on the work of Wagner et al. (2017) that, as stated before, created a coding instrument with twelve emotional appeals and twelve functional appeals. In their study, post appeals emerged from their coding instrument and their sample of posts didn't influence it. On the contrary, Wang et al. (2017), in order to define the coding instrument, firstly read their sample of posts and after developed eleven post appeals. Swani et al. (2017), although only distinguish between emotional and functional appeals, did suggest categories of both such as humor, romance and contest, among others. In this study, on both cases of Facebook and Instagram, a mix approach was used. A reading of the whole sample was performed before developing the appeals, but the processing of the appeals also followed the procedures suggested by the literature when generating a coding instrument.

In order to construct a valid coding instrument, it is desirable that the appeals represent wide topics because otherwise it would be difficult to distinguish clearly the categories. As a consequence, while reading through the sample this concern was already present. After having the initial list of potential post appeals, a more detailed analysis to that list was performed to secure that similar categories were grouped. As a final step all categories that weren't immediately perceived, were eliminated. This is important because during the coding procedure it should be easy to comprehend and to code each post without questions. Moreover, the name of the appeals should also be straightforward and created using understandable language. To complete, a description of each appeal should be developed to ensure the minimum level of ambiguity (Wagner et al., 2017).

Afterwards, the list was compared to the coding instruments of previous studies. From the eight post appeals proposed by this study, six of them correspond to post appeals previously used by Wang et al. (2017), Wagner et al. (2017) and Swani et al. (2017).

The control variables, day of the week and length of the caption of the post, were also coded. Each post was coded as "1 = weekday" if they corresponded to days from Monday to Friday and "0 = weekend" if Saturday and Sunday were the day of publication. Regarding the length of the caption an Excel function was used (LEN) in order to facilitate the process and to ensure the accuracy of this variable. Every caption was copied to an Excel file and then the function was executed.

The number of likes, reactions, comments and shares were documented by reading the information provided on the screenshots.

From a total of 382 posts from Facebook, it was concluded that some had to be excluded. Three of them were milestones, which don't fall into neither of the post types in this study and therefore were excluded. Another three were GIFs, and for the same reason were also excluded. One of the posts, for an unknown reason, didn't had an available URL. As a content analysis will be performed, this post was also excluded, once it is not possible to perform a rigorous content analysis in order to identify the post appeal. Concerning Instagram, only one post was eliminated as it didn't fall into any post appeal. Additionally, only brand posts were considered on both SNSs.

To conclude, the sample is composed of 375 posts from Facebook and 52 from Instagram.

SOLUTIONS AND RECOMMENDATIONS

In this study, factors such as post type, time frame, message interactivity and post appeal were analyzed in order to investigate its effect on customer engagement through social media.

The first factor proposed by the framework of this study was post type and the goal was to identify which post type had more influence on customer engagement. This is an important issue, since each post type requires significantly different amount of time in order to be created. As time is a valuable asset, it is relevant for brands to know which is the best post type in terms of customer engagement. On Facebook, video was significantly and positively related to all of the metrics whereas images were only significant on the number of likes, reactions and comments. In addition, images were negatively related to the number of comments. Furthermore, it is noteworthy that video was the most important variable in every model except in the comments one, showing its relevance. The model for the number of likes is significant as a whole (F-value = 4.907, *p*-value <0.05) and has an explanatory power of 18% (R^2 = 22.6%, adj. R^2 = 18%).

Concerning post type, both image and video are significantly related with the number of likes. Image posts have a positive effect (β = 0.462, *p*-value < 0.05) as well as videos (β = 1.234, *p*-value < 0.05). However, attention should be paid to the greater impact of videos when comparing to images. Although both of them have a positive effect, video exert a more powerful effect.

The message interactivity is also significantly and positively related with the number of likes (β = 0.313, *p*-value < 0.05). Consequently, from these findings, it is suggested that video is the post type that has more influence on customer engagement on social media, followed by images.

On Instagram, results were different since video had a negative impact on the number of likes. Concerning post type, video (β = -0.217, p-value < 0.10) showed to be significantly and negatively related to the number of likes on Instagram. This could be considered a normal result since Instagram is mostly known by the share of images. Videos are also a post type possible, but not the most commonly used by users. Nevertheless, the platform has already updated the video features. In the beginning only 15 second were allowed and currently videos can be uploaded up to 60 seconds. This could be an improvement from the brand in order to promote the use of videos among users. However, from the results of this work, it is suggested that images are preferred over videos on Instagram.

Regarding time frame, results were very surprising. The aim of this study was to analyze which months had a positive effect on customer engagement but instead, findings only contemplate months with a negative impact. On Instagram, it wasn't possible to analyze this issue once none of the months was a significant variable. Concerning Facebook, December was negatively related with likes and comments, August with reactions and October with the number of reactions and comments. Although on the work of Coelho et al. (2016), the positive impact of some months were justified by the presence of national holidays, it is believe in this study, that the activity of users on social media is increased during work hours as showed by some studies. As a consequence, on periods of holidays and vacations as the case of December and August, it would be normal for the metrics of customer engagement to decrease.

With respect to message interactivity, the results of this study suggest different conclusions regarding the nature of the SNS. was expected that the number of comments would be increased by the response-inviting characteristic and this was empirically proved. Additionally, it was expected that the other variables (likes, reactions and shares) would be negatively impacted by the interactivity. However, the contrary was observed. Both likes and reactions were positively related to message interactivity. It can be concluded that brands have a crucial role when creating their content because this independent variable has an effect on the majority of the metrics of customer engagement.

These findings are partially in accordance with the previous work of Kim and Yang (2017) since in their study, the positive effect was only on the number of comments. Additionally, both this study and past studies confirm that having posts encouraging the response from users can increase the number of comments which is an expected result since it is the action the post aims for. Nevertheless, through the work of the present study it was proven that the number of likes and reactions were also positively affected by the response-inviting aspect of the message. This could mean that users also feel more encouraging to demonstrate their feelings about a post when the brand asks for their opinion. It is visible that it was very frequently that the brand simply asks if the users agreed with the message on the post. Consequently, as it could be only a yes or no answer, the yes could be demonstrated simply by a like on the post, leading to the increased of the number of likes and reactions.

On Instagram, message interactivity had no influence on the number of likes and as the model for the number of comments wasn't significant as a whole.

Regarding the study of post appeals, interesting findings were observed. On Facebook, both challenge and family were significant for all customer engagement metrics on social media.

Challenge was only positively related to the number of comments which is an understandable result. It was expected that, as the behavior stimulated by the response-inviting aspect is commenting, this variable would be the only one positively influenced as the other ones would be cannibalized. This wasn't what happened to interactivity. However, it happened for the challenge appeal. The difference, as discussed above is that the response-inviting aspect can indeed encourage different types of responses from the users. In the case of challenges, as the only way of participating is through comments, it is natural that this behavior is increased while others are decreased.

Family, on the other hand, was a positive influence in every metric, proving that it is an important and crucial appeal. The explanation behind this result could be related to the fact of relatability and identification. It is easy to establish connections with users through the thematic of family, once it is one of the most powerful memories and it is a big part of one's life. The great majority of the fans are women between the age of 35 to 44 that, most probably, are moms interested in the education of their children. Consequently, the topic of family is also of their interest and it is close to their hearts.

The metric that was influenced by more appeals were the reactions. Challenge, family, humor, pride and sad were those appeals and in exception from challenge, all the remaining ones had a positive influence on the number of reactions. Interestingly, these appeals can be easily related to the options for reactions on Facebook. For instance, humor is translated as the *Haha* reaction and sad by the *Sad* one. In addition, family and pride can both be associated to the love feeling represented by the *Love* reaction, which through the reading of the sample from Facebook, was one of the most frequent reaction. These results also prove that, in fact, users perceive the main appeal of the post as they have associated them to corresponding reactions as suggested by the framework of Wagner et al. (2017).

Parenting was only significant on the comments model and had a negative influence on this variable.

In summary and in response to the third research question, the post appeals that have a positive effect on customer engagement can be seen on Table 1.

Table 1. The impact of each post appeal on the dependent variables

	Facebook				Instagram
	Likes	Reactions	Comments	Shares	Likes
Challenge	(-)	(-)	(+)	(-)	-
Family	(+)	(+)	(+)	(+)	(+)
Humor	-	(+)	-	-	-
Pride	-	(+)	-	-	-
Sad	-	(+)	-	-	-
Parenting	-	-	(-)	-	-

(-) post appeals with a negative effect; (+) post appeals with a positive affect

A frequency analysis was performed in order to analyze if the post appeals with a positive effect on customer engagement were the most frequently used as formulated on the fourth research question. This study reports mixed results depending on the type of SNS. On Facebook, more than half of the post are only about two topics: education and parenting. As stated previously, the second one is related to the decrease on the number of comments. Additionally, family, which the only appeal that impacts positively all customer engagement metrics, is solely used 9.6% of the times, which is reasonably low. Humor and pride are also seldom used. Sad, which accounts for less than 1% also proved to be positively related with the number of reactions. It could be though by brands that using sad emotions is prejudicial for customer engagement, however, when used properly, it can have a positive impact. Additionally, the challenge appeal which is the most important variable in the comments model, meaning that it is the most powerful factor, is barely used. Towards these findings, it could be argued that brands could be more data driven and should include the study of post appeal on their analysis. Moreover, making use of the appeals that are similar to reactions is also a behavior that could be beneficial to improve customer engagement on social media.

On Instagram, humor showed to be a positive influence on the number of likes and it is, in fact, the most used appeal. The appeals used on each SNS aren't the same, however, the one they have in common, humor, when significant, has a positive effect on both Facebook and Instagram. Thus, attention should be paid to this appeal by brands.

In terms of managerial implications, it is advised for brands and their managers to consider each SNS as independent. This is, while it is true that having presence in multiple platforms is beneficial (depending off course on the type of company and its goals), it is necessary to recognize that the same strategies or the same content won't have the same results on both platforms. For instance, if on Facebook users potentially prefer videos, on Instagram, the best way to reach the audience is through images. While on Facebook, response-inviting content seems to be relevant and have a positive impact on customer engagement, on Instagram this aspect doesn't appear to be significant. In fact, on Facebook, response-inviting was relevant for both the number of likes, reactions and comments which turns this factor into one of the most important of the framework presented in this work. For brands, this is important, once they can really focus on developing the ability of establishing a of and it will have a positive impact on most of the metrics of customer engagement on social media.

The framework proposed by this study also contributes for the literature and future research as it showed to be relevant and therefore can be applied to different situations. Additionally, it incorporates both soft and hard criterion which is an important contribution since both types of factors should be taken into consideration when studying customer engagement on social media.

CONCLUSION

The findings of this study suggest that all four factors, namely post type, time frame, message interactivity and post appeal have influence on customer engagement.

Through the results from the message interactive factor, it is important to notice that brands play a crucial role in setting the tone and the type of communication that is establish with users. This was a factor that had an influence on 3 out of 4 metrics of customer engagement on Facebook, proving its relevance. Not only brands encourage comments by posting response-inviting content but also encourage likes and reactions from users. This proves that brands should promote an open dialogue between them and customers (Mollen & Wilson, 2010) and that they should be the first showing they are open and interested in having a dialogue and caring about the opinions of customers.

Post appeal also proved to be of extreme importance. Users want to be involved and connected with brands and they want to have unique experiences. Creating such a feeling and a connection is not easy, and thus, understanding what post appeals work best in terms of customer engagement is important. From the results of this study, it is possible to conclude that family and challenge are the most salient appeals regarding Facebook. This is interesting because the challenge appeal is related to the message interactivity. In other words, it could be argued that users, indeed, like and have a positive response to content that requires their active participation. This is also in agreement with what is thought about the new role of customers as they seek for a more active role in the buying process and their desire to co-create value with the brand (Gambetti & Graffigna, 2010). Consequently, brands should definitely take these results into account and try to incorporate message interactivity in their content and make customers feel that their opinion is valued. Regarding Instagram, humor proved to be a positive influence on the number of likes which also impacted positively the number of reactions on Facebook. Thus, when significant, this appeal also stood out by being a positive influence on customer engagement. It is also important to notice, that this work contributes to enrich literature about post appeals. Traditionally, the majority of studies only distinguished between emotional or functional appeals, without incorporating the different cues within each category. This work confirms some results proposed by Wagner et al. (2017)and Wang et al. (2017) and proposes new cues that haven't been studied yet, such as parenting, motivation and sad.

Furthermore, this work showed that depending on the SNS, factors have a different impact on customer engagement, and so, the conclusions withdrawn for Facebook aren't the same for Instagram. Coelho et al. (2016) has already pointed out the potential mediating role that distinct SNSs could have on results and with the findings of this study, it is possible to corroborate its suspicion and contribute to the literature on this topic. Although every SNS such as Facebook, Instagram, Twitter and LinkedIn have a common base, the goals, the audience that brands can reach and the features within the platforms are different. Therefore, due to these aspects it is possible that the impact of certain factors can differ. Thus, this is also a managerial implication since it is important for managers and brands to understand that their strategies must be adapted for each social media or that, even having the same content on multiple platforms, it would be normal not to have the same results in terms of customer engagement.

Regarding post type, as stated before, the existent literature reports mixed results. In this study, it can be inferred that on Facebook, video is always more significant than images and thus it is recommended for brands to make use of videos. This is a conclusion that agrees with the most recent studies, which could signal that through time, videos have gained more relevance and importance within Facebook and its users. On Instagram, the implication isn't the same as the impact of video on the number of likes is negative. Thus, in order to increase customer engagement on Instagram it is recommended to brands to use images.

With respect to the time frame, the goal of this study was to identify which months had a positive effect on customer engagement. On the contrary, only months with a negative influence were identified. Given that those months were August and December, which are characterized by being a period of vacations and holidays, it could be argued that users have more online presence and activity during the work period.

Attention should be paid to the importance of the reactions as they are gaining relevance and use among users. As stated before, it can be a powerful measure for brands, as they can better understand how their customers feel and how they react towards their content and products. Additionally, as showed by this study, it was one of the metrics of customer engagement that suffered more impact from the factors included in the framework, specially by post appeals. This emphasizes its relevance as a powerful data that should be analyzed by brands. For the academic research this is also an interesting contribution since, at the time, there is barely any literature that considers the number of reactions as a metric of customer engagement on social media.

To summarize, in order for brands to increase their customer engagement, it is suggested that, on Facebook, they make use of videos, response-inviting content and utilize both family and challenge appeal. On Instagram, images should be the first option combined with the humor appeal.

FUTURE RESEARCH DIRECTIONS

This study showed that results were different between Facebook and Instagram which opens the way for questioning if other social networking sites would also have different results or if they would have a similar behavior to one of these. Thus, it is also encouraged, that future researchers study other social networking sites such as LinkedIn or Pinterest. Additionally, more evidences are needed regarding Instagram, once that there are few studies concerning customer engagement on this platform. Consequently, future work could apply the framework presented in this study to other companies on Instagram and compare the results obtained.

REFERENCES

Ahmad, N. S., Musa, R., & Harun, M. H. M. (2016). The impact of social media content marketing (SMCM) towards brand health. *Procedia Economics and Finance*, *37*, 331–336. doi:10.1016/S2212-5671(16)30133-2

Ariel, Y., & Avidar, R. (2015). *Information, Interactivity, and Social Media.*, *23*, 19.

Bagozzi, R. P., Gopinath, M., & Nyer, P. U. (1999). The role of emotions in marketing. *Journal of the Academy of Marketing Science*, *27*(2), 184–206. doi:10.1177/0092070399272005

Bowden, J. L.-H. (2009). The process of customer engagement: a conceptual framework. *Journal of Marketing Theory and Practice*, *17*(1), 63–74. doi:10.2753/MTP1069-6679170105

Carah, N., & Shaul, M. (2015). Brands and Instagram: Point, tap, swipe, glance. *Mobile Media & Communication*, *4*(1), 69–84. doi:10.1177/2050157915598180

Coelho, R. L. F., Oliveira, D. S. D., & Almeida, M. I. S. D. (2016). Does social media matter for post typology? Impact of post content on Facebook and Instagram metrics. *Online Information Review*, *40*(4), 458–471. doi:10.1108/OIR-06-2015-0176

Cvijikj, I. P., & Michahelles, F. (2013). Online engagement factors on Facebook brand pages. *Social Network Analysis and Mining*, *3*(4), 843–861. doi:10.100713278-013-0098-8

De Vries, L., Gensler, S., & Leeflang, P. S. H. (2012). Popularity of brand posts on brand fan pages: an investigation of the effects of social media marketing. *Journal of Interactive Marketing, 26*(2), 83–91. doi:10.1016/j.intmar.2012.01.003

Dessart, L., Veloutsou, C., & Morgan-Thomas, A. (2016). Capturing consumer engagement: Duality, dimensionality and measurement. *Journal of Marketing Management, 32*(5-6), 399–426. doi:10.1080/0267257X.2015.1130738

Erkan, I. (2015). Electronic word of mouth on Instagram: Customers' Engagements with Brands in Different Sectors. *International Journal of Management, Accounting, and Economics, 2*(12), 1435–1444.

Gambetti, R., & Grafigna, G. (2010). The concept of engagement: A systematic analysis of the on-going marketing debate. *International Journal of Market Research, 52*(6), 801–826. doi:10.2501/S147078531020166

Go, E., & Bortree, D. S. (2017). What and how to communicate CSR? The role of CSR fit, modality interactivity, and message interactivity on social networking sites. *Journal of Promotion Management*, 1–21.

Hollebeek, L. D., Glynn, M. S., & Brodie, R. J. (2014). Consumer brand engagement in social media: conceptualization, scale development and validation. *Journal of Interactive Marketing, 28*(2), 149–165. doi:10.1016/j.intmar.2013.12.002

Holliman, G., & Rowley, J. (2014). Business to business digital content marketing: Marketers' perceptions of best practice. *Journal of Research in Interactive Marketing, 8*(4), 269–293. doi:10.1108/JRIM-02-2014-0013

Kim, C., & Yang, S.-U. (2017). Like, comment, and share on Facebook: How each behavior differs from the other. *Public Relations Review, 43*(2), 441–449. doi:10.1016/j.pubrev.2017.02.006

Kim, J. K., & Hull, K. (2017). How fans are engaging with baseball teams demonstrating multiple objectives on Instagram. *Sport, Business, and Management International Journal (Toronto, Ont.), 7*, 216–232.

Lee, H., & Park, H. (2013). Testing the impact of message interactivity on relationship management and organizational reputation. *Journal of Public Relations Research, 25*(2), 188–206. doi:10.1080/1062726X.2013.739103

Liu, J., Li, C., Ji, Y. G., North, M., & Yang, F. (2017). Like it or not: The Fortune 500's Facebook strategies to generate users' electronic word-of-mouth. *Computers in Human Behavior, 73*, 605–613. doi:10.1016/j.chb.2017.03.068

Malthouse, E. C., Calder, B. J., Kim, S. J., & Vandenbosch, M. (2016). Evidence that user-generated content that produces engagement increases purchase behaviours. *Journal of Marketing Management, 32*(5-6), 427–444. doi:10.1080/0267257X.2016.1148066

Mollen, A., & Wilson, H. (2010). Engagement, telepresence and interactivity in online consumer experience: Reconciling scholastic and managerial perspectives. *Journal of Business Research, 63*(9-10), 919–925. doi:10.1016/j.jbusres.2009.05.014

Ngai, E. W. T., Tao, S. S. C., & Moon, K. K. L. (2015). Social media research: Theories, constructs, and conceptual frameworks. *International Journal of Information Management*, *35*(1), 33–44. doi:10.1016/j.ijinfomgt.2014.09.004

Phua, J., Jin, S. V., & Kim, J. (2017). Gratifications of using Facebook, Twitter, Instagram, or Snapchat to follow brands: The moderating effect of social comparison, trust, tie strength, and network homophily on brand identification, brand engagement, brand commitment, and membership intention. *Telematics and Informatics*, *34*(1), 412–424. doi:10.1016/j.tele.2016.06.004

Sabate, F., Berbegal-Mirabent, J., Cañabate, A., & Lebherz, P. R. (2014). Factors influencing popularity of branded content in Facebook fan pages. *European Management Journal*, *32*(6), 1001–1011. doi:10.1016/j.emj.2014.05.001

Sashi, C. M. (2012). Customer engagement, buyer-seller relationships, and social media. *Management Decision*, *50*(2), 253–272. doi:10.1108/00251741211203551

Swani, K., & Milne, G. R. (2017). Evaluating Facebook brand content popularity for service versus goods offerings. *Journal of Business Research*, *79*, 123–133. doi:10.1016/j.jbusres.2017.06.003

Swani, K., Milne, G. R., Brown, B. P., Assaf, A. G., & Donthu, N. (2017). What messages to post? Evaluating the popularity of social media communications in business versus consumer markets. *Industrial Marketing Management*, *62*, 77–87. doi:10.1016/j.indmarman.2016.07.006

Van Doorne, J., N. Lemon, K., Mittal, V., Nass, S., Pick, D., Pirner, P., & Verhoef, P. (2010). *Customer engagement behavior: theoretical foundations and research directions*.

Verhoef, P. C., Reinartz, W. J., & Krafft, M. (2010). Customer engagement as a new perspective in customer management. *Journal of Service Research*, *13*(3), 247–252. doi:10.1177/1094670510375461

Wagner, T. F., Baccarella, C. V., & Voigt, K.-I. (2017). Framing social media communication: Investigating the effects of brand post appeals on user interaction. *European Management Journal*, *35*(5), 606–616. doi:10.1016/j.emj.2017.05.002

Wang, R., Kim, J., Xiao, A., & Jung, Y. J. (2017). Networked narratives on Humans of New York: A content analysis of social media engagement on Facebook. *Computers in Human Behavior*, *66*, 149–153. doi:10.1016/j.chb.2016.09.042

KEY TERMS AND DEFINITIONS

Content Marketing: It is used to attract, acquire and engage with a well-defined public through the distribution of relevant content. The final goal is to lead to a desirable customer action which could be seen as the purchase of the product of service of the brand that employed the content marketing strategy.

Customer Engagement: Emotions and relationships customers have with brands, representing loyalty.

Post Types: Image, link and video.

This research was previously published in Managing Social Media Practices in the Digital Economy; pages 45-66, copyright year 2020 by Business Science Reference (an imprint of IGI Global).

Chapter 17
Influence of Web Attributes on Consumer Purchase Intentions

Rama Mohana Rao Katta

Department of Commerce and Management Studies, Andhra University, India

Chandra Sekhar Patro

iD https://orcid.org/0000-0002-8950-9289

Department of Management Studies, Gayatri Vidya Parishad College of Engineering (A), India

ABSTRACT

The rise in the number of households possessing computers and the ease of internet access has led to widespread acceptance of B2C e-commerce, and has rapidly evolved into a global phenomenon. The competition among e-commerce vendors is getting intensified year by year and all of them are adopting innovative and creative approaches to attract, satisfy and retain customers. Web attributes are considered as one of the key influencers of consumer purchase intentions. With the support of existing literature, an attempt is made in this research paper to identify the list of attributes of online shopping websites that influence consumers' purchase intentions. The findings of the study are based on empirical data collected using online survey method.

INTRODUCTION

Over the years, the evolution of internet as a marketing medium has become a global phenomenon, leading to a rapid escalation of e-commerce in the past decade. The rapid growth of internet has given rise to online marketing where firms can promote and enhance images of product and services through website. Internet is changing the way consumers shop and buy goods and services. Many companies have started using the Internet with the aim of cutting marketing costs, thereby reducing the price of their products and services. Customers use the Internet not only to buy the product online, but also to compare prices, product features and after sale service facilities they will receive if they purchase the product from a particular store (Shergill & Chen, 2005). Therefore, detailed product information and

DOI: 10.4018/978-1-7998-9020-1.ch017

improved service attracts more and more people and as a result, customers are shifting from traditional purchase to online purchase.

Online shopping has been on rise with the advancement of mobile technology. Adoption of e-commerce by the consumers is much faster in Tier-2 cities as compared to Tier-1 cities (Prabhudesai, 2014). The mobile apps present a new way of fostering brand loyalty within customers. Almost 41 per cent of Indian e-commerce sales are from mobile as it is the most mobilized way of shopping (Vikas, 2015). India Ranks 3rd after China and Germany in terms of increasing online shopping trend, and is expected to go high in the coming years (Reddy & Jayalaxmi, 2014). The overall Indian e-commerce industry is valued at USD 17 billion, and has been growing at a compounded annual growth rate of about 35 percent per year (PTI, 2014). The key growth drivers are greater Internet penetration, rise in the number of online shoppers and an increase in per capita income. It is estimated that India will have almost 320 million online shoppers by 2020 compared with 50 million in 2015 (Maheshwari, 2016).

The major players of Indian e-commerce industry, catering myriad needs of tangible products are Amazon, Flipkart, Snapdeal, Shopclues, etc. Similarly, Bigbasket is the most popular and leading e-retail stores in groceries department, Myntra in fashion, Babyoye in baby care, Quikr in online classifieds and the list goes on (Bose, 2015). The Travel industry comprised almost 61 per cent of the total e-commerce market (Sirohi, 2015). Other categories like apparels, computer and electronics are also fueling the overall online market growth. According to a report of PTI (2014) on an average the consumers in India spend around Rs. 6,000 each annually on online purchases and is expected to rise by 67 per cent i.e. Rs.10,000 per year by next year. About 40 million consumers purchased something online in 2014 and the number is expected to grow to 65 million with better infrastructure in terms of logistics, broadband and Internet-ready devices. Consumers increasingly being educated on how to safely shop online together with improved security technology, resulted in more consumers making online purchases.

LITERATURE REVIEW

The study focuses on the website attributes which are more frequently found in the literature. This includes: website design and quality, security and privacy, reliability and trust, website popularity, accessibility, compatibility with social media, and search engine optimization of the website. In the following paragraphs, the key website attributes are elaborated.

Website Design and Quality

Website design is one of the important factors in motivating consumers for online shopping. The quality of website design is crucial for any e-store to attract the customers. Website design describes the appeal that user interface design presents to customers (Kim & Lee, 2002). According to Ranganathan and Grandon (2002), website design represents the way in which the content is arranged in the website and positively influences purchase intention. Cho and Park (2001) found that customer satisfaction in e-commerce is related to the quality of website design. Design characteristics of a web page were found to affect consumers' online buying decision. Vijayasarathy (2004); Richard and Chandra (2005) stated that website design affects online purchase intention. Technology factors comprise the quality of the website that facilitates online transactions, and considers security, privacy, and usability to be the key attributes of website quality (Schaupp & Belanger, 2005). Anand (2007) pointed out that customized content is important in enhancing usability. Likewise, Hausman and Siekpe (2009) emphasized the importance of informational content. Search functions, download speed and navigation also improve website usability (Zeithaml, Parasuraman, & Malhotra, 2002). According to Park and Kim (2000) interaction represents the way the user can surf the web pages with maximum ease. The presentation aspect of the design represents the emotional appeal of the website, like the presence of visual aids, etc. Therefore, the design of the website, which acts as the interface, plays an important role in influencing customers' purchase intentions.

Security and Privacy

Website security is one of the factors that influence customers' online purchasing intentions. Security provided by a website refers to the safety of the computer and credit card or financial information (Bart, Shankar, Sultan, & Urban, 2005). Customers believe that the internet payment channels are not always secure and could potentially be intercepted (Jones & Vijayasarathy, 1998). This reduces the customer's level of trust, discouraging them from providing personal information and making online purchases. Ranganathan and Ganapathy (2002) emphasize the use of secure modes by online companies for transaction. Chen and Barns (2007) stated that improvement in security results in increase in trust with the online vendor. Even if retailers adhere to a scientific assessment of security and privacy based on technological solutions and legal guidelines, customers' perceived sense of privacy and security would still be necessary to create the required level of trust to enable online transactions (Patro, 2016). The protection of privacy is imperative for online transactions. Liu, Marchewka, Lu, and Yu (2004) opined that the protection of privacy signifies transaction integrity and thus influences transaction decisions. Belanger, Hiller, and Smith (2002) suggested that a privacy statement can enhance the perceived trustworthiness of e-vendors. To eliminate consumer privacy concerns, many online shopping websites have developed privacy policies.

Reliability and Trust

Reliability represents the ability of the website to fulfill orders correctly, deliver promptly, and keep personal information secure (Janda, Trocchia, & Gwinner, 2002; Kim & Lee, 2002). The importance of reliability has been emphasized by the information technology-based service. Zhu, Wymer, and Chen (2002) stated that reliability dimension has a direct positive effect on perceived service quality and customer satisfaction by electronic banking systems. Online stores must provide mistake-free service and secure online transactions to make customers feel comfortable using online shopping. According to Goode and Harris (2007), perceived online reliability as the extent to which the site consistently responds and functions as expected (without broken links, broken pages or dead-end links). Service reliability is one of the major e-service quality dimensions leading to overall customer satisfaction (Kim, Kim, & Kandampully, 2009). To attract new customers and to retain existing customers, the perceived reliability of websites is of pivotal importance (Ndubisi,2011). Trust encourages online customer purchasing activity and affects customer attitudes toward purchasing from an online store (Gefen, Karahanna, & Straub, 2003). Trust is important in developing long-term online B2C relationships (Eastlick, Lotz, & Warrington, 2006). According to Chiu, Chang, Cheng, and Fang (2009), trust is viewed as a set of specific beliefs dealing primarily with the benevolence, competence and integrity of another party. Research studies in this area indicate that trust plays a pivotal role in driving customer repurchase intentions.

Website Popularity

Popularity refers to belief of customers that a seller/website is honest and concern about its customer (Doney & Cannon, 1997). Reputation has often been associated with brand equity or organization credibility (Gosschalk & Hyde, 2005). Perceived reputation may be seen as a consequence of the interactions of business with its environment. This set of interactions between the company and its customers will be a source of information which enables customers to appreciate more deeply the quality of the offer (Yoon, Guffey, & Kijewski, 1993). Thus, popularity shows how honest the company is and how much it cares for its environment. Dholakia and Rego (1998) found that a high daily hit-rate is strongly influenced by the number of updates made to the website in the preceding three-month period. The number of links to other websites was also found to attract visitor traffic. Reputation is considered as the crucial factor affecting trust development (Li, Hess, & Valacich, 2008; Pennington, Wilcox, & Grover, 2004). This is because customers can infer the trustworthiness of a seller or a website through rating and comments in the feedback-based systems (Ba & Pavlou, 2002). Furthermore, a website or a seller must make significant investment to develop a favorable reputation and a website or a seller is reluctant to jeopardize its reputation by acting opportunistically (Teo & Liu, 2007).

Accessibility

Accessibility refers to the services and practices of online shopping websites that reduce consumer time and effort in the transaction process. Services, such as product search (Richard, 2005) and payment options (Liang & Lai, 2002) can reduce the effort consumers expend and increase online purchase intention. Seiders, Voss, Godfrey, and Grewal (2007) revealed that access convenience interacted with satisfaction in terms of influencing consumers' future intentions. One of the most significant attractions of e-shopping is perceptions of convenience (Evanschitzky, Iyer, Hesse, & Ahlert, 2004). Convenience in e-commerce refers to the practices and services of online shopping websites that reduce customer effort and time in the transaction process (Yen & Gwinner, 2003). Online shoppers will enjoy multiple forms of convenience. These include less physical effort involved, flexibility in terms of when they want to shop, easiness in responding to promotions and advertising, and simple and user-friendly websites (Soopramanien & Robertson, 2007; Suki, Ramayah, & Suki, 2008). Many of the studies in past have identified that convenience as an important factor contributing to online shopping. Convenience orientation has been widely supported as one of the motivational elements that influence customers' preferences and perception to shop online (Choudhury & Karahanna, 2008; Rohm & Swaminathan, 2004).

Compatibility with Social Media

The social relationship of consumers generated through social media significantly affects the perceived trust of consumers (Pan & Chiou, 2011). The interactions on these platforms generate social support. Social support generated through social media therefore influences trust (Weisberg, Te'eni, & Arman, 2011). In addition, more positive comments, feedback and higher ratings lead to a higher level of trust in a vendor (Ba & Pavlou 2002). The quality and quantity of information produced by customer reviews influence intention to buy through increased trust (Do-Hyung, Jumin, & Ingoo, 2007). People spend more than one third of their waking day consuming social media (Lang, 2010). Due to the advantages of social media in connecting businesses to end-consumers directly, in a timely manner and at a low cost in influencing customer perceptions and behavior (Williams & Cothrell, 2000), and in bringing together different like-minded people (Wellman & Gulia, 1999), it has become the center of attention in different industries. The much higher level of efficiency of social media compared to other traditional communication channels prompted industry leaders to state that companies must participate in Facebook, Twitter, etc., in order to succeed in online environments (Kaplan & Haenlein, 2010). Thus, more industries try to benefit from social media as they can be used to develop strategy, accept their roles in managing others' strategy or follow others' directions (Williams & Williams, 2008). In joining social media, people fulfill their need for belongingness and their need for cognition with those who have shared norms, values and interests (Gangadharbhatla, 2008; Ahmed, 2015).

Search Engine Optimization

Search Engine Optimization (SEO) is a natural or an organic way of ensuring that a website comes out on top when someone searches for a particular product or a particular keyword. Search Engine Optimization is a set of techniques used by websites in order to be better indexed by search engines (Aurélie & Amanda, 2011). Consumers, who are expressing their immediate purchasing needs using search engines, often resulting in their purchase of products and services (Batista, 2008). Business firms are quickly realizing that search engines are a prime source for these new leads and customers (Olbrich & Schultz, 2008), that's why search engines are considered to be the most dynamic marketing newest online communication channels (Barnes, 2007). SEO can take into account how search algorithms work and what exactly online customers search for, in terms of user-centered design and online customer value (McMahon & Griffy-Brown, 2009) and cost-effectiveness (Kennedy & Kennedy, 2008). The basic business constructs within the scope of website design, addressing the needs of the users could introduce an array of intricate issues because of the diversity of the potential site visitors, in terms of e-commerce activities (Falk, Sockel & Chen, 2005).

SIGNIFICANCE OF THE STUDY

It is significance to note that there is a noticeable shift from conventional shopping to e-shopping either totally or partially in many parts of the world. This kind of change in priorities of shopping options and increasing connectivity of consumers to internet necessitating a greater penetration in to the study of consumer behavior. the study of web attributes is one such area that has been identified as the factor influencing consumers purchase intentions and thereby consumers purchase decision process. The determination of key factors of e-retailer websites and their relative influence on consumers purchase intentions are necessary for designing e-retailer websites effectively and also to achieve greater consumer connectivity with websites. This study is designed to determine web attributes and their impact on consumer purchase intentions.

RESEARCH OBJECTIVE

The present study aims to identify and analyze the impact of different website attributes on the consumers' online purchase intentions.

RESEARCH FRAMEWORK AND HYPOTHESES

Online shopping has been fundamentally changing the way consumers buy the goods and services. A study on how online buyers act in an ever-changing e-marketing environment, therefore, becomes necessary. This paper investigates how the website attributes affect the online consumers' purchase intentions? The model shown in Figure 1 clearly explains how the website attributes influences the online consumers' purchase intentions.

Figure 1. Research framework

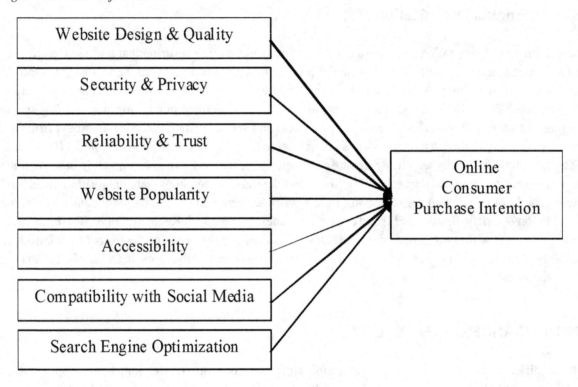

Hypotheses

The null hypotheses formulated for the study are – the consumers' online purchase intentions are not significantly impacted by website attributes such as: Website Design and Quality (H_{01}), Security and Privacy (H_{02}), Reliability and Trust (H_{03}), Website Popularity (H_{04}), Accessibility (H_{05}), Compatibility with Social Media (H_{06}), and Search Engine Optimization (H_{7}). The alternative hypotheses related to the seven website attributes are formulated as having a significant impact on the consumers' online purchase intentions. The summary of the website attributes key findings and sources through which the questionnaire constructs are derived are shown in Table 1.

Table 1. Summary of web attributes key findings and sources

Attributes	Findings	Sources
Website Design & Quality	Consumer perception of degree of quality and user friendliness in using an online website influences purchase intentions.	Kim and Lee (2002) Vijayasarathy (2004) Richard and Chandra (2005) Hausman and Siekpe (2009)
Security & Privacy	The degree to which the online shopping website is safe and protects the consumers' information has a significant impact on purchase intentions.	Bart, et al (2005) Chen and Barns (2007) Patro (2016) Liu, et al (2004)
Reliability & Trust	Consumer perception of the reliability and trust of the service provided by an online website significantly influences purchase intentions.	Goode and Harris (2007) Kim, et al (2009) Ndubisi (2011) Eastlick et al. (2006)
Website Popularity	Consumers perceptions of how well a firm take care of customers and are genuinely concerned about their welfare influences purchase intentions.	Gosschalk and Hyde (2005) Li, Hess, and Valacich (2008) Pennington, et al (2004) Teo and Liu (2007)
Accessibility	Convenience has been widely supported as one of the motivational elements that influence customers' intentions to shop online.	Richard (2005) Liang and Lai (2002) Yen and Gwinner (2003) Suki, et al. (2008)
Compatibility with Social Media	The advantages of social media in connecting businesses to consumers directly, in a timely manner and at low cost influences the consumer intentions.	Pan and Chiou (2011) Lang (2010) Ahmed (2015) Kaplan and Haenlein (2010)
Search Engine Optimization	Consumers' who express their immediate purchase needs using search engines, often result in their purchase of products and services and has become a prime source for these new leads and customers.	Olbrich and Schultz (2008) McMahon and Griffy (2009) Kennedy and Kennedy (2008) Aurélie and Amanda (2011)

METHODOLOGY

A consumer survey was carried out to study the influence of website attributes on purchase intentions towards online shopping. For the purpose, the data was collected from primary sources with the help of a structured questionnaire. The top websites in terms of turnover have been selected for the study. As such Flipkart and Amazon are the two e-retailers selected. The study was limited to the students studying their graduation and post-graduation courses in different colleges of Andhra Pradesh state, India. The questionnaires campaign was done through emails among the selected students randomly based on the data provided by the educational institutions. A total of 260 responses were considered for the analysis after the scrutiny. The respondents were asked to rate on an agreement scale. The Cronbach's alpha reliability statistics test on the standardized items was calculated for each construct which is 0.96. The results indicate internal consistencies and reliability of the research as the test valueof the sample size is above 0.70. The mean values, standard deviation and one sample t-test is computed for the data. To evaluate the relative significance of each variable on the consumer purchase intentions, ANOVA test is conducted using SPSS 20.0 software.

STATISTICAL DATA ANALYSIS

The seven attributes identified as the website factors influencing consumer purchase intentions are proved to be significant as per the findings of the study. The Table 2 shows the mean, standard deviation, and t-values of all the attributes for both Flipkart and Amazon. Table 3 shows the mean and t-values of all the seven attributes gender wise. Table 4 shows the significant f-statistic values for all website attributes that influence online shoppers' purchase intentions.

Table 2. Influence of website attributes on consumer purchase intentions

Website Attributes	Flipkart (n = 130)			Amazon (n = 130)			Total (n = 260)		
	Mean (μ)	SD	t-value	Mean (μ)	SD	t-value	Mean (μ)	SD	t-value
Website Design & Quality	**3.83**	**0.80**	**12.39**	**3.89**	**0.74**	**14.28**	**3.86**	**0.77**	**18.81**
Visually attracting & harmonious appearance	3.97	0.73	15.23	4.03	0.67	17.55	4.00	0.70	23.12
User-friendly interface with easy navigation	3.68	0.90	8.69	3.75	0.83	10.40	3.72	0.86	13.45
Rich content and Interactive mechanisms	3.58	0.94	7.10	3.66	0.87	8.69	3.62	0.90	11.13
Updates the latest information frequently	3.90	0.79	13.06	3.95	0.71	15.24	3.93	0.75	19.93
Loads all text and graphics quickly	4.03	0.66	17.86	4.07	0.62	19.51	4.05	0.64	26.42
Security & Privacy	**3.77**	**0.80**	**11.82**	**3.82**	**0.75**	**13.47**	**3.80**	**0.78**	**17.85**
Provides error-free transactions	3.65	0.87	8.58	3.72	0.81	10.08	3.68	0.84	13.16
Protects personal information	3.56	0.91	7.06	3.63	0.85	8.41	3.60	0.88	10.92
Use various payment gateway mechanism	4.10	0.63	19.81	4.12	0.58	21.92	4.11	0.61	29.48
Reliability & Trust	**3.87**	**0.76**	**13.21**	**3.92**	**0.71**	**14.96**	**3.90**	**0.74**	**19.89**
Delivers orders to right place and time	4.02	0.70	16.70	4.05	0.66	18.15	4.03	0.68	24.64
Notifies about the order status	3.92	0.79	13.26	3.98	0.73	15.24	3.95	0.76	20.11
Exchange and Replacement Policy	3.68	0.80	9.66	3.75	0.74	11.50	3.71	0.77	14.91
Website Popularity	**3.85**	**0.76**	**13.05**	**3.89**	**0.71**	**14.73**	**3.87**	**0.74**	**19.61**
Offer good services compared to others	3.92	0.72	14.58	3.97	0.67	16.50	3.95	0.70	21.94
Website image meets my expectation	3.82	0.81	11.57	3.85	0.76	12.83	3.84	0.78	17.24
Offers quality products and services	4.02	0.64	18.21	4.06	0.59	20.38	4.04	0.62	27.25
Website offers branded products	3.84	0.78	12.33	3.87	0.70	14.21	3.85	0.74	18.70
Fair relationship with users	3.65	0.86	8.55	3.71	0.83	9.72	3.68	0.85	12.92
Accessibility	**4.03**	**0.64**	**18.89**	**4.06**	**0.62**	**19.91**	**4.04**	**0.63**	**27.70**
Provides services 24-hours a day	4.26	0.52	27.57	4.30	0.51	29.17	4.28	0.51	41.09
Provides In-depth information on products	3.94	0.69	15.50	3.96	0.68	16.24	3.95	0.68	22.47
Products can be ordered easily and quickly	3.94	0.67	16.03	3.95	0.67	16.00	3.94	0.67	22.69
Categorizes products for ease of shopping	3.98	0.68	16.48	4.02	0.63	18.24	4.00	0.66	24.54

continues on following page

Table 2. Continued

Website Attributes	Flipkart (n = 130)			Amazon (n = 130)			Total (n = 260)		
	Mean (μ)	SD	t-value	Mean (μ)	SD	t-value	Mean (μ)	SD	t-value
Compatibility with Social Media	**3.72**	**0.81**	**10.27**	**3.77**	**0.76**	**11.70**	**3.75**	**0.78**	**15.52**
Keeps up with new trends	3.67	0.83	9.20	3.74	0.77	10.89	3.70	0.80	14.17
Interactive descriptions and reviews	3.65	0.82	9.06	3.71	0.78	10.32	3.68	0.80	13.69
Advantage of sweepstakes and promotions	3.75	0.81	10.50	3.78	0.76	11.81	3.77	0.78	15.77
Enable customers to share information	3.82	0.76	12.31	3.86	0.71	13.78	3.84	0.74	18.44
Search Engine Optimization	**3.83**	**0.79**	**12.07**	**3.87**	**0.73**	**13.59**	**3.85**	**0.76**	**18.13**
Provides only relevant information	3.87	0.78	12.68	3.92	0.72	14.58	3.90	0.75	19.23
Minimum effort to find required product	3.90	0.76	13.58	3.94	0.71	15.02	3.92	0.73	20.21
Provides related links to products	3.72	0.82	9.96	3.75	0.77	11.19	3.73	0.79	14.95

All t-values are significant at the 0.05 level.

Table 3. Influence of website attributes on consumer purchase intentions (gender wise)

Website Attributes	Flipkart				Amazon				Total			
	Female (n = 56)		Male (n = 74)		Female (n = 61)		Male (n = 69)		Female (n = 117)		Male (n = 143)	
	Mean (μ)	t-value	Mean (μ)	t-value	Mean (μ)	t-value	Mean (μ)	t-value	Mean (μ)	t-value	Mean (μ)	t-value
Website Design & Quality	**3.74**	**5.64**	**3.91**	**14.33**	**3.64**	**9.92**	**4.12**	**11.99**	**3.69**	**9.62**	**4.01**	**17.85**
Visually attracting and harmonious appearance	3.89	7.05	4.03	17.82	3.75	13.56	4.28	14.22	3.82	12.22	4.15	21.47
User-friendly interface with easy navigation	3.54	3.41	3.80	11.50	3.59	7.18	3.90	7.93	3.56	6.55	3.85	12.96
Rich content and Interactive mechanisms	3.46	3.00	3.68	8.03	3.44	4.97	3.86	7.41	3.45	5.20	3.76	10.76
Updates the latest information frequently	3.86	6.31	3.93	14.40	3.67	10.35	4.20	12.84	3.76	10.35	4.06	18.58
Loads all text and graphic quickly	3.95	8.43	4.09	19.90	3.75	13.56	4.35	17.56	3.85	13.77	4.22	25.49
Security & Privacy	**3.64**	**5.39**	**3.87**	**12.73**	**3.62**	**9.45**	**4.00**	**11.27**	**3.74**	**9.36**	**3.84**	**16.56**
Provides error-free transactions	3.48	3.29	3.78	10.78	3.57	6.69	3.84	7.75	3.65	6.40	3.71	12.62
Protects personal information	3.39	2.70	3.69	8.23	3.48	5.15	3.77	6.78	3.53	5.16	3.64	10.45
Use various payment gateway mechanism	4.04	10.17	4.15	19.18	3.82	16.51	4.39	19.28	4.03	16.53	4.17	26.62

continues on following page

Table 3. Continued

Website Attributes	Flipkart				Amazon				Total			
	Female (n = 56)		Male (n = 74)		Female (n = 61)		Male (n = 69)		Female (n = 117)		Male (n = 143)	
	Mean (μ)	t-value	Mean (μ)	t-value	Mean (μ)	t-value	Mean (μ)	t-value	Mean (μ)	t-value	Mean (μ)	t-value
Reliability & Trust	**3.78**	**5.99**	**3.95**	**15.23**	**3.68**	**11.37**	**4.14**	**11.95**	**3.82**	**10.47**	**3.95**	**18.38**
Delivers orders to right place and time	3.93	7.62	4.09	19.90	3.75	13.56	4.30	15.19	3.92	12.82	4.10	23.51
Notifies about the order status	3.86	6.31	3.97	14.61	3.69	11.52	4.23	12.40	3.85	10.65	4.01	18.36
Exchange and Replacement Policy	3.54	4.05	3.78	11.18	3.61	9.02	3.87	8.27	3.69	7.94	3.73	13.26
Website Popularity	**3.77**	**6.06**	**3.91**	**14.80**	**3.67**	**10.32**	**4.09**	**12.18**	**3.71**	**10.25**	**4.00**	**18.25**
Offer good services compared to others	3.91	7.41	3.93	15.08	3.69	11.52	4.22	13.95	3.79	11.85	4.07	19.80
Website image meets my expectation	3.73	5.12	3.89	14.26	3.66	9.41	4.03	9.78	3.69	8.97	3.96	15.90
Offers quality products and services	3.96	8.93	4.07	19.22	3.75	13.56	4.33	18.91	3.85	14.29	4.20	26.13
Website offers branded products	3.77	5.70	3.89	14.26	3.67	10.35	4.04	10.92	3.72	9.88	3.97	17.08
Fair relationship with users	3.46	3.17	3.78	11.18	3.56	6.74	3.84	7.36	3.51	6.25	3.81	12.33
Accessibility	**4.02**	**10.32**	**4.04**	**17.40**	**3.80**	**15.13**	**4.34**	**16.57**	**3.99**	**16.27**	**4.12**	**23.95**
Provides services 24-hours a day	4.20	15.48	4.31	24.20	4.13	25.96	4.67	22.38	4.27	25.96	4.46	34.60
Provides In-depth information on products	3.95	8.43	3.93	14.40	3.69	11.52	4.20	13.52	3.89	12.89	3.99	19.17
Products can be ordered easily and quickly	3.96	8.93	3.92	14.56	3.69	11.52	4.17	13.06	3.90	13.35	3.96	18.90
Categorize products for ease of shopping	3.95	8.43	4.00	16.43	3.69	11.52	4.30	17.32	3.91	12.89	4.05	23.13
Compatibility with Social Media	**3.61**	**4.49**	**3.81**	**11.87**	**3.64**	**9.13**	**3.89**	**8.43**	**3.62**	**8.40**	**3.85**	**13.70**
Keeps up with new trends	3.50	3.58	3.80	11.50	3.62	8.36	3.84	7.75	3.56	7.31	3.82	12.93
Interactive descriptions and reviews	3.48	3.51	3.78	11.18	3.57	7.25	3.83	7.71	3.53	6.85	3.80	12.77
Advantage of sweepstakes and promotions	3.66	4.79	3.81	11.84	3.66	9.41	3.90	8.35	3.66	8.78	3.85	13.60
Enable customers to share information	3.79	6.08	3.85	12.95	3.69	11.52	4.01	9.93	3.74	10.64	3.93	15.48

continues on following page

Table 3. Continued

Website Attributes	Flipkart				Amazon				Total			
	Female (n = 56)		Male (n = 74)		Female (n = 61)		Male (n = 69)		Female (n = 117)		Male (n = 143)	
	Mean (μ)	t-value	Mean (μ)	t-value	Mean (μ)	t-value	Mean (μ)	t-value	Mean (μ)	t-value	Mean (μ)	t-value
Search Engine Optimization	**3.76**	**5.75**	**3.88**	**13.13**	**3.67**	**10.71**	**4.05**	**10.26**	**3.72**	**10.02**	**3.96**	**15.83**
Provides only relevant information	3.82	6.08	3.91	14.08	3.69	11.52	4.13	11.20	3.75	10.49	4.01	17.03
Minimum effort to find required product	3.86	6.81	3.93	13.80	3.69	11.52	4.16	11.81	3.77	11.31	4.04	17.53
Provides related links to products	3.61	4.37	3.80	11.50	3.64	9.10	3.86	7.79	3.62	8.26	3.83	12.94

All t-values are significant at the 0.05 level.

Table 4. ANOVA test (significant website attributes)

Website Attributes	F-Statistic	Sig.
Website Design & Quality	*12.614*	*.000*
Loads all text and graphics quickly	23.388	.000
Visually attracting and harmonious appearance	14.840	.000
Updates the latest information frequently	10.855	.001
Rich content and Interactive mechanisms	7.749	.006
User-friendly interface with easy navigation	7.048	.008
Security & Privacy	*7.176*	*.008*
Use various payment gateway mechanism	22.099	.000
Provides error-free transactions	7.419	.007
Protects personal information	7.223	.008
Reliability & Trust	*8.557*	*.004*
Delivers orders to right place and time	19.289	.000
Notifies about the order status	12.507	.000
Exchange and Replacement Policy	7.093	.008
Website Popularity	*11.073*	*.001*
Offers quality products and services	21.216	.000
Offer good services compared to others	10.435	.001
Fair relationship with users	8.251	.004
Website image meets my expectation	7.580	.006
Website offers branded products	7.425	.007

continues on following page

Table 4. Continued

Website Attributes	F-Statistic	Sig.
Accessibility	*12.493*	*.000*
Provides services 24-hours a day	27.994	.000
Categorize products for ease of shopping	17.941	.000
Provides In-depth information on products	8.992	.003
Products can be ordered easily and quickly	7.206	.008
Compatibility with Social Media	*5.518*	*.020*
Interactive descriptions and reviews	7.726	.006
Keeps up with new trends	6.614	.011
Enable customers to share information	4.573	.033
Advantage of sweepstakes and promotions	4.042	.045
Search Engine Optimization	*5.431*	*.021*
Minimum effort to find required product	9.180	.003
Provides only relevant information	8.029	.005
Provides related links to products	4.200	.041

The design and quality of the website is assessed based on the rating of the respondents on the five variables viz., visually attracting and harmonious appearance, user-friendly interface with easy navigation, rich content and interactive mechanisms, updates the latest information frequently, and loads all text and graphics quickly. All the five variables found to be significant as per results of f-statistic. The variable 'website loads all text and graphics quickly' got highest mean value of 4.05 out of 5 followed by the variables 'visually attracting and harmonious appearance (μ=4.00)', 'updates the latest information frequently (μ=3.93)', and 'user-friendly interface with easy navigation (μ=3.72)'. The variable 'Rich content and interactive mechanisms' got the lowest mean value of 3.62. The overall mean value of the factor website design and quality is 3.86 out of 5. The mean value of this factor in case of amazon is 3.89 while the mean value of Flipkart is 3.83. Thus, amazon scored relatively higher rating compared to flipkart with regard to website design and quality. The Gender wise analysis further reveals that the male respondents gave higher rating both in the case of amazon and flipkart for the attribute website design and quality than female respondents. Therefore, the findings of the study reject the hypothesis H_{01}.

For the purpose of assessing the influence of security and privacy as website attribute on consumer purchase intentions five variables are used to obtain ratings from the selected consumers. The data obtained is tested using ANOVA and based on the f-statistic only three variables are qualified. The variables 'website has a privacy statement', and 'website uses a certified transaction platform', are found to be not significant and hence they were dropped from the study. The three variables viz., website provides error-free transactions, protects personal information, use various payment gateway mechanism, are qualified as the values are positively significant. The variable 'website uses various payment gateway mechanism' got highest mean value of 4.11, followed by 'provides error-free transactions (μ=3.68)'. The variable website protects personal information got a lowest mean value of 3.60. The overall mean value of the attribute security and privacy is 3.80. The mean value of this attribute in case of amazon is 3.82 while the mean value of flipkart is 3.70. Thus, amazon scored relatively higher rating compared to flipkart with regard to security and privacy. The gender wise analysis further reveals that the male respondents gave higher rating in both the case of amazon and flipkart than female respondents for the attribute Security and Privacy. The findings of the study thus reject the null hypothesis H_{02}.

The influence of reliability and trust attribute of website on consumer purchase intentions is assessed based on the five variables and the f-statistic shows that the variables, 'instantaneous assistance to transaction problems' and 'unbiased product recommendations' are not significant and therefore they were dropped from the study. The three variables viz., delivers orders to right place and time, notifies about the order status, and exchange and replacement policy are found to be positively significant. The variable 'delivers orders to right place and time' got highest mean value of 4.03, followed by 'notifies about the order status ($\mu = 3.95$)'. And the variable exchange and replacement policy got a lowest mean value of 3.71. The overall mean value of the attribute reliability and trust is 3.90. The mean value of this attribute in case of amazon ($\mu = 3.92$) is relatively higher compared to the mean value of flipkart ($\mu = 3.87$). Further, the gender wise analysis reveals that the male respondents gave higher rating in both the case of amazon and flipkart for the attribute security and privacy. The findings of the study thus reject the hypothesis H_{03}.

The attribute website popularity is assessed based on the rating of the respondents on five variables viz., offer good services compared to others, website image meets my expectations, offers quality products and services, website offers branded products, and fair relationship with users. All the five variables found to be significant as per results of f-statistic. The variable 'offers quality products and services' got highest mean value of 4.04 followed by the variables 'offer good services compared to others ($\mu = 3.95$)', 'website offers branded products ($\mu = 3.85$)', and 'website image meets my expectations ($\mu = 3.84$)'. The variable 'fair relationship with users' got a lowest mean value of 3.68. The overall mean value of the attribute is 3.87, and the mean value in case of amazon is 3.89 while the mean value of flipkart is 3.85. Thus, amazon scored relatively higher rating compared to flipkart. The gender wise analysis reveals that the male respondents gave higher rating both in the case of amazon and flipkart than the female respondents. The findings of the study thus reject the hypothesis H_{04}.

For the purpose of assessing the influence of accessibility as website attribute on consumer purchase intentions the five variables are used to obtain ratings from the selected consumers. Based on the f-statistic test values only four variables are qualified. The variable 'timely notification of required products' is found to be not significant and hence dropped from the study. The four variables viz., provides services 24-hours a day, provides in-depth information on products, products can be ordered easily and quickly, and categorize products for ease of shopping, are qualified as the values are positively significant. The variable 'provides services 24-hours a day' got highest mean value of 4.28, followed by 'categorizes products for ease of shopping ($\mu = 4.00$)', 'provides in-depth information on products ($\mu = 3.95$)', and 'products can be ordered easily and quickly ($\mu = 3.94$)'. The overall mean value of the attribute is 4.04. The mean value in case of amazon ($\mu = 4.06$) is higher compared to flipkart ($\mu = 4.03$). The gender wise analysis further reveals that the male respondents gave higher rating in both the case of amazon and flipkart than female respondents. The finding of the study for the hypothesis H_{05} is thus rejected.

The influence of the attribute compatibility with social media on consumer purchase intentions is assessed based on five variables and the f-statistic shows that the variable 'helps to learn more about products' is not significant and therefore dropped from the study. The four variables viz.,keeps up with new trends, interactive descriptions and reviews, advantage of sweepstakes and promotions, and enable customers to share information, are found to be positively significant. The variable 'enable customers to share information' got highest mean value of 3.84, followed by 'advantage of sweepstakes and promotions

($\mu = 3.77$)', and 'keeps up with new trends ($\mu = 3.70$)'. The variable interactive descriptions and reviews got a lowest mean value of 3.68. The overall mean value of this attribute is 3.75. The mean value of this attribute in case of amazon ($\mu = 3.77$) is relatively higher compared to the mean value of flipkart ($\mu = 3.72$). Further, the gender wise analysis reveals that the male respondents gave higher rating in both the case of amazon and flipkart. The findings of the study thus reject the hypothesis H_{06}.

To assess the influence of search engine optimization as website attribute on consumer purchase intentions, the five variables are used to obtain ratings from the selected consumers. Based on the f-statistic test values only three variables are qualified. The variables 'fast and accurate search capability' and 'ease in sorting of products' are found to be not significant and hence dropped from the study. The three variables viz., provides only relevant information, minimum effort to find required product, provides related links to products are qualified as the values are positively significant. The variable 'minimum effort to find required product' got highest mean value of 3.92, followed by 'provides only relevant information ($\mu = 3.90$)' and 'provides related links to products ($\mu = 3.73$)'. The overall mean value of the attribute is 3.85. The mean value in case of amazon ($\mu = 3.87$) is higher compared to flipkart ($\mu = 3.83$). The gender wise analysis further reveals that the male respondents gave higher rating in both the case of amazon and flipkart than female respondents. The finding of the study for the hypothesis H_{07} is thus rejected.

CONCLUSION

Website attributes will play an important role in influencing the purchase intentions of the consumers shopping online. The seven website attributes identified for the study such as: website design and quality, security and privacy, reliability and trust, website popularity, accessibility, compatibility with social media, and search engine optimization are found to be significant as per the findings of the study. The study therefore satisfied the alternative hypothesis in the case of all the seven website attributes. An analysis of relative significance on the seven identified factors reveals that accessibility is the most influencing factor which secured relatively highest mean value of 4.04. Reliability and trust is found as the second most influencing factor with a mean value of 3.90, while website popularity is in third place with a mean value of 3.87 as the factor influencing purchase intention of the online shoppers. The factor compatibility with social media got relatively low mean value ($\mu=3.75$). Thus, the findings of the study rejects the null hypotheses formulated against each of the identified website attributes. Accessibility and Reliability, and Trust are the two factors in the top positions respectively for both amazon and flipkart. The third factor of amazon was share by two factors such as website popularity and website design and quality. The third place in case of Flipkart is website popularity.

The study concludes therefore that the companies in online retailing should give special focus on the identified seven factors to influence the purchase intentions of the online shopper. They should invest adequately in research and development to create new ways of enhancing accessibility and build positive website popularity. The other factors identified should also be given special focus because the consumers perceive the quality of the website based on the performance related to all attributes though, the influence of each attribute vary in influencing the perceptions. The marketer of online retailers need to ensure positive perceptions of service quality and relatively better perceptions compared to competitors.

Online shopping is expanding its wings worldwide and connecting larger population year by year. Many marketing experts are describing online marketing as the future of the industry. Therefore, the competition in this business domain is going to be intense and each player needs to become dynamic and unique in attracting and retaining customers to gain competitive advantage. Website attributes play pivotal role in influencing purchase intentions. Thus, providing superior quality website attributes may give distinctive advantage to online marketers.

FUTURE RESEARCH DIRECTIONS

The study was about the influence of web attributes on the consumer purchase intentions. As the e-retailers are facing stiff competition, the study focuses on the various web attributes influencing the consumers purchase intentions to shop online. However, the study tried to identify the main attributes influencing the online consumer and differs depending on what products they purchased. Therefore, this research it limited itself to products only. This research is expected to help other researchers to concern deeper about the dimensions which influence the consumers purchase intentions in web shopping. The results of the study could be used by the researchers and practitioners for conducting future studies in the similar area. It would encourage thinking more about the various benefits and risks that affect customers to shop online and further benefit to the e-retailer.

REFERENCES

Ahmed, M. (2015). Is Social Media the Biggest Influencer of Buying Decisions? *Socialmediatoday. com*. Retrieved July 14, 2016, from http://www.socialmediatoday.com/marketing/masroor/2015-05-28/social-media-biggest-influencer-buying-decisions#sthash.wow60EN3.dpuf

Anand, A. (2007). E-satisfaction - A comprehensive framework. In *Proceedings of 2ⁿᵈ International Conference on internet and web applications and services (ICIW'07)* (pp. 13-19:55-60).

Aurélie, G., & Amanda, R. (2011). Web site search engine optimization: A case study of Fragfornet. *Library Hi Tech News*, *28*(6), 6–13. doi:10.1108/07419051111173874

Ba, S., & Pavlou, P. A. (2002). Evidence of the effect of trust building technology in electronic markets: Price premiums and buyer behavior. *Management Information Systems Quarterly*, *26*(3), 243–268. doi:10.2307/4132332

Barnes, T. (2007). RSS: Marketing newest communication channel. *Journal of Website Promotion*, *1*(4), 15–30. doi:10.1300/J238v01n04_03

Bart, Y., Shankar, V., Sultan, F., & Urban, G. L. (2005). Are the drivers and role of online trust the same for all web sites and consumers? A large-scale exploratory empirical study. *Journal of Marketing*, *69*(4), 133–152. doi:10.1509/jmkg.2005.69.4.133

Batista, H. (2008). Techniques for growing small search engine marketing firms. *SEMJ.org*. Retrieved June 21, 2016, from http://www.semj.org/documents/SEMJ_2008_supplemental.pdf

Belanger, F., Hiller, J. S., & Smith, W. J. (2002). Trustworthiness in electronic commerce: The role of privacy, security, and site attributes. *The Journal of Strategic Information Systems*, *11*(3-4), 245–270. doi:10.1016/S0963-8687(02)00018-5

Bose, P. (2015). E-Commerce Industry in India worth $13.5 Billion in 2014: Will Cross $16 Billion in 2015. *Dazeinfo.com*. Retrieved June 14, 2016, from http://dazeinfo.com/2015/03/19/e-commerce-industry-india-worth-13-5-billion-2014-will-cross-16-billion-2015

Chen, Y. H., & Barns, S. (2007). Initial Trust and Online Behavior. *Industrial Management & Data Systems*, *107*(1), 21–36. doi:10.1108/02635570710719034

Chiu, C. M., Chang, C. C., Cheng, H. L., & Fang, Y. H. (2009). Determinants of customer repurchase intention in online shopping. *Online Information Review*, *33*(4), 761–784. doi:10.1108/14684520910985710

Cho, N., & Park, S. (2001). Development of electronic commerce user – consumer satisfaction index (ECUSI) for internet shopping. *Industrial Management & Data Systems*, *101*(8), 400–405. doi:10.1108/EUM0000000006170

Choudhury, V., & Karahanna, E. (2008). The relative advantage of electronic channels: A multidimensional view. *Management Information Systems Quarterly*, *32*(1), 179–200.

Dholakia, U. M., & Rego, L. L. (1998). What makes commercial web page popular: an empirical study of online shopping. In *Proceedings of 32nd Hawaii International Conference on System Sciences* (pp. 5-8). New York, NY: IEEE.

Do-Hyung, E., Jumin, L., &Ingoo, H. (2007). The effect of on-line consumer reviews on consumer purchasing intention: the moderating role of involvement. *International Journal of Electronic Commerce*, *11*(4), 125-148.

Doney, P. M., & Cannon, J. P. (1997). An examination of the nature of trust in buyer–seller relationships. *Journal of Marketing*, *61*(2), 35–51. doi:10.2307/1251829

Eastlick, M. A., Lotz, S. L., & Warrington, P. (2006). Understanding online B-to-C relationships: An integrated model of privacy concerns, trust, and commitment. *Journal of Business Research*, *59*(8), 877–886. doi:10.1016/j.jbusres.2006.02.006

Evanschitzky, H., Iyer, G. R., Hesse, J., & Ahlert, D. (2004). E-satisfaction: A re-examination. *Journal of Retailing*, *80*(3), 239–247. doi:10.1016/j.jretai.2004.08.002

Falk, L., Sockel, H., & Chen, K. (2005). E-commerce and consumer's expectations: What makes a website work? *Journal of Website Promotion*, *1*(1), 65–75. doi:10.1300/J238v01n01_06

Gangadharbhatla, H. (2008). Facebook me: Collective self-esteem, need to belong and internet self-efficacy as predictors of the I-generations attitudes toward social networking sites. *Journal of Interactive Advertising*, *8*(2), 5–15. doi:10.1080/15252019.2008.10722138

Gefen, D., Karahanna, E., & Straub, D. W. (2003). Trust TAM in online shopping: An integrated model. *Management Information Systems Quarterly*, *27*(1), 51–90.

Goode, M. M. H., & Harris, L. C. (2007). Online behavioral intentions: An empirical investigation of antecedents and moderators. *European Journal of Marketing*, *41*(5/6), 512–536. doi:10.1108/03090560710737589

Gosschalk, B., & Hyde, A. (2005). The business world will never be the same-The contribution of research to corporate governance post-Enron. *International Journal of Market Research*, *47*(1), 29–44.

Hausman, A. V., & Siekpe, J. S. (2009). The effect of web interface features on consumer online purchase intentions. *Journal of Business Research*, *62*(1), 5–13. doi:10.1016/j.jbusres.2008.01.018

Janda, S., Trocchia, P. J., & Gwinner, K. P. (2002). Customer perceptions of internet retail service quality. *International Journal of Service Industry Management*, *13*(5), 412–431. doi:10.1108/09564230210447913

Jones, J. M., & Vijayasarathy, L. R. (1998). Internet consumer catalog shopping: Findings from an exploratory study and directions for future research. *Internet Research*, *8*(4), 322–330. doi:10.1108/10662249810231069

Kaplan, A. M., & Haenlein, M. (2010). Users of the world, unite! The challenges and opportunities of social media. *Business Horizons*, *53*(1), 59–68. doi:10.1016/j.bushor.2009.09.003

Kennedy, K., & Kennedy, B. (2008). A small company's dilemma: Using search engines effectively for corporate sales. *Management Research News*, *31*(10), 737–745. doi:10.1108/01409170810908499

Kim, J., & Lee, J. (2002). Critical design factors for successful e-commerce systems. *Behaviour & Information Technology*, *21*(3), 185–199. doi:10.1080/0144929021000009054

Kim, J. H., Kim, M., & Kandampully, J. (2009). Buying environment characteristics in the context of e-service. *European Journal of Marketing*, *43*(9/10), 1188–1204. doi:10.1108/03090560910976438

Lang, B. (2010). *Ipsos OTX study: People spend more than half their day consuming media.* Retrieved July 14. 2016, from http://www.thewrap.com/node/21005

Li, X., Hess, T. J., & Valacich, J. S. (2008). Why do we trust new technology? A study of initial trust formation with organizational information systems. *The Journal of Strategic Information Systems*, *17*(1), 39–71. doi:10.1016/j.jsis.2008.01.001

Liang, T. P., & Lai, H. J. (2002). Effect of store design on consumer purchases: Van empirical study of online bookstores. *Information & Management*, *39*(6), 431–444. doi:10.1016/S0378-7206(01)00129-X

Liu, C., Marchewka, J. T., Lu, J., & Yu, C. S. (2004). Beyond concern: A privacy-trust-behavioral model of electronic commerce. *Information & Management*, *42*(1), 127–142. doi:10.1016/j.im.2004.01.002

Maheshwari, R. (2016). *Indian ecommerce market to grow fastest globally over 3 years: Morgan Stanley.* Retrieved September 14, 2016, from http://economictimes.indiatimes.com/articleshow/51031652.cms?utm_source=contentofinterst&utm_medium=text&utm_campaign=cppst

McMahon, D., & Griffy-Brown, C. (2009). Developing an effective and affordable search engine marketing strategy for nonprofits. *International Journal of Internet Marketing and Advertising*, *5*(1-2), 113–130. doi:10.1504/IJIMA.2009.021953

Ndubisi, N. O. (2011). Conflict handling, trust and commitment in outsourcing relationship: A Chinese and Indian study. *Industrial Marketing Management*, *40*(1), 109–117. doi:10.1016/j.indmarman.2010.09.015

Olbrich, R., & Schultz, C. (2008). *Search engine marketing and click fraud* (Research Paper No. 5). FernUniversität, Hagen. Retrieved July 10, 2016, from http://www.fernuni-hagen.de/MARKETING/ material/downloads/ no5_web.pdf

Pan, L. Y., & Chiou, J. S. (2011). How much can you trust online information? Cues for perceived trustworthiness of consumer-generated online information. *Journal of Interactive Marketing, 25*(2), 67–74. doi:10.1016/j.intmar.2011.01.002

Park, J., & Kim, J. (2000). Contextual navigation aids for two World Wide Web systems. *International Journal of Human-Computer Interaction, 12*(2), 193–217. doi:10.1207/S15327590IJHC1202_3

Patro, C. S. (2016). Attitudes of E-Shoppers and Non E-Shoppers towards E-Shopping: A Comparative Study. *International Journal of Cyber Behavior, Psychology and Learning, 6*(2), 95–107. doi:10.4018/ IJCBPL.2016040106

Pennington, R., Wilcox, H. D., & Grover, V. (2004). The role of system trust in business-to-consumer transactions. *Journal of Management Information Systems, 20*(3), 197–226. doi:10.1080/07421222.20 03.11045777

Prabhudesai, A. (2014). *Indian E-Commerce Stats: Online Shoppers &Avg Order Values to Double In Next 2 Years.* Retrieved June 14, 2016, from http://trak.in/tags/business/2014/04/04/indian-e-commerce-growth-stats

PTI. (2014). *Indian online shopping to increase to 67 percent in 2015.* Retrieved June 14, 2016, from http://tech.firstpost.com/news-analysis/indian-online-shopping-to-increase-to-67-percent-in-2015-report-247318.html

Ranganathan, C., & Ganapathy, S. (2002). Key dimensions of business-to-consumer websites. *Information & Management, 39*(6), 457–465. doi:10.1016/S0378-7206(01)00112-4

Ranganathan, C., & Grandon, E. (2002). An exploratory examination of factors affecting online sales. *Journal of Computer Information Systems, 42*(3), 87–93.

Reddy, K. S. L., & Jayalaxmi, S. (2014). A comparative study of Traditional shopping Vs Online shopping. *ANNQUEST, 3*(1), 37–51.

Richard, M. O. (2005). Modeling the impact of internet atmospherics on surfer behavior. *Journal of Business Research, 58*(12), 1632–1642. doi:10.1016/j.jbusres.2004.07.009

Richard, M. O., & Chandra, R. (2005). A model of consumer web navigational behavior: Conceptual development and application. *Journal of Business Research, 58*(8), 1019–1029. doi:10.1016/j. jbusres.2004.04.001

Rohm, A. J., & Swaminathan, V. (2004). A typology of online shoppers based on shopping motivations. *Journal of Business Research, 57*(7), 748–758. doi:10.1016/S0148-2963(02)00351-X

Schaupp, L. C., & Belanger, F. (2005). A conjoint analysis of online consumer satisfaction. *Journal of Electronic Commerce Research, 6*(2), 95–111.

Seiders, K., Voss, G. B., Godfrey, A. L., & Grewal, D. (2007). SERVCON: Development and Validation of a Multidimensional Service Convenience Scale. *Journal of the Academy of Marketing Science, 35*(1), 144–156. doi:10.100711747-006-0001-5

Shergill, G. S., & Chen, Z. (2005). Web-based shopping: Consumers' attitudes towards online shopping in New Zealand. *Journal of Electronic Commerce Research, 6*(2), 79–94.

Sirohi, G. (2015). *E-Commerce (Online Shopping) Industry in India To Cross 1 Lakh Crore In 2015*. Retrieved July 10, 2016, from https://www.linkedin.com/pulse/e-commerce-online-shopping-industry-india-cross-1-lakh-gulshan-sirohi

Soopramanien, G. R., & Robertson, A. (2007). Adoption and usage of online shopping: An empirical analysis of the characteristics of 'buyers' 'browsers' and 'non-internet shoppers'. *Journal of Retail Customer Service, 14*(1), 73–82. doi:10.1016/j.jretconser.2006.04.002

Suki, N. M., Ramayah, T., & Suki, N. M. (2008). Internet shopping acceptance: Examining the influence of intrinsic versus extrinsic motivations. *International Journal of Direct Marketing, 2*(2), 97–110. doi:10.1108/17505930810881752

Teo, T. S. H., & Liu, J. (2007). Consumer trust in electronic commerce in the United States, Singapore and China. *Omega, 35*(1), 22–38. doi:10.1016/j.omega.2005.02.001

Vijayasarathy, L. R. (2004). Predicting consumer intentions to use on-line shopping: The case for an augmented technology acceptance model. *Information & Management, 41*(6), 747–762. doi:10.1016/j.im.2003.08.011

Vikas, S. N. (2015). *41% of India E-commerce sales is from Mobile; Mobile wallet usage surging: Meeker's 2015 Internet Trends*. Retrieved June 10, 2016, from https://www.meekers.com/41-percent-of-India-E-commerce-sales-is-from-Mobile-;-Mobile-wallet-usage-surging-Meeker's-2015-Internet-Trends

Weisberg, J., Te'eni, D., & Arman, L. (2011). Past purchase and intention to purchase in e-commerce: The mediation of social presence and trust. *Internet Research, 21*(1), 82–96. doi:10.1108/10662241111104893

Wellman, B. (1999). The network community: An introduction to networks in the global village. In *Networks in the global village*. Boulder, CO: Westview.

Williams, L., & Cothrell, J. (2000). Four smart ways to run online communities. *Sloan Management Review, 41*, 81–91.

Williams, T., & Williams, R. (2008). Adopting social media: Are we leaders, managers or followers? *Communication World, 25*(4), 34–37.

Yen, H. J. R., & Gwinner, K. P. (2003). Internet retail customer loyalty: The mediating role of relational benefits. *International Journal of Service Industry Management, 14*(5), 483–500. doi:10.1108/09564230310500183

Yoon, S. J. (2002). The antecedents and consequences of trust in online purchase decisions. *Journal of Interactive Marketing, 16*(2), 47–63. doi:10.1002/dir.10008

Zeithaml, V. A., Parasuraman, A., & Malhotra, A. (2002). Service quality delivery through web sites: A critical review of extant knowledge. *Journal of the Academy of Marketing Science*, *30*(4), 362–375. doi:10.1177/009207002236911

Zhu, F. X., Wymer, W., & Chen, I. (2002). IT-based services and service quality in consumer banking. *International Journal of Service Industry Management*, *13*(1), 69–90. doi:10.1108/09564230210421164

Chapter 18
Factors Influencing Intention of Facebook Fans of Companies to Convert into Actual Buyers

Hsiu-Yuan Wang
Department of Hospitality Management, Chung Hua University, Hsinchu City, Taiwan

Jian-Hong Wang
School of Computer Science and Engineering, Yulin Normal University, Yulin, Guangxi, China

Hsing-Wen Wang
Department of Business Administration, National Changhua University of Education, Changhua County, Taiwan

Chi-Chun Chen
Department of Electronic Engineering, National Chin-Yi University of Technology, Taichung, Taiwan

ABSTRACT

Recently, a new wave of business opportunities has emerged by integrating social media and commerce. Although many hospitality organizations have considered online social communities as potential channels for promotion, most of them have failed to obtain sales from community members. Therefore, the purpose of this study was to propose and examine a new research model that can capture cognitive- and affective-based trust elements influencing fans' behavioral intention to purchase by affecting their firm commitment. A survey of 393 Facebook participants found strong support for the model. The results indicated that Facebook fans' perceptions of firm commitment could be a strong predictor of their buying intention. Factors of building cognitive trust (i.e. perceived reputation, perceived ability, and information quality) as well as affective trust (i.e. perceived benevolence, perceived integrity and perceived social presence) were the critical components significantly influencing fans' firm commitment. Theoretical and practical implications of the results are discussed.

DOI: 10.4018/978-1-7998-9020-1.ch018

1. INTRODUCTION

Social networking sites (SNSs), defined as web-based services, have been around since the mid-90's, but in recent years, social networking has exploded across the Internet, providing people with three major capabilities (Boyd & Ellison, 2007): First, the capability to build a public or semi-public profile; second, the capability to find a list of other users with whom a connection is shared; and third, the capability of individuals to observe and track their connections as well as those made by others. Popular SNSs include Facebook, MySpace, Friendster, Twitter, and so on.From 2012 to 2019, Facebook surged past MySpace to become the most popular social network (Nations, 2013). Due to the continuous innovation of social networking technology (Mitra et al., 2007; Long & Siau, 2007). According to Rouse et al. (2010), a Facebook "fan" is a user who "likes" a particular page. If users choose to click "likes" for a page, they are then able to get updates from that page's administrator through status updates, link posts and event invitations. Fans display lists of pages they have "liked" on their profile, under the "interests" section of their information tab. Furthermore, a Facebook company fan page is a Facebook page specific to a business/organization, as opposed to a personal page (Squidoo, 2013). Those who launch a Facebook company fan page do so in order to market a business or to collect interested fans in one place online. Then once a hospitality firm makes a Face book company fan page, it can communicate to all fans regularly on their personal feed.

In today's highly competitive environment, hospitality practitioners have responded to the opportunities offered by the Internet by reducing costs and providing real time information to promote and sell their products to consumers (Corritore et al., 2003; Kim et al., 2013; Pernsteiner & Rauseo, 2000). SNSs are having a great impact on the development of businesses. To stay competitive and increase revenue, organizations, especially hospitality organizations, are increasingly learning to exploit the potential of SNSs, such as Facebook, for marketing and growth (Hutchings,2012). Therefore, many hospitality firms create and make use of their own Facebook company fan page in order to collect fans and maintain their relationships with their fans. As a practitioner, through the Facebook fan/business page, you can put the photos, videos, articles, links, discussions, events, news, offers, and all forms of information-related to your business in one place, your Facebook business page. Your customers will get updated with the latest offers and news related to your products/services. You can directly interact with your customers, ask for their feedback/suggestions about your products/services and also create a pre-launch offer on your page to test your product or service with them before launching it on the market. You will thereby get genuine feedback from your loyal customers.

Because the value of social networking continues to increase, a new wave of opportunities has resulted from the integration of social media and commerce. Hospitality organizations are learning how to embrace social media and combine it with commerce to fully monetize their online initiatives. Although many organizations have considered online social communities as potential channels for promotion, most of them have failed to obtain sales from community members (Shan et al., 2005). This phenomenon raises questions, such as: What factors will actually contribute to fans' intention to convert into actual buyers? Understanding the factors which influence fans' intention to transform into online buyers is indispensable for achieving the successful implementation of the company fan page. The answers to the question related to the relevant factors may be useful for hospitality organizations to develop broader relationships with their fans, facilitate hospitality firms in their endeavor to benefit from their fans and finally increase their sales.

While some studies have examined the influence of Facebook in various ways (Baek et al., 2011; Mehdizadeh, 2010; Tong et al., 2008; Zhao et al., 2008), limited efforts have been made to explore factors influencing hospitality company fans' intentions to convert into actual buyers in the context of Facebook. Related research asserts that fan commitment to a virtual community is important for cyber firms to gain benefits from the community (Gupta & Kim, 2007). Also, researchers in marketing have pointed out that trust leads to a high level of firm commitment, i.e. a strong desire to maintain a relationship (Crosby et al., 1990; Crosby et al., 1996). One useful perspective posits that two major types of trust can be recognized: cognitive trust and affective trust (McAllister, 1995). Therefore, the purposes of this study are twofold: 1. to propose and examine a new research model that can capture cognitive- and affective-based trust elements influencing fans' firm commitment; and 2. to investigate the impact of commitment on fans' behavioral intention to purchase.

2. Problem Formulation

2.1 Social Commerce (s-commerce)

S-commerce was officially created by David Beach (Beach, 2005), the product manager of Yahoo! Shopping. Yahoo! Shopping released two essential applications, Shop sphere and Pick Lists, to enhance the company's core shopping search capabilities. The Shop sphere is a place to look for interesting and useful products thematically arranged into Pick Lists by other shoppers. Pick Lists are lists of products on any topic. With Pick Lists, customers can share their knowledge about products which they have investigated, for the advantage of the community. Customers can see a Pick List in the Shop sphere, rank it and comment on it. The implementation of these two applications offers an effective source for shoppers by sharing the shopping experience with other members of the community.

The emergence of s-commerce takes us back to the beginning of electronic commerce (e-commerce) ten years ago. At that time, e-commerce illustrated both a new approach and a new channel for communicating brand promise to a customer. In recent years, many researchers have offered definitions for s-commerce. For example, Kim et al. (Kim & Park, 2013) stated that s-commerce is a type of online business that integrates social media (e.g., SNSs) with e-commerce to offer daily deals for customers. Stephen et al. (Stephen & Toubia, 2010) considered s-commerce as a relation- and group-based open online market. Marsden (Marsden, 2010) proposed that s-commerce is a portion of e-commerce operating through social media to facilitate the online shopping experience and enhance social interactions. Therefore, s-commerce is similar to e-commerce, and offers a new way of doing business. It is changing how customers purchase and also reshaping customer expectations about their interactions with firms. Poston et al. (Poston & Kettinger, 2014) observe that following a mindful introduction process reaps some of the benefits of experimentation, such as greater stakeholder satisfaction and organization-wide learning and understanding of the technology's potential.

Although the growth of s-commerce has been rapid, only a limited number of studies have tried to investigate the influence of s-commerce on marketing. Among these relatively few studies, Trusov et al. (2009) conducted a search to understand the effect of word-of-mouth (WOM) marketing on member growth at an Internet SNS, and compared it with traditional marketing vehicles. Their findings demonstrated the effectiveness of WOM made by the SNS both in the short and long run. Stephen et al. (Stephen & Toubia, 2010) examined the economic value implications of a social network for sellers in a large online s-commerce marketplace. The results presented three points: First, allowing sellers to connect creates substantial economic value. Second, the network's value lies mainly in making shops more accessible to customers browsing the marketplace. Third, the sellers who benefit the most from the network are not necessarily those who are central to the network, but rather those whose accessibility is most enhanced by the network. Weijun et al. (2011) presented a review of s-commerce studies and investigated the rise of s-commerce by utilizing documentary and comparative methods; they analyzed s-commerce and explored the possible future of s-commerce to offer an essential understanding of s-commerce.

Based on the above, hospitality firms must know that their consumers are moving online in increasing numbers and that in the realm of SNSs, these consumers are likely affected by many SNSs devoted to the discussion of purchasing products and services. Hospitality or tourism managers should take the lead in understanding the emerging technologies and then applying them to promote their deals.

2.2 Theories of Trust

The extensive adoption of online shopping, despite the implied risks, depends not only on the predictable advantage they provide, but also on customers' trust in online commerce. Matemba and Maiseli (2018) reveal that perceived availability of merchant support, convenience and social influence preference promote consumers' stickiness behaviors to wallet. In addition, perceived security insignificantly moderates the relationships between convenience/social influence and consumers' stickiness. Beldad et al. (2010) conducted a literature review to understand more about people's trust in, and adoption of, computer-mediated services. Traditionally, trust can be conceptualized from two different perspectives (Beldad et al., 2010). The first considers trust as an expectation regarding the behavior of an interaction partner, while the second relates trust with acceptance of and exposure to, vulnerability. On the other hand, several earlier research studies tried to interpret trust from different ways in the brick-and-mortar shopping environment. For instance, Moorman et al. (1992) defined trust as one's dependence on one's opponent in the hopes that the opponent's words or appointments are trustworthy. McKnight et al. (2002) suggested that trust is individuals' willingness to depend on their interactional partners. Mayer et al. (1995) saw trust as an expression for enduring beliefs from the opponent's action. In addition, Currall et al. (1995) claimed that trust is one's behavioral reliance on others in facing risk. Based on the above, there is no universally accepted definition in terms of trust in a face-to-face shopping context (Beldad et al., 2010).

As Internet-related technology continues to grow in importance, it allows potential customers to interact and transact with others without the constraints of space and time. Studies have employed the term "online trust" in online business contexts (Corritore et al., 2003). Are there any differences between online and offline trust? Corritore et al. (Corritore et al., 2003) pointed out the common point between the two is their rootedness on exchange. Similar to offline interactions, the aim of trust in an online shopping context also has the necessity of showing online firms as trustworthy parties. Shankar et al. (2002) mentioned that online and offline trust varies in the light of their targets of trust. In an offline commerce environment, the target of trust is typically a firm/organization (Doney & Cannon, 1997); whereas online, how the Internet and the firm deploy the Internet-related technology is the primary target of trust. From a customer viewpoint, in online commerce, customers have to trust not only the website and the description of why this website is reliable, but also the firm behind the site.

Moreover, to better understand the true concept of trust, related research states that trust can be theorized from both cognitive and affective perspectives (McAllister, 1995). According to studies on marketing and social psychology (Moorman et al., 1992; Rempel et al., 1985), the distinction between cognitive and affective types of trust is illustrated as follows: Cognitive trust is defined as the degree to which customers believe in, or are willing to depend on, a firm. People normally form cognitive trust arising from their reasoned interpretation regarding firms' performance and information presented. On the other hand, affective trust refers to an individual's feelings related to the level of care, kindness and honesty shown by the firm. Thus, cognitive trust is accrued by regularly examining a company's behaviors, while affective trust is accumulated by affective relationships between customers and companies. The following section describes the research model and hypotheses.

2.3 Research Model

Taking into account the nature of human behavior, fans assess their intention of converting into actual buyers by considering all the relevant cognitive and affective trust factors. Accordingly, this study hypothesizes that two main groups of variables influence fans' buying intention by affecting their commitment toward online hospitality companies: 1. cognitive trust factors (perceived reputation, perceived ability and information quality) and 2. affective trust factors (perceived benevolence, perceived integrity and perceived social presence). For the sake of covering some important features that can account for most of the variance in the context of Facebook, this study proposes a new research model, as shown in Figure 1. In this model, behavioral intention, a person's subjective probability of performing a specified behavior, was chosen as the dependent variable for theoretical and practical reasons. According to related studies (Ajzen & Fishbein, 1980; Legris et al., 2003; Venkatesh & Davis, 2000; Venkatesh & Morris, 2000), intention has a major influence on actual behavior. Also, even though people becoming fans on Facebook is now more common, it is difficult to gather a large sample of participants conducting buying actions while they are visiting a certain online hospitality firm's page. Thus, the choice of intention instead of actual behavior as a dependent variable is desirable; it allows a timely investigation of fans' acceptance to convert into actual shoppers and seems to be more meaningful. The author expected that this narrower model could be useful and helpful in understanding and predicting Facebook fans' intention to convert into actual buyers.

The literature on marketing has extensively discussed the importance of customer commitment. Commitment in this study refers to the extent to which fans desire to maintain their relationship with a hospitality firm via its company page. For example, 1. fans like to offer their suggestions related to products or services through the company's page; 2. fans are willing to put in more effort on WOM marketing of the company; 3. fans care about the company's future development; and 4. fans devote themselves to maintaining their relationship with the company through its Facebook page. From the perspective of customer choice, researchers have demonstrated that potential firm commitment could be a predictor of customers' behavioral intention to purchase (Gupta et al., 2010; Hsu et al., 2010). Therefore, in regard to Facebook, this study infers that high evaluation of firm commitment will fortify fans' behavioral intention to purchase. The following hypothesis is presented:

H1. Firm commitment has a positive effect on behavioral intention to purchase.

Figure 1. Research model

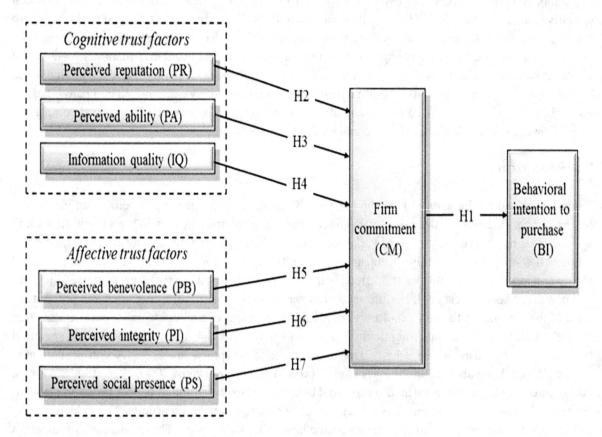

2.3.1 Cognitive Factors

Based on a literature review (Matemba & Maiseli, 2017), this study suggests that there are three primary cognitive trust components related to Facebook fans' firm commitment: perceived reputation, perceived ability and information quality.

2.3.1.1 Perceived Reputation

Perceived reputation in this study is defined as the extent to which a fan perceives a hospitality firm page's popularity. For a long time, firms' reputation has been considered as an important factor in building customer trust (Barber, 1983), especially in cyberspace (McKnight et al., 2002). According to Singh et al. (Singh & Sirdeshmukh, 2000), companies with a good reputation offer quality guarantees in customers' impressions. In the context of Facebook, companies' reputation may, through WOM among Internet users, influence fans' perception of quality before requesting services or purchasing products. Related research has indicated that firms' reputation may decrease customers' uncertainty about consumer risk when making purchase decisions for products or services (Robertson & Gatignon, 1986). Therefore, this study believes that, if a positive firm reputation can make fans perceive reliability, fans' firm commitment may be established. The following hypothesis is offered:

H2. Perceived reputation has a positive effect on firm commitment.

2.3.1.2 Perceived Ability

Ability has been defined as the trustor's comprehension of a trustee's capability and knowledge relevant to the expected behavior (Mayer et al., 1995). For example, people trust professionals with specific domain knowledge and background, such as 1. physicians with medical competence, and 2. computer experts with excellent software knowledge and skill. Basically, trust has a trusting and a trusted side. Perceived ability is the assessment that the trusted side understands its task and that this knowledge decreases the uncertainty regarding the trusting side obtaining its expected outcomes from the relationship, as a result of decreasing the possible range of undesirable behaviors regarding insufficient ability that the trusted side may present. In this study, perceived ability refers to the degree to which fans perceive that a hospitality firm is competent, knows how to provide excellent service, understands the market it works in and is capable of providing professional knowledge related to its service field. Numerous studies have argued that ability is a critical element of online trust (Gefen et al., 2003; Gefen & Straub, 2004; McKnight et al., 2002). Therefore, in the context of Facebook, the greater the competence that fans perceive, the more likely it is that they will become committed, active and helpful members of the hospitality firm. The following hypothesis is examined:

H3. Perceived ability has a positive effect on firm commitment.

2.3.1.3 Information Quality

Information quality in this study is defined as the degree to which fans perceive that a hospitality firm's company page is well-arranged and can help them to get complete, detailed, timely, accurate and reliable information so that they can gain better quality products/services. Research on e-commerce has found that the content quality of an online vendor's website (referring to the usefulness, completeness and accuracy of the information offered) may raise customers' trust in online transactions (Gefen & Straub, 2006). Several studies on online hotel reservation have found that information quality is a crucial factor for increasing Internet sales (Kim et al., 2006; Perdue, 2001; Ranganathan & Grandon, 2002). Again, the quality of information on e-health websites has been demonstrated to be important for the development of trust in the e-health services (Sillence et al., 2007). As a result, in this study, the authors infer that fans' perceived information quality toward a hospitality company's page has a positive effect on their commitment. This leads to the following hypothesis:

H4. Information quality has a positive effect on firm commitment.

2.3.2 Affective factors

Apart from cognitive trust factors, online firms in transactions may be assessed as trustworthy based on customers' emotions formed by the level of sincere concern and care demonstrated by the firms (Kim & Park, 2013; Rempel et al., 1985). According to marketing- and technology-related literature, this study assumes that the possible affective trust determinants of influencing fans 'firm commitment include aspects such as perceived benevolence, perceived integrity and perceived social presence.

2.3.2.1 Perceived Benevolence

Based on Gefenet al. (2004), benevolence in this study refers to a hospitality firm's actions that shape fans' beliefs about the firm. These actions include those behaviors affecting fans' welfare. For example: a hospitality firm: 1. puts fans' interests before its own; 2. will consider how its actions affect fans; 3. is perceived to be benevolent by its fans; 4. is well meaning; and so forth. Previous studies have demonstrated that caring is viewed as symbolic of good service, and generally augments customer satisfaction and retention (Gefen, 2002; Zeithaml et al., 1996). In the environment of a Facebook hospitality company's page, benevolent behavior decreases transactional uncertainty related to undesirable behavior, i.e. the likelihood that the firm will act based on a temporary opportunistic motive, while its fans are acting with a long-term orientation. From a fan's point of view, this study anticipates that a higher level of perceived benevolence is associated with a stronger commitment. Thus, the following hypothesis is tested:

H5. Perceived benevolence has a positive effect on firm commitment.

2.3.2.2 Perceived Integrity

Perceived integrity is another variable concerning affective-based trust; in this study it refers to the extent to which fans do not doubt the honesty of a hospitality firm, as well as feel confident that the firm will keep the promises it makes. A dishonest online firm may: 1. cheat customers by inducing them to buy poor quality products/services, 2. make inappropriate use of credit card and personal information, and 3. track customers' purchase activity without obtaining prior approval. Related research has mentioned the reality of such threats as automatically tracking e-commerce shopping and illegal usage of the customers' personal information (Lenard & Rubin, 2007). Tan et al. (2008) conducted an online survey with a panel of e-government participants and made them recall an e-government website based on their transactional experience with the website. The results showed that perceived integrity is an important factor in creating online trust. An interesting example related to online trust was reported by Gefen et al (2004). The authors directed MBA students to check for flights online and then book but not purchase them. The findings also supported that perceived integrity was essential in shaping participants' trust toward e-commerce vendors. Accordingly, the belief in the integrity of an online firm should be a central belief convincing the customers that their expected outcomes from the transaction will be fulfilled. It is anticipated that the more perceived integrity an online hospitality firm presents, the more likely that the fans will have a high tendency of developing committed participation. The following hypothesis is proposed:

H6. Perceived integrity has a positive effect on firm commitment.

2.3.2.3 Perceived Social Presence

Based on related research (Gefen & Straub, 2004; Tu & McIsaac, 2002), perceived social presence in this study refers to the degree of Facebook fans' feelings, perceptions and reactions to being connected by computer-mediated communication to a hospitality company page. High social presence is usually found in face-to-face communication, while low social presence is found in technology-based environments. Due to the fact that an e-commerce website typically implies no real interaction with other people, social presence cannot be established in a website. Gefen et al. (Gefen & Straub, 2004) indicated that if photos of a person can express a sense of sociable and sensitive human contact, so too should online firms' website. The perception of social presence can still be generated despite the lack of real human contact. For example, an online company could welcome customers by name when they visit the website and enable website communications to become more personalized. Although e-commerce websites inherently possess lower levels of social presence, technology-related research has provided evidence that websites embedded with a high level of social presence are more welcome by customers and more easily earn their trust (Gefen & Straub, 2004). Again, higher perceived social presence may improve the feeling of trust via its effect on regular interactions through electronic communication (Gefen & Straub, 1997). Therefore, in the context of Facebook, this study infers that high evaluation of perceived social presence by a hospitality company's fans will enhance their committed participation in the company's activities. The following hypothesis is presented:

H7. Perceived social presence has a positive effect on firm commitment.

3. Problem Solution

3.1 Measures

To ensure the content validity of the scales, the items selected must represent the concepts which generalizations are to be made. Therefore, validated instruments adapted from studies were used to measure the constructs of perceived reputation, perceived ability, information quality, perceived benevolence, perceived integrity, perceived social presence, commitment and behavioral intention to purchase. Those items for perceived reputation, perceived ability, perceived benevolence, and perceived integrity were adapted from Gefen (Gefen, 2002), Gefen et al. (Gefen & Straub, 2004), and Wang et al. (2005). The items for information quality were adapted from Wang et al. (2010). The measures for perceived social presence were based on Cyr et al. (2007). Commitment was based on the studies of Koh et al. (2004), and Hsu et al. (2010). Finally, the items of purchase intention were mainly developed by this study.

To confirm the content validity of the questionnaire developed by this study, discussions were carried out from the 20th through the 24th of October 2014 with three professionals and three graduate students who are specialized in technology as well as the hospitality field. They were asked whether the items were appropriate for the questionnaire. As a result, only suitable items were retained to constitute a complete range for this study. Consistent with research on social and human behavior, the questionnaire also contained demographic questions. Likert-type scales with anchors ranging from 1, "strongly disagree" to 7, "strongly agree", respectively, were used for all construct items. Moreover, the authors developed the original questionnaire in English, which was then translated into Chinese by a professional academician who is bilingual. The Chinese questionnaire was translated back into English by another bilingual academician. Two researchers and one bilingual academician compared the two English versions to resolve discrepancies in order to confirm translation equivalence and consistency. The final list of items for each construct is provided in the Appendix.

3.2 Data Collection

The target population was Facebook users. Similar to web-related studies, this study intended to recruit participants via an Internet survey. A panel of experts was assembled to determine how long the Internet survey would take. By referring to relevant literature (Hsu & Lin, 2008; Wang, 2012), the experts suggested that survey messages should be sent to several popular online communities in Taiwan for about 10 weeks (including Yahoo-Kimo, Yam, Sina, PChome Online, and campus bulletin board systems [BBS], such as PTT and Formosa) to invite online potential Facebook users to fill out the questionnaire. In order to exclude invalid participants from the study (i.e. only the fans of hospitality firms were would be participants), two screening questions would be included in the survey (Are you a Facebook user? and Are you a fan of a hospitality company page on Facebook? e.g., a fan of certain restaurants, hotels, and so on). In the questionnaire, the authors requested participants to answer all the items from a fan's point of view, and mentioned that "this hospitality company" indicated one of the hospitality companies they liked and had joined as a fan. This ensured that the authors successfully made the participants' recall one particular hospitality company page for which they chose to be a fan prior to completing the instrument. At any time during the 10 weeks, participants could respond to the online questionnaire by clicking the URL provided on the message, which also summarized the purpose of this study, provided a hyperlink to the electronic survey form and illustrated that there were 60 NT$100 gift coupons as a reward for respondents in a drawing at the completion of this survey. In the ten-week period, a total of 458 responses were received. Of the 458 responses, 65 questionnaires were invalid or repeated (duplicate IP addresses), which amounted to 393 usable responses, for a valid response rate of 86%.

Among those responding, 48.1% of the respondents were male, 51.9% were female. The respondents had an average of 9.08 years of computer experience (standard deviation [SD] = 4.57) and 8.37 years of Internet experience (SD = 4.24). Also, 38.9% of respondents had a bachelor's degree. The characteristics of the respondents are shown in Table 1.

Table 1. Demographic attributes of the respondents

	Frequency	Percentage	Cumulative
Gender			
Female	204	51.9	
Male	189	48.1	
Age			
< 20	110	28.0	28.0
21-30	181	46.1	74.1
31-40	72	18.3	92.4
41-50	21	5.3	97.7
> 51	9	2.3	100.0
Education level			
Senior high school	74	18.8	18.8
Some college	131	33.3	52.1
Bachelor's degree	153	38.9	91
Graduate degree (or above)	35	9.0	100.0
Industry			
Manufacturing	76	19.3	
Service	158	40.2	

continues on following page

Table 1. Continued

	Frequency	Percentage	Cumulative
School	90	22.9	
Government agencies	23	5.9	
Self-employed	32	8.1	
Others	14	3.6	
Machine utilized to log into Facebook (multiple responses)			
Desktop computer	85	10.4	
Laptop computer	178	21.9	
Tablet computer	197	24.2	
Smartphone	354	43.5	
Time in using Facebook each time			
Under 1 h	83	21.1	21.1
1-2 h	121	30.8	51.9
2-3 h	71	18.1	70.0
Over 3 h	118	30.0	100.0
Experience in using Facebook			
Under 3 months	41	10.4	10.4
3 months-6 months	62	15.8	26.2
6 months-1year	56	14.3	40.5
1 year-2 years	83	21.1	61.6
Over 2 years	151	38.4	100.0
Experience in being a fan of Facebook business pages			
Under 3 months	49	12.5	12.5
3 months-6 months	118	30.0	42.5
6 months-1year	134	34.1	76.6
Over 1 years	92	23.4	100.0

4. Data analysis and results

4.1 Assessment of Measurement Model

A confirmatory factor analysis via AMOS 17.0 was conducted to test the measurement model. Six common model-fit measures were employed to measure the model's overall appropriateness of fit: the ratio of $\chi2$ to degrees-of-freedom (*df*), goodness-of-fit index (GFI), adjusted goodness-of-fit index (AGFI), normalized fit index (NFI), comparative fit index (CFI) and root mean square residual (RMSR). To attain a better model fitness, two items, 6 and 15 (see Table 6), were eliminated due to low or cross factor loadings. As shown in Table 2, all the model-fit indices exceeded their respective common acceptance levels suggested by previous research, thus demonstrating that the measurement model revealed a fairly good fit with the data collected. Moreover, the authors examined common method variance bias by Harman's single-factor test (Aulakh & Gencturk, 2000) and found the value for explainable variance to be 38.7% (i.e. not over 50%), so there was no common method variance bias. This study could therefore proceed to evaluate the psychometric properties of the measurement model in terms of reliability, convergent validity and discriminated validity.

Reliability and convergent validity of the factors were calculated by composite reliability, and by the average variance extracted (see Table 3). The composite reliabilities can be calculated as follows: (square of the summation of the factor loadings)/ {(square of the summation of the factor loadings) + (summation of error variables)}. The interpretation of the resultant coefficient is similar to that of Cronbach's alpha. Composite reliability for all the factors in the measurement model was above 0.80. The average extracted variances were all above the recommended 0.50 level (Hair et al., 1992), which implied that more than one-half of the variances observed in the items were accounted for by their hypothesized factors. Convergent validity can also be evaluated by observing the factor loadings and squared multiple correlations from the confirmatory factor analysis (see Table 4). Based on Hair et al.'s suggestion (Hair et al., 1992), factor loadings greater than 0.50 were deemed as very significant; all the factor loadings of the items in the research model were greater than 0.70. Thus, all factors in the measurement model had adequate reliability and convergent validity.

To test discriminate validity, this study compared the shared variance between factors with the average variance extracted of the individual factors. This analysis exhibited that the shared variances between factors were lower than the average variance extracted of the individual factors, thus confirming discriminate validity (see Table 3). In brief, the measurement model demonstrated adequate reliability, convergent validity and discriminate validity.

Table 2. Fit indices for measurement and structural models

Goodness-of-fit measure	Recommended value	Measurement model	Structural model
χ^2/degree of freedom	≤3.00	1.400	1.421
Goodness-of-fit index (GFI)	≥0.90	0.903	0.901
Adjusted goodness-of-fit index (AGFI)	≥0.80	0.860	0.859
Normed fit index (NFI)	≥0.90	0.940	0.938
Comparative fit index (CFI)	≥0.90	0.987	0.987
Root mean square residual (RMSR)	≤0.10	0.015	0.016

4.2 Structural Model Estimation and Hypotheses Testing

A similar set of model-fit indices was used to examine the structural model (see Table 3). The six common model-fit measures of the structural model also exceeded their respective common acceptance levels, as suggested by previous research. This result provided firm evidence of a good model-data fit. Thus, this study could proceed to investigate the path relationships hypothesized by this study. Figure 2 shows the standardized path coefficients for all of the respondents in the hypothesized model. As predicted in Hypothesis 1, firm commitment was found (at the 0.001 level) to be a significant factor in determining purchase intention ($\beta = 0.638$, $p < 0.001$). Also, as predicted in Hypothesis 2, perceived reputation had a significant positive influence (at the 0.001 level) on firm commitment ($\gamma = 0.302$, $p < 0.001$). Perceived ability had a significant positive impact (at the 0.01 level) on firm commitment ($\gamma = 0.213$, $p < 0.01$), supporting Hypothesis 3. The proposed model further conjectured that information quality would directly influence firm commitment (Hypothesis 4). The result provided support (at the 0.001 level) for this as well ($\gamma = 0.351$, $p < 0.001$). Furthermore, the positive relationship between perceived benevolence and firm commitment, predicted by Hypothesis 5, was also supported at the critical 0.01 level ($\gamma = 0.204$, $p < 0.01$). As anticipated, perceived integrity was found to have a significant positive influence on firm commitment ($\gamma = 0.199$, $p < 0.01$), supporting Hypothesis 6 at the 0.01 level. Finally, perceived social presence was found (at the 0.001 level) to be a significant factor in determining firm commitment ($\beta = 0.367$, $p < 0.001$). Altogether, the model accounted for around 70.5% of the variance in firm commitment and 48.6% of the variance in behavioral intention to purchase. Table 5 summarizes the results of the hypotheses testing.

Up to now, this article has delineated the results of the research model. Next, the authors are going to discuss the theoretical and practical implications of the results.

Table 3. Reliability, average variance extracted, and discriminate validity

Factor	CR	1	2	3	4	5	6	7	8
1. Perceived reputation	0.858	0.668							
2. Perceived ability	0.906	0.516	0.762						
3. Information quality	0.913	0.388	0.403	0.724					
4. Perceived benevolence	0.898	0.384	0.373	0.296	0.747				
5. Perceived integrity	0.907	0.389	0.283	0.336	0.582	0.765			
6. Perceived social presence	0.958	0.301	0.426	0.300	0.434	0.520	0.851		
7. Firm commitment	0.916	0.403	0.284	0.271	0.201	0.117	0.287	0.731	
8. Behavioral Intention	0.975	0.410	0.306	0.151	0.182	0.163	0.135	0.319	0.928

CR = Composite Reliability

Diagonal elements are the average variance extracted. Off-diagonal elements are the shared variance.

4.3 Discussion

This research aimed to propose and test a new research model that can capture cognitive and affective trust factors influencing Facebook fans' firm commitment. Consistent with related studies (Blanchard & Markus, 2004; Gupta et al., 2010; Hsu et al., 2010; Koh & Kim, 2004), firm commitment was found to be a strong predictor of behavioral intention to purchase for the respondents. The results also indicated that three cognitive trust variables (perceived reputation, perceived ability and information quality), and three affective trust variables (perceived benevolence, perceived integrity and perceived social presence) were significant determinants that can influence Facebook fans' firm commitment. Policy makers and hospitality marketing managers should explore the main trust-related factors identified here, and look for a means to improve fans' perceptions in order to help them become committed members of their firms. The findings of this study provide several important implications for Facebook-related research and practice.

Table 4. Factor loadings and squared multiple correlations of items

	Factor loadings	Squared multiple correlations
Perceived reputation		
PR1	0.790	0.624
PR2	0.839	0.704
PR3	0.822	0.676
Perceived ability		
PA1	0.855	0.731
PA2	0.845	0.714
PA4	0.917	0.841
Information quality		
IQ1	0.887	0.787
IQ2	0.864	0.746
IQ3	0.817	0.667
IQ4	0.833	0.694
Perceived benevolence		
PB1	0.873	0.762
PB2	0.870	0.757
PB3	0.849	0.721
Perceived integrity		
PI1	0.853	0.728
PI2	0.930	0.865
PI3	0.838	0.702
Perceived social presence		
PS1	0.945	0.893
PS2	0.866	0.75
PS3	0.925	0.856
PS4	0.951	0.904
Firm commitment		
CM1	0.862	0.743
CM2	0.919	0.845
CM3	0.786	0.618
CM4	0.848	0.719
Behavioral intention to purchase		
BI1	0.966	0.933
BI2	0.978	0.956
BI3	0.945	0.893

PR, perceived reputation; PA, perceived ability; IQ, information quality; PB, perceived benevolence; PI, perceived integrity; PS, perceived social presence; CM, firm commitment; BI, behavioral intention to purchase.

Table 5. Summary of testing results

	Relationship	Hypothesis	Testing result
H1	CM -> BI	Positive	Supported
H2	PR -> CM	Positive	Supported
H3	PA -> CM	Positive	Supported
H4	IQ -> CM	Positive	Supported
H5	PB -> CM	Positive	Supported
H6	PI -> CM	Positive	Supported
H7	PS -> CM	Positive	Supported

H, hypothesis; PR, perceived reputation; PA, perceived ability; IQ, information quality; PB, perceived benevolence; PI, perceived integrity; PS, perceived social presence; CM, firm commitment; BI, behavioral intention to purchase.

Figure 2. Results of structural modeling analysis

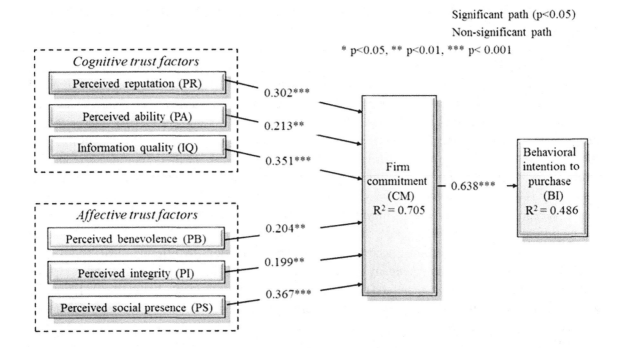

4.4 Implications of Cognitive Trust

From the perspective of cognitive factor, all three proposed trust-based constructs (perceived reputation, perceived ability and information quality) had significant, positive effects on firm commitment. This is consistent with the research on traditional marketing (Crosby et al., 1990; Farrent, 1996; Garbarino & Johnson, 1999) and electronic marketing (Hsu et al., 2010) that had interpreted trust as a critical factor when shaping customers' firm commitment. That means that the majority of our respondents care about whether or not the page of a hospitality firm has been known for a long time; if so, it can generate good impressions and even persuade them. Meanwhile, it is believed that a firm's page that can make fans believe the firm is competent and has professional knowledge in its service field is more likely to help in establishing firm commitment, which in turn encourages a high intention to purchase its products or services. Also, well-arranged, accurate, reliable, complete and detailed information presented on a hospitality firm's page attracts customers and plays a critical motivational role leading to their commitment toward the firm. Facebook makes it easy for business owners to set up pages. There are several ways to make hospitality company Facebook pages more capable and informative: 1. hospitality owners could inform their fans about activities on company pages, such as creating events, posting photos of their products, updating their status, and announcing a new service or deal; 2. managers could allow their fans to tag photos of themselves using the firm's product, on your page; 3. companies could construct their page for one-stop shopping for customers to interact, engage and buy their product; and 4. firms could add a product tab to their page to allow fans to view all of their products and easily purchase them without having to leave Facebook.

4.5 Implications of Affective Trust

In considering the effects of the affective factor, this study found that all the three trust-based variables (perceived benevolence, perceived integrity and perceived social presence) had a significant positive influence on firm commitment. This is consistent with e-service-related research that has identified perceived benevolence, perceived integrity and perceived social presence as major elements of trustworthiness (Cyr et al., 2007; Gefen & Straub, 2004; Yousafzai et al., 2003). When purchasing, people first search for needed purchase information. With the progress of web technology, Facebook business pages have become a vital resource to get useful purchase guides. This study provided evidence that our respondents place importance on verifying if a hospitality firm's page can assist in establishing fans' affective trust by presenting benevolent behaviors, such as caring about them, putting their interests before its own, considering how its actions affect them, and so forth. To increase fans' perception that a company is benevolent, company page owners could endeavor to collect some relevant content that their fans expect to see on their page; they may "like" the post, "comment" on the post, answer a question on the page, click a link on the post, share the post, and so on. Plus, hospitality managers could use Facebook as an exclusive, fans-only access to specials and promotions by offering meals and deals to fans loyally connected with their company on Facebook. To improve fans' firm commitment, companies could differentiate between what fans and non-fans see on their company page. For example: 1. hoteliers could give incentives (e.g., coupon codes, special offers, or fan-only content) for fans; 2. hospitality managers could inform fans of current events related to their interests (both local and national/global); and 4. firms could stimulate fans by using funny, entertaining, or beautiful pictures and videos, info graphics, etc. The more benevolent the approach, the more likely the fans and followers will be thankful, spreading their own massive social networks, which in turn improves the fans' commitment to the firm.

As for perceived integrity, integrity ensures that fans intend to pay for what they are committed to buy in an appropriate and timely manner. Meanwhile, it is necessary to ensure that the hospitality firms deliver products/services of promised characteristics within the agreed period of time after the receipt of payment. In the context of Facebook, 1. maintaining the integrity of companies requires that the companies actually enforce the rules of the transaction without any bias; 2. fans should be given notification as to uses of any personal information collected from them, especially for secondary uses that are unrelated to complete the original transaction; and 3. managers should take reasonable steps to destroy fans' untimely data and convert them into an anonymous form before using them for secondary purposes.

Additionally, social presence reflects the feeling of warmth and sociability that a technology-based medium provides (Kumar & Benbasat, 2006). Previous research has demonstrated that higher perceived social presence is an important trust factor in an e-mail interaction context (Gefen & Straub, 1997). Actually, no one wants to talk to a business; people like to talk to a person. So, on Facebook, hospitality companies should let their fans know the people who are behind the company page. People who care and share on your page may be those who love your products/services, or love to say something about the niche you share with them. There are several ways that hospitality managers can enhance fans' perceptions of social presence. For example: 1. submitting questions is a good way to spark dialogue with fans because this method can get people to respond to your posts and increase interactivity; 2. making use of emoticon icons enables you to provide more vivid responses and information about opinions arising from your fans; 3. posting interesting photos and videos could also be a good way to get your fans' attention and encourage your fans to interact with you; and 4. instead of answering questions, you could get your fans to help others who are in need of tips, because it enables potential customers to sense one another's presence (Yadav & Varadarajan, 2005); this way, customers will consider their online activities two-way rather than one-way communication. Moreover, managers should regularly check their page in order to give responses to new comments and questions because the best motivation and reward for fans is human interaction.

5. CONTRIBUTIONS

In summary, Comparing this research work to other prior works (Kim & Ko, 2010; Weisberg et al., 2011; Powers et al., 2012; Habibi et al., 2014; See-Toa & Hob, 2015; Lu et al., 2016; Hajli et al., 2017), the major contributions of this study in theoretical and practical can be described as follows: First, this study proposed a research model consisting of two categories of variables that seem to be highly relevant to the perceptions of Facebook participants. Second, the results have shown the importance of proposed trust-based factors in influencing potential hospitality companies' fans 'firm commitment and behavioral intention to purchase. Third, fans' firm commitment could be a strong predictor of their buying intention. All the proposed variables: perceived reputation, perceived ability, information quality, perceived benevolence, perceived integrity and perceived social presence were found to be critical factors significantly influencing fans' firm commitment. Finally, all the significant factors explained about 70.5% of the variance in commitment and 48.6% of the variance in behavioral intention to purchase. This demonstrated that they adequately describe the feelings of Facebook fans. The findings of this study will not only help hospitality practitioners in understanding the perceptions of Facebook fans, but also provide insights into research on technology's influence on the hospitality industry.

6. CONCLUSION AND FUTURE RESEARCH

This study's results should be interpreted with caution since the survey data have certain inherent limitations. First and foremost, the number of active Facebook users in Taiwan reached 15 million per month in the fourth quarter of 2013 (Taipei Times, 1986) and it already has 97% of Taiwan's Internet users in 2018 (Jennings, 2018). Therefore, bias exists since the sample was self-selected. Second, the research subjects were Facebook hospitality company fans in Taiwan. Lifestyle and culture may differ among countries; therefore, a cross-cultural validation using another large sample gathered elsewhere is required for further generalization of this study's findings. Third, this study was conducted with a snapshot research approach, so that longitudinal research efforts are needed to evaluate the validity of the proposed model and the findings. Thus, conducting a longitudinal observation inside the social networking site Facebook is a good way to enhance our understanding of causality among the variables that are important to influencing hospitality companies' fans 'intention to convert into actual buyers. Moreover, conducting such a longitudinal observation may help to identify what types of fans are more likely to conduct committed behaviors and also actually purchase the products/services offered by those hospitality companies they have joined as fans. Relevant view of points can also be seen in the Poston et al. (2014), Matemba et al. (2018), Wang et al. (2015), and Wang (2015).

In the future, as the analyzed result by Wang et al. (2019), the artificial intelligence, machine learning, automation, robotics Factors would play more important role on influencing intention of Facebook fans of hospitality companies to convert into actual buyers. It is also the great future research direction for this research.

ACKNOWLEDGMENT

This study was supported by grants from the Ministry of Science and Technology of the Republic of China under Contract Number MOST 103-2410-H-216 -007 -.This study also was supported by grants from the Ministry of Science and Technology of the Republic of China under Contract Number MOST 103-2410-H-216 -007 -.We also would like to thank to the Contract Number MOST 94-2516-S-018 -017,- 93-2516-S-018 -008 -, and the support from the Research Centre for Global Creativity, Innovation, Entrepreneurship and Management Technology, National Changhua University of Education.

REFERENCES

Ajzen, I., & Fishbein, M. (1980). *Understanding attitudes and predicting social behavior.* Englewood Cliffs, NJ: Prentice-Hall.

Aulakh, P. S., & Gencturk, E. F. (2000). International principal – agent relationships – control, governance and performance. *Industrial Marketing Management, 29*(6), 521–538. doi:10.1016/S0019-8501(00)00126-7

Baek, K., Holton, A., Harp, D., & Yaschur, C. (2011). The link that bind: Uncovering novel motivations for linking on Facebook. *Computers in Human Behavior, 27*(6), 2243–2248. doi:10.1016/j.chb.2011.07.003

Barber, B. (1983). *The logic and limits of trust.* Brunswick, NJ: New Rutgers University Press.

Batra, D. (2017). Adapting Agile Practices for Data Warehousing, Business Intelligence, and Analytics. *Journal of Database Management, 28*(4), 1–23. doi:10.4018/JDM.2017100101

Beach, D. (2005, October 5). Social commerce via the shop sphere& pick lists. Ysearch Blog. Retrieved from http://www.ysearchblog.com/2005/11/14/social-commerce-via-the-shoposphere-pick-lists/

Beldad, A., Jong, M., & Steehouder, M. (2010). How shall I trust the faceless and the intangible? A literature review on the antecedents of online trust. *Computers in Human Behavior*, *26*(5), 857–869. doi:10.1016/j.chb.2010.03.013

Blanchard, A. L., & Markus, L. M. (2004). The experienced "sense" of a virtual community: Characteristics and processes. *The Data Base for Advances in Information Systems*, *35*(1), 65–79. doi:10.1145/968464.968470

Boyd, D. M., & Ellison, N. B. (2007). Social network sites: Definition, history and scholarship. *Journal of Computer-Mediated Communication*, *13*(1), 210–230. doi:10.1111/j.1083-6101.2007.00393.x

Connolly, D. J., Olsen, M. D., & Moore, R. G. (1998). The Internet as a distribution channel. *The Cornell Hotel and Restaurant Administration Quarterly*, *39*(4), 42–54. doi:10.1177/001088049803900408

Corritore, C. L., Kracher, B., & Wiedenbeck, S. (2003). Online trust: Concepts, evolving themes, a model. *International Journal of Human-Computer Studies*, *58*(6), 737–758. doi:10.1016/S1071-5819(03)00041-7

Crosby, L. A., Evans, K. R., & Cowles, D. (1990). Relationship quality in services selling: An interpersonal influence perspective. *Journal of Marketing*, *21*(3), 68–81. doi:10.1177/002224299005400306

Currall, S. C., & Judge, T. A. (1995). Measuring trust between organizational boundary role persons. *Organizational Behavior and Human Decision Processes*, *64*(2), 151–170. doi:10.1006/obhd.1995.1097

Cyr, D., Hassanein, K., Head, M., & Ivanov, A. (2007). The role of social presence in establishing loyalty in e-service environments. *Interacting with Computers*, *19*(1), 43–56. doi:10.1016/j.intcom.2006.07.010

Doney, P. M., & Cannon, J. P. (1997). An examination of the nature of trust in buyer-seller relationships. *Journal of Marketing*, *61*, 35–51.

Farrent, D. (1996). How is your trust rating. *American Salesman*, *41*, 3–7.

Garbarino, E., & Johnson, M. S. (1999). The different roles of satisfaction, trust, and commitment in customer relationship. *Journal of Marketing*, *63*(2), 70–87. doi:10.1177/002224299906300205

Gefen, D. (2002). Customer loyalty in e-Commerce. *Journal of the Association for Information Systems*, *3*(1), 27–51. doi:10.17705/1jais.00022

Gefen, D., Karahanna, E., & Straub, D. W. (2003). Trust and TAM in online shopping: An integrated model. *Management Information Systems Quarterly*, *27*(1), 51–90. doi:10.2307/30036519

Gefen, D., & Straub, D. W. (1997). Gender differences in perception and adoption of e-mail: An extension to the technology acceptance model. *Management Information Systems Quarterly*, *21*(4), 389–400. doi:10.2307/249720

Gefen, D., & Straub, D. W. (2004). Consumer trust in B2C e-Commerce and the importance of social presence: Experiments in e-Products and e-Services. *Omega*, *32*(6), 407–424. doi:10.1016/j.omega.2004.01.006

Gupta, S., Kim, H., & Shin, S. (2010). Converting virtual community members into online buyers. *Cyberpsychology, Behavior, and Social Networking*, *13*(5), 513–520. doi:10.1089/cyber.2009.0202

Gupta, S., & Kim, H. W. (2007). Developing the commitment to virtual community: The balanced effects of cognition and affect. *Information Resources Management Journal, 20*(1), 28–45. doi:10.4018/irmj.2007010103

Habibi, M. R., Laroche, M., & Richard, M. O. (2014). The roles of brand community and community engagement in building brand trust on social media. *Computers in Human Behavior, 37*, 152–161. doi:10.1016/j.chb.2014.04.016

Hair, J. T., Anderson, R. E., Tatham, R. L., & Black, W. C. (1992). *Multivariate data analysis with readings.* New York: Macmillan.

Hajli, N., Sims, J., Zadeh, A. H., & Richard, M. O. (2017). A social commerce investigation of the role of trust in a social networking site on purchase intentions. *Journal of Business Research, 71*, 133–141. doi:10.1016/j.jbusres.2016.10.004

Hsu, C., & Lin, J. C. (2008). Acceptance of blog usage: The roles of technology acceptance, social influence and knowledge sharing motivation. *Information & Management, 45*(1), 65–74. doi:10.1016/j.im.2007.11.001

Hsu, C., Liu, C., & Lee, Y. (2010). Effect of commitment and trust towards micro-blogs on consumer behavioral intention: A relationship marketing perspective. *International Journal of Electronic Business Management, 8*(4), 292–303.

Hutchings, C. (2012). Commercial use of Facebook and Twitter – risks and rewards. *Computer Fraud & Security, 2012*(June), 19–20. doi:10.1016/S1361-3723(12)70065-9

Kim, A. J., & Ko, E. (2010). Impacts of luxury fashion brand's social media marketing on customer relationship and purchase intention. *Journal of Global Fashion Marketing, 1*(3), 164–171. doi:10.1080/20932685.2010.10593068

Kim, S., & Park, H. (2013). Effects of various characteristics of social commerce (s-commerce) on consumers' trust and trust performance. *International Journal of Information Management, 33*(2), 318–332. doi:10.1016/j.ijinfomgt.2012.11.006

Kim, W. G., Ma, X., & Kim, D. J. (2006). Determinants of Chinese hotel customers' e-satisfaction and purchase intentions. *Tourism Management, 27*(5), 890–900. doi:10.1016/j.tourman.2005.05.010

Koh, J., Kim, Y. G., & Kim, Y.-G. (2004). Sense of virtual community: A conceptual framework and empirical validation. *International Journal of Electronic Commerce, 8*(2), 75–93. doi:10.1080/10864415.2003.11044295

Kumar, N., & Benbasat, I. (2006). The influence of recommendations and consumer reviews on evaluations of websites. *Information Systems Research, 17*(4), 425–439. doi:10.1287/isre.1060.0107

Legris, P., Ingham, J., & Collerette, P. (2003). Why do people use information technology? A critical review of the technology acceptance model. *Information & Management, 40*(3), 191–204. doi:10.1016/S0378-7206(01)00143-4

Lenard, T. M., & Rubin, P. H. (2007, October 7). Privacy and the commercial use of personal information: The case of customer proprietary network information. Tech Policy Institute. Retrieved from www.techpolicyinstitute.org/files/3.pdf

Liao, C., Palvia, P., & Lin, H. N. (2006). The roles of habit and website quality in e-commerce. *International Journal of Information Management*, 26(6), 469–183. doi:10.1016/j.ijinfomgt.2006.09.001

Long, Y., & Siau, K. (2007). Social Network Structures in Open Source Software Development Teams. *Journal of Database Management*, 18(4), 25–40. doi:10.4018/jdm.2007040102

Lu, B., Fan, W., & Zhou, M. (2016). Social presence, trust, and social commerce purchase intention: An empirical research. *Computers in Human Behavior*, 56, 225–237. doi:10.1016/j.chb.2015.11.057

Marsden, P. (2010, October 8). Social commerce: Monetizing social media. Digital Innovation Today. Retrieved from http://digitalinnovationtoday.com/documents/Syzygy_2010.pdf

Matemba, E. D., Li, G., & Maiseli, B. J. (2018). Consumers' Stickiness to Mobile Payment Applications: An Empirical Study of WeChat Wallet. *Journal of Database Management*, 29(3), 43–66. doi:10.4018/JDM.2018070103

Mayer, R. C., Davis, J. H., & Schoorman, F. D. (1995). An integrative model of organization trust. *Academy of Management Review*, 20(3), 709–734. doi:10.5465/amr.1995.9508080335

McAllister, D. J. (1995). Affect and cognition-based trust as foundations for interpersonal cooperation in organizations. *Management Journal*, 38, 24–59.

McKnight, D. H., Choudhoury, H., & Kacrmar, C. (2002). Developing and validating trust measures for E-commerce: An integrative typology. *Information Systems Research*, 13(3), 334–359. doi:10.1287/isre.13.3.334.81

Mehdizadeh, S. (2010). Self-presentation 2.0: Narcissism and self-esteem on Facebook. *Cyberpsychology, Behavior, and Social Networking*, 13(4), 357–364. doi:10.1089/cyber.2009.0257

Mitra, S., Bagchi, A., & Bandyopadhyay, A. K. (2007). Design of a Data Model for Social Network Applications. *Journal of Database Management*, 18(4), 51–79. doi:10.4018/jdm.2007100103

Moorman, C., Zaltman, G., & Deshpande, R. (1992). Relationships between providers and users of market research: The dynamics of trust within and between organization. *Journal of Marketing*, 29(3), 314–328. doi:10.1177/002224379202900303

Nations, D. (2013, October 10). The top social networking sites. Webtrends. Retrieved from http://webtrends.about.com/od/socialnetworking/a/social_network.htm

Perdue, R. R. (2001). Internet site evaluations: The influence of behavioral experience, existing images, and selected website characteristics. *Journal of Travel & Tourism Marketing*, 11(2-3), 21–38. doi:10.1300/J073v11n02_02

Pernsteiner, C., & Rauseo, N. (2000). Transforming the hospitality industry into e-business. *FIU Hospitality Review*, 18(2), 10–21.

Poston, R. S., & Kettinger, W. J. (2014). Mindfully Experimenting with IT: Cases on Corporate Social Media Introduction. *Journal of Database Management, 25*(2), 29–51. doi:10.4018/jdm.2014040102

Powers, T., Advincula, D., Austin, M. S., Graiko, S., & Snyder, J. (2012). Digital and social media in the purchase decision process: A special report from the Advertising Research Foundation. *Journal of Advertising Research, 53*(4), 479–489. doi:10.2501/JAR-52-4-479-489

Prasad, S., Gupta, I. C., & Totala, N. K. (2017). Social media usage, electronic word of mouth and purchase-decision involvement. *Asia-Pacific Journal of Business Administration, 9*(2), 134–145. doi:10.1108/APJBA-06-2016-0063

Ranganathan, C., & Grandon, E. (2002). An exploratory examination of factors affecting online sales. *Journal of Computer Information Systems, 42*(3), 87–93.

Rempel, J. K., Holmes, J. G., & Zanna, M. P. (1985). Trust in close relationships. *Journal of Personality and Social Psychology, 49*(1), 95–112. doi:10.1037/0022-3514.49.1.95

Robertson, T. S., & Gatignon, H. (1986). Competitive effects on technology diffusion. *Journal of Marketing, 50*(3), 1–12. doi:10.1177/002224298605000301

Rouse, M. (2010, October 1). Facebook fan. Techtarget. Retrieved from http://whatis.techtarget.com/definition/Facebook-fan

See-Toa, W. K., & Hob, K. W. (2015). Value co-creation and purchase intention in social network sites: The role of electronic Word-of-Mouth and trust–A theoretical analysis. *Computers in Human Behavior, 53*, 627. doi:10.1016/j.chb.2015.05.003

Shan, L. M., Sutanto, J., & Kankanhalli, A. (2005). Converting online community visitors into online consumers. In S. Dasgupta (Ed.), *Encyclopedia of virtual communities and technologies* (pp. 54–60). Hershey, PA: IGI Global.

Shankar, V., Urban, G. L., & Sultan, F. (2002). Online trust: A stakeholder perspective, concepts, implications, and future directions. *The Journal of Strategic Information Systems, 11*(3-4), 325–344. doi:10.1016/S0963-8687(02)00022-7

Sillence, E., Briggs, P., Harris, P., & Fishwick, L. (2007). Health websites that people can trust – The case of hypertension. *Interacting with Computers, 19*(1), 32–42. doi:10.1016/j.intcom.2006.07.009

Singh, J., & Sirdeshmukh, D. (2000). Agency and trust mechanisms in consumer satisfaction and loyalty judgments. *Journal of the Academy of Marketing Science, 28*(1), 150–167. doi:10.1177/0092070300281014

Squidoo. (2013, October 3). Facebook fanpage promotion. Retrieved from http://www.squidoo.com/facebook-fanpage-promotion

Stephen, A. T., & Toubia, O. (2010). Deriving value from social commerce networks. *JMR, Journal of Marketing Research, 42*(2), 215–228. doi:10.1509/jmkr.47.2.215

Taipei Times. (2014, October 9). Taiwan likes Facebook, has highest penetration. Retrieved from http://www.taipeitimes.com/News/biz/archives/2014/02/28/2003584495

Tan, C., Benbasat, I., & Cenfetelli, R. T. (2008). Building citizen trust towards e-government services: Do high quality websites matter? In *Proceedings of the 41st Hawaii international conference on system sciences*, Hawaii. IEEE Press. 10.1109/HICSS.2008.80

Tong, S. T., Heide, B. V. D., & Langwell, L. (2008). Too much of a good thing? The relationship between number of friends and interpersonal impressions on Facebook. *Journal of Computer-Mediated Communication*, *13*(3), 531–549. doi:10.1111/j.1083-6101.2008.00409.x

Trusov M., Bucklin R.E., &Pauwels K. (2009). Effects of word-of-mouth versus traditional marketing: Findings from an Internet social networking site. *Journal of Marketing, 73*(5), 90-102.

Tu, C. H., & McIsaac, M. (2002). The relationship of social presence and interaction in online classes. *American Journal of Distance Education*, *16*(3), 131–150. doi:10.1207/S15389286AJDE1603_2

Venkatesh, V., & Davis, F. D. (2000). A theoretical extension of the technology acceptance model: Four longitudinal field studies. *Management Science*, *46*(2), 186–204. doi:10.1287/mnsc.46.2.186.11926

Venkatesh, V., & Morris, M. G. (2000). Why don't men ever stop to ask for directions? gender, social influences, and their role in technology acceptance and usage behavior. *Management Information Systems Quarterly*, *24*(1), 115–139. doi:10.2307/3250981

Wang, H. (2012). Investigating the determinants of travel blogs influencing readers' intention to travel. *Service Industries Journal*, *32*(2), 231–255. doi:10.1080/02642069.2011.559225

Wang, H., & Wang, S. (2010). Predicting mobile hotel reservation: Insight from a perceived value standpoint. *International Journal of Hospitality Management*, *29*(4), 598–608. doi:10.1016/j.ijhm.2009.11.001

Wang, H. W. (2015). An explorative study of continuance intention with applying social networks blended cloud service in new era of internet technology applications. *Journal of Internet Technology*, *16*(3).

Wang, H. W. (2015). An Explorative Study of Continuance Intention with Applying Social Networks Blended Cloud Service in New Era of Internet Technology Applications. *Journal of Internet Technology*, *16*(3).

Wang, H. W., Wu, Y. C. J., & Dong, T. P. (2015). Exploring the Impacts of Social Networking on Brand Image and Purchase Intention in Cyberspace. *Journal of Universal Computer Science*, *21*(11).

Wang, W., & Benbasat, I. (2005). Trust in and adoption of online recommendation agents. *Journal of the Association for Information Systems*, *6*(3), 72–101. doi:10.17705/1jais.00065

Wang, W., & Siau, K. (2019). Artificial intelligence, machine learning, automation, robotics, future of work and future of humanity: A review and research agenda. *Journal of Database Management*, *30*(1), 61–79. doi:10.4018/JDM.2019010104

Weijun, W., & Lin, L. (2011). Research on social commerce in web 2.0 environment. In *Proceedings of the International Conference on E-Business and E-Government (ICEE)*, Shanghai, China. Academic Press.

Weisberg, J., Te'eni, D., & Arman, L. (2011). Past purchase and intention to purchase in e-commerce: The mediation of social presence and trust. *Internet Research*, *21*(1), 82–96. doi:10.1108/10662241111104893

Yadav, M. S., & Varadarajan, R. (2005). Interactivity in the Electronic Marketplace: An Exposition of the Concept and Implications for Research. *Journal of the Academy of Marketing Science, 33*(4), 585–603. doi:10.1177/0092070305278487

Yousafzai, S. Y., Pallister, J. G., & Foxall, G. R. (2003). A proposed model of e-trust for electronic banking. *Technovation, 23*(11), 847–860. doi:10.1016/S0166-4972(03)00130-5

Zeithaml, V. A., Berry, L. L., & Parasuraman, A. (1996). The behavioral consequence of service quality. *Journal of Marketing, 60*(2), 31–46. doi:10.2307/1251929

Zhao, S., Grasmuck, S., & Martin, J. (2008). Identity construction on Facebook: Digital empowerment in anchored relationships. *Computers in Human Behavior, 24*(5), 1816–1836. doi:10.1016/j.chb.2008.02.012

This research was previously published in the Journal of Database Management (JDM), 30(4); pages 1-23, copyright year 2019 by IGI Publishing (an imprint of IGI Global).

APPENDIX

Table 6. The items list used in the study

Variable	Item		Description
Perceived Reputation	1.	PR1	I think this hospitality company has been known for a long time.
	2.	PR2	I think this hospitality company is extensively known for having a good reputation.
	3.	PR3	I think this hospitality company is very popular.
Perceived Ability	4.	PA1	I think this hospitality company is competent.
	5.	PA 2	I think this hospitality company knows how to provide excellent service.
	6.	PA 3	I think this hospitality company understands the market it works in.
	7.	PA4	I think this hospitality company is capable of providing fans' with professional knowledge related to its service field.
Information Quality	8.	IQ1	I think the features of this hospitality company page meet my needs.
	9.	IQ 2	I think this hospitality company page can provide accurate information.
	10.	IQ 3	It is easy to find the information I want on this hospitality company page.
	11.	IQ 4	Overall, this hospitality company page is well-designed.
Perceived Benevolence	12.	PB1	I think this hospitality company is benevolent.
	13.	PB 2	I think this hospitality company puts fans' interests before its own.
	14.	PB 3	I think this hospitality company will consider how its actions affect me.
	15.	PB 4	I think this hospitality company is well meaning.
Perceived Integrity	16.	PI1	I think this hospitality company will not cheat its fans into buying poor quality products.
	17.	PI 2	I think this hospitality company will not disseminate fake customer experiences to promote itself.
	18.	PI 3	I think this hospitality company is honest with its fans.
Perceived Social Presence	19.	PS1	I think this hospitality company page could provide fans with a sense of human contact.
	20.	PS 2	I think this hospitality company page could provide fans with a sense of human warmth.
	21.	PS 3	I think this hospitality company page could provide fans with a sense of sociability.
	22.	PS 4	I think this hospitality company page could provide fans with a sense of human sensitivity.
Commitment	23.	CM1	I am proud to become one of the fans of this hospitality company page.
	24.	CM 2	I am willing to put my efforts into promoting this hospitality company page.
	25.	CM 3	I would encourage others to be fans of this hospitality company page.
	26.	CM 4	I hope my relationship with this hospitality company page can last long.
Behavioral Intention to Purchase	27.	PI1	The probability that I would consider buying product(s) from this hospitality company is high.
	28.	PI 2	If I were to buy a product, I would consider buying it from this hospitality company.
	29.	PI 3	My willingness to buy a product from this hospitality company is high.

Chapter 19
CommuniMents:
A Framework for Detecting Community Based Sentiments for Events

Muhammad Aslam Jarwar

Department of Computer Sciences, Quaid-i-Azam University, Islamabad, Pakistan & Department of Information and Communications Engineering, Hankuk University of Foreign Studies (HUFS), Seoul, South Korea

Rabeeh Ayaz Abbasi

Faculty of Computing and Information Technology, King Abdulaziz University, Jeddah, Saudi Arabia & Department of Computer Sciences, Quaid-i-Azam University, Islamabad, Pakistan

Mubashar Mushtaq

Department of Computer Science, Forman Christian College (A Chartered University), Lahore, Pakistan & Department of Computer Sciences, Quaid-i-Azam University, Islamabad, Pakistan

Onaiza Maqbool

Department of Computer Sciences, Quaid-i-Azam University, Islamabad, Pakistan

Naif R. Aljohani

Faculty of Computing and Information Technology, King Abdulaziz University, Jeddah, Saudi Arabia

Ali Daud

Faculty of Computing and Information Technology, King Abdulaziz University, Jeddah, Saudi Arabia & Department of Computer Science and Software Engineering, International Islamic University, Islamabad, Pakistan

Jalal S. Alowibdi

Faculty of Computing and Information Technology, University of Jeddah, Jeddah, Saudi Arabia

J.R. Cano

Department of Computer Science, University of Jaén, Jaén, Spain

S. García

Department of Computer Science and Artificial Intelligence, University of Granada, Granada, Spain

Ilyoung Chong

Department of Information and Communications Engineering, Hankuk University of Foreign Studies (HUFS), Seoul, South Korea

DOI: 10.4018/978-1-7998-9020-1.ch019

ABSTRACT

Social media has revolutionized human communication and styles of interaction. Due to its effectiveness and ease, people have started using it increasingly to share and exchange information, carry out discussions on various events, and express their opinions. Various communities may have diverse sentiments about events and it is an interesting research problem to understand the sentiments of a particular community for a specific event. In this article, the authors propose a framework CommuniMents which enables us to identify the members of a community and measure the sentiments of the community for a particular event. CommuniMents uses automated snowball sampling to identify the members of a community, then fetches their published contents (specifically tweets), pre-processes the contents and measures the sentiments of the community. The authors perform qualitative and quantitative evaluation for a variety of real world events to validate the effectiveness of the proposed framework.

INTRODUCTION

Social media applications provide easy and effective ways for communication, sharing of opinions and exchange of information. These applications enable people to communicate with a large and diverse set of people for different purposes. For example, people may communicate and share their problems directly with their representatives in government and parliament. They may also give their opinion and show their sentiments on social problems, events, political movements, and government policies. Active participation of a large number of users results in abundance of information, and most of this information is unstructured and unmanageable. The huge amount of information in social media leads to the problem of "Social media information overload" (Bright et al., 2015). Social media information overload and the diversity of information create difficulties and challenges in information processing, presentation and analysis (Batrinca and Treleaven, 2015, Schuller et al., 2015).

In social media, the information which is created, shared and exchanged has importance for the public, news agencies, governments, oppositions and political parties because this information contains public opinion and sentiments. News agencies these days often select the subject of talk shows and the trends of news as per opinion and sentiments of public in social media. The government may also be able to benefit from the social media while making policies and taking decisions about the country and the general public, as users on social media discuss and express their opinions about the government policies, decisions and its governance with their friends, colleagues, and community. Through the effective monitoring and analysis of social media posts, government may make their policies and take decisions in a more informed way (WeGov, 2016).

Nowadays many communities, e.g. lawyers, politicians, journalists, doctors, and researchers are aware about the importance of social media and they use social media services to express their opinions on various issues in their daily lives (Manaman et al., 2016). Among these communities, the journalist community actively participates in discussions on social media like twitter, and expresses its opinions about the events occurring in the surroundings. Journalists and media also have an influential role on government policies and they affect the mindset of the public, which also effects the election results (Takahashi et al., 2015, Bekafigo and McBride, 2013). Journalists are using social media services increasingly (Zubiaga et al., 2013) to gather the news about the major events.

Due to the important role of communities in society and social media, in our study we propose a framework *CommuniMents*, for identifying targeted communities and analyzing their event based sentiments. It is a challenging task to identify a community which contains members from all the demographic locations of a country and not certain selected members only. We test our framework by identifying the Pakistani journalist community and finding its event based sentiments. Our framework has three components, the first component identifies members of a community. The second component gathers publicly available tweets of community members and filters event specific tweets. The third component measures collective sentiments of the community for a particular event. To evaluate our framework, we use real data related to important events within Pakistan.

Figure 1. Example of a hashtag (#BBSaid) and a mention (@SaeedGhani1) in a tweet

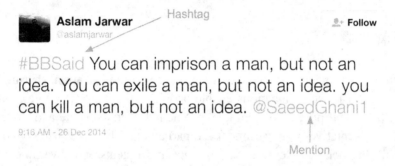

BACKGROUND AND RELATED WORK

Twitter was launched officially on 13th July, 2006 (Kumar et al., 2014). It facilitates its users to communicate in real time and create, send, receive and read posts known as "Tweets". The length of a tweet is limited to 140 characters (Mollett et al., 2011) and averages eleven words per tweet (O'Connor et al., 2010). Twitter is popular with academic researchers (Mollett et al., 2011), because most of the tweets are publicly available and are accessible through the twitter API (Makice, 2009). Different activities are performed by twitter users, such as to post a tweet publicly or specially to a user by mentioning his address as "@userid", read a tweet, and forward a tweet known as "Retweet". The retweet mechanism of twitter gives the strength to users to spread a tweet to many users who are not followers of the original user who created the tweet. Due to its specific structure and features, twitter has emerged as a new medium of communication and a channel of rapidly spreading information (Khan Minhas et al., 2015, Kwak et al., 2010, Honey and Herring, 2009).

Twitter users use the hash symbol "#" followed by a word called "hashtag" (Figure 1) in their posts to categorize posts or follow posts related to a specific topic. Sometimes users overlap topics by using a hashtag not in the context of the topic (Bastos et al., 2013). Hashtags further help users in searching posts. Hashtags, simple words, and phrases are used by many users in their tweets and are also tracked by twitter for detecting trending topics.

In twitter, users may create new lists or subscribe to existing lists. A lists has the ids of users who are mostly related to the theme of the list. By using lists, users can see a tailored stream of tweets of the users present in the list. The list can be private or public. The public lists of a user @rabeeh are shown in Figure 2.

Figure 2. Public lists of the user @rabeeh

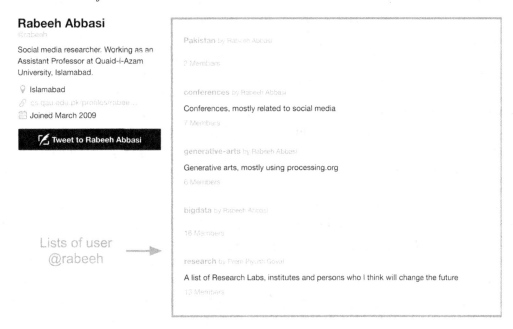

Snowball sampling or "chain-referral sampling" is a non-probabilistic sampling technique where existing study subjects recruit future subjects from their acquaintances. This technique is used for identifying specific communities in twitter, e.g., celebrities, media, organizations, and blogs (Wu et al., 2011). It starts with seed users U_0 belonging to a specific community. The seed users U_0 are mostly famous personalities within a community. All lists having the users U_0 are retrieved. The retrieved lists for each user are filtered on the basis of manually chosen keywords. The filtered lists L_0 contain only those lists whose names match the manually chosen keywords. In a recent study (Khan et al., 2014), the researchers have used snowball sampling for spell checking in English tweets.

An event represents an action occurring in our surroundings. Due to the simplicity, popularity, and adhoc usage of Twitter, many people report events on Twitter. In recent years, the demand of event based analysis of tweets has led to an increase in the interest of researchers to explore event extraction mechanisms from twitter. An extensive survey of event detection methods on twitter is presented in (Atefeh and Khreich, 2015). It discusses the event detection methodologies for both specified (for known) and unspecified (for unknown) events. (Abdelhaq et al., 2016) extract events from a real-time stream of tweets. The extracted events are described using keywords, time and location. (Zhou et al., 2015) use a Bayesian modelling approach to extract event-related keywords from tweets without supervised learning. (Lin et al., 2016) compare behavior of users on two different micro-blogging platforms, Twitter and Weibo.

Tweets contain metadata and unstructured text which includes URLs, user ids and special characters, abbreviations, hashtags, and non-stem words which affects the accuracy of sentiment analyzers inversely (Pang and Lee, 2008). In recent studies (Khan et al., 2014, Gupta and Sharma, 2016) WordNet is used for the identification of abbreviations and spelling correction. Before discussing the recent literature on sentiment analyzers, let us discuss what a sentiment analyzer is. The phrase "sentiment analysis" was first used in (Nasukawa and Yi, 2003). In textual natural language processing (Khan et al., 2016) "Sentiment analysis" is the process of finding the opinion of the writer. (Medhat et al., 2014) describes "sentiment analysis" or "opinion mining" as the study of knowing the people's opinions, attitudes and emotions towards objects (Balazs and Velsquez, 2016, Bravo-Marquez et al., 2016, Khan et al., 2017, Liu, 2012, Muhammad et al., 2016, Wang et al., 2016).

In sentiment analysis, the first step is the selection of text features. These features include the frequency of terms present, use of adjectives (parts of speech), phrases, and negations (Liu and Zhang, 2012). The features are selected using two methods: lexicon-based statistical measures-based. The lexicon-based method is a manual method, in which the human annotator annotates the features manually. The statistical method is fully automatic and widely used (Medhat et al., 2014). However, the chances of novice features in this case are much greater as compared with the lexical method. Most of the sentiment analysis methods work on whole documents, with exception of a few methods that work at sentence level (Appel et al., 2016).

The CoreNLP sentiment annotator uses the supervised methodology to train the classifier. For accurate results the classifier uses the sentiment treebank, which includes 215,154 phrases labeled with fine-grained sentiment labels in 11,855 parse tree sentences. Recursive Neural Tensor Network (Hammer, 2002) is used to reduce the complexity in sentiment composition. This sentiment annotator classifies the sentence into positive/negative polarity with accuracy ranging from 80% to 85.4% and in fine-grained classification up to 80.7% (Socher et al., 2013). Another sentiment analysis tool SyneSketch uses the word lexicon based on WordNet, lexicon of emoticons, common slang words and a set of heuristic rules for extracting the fine-grained Ekman emotion classes (i.e. happiness, sadness, anger, fear, disgust, and surprise) and classifies the sentence in positive with value (+1) and negative with value (-1) polarity (Krcadinac et al., 2013). Sentiments related to events on twitter are discussed by (Thelwall et al., 2011, Gaspar et al., 2016, Rill et al., 2014). Researchers have also used machine learning algorithms to detect deception (Alowibdi et al., 2015) and sentiments (Katz et al., 2015) on twitter.

Communities in Twitter have been addressed to solve various problems by researchers. In (Takahashi et al., 2015), authors investigate how different types of communities use Twitter in a situation of disaster and emergency. They particularly focus the typhoon Haiyan in the Philippines. The social media usage patterns were also investigated among those who were directly affected by the typhoon, and those who were coordinating the relief efforts or disseminating information. The results of this study show that different communities use social media for the promulgation of second-hand information in mobilizing relief efforts. The authors manually found different types of communities (i.e. ordinary citizen, journalists, NGO, Government officials, and celebrities), by analyzing a random sample of 1000 tweets, whereas our proposed framework *CommuniMents* enables identification of community members using snowball sampling technique.

PROPOSED FRAMEWORK: COMMUNIMENTS

We propose a framework, *CommuniMents*, to detect the sentiments of a specific community for a particular event. The framework has the following three components (Figure 3):

1. **Identifying Community Users:** This component receives a list of seed community members and based on these seed members, gathers more members using snowball sampling described in the previous section;

2. **Collecting and Filtering Tweets:** This component receives input (collection of community members) from the first component as well as from keys related to an event and then collects all the publicly available tweets of the community members and filters the tweets that are related to the event;

3. **Sentiment Analysis:** This component takes input (tweets of a community against an event) from the second component and analyzes the sentiments of these tweets after pre-processing them.

Figure 3. The CommuniMents framework

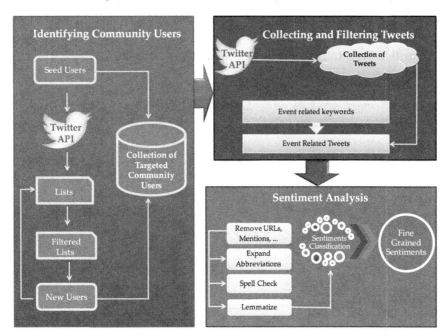

We detail working of the components in the following sections.

Identifying Community Users

This first component of the proposed framework *CommuniMents* identifies members (U_c) of a particular community c. It does so by starting with a set of seed users U_s. All lists having one of the users in U_s are retrieved. The rationale behind getting these lists is that they will contain similar types of users as in the set U_s.

These lists are then filtered and only those lists are retained which contain words from a set of predefined keywords K_l in their names. For example, if K_l contains keywords {"journalist", "journalists", "analysts"}, and the lists fetched (L_0) contains lists {"Journalists of Pakistan", "Political Analysts", "Pakistani Sportsmen"} then only first and second lists in L_0 are considered for further steps.

Once the lists are filtered, users present in these lists are fetched. The users are filtered (in a way similar to how lists are filtered), such that only those users are kept which have one of the keywords from the set K_u in their profile description.

This process is repeated until no new users are found or a maximum number (max_c) of users belonging to a community are fetched. The process taking place in this component is explained in Algorithm 1. The function *GetLists* calls a Twitter API[1] to get all the lists in which users U_s are present. Similarly, *GetUsers* also calls a Twitter API[2] to get all the users present in the lists *L*. The *FilterLists* and *FilterUsers* functions are used to filter lists and users based on the keywords K_l and K_u respectively.

In comparison to other sampling methods (like stratified or random sampling), identifying users of a community using hashtags (Lin et al., 2016), looking at top *n* user related to a topic (Sligh et al., 2016), or clustering users in a community (Guo et al., 2016), snowball sampling allows to start with a limited set of items, and grows the number of items in the sample. *CommuniMents* uses snowball sampling in a semi-automated way, in which all the members of a community are not required to be known beforehand.

Algorithm 1. Algorithm for getting members belonging to a community

```
function GetCommunityMembers(U_s, K_l, K_u, max_c)
 •U_s is the set of seed users   •K_l is the set of keywords for filtering lists
•K_u is the set of keywords for filtering users   •max_c is the maximum number of
community members
  L ← GetLists(U_s)
  L_0 ← FilterLists(L)
  U ← GetUsers(L_0)
  U_0 ← FilterUsers(U)
  i ← 1
  repeat
  L ← GetLists(U_{i-1})
  L_i ← FilterLists(L)
  U ← GetUsers(L_{i-1})
  U_i ← FilterUsers(U)
  i ← i + 1
  until |U_i| = |U_{i-1}| or |U_i| ≥ max_c
  return U_c                               ◊ Set of users U
belonging to community c)
 end function
```

Collecting and Filtering Tweets

The second part of the proposed framework acquires tweets (T_c) of the targeted community (c) and filters these tweets based on an event (e). Algorithm 2 is used for getting the tweets. The *GetTweets* function gets all the publicly available[3] tweets of the user *u* using the Twitter API[4].

Algorithm 2. Algorithm for getting tweets of community members U_c

```
function GetCommunityTweets(U_c)
  T_c ←∅
```

```
   for all u ∈ U_c do
      T_c ← T_c ∪ GetTweets(u)
   end for
   return T_c
end function
```

For identifying the tweets (T_{ce}) that belong to a particular event, *CommuniMents* uses a set of keywords K_e that represent the event e. Currently, this list is maintained semi-automatically, in such a way that seed keywords representing the event are used to fetch a set of tweets belonging to the event (Abdelhaq et al., 2016). The list of the seed keywords in extended by adding most frequent keywords from the tweets to the list K_e and the processes of adding frequent keywords is repeated until no more frequent and relevant word is found. The process is described in Algorithm 3.

Algorithm 3. Algorithm for filtering tweets T_c related to an event e based on the set of keywords K_e

```
function FilterCommunityTweets(T_c, K_e)
  T_ce ←∅
  L ←∅                                          • L is the
list of frequent words
  repeat
  KTemp_e ← K_e
  for all t ∈ T_c do
  if t contains a keyword from K_e and t not in T_ce   then
  T_ce ← T_ce ∪{t}
    for all words w in t do
    if L contains w then
    freq(w) ← freq(w) + 1
    else
    freq(w) ← 1
    L ← L ∪{w}
    end if
    end for
  end if
  end for
  Add most frequent relevant words to K_e
  until |KTemp_e|≠|K_e|
  return T_ce
end function
```

Sentiment Analysis

The third component of *CommuniMents* pre-processes the tweets filtered by Algorithm 3 (T_{ce}) and finds sentiment score of each tweet. The sentiment scores of individual tweets are aggregated to obtain an overall sentiment score (SS_{ce}) which indicates the sentiments of the community c for the event e. Before finding sentiment scores for individual tweets, it is important to pre-process the tweets, because tweets have limited length (140 characters) and this limited length forces users to use slang words and abbreviations. Twitter users also use mentions, URLs, and hash-tags. It is also quite possible that users make intentional (to keep to tweet short) or unintentional spelling mistakes. These twitter specific features affect the accuracy of the sentiment analysis algorithms, since most sentiment analysis tools are not specially built for twitter. Therefore, it may be better to extract twitter specific features before extracting features for sentiment analysis. Addressing these issues facilitates in achieving higher accuracy (Bao et al., 2014). Effectiveness of these pre-processing steps for sentiment analysis has already been reported in (Khan et al., 2014). Algorithm 4 shows the pre-processing steps.

Algorithm 4. Algorithm for pre-processing tweets T_{ce}

```
function PreProcessTweets(T_ce)
  TP_ce ←∅
  for all t ∈ T_ce do
  tTemp ← RemoveURLs(t)
  tTemp ← RemoveMentions(tTemp)
  tTemp ← RemoveHashSymbols(tTemp)
  tTemp ← ExpandAbbriviations(tTemp)
  tTemp ← SpellCheck(tTemp)
  tTemp ← Lemmatize(tTemp)
  TP_ce ← TP_ce ∪{tTemp}
  end for
  return TP_ce
end function
```

Each function used in Algorithm 4 is described below:

- **RemoveURLs:** Removes all the strings matching the following regular expression (representing a URL);
- **RemoveMentions:** Removes the user ids (user screen names followed by an @ symbol) in a tweet by using the following regular expression;
- **RemoveHashSymbols:** Removes the hash symbols (#) in a tweet. The hashtag (word followed by # symbol) is kept. Without removing hash symbols, the sentiment analyzer cannot identify the polarity of the hash tag;
- **ExpandAbbreviations:** Identifies the abbreviations and slang words by looking at each word of the tweet in *WordNet*[6]. If a word is not found in WordNet, it is considered as slang or an abbreviation. Then the function looks up such a word in a customized *Netlingo*[5] acronyms dictionary.The words found in the custom dictionary are replaced by their expanded form;
- **SpellCheck:** Corrects the spellings of the words not found in WordNet and the customised NetLingo dictionary. Microsoft COM API[6] is used for correcting the spellings mistakes;
- **Lemmatize:** Replaces the words with their roots. For the current implementation of *CommuniMents*, we use the *lemasharp* library[7].

Remove URLs

\b(((https?)\:\/\/)|(www\.))\S+\b

Remove mentions

\@\S+\b

After pre-processing the tweets, *CommuniMents* assigns a sentiment score to each tweet. These scores are aggregated to measure the sentiment polarity of the community c for the event e. Algorithm 5 shows the process of finding sentiments. *GetSentimentScore* uses a sentiment analysis library for measuring the sentiment score of an individual tweet t. min_s is the minimum score returned by the *GetSentimentScore* function, representing the most negative sentiment and max_s is the maximum score returned by the *GetSentimentScore* function, representing the most positive sentiment.

As there are many sentiment analysis tools and libraries available, we evaluated two popular libraries *CoreNLP* and *SyneSketch*. Based on empirical analysis, we found that the results of CoreNLP are better than that of SyneSketch therefore the current implementation of *CommuniMents* uses *CoreNLP* for finding sentiments. Stanford CoreNLP toolkit (Manning et al., 2014) classifies a phrase into five integer values ranging from 0 to 4 that describe the fine-grained sentiment classes i.e. "Very Negative" (0), "Negative" (1), "Neutral" (2), "Positive" (3), and "Very Positive" (4). The values are re-scaled between -2 and 2 for aggregation, such that 0 becomes -2 and 4 becomes 2. In case of *CoreNLP*, $min_s = 0$ and $max_s = 4$.

Algorithm 5. Algorithm for finding sentiments of tweets TP_{ce}

```
function FindSentiments(TP_ce)
  TS_ce ←∅
  SS ← 0
  for all t ∈ TP_ce do
  sTemp ← GetSentimentScore(t)
```
$$s \leftarrow \left(\frac{sTemp - min_s}{\max_s - min_s} \right) \times 4 - 2$$
```
  SS ← SS + s
  TS_ce ← TS_ce ∪{(t,s)}
  end for
```
$$SS_{c_e} \leftarrow \frac{SS}{\left| TP_{c_e} \right|}$$
```
  return (TS_ce,SS_ce)
end function
```

RESULTS

For testing *CommuniMents*, we chose the Pakistani Journalist community, because this community is active on social media and has great impact on the Pakistani society and government. By using the first part of the framework, we identified 969 user ids of Pakistani journalists. For getting event based community sentiments, we downloaded 2,107,374 tweets with metadata belonging to these users. Then tweets were filtered into three distinctive events. These events include "Zarb-e-Azab", "Azadi and Inqlab March" and "Hockey Champions Trophy for Men 2014". Zarb-e-Azab is a joint military operation conducted by Pakistan armed forces against Tehrik-i-Taliban Pakistan (TTP) and others militant groups in North Waziristan area. This operation started on 15 June 2014, and was in progress when we started to retrieve tweets in 2015. The Azadi (freedom) and Inqilab (revolution) marches were launched by two political parties Pakistan Tehrik-e-Insaf (PTI) and Pakistan Awami tehrik (PAT) from Lahore to Islamabad for getting their demands met from the government. Azadi march continued from 14th August 2014 to 17th December 2014 and Inqilab march continued from on 14th August 2014 to 21st October 2014. The Hockey Champions Trophy for Men 2014 sports event was held from 6 to 14th December 2014 in Bhubaneswar, India. In the semi-final Pakistan won against India by 4 goals to 3 and Germany won against Australia by 3 goals to 2. The final was won by Germany, which defeated Pakistan by 2 goals to 0.

Table 1 shows the number of event wise tweets and journalists' participation. It also shows the polarity of sentiments for the whole community for the three events as computed by Algorithm 5 (SS_{ce}). Overall sentiments of journalists' community are negative for all the events.

Table 1. Polarity of sentiments of journalists community participating in three events

Event	Tweets	Participating Journalists	Polarity
Zarb-e-Azab	11007	605 (65.55%)	-0.71
Azadi and Inqlab March	144845	796 (86.24%)	-0.62
Hockey Champions Trophy for Men 2014	13222	597 (64.68%)	-0.52

As the Algorithms 3 and 1 filter users and tweets on the basis of keywords, there is a chance irrelevant users and tweets are included during the process. To count the exact number of tweets that are irrelevant, we need to label the complete dataset, which is not possible due to the large size of the dataset. Instead we created a random sample of 30 event-related ("Zarb-e-Azab") tweets. These tweets are shown in Table 2 along with their user ids. Analysis of Table 2 shows that 23 out of 25 (92%) users are either journalists or often participate in discussions with journalists. Users at serial numbers 10 and 23 are not actually journalists, but news related accounts. Irrelevant accounts are included because many users keep the journalists and news related accounts in the same twitter list, which affects the process of snowball sampling, and causes irrelevant users to be included in the targeted community. When we look at the number of relevant tweets, we find that 27 out of 30 (90%) tweets are relevant to the event. The reason behind inclusion of irrelevant tweets is the different context of the keywords that journalists use. For example, tweets at serial numbers 4, 10, and 17 in Table 2 are not related to the event "Zarb-e-Azab" but these are included in the dataset due to related keywords.

Event Based Sentiments Classification

The sentiments analysis has certain limitations, for example, if some events have more negative tweets, it does not mean that people are talking against the event, because sometimes there are circumstances, in which people are talking in the favor of the event and criticizing the opposite side/view. To focus on this problem, in this section we discuss the sentiment results of each of the three events individually.

Table 2. Random sample of tweets for the event "Zarb-e-Azab"

S	Twitter ID	Tweet
1	Aak0	#ZarbEAzb The other side of peace: scared residents flee the war zone
2	Adnanrandhawa	Wondering when CIA senate committee members disappear and reports "leaked" to media they have gone to N. Waziristan wilfully.
3	adilshahzeb	See how good he sounds here MT "@MurtazaGeoNews: TuQ says he'll dispatch 14 truckloads of food/medicine today4 IDPs in Bannu,more2 follow"
4	ajmaljami	—-RT @ReesEdward: The British in N. Waziristan. Sometime in early 20th century.
5	alisalmanalvi	Dear COAS, the killers of these innocent school children are not restricted to North Waziristan only. They are everywhere in #Pakistan.
6	AmirMateen2	need to something fast What started as a mass exodus of locals is now humanitarian crisis" http://t.co/rokEZDExKz Waziristan @DalrympleWill
7	madihariaz	Samaa ran a report mocking the cricket team about the amount of their donation for IDPs. Then asked a moulvi's opinion who deplored it too
8	MahsudFarooq	Effect of Terrorism on music in South waziristan . @AnserAbbas @alex_gilchrist @FATANews @IftikharFirdous @pirroshan
9	MahsudFarooq	Clash b/w security forces and millitants, 5 Millitants killed in sarvakai area #south #waziristan agency, security sources
10	ApnaWaziristan	New Delhi: Kashmir Bharat Ka Atoot Hissa Tha, Hissa Hein Aur Rahay Ga, Pakistan Ko Sirf Apni Fikar Karni Chahiye:#BJP
11	ApnaWaziristan	*Peshawar: Kpk Hakumat Ny IDPs Ky Liye Shikayat Cell Qaim Kr Diya, IDPs Peer Sy Hafta Subha 9 Bajay Tak Shikayat Darj Kara Saktay Hyn:
12	AtikaRehman	RT @TahaSSiddiqui: Since we've SO MUCH of aid coming in for #Waziristan IDPs, why not waste some thru poor logistics and arrangements! http
13	BenazirMirSamad	RT @PTIofficial: Khyber Pakhtunkhwa Govt making adequate arrangements for IDPs. Instructions passed to all relevant departments.
14	SaeedShah	RT @asadmunir38: Suicide attack kills four soldiers in North Waziristan http://t.co/eGRQNMpXBT
15	DawarSafdar	Afghan gov will teach IDPs children,and here KP Gov ordered to vacate the schools
16	DawarSafdar	In thousands IDPs in government schools going to IDPs again.
17	FarooqHKhan	RT @Shahidmasooddr: We pay taxes to Govt for IDPs/flood victims etc.We dont pay taxes to opposition! And its better to beg than to Rob jana
18	FauziaKasuri	RT @imran_sidra: Ma'am @FauziaKasuri & team while doing clothes shopping for IDPs sisters in Bannu KP. #HelpIDPs #Donate #IKF #PTI http://t
19	FauziaKasuri	@ArshadSidiqi Thank u for thinking of the IDPs..Allah bless you all.
20	taahir_khan	@Jan_Achakzai JUI-F should start protest to force the gov't, military to send back 1 million North Waziristan people instead political Jirga
21	MinaSohail	RT @asadmunir38: #PakArmy soldier #ZarbeAzb
22	P_Musharraf	I vehemently condemn the suicide attack on our troops in North Waziristan. The ultimate sacrifice offered by our... http://t.co/nM4MXtXcwt
23	PakMilitaryNews	RT @AsimBajwaISPR: #ZarbeAzb:A pic taken in #IDP Camp Bannu today. Let us join hands to bring back their smiles#helpidps
24	PakMilitaryNews	Pakistan plans military operation in North Waziristan, targeting extremist groups
25	KlasraRauf	RT @Dr_Afaq: @KlasraRauf doesn't talk of utopia in his Urdu column.He talks about real life solution to #IDPs problem.
26	penpricker	For me those nameless innocent kids of Waziristan, who die in drone strikes r no less than Malala. All of 'em are victim of a war not ours

continues on following page

Table 2. Continued

S	Twitter ID	Tweet
27	muniraqazi	@dunyanetwork @BBhuttoZardari Good one! The PPP's support for #ZarbEAzb is vital for a stable & secure #Pakistan. #PPP
28	MudassarGEO	RT @NazranaYusufzai: What would be the meeting point of #drones and #Fazluallah - would he go to Waziristan or drone would come to swat.
29	nadia_a_mirza	In #Bannu everything trickles down to army to serve n manage #IDPs, No Federal neither Provincial Govt presence, only photo sessions.
30	QuatrinaHosain	RT @Khawar69: Media shud rather demonise the ideology of TTP and Jandullah that preach killing of humans for political goal. #zarbeazb will

Figure 4. Distribution of tweets by the sentiment classifier. Figure (a) For the event "Zarb-e-Azab"; (b) For the event "Azadi and Inqlab March"; and (c) For the event "Hockey Champions Trophy for Men 2014".

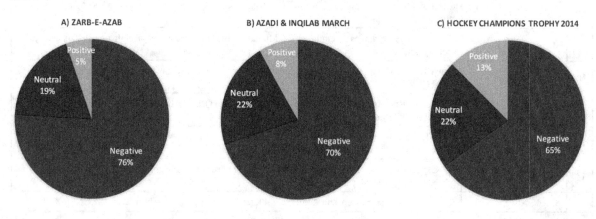

Figure 4a shows that there are 76% tweets classified as negative, in the event "Zarb-e-Azab". The operation "Zarb-e-Azab" was against the militants. The majority of negative tweets prove that the targeted community (Pakistani journalists) were against the operation "Zarb-e-Azab". In tweets these journalists expressed their opinions regarding the issues in operation, militants, and problems faced by IDPS (internally displaced persons). Tweets at serial no 1, 3, 6, 7, 14, 16, and 17 in Table 3 show that the majority of the journalists are not in favour of the operation. The tweets in Table 3 are randomly selected from all the negative tweets of this event. There are also 5% tweets, which are classified as positive. In the positive tweets, journalist are praising the operation and bravery of the law enforcement agencies. For example, tweets at serial no 1 and 7 in Table 4 support our argument. The tweets in Table 4 are randomly selected from the positive set.

Figure 4b shows the sentiment analysis of the event "Azadi and Inqlab March". As discussed in previous sections, this movement by two political parties PTI and PAT was against the government. As shown in the pie chart, 70% tweets are classified as negative, 22% are neutral and only 8% tweets are classified as positive. We randomly chose 20 negative tweets shown in Table 5 to study why majority of the tweets are classified as negative. In the tweets at serial no 1, 6 and 20 journalists give opinion with negative sentiments about the said event and in tweet at serial no 10 compare the march with previous movements. In other tweets, peoples are expressing their support for the march while criticizing the government and others. Thus, a majority of negative tweets does not mean that majority of journalists were against the "Azadi and Inqlab March". A random sample of tweets having positive sentiments is shown in Table 6. In these tweets journalist express their opinion directly in favor of the event. The examples of these type tweets are serial no 2, 3, 4, 8 and 9 in Table 6.

Table 3. Tweets with negative sentiments from the event "Zarb-e-Azab"

S	Twitter ID	Tweet	Polarity
1	AtifSal	#Pakistan rulers claims of #ZarbeAzb n #Waziristan exposed wth #PeshawarAttack.Fighting paid US War of Terror is bringing mayhem inside Pak.	Negative
2	KhSaad Rafique	Attended High level meeting chaired by Prime Minister. Current political situation, Operation, IDPs were discussed	Negative
3	MariumCh	RT @YusraSAskari: 'So far 572,529 people, belonging to 44,633 families have been registered as Internally Displaced Persons' #ZarbEAzb #Pak	Negative
4	arsched	#PMSharif refused to authorise operation against militants when #GenSharif Gen sought authorisation in Feb & March #ZarbEAzb	Negative
5	DawarSafdar	RT @washingtonpost: Pakistan military advances against Taliban, kills 27 militants in North Waziristan http://t.co/3gMo14Rnbn	Negative
6	TahaSSiddiqui	#PakArmy commences op in #NorthWaziristan by name of #ZarbeAzb (Prophet's sword name). Will it b a failure like Swat & South Waziristan ops?	Negative
7	Mustafa Qadri	Pakistan authorities must ensure mil operations in N Waziristan respect laws of war, no collective punishment & provide for IDPs	Negative
8	wasi78	Terrorists' network worth Rs 2 billion 49 crore 80 lakh destroyed as Zarb-e-Azb continues —... http://t.co/bYaDYGgk65	Negative
9	taahir khan	Blast at marketplace in North Waziristan's headquarters Miranshah killed two people on Tuesday, tribesmen said.	Negative
10	PATofficialPK	#ZarbEAzb #ZarbeHaq rally by #PAT in Lahore to show solidarity with #PakArmy operation #Pakistan http://t.co/qgpa5i5SQk	Negative
11	MahsudFarooq	2 soldiers wer killed,4 injd wen n IED planted by Terrorists, exploded on roadside in area vill Jatarai barwand n South Waziristan Agency,	Negative
12	asmashirazi	RT @fareedraees: TTP's Hafiz Gul Bahadur instructions to the people of #Waziristan. He has advised people to migrate before 10th June. http	Negative
13	ZaaraAbbasKhar	RT @AsimBajwaISPR: Army #Chief visited CMH,met injured students.Students said,we are in high spirits,consider us soldiers of ZarbeAzb,don't	Negative
14	shaistaAziz	How many people people remain in north Waziristan and which groups is the army targeting? http://t.co/AIiBjqUYCk via #Pakistan #ZarbeAzb	Negative
15	aliarqam	RT @mjdawar: Waziristan has been Razed to the ground by PAF Jets and none of the terrorists killed. #StateFranchisedTerror	Negative
16	DawarSafdar	Till curfew in waziristan,I think and worry that with curfew uplifting the war will start among military and militancy .	Negative
17	SanaTGulzar	RT @iramabbasi: Tribal customs making it difficult for some women IDPs to get access to all the help the need:My Video Story @BBCUrdu http:	Negative
18	arsched	RT @javerias: Chief of Army Staff General Raheel Sharif at MiranShah . #ZarbEAzb #MilataryOperation #NorthWazirstan #TTP #Pakistan http://t	Negative
19	Rabail26	Extremist religious outfits have access to #IDPs in Bannu to provide "relief": by @TahaSSiddiqui. http://t.co/SbAGoPBYwu#ZarbeAzb #Pakistan	Negative
20	kazmiwajahat	BREAKING: #PakArmy troops are deployed in all the major cities of #Pakistan including #Karachi, #Lahore & #Islamabad. #ZarbeAzb #TTP	Negative

Figure 4c shows the tweets classification of the event "Hockey Champions Trophy for Men 2014". The tweets of this event are classified as 65% negative, 13% positive and 25% neutral. More negative sentiments are because of the criticism on International Hockey Federation (FIH). FIH banned two Pakistani hockey players due to violation of discipline. For further analysis, we randomly choose 20 tweets as shown in Table 7 from negatively classified tweets. In tweets at serial no 5, 6, 8, 15, 18 and 19 the people express their disgust about the decision of FIH, Indian media and others. These are the major reasons that majority of sentiments of this event are classified as negative.

Table 4. Tweets with positive sentiments from the event "Zarb-e-Azab"

S	Twitter ID	Tweet	Polarity
1	khushnood2020	RT @amarbail1: I am sure helpin IDPs in holy month of #Ramzan will bring peace and satisfaction to ur heart. #HelpIDPs @ErumManzoor http://	Positive
2	MishalHusainBBC	Happy Christmas, wherever you are RT @Razarumi: Church in South Waziristan celebrates http://t.co/wK07ymz2	Positive
3	FauziaKasuri	RT @syedsuhaibshah: Mrs. @FauziaKasuri distributing relief goods among the IDPs of North Waziristan with team@GVPakistan. @rameez_mumtaz ht	Positive
4	sharmeenochinoy	Now would be a good time to address the nation! #PM #ZarbEAzb	Positive
5	NadiaaQasim	Plz Allah protect our soldiers who r in #WaziristanOperation as they always protect us.Allah Bless U and may you come home safe & sound,,	Positive
6	AtifSal	How many $$$?"@AsimBajwaISPR: #ZarbeAzb:Whole of nation approach will help us succeed vs terrorism,extremism in st http://t.co/VEQWUrZEHG"	Positive
7	taahir_khan	Air strikes in Waziristan 'effective and successful': Sartaj Aziz http://t.co/9e81NV21el	Positive
8	TheHaroonRashid	A selfie with lovely Waziristan orphans at Sweet Home. Watch report now on @BBCurdu on Aaj TV http://t.co/QOzuwQnpB6	Positive
9	omar_quraishi	RT @Majid_Agha: Dear @AsimBajwaISPR #ZarbEAzb is hope of the nation.#BringBack TaseerAndGillani http://t.co/kdUJ8cW2k9	Positive
10	praveenswami	Jibran Ahmad has a great piece on refugees fleeing Pakistans war-torn North Waziristan — http://t.co/VyfkEskSIt	Positive

To measure the effectiveness of the proposed framework, we computed its precision. Although it is desired to measure precision on the complete dataset, but in absence of a labeled dataset, we computed precision based on random samples. We calculate two types of precisions, first P_t for the tweets retrieved by the framework and second P_u for the users retrieved by the framework. $P_t = 1$ if all the tweets retrieved by the framework are relevant to the event, and $P_u = 1$ if all the users retrieved by the framework belong to the community. To compute each of the precisions, we take 3 random samples of 50 tweets each, and measure the average precision for all the samples. We compute P_t and P_u using the following equations:

$$P_t = \frac{Relevant\ Tweets\ in\ the\ Sample}{Total\ Number\ of\ Tweets\ in\ the\ Sample} \tag{1}$$

$$P_u = \frac{Relevant\ Users\ in\ the\ Sample}{Total\ Number\ of\ Users\ in\ the\ Sample} \tag{2}$$

Table 5. Tweets with negative sentiments from the event "Azadi and Inqlab March"

S	Twitter ID	Tweet	Polarity
1	NasimZehra	Maulana Fazlur Rehman makes terrible/incorrect accusation of fa'hashi against PTI's protests.Stick to pol, Constitutional issues,Maulana sb	Negative
2	Mahamali05	Will the reforms include making one joint electorate for all? Will you ask for this reform Imran Khan?	Negative
3	ZaidZamanHamid	That is why Altaf the toad and beaten up, corrupt politicians are supporting Dr. TUQ. They want their share in the National govt ! Got it ?	Negative
4	MominaKhawar	Life. "@fasi_zaka: A day after meeting his hero, Imran Khan's biggest fan passes away http://t.co/qdPnLuaNyX"	Negative
5	shabbeerwahgra	RT @saleemiss: Imran Khan releasing his workers from the Police Station, making a video & uploading it from his official page too https://t	Negative
6	ImaanZHazir	RT @mazdaki: After calling off his dharna Dr.Tahir-ul-Qadri walks straight into the dustbin of history; Aabpara will retrieve him if & when	Negative
7	mushtaqminhas	RT @Maria95PTI: @Asad_Umar @ImranKhanPTI Almost many many pti girl wing ISB are upset ...We will not come in azadi march if its in allian	Negative
8	FaisalJavedKhan	VIDEO: Imran Khan's speech on 41st day of the protest at #AzadiSquare 23rd Sep, 2014 http://t.co/28coSjml5r	Negative
9	SikanderBalouch	@AnsarAAbbasi or Ulma Counsal ny wese bhe pehle bewi sy ijzat walee shart bhee khatm kardee,,ab tu Naya Pakistan with New Wife #AzadiSquare	Negative
10	tariqbutt_	Particularly sacrifices of interior Sindh ppl in MRD movement were matchless Then many revolutionaries of 2day weren't even born in politics	Negative
11	KlasraRauf	RT @aslammuz: @Uzma_Views @KlasraRauf @arsched media is also responsible for this, promoting a criminal as a hero like @ImranKhanAnchor	Negative
12	AzazSyed	Met two doctors both support @ImranKhanPTI and both admit he has lack of vision.	Negative
13	sanabucha	Resignations? PTI in an effort to prove 'we mean business' by going 'out of business'! Only 'business as usual' in KPK. Vah!	Negative
14	SaeedShah	RT @MurtazaGeoNews: Leading female reporters @Fereeha and @asmashirazi threaten to boycott #PTI coverage if attacks on journalists by #PTI	Negative
15	mohsinrz	RT @KamranShafi46: 9,000 in one DHARNA and 11,000 in another ain't makin' Nawaz/ Shahbaz Sharif to 'GO' and the assemblies to be dissolved.B	Negative
16	ShahidMursaleen	RT @RaheeqAbbasi: One of the reason for #DrQadri to go abroad: Govt denied right of treatment in Pakistan for #DrQadri #LongLiveDrQadri htt	Negative
17	Khalil_a_hassan	RT @TahirulQadri: We condemn the death of a protesting #PTI worker in Faisalabad and the state brutality towards them. #PAT	Negative
18	wajih_sani	RT @HamidMirGEO: Imran Khan mentioned missing persons after a long time good to hear that from him	Negative
19	DrAwab	RT @ArsalanGhumman: Dharna has ended but uprising movement has stated ! #RespectForIK	Negative
20	kdastgirkhan	MT @AnsarAAbbasi:Breaking DI Khan & Bannu Jails was terrorism. Removing prisoners forcibly from police van was political activity?	Negative

Table 8 shows the average precisions for tweets and the users. The high precision rates show the effectiveness of *CommuniMents*. Even for totally different types of events, at least 76% of the tweets fetched by the framework are related to the event. Moreover, the framework performs even better in terms of user precision (P_u), where the least precision is 81% for the event *Azadi and Inqilab March*.

Table 6. Tweets with positive sentiments from the event "Azadi and Inqlab March"

S	Twitter ID	Tweet	Polarity
1	NazBalochPTI	Musarrat Misbah joins PTI. Great to have a leading woman in the field of social welfare become part of #PTIFamily. http://t.co/QE5aNGOgSo	Positive
2	Fereeha	Just finished a very interesting meeting with @TahirulQadri at his home. He categorically denied rumours of a deal. http://t.co/Hwii2BJubK	Positive
3	mosharrafzaidi	This is the finest piece you will read on Imran Khan's Plan C. Even Insafians may like it (if you read to the end). http://t.co/ruybDf9lf1	Positive
4	jasmeenmanzoor	RT @AmnaKhanPTI: And the hilarious moment when IK cleans his sweating with his kameez....Baqio k tou tissues hi nahi khatam hote	Positive
5	kazmiwajahat	An attempt to get celebrities like Shahid Afridi & Wasim Akram & in return a good number of crowd. #ShameOnIK #PTI http://t.co/7gaItCQ59G	Positive
6	NadeemMalikLive	@ImranKhanPTI talking with @nadeemmalik, right now @SAMAATV http://t.co/9Cfg9tgsFK	Positive
7	Mubashirlucman	@AsimBajwaISPR sir when will you gives us good news of Nawaz Sharif arrest? #AzadimarchPTI #InqilabmarchwithDrQadri #DrQadri	Positive
8	FarahnazZahidi	Thank you Sargodha! Massive! And well done #PTI for such an organzied jalsa.	Positive
9	arsched	The rich man stops laughing when the revolution comes. Quote #RevolutionMarch	Positive
10	NazBalochPTI	RT @syedarr: @RNYousuf @NazBalochPTI nice to meet the enthusiastic PTI couple .. Like My brother and sister .. #GoNawazGo http://t.co/zp	Positive

DISCUSSION

To know the opinion of targeted community about the events under study, we identified the members of community by using the snowball sampling technique. During this process, it is possible that irrelevant users are also fetched along with actual members. To reduce this risk, an effective filtering mechanism is necessary. To filter irrelevant users, we carried out a semi-manual process.

For knowing the opinions of journalists about events under study, we performed event based sentiment analysis of their tweets. Popular sentiment analyzer (Stanford CoreNLP) classified the tweets into very positive, positive, neutral, negative, and very negative.

It is difficult to completely rely on sentiments in forming an opinion about an event, because the meaning of positive and negative depends on the context. For example, in the event "Azadi and Inqlab March" journalists condemn the federal government and election commission of Pakistan for the rigging in general election 2013 and the way the federal government handled the issue of protest and sit-in (dharna) by using the paramilitary forces. In the same way journalists also criticized the Punjab government due to the incident of Model town, Lahore. Due to the condemning and criticism, a large part of event related tweets are classified as negative. Upon the analysis of these negative tweets, we reached the conclusion that the targeted community was actually supporting these protests in their tweets.

On the other hand, in "zarb-e-azb" event related tweets, those classified as negative, were really negative tweets. The community under study was reluctant that this war was not ours, and they were worried regarding the displacement of the common residents of area, where the operation was started.

Table 7. Tweets with negative sentiments from the event "Hockey Champions Trophy for Men 2014"

S	Twitter ID	Tweet	Polarity
1	JavedAzizKhan	Indian hockey chief announces ending ties with #Pakistan: TV reports ... WTH ? .. #Hockey #ChampionsTrophy	Negative
2	SaadiaAfzaal	RT @usmanmanzoor: When will Malik Riaz announce plots and cash for the poor Hockey players ??? #Waiting	Negative
3	alisalmanalvi	Some asses are set on fire... Sore losers. https://t.co/ sh9w6CAkXC#ChampionsTrophy2014 #PakvInd #Hockey	Negative
4	shakirhusain	RT @faizanlakhani: BLAST FROM THE PAST: This is India's Prabhjot Singh during WC2010, after Indian's loss to Argentina. cc: @FIH_Hockey htt	Negative
5	AsmatullahNiazi	congratulations #Indian #Media for success in getting ban from #FIH is it not a biased decisions #fihockey ???????????	Negative
6	ApaAlii	RT @SalaamHockey: It was only 5 members of the 7k crowd who'd said derogatory things & unfortunately got the better of our boys, spoiling t	Negative
7	IffatHasanRizvi	RT @Anujmanocha: @iffathasanrizvi @imvkohli cricket ka badla hockey me ! wah!! . see u in the world cup 2015	Negative
8	MuhamadAfzalECP	RT @AQpk: After years of #Indian abuse and pettiness, finally someone from #Pakistan pays them in kind. #PakistanHockeyTeam #TitForTat #We	Negative
9	yasmeen_9	RT @faizanlakhani: Nadeem Omar, the businessman who helped Pakistan Hockey team financially, announces gold medals for the players of Pakis	Negative
10	ArifAlvi	Sorry! I opted out of @arsched ARY show because did not want to give up a double whammy show of cricket and hockey @KlasraRauf	Negative
11	SikanderRJ	Congrats Pakistan Hockey team on reaching the final of the #CT2014 beating India 4-3	Negative
12	khalidkhan787	pics: Muhammad Tousiq, left and Ammad Shakeel Butt performing Sajda after beating Netherlands in Hockey Quarterfinals http://t.co/WYttkzw4vg	Negative
13	AnsarAAbbasi	Report- Hockey India calls off bilateral series with Pakistan. #RoIndiaRo #RoIndiaRo #RoIndiaRo #RoIndiaRo #RoIndiaRo #RoIndiaRo	Negative
14	AdilNajam	Congrats #Pakistan for #Silver in #Hockey #ChampionsTrophy.But uneeded controversy bad for #SouthAsia + for #Hockey. http://t.co/0zHxzYQ6Wq	Negative
15	AqilSajjad	India's behavior in hockey after yesterday's game & how its been behaving in cricket for the last few years. totally shameful	Negative
16	khawajaNNInews	Report Decision PAK Player #22 Ali Amjad https://t.co/7HToKfnPUu#CT2014 #Bhubaneswar #fihockey"	Negative
17	faizanlakhani	Nadeem Omar, the businessman who helped Pakistan Hockey team financially, announces gold medals for the players of Pakistan team. #CT2014	Negative
18	asadrana74	RT @Khan_Arsalan: That awkward moment when World's Largest Democracy cries over a Hockey Match Defeat..#RoIndiaRo #CT2014 http://t.co/uQLj	Negative
19	ApaAlii	Why has @FIH_Hockey not made Youtube live streaming available in England!?	Negative
20	AQpk	#Pakistan remember: Our hockey team defeated in semifinals Champions Trophy becuz #India lobbied @FIH_Hockey to wrongfully ban 2 key players	Negative

Table 8. Precision of framework in terms of relevant tweets (Pt) and relevant users (Pu)

Event	P_t	P_u
Zarb-e-Azab	0.79	0.93
Azadi and Inqlab March	0.77	0.81
Hockey Champions Trophy for Men 2014	0.76	0.83

In event "Hockey Champions Trophy for Men 2014", a large part of relevant tweets were also classified as negative. The Pakistani journalist community expressed their opinion in support of Pakistani players and team while condemning and criticizing the decision of ban by the International Hockey Federation (IHF).

From the experiments and evaluation it has been observed that sentiment analysis i.e. Polarity of tweets is only helpful in primary and rapid opinion making about any specific event. To know the complete opinion of community about a specific event, qualitative analysis of tweets is necessary.

CONCLUSION AND FUTURE WORK

In this paper, we discussed the significance and role of social media among various communities and highlighted the influential role of communities which is powered by social media. Due to the importance of communities, a generic framework has been proposed to identify a specific community and also find out the event based sentiments of the community. *CommuniMents* consists of three main parts, which includes identification of members of targeted community, acquiring and filtering tweets in required events and cleansing event based tweets, and finding out the sentiments. For testing the framework, we chose the Pakistani journalist community as the targeted community and three different real events in the Pakistani context. The precision and recall of the obtained tweets and their sentiments proves the effectiveness of the proposed framework.

The direction of future research includes the requirement of a fully automatic filtering algorithm, which filters the relevant members of a targeted community from irrelevant members. Also in this study, the keywords lists are prepared manually and extended semi-automatically, but in the future, the process of creating keywords lists can be automated. For the current evaluation, the tweets other than English language are excluded, because the sentiment analyzers do not understand the local Pakistani languages, especially Urdu and Roman Urdu. So work in the future may be directed to provision of sentiment analysis facility of Urdu and Roman Urdu tweets in the proposed framework.

REFERENCES

Abdelhaq, H., Gertz, M., & Armiti, A. (2016). Efficient online extraction of keywords for localized events in twitter. *GeoInformatica*.

Alowibdi, J. S., Buy, U. A., Yu, P. S., Ghani, S., & Mokbel, M. (2015). Deception detection in twitter. *Social Network Analysis and Mining*, *5*(1), 1–16. doi:10.100713278-015-0273-1

Appel, O., Chiclana, F., Carter, J., & Fujita, H. (2016). A hybrid approach to the sentiment analysis problem at the sentence level. (New Avenues in Knowledge Bases for Natural Language Processing.). *Knowledge-Based Systems*, *108*, 110–124. doi:10.1016/j.knosys.2016.05.040

Atefeh, F., & Khreich, W. (2015). A survey of techniques for event detection in twitter. *Computational Intelligence*, *31*(1), 132–164. doi:10.1111/coin.12017

Balazs, J. A., & Velsquez, J. D. (2016). Opinion mining and information fusion: A survey. *Information Fusion*, *27*, 95–110. doi:10.1016/j.inffus.2015.06.002

Bao, Y., Quan, C., Wang, L., & Ren, F. (2014). The role of pre-processing in twitter sentiment analysis. In D.-S. Huang, K.-H. Jo, & L. Wang (Eds.), Intelligent Computing Methodologies, LNCS (Vol. 8589, pp. 615–624). Springer International Publishing. doi:10.1007/978-3-319-09339-0_62

Bastos, M. T., Puschmann, C., & Travitzki, R. (2013). Tweeting across hashtags: Overlapping users and the importance of language, topics, and politics. *Proceedings of the 24th ACM Conference on Hypertext and Social Media HT '13* (pp. 164–168). New York, NY, USA. ACM. 10.1145/2481492.2481510

Batrinca, B., & Treleaven, P. C. (2015). Social media analytics: A survey of techniques, tools and platforms. *AI & Society, 30*(1), 89–116. doi:10.100700146-014-0549-4

Bekafigo, M. A., & McBride, A. (2013). Who tweets about politics? political participation of twitter users during the 2011 gubernatorial elections. *Social Science Computer Review, 31*(5), 625–643. doi:10.1177/0894439313490405

Bravo-Marquez, F., Frank, E., & Pfahringer, B. (2016). Building a twitter opinion lexicon from automatically-annotated tweets. *Knowledge-Based Systems, 108*, 65–78. doi:10.1016/j.knosys.2016.05.018

Bright, L. F., Kleiser, S. B., & Grau, S. L. (2015). Too much Facebook? an exploratory examination of social media fatigue. *Computers in Human Behavior, 44*, 148–155. doi:10.1016/j.chb.2014.11.048

Gaspar, R., Pedro, C., Panagiotopoulos, P., & Seibt, B. (2016). Beyond positive or negative: Qualitative sentiment analysis of social media reactions to unexpected stressful events. *Computers in Human Behavior, 56*, 179–191. doi:10.1016/j.chb.2015.11.040

Guo, L., Ding, Z., & Wang, H. (2016). Database Systems for Advanced Applications. In *Behavior-Based Twitter Overlapping Community Detection* (pp. 371–376). Springer International Publishing, Cham.

Gupta, S., & Sharma, S. (2016). A spelling mistake correction (smc) model for resolving real-word error. In H.S. Behera, & D.P. Mohapatra (Eds.), Computational Intelligence in Data Mining, AISC (Vol. 410, pp. 429–438). Springer India.

Hammer, B. (2002). Recurrent networks for structured data a unifying approach and its properties. *Cognitive Systems Research, 3*(2), 145–165. doi:10.1016/S1389-0417(01)00056-0

Honey, C., & Herring, S. (2009). Beyond microblogging: Conversation and collaboration via twitter. *Proceedings of the 42nd Hawaii International Conference on System Sciences HICSS '09* (pp. 1–10).

Katz, G., Ofek, N., & Shapira, B. (2015). Consent: Context-based sentiment analysis. *Knowledge-Based Systems, 84*, 162–178. doi:10.1016/j.knosys.2015.04.009

Khan, F. H., Bashir, S., & Qamar, U. (2014). Tom: Twitter opinion mining framework using hybrid classification scheme. *Decision Support Systems, 57*, 245–257. doi:10.1016/j.dss.2013.09.004

Khan, H. U., Daud, A., Ishfaq, U., Amjad, T., Aljohani, N., Abbasi, R. A., & Alowibdi, J. S. (2017). Modelling to identify influential bloggers in the blogosphere: A survey. *Computers in Human Behavior, 68*, 64–82. doi:10.1016/j.chb.2016.11.012

Khan, W., Daud, A., Nasir, J. A., & Amjad, T. (2016). A survey on the state-of-the-art machine learning models in the context of NLP. *Kuwait Journal of Science, 43*(4), 95–113.

Khan Minhas, M. F., Abbasi, R. A., Aljohani, N. R., Albeshri, A. A., & Mushtaq, M. (2015). Intweems: A framework for incremental clustering of tweet streams. *Proceedings of the 17th International Conference on Information Integration and Web-based Applications & Services iiWAS '15* (pp. 87:1–87:4). New York, NY, USA: ACM. 10.1145/2837185.2843853

Krcadinac, U., Pasquier, P., Jovanovic, J., & Devedzic, V. (2013). Synesketch: An open source library for sentence-based emotion recognition. *IEEE Transactions on* Affective Computing, *4*(3), 312–325.

Kumar, S., Morstatter, F., & Liu, H. (2014). Visualizing twitter data. In *Twitter Data Analytics* (pp. 49–69). Springer. doi:10.1007/978-1-4614-9372-3_5

Kwak, H., Lee, C., Park, H., & Moon, S. (2010). What is twitter, a social network or a news media? *Proceedings of the 19th International Conference on World Wide Web WWW '10* (pp. 591–600). New York, NY, USA: ACM. 10.1145/1772690.1772751

Lin, X., Lachlan, K. A., & Spence, P. R. (2016). Exploring extreme events on social media: A comparison of user reposting/retweeting behaviors on twitter and weibo. *Computers in Human Behavior, 65*, 576–581. doi:10.1016/j.chb.2016.04.032

Liu, B. (2012). Sentiment analysis and opinion mining. *Synthesis Lectures on Human Language Technologies, 5*(1), 1–167. doi:10.2200/S00416ED1V01Y201204HLT016

Liu, B., & Zhang, L. (2012). *A Survey of Opinion Mining and Sentiment Analysis.* Boston, MA: Springer US. doi:10.1007/978-1-4614-3223-4_13

Makice, K. (2009). *Twitter API: Up and Running.* O'Reilly Media.

Manaman, H. S., & Jamali, S. (2016). Online reputation measurement of companies based on user-generated content in online social networks. *Computers in Human Behavior, 54*, 94–100. doi:10.1016/j.chb.2015.07.061

Manning, C. D., Surdeanu, M., Bauer, J., Finkel, J., Bethard, S. J., & McClosky, D. (2014). The stanford corenlp natural language processing toolkit. *Proceedings of 52nd Annual Meeting of the Association for Computational Linguistics: System Demonstrations* (pp. 55–60). 10.3115/v1/P14-5010

Medhat, W., Hassan, A., & Korashy, H. (2014). Sentiment analysis algorithms and applications: A survey. *Ain Shams Engineering Journal, 5*(4), 1093–1113. doi:10.1016/j.asej.2014.04.011

Mollett, A., Moran, D., & Dunleavy, P. (2011). Using twitter in university research, teaching and impact activities. Retrieved from http://eprints.lse.ac.uk/38489/

Muhammad, A., Wiratunga, N., & Lothian, R. (2016). Contextual sentiment analysis for social media genres. (New Avenues in Knowledge Bases for Natural Language Processing.). *Knowledge-Based Systems, 108*, 92–101. doi:10.1016/j.knosys.2016.05.032

Nasukawa, T., & Yi, J. (2003). Sentiment analysis: Capturing favorability using natural language processing. *Proceedings of the 2Nd International Conference on Knowledge Capture K-CAP '03* (pp. 70–77). New York, NY, USA: ACM.

O'Connor, B., Balasubramanyan, R., Routledge, B. R., & Smith, N. A. (2010). From tweets to polls: Linking text sentiment to public opinion time series. *Proceedings of the Fourth International AAAI Conference on Weblogs and Social Media (ICWSM)* (pp. 122–129).

Pang, B., & Lee, L. (2008). Opinion mining and sentiment analysis. *Found. Trends Inf. Retr.*, *2*(1-2), 1–135. doi:10.1561/1500000011

Rill, S., Reinel, D., Scheidt, J., & Zicari, R. V. (2014). Politwi: Early detection of emerging political topics on twitter and the impact on concept-level sentiment analysis. *Knowledge-Based Systems*, *69*, 24–33. doi:10.1016/j.knosys.2014.05.008

Schuller, B., Mousa, A. E.-D., & Vryniotis, V. (2015). Sentiment analysis and opinion mining: On optimal parameters and performances. *Data Mining and Knowledge Discovery*, *5*(5), 255–263.

Sligh, J., Abedtash, H., Yang, M., Zhang, E., and Jones, J. (2016). A novel pipeline for targeting breast cancer patients on twitter for clinical trial recruitment.

Socher, R., Perelygin, A., Wu, J., Chuang, J., Manning, C. D., Ng, A., & Potts, C. (2013). Recursive Deep Models for Semantic Compositionality Over a Sentiment Treebank. *Proceedings of the 2013 Conference on Empirical Methods in Natural Language Processing* (pp. 1631–1642). Seattle, Washington, USA. Association for Computational Linguistics.

Takahashi, B. Jr, Tandoc, E. C. Jr, & Carmichael, C. (2015). Communicating on twitter during a disaster: An analysis of tweets during typhoon Haiyan in the Philippines. *Computers in Human Behavior*, *50*, 392–398. doi:10.1016/j.chb.2015.04.020

Thelwall, M., Buckley, K., & Paltoglou, G. (2011). Sentiment in twitter events. *Journal of the American Society for Information Science and Technology*, *62*(2), 406–418. doi:10.1002/asi.21462

Wang, Y., Rao, Y., Zhan, X., Chen, H., Luo, M., & Yin, J. (2016). Sentiment and emotion classification over noisy labels. *Knowledge-Based Systems*, *111*, 207–216. doi:10.1016/j.knosys.2016.08.012

WeGov. (2016). Where eGovernment meets the eSociety. Retrieved from http://www.wegov-_project.eu

Wu, S., Hofman, J. M., Mason, W. A., & Watts, D. J. (2011). Who says what to whom on twitter. *Proceedings of the 20th International Conference on World Wide Web WWW '11* (pp. 705–714). New York, NY, USA. ACM. 10.1145/1963405.1963504

Zhou, D., Chen, L., & He, Y. (2015). An unsupervised framework of exploring events on twitter: Filtering, extraction and categorization. *Proceedings of AAAI Conference on Artificial Intelligence* (pp. 2468–2474).

Zubiaga, A., Ji, H., & Knight, K. (2013). Curating and contextualizing twitter stories to assist with social newsgathering. *Proceedings of the 2013 International Conference on Intelligent User Interfaces IUI '13* (pp. 213–224), New York, NY, USA. ACM. 10.1145/2449396.2449424

ENDNOTES

[1]   https://dev.twitter.com/rest/reference/get/lists/memberships
[2]   https://dev.twitter.com/rest/reference/get/lists/members
[3]   Currently Twitter API returns last 3200 publicly available tweets of a user
[4]   https://dev.twitter.com/rest/reference/get/statuses/user_timeline
[5]   http://www.netlingo.com/acronyms.php
[6]   https://msdn.microsoft.com/library?url=/library/en-us/off2000/html/woobjproofreadingerrors.asp
[7]   http://lemmagen.ijs.si/

This research was previously published in the International Journal on Semantic Web and Information Systems (IJSWIS), 13(2); pages 87-108, copyright year 2017 by IGI Publishing (an imprint of IGI Global).

Section 3
Tools and Technologies

Chapter 20
Social Networking Data Analysis Tools and Services

Gopal Krishna

Aryabhatt Knowledge University, India

ABSTRACT

Social networks have drawn remarkable attention from IT professionals and researchers in data sciences. They are the most popular medium for social interaction. Online social networking (OSN) can be defined as involving networking for fun, business, and communication. Social networks have emerged as universally accepted communication means and boomed in turning this world into a global town. OSN media are generally known for broadcasting information, activities posting, contents sharing, product reviews, online pictures sharing, professional profiling, advertisements and ideas/opinion/sentiment expression, or some other stuff based on business interests. For the analysis of the huge amount of data, data mining techniques are used for identifying the relevant knowledge from the huge amount of data that includes detecting trends, patterns, and rules. Data mining techniques, machine learning, and statistical modeling are used to retrieve the information. For the analysis of the data, three methods are used: data pre-processing, data analysis, and data interpretation.

INTRODUCTION

This Chapter on Social Networking Data Analysis Tools and Services introduces the various perspectives of the online social networking sites(OSNs), its various aspects such as its applications, types of data available on OSN, different types of analysis for these huge amount of data, the tools used to analysis these data, the platform components, system architecture and research issues on OSN. It will help the academician, researchers and practitioners to improve their capacity to gain an accurate and deep understanding of about OSN. The term social network or online social network or social media is referred to depict web-based services that permit persons to make a profile inside a certain domain so that they may interact with other users in the specified network. Graph theory is applied in the social network that consist of *vertices* and *edges* employed to symbolize social relations on OSN sites. A huge number of domains and sectors, ranging from business analysis and economic to public administration,

DOI: 10.4018/978-1-7998-9020-1.ch020

from governance to scientific researches in many fields, involve with social networking data analysis tools and techniques. On the one hand, social networking data is enormously important to increase the productivity in businesses and progressive discovery in research disciplines, that provide a lot of opportunities for the enormous development in many areas. OSN data are very complex because of its three features named as size, noise and dynamism. For the analysis of these data, data mining techniques are used for identifying the relevant knowledge from the huge amount of data that includes detecting trends, patterns and rules. Data, information and knowledge are three important data mining paradigms. The huge amount data in social networks datasets are needed for automated processing and analyzing of information within a realistic time.

Fascinatingly, huge data sets are required to mine significant model from data in data mining techniques. OSN sites emerged as an ideal platform to mine with data mining techniques and tools. Data mining tools may have varieties from unsupervised or semi supervised machine learning techniques to supervised machine learning techniques. Sometimes users make decisions based on contents shared by unknown person on OSN sites. These escalating the level of dependence on the trustworthiness of these sites. OSN has also provided users the freedom to give opinions and reviews in real time with very little or no restriction.

BACKGROUND

Social networking provides facilities to the users to share their views, photos, posts, videos and others contents such as their events and activities to connect with people in their network. It is similar to the inter personal social gathering in villages, markets, towns to discuss on the various issues and events.

But the main difference is that OSN enables users to connect with other users at difference locations, across the globe. Generally social networking can be noticed in different views first as which main purpose is to socializing with friends like facebook and instagram other can be networking for non-social interpersonal communication such as LinkedIn for a career and employment oriented site. So, there are many OSN sites through which people can be interlinked via cross-posting without invading the personal privacy.

The history and background of social networking is very interesting since the evolution of human civilization. It refers to the evolution of personal communication among the people. The medium of personal communication has changed a lot from the evolution of human civilization. The hand written letter was the oldest practice of communication across long distance from one person to another. It was started in 500 B.C., and became popular and broad medium in future centuries. In the year 1792, the telegraph was invented through which messages was delivered for the far distance than previous methods. Since through telegraph messages were short, it was a tremendous change in the communication in the society for the long period of time to convey news and information. Another way of communication started in the year 1865 was postal services for the personal, professional, and other communication. After that telephone and radio was another revolutionary invention in 1890 and 1891 respectively that are still in use today and developing day by day. Both has changed the lifestyle of people in the communication across the long distances immediately that was a new and amazing experience for mankind. In the 20th century, technology started to change immediately after the development of computers. Scientists and engineers started to develop the techniques to connect the computers that later lead to the birth of Internet. CompuServe was the earliest form of Internet in 1960s. Fundamental form of emails were developed during this period. After the evolution of internet networking technology has upgraded by 1970s, through UseNet allowed users communicate in the form of virtual newsletter. By 1980s, personal computers were becoming more popular and social media were being used on large scale. In 1988, Inter relay chats or IRCs were used firstly and continued to be used widely into 1900s. Six Degrees was the first online social networking site that was created in 1997. Using this user enabled to create a profile and making other user friends. In the year 1999, blogging sites evolved and made online social media became sensational and popular. In 2000s sites like Orkut, LinkedIn, MySpace achieved tremendous attention and response from users. Photobucket and Flickr promoted online photo sharing. In 2005, You-Tube came into existence which became the excellent medium for online video sharing and becoming popular day by day. Facebook and Twitter came out in 2006 and became most popular and successful across the globe on internet in the present era. There are many more online social media sites Spotify, Tumblr, Foursquare and Pinterest are also giving remarkable presence in the social networking world. In this age there are large variety of online social networking sites that are linked to each other to allow cross-posting through which users can reach the maximum numbers of people according to their choice and requirements without disturbing the personal confidentiality.

ISSUES, CONTROVERSIES, AND PROBLEMS

How Online Social Networking Sites (OSNs) Work

Social networking sites has millions of users and their millions of updates per second. So the question arises that how these data managed by the social networking sites? What software and servers are there to manage all these? What are the tools and services to maintain and manage all these? The answers behind these questions are open-source software and thousands of servers. The operating system behind the most of the social networking sites such as MySpace, Twitter and LinkedIn are all Linux. F5 Big-IP is used by Facebook, which is a member of Linux appliances used for the network management. The web servers used is Apache and ONE Web Servers is used by LinkedIn in along with Apache. Sun's MySQL is used by most of the Social networking sites for database management system to manage the user's messages and status updates. So, the most part of the social networking sites consist of the Linux, Apache, MySQL, PHP/Python/Perl. The APIs (Application Programming Interface) are there for the developers to develop the applications that will run on their network and to add the new features to the sites. OSN Sites has maintain the secrecy on their overall functionality suc as Twitter uses Ruby on Rails an open source web framework. Jabber/XMPP (Extensible Messaging and Presence Protocol) is used by Twitter for the routing of millions of the instant messages. Facebook handle 260 billion-page views per month according to the Royal Pingdom, a Swedish site that track Internet sites uptime. For this at present it runs 30K servers. From the hardware point of view, expensive and high-tech equipment (servers) is required for the better management of the social network. Each server acts as high-speed memory ranges from 256 GBs to 512GBs of RAM. All these servers are linked together into clusters. Servers are placed in data centers with major Internet's Network Points(NAPs). NAPs are at the major Internet Service Providers(ISPs) are connected to each other and direct access are provided for the Internet's fastest connections. After all these next step is to work out exactly how to change all these technologies into money.

Social Network Analysis

The analysis of social network can be viewed from individualism in the sociology to the structural analysis that defines the primary unit of analysis of new analytical methods development such as friendship relationship among persons, communication links among employees in an organization etc. The interesting features of a relation is patterns and structures. There are attributes of the users among whom the relationship exits. A structure list is the degree of friendship is transitive. Relations(*strands*) are defined by the strength, direction and content. The information exchanged among the user in a relation referred as resources.

A relation can be categorized as directed or undirected such as one person may connected with a second person can be termed as support. Support cab be of two type, one can take or give support or both. Alternately, users can maintain an undirected relationship or friendship in which they both maintain the friendship or relationship without following any particular direction. In course of maintaining the relationship or friendship, there may be chance of unbalanced relationship. Unbalance in the relationship refers that one user may claim a close friendship but in return other a weaker friendship or one is more active and other is less or there may be difference in the communication frequency. It can termed as asymmetrical relation.

Relation can also be defined in terms of strength. It can be defined i terms of the frequency of the communication among the user's weather on once in a day, work days, weekends, weekly, monthly, yearly or rarely. The strength of relationships can be measured in various aspects. These measurement criteria may be social capital shared among the users such as services, money or goods for the exchange of trivial or vital information.

It is required to connect users to be in relationship through a tie. A tie based relationship can be maintained by the pair on the basis of one to one relationship that may of similar background, or in same firm. A multiplex tie is maintained based on the relationship that may share on the basis of the other criteria such as information being shared, attending events together, visiting the places together etc. Ties can be differing in strength content and direction. It may be weaker or stronger in terms of context. Weak ties refer to the infrequent communication, less intimacy such as for those users who are connected with each other but their interest is not similar. In the strong ties the frequency of communication is higher, there is fine scope of content and idea sharing such as among college friends or batch mates. Since, both category of ties is important for the exchange of resources in the networks. More resources are shared in the network where strong ties are there whatever users want. In contrast in the weakly tied networks, users have less scope for the frequent content and resource sharing. They provide more access to the different resources of the social network. The users who never communicated with each other within a circle or organization, there is provision of electronic tie for the efficient flow of resources, data, content and information. There may be activity sharing to maintain the proper connectivity among them.

Multiplexity

The multiplex or multi-stranded is a tie that may be defined as multiple relations among the users in the network. It is found by the social network analysts that there is more scope for the connectivity, intimacy, support, and durability if multiplexity is used in network. But there are still some issues among the social network analysts that the internet, emails, personal messaging etc do not fulfill the criteria of multiplexity. This issue is more extended by the boutique approach. This approach is applied to online that encourages the specifications in ties. This trend demonstrates the multiple communication among the various user groups in the online social networking. It results in the broad sustainability, multiplexity and supportive among the internet participants. However, there is little scope for the research in terms of multiplexity ties over specialization, online, social network relations grow during time.

Functionalities and Features of Online Social Networking

There are large variety of online social networking sites for the different purposes. But there are some core features of every OSNs. The features of OSNs are mentioned as follows:

As OSN can be represented digitally for its users(nodes) and relationships or connections among them in real world along with networking services for conversations/chatting. It provides the medium to:

1. Allow individual to create a digital representation of themselves (generally called profiles or account) and establish their online social relation with other users (i.e., contact list or friend list).
2. To update and enhance the previous and pre-existing relation among users also provide support and maintenance of real world relations in the digital world.
3. Based on common activities, common interest, locations new online relationships can be established just like real world relationships. Following functionalities are provided by the online social networking sites to their users for the online social interactions and self-representation:

Personal Space Management

An online social networking sites should support a user to:

1. Create or delete a profile or an account.
2. Edit or update personal and general information in the account or profile.
3. Upload or edit user generated contents or posts like blog- postings, status update, photos, locations, interests etc.

Note that, generally in most of the online social networking sites, a user's activities in his personal space will be displayed to his friend list automatically. Therefore, any activity like uploading and editing user post or information are the important communication primitive between a user's and their friend list or contact list.

Social Connection Management

Online Social Networking sites connect individuals or users to through the formal means to establish their relationship (e.g.- friend lists) with each other represented by the social ties. New social ties or links can be established for those who share common interests and hobbies. These can have maintained or invoked through a social connection for which online social graph or simple labeled graph is used to create all data stored in the OSN sites. In the social graph the nodes or vertices denote the user and the edges represent the relationship between users. The user's profile is maintained by nodes and each link is tagged with a social link *label*. A few OSN sites provide not only a simple relationship but also establishes the trust relationships, categorize the relationships, and also make the various access without compromising the privacy and security of the users. The space in which the user's profile and social edges or connections are refer as digital personal space and collection of registered user's personal spaces are referred as the digital social space.

Means of Communication

There are various means of communications for users, since communication is the main theme or idea of any OSN sites. Public messages that is blogging and private messages in the various modes such as photos, audio, texts, video, and so on using personal spaces. Another mode may be the asynchronous communication and asynchronous communication. Many other OSNs also provide facilities to play real time online games in pair or group wise.

Exploring Digital Social Space

There is restriction for the existing users to interact with another users that encourages users to build new social relations can be termed as socialization. Searching the new or unknown users in the OSNs is also the main feature that can be authenticated and authorized in the two steps. The two-important means through which the personal space of an unknown users can be reached as:

1. **Global Keyword Search (or Social Search):** The Global keyword search is the first mean of search. For the successful search accessing the search list is the main task. Search policy can be specified by the users to be access through a global name search.
2. **Social Graph Traversal (or Social Traversal):** The Social Graph traversal is the second mean to access the search listing through traversing online social graph. Users can search the new users by traversing or accessing the contact list or friend list of new users or person. An user can restrict other user to view his account by the traversal policy that specifies the set rules. Usability and sociability is the main traditional goal of OSNs that can be achieved by supporting all the functionalities in the design of new secured and privacy preserving OSNs.

System Architectures of Online Social Networking

There are two standard for the implementation of an OSN are Peer-to-Peer Architecture Client Server Architecture that provide distribute system and Centralized system respectively.

1. **Peer-to-Peer Architecture:** This is based on the decentralized architecture for the design of next-generation OSNs carry on the cooperation among the user also called independent parties. The database of in the personal space of the users are stored and maintained in the distribute form. It may take support of real social networks and geographical proximity to support local services in the unavailability of Internet. Global search is the example of the P2P architecture in a distributed manner is an challenging task.
2. **Client Server Architecture:** This is based on the centralized system and web-server. This is followed by the commercial social media such as LinkedIn Corp., Facebook Inc, XING AG etc. in which all functionalities are there like storage, maintenance, and access. It's a basic and conventional

architecture. It is easier to implement and has an benefit of being genuine and while it also suffers from some defect like any single entity can cause an issue for the failure.

Figure 1. A three-tiered OSN Architecture: Client server architecture and Peer-to-peer architecture

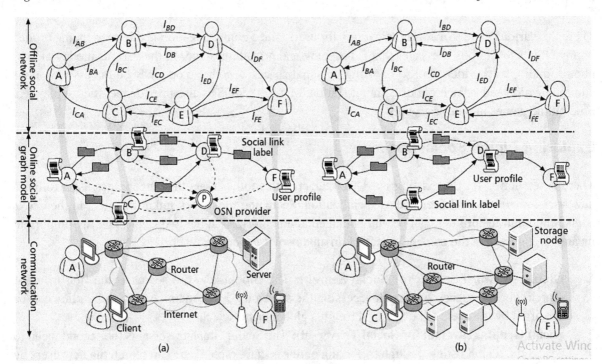

Trust, Privacy, and Security Concerns in Online Social Networking

Privacy and security issues with the trust impact is the main concern in the online social networking sites. To maintain the balance between the privacy and security in the OSNs for the better implementation of usability and sociability, various standard principles of network security are there such as confidentiality, integrity and availability. After the joining OSNs, users create their profiles to connect with their existing friends as well as new people. In the profile they include their general information such as name(real name or pseudonym), age, profession, personal interest, hometown etc. There are facilities to post their status, activities, photos, videos, chatting, personal messaging, public testimonials etc in order to stay connected with each other and make them updated Users send friend request or follow request through messages and other ways to connect with their friends and to add them to the social network. The main purpose of joining the social network is the communication and establish the relationships. Trust can be defined as "the willingness of a person to be accessible to the activities of the other person based on the expectation that the other will perform the specific activity to the user.

Trust is the major and critical determinant of sharing information and establishing new relationships. Trust is main component that is to be believed in the perception of social and interpersonal exchange that confirm the precondition for self disclosure. Electronic commerce research has found trust to be strongly related to information disclosure. Privacy issue in the OSNs sites is generally is undefined since it maintains all records of interactions, posts, updates and preserve them for potential use in data mining and data analysis. The unwanted, illegal disclosure and improper use personal data of someone can cause hazard or damaging their lives. To the security of these data and information these OSNs sites require explicit policies and data safety techniques in order to achieve social network privacy and security goal that ensures a higher level of cyber security.

Security Issues Can Identified As

- **Identity Theft:** The identity misuse or identity theft happens when someone uses personal information of other persons without his or her knowledge for some intentional harm. It is one of the most committed cybercrime. For example a cybercriminal can access online banking of any customer through social media or application and perform the online transaction that leads to loss. Another example is that an attacker or cybercriminal who create a fake profile of HR of any organization on a social networking site and post an attractive job opening. The users may become the victims by posting their personal information and resumes. The attacker or cybercriminal can share the personal information with the third party advertising or job consultancy companies. The uncontrolled features of social networking platform provides the attackers, fraudsters, cybercriminals a factual opportunities of criminal activities.

- **Malwares, Viruses and Phishing Attacks:** These kinds of attacks can occur through the email communication, user posts, link sharing, direct messages and harmful tweets on social media. There are various methods used by the cyber-attackers to spread the malicious software on social media. The purpose of this attack is to obtain the personal information of users and get access to the network. After getting the access to the network, the attacker get the valuable and confidential information of victims. Phishing refers to a fraud in which intruder tries to access the login credential, personal information and account information by masquerading as a reputable entity.

- **Threats From Third Party Applications:** Many third party websites and mobile application are integrated with the social networking sites for the user convenience to avoid the multiple registrations. Users easily allow these applications to get the personal information and likely to provide access to the personal data.

Privacy Issues has Several Broad Categories

- **User's Identity Anonymity:** For the safety of user's identity, different social networking sites has different mechanisms. In Facebook real name or user id is used for the representation of an user's profile or account. There is no validation for the user identification in the Facebook for creating profile or account. Friendster, a dating site has weak pseudonymity in which account is created by using only the first name of the user visible to others users, not the last name. Other dating websites like Match.com, the use of real names and real personal information is not encouraged. To protect the public identity of a person a random identifier is used.

- **User's Personal Space Privacy:** To access of the user's profile or to view the user's profile, different mechanisms are there for the different online social networking sites. The OSNs like Friendster and Tribe.net have feature in which profile can be viewed publically. In Facebook, there is customization for the view of profiles, where user can restrict other users to view his profile based on the category or group. In MySpace also users have their choice or option either they want to show their profile or not to public or friends. Except few OSN sites most of them have feature for the customization of viewing of profile or general information. LinkedIn allows users to select hiding their friend lists.

- **User's Communication Privacy**: There are various information other than personal information such as length and time of the established connection, IP address of the network, no. of profiles visited, sent and received messages and so on may also be disclosed by the OSNs in the digital space of the users. So, there is need for the privacy in these areas. To achieve this, unauthorized entities should not be granted directly by the users. This leads to the access control in terms of data privacy. Also unauthorized and unauthenticated entities should not be linked up with the multiple private information databases.

- **Authentication and Data Integrity:** Authentication and Data Integrity is the main aspect of any digital communication. Since social networking reestablishes the preexisting social relationship. So, formally OSN can be said as a digital representation of an Real Life Social(RSN) Network or Offline Social Network. There is one to one mapping in social graph to represent the RSN. Data integrity in the context of OSNs means that this consistency should be kept; that is, any attempt of deviating an online social graph model from its corresponding RSN is a kind of attack, and should be detected and corrected with appropriate mechanisms.

Generally, there are two categories of attacks on social graph:

1. Forging nodes/identities and
2. Forging social links/connections

Forging is one of the main mechanism through which many security issues can be solved. It is primary issue in the most of the OSN sites. Forging a node refers to identifying the theft or intrusion in the network. The most common example of forging is that an intruder or attacker may create a fake profile or account of any famous or important personality or celebrity or brand for their own sake or benefits or distract the attentions. Also to disturb the digital image of any OSN sites, an attacker can create multiple fake identities. Thus, legitimacy is very important to prevent all these activities. It refers to the key used between the trusted parties who are authorized and authenticate their identities. Authentication can be achieved by using an entity through which the real identity of the party can be claimed. In OSN sites availability and accountability must be satisfied to fulfill the security requirements. Availability refers to the published data that should be continuously available. Accountability refers to the misbehavior of the data should be detectable.

Classes of Adversaries

It is incomplete discussion of security if, the adversary model is not discussed. There are many categories of adversaries but in Social network context it can be of two types:

- **Inside Attackers or Intruder:** Inside attackers are those adversaries whose primarily role is to be seems as legitimate player in the OSN but in some cases malicious acts are done by them; for example, a malicious OSN provider, a malicious third-party application provider, a malicious user of the OSN, or a malicious party that has access to the network infrastructure (e.g., an eavesdropper of a wireless link or a malicious ISP).

- **External Attackers or Intruders:** An eternal intruder or attacker is not a legitimate player in the OSN, but can carry out attacks on the OSN system or on the network infrastructures used by the OSN.

Measurements and Structure of Online Social Network

In online social network, the density of the network measures the amount of interconnections between the users that is unexpectedly pursued in the all categories of network classified as: rapid growth, decline and the slow but steady growth. The members in these networks can be categorized into three groups: the singletons, the giant component and the middle region.

- **Singletons:** The users in this group who have joined the social network but never established the connectivity with other users. The degree of these users is zero. Their participation is negligible and viewed as loners.
- **Giant Component:** This group represents the users on the large scale whose connectivity is through the paths in the social network. The users in this network find themselves as strongly connected with each other either directly or indirectly. Users are very active in this group.
- **Middle Region:** This group consists of different small and isolated subgroups in which users interact with each other but not within network on the large scale. It may represents the both active and inactive users of the total fraction of users.

Data Mining vs. Privacy

For the social and marketing analysis of data collected or aggregated in the social media is a major source that provide the useful and important information regarding the evolution of a social group in the collaborative solution of problems. Data mining is also used for the optimized use of OSN services based on the specification of user's group such as interests and preferences. There may be possibilities of conflicts between Privacy requirements in OSN and the social data mining. The adversaries can attack on the personal information of the users declared on the OSN and some background knowledge that can be prevented by node anonymization. It refers to the replacement corresponding users name with meaningless random identities. On the basis of graph topology, adversaries still can discover user's identities. So to overcome this problem age perturbation is introduced in the graph for anonymization procedure.

Social Network Analytics Tools

- **Scientific Programming Tools:** Provides platform for searching, sourcing and examining text. Tools include: R(statistical programming), MATLAB(used for numeric scientific programming) and Mathematica(used for symbolic scientific programming). Python is used for the natural language detection. Apache UIMA (Unstructured Information Management Applications) is another open-source tool through which big data analysis and data mining is done.
- **Business Toolkits:** It is the collection of tools and services used for sourcing, searching and analyzing the text for a variety of commercial uses. SAS (Sentiment Analysis Manager), a sub-

domain of the SAS Text Analytics program, are used for scraping content sources, including conventional websites and social media channels, as well as internal organizational text sources, and creates reports that describe the expressed feelings of consumers, customers and competitors in real time. RapidMiner is a well-known toolkit provides an open-source community that provides data mining and machine learning tasks. Lexalytics is also a tool used for the commercial sentiment analysis engine and IBM SPSS Statistics is one of the most used programs for statistical analysis in social science.

- **Social Media Monitoring Toolkits:** These tools include sentiment analysis tools for tracking and measuring the customers review about company or its products and services. The examples of social media monitoring include: Social Mention, Amplified Analytics, Lithium Social Media Monitoring and Trackur

- **Text Analysis Toolkit:** These tools used for text analysis and NLP. Vendors in the text analysis area are: OpenAmplify and Jodange whose tools are used in sentiment analysis. . Lexalytics Sentiment Toolkits is also a powerful toolkit that performs the automatic sentiment analysis on input documents. Especially efficient when the input document is too large, but data scraping is not performed. Python NLKT(Natural Language Toolkit) is an open-source python analysis tool based Python module. Another examples of commercial software for text mining are AeroText, Attensity, Clarabridge, IBM LanguageWare, SPSS Text Analytics for Surveys, Language Computer Corporation, STATISTICA Text Miner and WordStat.

- **Social Media Analytics Platforms:** This include social media archive, data feeds, data mining and data analysis tools. They can be categorized into two categories:
  - **Social Network Media Platform:** Provides data mining and analytics on Twitter, Facebook, and other social network media.
  - **News Platforms:** Platforms such as Thomson Reuters providing news archives/feeds and associated analytics and targeting companies such as financial institutions seeking to monitor market sentiment in news.

- **Data Visualization Tools:** These tools offer business intelligence(BI) capabilities and allow users of different field to expand the approaches in Big Data. SAS Sentiment Analysis and SAS Social Media Analytics have a user-friendly interface for developing models; users can upload sentiment analysis models directly to the server in order to minimize the manual model deployment. More advanced users can use the interactive workbench to refine their models.

FUTURE RESEARCH DIRECTIONS

Research Issues on Social Network Analysis

- **Linkage-Based and Structural Analysis:** Refers to the linkage manners of the ONS so as to establish appropriate edges, links, groups and relevant fields.
- **Dynamic Analysis and Static Analysis:** Static analysis is supposed to be used in streaming networks. It changes gradually over time and batch mode analysis is done. Conversely, it is very difficult to carry out dynamic analysis for streaming networks like YouTube and Facebook due to the high speed data and large capacity.

- **Recommender System in Social Network Community**: In social network recommendations for a user are based on the ranking of her/his mutual connections among nodes in social network groups.
- **Semantic Web of Social Network:** It is the domain for information sharing and its feasible reuse over different tools and groups. Semantic web improves the facts of the fame of Semantic Web Community.
- **Aspect-Based/Feature-Based Opinion Mining:** It is the process of mining the customers review field. It is important to sum up the opinion as the review to determine the divergence of the overall reviews either positive or negative or ambiguous.
- **Topic Detection and Tracking on Social Network(TDT):** *TDT* utilizes diverse methods for determining the evolution of new topics (or events) and for tracking their successive evolvements over a period of time.
- **Natural Language Processing(NLP):** It is a field of linguistics, computer science and artificial intelligence that is related with the communication between computers and human(natural) languages. Specially, it is the method of mining significant.
- **News Analytics of Social Network:** Refers to the different quantitative and qualitative measurement of unstructured data whose attributes are novelty, sentiments and relevance.
- **Scraping:** Online data(unstructured text) collection from OSNs and other websites and also known as site scraping, web data extraction and web harvesting.
- **Sentiment Analysis on Social Network:** Refers to the application of NLP, text analytics and computational linguistics to recognize and mine biased information. It consists of following analysis:
  - Sentiment Orientation (SO)
  - Product Ratings and Reviews
  - Reviews and Ratings (RnR) Architecture
  - Aspect Rating Analysis
- **Text Analytic on Social Network:** It deals with information retrieval (IR), lexical analysis for the study of word frequency distributions, data mining techniques including link and association analysis, pattern recognition, information extraction, visualization, tagging/annotation, and predictive analytics.
- **Opinion Mining / Opinion Mining Analysis on Social Network:** Refers t, opinion/sentiment mining. It is the field of research that endeavor to build automated model to find out human sentiments and ideas from the text written in natural language.

Major Components in the Experimental Computational Environment in Social Networks

1. **Data:**
   a. **Data Storage:** For the data aggregation and data mining it provide facilities of principle data storage in specified area.
   b. **Data Protection/Security:** It can be achieved through applying certain mechanism to stop the user to access particular information.
   c. **Data Streaming:** Refers to access and combine real-time feeds and archived data for analytics.
   d. **Programmable Interfaces:** APIs(application Programming Interfaces) are used for scrapping and storing certain data available that cannot be collected automatically.

e. **Data Scraping:** Method of scraping any new type of social media such as news, blogs, RSS feeds, wikis, etc.

2. **Analysis:**

a. **Analytics Dashboards:** For the deep access to the raw data non-programming interfaces are required.

b. **Programmable Analytics:** To deploy advanced data mining and other simulation using simulator tools and languages like MATLAB, Java and Python, programming interfaces are required.

c. **Stream Processing:** For the stream processing of real-time data feeds in OSNs facilities are required.

d. **High-Performance Computing:** At last the platform required to support non-programming interfaces to NoSQL databases, MapReduce/Hadoop and Grids of processors.

e. **Decentralized Analytics:** Decentralized analytics is needed to if more valuable/sensitive data owned by financial institutions, governments, retailers and other commercial organization in a highly secure way.

3. **Platform Component:** The platform comprises the following modules, which are

a. **Back-End Services:** Back-end services consists of various services which allow connections to data providers, helps in managing, executing and maintaining the data in models. Hence we can say it is the core of platform functionalities.

b. **Front-end Client APIs:** Front-end client APIs is a set of graphical and programmatic interfaces which can be used to communicate, execute and test analytical models. For the simplification of the functionalities and to define the same structure of the analytical method the programmatic interface is required. Enabling the users to visualizing the data in different format, users should be allowed to detect the concerned events and information.

c. **Connectivity Engine:** Connectivity engine is a means through which we can communicate throughout the world like data providers, financial brokers etc. The control of communication of the outside venues is controlled by a dedicated connector utilized by the platform. This is possible because the outside institutions provide either a dedicated API or uses a communication protocol such as the FIX protocol and the JSON/XML-based protocol). The platform provides a generalized interface to allow standardization of a variety of connectors.

d. **Internal Communication Layer:** Internal messaging system is used obtained from the idea of event driven programming. It is allowed in the internal layer in which analytical platform utilizes variety of events as a major medium of interaction among the various entities either for producer or consumer of events.

e. **Aggregation Database:** In the aggregation database there is fast and vigorous aggregation of data at the entry level. Different mechanisms in the aggregation of data are filtrations, reconstruction and storage of data in big data style. The analytical platforms is facilitated by the aggregation database for the storage, extraction and management of large amount of data. Along with the replay of historical data, complex functionalities are allowed to perform various analysis and evolution.

f. **Client SDK:** It is the collection of Application Programming Interfaces(APIs) through which various operations can be performed such as designing, development, implementation, testing and maintenance of the analytical model by using the Integrated Development

Environment(IDEs). IDEs are used for the connection establishment at the server side also to develop and execute models for the platform required by the users.

g. **Shared Memory:** Memory usage requirement is reduced by the buffer type functionality that speeds up the delivery of temporal/ historical data to models and the analytics-related elements of the platform. The aim is to have a central point in the memory (RAM) which will manage and provide a temporal/historical data from the current point of time up to a specified number of time stamps back in history). Since the memory is shared, and kept in RAM rather than in the files or the DBMS, Therefore the access to it is instant and bounded only by the performance of hardware and no model will have to keep and manage history by itself.

h. **Model Templates:** Two generic types of models are supported by model templates: push and pull. Push specifies set of data stream which are registered during initialization, and each time a new data feed arrives to the platform execution of the model logic is triggered. This is quick, have low latency, high frequency models and the feed is achieved at the cost of small shared memory buffers. In pull it is based on a schedule templates and are executed and requested.. It has a direct connection to the big data facilities and hence can request as much historical data as necessary, at the expense of speed.

4. **System Architecture:** The following section outlines the key components of the overall system. The basic idea is that each external feed has a dedicated connectivity engine (API) and this streams data to the message bus, which handles internal communication, analytics and storage.

a. **Connectivity Engines:** The main functionality of connectivity engines is to establish the connection between external data sources and the APIs, blogs, news feeds of OSN sites. as per the requirements of social media the APIs platform are expanding constantly and data is also increasing day by day as the number of users and their posts are increasing continuously.

b. **Messaging Bus:** The incoming messages or data streams from various sources and connectivity engines for the representation of internal data and information across the different modules at the platform are served by the message bus as the internal communication layer. To maintain all these information and data an efficient database is maintained.

c. **Data Warehouse:** The data warehouse refers to the collection of historical data in which terabytes of text based entries are supported. There is large variety of metadata are there which is increasing the scope in the field of research and development. Entries are organized by source and accurately time-stamped with the time of publication, as well as being tagged with topics for easy retrieval by simulation models. HBase is currently used as the platform, but Apache Cassandra or Hive may be used in future.

d. **Simulation Manager:** Simulator manager is a web based GUI through which users can select various filters to apply the different data sets for uploading them in an external API for clients to interact with data is provided by simulation manager. All client-access to the data warehouse and the data sets uploaded by the user for aggregation with UCL's social data for particular simulation are facilitated. We can also switch between historical mode and live mode.

CONCLUSION

The social networking is of one of the important theme of many popular websites after the evolution of data science. There are many applications of online social networking that can be seen in our daily life. In the near future the online social networking will play a vital role in the online commercial and personal transactions and communication. Online social networks are consist of huge number of nodes or clusters connected to each other with a high-degree of nodes. Many research issues such as sentiment analysis, data scraping, semantic web, opinion mining etc led to the data explosion and data services for which different variety of software tools are required. Social media analytics platforms are used in sentimental analysis. Many Data mining tools and technique are also required in the social networking data analysis tools and services. Privacy and security is also important concern. Various aspects and strategies for maintaining the security and privacy are user's identity anonymity, user's personal space privacy, user's communication privacy. and authentication and data integrity. The impact of social networking in everyday life can be easily noticed for the people of every age group and almost every sectors and domains ranging from scientific research to administration, education to corporate sector, governance to entertainment, business analysis and economic to public administration etc. Graph theory is the main technique applied in the social network for the representation of social relations in online social networking that involve with social networking data analysis tools and techniques. But still there is scope in future for research and development for many domains of social networking that will provide good and bright opportunities business, research, academics and many other areas. title should be "Conclusion", not "Conclusions". Provide discussion of the overall coverage of the chapter and concluding remarks.

ACKNOWLEDGMENT

This work is supported by many intellectual persons. I would like to express my deep gratitude towards the Mr. Krishna Murari, Registrar of Netaji Subhas Institute of Technology, Patna, Bihar, India for providing good academic environment. Dr. Prabhat Kumar, HoD, Department of Computer Science & Engineering, National Institute of Technology Patna, India, Dr. J. P. Singh, Assistant Professor, Department of Computer Science & Engineering, National Institute of Technology Patna, India for his motivation and inspiration. I would also take this opportunity to express my deep sense of thankfulness to Dr. S. B. Singh, Principle, of Netaji Subhas Institute of Technology, Patna, Bihar, India and Mrs. Soni Sweta, HoD and all Teaching Faculties of Department of Computer Science & Engineering, Netaji Subhas Institute of Technology, Patna, Bihar, India. In addition, I would also like to thank my parents and friends for their support and motivation. throughout the entire course of time. At last but not least I am grateful to IGI Global publication for giving this opportunity to explore my knowledge and ideas in Social Networking.

REFERENCES

Batrinca, B., & Treleaven, P. C. (2015). Social media analytics: A survey of techniques, tools and platforms, *Open access at springer*. *AI & Society*, *30*(1), 89–116. doi:10.100700146-014-0549-4

Dwyer, C., Hiltz, S. R., & Passerini, K. (2007). Trust and Privacy Concern Within Social Networking Sites: A Comparison of Facebook and MySpace. *Proceedings: Americas Conference on Information System.*

Handrick, D. (n.d.). *Complete History of Social Media: Then and Now.* Retrieved from https://smallbiztrends.com/2013/05/the-complete-history-of-social-media-infographic.html

Miles, Huberman, & Lotto. (1986). Qualitative Data Analysis: A Sourcebook of New Methods. *Educational Evaluation and Policy Analysis, 8* (3), 329-331.

Mislove, A., Macron, M., Gummadi, K. P., & Druschel, P. (n.d.). Measurement and Analysis of Online Social Networks. *Proceedings of the 7th ACM SIGCOMM conference on Internet measurement.* DOI:10.1145/1298306.1298311

Zhang, Sun, Zhu, & Fang. (2010). Privacy and Security for Online Social Networks: Challenges and Opportunities. *IEEE Network, 24*(4). DOI: doi:10.1109/MNET.2010.5510913

This research was previously published in Social Network Analytics for Contemporary Business Organizations; pages 19-34, copyright year 2018 by Business Science Reference (an imprint of IGI Global).

Chapter 21
The Role of Social Media Tools in the Knowledge Management in Organizational Context:
Evidences Based on Literature Review

Marcello Chedid

https://orcid.org/0000-0003-0435-6568

University of Aveiro, Portugal

Leonor Teixeira

https://orcid.org/0000-0002-7791-1932

University of Aveiro, Portugal

ABSTRACT

The advancement of the economy based on knowledge makes knowledge management critical for organizations. The traditional knowledge management systems have presented some shortcomings on their implementation and management. Social media have demonstrated that are not just a buzzword and have been used increasingly by the organizations as a knowledge management component. This chapter was developed aiming at exploring and critically reviewing the literature of social media use in organizational context as a knowledge management component. The review suggests that, while traditional knowledge management systems are static and often act just as knowledge repositories, social media have the potential for supporting different knowledge management processes that will impact on the organizational culture by encouraging on participation, collaboration and knowledge sharing. Despite their recognized impact on knowledge management processes, some uncertainty remains amongst researchers and practitioners and is associated to the difficulty in understanding and measuring their real impact.

DOI: 10.4018/978-1-7998-9020-1.ch021

INTRODUCTION

In the last twenty years knowledge management emerges as a distinct area of study, consolidating as a significant source of competitive advantage and as one of the most important resources in the capacity of progress of modern organizations (Mårtensson, 2000; Pekka-Economou & Hadjidema, 2011). The ability to define, implement and manage business opportunities depends largely on the availability and quality of knowledge.

To meet the challenge of capturing, organizing and disseminating knowledge, the organizations have undertaken heavy investments in technology, however, with "significant failure rates" (Malhotra, 2005, p. 8). In general, the system was not appropriated or the organization was not prepared for the required cultural change.

Despite the wide agreement that knowledge management occurs within a social context, some authors have the opinion that organizations have been focused primarily on the technology and little on people and process (Kakabadse, Kakabadse, & Kouzmin, 2003), and most of the solutions were centralized within the organization with lack of interactivity (Panahi, Watson, & Partridge, 2012).

Social media became a global phenomenon (Schlagwein & Hu, 2016) and have been used increasingly by the organizations. There are several examples of social media use in line with different organization objectives across countries and different types of industries. According to Von Krogh (2012, p. 154), "the increased use of social software by firms is often the result of a strategic imperative for more openness toward the outside", including, for example, universities, suppliers, customers, and users.

Social media, also called social software, has become in a driving force by exploiting the collective intelligence (Chatti, Klamma, Jarke, & Naeve, 2007). Social media are a set of features, grouped into software applications, which enables to recreate online various types of social interactions that are possible to find in physical environments.

The strategically chosen social media can be internal or external to organization and its use can have as objective to achieve internal or external goals. Schlagwein and Hu (2016, p. 3) add that "technologically different social media tools might achieve the same organizational purpose, or technologically similar social media tools might achieve very different organizational purposes". These purposes can be such as to improve productivity, increase the interaction between departments and team workers, create a channel with consumers or enhance the management of knowledge.

Truly, almost none of the social media acts alone. The combination of different tools in an appropriate measure can produce excellent results for organizations. However, often identifying the perfect match of tools can be somewhat difficult due to the dynamism and versatility of social media tools (Schlagwein & Hu, 2016).

Social media are very close in its principle and attributes to knowledge management (Levy, 2009), providing inexpensive alternatives and solutions that can overcome many failures of traditional knowledge management models (von Krogh, 2012). These tools have also shown to be an efficient mechanism in supporting knowledge sharing, particularly tacit knowledge, helping organizations to capture knowledge based on the knowledge from different stakeholders (Al Saifi, Dillon, & McQeen, 2016; Clark et al., 2015; Costa et al., 2009; Panahi et al., 2012; Paroutis & Al Saleh, 2009; Tee & Karney, 2010). Based on the crowd-wisdom, the social media enable to keep knowledge relevant and up-to-date (Chatti et al., 2007).

According to Kane et al. (2014, p. 276) "the impact of social media on and for organizations, represents an important area for information systems research".

Given that knowledge management is critical for organizations and social media tools have the potential to be enablers for knowledge management processes, through a literature review, the chapter's authors aim to explore and contribute to understanding the possible impacts and consequences in the use of these tools in knowledge management in organizational context, and highlight the factors that can be determining to the eventual success of a knowledge management based on social media. The chapter also aims to address some further research directions.

This chapter is to be understood as being exploratory in its nature and is organized as follows. In the next section, the authors through the theoretical background introduce social media and knowledge management. The following section, based on the literature reviewed, provides a critical discussion of the role of social media in the knowledge management processes. Following this section, the authors discuss about the main benefits and threats of social media in the knowledge management context. Conclusion and directions for future research are in the final part of this chapter.

BACKGROUND

Initially, it is important to make a brief theoretical background of the study. In this section, the authors provide an overview of social media tools and traditional knowledge management.

Social Media Tools

Social media have demonstrated that is not just a buzzword. After influencing how organizations and society operate (Ford & Mason, 2013b), social media in the organization have been boosting collaboration and participation among knowledge workers, helping to create a social network in which people are more connected and knowledge can flow more efficiently between participants (Gaál, Szabó, Obermayer-Kovács, & Csepregi, 2015; Levy, 2009).

Kaplan and Haenlein (2010, p. 59) argue that in the literature "there seems to be very limited understanding of what the term "social media" exactly means", and what exactly should be included under this term (Kaplan & Haenlein, 2010). Practitioners and researchers have used the term social media interchangeably and as synonym for Web 2.0 (Kaplan & Haenlein, 2010; O'Reilly, 2007). This situation causes some confusion, so it is necessary to clarify the terms. The term Web 2.0 is credited to O´Reilly (Paroutis & Al Saleh, 2009) and it refers to a set of technology of online tools that supports social interaction among users. Social media are the platforms created using the Web 2.0 technologies being, according to Kaplan and Haenlein (2010, p. 61), defined as "a group of Internet-based applications that build on the ideological and technological foundations of Web 2.0, and that allow the creation and exchange of User Generated Content". Also De Wever et al. (2007, p. 512) define social media as "software that enables communication through digital technologies during which people connect, converse, collaborate, manage content and form online networks in a social and bottom-up fashion".

Harrysson et al. (2016) state that, based on their survey "The evolution of social technologies" carried out among 2750 global executives over each year from 2005 to 2015, since the beginning of the social-technology era, organizations have recognized potential of social media in strengthen lines of company communication and collaboration, and to boost knowledge sharing. In their article, Kane et al. (2014) support that the adoption of social media by organizations has just begun. Interestingly though, a more recent survey of McKinsey&Company (Bughin, 2015) points out that organizational use of social media grew rapidly, but currently growth is flattening.

The availability of popular, and free, open source software, that are simpler, smarter and more flexible has fostered the increased use of social media (Avram, 2006; Leonardi, Huysman, & Steinfield, 2013).

Social media are based on integration between people and comprise a set of technological tools that support organizational purpose enabling people to connect, communicate, and collaborate by self-organizing social networks and engaging in conversational interactions and social feedback (Hemsley & Mason, 2011; Schlagwein & Hu, 2016; Sigala & Chalkiti, 2015).

According to Levy (2009), the decision to use social media tools by the organizations is taken based on two dimensions: technology adoption (software infrastructure or software application), and user orientation (use by and for organizational members, or use by organization facing stakeholders - customers, partners and suppliers). These tools typically consist in: blogs and micro-blogs, discussion forums, social networks or relationship maps, document or media sharing, and wikis (Ford & Mason, 2013b; Hemsley & Mason, 2011).

At the strategic level, according to the Harrysson et al.'s survey (2016), around 30% of the organizations use social tools for strategy development, and 25% of organizations make decisions and setting strategic priorities from bottom up. The survey results also point to the fact that, according to the 47% of surveyed executives, the strategy of priorities from the bottom up would intensify over the next three to five years, with organizations using mainly social networks that have their use expanded and become better integrated.

However, organizations do not work the same way the Internet community does, and a model that is working out there could fail in the organizational context. Consequently, social media use in organizations faces two main barriers. The first on the part of organizations that are concerned about the risks and consequences of a potential misuse, and the second on the part of workers and managers that are not motivated or are not aware of the benefits of using these tools for work purposes (Gaál et al., 2015).

The same social media tool can be used for very different organizational purposes (Schlagwein & Hu, 2016). However, this versatile characteristic brings a challenge. According to McAfee (2006) the challenge lies in ability of each organization to exploit these tools, and he adds that the significant difference in organizations' abilities that will make all the difference.

Due to the combination of their main characteristics, such as user-generated content, peer to peer communication, networking, multimedia oriented, and user friendly (Panahi et al., 2012), these tools represent a successful mechanism that enables knowledge sharing and knowledge creation, keeps people connected, can supply endless reusable knowledge, or even facilitates to access expert's knowledge (Bharati, Zhang, & Chaudhury, 2015).

Traditional Knowledge Management

After the information management, a neutral and normative system in the organizations (Gloet & Terziovski, 2004), knowledge management emerges as a distinct area of study, establishing as a significant source of competitive advantage and as one of the most important resources in the capacity of progress of organizations in today's hypercompetitive and globalized marketplace (Ford & Mason, 2013b; Mårtensson, 2000; Pekka-Economou & Hadjidema, 2011).

The advancement of an economy based on knowledge has increased the visibility and importance of organizations that create and disseminate knowledge. Through knowledge, organizations can disrupt limitations, enhancing development and create new opportunities (Pekka-Economou & Hadjidema, 2011). Several authors consider that new knowledge and innovation are heavily dependent on knowledge management practices (Gaál et al., 2015; Gloet, 2006; Inkinen, 2016), thus constituting knowledge management practices as a key driver of innovation performance.

According to the classical division introduced by Polanyi (1966), and widely spread by Nonaka et al. (1996) knowledge can be explicit or tacit.

Explicit knowledge is a type of knowledge that can be easily codified, articulated, documented and archived, and usually, it is stored and expressed in the form of text, data, scientific formulae, maps, manuals and books, websites, etc. (Alavi & Leidner, 2001; Iacono, Nito, Esposito, Martinez, & Moschera, 2014; Nonaka & Konno, 1998; Polanyi, 1966; Santoro & Bierly, 2006; Seidler-de Alwis & Hartmann, 2008).

Tacit knowledge is the basis of knowledge creation, it is complex and not codified, and presents some difficulty in its reproduction in document or database. Smith (2001) reported that ninety percent of the knowledge in any organization is tacit knowledge and it is embedded and synthesized in peoples' heads.

Among several authors knowledge management is a multidimensional concept (e.g., Gaál et al., 2015). In the present chapter the authors adopt the Davenport and Prusak's (1998) definition, that is one of the most cited in the literature: "knowledge management is concerned with the exploitation and development of the knowledge assets of an organization with a view to furthering the organization's objectives."

Knowledge management is based on three main pillars (technology, people and process), and occurs within a social context (Kalkan, 2008; Prieto, Revilla, & Rodríguez-Prado, 2009) (Figure 1).

Figure 1. Knowledge Management Pillars

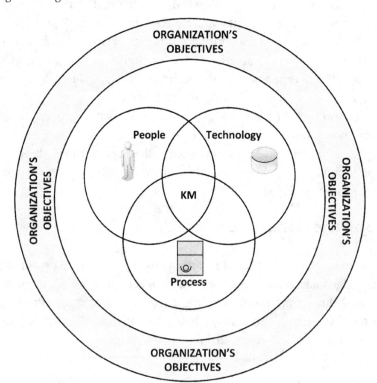

With substantial investments in highly structured technological solutions, organizations have been carried to focus primarily on the technology and little on people and process (Kakabadse et al., 2003), not enabling the interactivity and opportunity of the people in influencing (McAfee, 2006; Panahi et al., 2012). According to Sultan (2013, p. 162) "working people are more likely to seek work-related advice from fellows workers than from a knowledge-based system".

Technologies are not creator of knowledge, but are considered as one of the key enablers in the knowledge management process (Malhotra, 2005).

Knowledge management describes the processes of sharing and transfer, capture, and application of organizational knowledge to improve organizations' competitiveness.

Kang et al.'s (2010) state that knowledge by itself is not a useful resource that creates value and competitive advantage until it can be shared and transferred. Knowledge emerges from sharing knowledge in a social context (Jakubik, 2008) resulting of interactions between people. However, several authors (e.g., Ford & Mason, 2013b; Sigala & Chalkiti, 2015; von Krogh, 2012) identify the knowledge sharing process, a weak point of traditional models of knowledge management.

The successful sharing and transfer of knowledge is an important factor in knowledge management performance (Gaál et al., 2015; Wang & Noe, 2010), and according to Gaál et al. (Gaál et al., 2015, p. 185) "actually, the organizations are faced with the challenge how to get people to share their knowledge". Faced with this challenge, organizations have been forced to improve their knowledge sharing practices and to adopt new technologies.

Knowledge needs to be captured, stored and then disseminated (Huzita et al., 2012). The knowledge capture is a key process of preserving and formalizing knowledge (Becerra-Fernandez & Sabherwal, 2010) and the result is the inclusion of the knowledge into the stock of knowledge. The process of capture has various methods and the selected method depends on the type of knowledge. The process of capture must be disposed of properly, responding to the challenge of capturing only the relevant and valuable knowledge (Nielsen, 2006). Once captured, knowledge should be continuously evaluated to ensure their quality and relevance.

Knowledge application is the process management that justifies the existence all of others processes. It makes no sense to create knowledge, capture it, share it and download it, if not be disseminated and applied. Starbuck (1992) argued that merely storing knowledge does not preserve it.

New knowledge is disseminated through several channels available among the members of a social system (Graham et al., 2006) promoting their application (Becerra-Fernandez & Sabherwal, 2010). Social system is considered a set of interactions between people who have connection between themselves and that belong to the same context (Figure 2).

Traditional knowledge management are complex environments which have as organizational purposes to capture knowledge through documents repositories, share that knowledge with groupware tools, and make it accessible via corporate portals (von Krogh, 2012). These solutions often require an effort of investment and presents some difficulty in its application (Sultan, 2013).

In general, traditional knowledge management system consist in a collection of knowledge management technologies (Figure 3), which support the knowledge management processes, and a set of communication media widely diffused in the organizations, such as e-mail, person-to-person instant messaging, and telephone (McAfee, 2006; von Krogh, 2012). The usage of communication media use, according to McAfee (2006, p. 22), enable that digital knowledge "can be created and distributed by anyone, but the degree of commonality of this knowledge is low", i.e., it's only viewable by the few people who are part of the subject.

Figure 2. Social System

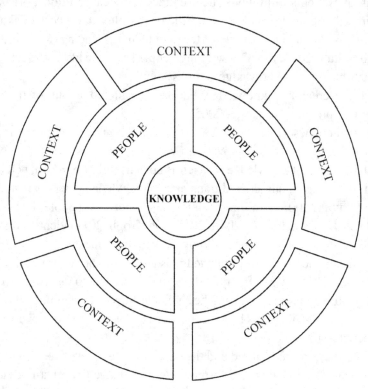

Figure 3. Knowledge Management Technologies

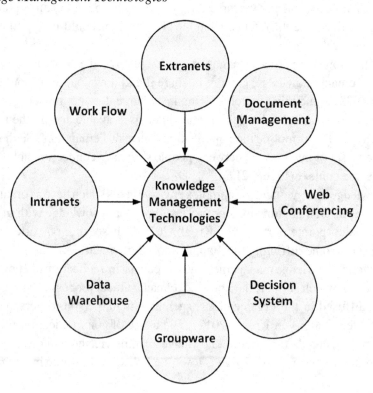

THE ROLE OF SOCIAL MEDIA TOOLS IN THE KNOWLEDGE MANAGEMENT IN ORGANIZATIONAL CONTEXT

Knowledge Management 2.0

The expression "knowledge management 2.0" refers to the knowledge management system that enables self-organization of people, by utilization of appropriate social media tools (Becerra-Fernandez & Sabherwal, 2010; Levy, 2009). In contrast to the traditional knowledge management models, knowledge management 2.0 is characterized by the content that is generated in decentralized and distributed way and in a bottom-up condition, from workers (internal social media use) and stakeholders (external social media use) (Avram, 2006; Schlagwein & Hu, 2016; von Krogh, 2012). Ford and Mason (2013a, p. 8) highlight that "the two types may have different risks, costs, and benefits for organizations".

As well as with the knowledge management, the use of social media by organizations has become a global phenomenon (Schlagwein & Hu, 2016). Bharati et al. (2015) cite in their study that, based on the 2011 McKinsey's survey, around 70% of the organizations use social media tools to increase speed to access knowledge.

The social media tools, that organizations can buy or develop, are close to some principles of knowledge management (Ford & Mason, 2013b; Levy, 2009; McAfee, 2006; von Krogh, 2012), since both involve people using technology to capture or acquire knowledge, create knowledge, and share this knowledge (Bradley & McDonald, 2011).

According to von Krogh (2012) social media have three aspects of relevance to knowledge management: (i) it is founded on socially oriented principles; (ii) it consists of a series of intuitive and easy to use applications (e.g., blogs and wikis); (iii) it is based on infrastructures (e.g. open platforms and enabling services) that make possible to reach considerable economies of scale.

The significant difference consists in the centralization and controlled attitude of knowledge management, in contrast to the uncontrolled and decentralized one of social tools (Levy, 2009).

The traditional knowledge management systems are technology-centric with a rigid and hierarchic knowledge structure. However, Malhotra (2000) in his work "Knowledge management and new organization forms: a framework for business model innovation" points to the fact that knowledge management technologies, in itself, do not assure knowledge creation and knowledge evolution. In this era characterized by discontinuous change, there is an increasing importance of the "human function of ensuring the reality check - by means of repetitive questioning, interpretation and revision of the assumptions underlying the knowledge system" (Malhotra, 2000, p. 11).

Social media technologies are people-centric with priority to the relationship and collaborative knowledge management processes (Sigala & Chalkiti, 2015). This second generation of knowledge management solutions puts technology in the background and focuses on people, promoting the participation of knowledge workers, who will be more willing to share and innovate by using tools they already know and like (Levy, 2009).

Figure 4 illustrates the difference between these two approaches.

McAfee (2006) alerts to the fact that social technologies are not incompatible with traditional knowledge management systems. Existing channels and platforms can be enhanced, improving and reducing gaps in processes and technologies, by adoption of social tools that provide the essential ingredients needed to succeed in the organizations. These ingredients are summarized in an acronym formulated by McAfee (2006) (see Figure 5).

Figure 4. Technology-Centric and People-Centric Approaches

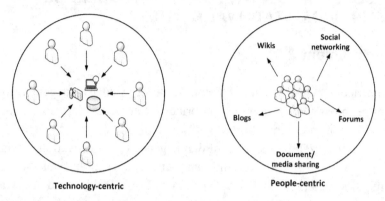

Figure 5. SLATES Infrastructure – Based on McAfee (2006)

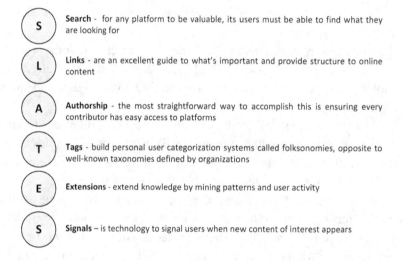

Knowledge management 2.0, with structures more open and informal with short communication lines, arises to answer the request for effective ways to support knowledge sharing, and collaborative work. Organizations have been looking for secure, flexible environments where workers can add, organize, share and socialize knowledge through close interpersonal relationships with higher degree of trust. Social media tools seem to be suited to increase knowledge sharing, and improve organizational competences.

Social Media as a Knowledge Management Component

The usage of social media as a component of the knowledge management system has a great potential to leverage the existing knowledge management initiatives in organizations (Ford & Mason, 2013a; Richter, Stocker, Müller, & Avram, 2011), and to foster and to support the human participation in the processes. It is important that organizations embrace them and consciously utilize them to support their knowledge management initiatives (Levy, 2009; von Krogh, 2012).

The social media use as a knowledge management component can facilitate communication and collaboration between users within and outside an organization (Bharati et al., 2015), enabling users to easily share what they have learned, created and experienced, creating opportunities and conditions that promote the flow of tacit knowledge (Panahi et al., 2012), as well as allowing the storage of knowledge directly on social media or the use of social media to post links to knowledge management system (Schlagwein & Hu, 2016).

The Figure 6 represents a conceptual model of tacit knowledge sharing in social media according Panahi et al. (2012).

Figure 6. Tacit Knowledge Sharing in Social Media From Panahi et al. (2012)

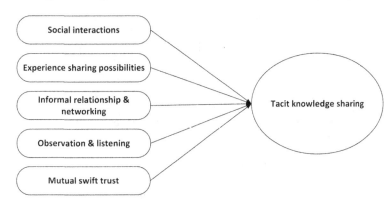

Citing Bebensee et al. (2011), von Krogh (2012) argues that social media have three layers of relevance to knowledge management, namely, they are based on socially oriented principles, the tools are intuitive to understand and easy to use, and they are infrastructures as open platforms that achieve considerable economics scale. Dave and Koskela (2009) add two other relevant aspects. They mention search capabilities, that make easy to retrieve knowledge, and anytime/anywhere and widespread availability.

The knowledge management evolution is characterized by the adoption of appropriate social media tools including, among others, wikis, blogs and social networks. The use of one or a combination of these tools as a knowledge management component has been providing to the organizations a new knowledge environment (Hemsley & Mason, 2011) with enhancement of organizational knowledge management and collaborative sharing of knowledge (Bharati et al., 2015; O'Reilly, 2007; von Krogh, 2012).

The paradigm shift taking place in the new forms of interaction and knowledge sharing requires that organizations will adopt more flexibility in roles and control, with greater individual responsibilities (Ford & Mason, 2013a). Social media tools can facilitate this shift, supporting and providing fundamental changes in traditional knowledge management processes (Bharati et al., 2015; Richter et al., 2011).

Social media embodied with a business mindset can move organizational knowledge management, with impacts within and outside the organizations (Dave & Koskela, 2009), towards to a more flexible structure, thereby leading to fundamental change in such a way that enables interactions among individuals with rich and diverse types and contents knowledge (Richter et al., 2011; Sigala & Chalkiti, 2015). This change enable self-organization of workers, promote social interactions, networking and different ways of knowledge sharing (Bharati et al., 2015; Dave & Koskela, 2009; Sigala & Chalkiti, 2015), in particular regarding the tacit knowledge (Dave & Koskela, 2009).

Sigala and Chalkiti (2015) suggest that according the existing literature, social media can support all the four circles of the SECI model (Nonaka et al., 1996) by empowering people to create and renew knowledge in a dynamic, conversational and flexible way (Figure 7). The SECI model is based on the assumption that the creation and expansion of organizational knowledge occur by the continuing interaction between tacit and explicit knowledge resulting from the interactions between groups or individuals.

Figure 7. Knowledge Conversion Circles Enabled by Social Media – Based on Nonaka et al. (2000) and Adapted From Sigala and Chalkiti (2015)

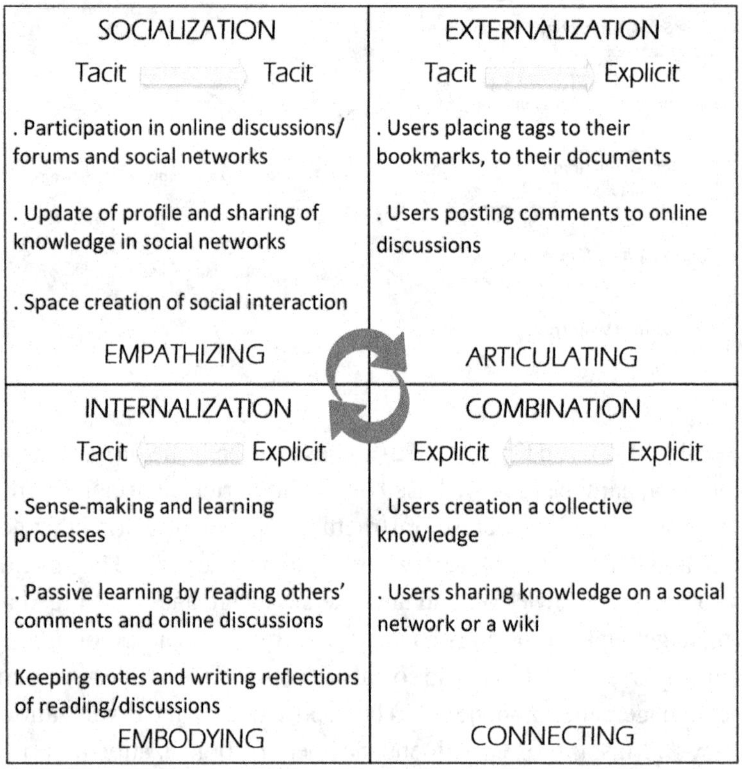

Although their significant impact, some organizations remain uncertain of their usage (Ford & Mason, 2013a). This uncertainty, according to several authors (Kane et al., 2014; Richter et al., 2011; Schlagwein & Hu, 2016), is associated to the difficulty amongst researchers and practitioners in understanding the real impact of the social media adoption in the organizations. In recent study Schlagwein and Hu (2016) discuss about this issue and identify three social media characteristics that can hinder this understanding. Social media are continuously in development, encompass a wide range of different tools and content, and the same social media tool at the same time can be used for very different organizational purposes or different social media tools might achieve the same organizational purpose (Schlagwein & Hu, 2016).

Based on the literature reviewed, the Table 1 presents several empirical studies about the usage of social media in the knowledge management context.

Table 1. Social Media in Knowledge Management Context

Author	Study	Method
Al Saifi et al. (2016)	This paper explores the relationship between face-to-face social networks and knowledge sharing. The results reveal that face to face social networks facilitate knowledge sharing in diverse ways.	Semi- structured interview
Schlagwein & Hu (2016)	This study examines the relation between social media use and the absorptive capacity of organizations.	Semi- structured interview
Bharati et al. (2015)	This study highlights both the potential and limitations of social media in promoting organizational knowledge management.	Case study
Gaál et al. (2015)	This research investigates how internal or external social media technologies are being used for knowledge sharing during work or for professional development.	Survey
Sigala & Chalkiti (2015)	The study investigates the relation between social media use and employee creativity by adopting a knowledge management approach in order to consider the influence of social networks and interactions on individuals' creativity.	Case study
Soto-Acosta et al. (2014)	This paper extends previous studies on the use of internet technologies and knowledge management by analyzing factors affecting knowledge sharing through Web 2.0 technologies within small and medium-sized enterprises.	Survey
Giuffrida & Dittrich (2013)	This paper reviews and map empirical studies on the usage of social software in Software Engineering projects and in distributed teams. Social software is reported as being chiefly used as a support for collaborative work, fostering awareness, knowledge management and coordination among team members.	Systematic mapping study
Bebensee et al. (2011)	This article aims at identifying Web 2.0 applications for bolstering up organizations' knowledge management practices.	Case study
García et al. (2011)	The aim of this work is to provide a set of guidelines to develop knowledge-based Process Asset Libraries to store software engineering best practices, implemented as a Wiki.	Fieldwork case study
Richter et al. (2011)	This study analyzed social software adoption in 23 companies and derived six main goals of corporate social software adoption. These goals were compared with the goals of knowledge management projects and initiatives, as identified in a series of well-known knowledge management studies.	Case study
Costa et al. (2009)	This case study describes the effects of using a Web Based Social Network approach to Knowledge Management in a Brazilian software development organization.	Case study
Dave & Koskela (2009)	This paper discusses a range of solutions and presents a case study where a collaborative knowledge management solution is implemented across a multi-functional construction company.	Case study
Paroutis & Al Saleh (2009)	The purpose of this paper is to investigate the key determinants of knowledge sharing and collaboration using Web 2.0 technologies by exploring the reasons for and barriers to employees' active participation in its various platforms.	Case study design

Benefits of Using Social Media as Knowledge Management Component

Considering that organizations do not have the mass of people as the Web does (Levy, 2009), the collaborative use of social media by organizations assumes an important role in the development of a collective intelligence knowledge environment which can represent a competitive advantage (Charband & Navimipour, 2016; Hemsley & Mason, 2011).

Knowledge management 2.0 with structures more open and informal with short communication lines, can provide workers close interpersonal relationships with higher degree of trust. This context is extremely favorable to knowledge sharing activities (Al Saifi et al., 2016).

Social media enable that knowledge becomes more articulated and explicit through discussions within workers and different stakeholders with creation of particular knowledge outputs as well as products and services (Schlagwein & Hu, 2016), overcoming many of failings of traditional knowledge management solutions (Chatti et al., 2007).

Leonardi et al. (2013) highlight that social media are distinguished with respect to other communication technologies since maintain the visibility and persistence of communicative actions, expanding the environment whom workers can learn. Social media also promotes the knowledge reuse, or as Schlagwein and Hu (2016, p. 19) say "may prevent that organization from forgetting what it already knows", with workers taking advantage of past experiences and learning from what others already know within and outside organization. As well as, compared to traditional knowledge management systems, social media enable easily that knowledge be edited, updated and searched, what encourages workers to participate in creation and use of relevant knowledge, fostering and enriching the individual and collective processes of cognitive interactions. (Harrysson et al., 2016; Schlagwein & Hu, 2016; Sultan, 2013).

McAfee (2006, p. 26) address another important issue related to the integration capability of social media in large organizations, that makes organizations "in some ways more searchable, analyzable and navigable than smaller ones". The workers are able to find knowledge more readily and to identify experts on various topics.

Due to their characteristics, social media also emerge as an opportunity for the small and medium enterprises. These organizations work in a scenery of shortage of resources, and in the knowledge era they will be competitive if they take advantage of their peculiarities and peculiarities of their environment (Starbuck, 1992). Social media can meet the knowledge management needs of these type of organizations (Sultan, 2013).

Richter et al. (2011) in their study "Knowledge management goals revisited - A cross-sectional analysis of social software adoption in corporate environments" identify the main benefits that organizations expect to reach with the adoption of social media (Table 2).

Social media have also shown to be an important and efficient mechanism in supporting tacit knowledge sharing, helping organizations to capture knowledge based on the knowledge from different stakeholders (Al Saifi et al., 2016; Clark et al., 2015; Costa et al., 2009; Tee & Karney, 2010). With the creation of social interactive and collaborative spaces - so-called *Ba* by Nonaka et al. (2000), provided by these technologies, the individual and collective cognitive processes are facilitated (Sigala & Chalkiti, 2015), occurring great opportunity for effective flow of tacit knowledge between workers or communities of experts (Chatti et al., 2007; Panahi et al., 2012).

Threats of Using Social Media as Knowledge Management Component

The flexibility seems to be the watchword of social media. The new forms of communication and knowledge sharing, arising from the adoption of social media as a knowledge management component, require greater flexibility by organizations with impact on organizational culture of control and management.

However, Richter et al. (2011, p. 8) highlight that "flexibility in use does not come without threats".

Based on the literature reviewed, the chapter's authors identify some threats related with knowledge protection, knowledge quality, and management approach.

Table 2. Main Goals for the Adoption of Social Media - Adapted From Richter et al. (2011)

Main Goal	Characteristics of the Goal
Efficient, goal-oriented employee communication and avoidance of information overload	Implementation of open communication channels, support of employees' goal orientation by enhancing communication, improvement of employee- to-employee communication, prevention and control of information overload, decrease of e-mail usage
Efficient knowledge transfer	Preservation and restoration of internal knowledge, break up of knowledge silos, facilitation of intra-organizational knowledge transfer, better access to best practices
The establishment of networks of experts	Improvement of networking among employees and identification of experts, connecting people with similar contexts, development of expert communities (e.g. yellow pages), support for wisdom of crowds
Participation of employees and creation of open corporate culture	Sustainable involvement of employees i.e. each employee should be able to contribute actively, prevent employee anonymity within the organization, improve exchange and discussion among the employees to get better insights to support the corporate culture, development of a creative climate, openness of corporate culture allowing employees to participate more
Increased awareness and transparency	Provide better visibility to common tasks and competences, more transparency within decisions and processes, employees and management are aware of each other, cross-cutting issues can be revealed
Support for the innovation potential and secure the future viability of the enterprise	Innovation can be communicated faster and will be better understood, innovation can be started from inside and outside, new systems guarantee future-orientation and flexibility, sustainability is demonstrated by including the younger generations

Knowledge Protection

The advent of social media as a knowledge management component may represent large efficiency gains, and knowledge sharing within and across organization boundaries (von Krogh, 2012) stands out as one of the most significant benefit. However, knowledge sharing achieved with the use of social media can turn into a relevant threat for the organizations.

Due to the ease with that knowledge can be disseminated and shared, result of social media characteristics, such as speed of knowledge distribution, blurry audience, and easily collectible (Ford & Mason, 2013b; Richter et al., 2011), and the way that organization perceive knowledge in this new environment, social media could represent as a knowledge protection threat (Ford & Mason, 2013b).

This threat may mean potential loss in the organization's value resulting from disclosure of critical knowledge assets (Ford & Mason, 2013b; von Krogh, 2012), misuse of knowledge (Ford & Mason, 2013b), or risk of exposure of existing gaps in organizational knowledge (von Krogh, 2012).

The philosophy of traditional knowledge management concerning the notion of knowledge protection seems to be conflicting with knowledge management 2.0's philosophy. Restrictive rules, and monitoring at the individual level may be impractical and counterproductive (von Krogh, 2012), and can seriously inhibit or even stop spontaneous workers' interactions and collaborations.

Knowledge Quality

The quality of knowledge created in this new environment derived of the adoption of social media is often questioned in the literature (von Krogh, 2012). Whereas knowledge quality is essential to manage business opportunities, this issue may be also viewed as a possible threat.

The environment that enables quality of knowledge should be rich and diverse in sources of knowledge in order to benefit knowledge creation, thus avoiding the influence of existing biases within and among of small groups of workers (Kane, 2015). McAfee (2006) also alerts for the fact of that, due to the versatility of social media, despite the correct use of them by the workers, the knowledge reached by the organization may not being the intended.

Another issue which arises when talking about quality of knowledge is the overload of knowledge that results from the diversity in the knowledge sharing process fostered by the social media use in knowledge management. It will therefore be fundamental for the organizations to ensure the increased efficiency and effectivity at knowledge sharing (Charband & Navimipour, 2016; Richter et al., 2011).

The overload knowledge effect may cause some difficulty to workers in processing a vast quantity of knowledge (Kane et al., 2014) or in differentiating the relevant knowledge (Kane et al., 2014; Leonardi et al., 2013). Which, according to Leonardi et al. (2013, p. 12), "could force workers to become even more insulated and in-group focused than they were before of social media use".

The business emphasis of knowledge management plays a central role in bridging the threat of knowledge quality in the social media use (Bharati et al., 2015; Dave & Koskela, 2009).

Management Approach

Ford and Mason (2013b) highlight that the adoption of social media causes emergence of some tensions between these technologies and knowledge management initiatives arise. The tensions arise from the necessity to redefine previously accepted organizational mechanisms (e.g., roles, control) that become difficult to maintain in what is emerging as a dynamic, complex knowledge environment (Ford & Mason, 2013a, 2013b). The formality will not disappear entirely, however management style will play an important role in this process, and their involvement in the adoption and utilization of social media as a component of knowledge management practices will be crucial (Bharati et al., 2015). The management should clearly support the adoption of new technologies, explicit expectations about the outcomes (Paroutis & Al Saleh, 2009), and embrace social media as a part of organization's knowledge strategic component (von Krogh, 2012).

In the literature several authors point out some issues that the management faces when organizations adopt social media. For example, McAfee (2006) has the opinion that knowledge workers, in general, are busy, do not help to development social media platforms, and just use them as user. Ford and Mason (2013a) comment that when organization supports empowerment and engagement, these initiatives may fail if they are seen as attempts to control the knowledge and to make workers expendable. According to Sultan (2013, p. 164) "a large proportion of the content created on social media platforms is the contribution of a small proportion of the people who use those tools", making it necessary to encourage as many of workers as possible to engage and contribute to knowledge creation process in a collaborative manner (Al Saifi et al., 2016; Richards, 2007).

FUTURE RESEARCH DIRECTIONS

The adoption of social media by organizations has increased quickly and the implementation approaches vary from organization to organization (Bharati et al., 2015; Richter et al., 2011; von Krogh, 2012). The research opportunities are vast on the usage impact of these tools for knowledge management into organizations. It is possible to find in the existing literature studies which are devoted to the opportunities or needs of research on this subject (e.g., Kane et al., 2014; Leonardi et al., 2013; von Krogh, 2012).

The chapter's authors highlight some questions which should be addressed in future research:

- First of all, does exist difference among the types of organization that social media is more suitable than traditional knowledge management?
- How does organization balance the social media and traditional knowledge management uses to enable knowledge processes?
- How does organization protect their knowledge exploiting the benefits and mitigating the threats?
- It seems to be consensus among authors that capture and sharing of knowledge may become easier with social media use. What are the best practices to boost them?
- Finally, due to the phenomenon of globalization of organizations, would be interesting further researches on the identification of the impact of cultural differences in social media adoption.

CONCLUSION

This chapter was developed aiming at exploring and critically reviewing the literature of social media use in organizational context as a knowledge management component, and highlight which roles that these tools have played enabling and improving the development of knowledge management in the organizations.

In the extensive literature the term "easy" is the most commonly used by different authors in relation to social media (e.g., Avram, 2006; Leonardi et al., 2013; Levy, 2009; von Krogh, 2012). However, the abilities to exploit these tools will make significant difference among organizations.

Despite some authors claim that social media oriented to knowledge management will require much less of the "management" component, the chapter's authors have the opinion that the adoption of these tools often requires management actions more intense than in the traditional knowledge management, since the workers are used to use social media in a very spontaneous way and in accordance with their interests. According to Gaál et al. (2015, p. 196), "it is recommended for management to support introducing social media tools, establish the terms and conditions of usage, communicate the benefits and provide the necessary trainings".

The review suggests that, while traditional knowledge management systems are static and often act just as knowledge repositories, social media have the potential for supporting different knowledge management processes that will impact on the organizational culture by encouraging on participation, collaboration and knowledge sharing. This impact provides capabilities, which are difficult in traditional model that can make knowledge management processes, mainly knowledge creation and sharing, more effectively and efficiently.

Social media, probably due to its continuous change and variety of platforms, have not yet been fully exploited, but it seems be clear their potential as a significant component of knowledge management system.

REFERENCES

Al Saifi, S. A., Dillon, S., & McQeen, R. (2016). The relationship between face to face social networks and knowledge sharing: An exploratory study of manufacturing firms. *Journal of Knowledge Management*, *20*(2), 308–326. doi:10.1108/JKM-07-2015-0251

Alavi, M., & Leidner, D. E. (2001). Review: Knowledge management and knowledge management systems: Conceptual foundations and research issues. *Management Information Systems Quarterly*, *25*(1), 107–136. doi:10.2307/3250961

Avram, G. (2006). At the crossroads of knowledge management and social software. *Electronic Journal of Knowledge Management*, *4*(1), 1–10.

Bebensee, T., Helms, R., & Spruit, M. (2011). Exploring Web 2.0 applications as a means of bolstering up knowledge management. *Electronic Journal of Knowledge Management*, *9*(1), 1–9.

Becerra-Fernandez, I., & Sabherwal, R. (2010). *Knowledge management: systems and processes*. Armonk, NY: M.E. Sharpe, Inc.

Bharati, P., Zhang, W., & Chaudhury, A. (2015). Better knowledge with social media? Exploring the roles of social capital and organizational knowledge management. *Journal of Knowledge Management*, *19*(3), 456–475. doi:10.1108/JKM-11-2014-0467

Bradley, A. J., & McDonald, M. P. (2011). Social media versus knowledge management. *Harvard Business Review*, 1–4. Retrieved from https://hbr.org/2011/10/social-media-versus-knowledge

Bughin, J. (2015). Taking the measure of the networked enterprise. *McKinsey Quarterly Survey*. Retrieved from http://www.mckinsey.com/business-functions/business-technology/our-insights/taking-the-measure-of-the-networked

Charband, Y., & Navimipour, N. J. (2016). Online knowledge sharing mechanisms: A systematic review of the state of the art literature and recommendations for future research. *Information Systems Frontiers*, 1–21.

Chatti, M. A., Klamma, R., Jarke, M., & Naeve, A. (2007). The Web 2.0 driven SECI model based learning process. In *Seventh IEEE International Conference on Advanced Learning Technologies (ICALT 2007)* (Vol. 5, pp. 780–782). IEEE. 10.1109/ICALT.2007.256

Clark, S. S., Berardy, A., Hannah, M. A., Seager, T. P., Selinger, E., & Makanda, J. V. (2015). Group tacit knowledge and globally distributed virtual teams: Lessons learned from using games and social media in the classroom. *Connexions - International Professional Communication Journal*, *3*(1), 113–151.

Costa, R. A., Silva, E. M., Neto, M. G., Delgado, D. B., Ribeiro, R. A., & Meira, S. R. L. (2009). Social knowledge management in practice: A case study. In L. Carriço, N. Baloian, & B. Fonseca (Eds.), *Groupware: Design, Implementation, and Use* (Vol. 5784, pp. 94–109). Springer Berlin Heidelberg. doi:10.1007/978-3-642-04216-4_8

Dave, B., & Koskela, L. (2009). Collaborative knowledge management - A construction case study. *Automation in Construction, 18*(7), 894–902. doi:10.1016/j.autcon.2009.03.015

Davenport, T. H., & Prusak, L. (1998). *Working knowledge: How organizations manage what they know.* Boston, MA: Harvard Business School Press.

De Wever, B., Mechant, P., Veevaete, P., & Hauttekeete, L. (2007). E-learning 2.0: Social software for educational use. *Ninth IEEE International Symposium on Multimedia Workshops (ISMW 2007),* 511–516. 10.1109/ISM.Workshops.2007.91

Ford, D. P., & Mason, R. M. (2013a). A multilevel perspective of tensions between knowledge management and social media. *Journal of Organizational Computing and Electronic Commerce, 23*(1–2), 7–33. doi:10.1080/10919392.2013.748604

Ford, D. P., & Mason, R. M. (2013b). Knowledge management and social media: The challenges and benefits. *Journal of Organizational Computing and Electronic Commerce, 23*(1–2), 1–6. doi:10.1080/10919392.2013.748603

Gaál, Z., Szabó, L., Obermayer-Kovács, N., & Csepregi, A. (2015). Exploring the role of social media in knowledge sharing. *Electronic Journal of Knowledge Management, 13*(3), 185–197.

García, J., Amescua, A., Sánchez, M. I., & Bermón, L. (2011). Design guidelines for software processes knowledge repository development. *Information and Software Technology, 53*(8), 834–850. doi:10.1016/j.infsof.2011.03.002

Giuffrida, R., & Dittrich, Y. (2013). Empirical studies on the use of social software in global software development - A systematic mapping study. *Information and Software Technology, 55*(7), 1143–1164. doi:10.1016/j.infsof.2013.01.004

Gloet, M. (2006). Knowledge management and the links to HRM. *Management Research News, 29*(7), 402–413. doi:10.1108/01409170610690862

Gloet, M., & Terziovski, M. (2004). Exploring the relationship between knowledge management practices and innovation performance. *Journal of Manufacturing Technology Management, 15*(5), 402–409. doi:10.1108/17410380410540390

Graham, I. D., Logan, J., Harrison, M. B., Straus, S. E., Tetroe, J., Caswell, W., & Robinson, N. (2006). Lost in knowledge translation: Time for a map? *The Journal of Continuing Education in the Health Professions, 26*(1), 13–24. doi:10.1002/chp.47 PMID:16557505

Harrysson, M., Schoder, D., & Tavakoli, A. (2016). *The evolution of social technologies.* McKinsey Quarterly Survey. Retrieved from http://www.mckinsey.com/industries/high-tech/our-insights/the-evolution-of-social-technologies

Hemsley, J., & Mason, R. M. (2011). The nature of knowledge in the social media age: Implications for knowledge management models. *Proceedings of the Annual Hawaii International Conference on System Sciences,* 3928–3937.

Huzita, E. H. M., Leal, G. C. L., Balancieri, R., Tait, T. F. C., Cardoza, E., Penteado, R. R. D. M., & Vivian, R. L. (2012). Knowledge and contextual information management in global software development: challenges and perspectives. In *2012 IEEE Seventh International Conference on Global Software Engineering Workshops* (pp. 43–48). IEEE. 10.1109/ICGSEW.2012.12

Iacono, M. P., De Nito, E., Esposito, V., Martinez, M., & Moschera, L. (2014). Investigating the relationship between coordination mechanisms and knowledge in a wine firm. *Knowledge and Process Management*, *21*(4), 280–291. doi:10.1002/kpm.1436

Inkinen, H. (2016). Review of empirical research on knowledge management practices and firm performance. *Journal of Knowledge Management*, *20*(2), 230–257. doi:10.1108/JKM-09-2015-0336

Jakubik, M. (2008). Experiencing collaborative knowledge creation processes. *The Learning Organization*, *15*(1), 5–25. doi:10.1108/09696470810842475

Kakabadse, N. K., Kakabadse, A., & Kouzmin, A. (2003). Reviewing the knowledge management literature: Towards a taxonomy. *Journal of Knowledge Management*, *7*(4), 75–91. doi:10.1108/13673270310492967

Kalkan, V. D. (2008). An overall view of knowledge management challenges for global business. *Business Process Management Journal*, *14*(3), 390–400. doi:10.1108/14637150810876689

Kane, G. C. (2015). Enterprise social media: Current capabilities and future possibilities. *MIS Quarterly Executive*, *14*(1), 1–16.

Kane, G. C., Labianca, G., & Borgatti, S. P. (2014). What's different about social media networks? A framework and research agenda. *Management Information Systems Quarterly*, *X*(X), 1–30.

Kang, J., Rhee, M., & Kang, K. H. (2010). Revisiting knowledge transfer: Effects of knowledge characteristics on organizational effort for knowledge transfer. *Expert Systems with Applications*, *37*(12), 8155–8160. doi:10.1016/j.eswa.2010.05.072

Kaplan, A. M., & Haenlein, M. (2010). Users of the world, unite! The challenges and opportunities of social media. *Business Horizons*, *53*(1), 59–68. doi:10.1016/j.bushor.2009.09.003

Leonardi, P. M., Huysman, M., & Steinfield, C. (2013). Enterprise social media: Definition, history, and prospects for the study of social technologies in organizations. *Journal of Computer-Mediated Communication*, *19*(1), 1–19. doi:10.1111/jcc4.12029

Levy, M. (2009). WEB 2.0 implications on knowledge management. *Journal of Knowledge Management*, *13*(1), 120–134. doi:10.1108/13673270910931215

Malhotra, Y. (2000). Knowledge management and new organization forms: A framework for business model innovation. *Information Resources Management Journal*, *13*(1), 5–14. doi:10.4018/irmj.2000010101

Malhotra, Y. (2005). Integrating knowledge management technologies in organizational business processes: Getting real time enterprises to deliver real business performance. *Journal of Knowledge Management*, *9*(1), 7–28. doi:10.1108/13673270510582938

Mårtensson, M. (2000). A critical review of knowledge management as a management tool. *Journal of Knowledge Management, 4*(3), 204–216. doi:10.1108/13673270010350002

McAfee, A. P. (2006). Enterprise 2.0: The dawn of emergent collaboration. *IEEE Engineering Management Review, 34*(3), 38–47. doi:10.1109/EMR.2006.261380

Nielsen, A. P. (2006). Understanding dynamic capabilities through knowledge management. *Journal of Knowledge Management, 10*(4), 59–71. doi:10.1108/13673270610679363

Nonaka, I., & Konno, N. (1998). The concept of ba: Building a foundation for knowledge creation. *California Management Review, 40*(3), 40–54. doi:10.2307/41165942

Nonaka, I., Takeuchi, H., & Umemoto, K. (1996). A theory of organizational knowledge creation. *International Journal of Technology Management, 11*(7–8), 833–845.

Nonaka, I., Toyama, R., & Konno, N. (2000). SECI, Ba and leadership: A unified model of dynamic knowledge creation. *Long Range Planning, 33*(1), 5–34. doi:10.1016/S0024-6301(99)00115-6

Nonaka, I., Toyama, R., & Nagata, A. (2000). A firm as a knowledge-creating entity: A new perspective on the theory of the firm. *Industrial and Corporate Change, 9*(1), 1–20. doi:10.1093/icc/9.1.1

O'Reilly, T. (2007). What is Web 2.0: Design patterns and business models for the next generation of software. *Communications & Stratégies, 1*(65), 17–37.

Panahi, S., Watson, J., & Partridge, H. (2012). Social media and tacit knowledge sharing : Developing a conceptual model. *World Academy of Science. Engineering and Technology, 64*, 1095–1102.

Paroutis, S., & Al Saleh, A. (2009). Determinants of knowledge sharing using Web 2.0 technologies. *Journal of Knowledge Management, 13*(4), 52–63. doi:10.1108/13673270910971824

Pekka-Economou, V., & Hadjidema, S. (2011). Innovative organizational forms that add value to both organizations and community: The case of knowledge management. *European Research Studies, 14*(2), 81–95.

Polanyi, M. (1966). The logic of tacit inference. *Philosophy (London, England), 41*(155), 1–18. doi:10.1017/S0031819100066110

Prieto, I. M., Revilla, E., & Rodríguez-Prado, B. (2009). Managing the knowledge paradox in product development. *Journal of Knowledge Management, 13*(3), 157–170. doi:10.1108/13673270910962941

Richards, D. (2007). Collaborative knowledge engineering: Socialising expert systems. In *11th International Conference on Computer Supported Cooperative Work in Design* (pp. 635–640).

Richter, A., Stocker, A., Müller, S., & Avram, G. (2011). Knowledge management goals revisited - A cross-sectional analysis of social software adoption in corporate environments. In *22nd Australasian Conference on Information Systems* (pp. 1–10).

Santoro, M. D., & Bierly, P. E. (2006). Facilitators of knowledge transfer in university-industry collaborations: A knowledge-based perspective. *IEEE Transactions on Engineering Management, 53*(4), 495–507. doi:10.1109/TEM.2006.883707

Schlagwein, D., & Hu, M. (2016). How and why organisations use social media: Five use types and their relation to absorptive capacity. *Journal of Information Technology*, (May): 1–28.

Seidler-de Alwis, R., & Hartmann, E. (2008). The use of tacit knowledge within innovative companies: Knowledge management in innovative enterprises. *Journal of Knowledge Management*, *12*(1), 133–147. doi:10.1108/13673270810852449

Sigala, M., & Chalkiti, K. (2015). Knowledge management, social media and employee creativity. *International Journal of Hospitality Management*, *45*(February), 44–58. doi:10.1016/j.ijhm.2014.11.003

Smith, E. A. (2001). The role of tacit and explicit knowledge in the workplace. *Journal of Knowledge Management*, *5*(4), 311–321. doi:10.1108/13673270110411733

Soto-Acosta, P., Perez-Gonzalez, D., & Popa, S. (2014). Determinants of Web 2.0 technologies for knowledge sharing in SMEs. *Service Business*, *8*(3), 425–438. doi:10.100711628-014-0247-9

Starbuck, W. H. (1992). Learning by knowledge-intensive firms. *Journal of Management Studies*, *29*(6), 713–740. doi:10.1111/j.1467-6486.1992.tb00686.x

Sultan, N. (2013). Knowledge management in the age of cloud computing and Web 2.0: Experiencing the power of disruptive innovations. *International Journal of Information Management*, *33*(1), 160–165. doi:10.1016/j.ijinfomgt.2012.08.006

Tee, M. Y., & Karney, D. (2010). Sharing and cultivating tacit knowledge in an online learning environment. *International Journal of Computer-Supported Collaborative Learning*, *5*(4), 385–413. doi:10.100711412-010-9095-3

von Krogh, G. (2012). How does social software change knowledge management? Toward a strategic research agenda. *The Journal of Strategic Information Systems*, *21*(2), 154–164. doi:10.1016/j.jsis.2012.04.003

Wang, S., & Noe, R. A. (2010). Knowledge sharing: A review and directions for future research. *Human Resource Management Review*, *20*(2), 115–131. doi:10.1016/j.hrmr.2009.10.001

KEY TERMS AND DEFINITIONS

Knowledge Capture: A fundamental process of preservation and formalization of knowledge.

Knowledge Management: The exploitation and development of the knowledge assets of an organization with a view to furthering the organization's objectives.

Knowledge Management 2.0: Knowledge management system that enables self-organization of people, by utilization of appropriate social media tools, such as wikis, blogs and social networks.

Knowledge Sharing: Sharing and transfer interchangeable, and commonly appear with the same sense in the literature. Knowledge sharing promotes the creation of new theories and ideas, and establishment of new research principles. It is a key driver of innovation process.

Social Media: A set of features, grouped into software applications and websites, which enables people and organizations to recreate online various types of social interactions that enable to create and share content.

Social Networks: Web sites that enable users to articulate a network of connections of people with whom they wish to share access to profile information, news, or other forms of content.

Tacit Knowledge: Knowledge that is complex, not codified, and presents some difficulty in its reproduction in a document or in a database. It can be get from experience, perceptions and individual values, and depends on the context in which is inserted.

Web 2.0: The second generation of the World Wide Web, that emphasizes the concept of exchange of information and collaboration through the Internet sites and virtual services. The idea is that the online environment becomes more dynamic and, in this way, users to collaborate to organize content.

This research was previously published in Social Media for Knowledge Management Applications in Modern Organizations; pages 31-57, copyright year 2018 by Business Science Reference (an imprint of IGI Global).

Chapter 22
Which is the Best Way to Measure Job Performance:
Self–Perceptions or Official Supervisor Evaluations?

Ned Kock

Department of International Business and Technology Studies, Texas A&M International University, Laredo, TX, USA

ABSTRACT

Among latent variables that can be used in e-collaboration research, job performance is a particularly important one. It measures what most e-collaboration tools in organizations aim to improve, namely the performance at work of individuals executing tasks collaboratively with others. The authors report on a comparative assessment of scores generated based on a self-reported job performance measurement instrument vis-à-vis official annual performance evaluation scores produced by supervisors. The results suggest that the self-reported measurement instrument not only presents good validity, good reliability and low collinearity; but that it may well be a better way of measuring job performance than supervisor scores.

INTRODUCTION

Structural equation modeling (SEM) methods and software tools make possible for researchers to simultaneously specify and test measurement and structural models involving latent variables. Mathematically, latent variables are aggregations of their indicators and measurement error. The indicators are quantitative responses, often provided along Likert-type scales, to question-statements in questionnaires.

Two main classes of SEM have been experiencing increasing use in e-collaboration research, as well as in empirical research in many other fields where multivariate statistical methods are typically used. One of these two main classes are SEM based on the partial least squares (PLS) method, a composite-based (as opposed to factor-based) method that does not explicitly account for measurement error. This class of SEM methods owes much of its existence to the work of Herman Wold, who devised a set of

DOI: 10.4018/978-1-7998-9020-1.ch022

computationally efficient and nonparametric algorithms that serve as an alternative to the more restrictive covariance-based approach to SEM.

Covariance-based SEM accounts for measurement error and yields fairly precise parameter estimates; also, it has been widely used in the past, although it is arguably experiencing some decline in recent years. Among the reasons for this decline are that covariance-based SEM is somewhat difficult to use and restrictive in its assumptions (i.e., it assumes multivariate normality); and, perhaps more importantly, covariance-based SEM does not estimate factors as part of its iterative parameter convergence process, which can be seen as a major limitation (Kock, 2015a, 2015b).

The other main class of SEM methods seeing increasing use is factor-based SEM (Kock, 2015b), which fully accounts for the measurement errors that are part of the factors in a model. This latter SEM class in some cases builds on coefficients generated by PLS algorithms, although it is very different from PLS-based SEM. The increasing use of this latter type of SEM is due in part to the ease-of-use and extensive features of software tools that implement it, such as WarpPLS (Kock, 2010, 2015a), which we use here in our analyses, building on an illustrative model. We use WarpPLS not only because it implements factor-based SEM, but also because it provides the most extensive set of features among comparable SEM software. Among these features is a comprehensive set of model fit and quality indices, as well as various coefficients that can be used in a variety tests – e.g., full collinearity variance inflation factors, used in multi-collinearity and common method bias tests.

Among latent variables that can be used in e-collaboration research, job performance is a particularly important one. After all, it measures what one usually wants to ultimately improve with the use of practically any e-collaboration tool in any organization – the job performance of individuals working in teams. In this study, we provide a comparative assessment of scores generated based on a self-reported job performance measurement instrument vis-à-vis official annual performance evaluation scores produced by immediate supervisors. The results discussed here suggest that the self-reported job performance measurement instrument is not only more than adequate, but may well be a better measure than official evaluation scores produced by supervisors.

ILLUSTRATIVE MODEL AND DATA

Our discussion is based on the illustrative model depicted in Figure 1. This illustrative model addresses the organizational effect of the use of social networking sites (SN), such as Facebook and LinkedIn, on job performance (JP). In the model, this effect (i.e., of SN on JP) is hypothesized to be indirect and mediated by intermediate effects on job satisfaction (JS) and organizational commitment (OC). These hypotheses are generally supported by the structural model coefficients; notable among these are the path coefficients and P values indicated next to each arrow in the model. This illustrative model is based on an actual study.

Note that in the model the effect of SN on OC also appears to be primarily indirect and mediated by JS. Our illustrative model is consistent with theoretical developments and past empirical studies relating the use of social networking sites and job performance (Moqbel et al., 2013; Kock & Moqbel, 2016; Kock et al., 2016). The impact of social networking site use on job performance is a topic that can be seen as falling within the broader scope of the e-collaboration research area (Kock, 2005, 2008; Kock & Lynn, 2012).

Figure 1. Illustrative model used. Notes: SN = social networking site use; JS = job satisfaction; OC = organizational commitment; JP = job performance; notation under latent variable acronym describes measurement approach and number of indicators, e.g., (R)5i = reflective measurement with 5 indicators

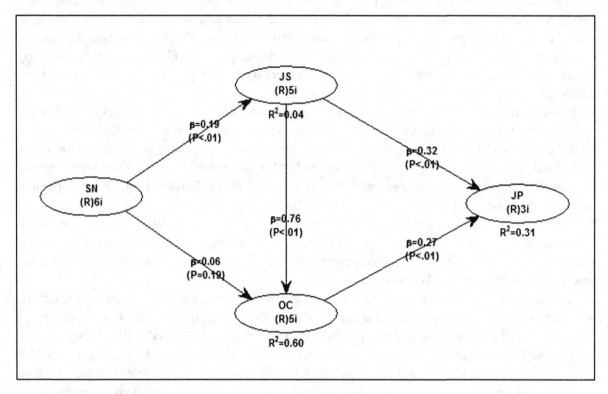

The figure has been created with the SEM analysis software WarpPLS (Kock, 2010, 2015a). As such the figure displays the software's standard notation for summarized latent variable description. In this notation, the alphanumeric combination under each latent variable's label (e.g., "JS") in the model describes the measurement approach used for that latent variable and the number of indicators. For instance, the alphanumeric combination "(R)5i" means reflective measurement with 5 indicators.

The latent variables have been measured through indicators based on the question-statements listed in Appendix A. The data was collected from 193 working professionals across the USA. These working professionals used social networking sites, with different degrees of use intensity. Use of social networking sites in general was considered in the data collection, not specifically use of social networking sites during business hours or while formally at work. The underlying theoretical basis of the model builds on the notion that social networking site use in general is likely to lead to positive emotions, with an overall positive effect on job performance. Therefore, the use of social networking sites is seen through this model as akin to mood-improving activities that could be performed within or outside work hours, such as recreational exercise and meditation, in terms of the activities' overall positive effect on one's performance at work.

ASSESSMENT OF SELF-PERCEIVED MEASURE: VALIDITY, RELIABILITY AND COLLINEARITY

In our analysis, we employed a factor-based SEM algorithm that estimates parameters based on the two-stage process described by Kock (2015b), with the key difference that the factor-based SEM algorithm used here employs a consistent reliability estimate developed by Theo K. Dijkstra during his Ph.D. work conducted under Herman Wold. Wold is widely regarded as the originator of the classic PLS-based methods for SEM, which does not build on factors and thus does not take measurement error into account when estimating model parameters.

Our factor-based SEM algorithm is implemented in WarpPLS starting in version 6.0. Dijkstra's "consistent PLS" reliability estimate, which is utilized by this factor-based SEM algorithm, itself uses coefficients generated via the PLS Mode A algorithm employing the centroid scheme. This is the basic scheme for PLS Mode A, developed by Wold, and also implemented in WarpPLS. The factor-based SEM algorithm we used here yields results that are very similar to those previously implemented in WarpPLS by factor-based SEM methods employing Cronbach's alpha, a more widely used measure of reliability – which nevertheless tends to underestimate the true reliability when factor-indicator correlations (i.e., loadings) are highly heterogeneous. All of these factor-based SEM algorithms implemented in WarpPLS generally display the same precision as covariance-based SEM with full-information maximum likelihood.

In Table 1 we show several coefficients associated with JP. Some of these coefficients were calculated with respect to other variables, following standard approaches for measurement instrument quality assessment. They include the loadings associated with each of JP's three indicators (top-left of table), the correlations with other latent variables in the model (top-right), the composite reliability and Cronbach's alpha coefficients associated with JP (bottom-left), the average variance extracted and its square root (bottom-right), and the full collinearity variance inflation factor associated with JP in the context of our illustrative model (also bottom-right). These coefficients illustrate the quality of the self-perceived measure used for JP.

Table 1. Validation of self-perceived measure

Loadings		Correlations with LVs	
JP1	0.843	SN	-0.006
JP2	0.933	JS	0.487
JP3	0.927	OC	0.490
Composite reliability		AVE and square root of AVE	
0.929		0.814	0.902
Cronbach's alpha		Full collinearity VIF	
0.924		1.390	

Notes: LVs = latent variables other than JP; AVE = average variance extracted; VIF = variance inflation factor; the square root of the AVE is normally used in discriminant validity tests.

The loadings for the three indicators associated with JP were equal to or greater than the threshold value of 0.5, and the P values associated with these loadings were all significant at the 0.001 level.

Moreover, the average variance extracted for JP was greater than the threshold value of 0.5. Taken as a whole, these results suggest that the measurement instrument used for JP presents good convergent validity (Kock, 2011, 2014, 2015a; Kock & Lynn, 2012). In fact, the lowest loading for JP was 0.843 and the average variance extracted was 0.814, both well above the generally accepted threshold of 0.5.

The square root of the average variance extracted for JP was 0.902. This is far greater than any of the three correlations involving JP and the other three latent variables in the model, which are shown in the table. Therefore, we can safely conclude that the measurement instrument used for JP displays good discriminant validity in the context of our model (Kock, 2011, 2014, 2015a; Kock & Lynn, 2012). The composite reliability and Cronbach's alpha coefficients were 0.929 and 0.924 respectively, both greater than the conservative threshold value of 0.7, suggesting that the measurement instrument used for JP has good reliability (Kock, 2011, 2014, 2015a).

Finally, the full collinearity variance inflation factor associated with JP was 1.390. This coefficient is a model-wide measure of multi-collinearity, calculated in a way that incorporates the variations in the other variables in the model, and that allows us to test whether respondents viewed JP as conceptually different from all of the other latent variables. This 1.390 value is well below the recommended threshold of 3.3 (Kock & Lynn, 2012), suggesting that JP is not collinear with any of the other latent variables in the model, and thus is perceived as conceptually unique within our model.

Moreover, this low 1.390 value is also below the recommended threshold of 3.3 for common method bias; this is the same threshold used for multi-collinearity assessment (for details, see: Kock, 2015c; Kock & Lynn, 2012). This suggests that JP is not contaminated with pathological common method variance (Kock, 2014, 2015a, 2015c). As previously demonstrated (Kock, 2015c), common method variance tends to lead to high model-wide collinearity levels, leading to biases that are often not captured by discriminant validity or other classic common method bias tests; but that are captured by the test based on full collinearity variance inflation factors proposed by Kock (2015c) and Kock & Lynn (2012). As can be inferred from the above discussion, this latter test is also used for multi-collinearity assessment.

ASSESSMENT OF SELF-PERCEIVED MEASURE AGAINST OFFICIAL SUPERVISOR EVALUATIONS

The measurement instrument for JP was also validated against actual performance evaluation scores received by employees from immediate supervisors. Two steps were used in this validation. In the first step, we created two models containing two variables, JPself and JPsupv, and conducted linear and non-linear analyses. JPself refers to self-perceived job performance, measured using the instrument for JP in Appendix A. JPsupv refers to official annual performance evaluation scores received from immediate supervisors. In the second step, we combined the indicators of these two variables into one latent variable, and again conducted validity and reliability assessments. These steps are discussed in more detail below.

First Step: Segregated Indicators

In the first step the following simple models, with only two variables each, were analyzed linearly and nonlinearly: JPself → JPsupv, and JPsupv → JPself. The reason for two models instead of one is that nonlinear results vary depending on the direction of a link; the linear results are the same. The linear and nonlinear path coefficients obtained were 0.502 (P < 0.001) and 0.546 (P < 0.001), respectively, for the model JPself → JPsupv. For the model with the link reversed, namely JPsupv → JPself, the linear and nonlinear path coefficients obtained were 0.502 (P < 0.001) and 0.503 (P < 0.001), respectively.

These results suggest that the association between the variables JPself and JPsupv is strong enough to justify using either of these two variables as a proxy for the other (Kock & Lynn, 2012). These results also suggest that, if only one of the two variables were to be used, the better choice would arguably be JPself, because it is the better predictor of the two (Kock & Gaskins, 2016; Pearl, 2009), as indicated by the nonlinear coefficients.

Second Step: Combined Indicators

In the second step, we combined the indicators of the two variables into one new latent variable to further assess the compatibility of the two variables, and thus their proxy potential. The indicators of the variable JPself refer to the three corresponding question-statements in Appendix A. The variable JPsupv has only one indicator, namely the annual performance evaluation scores received from immediate supervisors.

The new latent variable with four indicators passed the criteria for validity and reliability assessment discussed earlier. Its composite reliability was 0.916, its Cronbach's alpha was 0.874, and its average variance extracted was 0.736. The loadings obtained for each of the indicators were the following: 0.879, 0.936, 0.929 and 0.658. The first three loadings refer to the three corresponding question-statements in Appendix A; the last loading refers to the annual performance evaluation scores received from immediate supervisors.

As can be seen, the composite reliability and Cronbach's alpha coefficients suggest acceptable reliability in connection with the new latent variable with four indicators. The average variance extracted and loadings, the latter all significant at the P<0.001 level, suggest acceptable convergent validity. These results provide further evidence in favor of the conclusion that JPself and JPsupv are fairly compatible, and thus could be used as proxies for each other.

However, the loading for 0.658 was below the more conservative threshold of 0.7 for convergent validity (Kock, 2014, 2015a), and also significantly lower than those for JP1, JP2 and JP3. Moreover, both the variability and range of variation for JPself were greater than for JPsupv, which suggests that the former variable provides a more fine-grained measure of job performance. Interestingly, the means for the indicators of JPself were lower than the mean for the single JPsupv indicator, suggesting that self-evaluations might have been more realistic. These results, combined with the results from the first step, suggest that it might be advisable to use only JPself (made up of JP1, JP2 and JP3) in SEM analyses, instead of the expanded latent variable with four indicators.

CONCLUSION

The results of the assessments discussed here not only suggest that the self-reported job performance measurement instrument used in our illustrative study is more than adequate, but also that it is probably a better measure than official annual performance evaluation scores received from immediate supervisors. In other words, anonymous self-evaluations of job performance may be better, from a measurement instrument quality perspective, than official annual performance evaluation scores produced by supervisors.

Therefore, we recommend that researchers employ the measurement instrument for job performance provided in Appendix A, or an extended measurement instrument that builds on the question-statements provided in Appendix A. An extended measurement instrument can be generated by adding question-statements whose meaning is likely to be seen as redundant with the three existing question-statements (see Appendix B). An example would be: "I am proud of my performance in my current job."

Having more redundant question-statements in the measurement instrument for job performance means that more redundant indicators would be available, which would likely lead to greater reliability values and thus lower measurement error magnitudes. It should be noted that redundant indicators present high levels of collinearity among themselves, which is a desirable property in a reflective latent variable measurement instrument such as the one we used here for job performance. This desirable measurement model property, at the individual latent variable level, is undesirable at the structural model (i.e., the inner model). The structural model includes the latent variable scores (or factor scores) and the links among latent variables. A high level of collinearity among latent variables, indicated by one or more full collinearity variance inflation factors above a threshold (e.g., 3.3 or, less conservatively, 5), is generally undesirable in part because it tends to lead to path coefficient distortion and instances of Simpson's paradox (Kock & Gaskins, 2016).

A key reason why anonymous self-evaluations of job performance may be better than official annual performance evaluation scores produced by supervisors may be that the former are anonymous while the latter are not. That is, the identities of the supervisors are known to the employees they evaluate. As such, supervisors may tend to generate evaluation scores that are a poorer reflection of their employees' performance than the employees own self-reported job performance evaluations. More specifically, supervisors may be tempted to overstate their employees' performance, perhaps to avoid conflict and ensure their employees' loyalty.

ACKNOWLEDGMENT

The author is the developer of the software WarpPLS, which has over 7,000 users in more than 33 different countries at the time of this writing, and moderator of the PLS-SEM e-mail distribution list. He is grateful to those users, and to the members of the PLS-SEM e-mail distribution list, for questions, comments, and discussions on topics related to the use of WarpPLS.

REFERENCES

Kock, N. (2005). What is e-collaboration. *International Journal of e-Collaboration*, *1*(1), 1–7.

Kock, N. (2008). E-collaboration and e-commerce in virtual worlds: The potential of Second Life and World of Warcraft. *International Journal of e-Collaboration*, *4*(3), 1–13. doi:10.4018/jec.2008070101

Kock, N. (2010). Using WarpPLS in e-collaboration studies: An overview of five main analysis steps. *International Journal of e-Collaboration*, *6*(4), 1–11. doi:10.4018/jec.2010100101

Kock, N. (2011). Using WarpPLS in e-collaboration studies: Descriptive statistics, settings, and key analysis results. *International Journal of e-Collaboration*, *7*(2), 1–18. doi:10.4018/jec.2011040101

Kock, N. (2014). Advanced mediating effects tests, multi-group analyses, and measurement model assessments in PLS-based SEM. *International Journal of e-Collaboration*, *10*(3), 1–13.

Kock, N. (2015a). *WarpPLS 5.0 User Manual*. Laredo, TX: ScriptWarp Systems.

Kock, N. (2015b). A note on how to conduct a factor-based PLS-SEM analysis. *International Journal of e-Collaboration*, *11*(3), 1–9. doi:10.4018/ijec.2015070101

Kock, N. (2015c). Common method bias in PLS-SEM: A full collinearity assessment approach. *International Journal of e-Collaboration*, *11*(4), 1–10. doi:10.4018/ijec.2015100101

Kock, N., & Gaskins, L. (2016). Simpsons paradox, moderation, and the emergence of quadratic relationships in path models: An information systems illustration. *International Journal of Applied Nonlinear Science*, *2*(3), 200–234. doi:10.1504/IJANS.2016.077025

Kock, N., & Lynn, G. S. (2012). Lateral collinearity and misleading results in variance-based SEM: An illustration and recommendations. *Journal of the Association for Information Systems*, *13*(7), 546–580.

Kock, N., & Moqbel, M. (2016). A six-stage framework for evolutionary IS research using path models: Conceptual development and a social networking illustration. *Journal of Systems and Information Technology*, *18*(1), 64–88. doi:10.1108/JSIT-04-2015-0028

Kock, N., Moqbel, M., Barton, K., & Bartelt, V. (2016). Intended continued use of social networking sites: Effects on job satisfaction and performance. *International Journal of Virtual Communities and Social Networking*, *8*(2), 28–46. doi:10.4018/IJVCSN.2016040103

Moqbel, M., Nevo, S., & Kock, N. (2013). Organizational members use of social networking sites and job performance: An exploratory study. *Information Technology & People*, *26*(3), 240–264. doi:10.1108/ITP-10-2012-0110

Pearl, J. (2009). *Causality: Models, reasoning, and inference*. Cambridge, England: Cambridge University Press. doi:10.1017/CBO9780511803161

This research was previously published in the International Journal of e-Collaboration (IJeC), 13(2); pages 1-9, copyright year 2017 by IGI Publishing (an imprint of IGI Global).

APPENDIX A

Latent Variable Measurement Instrument

The question-statements below, answered on a Likert-type scale, were used for data collection related to the indicators of the latent variables in our illustrative model. The question-statements were answered on a Likert-type scale going from "1 – Strongly disagree" to "5 – Strongly agree".

Social Networking Site Use (SN)

SN1: My social networking sites' account/s are/is a part of my everyday activity.
SN2: I am proud to tell people I'm on social networking sites such as Facebook.
SN3: Social networking sites have become part of my daily routine.
SN4: I feel out of touch when I haven't logged onto social networking sites for a while.
SN5: I feel I am part of the social networking sites community.
SN6: I would be sorry if social networking sites shut down.

Job Satisfaction (JS)

JS1: I am very satisfied with my current job.
JS2: My present job gives me internal satisfaction.
JS3: My job gives me a sense of fulfillment.
JS4: I am very pleased with my current job.
JS5: I will recommend this job to a friend if it is advertised /announced.

Organizational Commitment (OC)

OC1: I would be very happy to spend the rest of my career with this organization.
OC2: I feel a strong sense of belonging to my organization.
OC3: I feel 'emotionally attached' to this organization.
OC4: Even if it were to my advantage, I do not feel it would be right to leave my organization.
OC5: I would feel guilty if I left my organization now.

Job Performance (JP)

JP1: My performance in my current job is excellent.
JP2: I am very satisfied with my performance in my current job.
JP3: I am very happy with my performance in my current job.

APPENDIX B

Extended Job Performance (JP) Measurement Instrument

The first three question-statements below are from Appendix A. The other question-statements are suggestions for an extended set, which could be expected to increase latent variable reliability if used (without compromising loadings).

JP1: My performance in my current job is excellent.
JP2: I am very satisfied with my performance in my current job.
JP3: I am very happy with my performance in my current job.
JP4: I am proud of my performance in my current job.
JP5: I contribute a lot to my current organization in terms of job performance.
JP6: I am a high-performing member of my current organization.

These question-statements may be answered based on Likert-type scales going from "1 – Strongly disagree" to "5 – Strongly agree", or from "1 – Strongly disagree" to "7 – Strongly agree". Broader scales (e.g., 1 to 100) would probably not add much useful variation due to the human cognitive limitations associated with the "magical number 7" notion proposed by the cognitive psychologist George A. Miller.

Chapter 23
Competitive Analysis Based on Social Media Mining

Roberto Marmo
University of Pavia, Italy

ABSTRACT

With the ever-inflating of information in Social Media, companies are working in a complex, open and mobilizing environment, they need to know their competitors if they need to survive in contemporary shrinking market, and identify opportunities to optimize their own content strategies. This chapter describes some technologies that can help to execute competitive analysis using social media mining, it also discusses background, knowledge, challenges and critical factors necessary for successful business.

INTRODUCTION

With the ever-inflating of information in Social Media, companies are working in a complex, open and mobilizing environment, they need to know their competitors if they need to survive in contemporary shrinking market, and identify opportunities to optimize their own content strategies.

This chapter describes some technologies that can help to execute competitive analysis using social media mining, it also discusses background, knowledge, challenges and critical factors necessary for successful business.

COMPETITIVE INTELLIGENCE

Competitive intelligence is defined to be "the art of defining, gathering and analyzing intelligence about competitor's products, promotions, sales etc. from external sources" (Dey et all, 2011), allowing a company to predict or forecast what is going to happen in its competitive environment (Bose, 2008). Competitive intelligence refers to the information collecting and analyzing conducted by a competitive party in order to maintain its advantage. The purpose of the study (Colakoglu,2011) is to investigate the literature and applications in business world about the competitive intelligence, and especially evaluating and develop-

DOI: 10.4018/978-1-7998-9020-1.ch023

ing competitive intelligence. Comparison between the literature and applications will be done and the results of comparison will be given as conclusion. Types of competitive intelligence include analysis of competitors, the competitive environment, competitive trends and strategy. In particular, competitive analysis regards a systematic process in order to gather and analyze information about competitors.

Competitive analysis help to compare your competitors' performance and uptime to your own search and ranking tools to understand how well competitors are viewed by the rest of the web, how test users interact with competitors' websites.

The competitive analysis section is a relevant section of business plan, because it is devoted to analyzing both your current competition and potential competitors who might enter your market.

To identify your current competitors there can be two ways of doing an analysis: look at them from a customer's point of view, look at them from their point of view. By looking at them from a customer's point of view, you are looking at their major strengths and flaws, think like a customer would. On the other hand looking at them from their point of view will help you try to see what their weaknesses are, how you would compensate for them their firm better, how you would play them in the marketing field.

Some suggestions on why do social competitive analysis:

- To get ideas for how brand can engage in the social media channel;
- To gauge the overall marketing for product or service engages in social media;
- To identify opportunities your competitors may be missing.;
- To study what type of content works on which network or even if a specific network is worth your effort, by seeing what is working for others, especially those in your niche or industry;
- Get ideas for how, your brand can engage in the social media channel.

Social Media

Social media is the collective of online communications channels dedicated to community-based input, interaction, content-sharing and collaboration. Social Network is a social structure composed of individuals, organizations, company etc. which are connected by relationships and interactions.

Social media are used intensely to communicate, to publish resources (personal data, photo, video, blog), to establish relationships of a different type share information, make decisions, and do business in many ways, with hundreds web platforms in the world collecting the information of more than one billion registered users. Categories of social media regards: blogs, discussion forums, blogs, social networking, news discussions, media sharing sites, collaborative websites. Well-known online platforms are: Facebook as generic social network, LinkedIn as business social network, Flickr about photo sharing, Google+ as solution from Google search engine, WordPress from hobby blogs to the biggest news sites online. Thus, today online social network is a relevant part of human life and it is truly the reflection of today's society.

Social media can be considered as economic environment in which brands are competing for a product market, companies that interact within a social media in which a certain agent persuades others to update or shift their brands; the brands of the products they are using.

Social Media Mining

Social media mining is the process of representing, analyzing, and extracting actionable patterns and trends from raw social media data. The term mining is an analogy to the resource extraction process of mining for rare minerals. It requires human data analysts and automated software programs to sift through massive amounts of raw social media data in order to discern patterns and trends. Social Media Mining integrates social media, social network analysis, and data mining to provide a coherent platform to understand the basics and potentials of social media mining (Zafarani, Abbasi, Liu, 2014).

Using Social media mining, it is possible media usage, online behaviors, sharing of content, connections between individuals, online buying behavior, etc. These patterns and trends are of interest to organizations that can use these patterns and trends to execute social competitive analysis based on publicly available data.

The key questions for social media mining, and at the same time the main questions for competitive analysis, are:

- How to derive information from unstructured textual data, image, video?
- How to form analysis to assist in decision making based on the information derived from the text documents?
- How to grasp opportunities for business success based on the generated report?

Answers can be provided through actively listening, reading, discussing and performing.

Legal Factors and Ethical

As suggested in (West, 2001) ethics, or what is deemed to be good or bad in human conduct, is a key issue in all types of research activity. Competitive analysis is particularly prone to ethical assessment and is also subject to legal constraints, because there are many who regard it as an invasion of privacy, and therefore inherently unethical, and partly because there have been widely publicized situations in which the methods used to collect information have been open to criticism.

The legal and ethical issues must be aware are:

- Copyright law, prevents the copying and redistribution of all written material without the permission of the author;
- Criminal law, protects companies and individuals from theft, fraud and trespass;
- Data protection legislation, protects the privacy of individuals by controlling the content and use of databases containing personal information.

METHODOLOGY

There are six main steps to achieving competitive analysis:

Step 1: Allocating resources;
Step 2: Preliminary analysis;

Step 3: Social metrics;
Step 4: Social analytics tool;
Step 5: Competitive report;
Step 6: Decision making.

The process can be think as a cycle, to re-start from the first point, if necessary, in order to obtain more in-depth results or to try another approach.

Microblog is one of the most convenient platforms since it is short, instantaneous, spontaneous and mobile and has become a great source of consumer opinions. The paper (Arrigo, 2016) is focused on microblog as a marketing intelligence tool, it provides a theoretical framework for microblog competitive intelligence and discusses its opportunities and limitations.

The paper (Dey et all, 2011) discusses methodologies to obtain competitive intelligence from different types of web resources including social media using a wide array of text mining techniques.

A methodology to integrate several techniques including quantitative analysis, text mining, and sentiment analysis for analyzing and comparing social media content from business competitors is detailed on (Wu et all, 2016).

Allocating Resources

As suggested in (Håkansson et all, 2015) important parts of the methodology are budgeting the process and allocating personnel and financial resources.

The ideal situation is to get high quality insight rapidly and at a low cost. However, the three parameters of quality, speed and cost are interdependently related and it is not possible to optimise one without sacrificing another. Therefore, this step requires the definition of ambition level of quality insight.

A timetable is needed to specify the deadlines for the different activities and for the final result, because information which comes too late is often useless.

Reporting occasions also serve as a trigger to ensure active and vital analysis work, as detailed on next section.

In this kind of analysis can be accumulating and analyzing a lot of data, the only way to make sense of it all is to keep it as organized as possible.

Preliminary Analysis

Before to embark on any competitive analysis, it is necessary to ask yourself why you care, to ask whether you care if your competitors know what you're up to. Only then can you decide what to collect and how to report it. Some possible questions you want to answer include:

- Do I have competitors I don't know about?
- Do competitors have a better reputation than I do?
- Are others getting more likes, comments, share etc. than me?
- Are others' marketing and brand awareness efforts more successful than mine?
- Have competitors made changes that I can use to my advantage?
- Is their marketing and branding working better?
- Have they made changes I can use?

- Do they have a better reputation?
- Are any of your competitors doing something unique or unconventional?
- Are any of your competitors running a type of campaign or contest that no one else is?

With social media platforms, competitors should be classed as any of the following:

- Your direct, traditional competitors;
- Those competing for the attention of a similar audience to you, even if in a different sector;
- Businesses with a similar content strategy, albeit for a different audience.

Before comparing metrics with competitors, start by analyzing your own communities to understand where the most growth occurred during your predetermined period of time and on which days.

At this point, there is an excellent base for building a competitor profile.

SOCIAL METRICS

Before conducting a competitive analysis, it's imperative to identify which metrics are important to your social media marketing strategy and why, across all regions and social channels. This starts with having a clear vision of your marketing goals, and deciding how social media channel fits into accomplishing them. Let's start with a few metrics, in order:

1. Community size and growth, to answer the following questions: "Which channels are my competitors seeing the most growth in terms of fans/followers?";
2. Volume of interactions and engagement rate, by a variety of different terms depending on the social channel, such as:
   a. Facebook: likes, comments, shares;
   b. Twitter: favorited, replies, retweets;
   c. Google+: replies, reshares;
   d. YouTube: views, likes, comments;
   e. LinkedIn: likes, comments;
   f. Instagram: likes, comments;
   g. Pinterest: likes, comments, repins;
3. Volume and type of publications, type of publications:
   a. Facebook: post;
   b. Twitter: tweet;
   c. Google+: post;
   d. YouTube: video;
   e. LinkedIn: post;
   f. Instagram: picture;
   g. Pinterest: pin.

Social Analytics Tool

There are three ways to begin conducting a competitive analysis based on publicly available social media data: manual operations, free or paid automated tools. Also in case of automated tools, humans are still needed to transform the data into actionable intelligence .

Choosing an analytics tool, it is relevant to prefer a tool that enables to analyze data for total community sizes in aggregate and at an individual level over a set period of time. This means having the ability to slice and dice data based on social accounts by media type, region, language, and brand.

To get more specific, it is necessary to drill down into data obtained by social channel or region to get a detailed snapshot of each community, segmenting data by region, language, or social account depending on which metrics are most important to the social marketing benchmarks you have set.

If the size and growth across social communities globally is a key metric, it is possible start by creating an overview of the brands within your competitive set. This will give an aggregate view of all social communities as a whole. A helpful indicator as to whether you're on the right track is to compare the growth rate across brands over time, in addition to overall share fans/followers.

Text mining is an extension of data mining to textual data that attempts to extract meaningful information, trends, patterns, or rules from unstructured textual data, such as: frequency counts of words, length of the sentence, presence/absence of certain words, etc. Case study and the power of text mining as an effective technique to extract business value are described on (Gémar, 2015).

Sentiment analysis (also known as opinion mining) refers to the use of natural language processing, text mining and computational linguistics to identify and extract subjective information in source materials. Sentiment analysis is widely applied to reviews and social media to determine the attitude of user with respect to some topic or the overall contextual polarity of a post, image, etc.

Tools based on text mining and sentiment analysis can provide an in-depth analysis of a particular situation. The book (Pozzi et all, 2016) explores both semantic and machine learning models and methods that address context-dependent and dynamic text in online social networks.

Manual Operations

It is possible to aggregate metrics from each social channel individually by visiting their pages regularly and copying data into a spreadsheet. This could be somewhat tedious, but it is an option for brands on a limited budget.

Google is an obvious place to start. Many competitive questions can be answered directly from Google. Searching on Google for specific terms adding keyword based on name of famous social media website, can shows what competitors sites come up, and see if there are others that are not yet know. Google Alerts on https://www.google.com/alerts can also be used to help with new content ideas, link acquisition for unlinked brand mentions, guest post opportunities, and to discover new topically relevant content to share with your community across your social media channels.

Looking at past versions of the competitor's social media on Wayback Machine https://archive.org/ can shed light on changes of direction in strategy, marketing and product development.

Press release sites have a search and it is possible search "social media campaign" to see what other brands are doing or have done. Reading about and follow the links to see what they did, it is possible to see what worked and adapt it to your industry.

Subscribe to competitors email newsletters and if possible use tools to determine what works best and follow their best practices, notice their sign up process, content and subject lines.

Learn about their Facebook fans and their interest by using graph search, to determine what kind of content your audience responds to. As example of Facebook graph search, on the top search box typing "Pages liked by people who like [name of competitor]" it is possible to obtain some interesting results.

Note what post work best, quantity of comments, sharing, likes etc. see what type of content is working for them and adapt it to your audience.

One of the easiest ways to ensure you're aware of your competitors is to find yourself in a directory, like as Facebook Directory Pages on http://www.facebook.com/directory/pages and see who else is listed there.

It is relevant to prepare a list of competitors, to keep continuously update, to visit competitors' sites regularly using browser on desktop and smartphone, to detect when there is a change to these sites

Follow key influencers that they are most active on competitor's social pages, to obtain a more complete picture of competitor and benefit from their best thinkers.

Free or Paid Automated Tools

While it often requires some monetary investment, you can expect to save time and gain actionable insights that may not find by manually monitoring pages or using free tools.

Digimind Social Analytics on https://www.digimind.com is a smart software to listen, engage, analyse, and report, allows brands to monitor hundreds of social accounts.

Fanpage Karma on http://www.fanpagekarma.com is useful to see where your competitors are succeeding in the social universe with the best analytics, statistics tool, insight reports.

Hootsuite on http://hootsuite.com can be used to follow your competitors' activity in real-time, how their customers perceive them, how many followers your competitors have on each network, if the number of followers trending up or down and how quickly.

HubSpot on https://www.hubspot.com is an inbound marketing and sales platform, the Analysis Competitor tool allows to run a competitor analysis in the most efficient and easy way, also recording social ranking over time.

SEM Rush on https://www.semrush.com is a great software to get a look into what other companies are ranking for your keyword and how you stack up against them. It is one of our favorite tools for flushing out the keywords your competition is targeting. Few examples of reports: Organic Keywords, Chart Tools.

Social Mention on http://www.socialmention.com is a social media search and analysis platform that aggregates user generated content from a large amount of web resources into a single stream of information. It allows to easily track and measure in real-time what people are saying about you, your company, a new product, or any topic.

Simply Measured on http://simplymeasured.com offers a complete social analytics solution, covering from brand reach to business value.

Trackur on http://www.trackur.com is a reliable, cost effective, usable measurement tools for gathering good content and listening to relevant conversations, with multiple ways to get results.

VOZIQ (He, 2015) on http://www.voziq.com can be used to glean industry-specific marketing intelligence, by first creating a social media sentiment benchmark.

Competitive Report

All this social data remains just that data, until you analyze it and transform it into insights. The purpose of a competitive report is to give your internal audience an at-a-glance understanding of key performance indicators you're tracking.

In this kind of report can be identify gaps and opportunities for creating and developing successful digital marketing campaigns, but to obtain considerable results it is necessary to provide comparable data on yourself. Use this report to help identify areas where you're either excelling above your competitors, or where you may not be meeting the standard and allocate resources accordingly. So, to report competitive data it is necessary to have comparable data on yourself.

The data represents metrics over a certain period of time, therefore keep track of the average rates of community growth, interactions, and publications in a separate report.

Using a social analytics tool is one of the easiest ways to not only quickly create a competitive analysis, but visualize the data in a meaningful way.

Information should include:

- A list of competitors you're tracking, with basic business information;
- Any newcomers to the list, as well as any who have been removed;
- A summary of activity for each competitor, including any changes detected in each one's online content as well as links to any important news picked up through alerts or feeds;
- Charts for each metric you're comparing;
- One series line for each competitor, and clearly show your own social organization for comparison;
- A table showing the score for each competitor, as well as the change from the previous reporting period;
- Community reports for any online profiles your competitors operate, such as the volume of Twitter messages, contributions to groups or forums, and so on.

SWOT is a structured planning method used to evaluate the Strengths, Weaknesses, Opportunities and Threats, it is a commonly used method of analysis, because relatively easy to understand and perform, for identifying and analyzing opportunities and threats and how well our own organization is equipped to meet them. Strengths and Weaknesses are factors inside the organization, Opportunities and Threats are external factors. These evaluations are typically shown using four elements in a 2×2 matrix. Some examples regarding competition can be found on (Håkansson et all, 2015).

Statistics are created to make better decisions, are essential and a powerful source of competitive advantage. As suggested in (Fraser, 2016), statistics must be easily and quickly produced using widely available software as Microsoft Excel. Therefore, to identify and analyze your position in the market can be used a competitive analysis Excel template designed as a spreadsheet, to report fundamentals metrics as above mentioned and to compute statistics and graphs. Searching on web using "Competitive Analysis Excel Template" you can find many useful files.

To write a good competitive analysis it is necessary: be objective, conduct fearless and thorough research, write well.

Once you start to publish regular competitive reports at regular intervals, an updated report can be sent via an internal mailing list, or an internal wiki so that it can be accessed by others doing research.

Breaking news, such as changes, product or marketing updates, or other alerts that can have a material impact on your company's business, should be communicated through a real-time model.

Depending on how important competitive intelligence is to your company, you may even want to capture and store competitive data within a community platform automatically.

DECISION MAKING

As final step, a business can compare its social media data to the social media data of their competitors to gain perspective on their performance. The comparison could help a business to identify weaknesses, find new opportunities and adjust their social media strategy.

Regarding the first metric, community size and growth, it is necessary to analyze data for total community sizes in aggregate and individual level over a set period of time, having the ability to slice and dice data based on social accounts by media type, region, language, and brand.

Start by analyzing your own communities to understand where the most growth occurred during your predetermined period of time and on which days, then comparing the same metrics with competitors. This will give you an aggregate view of all social communities as a whole. A helpful indicator is to compare the growth rate across brands over time, in addition to overall share fans/followers.

To get more specific insight, segment data by region, language, or social account depending on which metrics are most important to the social marketing benchmarks.

Regarding the second metric, volume of interactions and engagement rate, by measuring and comparing rates of interactions, it is possible quickly gauge how often people are engaging with your social media content alongside your competitors' content.

A specific analysis can be executed for each interactions on:

- **Passion:** The likelihood that individuals talking about a brand will do so repeatedly;
- **Reach:** The range of influence calculated by number of unique authors referencing a brand, divided by the total number of mentions;
- **Sentiment:** The ratio of mentions that are generally positive to those that are generally negative;
- **Strength:** The likelihood that a brand is being discussed, calculated by phrase mentions within the last 24 hours are divided by the total possible mentions;
- **Top Keywords:** Useful to check which keywords have more impact on searches and references to a brand;
- **Top Users:** The users mentioning a company the most, which is very useful to work with users and encourage loyalty;
- **Top Hashtag:** Main hashtags associated with brand mentions.

Analyzing these metrics can indicate which types of content and strategies are resonating with people, how often people are engaging, which social networks have had the highest levels of engagement overall, and which types are falling, comparing with how often people are engaging to know exactly how you stack up.

It is important to measure the interactions by day for a precise breakdown on each channel, also to pull hour and time related to competitors' engagement and take note of any major spikes in interactions, possibly indicating a campaign or a particularly engaging piece of content.

Regarding the third metric, volume and type of publications are similar to metrics regarding interactions, the publications metrics also differ based on which social channel you are analyzing. Take a look at your own volume and your competitors' volume of publications on different channels, analyzing the publications by media type will give you an idea of which social platforms they are prioritizing. An important is: "Which brands command the share of voice when it comes to their owned media strategy?". To understand this, create a competitive overview of the volume of publications and compare your own social posting strategy to competitors. The highest share of publications indicates the relevant voice. In addition, it's important to understand which types of content generated the highest rates of engagement among audiences. By looking at the top publications based on interaction rate, you can quickly compare which types of publications within each social channel are the most engaging.

Correlation between social media findings (consumer sentiments and opinions) and events (e.g., price changes, rival's promotional activities) and structured data like sales data need to be examined to understand how competition affects business and provide information for decision making (Dey, et all, 2011).

Finally, avoid copying what others have done and instead try to understand the why of competitor success, therefore the competitor is a source of inspiration, not duplication.

CASE STUDY

A case study which applies text mining to analyze unstructured text content on Facebook and Twitter sites is explained in (Wu et all, 2013), related to the three largest pizza chains: Pizza Hut, Domino's Pizza and Papa John's Pizza. The results reveal the value of social media competitive analysis and the power of text mining as an effective technique to extract business value from the vast amount of available social media data. Recommendations are also provided in the paper to help companies develop their social media competitive analysis strategy.

The tool named VOZIQ is used to analyze tweets associated with five large retail sector companies (Costco, Walmart, Kmart, Kohl's, and The Home Depot) and generating business insight reports and to generate meaningful business insight reports (Wu et all, 2015).

Some case-studies are shows on (Dey et all, 2011) to study the correlation of rival brand promotion events on sales data.

Analysis, similarities and differences and comparison of social media content on the Facebook sites of the three largest drugstore chains in the United States is discussed on (Wu et all, 2016).

FUTURE RESEARCH DIRECTIONS

The future research area focuses on to track real-time data and apply advanced data mining, text mining, sentiment analysis to analyze all social data, reasoning process for linking data, to generate intelligent alerts. Emphasis will also be given to assessment of data quality.

CONCLUSION

Social media have been adopted by many businesses. The competitive analysis based on social media mining is an effective way to get a competitive advantage, by providing insight and understanding of the competitors' products and services, as well as increased market knowledge, information useful to create a winning social media strategy.

Social trends and strategies are constantly evolving, therefore it is imperative to choice a set of metrics to segment the data by social media or geographic region, to get even deeper insights relative for benchmarks.

REFERENCES

Arrigo, E. (2016). Deriving Competitive Intelligence from Social Media: Microblog Challenges and Opportunities. *International Journal of Online Marketing*, *6*(2), 49–61. doi:10.4018/IJOM.2016040104

Bose, R. (2008). Competitive intelligence process and tools for intelligence analysis. *Industrial Management & Data Systems*, *108*(4), 510–528. doi:10.1108/02635570810868362

Colakoglu, T. (2011). The Problematic Of Competitive Intelligence: How To Evaluate & Develop Competitive Intelligence? *Procedia: Social and Behavioral Sciences*, *24*, 1615–1623. doi:10.1016/j.sbspro.2011.09.075

Dey, L., Haque, S. M., Khurdiya, A., & Shroff, G. (2011). Acquiring competitive intelligence from social media. *Proceedings of the 2011 joint workshop on multilingual OCR and analytics for noisy unstructured text data*. 10.1145/2034617.2034621

Fraser, C. (2016). *Business Statistics for Competitive Advantage with Excel 2016*. New York: Springer. doi:10.1007/978-3-319-32185-1

Gémar, G., & Jiménez-Quintero, J. A. (2015). Text mining social media for competitive analysis. *Tourism & Management Studies*, *11*(1), 84–90.

Håkansson, C., & Nelke, M. (2015). *Competitive Intelligence for Information Professionals*. Waltham, MA: Elsevier. doi:10.1016/B978-0-08-100206-3.00010-1

Pozzi, F. A., Fersini, E., Messina, E., & Liu, B. (2016). *Sentiment Analysis in Social Networks*. Burlington, MA: Morgan Kaufmann.

West, C. (2001). *Competitive Intelligence*. New York: Palgrave.

Wu, H., Harris, W., & Gongjun, Y. (2015). A novel social media competitive analytics framework with sentiment benchmarks. *Information & Management*, *52*(7), 801–812. doi:10.1016/j.im.2015.04.006

Wu, H., Shenghua, Z., & Ling, L. (2013). Social media competitive analysis and text mining: A case study in the pizza industry. *International Journal of Information Management*, *33*(3), 464–472. doi:10.1016/j.ijinfomgt.2013.01.001

Wu, H., Tian, X., Chen, Y., & Chong, D. (2016). Actionable Social Media Competitive Analytics For Understanding Customer Experiences. *Journal of Computer Information Systems*, *56*(2), 145–155. doi :10.1080/08874417.2016.1117377

Zafarani, R., Abbasi, M. A., & Liu, H. (2014). *Social Media Mining An Introduction*. Cambridge, UK: Cambridge University Press. doi:10.1017/CBO9781139088510

KEY TERMS AND DEFINITIONS

Competitive Analysis: An assessment of the strengths and weaknesses of current and potential competitors.

Competitive Intelligence: The action of defining, gathering, analyzing, and distributing intelligence about products, customers, competitors, and any aspect of business environment.

Social Analytics: The extraction of valuable hidden insights from vast amounts of social media data to enable informed and insightful decision making.

Social Media Marketing: The process of gaining website traffic or attention through social media sites. Social media marketing programs usually center on efforts to create content that attracts attention and encourages readers to share it with their social networks.

Social Media Mining: The process of representing, analyzing, and extracting actionable patterns and trends from raw social media data.

Social Network Analysis: Mathematical technique developed to understand structure and behaviour between members of social system, to map relationships between individuals in social network.

Word-of-Mouth: Passing of information from person to person by oral or written communication.

This research was previously published in the Handbook of Research on Global Enterprise Operations and Opportunities; pages 306-317, copyright year 2017 by Business Science Reference (an imprint of IGI Global).

Index

C

G

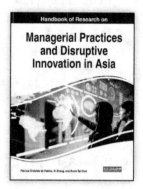
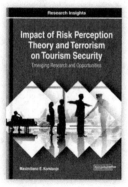

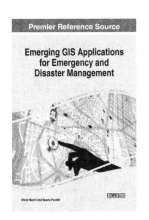
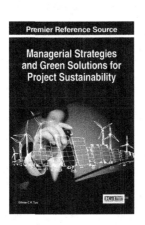

IGI Global Author Services

Providing a high-quality, affordable, and expeditious service, IGI Global's Author Services enable authors to streamline their publishing process, increase chance of acceptance, and adhere to IGI Global's publication standards.

Benefits of Author Services:

- **Professional Service:** All our editors, designers, and translators are experts in their field with years of experience and professional certifications.

- **Quality Guarantee & Certificate:** Each order is returned with a quality guarantee and certificate of professional completion.

- **Timeliness:** All editorial orders have a guaranteed return timeframe of 3-5 business days and translation orders are guaranteed in 7-10 business days.

- **Affordable Pricing:** IGI Global Author Services are competitively priced compared to other industry service providers.

- **APC Reimbursement:** IGI Global authors publishing Open Access (OA) will be able to deduct the cost of editing and other IGI Global author services from their OA APC publishing fee.

Author Services Offered:

English Language Copy Editing
Professional, native English language copy editors improve your manuscript's grammar, spelling, punctuation, terminology, semantics, consistency, flow, formatting, and more.

Scientific & Scholarly Editing
A Ph.D. level review for qualities such as originality and significance, interest to researchers, level of methodology and analysis, coverage of literature, organization, quality of writing, and strengths and weaknesses.

Figure, Table, Chart & Equation Conversions
Work with IGI Global's graphic designers before submission to enhance and design all figures and charts to IGI Global's specific standards for clarity.

Translation
Providing 70 language options, including Simplified and Traditional Chinese, Spanish, Arabic, German, French, and more.

Hear What the Experts Are Saying About IGI Global's Author Services

"Publishing with IGI Global has been an amazing experience for me for sharing my research. The strong academic production support ensures quality and timely completion." – **Prof. Margaret Niess, Oregon State University, USA**

"The service was very fast, very thorough, and very helpful in ensuring our chapter meets the criteria and requirements of the book's editors. I was quite impressed and happy with your service." – **Prof. Tom Brinthaupt, Middle Tennessee State University, USA**

Learn More or Get Started Here:

For Questions, Contact IGI Global's Customer Service Team at cust@igi-global.com or 717-533-8845

IGI Global
PUBLISHER of TIMELY KNOWLEDGE
www.igi-global.com

www.igi-global.com

Publisher of Peer-Reviewed, Timely, and
Innovative Academic Research Since 1988

IGI Global's Transformative Open Access (OA) Model:
How to Turn Your University Library's Database Acquisitions Into a Source of OA Funding

Well in advance of Plan S, IGI Global unveiled their OA Fee Waiver (Read & Publish) Initiative. Under this initiative, librarians who invest in IGI Global's InfoSci-Books and/or InfoSci-Journals databases will be able to subsidize their patrons' OA article processing charges (APCs) when their work is submitted and accepted (after the peer review process) into an IGI Global journal.

How Does it Work?

Step 1: **Library Invests in the InfoSci-Databases:** A library perpetually purchases or subscribes to the InfoSci-Books, InfoSci-Journals, or discipline/subject databases.

Step 2: **IGI Global Matches the Library Investment with OA Subsidies Fund:** IGI Global provides a fund to go towards subsidizing the OA APCs for the library's patrons.

Step 3: **Patron of the Library is Accepted into IGI Global Journal (After Peer Review):** When a patron's paper is accepted into an IGI Global journal, they option to have their paper published under a traditional publishing model or as OA.

Step 4: **IGI Global Will Deduct APC Cost from OA Subsidies Fund:** If the author decides to publish under OA, the OA APC fee will be deducted from the OA subsidies fund.

Step 5: **Author's Work Becomes Freely Available:** The patron's work will be freely available under CC BY copyright license, enabling them to share it freely with the academic community.

Note: This fund will be offered on an annual basis and will renew as the subscription is renewed for each year thereafter. IGI Global will manage the fund and award the APC waivers unless the librarian has a preference as to how the funds should be managed.

Hear From the Experts on This Initiative:

"I'm very happy to have been able to make one of my recent research contributions *freely available* along with having access to the *valuable resources* found within IGI Global's InfoSci-Journals database."

— **Prof. Stuart Palmer**,
Deakin University, Australia

"Receiving the support from IGI Global's OA Fee Waiver Initiative *encourages me to continue my research work without any hesitation*."

— **Prof. Wenlong Liu**, College of Economics and Management at Nanjing University of Aeronautics & Astronautics, China

For More Information, Scan the QR Code or Contact:
IGI Global's Digital Resources Team at eresources@igi-global.com.

IGI Global
PUBLISHER of TIMELY KNOWLEDGE

Printed in the United States
by Baker & Taylor Publisher Services